Social, Economic, and Environmental Impacts Between Sustainable Financial Systems and Financial Markets

Magdalena Ziolo
University of Szczecin, Poland

IGI Global
DISSEMINATOR OF KNOWLEDGE

A volume in the Practice, Progress, and Proficiency in Sustainability (PPPS) Book Series

Published in the United States of America by
IGI Global
Business Science Reference (an imprint of IGI Global)
701 E. Chocolate Avenue
Hershey PA, USA 17033
Tel: 717-533-8845
Fax: 717-533-8661
E-mail: cust@igi-global.com
Web site: http://www.igi-global.com

Library of Congress Cataloging-in-Publication Data

Names: Ziolo, Magdalena, 1976- editor.
Title: Social, economic, and environmental impacts between sustainable financial systems and financial markets / Magdalena Ziolo, editor.
Description: Hershey, PA : Business Science Reference, [2020] | Includes bibliographical references and index. | Summary: "This book explores sustainable financial systems, sustainable finance, blended finance, ESG risk, and individual and institutional motivations of financial managers in the sustainability. It also examines the link between finance, financial systems, financial markets, and externalities"-- Provided by publisher.
Identifiers: LCCN 2019023691 (print) | LCCN 2019023692 (ebook) | ISBN 9781799810339 (hardcover) | ISBN 9781799810346 (paperback) | ISBN 9781799810353 (ebook)
Subjects: LCSH: Sustainable development--Economic aspects. | Finance--Social aspects. | Finance--Environmental aspects.
Classification: LCC HC79.E5 S5674 2020 (print) | LCC HC79.E5 (ebook) | DDC 332--dc23
LC record available at https://lccn.loc.gov/2019023691
LC ebook record available at https://lccn.loc.gov/2019023692

This book is published in the IGI Global book series Practice, Progress, and Proficiency in Sustainability (PPPS) (ISSN: 2330-3271; eISSN: 2330-328X)

British Cataloguing in Publication Data
A Cataloguing in Publication record for this book is available from the British Library.

Practice, Progress, and Proficiency in Sustainability (PPPS) Book Series

Ayman Batisha
International Sustainability Institute, Egypt

ISSN:2330-3271
EISSN:2330-328X

Mission

In a world where traditional business practices are reconsidered and economic activity is performed in a global context, new areas of economic developments are recognized as the key enablers of wealth and income production. This knowledge of information technologies provides infrastructures, systems, and services towards sustainable development.

The **Practices, Progress, and Proficiency in Sustainability (PPPS) Book Series** focuses on the local and global challenges, business opportunities, and societal needs surrounding international collaboration and sustainable development of technology. This series brings together academics, researchers, entrepreneurs, policy makers and government officers aiming to contribute to the progress and proficiency in sustainability.

Coverage

- ICT and knowledge for development
- Knowledge clusters
- Environmental informatics
- Eco-Innovation
- Green Technology
- Global Content and Knowledge Repositories
- Sustainable Development
- Global Business
- Technological learning
- Innovation Networks

IGI Global is currently accepting manuscripts for publication within this series. To submit a proposal for a volume in this series, please contact our Acquisition Editors at Acquisitions@igi-global.com or visit: http://www.igi-global.com/publish/.

The Practice, Progress, and Proficiency in Sustainability (PPPS) Book Series (ISSN 2330-3271) is published by IGI Global, 701 E. Chocolate Avenue, Hershey, PA 17033-1240, USA, www.igi-global.com. This series is composed of titles available for purchase individually; each title is edited to be contextually exclusive from any other title within the series. For pricing and ordering information please visit http://www.igi-global.com/book-series/practice-progress-proficiency-sustainability/73810. Postmaster: Send all address changes to above address.

Titles in this Series

For a list of additional titles in this series, please visit:
https://www.igi-global.com/book-series/practice-progress-proficiency-sustainability/73810

Intellectual, Scientific, and Educational Influences on Sustainability Research
Rosario Adapon Turvey (Lakehead University, Canada) and Sreekumari Kurissery (Lakehead University, Canada)
Engineering Science Reference • copyright 2019 • 358pp • H/C (ISBN: 9781522573029) • US $195.00 (our price)

Driving the Development, Management, and Sustainability of Cognitive Cities
Kiran Ahuja (DAV Institute of Engineering and Technology, India) and Arun Khosla (Dr. B.R. Ambedkar National Institute of Technology, India)
Engineering Science Reference • copyright 2019 • 337pp • H/C (ISBN: 9781522580850) • US $225.00 (our price)

Technology-Driven Innovation in Gulf Cooperation Council (GCC) Countries Emerging Research and Opportunities
Anna Visvizi (Deree – The American College of Greece, Greece & Effat University, Saudi Arabia) Saad Bakry (King Saud University, Saudi Arabia) Miltiadis D. Lytras (Deree – The American College of Greece, Greece & Effat University, Saudi Arabia) and Wadee Alhalabi (Effat University, Saudi Arabia)
Business Science Reference • copyright 2019 • 180pp • H/C (ISBN: 9781522590125) • US $195.00 (our price)

Novel Technologies and Systems for Food Preservation
Pedro Dinis Gaspar (University of Beira Interior, Portugal) and Pedro Dinho da Silva (University of Beira Interior, Portugal)
Engineering Science Reference • copyright 2019 • 416pp • H/C (ISBN: 9781522578949) • US $345.00 (our price)

Bioeconomical Solutions and Investments in Sustainable City Development
José G. Vargas-Hernández (University of Guadalajara, Mexico) and Justyna Anna Zdunek-Wielgołaska (Warsaw University of Technology, Poland)
Engineering Science Reference • copyright 2019 • 306pp • H/C (ISBN: 9781522579588) • US $195.00 (our price)

Optimizing the Use of Farm Waste and Non-Farm Waste to Increase Productivity and Food Security Emerging Research and Opportunities
Leighton Naraine (Clarence Fitzroy Bryant College, St. Kitts-Nevis)
Engineering Science Reference • copyright 2019 • 223pp • H/C (ISBN: 9781522579342) • US $155.00 (our price)

Handbook of Research on International Collaboration, Economic Development, and Sustainability in the Arctic
Vasilii Erokhin (Harbin Engineering University, China) Tianming Gao (Harbin Engineering University, China) and Xiuhua Zhang (Harbin Engineering University, China)
Business Science Reference • copyright 2019 • 703pp • H/C (ISBN: 9781522569541) • US $235.00 (our price)

IGI Global
DISSEMINATOR OF KNOWLEDGE

701 East Chocolate Avenue, Hershey, PA 17033, USA
Tel: 717-533-8845 x100 • Fax: 717-533-8661
E-Mail: cust@igi-global.com • www.igi-global.com

Table of Contents

Detailed Table of Contents

Financial systems, which play a major role in the development of the economy, are primarily helping to fund flow and assist in capital increase. In this study, frequency domain causality test, which was developed by Geweke and Hosoya and developed by Breitung and Candelon, was used to analyze the causality relationship by short, medium, and long periods. This test, which provides periodical examination, was investigated to determine the effect of G7 countries on employment and growth of financial institutions and markets index used to calculate financial development index. Among the G7 countries, the development of financial markets and institutions has been affecting employment in Canada (short-medium), Germany (medium-long), Japan (short-medium-long), and the UK (medium-long); in addition, when the effects of economic growth on financial markets and institutions are investigated, Canada (short-medium), France (medium), Italy (medium-long), America (medium-long), Germany (medium-long), Japan (short-medium-long), and UK (short-medium-long) were determined by analysis.

The main purpose of this chapter is to identify the existing relations between the selected areas of sustainable development but carried out on the basis of the indicators describing the macroeconomic dimension of this development from the OECD countries' perspective. The theoretical basis for analyses is the concept of shared value, for the first time presented by Porter and Kramer in 2011. In this chapter, this proposition was applied to the studies carried out on the country level. For this purpose, the multidimensional statistical analysis was applied. The results of the study confirmed that on the current level of development, even in the case of the most developed countries, it is very difficult to find the shared space with the same level of development between these areas. In the same time, it is very important direction of further research and decisions undertaken on the macroeconomic level.

This chapter is an attempt to review the existing approaches in appraising sustainability projects using the conventional approaches of net present value (NPV) and introduce the modified forms of NPV (i.e., net present sustainable value [NPSV]). The chapter also elucidates on the prominent characteristics of sustainability projects and the inadequacy of traditional financial tools in appraising the same. Consequently, the need to transition from using only time value of money as in payback period approach to include opportunity costs as in NPV and furthering this approach to broaden the capital theory of sustainability by including both the time value of money and the opportunity costs has been strongly advocated. In addition to controlling the time value of money, risk-adjusted NPV measures are effective in evaluating sustainability projects. For assessment of renewable energy projects, real option analysis is suggested as an effective measure.

Public interest entities are socially and economically important elements of the economy. Since 2017 some of them have been obliged to prepare non-financial statements, which should contain among others a description of the policies pursued by the entity with regard to environmental issues. In this chapter, the authors analyzed the scope of environmental matters disclosed with non-financial statement and positively verified the hypothesis according to which the environmental issues in reporting of public interest entities increase the usefulness of the financial statement for stakeholders. Public interest entities fulfil their duties, but the scope and specificity of data contained in the statement on non-financial information differed between entities. Imposing requirement to annually present activities undertaken in environmental matters can make entities more sensitive to these issues and raise efficiently of implementation of the environmental policy. The research methods used in the study are a critical analysis of the literature, description, analysis, and synthesis methods.

The aim of the considerations is to assess the effectiveness of sustainable public procurement (SPP) as a tool for the implementation of sustainable development in the European Union. The chapter discusses the legal bases for the use of sustainable public procurement in the EU, the potential of the public sector in the implementation of sustainable development through public procurement in the EU, functioning of the market for sustainable public procurement, market potential of the public sector of the European Union in the implementation of sustainable development through public procurement, good practices and barriers related to green public procurement (GPP), and socially responsible procurement (SRPP). The chapter ends with conclusions from the research and practical recommendations regarding the use of sustainable public procurement in the European Union.

The EU has become a promoter of the idea of sustainable development and a defender of the global climate, which in many sectors results in ever higher and more ambitious ecological and efficiency requirements. State wants to protect the environment use various intervention instruments, including environmental taxes: "green taxes." In addition to the fiscal function, they are to stimulate various types of entities to undertake specific actions conducive to reducing pressure on the environment. The aim of the considerations (discussion) is to present changes in the approach to the use of "green taxes," as an important instrument of the public sector environmental policy in the impact on reducing pollution on the environment conducive to sustainable development. The research aims to verify the hypothesis and assumes the impact of environmental taxes on the public system of financing expenditure on environmental protection. The authors will also look for an answer to the question whether the policy of "green taxes" can contribute to the sustainable public financial system.

Public health, affecting the operations of the entity and its environment, plays an important role in the concept of sustainable development. Health condition affects the quality of life of the individual thus the condition of the economy. Taking into consideration the complex relationship of public health and the concept of Sustainable Development Goals, the analysis seems to be fully justified. The aim of the analysis is to determine challenges and opportunities of the sustainability of selected United Nations Member States healthcare sectors. Particular emphasis in the analysis was placed on the situation of the Polish sector against the background of the analyzed countries. The analysis was based on the Sustainable Development Goals and was carried out using one of the MCDA method.

The purpose of this chapter is connected with the rationale for the approach to understanding shock as an economic phenomenon in terms of its nature and forms of manifestation, the conditions of aging and the factors of realization, the mechanism of self-development, and the consequences for the sustainability of the national financial and economic systems. The author's interest is initially aimed at identifying the circumstances in which the system loses its ability to restore sustained structural relationships and to preserve integrity in the sphere of national finance and economy. An approach allowing the identification of the transmission mechanisms connected with market exchange that can generate marginal states of economic structural links as necessary and sufficient conditions for the destructive shocks impact on them is identified. Based on the obtained theoretical conclusions, it becomes possible to model the marginal states of different structural relationships and evaluate their impact on the sustainable state of economic systems as a whole on the base of shock theory.

The authors structure the main functions of the state in the economic system as the "famous triad" of R. Musgrave. They are connected with allocating resources, redistributing income (equality in income distribution), and stabilizing economy (economic efficiency). The aim is to find the causes of their low efficient implementation by the state. This is manifested in the fact that society itself does not have the ability to adequately control the current activities of the state created and put over it in order to protect its interests; in the contradictory essence of the state itself, which is the regulator, which forms the rules of behavior of economic agents and at the same time acts as the economic agent participating in market transactions. To model the options for the effective resolution of the problems of the "magic triangle," the authors formulated the Musgrave uncertainty principle by analogy with the Heisenberg uncertainty principle in physics. This makes it possible to assess the budget expenditures of the state in order to get out of its low efficiency trap.

The global financial crisis of 2007-2008 posed the problems of the slowing world economy growth rates that predetermined the necessity to investigate a national economy's structural characteristics associated not so much with the objective, easily modeled factors of its development as with the subjective ones, difficult to be understood but increasing in importance. The latter is connected with inequity in the simultaneously living generations' perception, which is fueled by the trends of accelerated income polarization of the population, the middle-class reduction, and decreasing possibilities of achieving higher living standards for the socially vulnerable groups. All the above predetermines the behavior of economic agents in society and ultimately the prospects for the long-run economic growth in the country. The author conducted a model experiment with the dynamics of intergenerational equity and economic growth on the basis of the sub-martingale. The results show the growing importance of the human factor in ensuring the stable growth of the global economy.

The author identifies the psychological and cognitive barriers (PCBs) in the students' consciousness in schooling as the very important factor of the contemporary education system crisis. Focusing on the unresolved "how to learn" problem, the author reveals the essence of PCBs, their causes, and models for overcoming them. At the same time, the main attention is paid to the social aspect of insurmountable

PCBs at school. It is about the education failure of schoolchildren, which predetermines their life and professional failure. And this, in turn, predetermines their negative value orientation in social exchange. As a result, the society receives a low-quality educational component of human capital, which is less and less in demand on the labor market due to the technological challenges of the future. The PCBs overcoming creates conditions for the success of schoolchildren as future carriers of high-quality human capital, able to ensure stable economic growth thanks to the activities of highly educated and intellectually autonomous professionals.

The chapter contains a methodology for formalized evaluation of the model of replacement of budget funds by private investment in the public infrastructure PPP projects for the purpose to ensure public finance sustainability. It can manifest itself only if the state could create appropriate conditions for private investors, including institutional players as its partners. The latter means primarily the stable formal institutional conditions for private investors, low transactional costs, attractive financial parameters, that could bring the ratio of budget and private financing of public infrastructure PPP projects to more than 1 to 1. It has become evident that accelerated development of many public infrastructure PPP projects is hampered by two factors: (1) inadequate institutional support for the design process itself and (2) absence of state-prepared acceptable financial models of public infrastructure PPP projects regarding the division of risks of infrastructure projects and delegating the proprietary rights of the state to private investors.

Enterprise Risk Management (ERM) is a comprehensive and holistic approach to risk management, requiring the determination, assessment and management of risks in an integrated and systematic manner. ERM has been considered as a financial, and accounting-based tool used to assess and manage the risks an organisation faces and to meet the compliance requirements of creditors, rating agencies, regulators and stock exchanges. Although ERM is widely examined by internal audit and finance scholars, ERM researches from management and strategy perspectives are limited in the literature. The purpose of this chapter is to provide a comprehensive overview of ERM including ERM concepts and definition of the risks and categorisation of risks surrounding the organisations. Moreover, the chapter handles how the risk management evolved into ERM. The distinguishing components of ERM (pillars) and the leading factors and motivation for ERM adoption (determinants) are presented.

This chapter examines a practical methodology for the assessment and control of market and liquidity risk exposures for financial trading portfolios that consist of certain equity assets. The applied technique is

Preface

The crisis of 2008 caused a broad discussion over the need to change the way of thinking about contemporary finance and financial markets. In view of the crisis phenomena with which the modern financial system struggled and struggles, the conventional finance paradigm based on efficient market theory proved to be failed and inadequate to the challenges contemporary financial markets are exposing. In the face of increasing climate change, social problems related to broadly understood social exclusion and a number of irregularities in the sphere of corporate governance, in particular in the field of ethics, transparency and risk management, the conventional finance requires thorough changes and reconstruction in the direction of sustainable finance. Sustainable finance is a three-dimensional concept, coherent with the three pillars (economic, environmental, social) of sustainable development, which helps eliminate negative externalities and influence non-financial factors, whose role is systematically growing in the context of (Environmental, Social, Governance) ESG risk.

The importance of non-financial factors (ESG) has clearly increased in public discussions and regulatory proposals that emerged after the 2008 crisis, including the Europe 2020 document contains references and recommendations regarding ESG, in the context of SRI and the need to repair the financial system after the 2008 crisis by changing the way of thinking about finances and financial markets. This change is expressed above all by emphasizing the social context of finance and the responsibility of financial markets for financial decisions towards society. At the same time, attention is paid to the key role of the environmental factor affecting finance.

Considering the growing relationship between finance and sustainability, especially in terms of the impact of finances on achieving sustainable development goals and overcoming negative externalities, the main questions have been: What are the key drivers of economic growth and financial development in the context of sustainability? What is the contemporary approach to creating of sustainable value? What is the role and how can state and sustainable public finance soften negative externalities? How to revise the assessment of sustainable project towards sustainability criteria? What's the role of risk management to address the problem of sustainability? Does human capital matter for stable economic growth? And finally how to deal with economic shocks, and what is the role of financial intermediaries in it?

The main goal of edited volume, *Social, Economic, and Environmental Impacts Between Sustainable Financial Systems and Financial Markets*, is to address contemporary challenges and prospects of the business, finance, and sustainability after post-crisis era. The volume reveals that the relation between finance and sustainable development is a relatively novel area. As a result the new approach is developed to assess the efficiency of sustainable finance, capital and risk evaluation, value perception, and a new approach to methodology and financial comparability. All of this issues and problems are in the scope of concern of this monograph. Finally, *Social, Economic, and Environmental Impacts Between Sustainable Financial Systems and Financial Markets* aims to points out the special role of sustainable development and sustainable finance in tackling the wider and socially harmful phenomena, namely the exclusion and increase of inequality.

The book's first chapter (Murat Gündüz and Yunus Özyıldırım) points out that financial systems play a major role in the development of the economy and are primarily helping to fund flow and assist in capital increase. Financial systems enable the savings by investors to be maximized from the minimum level, the savings to be used effectively and the companies for investment to be kept under control. They also contribute to recovery by allowing the investments to be made in different areas and the taken risks to be minimized or eliminated. In this context, the financial system is one of the components of the economic system. The study investigates the causal relationship between the level of development of financial institutions and financial markets of G7 countries and unemployment rate and economic growth. For this purpose, they use frequency domain causality analysis method, which allows to examine short, medium- and long-term causality.

The second chapter (Katarzyna Cheba) discusses both the theoretical and empirical aspects of the concept of creating a shared value considered from a macroeconomic perspective. The concept of shared value is usually presented as actions taken by enterprises to achieve mutual benefits for both the enterprise and for the society. However, the study proofs that the concept of shared value can also be explained as a scope of similar changes in different development areas of the countries across the globe. This development was considered through the prism of changes taking place in various areas of sustainable development (in the perspective of: human - economy - environment) and a relatively new area describing the support of this development from the public finance perspective.

The third chapter (Ria Sinha and Manipadma Datta) attempts to review the existing approaches in appraising sustainability projects using the conventional cash flow based measures such as net present value (NPV) and profitability based measures such as return on investment (ROI), accounting rates of return (ARR) and return on capital employed (ROCE).However, considering the typical characteristics of sustainability projects, these measures are inadequate and may lead to incorrect decisions. On the contrary, modified measures of NPV viz. net present sustainable value (NPSV) and NPV positive are capable of bridging the inherent caveats of traditional measures and provide a remedy.

The fourth chapter (Anna Spoz and Marian Żukowski) elaborates on the scope of environmental matters disclosed with non-financial statement and assumes that environmental issues in reporting of public interest entities increase the usefulness of the financial statement for stakeholders. Public interest entities fulfil their duties, but the scope and specificity of data contained in the statement on non-financial information differed between entities. Imposing requirement to annually present activities undertaken in environmental matters can make entities more sensitive to these issues and raise efficiently of implementation of the environmental policy.

The fifth chapter (Małgorzata Burchard-Dziubińska and Tomasz Jakubiec) examines the effectiveness of sustainable public procurement (SPP) as a tool for the implementation of sustainable development in the European Union. The chapter discusses, respectively; the legal bases for the use of SPP in the EU, the potential of the public sector in the implementation of sustainable development through public procurement in the EU; functioning of the market for SPP, market potential of the public sector of the European Union in the implementation of sustainable development through public procurement, good practices and barriers related to green public procurement (GPP) and socially responsible public procurement (SRPP).

The sixth chapter (Beata Zofia Filipiak and Dorota Wyszkowska) contributes to the relation between public financial system and green tax from the perspective of sustainable development. The study provides an original approach to sustainable financial system and the factor of determining the possibilities of intervention of public authorities through the public system towards sustainable development. The research presented in this chapter assumes that, the impact of environmental taxes occurs on the public system of financing expenditure on environmental protect. The chapter looks for an answer whether the policy of "green taxes" can contribute to the sustainable public financial system. The study aims to draw attention to the significant gap in the existing research referring to the impact of environmental taxes on the public system in the context of financing expenditure on environmental protection.

The seventh chapter (Małgorzata Miszczyńska) examines the multifaceted nature of relations between public health and the concept of sustainable development that is manifested in such aspects as improving the quality of life, efficiency and costs of the functioning of the economy or the impact of the environment on society's health. Sustainable socio-economic development is one of the most important challenges of the modern world and that is why it requires evaluating systems and implementing measures along with appropriate budget planning. The study aims to determine challenges and opportunities of the sustainability of selected United Nations Member States healthcare sectors. Particular emphasis in the analysis was placed on the situation of the Polish sector against the background of the analyzed countries.

The eighth chapter (Zoya Andreevna Pilipenko) is devoted to shocks as an economic phenomenon, which allows not only to anticipate the formation of necessary and sufficient conditions for its destructive impact, but also to use it for the purpose of a qualitative restructuring of the economic system, for example, in the context of expanding the potential of its growth. The synergistic effect of the shocks' theory is great, because it allows to get closer to understanding the self-development of economic systems, the role of financial intermediaries in it, the mechanisms for the emergence of the financial bubbles at the national level and their ability to influence other countries of the world, the role of impulse, called shocks as a trigger of the above phenomenon.

The ninth chapter (Olga Ivanovna Pilipenko) examines the problem of increasing the efficiency of the state in the national economy and identifying the factors that contribute to this. Despite significant progress in researching the factors that predetermine macroeconomic dynamics, many aspects of this fundamental scientific problem, especially in the context of the state's influence on the laws of its self-development, are far from understanding. To make some aspects of these two problems clear the study aims to investigate the interconnection of the government as a mega-regulator and its activities as the main factors capable to influence on the economic dynamics of national society.

Chapter 10 (Nataliya Sergeevna Makarova) proposes the new approach to the interpretation of the value orientations of individuals as the main motivational aspects in the process of turning human capital into the main driver of stable economic growth in the future. The study argues the "social and financial stability puzzle" is based on the idea that the growth of social budget expenditures can only keep the level of poverty unchanged, but not necessarily ensure the stability of economic development. However, the sense of justice, most clearly manifested in the assessment of equality between generations by the people themselves, gives a long-term economic return. The latter can be achieved through the adequate institutionalization by the state of formal and informal relations in society.

The eleventh chapter (Andrey Igorevich Pilipenko) presents a revision of the investigations dealing with human capital and education as its most important component; with the students "failure" in the learning process as the social manifestation of the modern education crisis. The study explains the Theory of Psychological and Cognitive Barriers in the Minds (PCBs theory) application to the problem of the schooling and learning mismatch and to the social consequences of its solution. Empirical part of the chapter is devoted to the main characteristics of future knowledge-based economy as a whole and of the model with high educated human capital and with their successful carriers, which is accompanied by estimates of raising the learning level of the "generation Z" in the process of learning as the PCBs overcoming.

The twelfth chapter (Irina Yurievna Vaslavskaya) proposes a model approach to the problem of financial design of the development of the public infrastructure PPP-projects allowing to justify new financial instruments and financial institutions to ensure the national economies' growth rates in the perspective to 2020. The chapter contains a methodology for formalized evaluation of the model of replacement of budget funds by private investment in the public infrastructure projects organized in the hybrid form of PPP contracts. As a result, it has been assessed the positive impact of the public finances consolidation on the growth rate of the national economy.

The thirteenth chapter (Ebru Oydag and Ozlem Senvar) provides an overview for Enterprise Risk Management (ERM) from management perspectives. This chapter emphasizes the links between strategy and ERM and involves discussions and recommendations for further directions. The study points out it is still interesting to see if there are any task environments, and industry specific commonalities between ERM designs as to the risks prioritised, and how they are managed. Likewise what the perceived and realised benefits have been after implementation is worth testing in different contexts, but preferably with similar methods. How the companies manage the biases, politics and bounded rationality issues when determining and managing their risks is also another area for future research. These aspects make ERM a new and interesting area not only for finance, accounting and risk scholars, but also for management and strategy scholars. With respect to the ERM implementation in practice, there are various frameworks and guidelines issued by professional organisations. However, it is not clear-cut and easy for practitioners to take a framework and apply it in the organisation. The study argues that ERM has the potential to be an investment with a positive pay-out when implemented in a holistic and carefully designed manner in line with the organisation's needs, size and resource base.

The fourteenth chapter (Mazin A. M. Al Janabi) lays out all the mathematical/quantitative infrastructures of LVaR method, and its limitations, and a robust modeling algorithm that incorporates the effects of illiquid assets in daily market risk management. The results of empirical tests and optimization of the maximum LVaR limits has been presented in empirical part of the chapter. The results of the study results suggest that in almost all tests, there are clear asymmetric behaviors in the distribution of returns of the sample indices and the two benchmark indices. The appealing outcome of this study suggests the inevitability of combining LVaR calculations with other methods such as stress-testing and scenario analysis to grasp a thorough picture of other remaining risks (such as, fat-tails in the probability distribution) that cannot be revealed with the plain assumption of normality.

The fiftieth, last chapter (Iwona Dorota Bąk, Beata Szczecińska) attempts to systematize the concept of economic value that takes into account elements of sustainable development. At the same time, it is the voice in the ongoing discussion on the purpose and methods of valuation of the company's value. The study emphasizes the importance of sustainable development in relation to the functioning of enterprises. The stages in the enterprise on the road to sustainable development as well as the benefits and costs resulting therefrom are indicated. Applying the principles of sustainable development in the functioning of enterprises may contribute to the increase of their value, as well as strengthening of the competitive position.

Acknowledgment

Research results presented in this volume are an element of research projects financed by the National Science Center Poland (NCN) under OPUS13 no UMO-2017/25/B/HS4/02172 and OPUS16 UMO-2018/31/B/HS4/00570.

Chapter 1
Does Financial Development Lead to Employment and Growth?
A Frequency Domain Causality Test for G7

Murat Gündüz
Usak University, Turkey

Yunus Özyıldırım
Usak University, Turkey

ABSTRACT

Financial systems, which play a major role in the development of the economy, are primarily helping to fund flow and assist in capital increase. In this study, frequency domain causality test, which was developed by Geweke and Hosoya and developed by Breitung and Candelon, was used to analyze the causality relationship by short, medium, and long periods. This test, which provides periodical examination, was investigated to determine the effect of G7 countries on employment and growth of financial institutions and markets index used to calculate financial development index. Among the G7 countries, the development of financial markets and institutions has been affecting employment in Canada (short-medium), Germany (medium-long), Japan (short-medium-long), and the UK (medium-long); in addition, when the effects of economic growth on financial markets and institutions are investigated, Canada (short-medium), France (medium), Italy (medium-long), America (medium-long), Germany (medium-long), Japan (short-medium-long), and UK (short-medium-long) were determined by analysis.

INTRODUCTION

Financial systems, which play a major role in the growth and development of the economy, perform functions such as providing funds flow initially and helping capital increase. Financial systems enable the savings by investors to be maximized from the minimum level, the savings to be used effectively

DOI: 10.4018/978-1-7998-1033-9.ch001

and the companies for investment to be kept under control. They also contribute to recovery by allowing the investments to be made in different areas and the taken risks to be minimized or eliminated. In this context, the financial system is one of the components of the economic system.

Financial development is the existence of all services which support the emergence of markets and intermediary institutions. Economies activated by the decisions taken in financial sector develop various mechanisms to minimize the effects of market imperfections. Governments offer a range of services varying from legal accounting systems to state banks with the purpose of reducing these imperfections and increasing resource allocation. Some economies became more successful in developing financial systems which lower such costs. It was however determined that they became less successful in some countries, which financial markets had great effects in economic development. For that reason, financial development is conceptually defined as the elimination of the effects of wrong information, limited applications and transaction cost of financial instruments, markets and institutions (World Bank, 2018). For example, the economies with effective legal and regulatory systems facilitate the development of equities and bond markets, which enable investors to hold more diversified portfolios without securities markets. Therefore, this may facilitate the capital flow to the investments with higher returns, accelerate the growth and increase the life standard (Demirgüç-Kunt, 2017). Financial institutions and markets in the world differ significantly in how well they provide services on the development of economies.

The aim of this study is to investigate the causal relationship between the level of development of financial institutions and financial markets of G7 countries and unemployment rate and economic growth. For this purpose, the frequency domain causality analysis method, which allows to examine short, medium and long term causality, was used.

Background

Analyzing the relationship between financial development and economic growth was regarded as highly attractive especially within the studies on development. Upon closer look at the literature we can see that many theoretical and empirical studies were carried out in this issue. The guide studies such as Schumpeter (1911), Goldsmith (1969), McKinnon (1973) and Shaw's (1973) set the theoretical framework of this relationship. Financial markets manage to direct the financial funds to the production by eliminating their unproductiveness and provide the productivity to increase. Therefore, they play an important role in providing economic growth. In this role especially the banking system is an important factor in growth with its success in effective use of savings, promoting innovative approaches and financing the production investments (Durusu-Ciftci, 2017). The support for economy through services such as data collection, analysis, risk spreading and fund-raising provided by financial institutions via Endogenous growth theory indicates that financial institutions have a positive impact on steady growth (Demetriades & Hussein, 1996).

In many studies it was suggested that financial development would provide more output and therefore, more developed financial markets would lead to economic growth. With reference to more output increase it is suggested that financial development would lead to employment increase by grounding upon the law of Okun. That being said, it is thought that companies would tend to capital-intensive technologies with the increase in financial development. There are also some views that this will increase the productivity and contribute to the growth positively but will not affect the employment positively. In this context, it is not certain that the relationship between financial development and economic growth can automatically be established between financial development and employment (Chen, 2016).

There are important discussions among economists concerning the role of financial development in decreasing poverty and improving economies. The evidences based on theoretical and empirical studies indicate that financial development has a main role in socio-economic development. The economies with higher financial development levels grow more rapidly and their poverty level decreases more rapidly (Demirgüç-Kunt, 2017).

Aslan and Korap (2006) divided the financial development two parts as financial expansion and financial depth. Financial expansion is called as the spread of financial services and the increase in the number of financial instruments or institutions. However, financial deepening is the increase in the number of financial services and institutions or the increase in the proportion of financial assets to per capita income.

At the same time, studies have been conducted in many areas which are thought to have an interaction with financial development. Jeanneney and Kpodar (2011) who brought a different perspective to the concept of financial development suggest that financial development resulted in the reduction of poverty in developing countries and effective use of banking system increased the access to financial services. The concept of financial development, which cannot be adequately explained by the number of financial instruments and institutions, is expressed by the effectiveness and availability of these financial instruments and institutions. In addition, Bayar et al. (2017) investigated the effect of financial development on total tax revenues. The findings of the study based on OECD countries showed that financial markets are one-way causality from development level to total tax revenues. Comin and Nanda (2019) examined the extent to which financial market development has influenced the spread of technology across 17 countries from 1870 to 2000. Researchers have found that in the near term of the invention of technology, more depth in financial markets for capital intensive technologies leads to faster technology diffusion. They also found that financial depth had no different impact on the diffusion of capital-intensive technologies in the final stages of diffusion.

GLOBAL FINANCIAL DEVELOPMENT

International banking does not guarantee the financial development and sustainability of the stability. Policy makers make efforts to maximize the benefits of international banking while controlling the risks. Researches indicate that institutionally developed countries tend to benefit more in terms of financial development and stability provided by the international banking system. Especially good information sharing and the significance of strong audit become important.

Financial development of countries around the world are shown on Figure 1. The attempts by policy makers to increase the financial development, foreign banks with strong institutions, domestic banks exposed to great competition, previously excluded SMEs may increase the access and participation for households and make the market sustainable. For financial development it is aimed to include the people from all strata into the market without the goal of focusing only on big customers as well as providing better access opportunity to banks, domestic financial institutions, SMEs and families (Global Financial Development Report, 2017/2018).

The financial development index and its sub-dimensions are shown in Figure 2. Financial development appears to be the recovery and improvement in the components of the financial system. Financial development indicators are defined as the instruments used for measuring the financial developments.

Figure 1. World Financial Development Index, 2016
Source: *IMF, Financial Development Index*

Financial Development Index (FDI), established by these indicators is a relative ranking on the depth, access and productivity of the financial institutions and markets of countries. FDI is an average of financial institutions index and financial markets index.

The Financial Development Index is obtained as the following by using the standard operation method: A number of indicators are used to measure the Depth, Access and Productivity values used in the formation of each sub-index (Financial Institutions and Financial Markets) under the pyramid. These indicators are used to measure the status of financial institutions and financial markets.

Each indicator was initially converted top the values between 0 and 1 through the normalization procedure. Therefore, the maximum value of a certain variable according to the time and the country

Figure 2. Financial Development Index Pyramid
Source: *IMF, Financial Development Data Base*

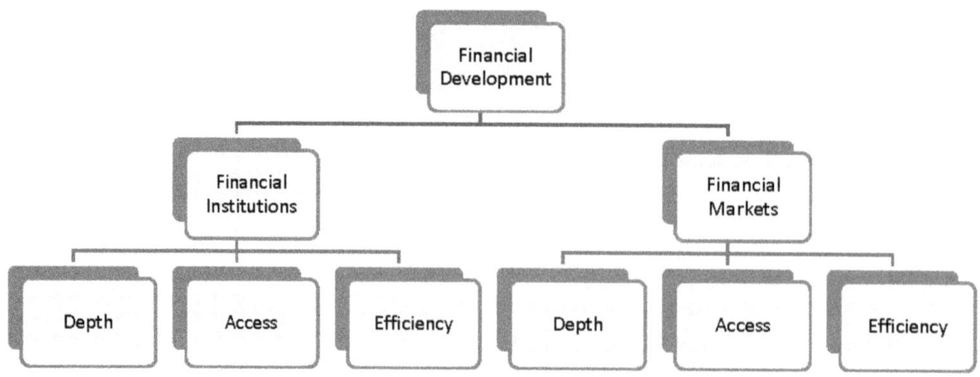

is equalized to 1 and the minimum value is equalized to 0 and all values are measured according to these maximum and minimum values. Indicators are defined as the fact that higher values point higher financial development. Then, the indicators gather under six sub-indices under the pyramid and at the highest level. The weights are obtained from the main component analysis and the weighted average of the basic index is taken. These weights reflect the effect of each sub-index on the change in financial institutions and financial markets index which forms the financial development (Sahay et al., 2015, p. 12).

Index Sizes of Financial Institutions and Financial Markets

Depth: The rate of pension fund assets, investment funds and insurance premiums to Gross National Product (GNP) is used in order to calculate the depth of financial institutions. In addition, the amount of credit allocated by deposit banks to private sector is another issue that helps to present the depth of financial institutions. However, the depth of financial markets is the proportion of stock market value to GNP. Stock market value equals to stock prices and the product of current shares. The companies listed on the stock market include domestic companies in country's stock market. Companies listed here do not include investment companies or other collective investment tools.

Access: The percentage of adults (over the age of 15) declaring that they have an account in a public financial institution is used in determining the access to financial institutions. The rate of the total market value to the GNP of other companies, except for the top 10 major companies, is used in order to measure the access to financial markets.

Efficiency: The difference between the interest rate on loans and the interest on the time deposits is used while calculating the efficiency of financial institutions. Loaning rate indicates the lending rate of banks to private sector. The deposit interest rate refers to the interest rate paid for savings deposits of commercial or similar banks. The efficiency in the financial markets is calculated by proportioning the total stocks traded throughout the period to the average market value of the period. The average market value is taken as the average of the period end values for the current period and the previous period.

Index of Financial Development- G7 Countries

Studies conducted to measure financial development formed the basis for the investigation of financial inclusion in a multidimensional way. When the countries with the highest financial development index value are analyzed in the conducted studies, it is seen that Switzerland is in the first rank. It was identified that Spain is in the second rank and the United States, one of the G7 countries, is in the third rank. When the top 20 ranks of financial development index is analyzed we can see that all of the G7 countries are in the top 20 countries. It was determined that the United States, Japan, Canada, United Kingdom, Italy and France are in the top 10 countries; however, Germany is at the16th rank in financial development index. The main components of this ranking are the financial institutions index and the financial markets index. Top 20 countries in Financial Development Index are indicated in Figure 3.

Financial institutions and financial markets indices of each G7 countries are indicated in Figure 4-10 along with the depth, access and efficiency dimensions.

In Canada the depth of the financial markets is remarkable as compared to access to financial markets and efficiency. We can also see that access to financial markets index has a very high value. However, efficiency of financial markets index stands out as the lowest dimension. While the depth index in Canadian financial institutions system is significant, the efficiency and access dimensions have pretty good values.

Figure 3. Financial development, top twenty countries
Source: *IMF, Financial Development Index*

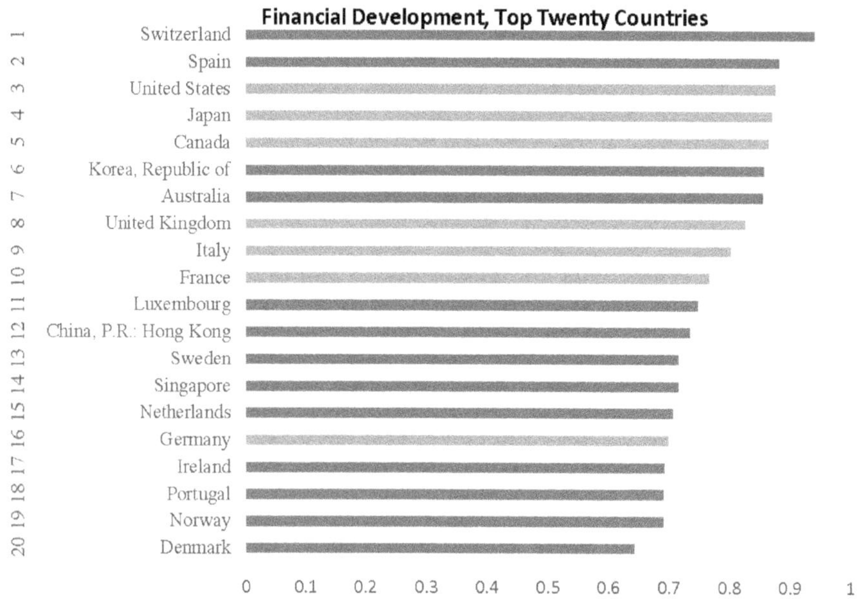

Although the access index in financial institutions system in France is remarkable, the efficiency and depth dimensions have pretty good values.

The depth of financial markets is quite high as compared to other market dimensions. While the efficiency dimension of financial markets have an average index value, it is remarkable that access to financial markets dimension has as a quite low value.

The efficiency of financial markets is more significant in Germany than the depth of and access to financial markets. It is remarkable that access to financial markets has the lowest value.

Although the efficiency index is the highest value in German financial institutions system, access and depth dimensions are very close to this value.

Index value of the efficiency of financial markets dimension in Italy has a value of 1. In other words, it can be said that financial markets in Italy are completely efficient. Although the access to financial markets dimension has a lower value than other dimensions, it is above the average.

It is remarkable that access index in Italian financial institutions system has a value close to 1. The efficiency index and depth index in financial institutions dimension have the values above the average.

Financial markets are completely efficient in Japan. We can see that the depth of financial markets has a good level with a value close to 1. Although access to financial markets index is at the average level, it stands out as the lowest value. It can also be seen that the efficiency index in Japanese financial institutions system is at the best level. In addition, access and depth dimensions have pretty high values.

With the value very close to 1 the depth of financial markets in United Kingdom is pretty high. Access and efficiency dimensions of the financial markets have the values close to the average values. It is remarkable that the efficiency of financial markets index has the lowest value within dimensions. The depth index value of United Kingdom in financial institutions system is full 1. In addition, it is seen that access and efficiency dimensions have pretty good values with the values above the average.

Figure 4. Financial Institutions and Markets Index Graphic of Canada for 2016
***Source**: Financial Development Index Database.*

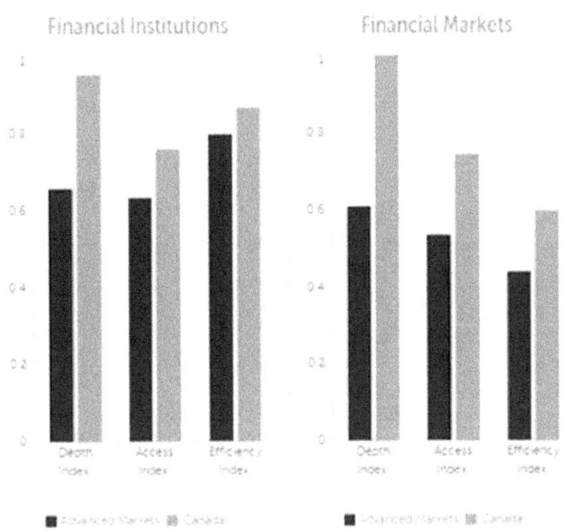

Figure 5. Financial Institutions and Markets Index Graphic of France, 2016
Source: *Financial Development Index Database*

Figure 6. Financial Institutions and Markets Index Graphic of Germany, 2016
Source: *Financial Development Index Database.*

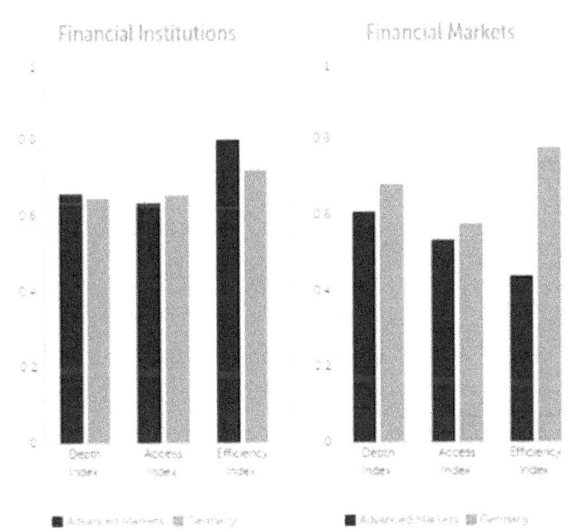

Figure 7. Financial Institutions and Markets Index Graphic of Italy, 2016
Source: *Financial Development Index Database*

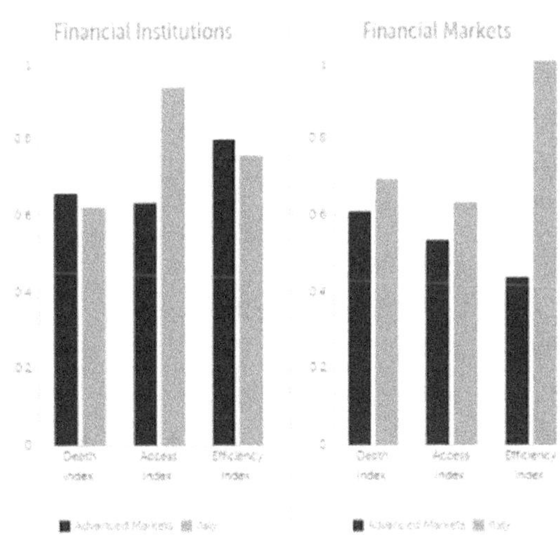

Figure 8. Financial Institutions and Markets Index Graphic of Japan, 2016
Source: *Financial Development Index Database*

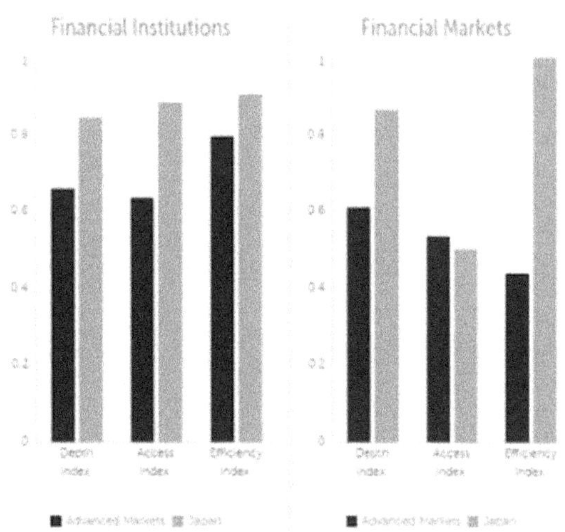

Figure 9. Financial Institutions and Markets Index Graphic of United Kingdom, 2016
Source: *Financial Development Index Database*

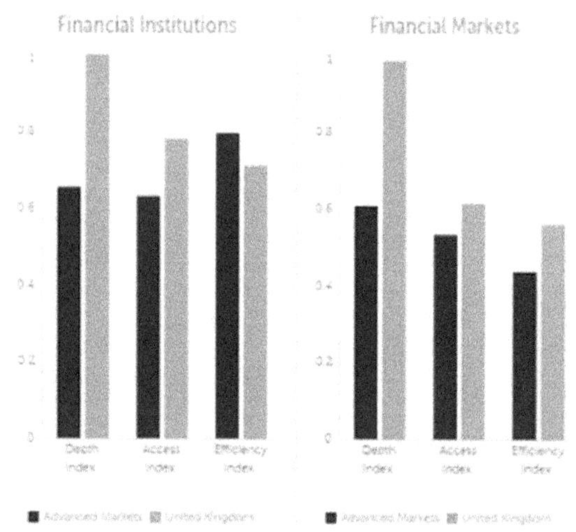

In the USA the depth and efficiency of financial markets indices are more remarkable than access to financial markets index. The index value of the depth and efficiency of financial markets is very close to 1. Although access to financial markets index has the lowest value, it has a value above the average. The dimension with the highest index value in American financial institutions system is the access dimension. Efficiency and depth dimensions have the values above the average.

Figure 10. Financial Institutions and Markets Index Graphic of United States, 2016
Source: *Financial Development Index Database*

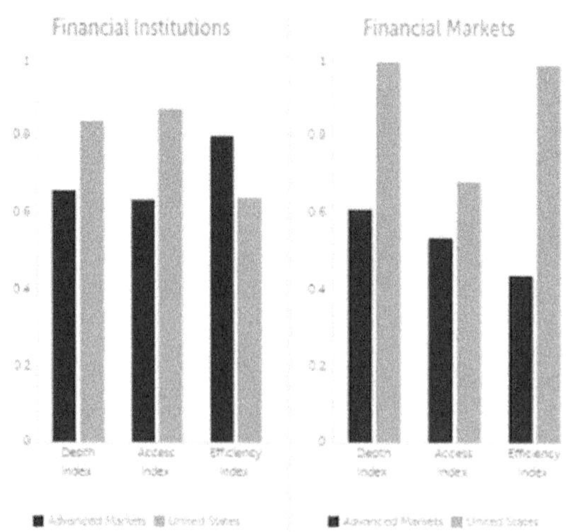

METHOD

Frequency Domain Causality Test

In traditional causality tests conducted by Granger (1969) and Toda-Yamamoto (1995), only one statistic is calculated for all terms and the causality analysis is carried out on this value. Through the frequency domain, causality test all terms are divided into three as short, mid and long term and the causality relationship is investigated. These terms are divided into three frequency terms and frequency value ranges are defined for long term between 0.01 and 0.05, for mid-term between 1.00 and 1.50 and for short term between 2.00 and 2.50. Since the causality is analyzed by dividing all terms into parts through this method, it presents the relationship between macro-economic variables more in detail (Taş et al., 2016, p. 11).

Within this context, based on the studies of Geweke (1982) and Hosoya suggesting the causality criteria in frequency domain we initially suppose that there is an observed two dimensional time series vector on $z_t=[x_t, y_t]$. It is assumed that the form of $t=1,\ldots,T, z_t$ has the finite order VAR representation (Breitung & Candelon, 2006).

$$\Theta(L)z_t=\varepsilon_t, \tag{1}$$

here

$$\Theta(L) = I - \Theta_p L^p, \quad L^k z_t = z_{t-k} \tag{2}$$

is 2x2 delayed polynomial.

It is assumed that the error vector with $\varepsilon_t E(\varepsilon_t)=0$ and $E(\varepsilon_t, \varepsilon_t') = \Sigma$ is white noise with, here Σ is positively defined. We ignore any of a determiner term in (1) for the ease of expression, but the model generally contains fixed, trend or artificial variables in empirical applications. Suppose that G is $G'G = \Sigma^{-1}$ sub-triangular matrix of Cholesky decomposition. so that it would $E(\eta_t, \eta_t') = I$ ve $\eta_t = G_{\varepsilon_t}$.
If it is assumed that the system is stable, MA representation of the system is:

$$z_t = \phi(L)\varepsilon_t = \begin{bmatrix} \phi_{11}(L) \phi_{12}(L) \\ \phi_{21}(L) \phi_{22}(L) \end{bmatrix} \begin{bmatrix} \varepsilon_{1t} \\ \varepsilon_{2t} \end{bmatrix} \tag{3}$$

$$= {}^{\cdot\cdot}(L)\eta_t = \begin{bmatrix} {}^{\cdot\cdot}{}_{11}(L) {}^{\cdot\cdot}{}_{12}(L) \\ {}^{\cdot\cdot}{}_{21}(L) {}^{\cdot\cdot}{}_{22}(L) \end{bmatrix} \begin{bmatrix} \eta_{1t} \\ \eta_{2t} \end{bmatrix}. \tag{4}$$

Here $\phi(L)=\phi(L)^{-1}$ and $\Psi(L)=\phi(L)G^{-1}$.

Using this demonstration x_t can be stated as the spectral density.

$$f_x(\omega) = \frac{1}{2\pi}\left\{\left|\Psi_{11}\left(e^{-i\omega}\right)\right|^2 + \left|\Psi_{12}\left(e^{-i\omega}\right)\right|^2\right\}. \tag{5}$$

e causality scale suggested by Geweke (1982) and Hosoya (1991) is:

$$M_{y\to x}\left(\omega\right) = log\left[\frac{2\pi f_x\left(\omega\right)}{\left|\Psi_{11}\left(e^{-i\omega}\right)\right|^2}\right]. \tag{6}$$

$$= log\left[1 + \frac{\left|\Psi_{12}\left(e^{-i\omega}\right)\right|^2}{\left|\Psi_{11}\left(e^{-i\omega}\right)\right|^2}\right]. \tag{7}$$

If it is $\left|\Psi_{12}\left(e^{-i\omega}\right)\right| = 0$., the scale is null, i.e $H_0 = M_{y\to x}\left(\omega\right) = 0$., in this case it can be sd that y does not lead to x in ω frequency.

EMPIRICAL ANALYSIS

Frequency domain causality test which was established by Geweke (1982) and Hosoya a developed by Breitung and Candelon (2006) and analyzed the causality relationship by dividing them into terms will be use in this study.

The causality relationship between Financial Institutions Development Index and Financial Markets Development Index taken from the Financial Development data base of IMF and economic growth and employment rate will be analyzed in the study. It is aimed to reveal thort, mid and long term causality between variables in the sample of G7 countries. Frequency domain causality analysis results for G7 are indicated below.

Canada

Frequency domain causality for Canada was analyzed and the results are indicated in Figure 11 using the graphs indicating the short, medium and long-term causality.

No short, medium and long term causality was found for Canada between the unemployment rate and financial institution development. When the causality between unemployment rate and financial markets, a long term causality from unemployment rate to financial markets was found. There is a short and midterm causality from financial markets to unemployment. From this point of view, it can be said that the development in financial markets influences the employment in short and midterm.

No short, mid and long term causality was found between growth and financial institution development. When the causality between growth and financial markets is analyzed, there is a short and midterm causality from financial markets to growth rate. Therefore, is was determined that the development in financial markets increased the growth in short and midterm.

Figure 11. Frequency Domain Causality Analysis Between Unemployment, Growth and Financial Development for Canada

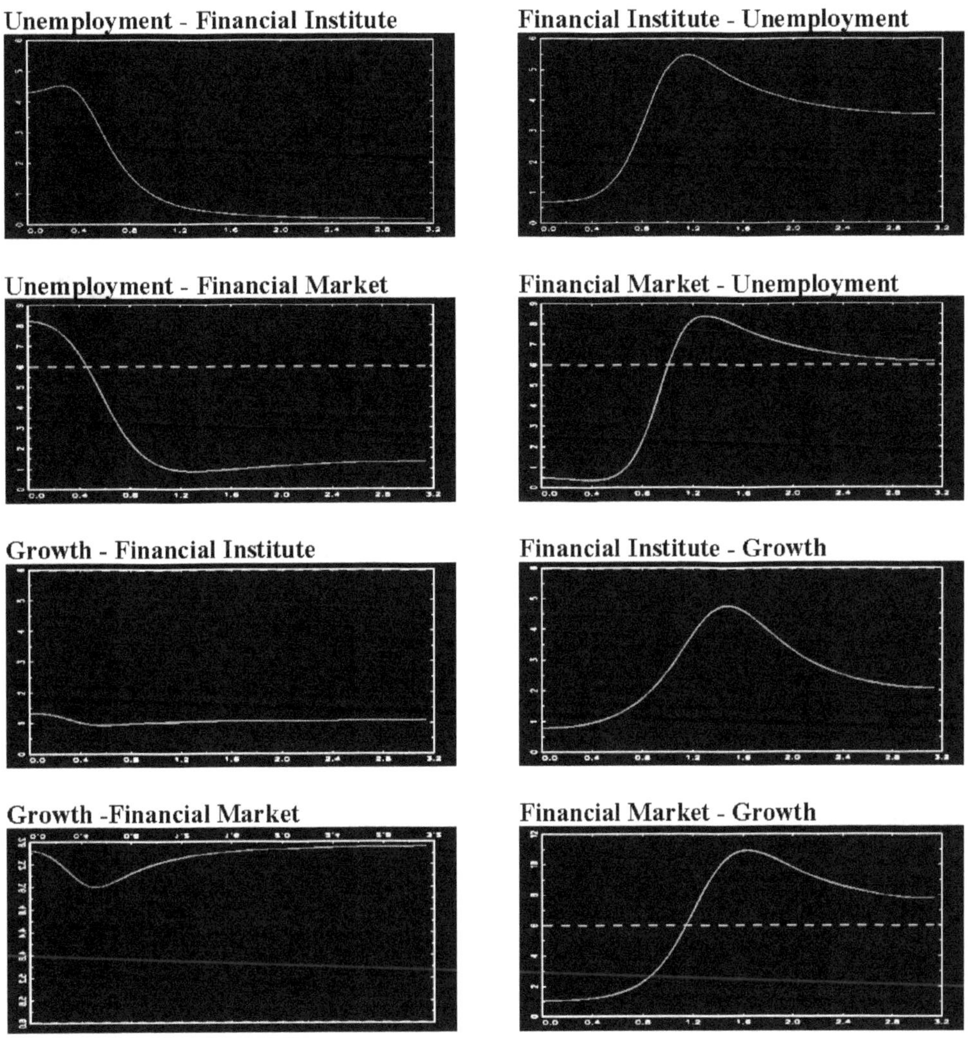

France

Frequency domain causality for France was analyzed and the results are indicated in Figure 12, which consists of graphs indicating short, medium and long-term causality.

No short, medium and long-term causality was found between unemployment rate and the development of financial institutions for France. When the causality between the unemployment rate and financial markets was analyzed, it was observed that no short, medium and long-term causality was found. From this point of view, it can be said that the development in financial markets and financial institutions does not affect the employment in short, medium and long-term in France.

Figure 12. Frequency Domain Causality Analysis Between Unemployment, Growth and Financial Development for France

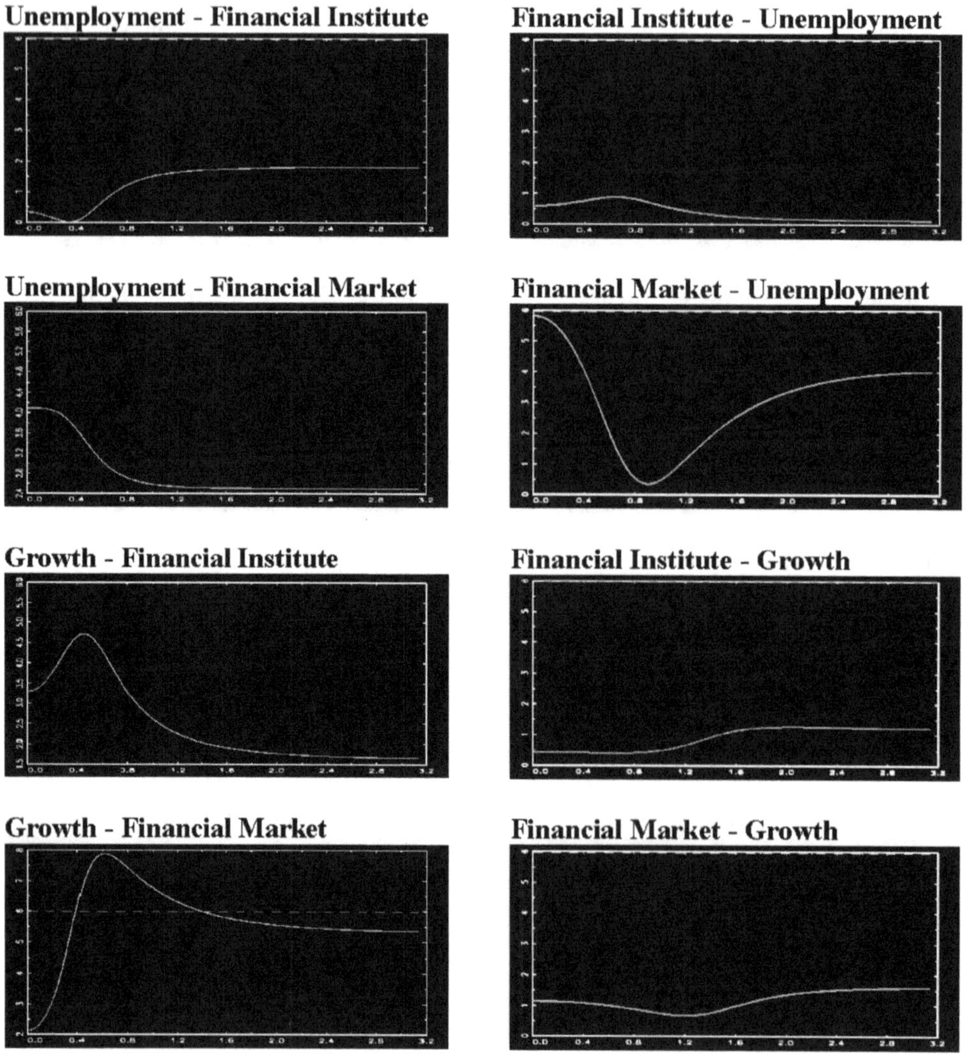

No short, medium and long-term causality was found between growth and development of financial institutions. When the causality between growth and financial markets is analyzed, there is medium-term causality from growth rate to financial markets. No short, medium and long-term causality was found from the financial markets to the growth rate. Therefore, it was identified that the development in economic growth contributed to the development of financial markets in medium-term.

Germany

Frequency domain causality for Germany was analyzed and the results are indicated in Figure 13, using the graphs indicating the short, medium and long-term causality.

Figure 13. Frequency Domain Causality Analysis Between Unemployment, Growth and Financial Development for Germany

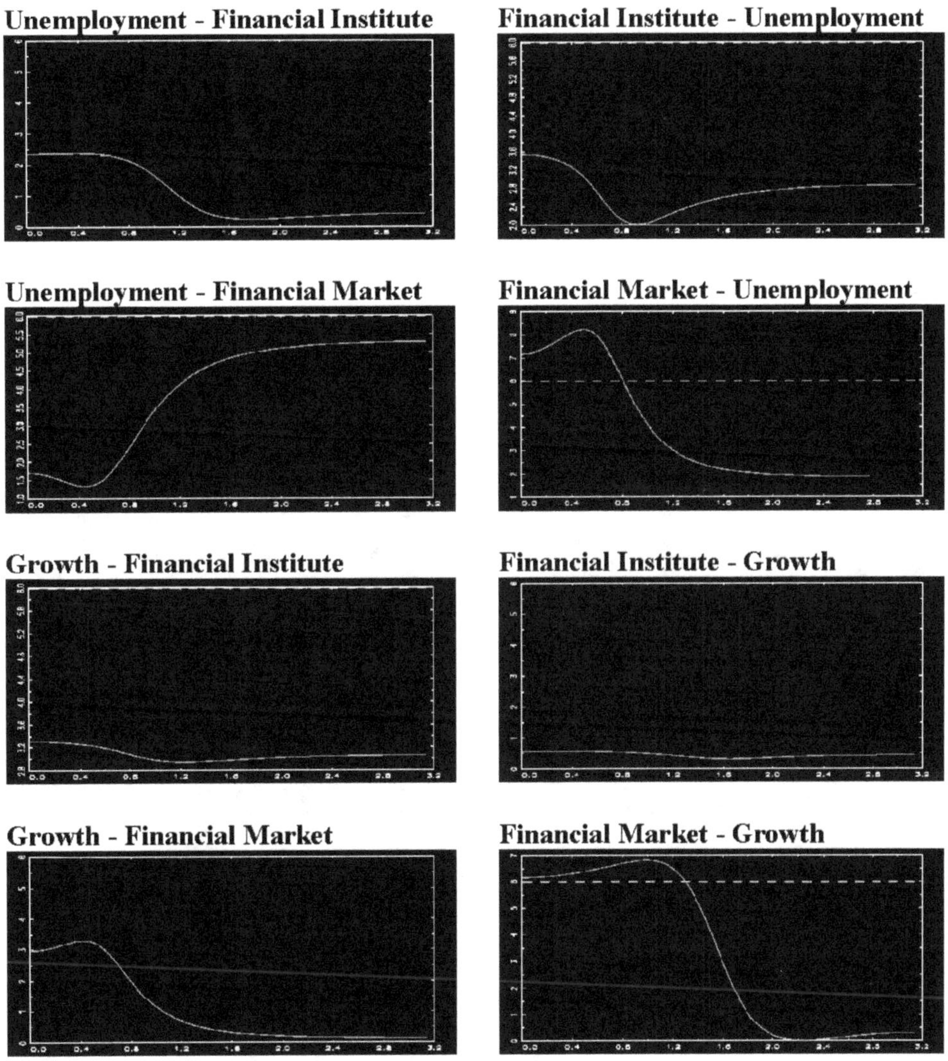

No short, medium and long-term causality was found between unemployment rate and the development of financial institutions for Germany. When the causality between unemployment rate and financial markets was analyzed, it was concluded that there was no causality from the unemployment rate to the financial markets; however, there was a long-term causality from the financial markets to the unemployment. From this point of view, it can be said that the development in financial markets affects the employment in long-term.

No short, medium and long-term causality was found between growth and development of financial institutions. When the causality between the growth and the financial markets is analyzed, there is medium and long-term causality from the financial markets to the growth. Therefore, it was determined that the development in financial markets increased the economic growth in medium and long-term.

Italy

Frequency domain causality indicating the short, medium and long-term causality for Italy was analyzed and the results from the graphs are indicated in Figure 14.

No short, medium and long-term causality was found between unemployment rate and the development of financial institutions for Italy. When the causality between employment rate and financial markets was analyzed, no causality could be determined for any terms. Similarly, there is no short, medium and long-term causality from the financial markets to the unemployment. From that point of view, we can say that the development in financial markets does not affect the employment.

Figure 14. Frequency Domain Causality Analysis Between Unemployment, Growth and Financial Development for Italy

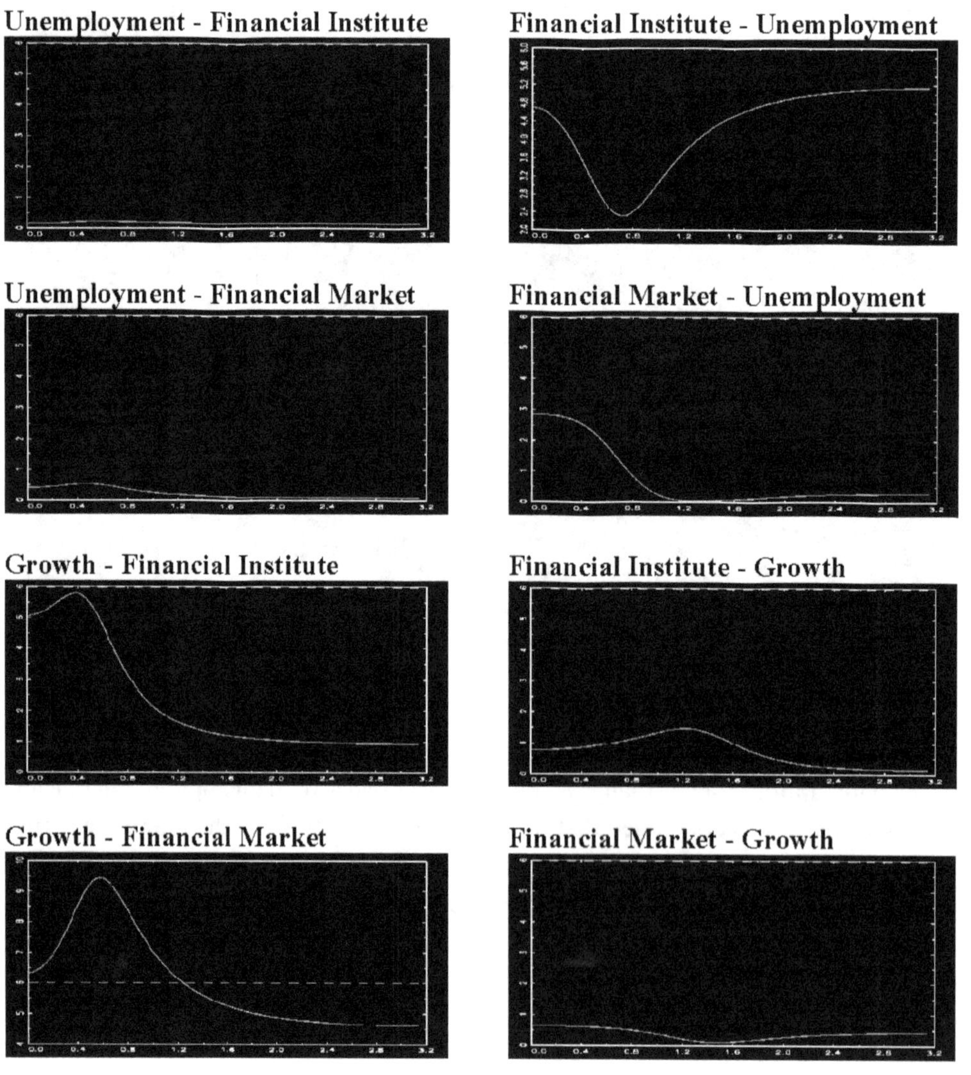

No short, medium and long-term causality was found between the growth and the development of financial institutions. When the causality between the growth and the financial markets is analyzed, there is a medium and long-term causality from the growth rate to the financial markets. There is no causality from the financial markets to the growth rate. Therefore, it was determined that the increase in economic growth contributed to the development of financial markets.

Japan

Frequency domain causality indicating the short, medium and long-term causality for Japan was analyzed and the results from the graphs are indicated in Figure 15.

Figure 15. Frequency Domain Causality Analysis Between Unemployment, Growth and Financial Development for Japan

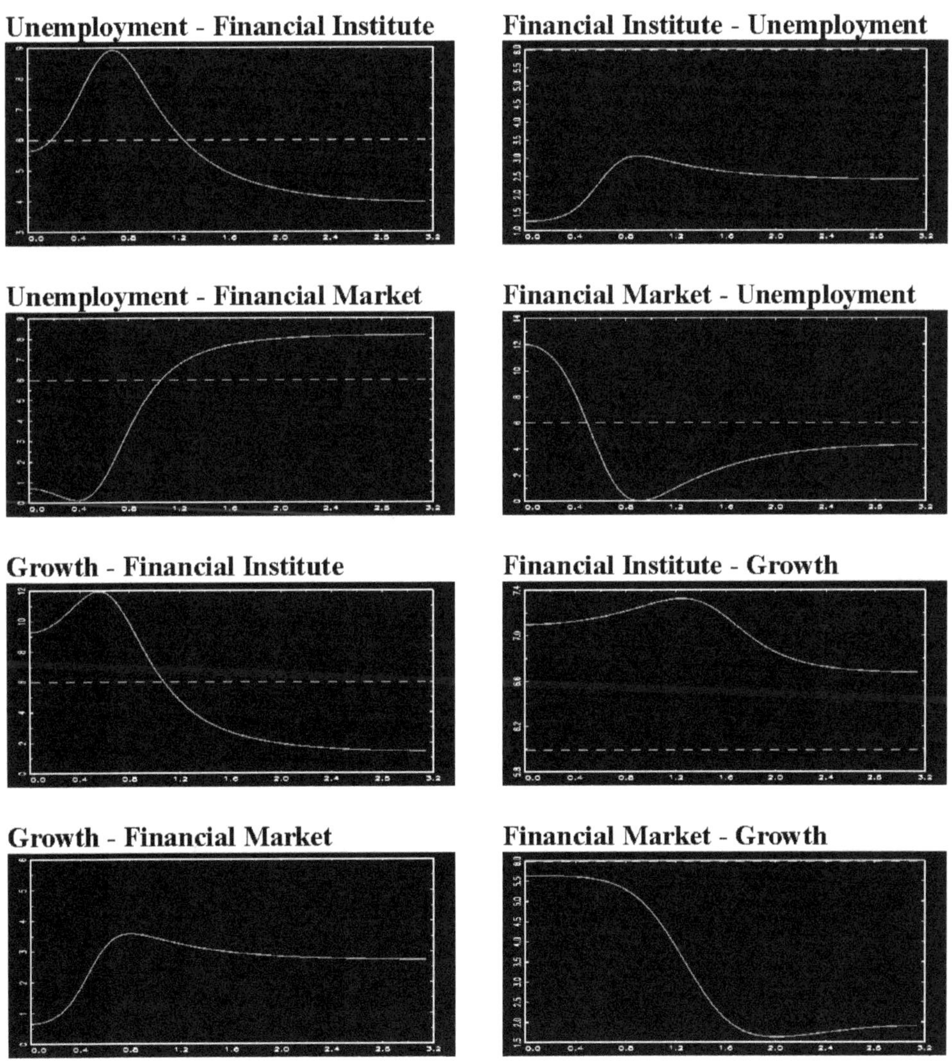

A medium and long-term causality from the unemployment to the development of financial institutions was found for Japan. However, no causality was determined from the development of financial institutions to the unemployment. When the causality between the unemployment rate and the financial markets was analyzed, a short and medium-term causality was found from the unemployment rate to the financial markets. There is a long-term causality from the financial markets to the unemployment. From this point of view, it can be seen that the development in financial institutions does not affect the unemployment; however, the change in unemployment affects the development in financial institutions in medium and long-term. Therefore, it can be said that the development in financial markets affects the employment in medium and long-term.

A medium and long-term causality was found between the growth and the financial institutions. When the causality between the growth and the financial markets is analyzed, there is no short, medium and long-term causality from the financial markets to the growth rate. Therefore, it can be said that the development in financial institutions affected the economic growth in short, medium and long-term. Although it was determined that the development in financial markets did not affect the economic growth.

United Kingdom

Frequency domain causality indicating the short, medium and long-term causality for United Kingdom was analyzed and the results from the graphs are indicated in Figure 16.

A long-term causality was found between the unemployment rate and the development of financial institutions for United Kingdom. When the causality between the unemployment rate and the financial markets was analyzed, it was concluded that there was no causality from the unemployment rate to the financial markets. There is no causality from the financial markets to the unemployment. From this point of view, it can be said that a change in employment affects the financial markets in medium-term.

Short, medium and long-term causality was found between the growth and the development of financial institutions. However, no causality was found from the development of financial institutions to the growth. When the causality between the growth and the financial markets is analyzed, there is no causality from the financial markets to the growth rate and from the growth rate to the financial markets. Therefore, it can be said that the development in financial markets does not affect the economic growth.

United States

Frequency domain causality indicating the short, medium and long-term causality for the United States was analyzed and the results from the graphs are indicated in Figure 17.

No causality was found in short, medium and long-term between the unemployment rate and the financial institutions for the United States. When the causality between the unemployment rate and the financial markets was analyzed, no causality was detected from the unemployment rate to the financial markets in any terms. From this point of view, it can be said that the development in financial markets did not affect the employment.

A long-term causality was found between the growth and the development of financial institutions. When the causality between the growth and the financial markets is analyzed, there is a medium and long-term causality from the growth rate to the financial markets. However, no short, medium and long-term causality was found from the financial markets to the growth rate. Therefore, it can be said that the increase in economic growth affects the development in financial markets in medium and long-term.

Figure 16. Frequency Domain Causality Analysis Between Unemployment, Growth and Financial Development for United Kingdom

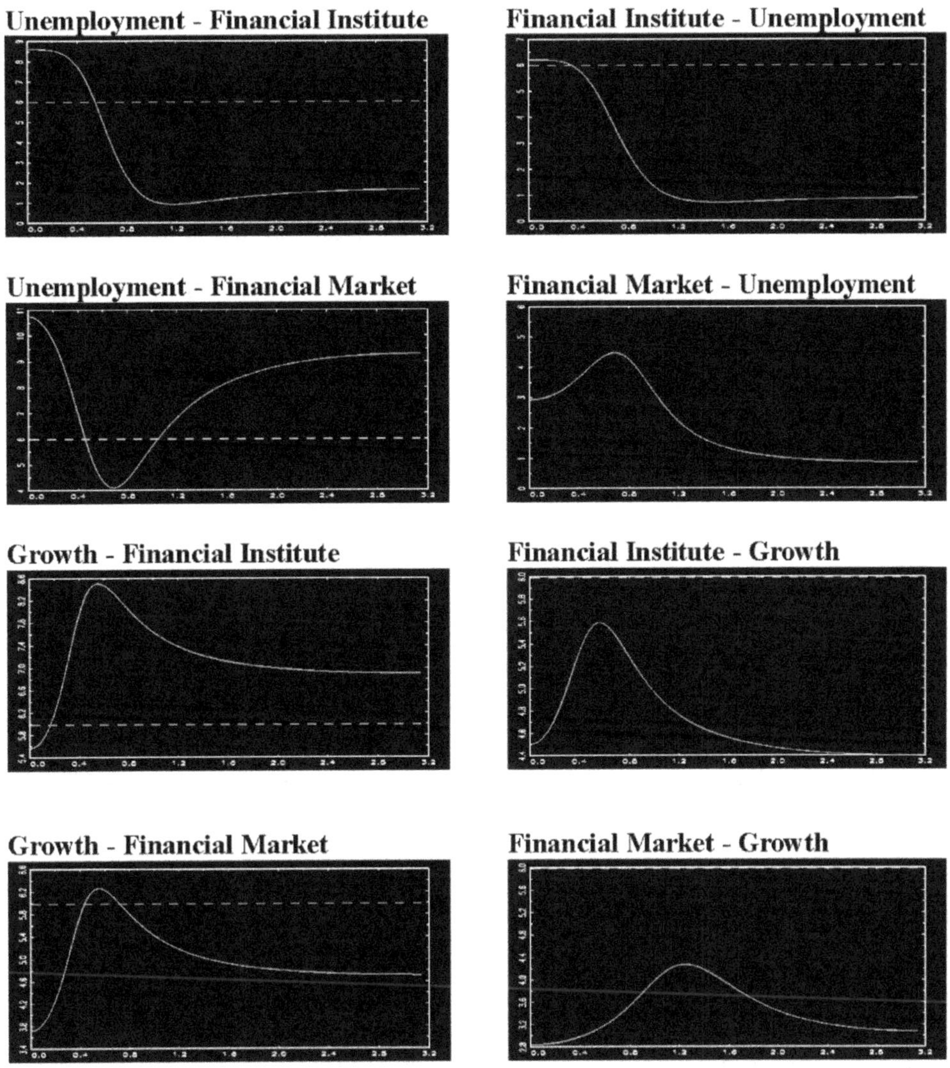

FUTURE RESEARCH DIRECTIONS

Developing economies, as part of their overall strategy, aim to increase the accessibility of financial services to low-income households and firms, namely financial services, for the stable development of financial markets (Morgan, 2014). Achieving savings through financial institutions in a highly inclusive financial market and increasing credit availability are seen as an important factor in sustainable economic development. In this respect, the impact of financial development on employment and growth for G7 countries was examined. As a result of the findings, short, medium and long-term causations were identified and brought into literature. In this context, it is aimed to provide a basis for the studies to be done in depth investigation on the reasons of financial development.

Figure 17. Frequency Domain Causality Analysis Between Unemployment, Growth and Financial Development for United States

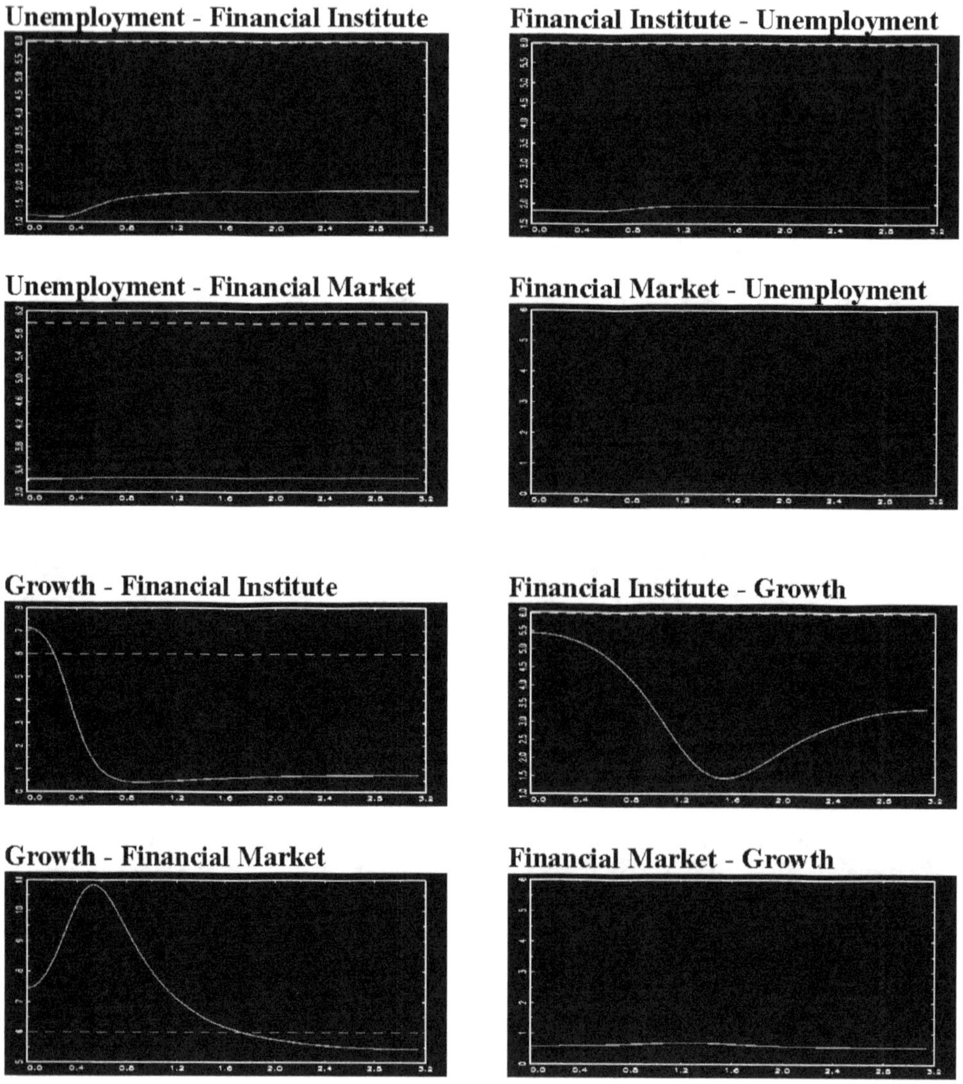

CONCLUSION

The importance of investment in the growth and development of economies has always been emphasized. It is commonly understood fact that the innovations promoting development become possible by the power of financing, when the economies run in their normal course. Hence, increasing financial support is in parallel with the development of financial markets. Accordingly, not only the development of financial markets contributes to the stable growth in economies, but also, they lead to a rapid increase in employment as well.

From this aspect, the causality relationship between the development level of financial institutions of G7 countries, the unemployment rate and the economic growth was then analyzed in short, medium and long-term, using frequency domain causality analysis. It was identified that the development in financial markets of Canada affected the employment and the economic growth in short and medium-term. We can see that the development in the financial markets and financial institutions of France did not affect the employment in short, medium and long-term; however, the development in economic growth contributed to the development of financial markets in medium-term. It was identified that the development in financial markets of Germany affected the employment in long-term and also the development in financial markets increased the economic growth in medium and long-terms.

While it can be said that the development in financial markets of Italy did not affect the employment in short, medium and long-term, we can see that the increase in economic growth contributed to the development of financial markets in medium and long-term. It was determined that the development of financial markets in Japan affected the employment in medium and long-term and also the development in financial markets affected the employment in short and medium-term. At the same time, it was identified that the development in financial institutions of Japan affected the economic growth in short, medium and long-term. It was concluded that the development in financial markets of United Kingdom increased the employment in long-term and also affected the employment in medium-term. Additionally, it was observed that the growth in economy in United Kingdom affected the development of financial institutions in short, medium and long-term. Finally, it was concluded that the development in financial markets of United States did not affect the employment; however, the development in economic growth affected the development in financial markets in medium and long-term.

REFERENCES

Aslan, Ö. & Korap, H. L. (2006). Financial Developments Economic Growth Relationship in Turkey. Muğla University Journal of the Institute of Social Sciences, 17.

Bayar, Y., Şaşmaz, M. Ü., & Öztürk, Ö. F. (2017). Financial Development and Tax Revenues: Evidence from OECD Countries. *Eurasian Academy of Sciences Eurasian Business & Economic Journal*, *12*, 51–63. doi:10.17740/eas.econ.2017-V12-4

Breitung, J., & Candelon, B. (2006). Testing for Short and Long-Run Causality: A Frequency-Domain Approach. *Journal of Econometrics*, *132*(2), 363–378. doi:10.1016/j.jeconom.2005.02.004

Chen, G., & Chen, S. (2016). Financial Development, Labor Participation, and Employment in Urban China. *Emerging Markets Finance & Trade*, *52*, 754–764. doi:10.1080/1540496X.2016.1116285

Comin, D., & Nanda, R. (2019). Financial development and technology diffusion. *IMF Economic Review*, *67*(2), 395–419. doi:10.105741308-019-00078-0

Demetriades, O. P., & Hussein, A. K. (1996). Does financial development cause economic growth? Time-series evidence from 16 countries. *Journal of Development Economics*, *51*(2), 387–411. doi:10.1016/S0304-3878(96)00421-X

Demirgüç-Kunt, A. (2017). Hot Off The Press. The Global Financial Development Report 2017/2018: Bankers without Borders.

Durusu-Ciftci, D., Ispir, M. S., & Yetkiner, H. (2017). Financial development and economic growth: Sometheory and More Evidence. *Journal of Policy Modeling*, *39*(2), 290–306. doi:10.1016/j.jpolmod.2016.08.001

Geweke, J. (1982). Measurement of Lineer Dependence and Feedback Between Multiple Time Series. *Journal of the American Statistical Association*, *77*(378), 304–324. doi:10.1080/01621459.1982.10477803

Goldsmith, R. W. (1969). *Financial structure and development*. New Haven, CT: Yale University Press.

Granger, C. W. J. (1969). Investigating Causal Relationship by Econometric Models and Cross-Spectral Methods. *Econometrica*, *37*(3), 424–438. doi:10.2307/1912791

Hosoya, Y. (1991). The Decomposition and Measurement of the Interdependency Between Second-Order Stationary Processes. *Probability Theory and Related Fields*, *88*(4), 429–444. doi:10.1007/BF01192551

IMF. (2016). Financial Development *Database*. IMF.

Jeanneney, S., & Kpodar, K. (2011). Financial Development and Poverty Reduction: Can There be a Benefit without a Cost? *The Journal of Development Studies*, *47*(1), 143–163. doi:10.1080/00220388.2010.506918

McKinnon, R. I. (1973). *Money and capital in economic development*. Washington, DC: The Brookings Institution.

Morgan, P. J., & Pontines, V. (2014). *Financial Stability and Financial Inclusion.* ADBI Working Paper Series, No.488.

Sahay, R., Cihak, M., N'Diaye, P., Barajas, A., & Bi, R. (2015). *Rethinking Financial Deepening: Stability and Growth in Emerging Markets*. IMF Staff Dıscussıon Note.

Schumpeter, J. A. (1911). *The Theory Of Economic Development: An İnquiry İnto Profits, Capital, Credit, İnterest, and The Business Cycle* (R. Opie, Trans.). Cambridge, MA: Harvard University Press.

Shaw, E. S. (1973). *Financial deepening in economic development*. Oxford, UK: Oxford University.

Taş, S., Ağır, H., & İğde, G. (2016). Causality Analysis of the Export and Economic Growth: The Case of Turkey. EconWorld, 2016, Barcelona, Spain.

Toda, H. Y., & Yamamoto, T. (1995). Statistical Inference in Vector Autoregressions With Possibly Integrated Processes. *Journal of Econometrics*, *66*(2), 225–250. doi:10.1016/0304-4076(94)01616-8

World Bank. (2018). *Global Financial Development Report 2017/2018*. Washington, DC: Bankers Without Borders.

Chapter 2
The Concept of Shared Value in the Theory of Sustainable Finance:
An Analysis From the OECD Countries' Perspective

Katarzyna Cheba
West Pomeranian University of Technology, Poland

Iwona Dorota Bąk
West Pomeranian University of Technology, Poland

ABSTRACT

The main purpose of this chapter is to identify the existing relations between the selected areas of sustainable development but carried out on the basis of the indicators describing the macroeconomic dimension of this development from the OECD countries' perspective. The theoretical basis for analyses is the concept of shared value, for the first time presented by Porter and Kramer in 2011. In this chapter, this proposition was applied to the studies carried out on the country level. For this purpose, the multi-dimensional statistical analysis was applied. The results of the study confirmed that on the current level of development, even in the case of the most developed countries, it is very difficult to find the shared space with the same level of development between these areas. In the same time, it is very important direction of further research and decisions undertaken on the macroeconomic level.

INTRODUCTION

The chapter presents both the theoretical and empirical aspects of the concept of creating a shared value but considered from a macroeconomic perspective. In the literature the concept of shared value is usually presented as actions taken by enterprises to achieve mutual benefits for both the enterprise and for the society. Some authors (Porter, Kramer, 2011) even indicate that this is another step in the evolution

DOI: 10.4018/978-1-7998-1033-9.ch002

of the concept of corporate social responsibility (CSR). However, it should be noted that in this chapter the concept of shared value can be explained as an area of similar changes in different areas of countries development. It means searching for areas characterized by a similar level of development in countries around the world. In the work, this development was considered through the prism of changes taking place in various areas of sustainable development (in the perspective of: human - economy - environment) and a relatively new area describing the support of this development from the side of public finance. An important area of these analyzes is the search for mutual dependencies between areas that make up a comprehensive assessment of the current level of sustainable development and the area describing the financing of this development. Such considerations and research results were already presented in the literature on the subject but only from the sustainable development perspective (Bąk, Cheba, 2018; Szopik-Depczyńska, Cheba, Bąk, Stajniak, Simboli, Ioppolo, 2018). In the work they were additionally expanded with analyzes related to the searching of similar direction of changes in sustainable development supported by finance.

Research on the relations between these areas considered in relation to OECD countries is the main goal of the work. For this purpose the data set published every year by World Economic Forum (WEF) was used. This database contains information on many different areas of development of over 150 economy of the world collected for over 10 years. The chapter compares the results of the last survey from 2017/2018.

The research used methods of multidimensional statistical analysis, including zero-unitarization method and correspondence analysis. These methods in the literature are commonly used to study the relationships between the appropriate categories of quantitative and qualitative variables (correspondence analysis) and to point out the best and the worst developed countries taking into account every considered area of analysis (the zero-unitarization method).

The added value of the methods used will be the classification of OECD countries due to the identified type of connections occurring between the factors included in the study, describing different dimensions of the created shared value in macroeconomic terms.

The chapter is divided into 7 sections. The first presents the aim of the research supported by theoretical background. In the next section a detailed literature review is presented. The next one is dedicated to the presentation of the statistical indicators that are the subjects of the study. The fourth section contains a description of the mathematical methods used. In the next two sections the research results are presented, and the last one contains conclusions and recommendations for further research.

LITERATURE REVIEW

In recent years, in the literature of the subject, more and more attention has been devoted to various types of corporate social responsibility concepts (Prahalad, Ramaswamy, 2004; Chapple, Moon, 2005; Aguilera, Rupp, Williams, Ganapathi, 2007; Carroll, 1991, 2008, 2015; Lindgreen, Swaen, Campbell, 2009). In the literature from early years of the twenty-first centuries the various business theories and models related to the long-term sustainable approach for inclusive growth started to appear, namely: sustainable value (Hart, Milstein, 2003; Laszlo, 2008), blended value (Bonini, Emerson, 2005), and firm-value maximization (Jensen, 2001). This interest is, among others, the effect of the crisis of social trust in commonly used corporate practices, very often focused primarily on maximizing profits for investors. Of course, many of today's corporations are also involved in social activities; however, it is usually classified as: cost in the company's budget, possibly charitable activity that can be deducted from the tax base, investment in the company's image or some kind of necessary expenditure, which lack can lead to break off business contacts.

Threats related to the perception in this way of expenses related to the activity that is part of the concept of corporate social responsibility in the subject literature for the first time are described by M.E. Porter and M.R. Kramer in the article entitled "Creating Shared Value", which was published by "Harvard Business Review" at the beginning of 2011. According to the authors of this new concept of creating a shared value also known as CSV, the search for business opportunities in such a way that it provides added value both for the company as well as its environment, in particular the local environment, is a better strategy of action than the solutions proposed so far created in accordance with the CSR concept. In this paper (Porter, Kramer, 2011), the shared value was defined as: „policies and operating practices that enhance the competitiveness of a company while simultaneously advancing the economic and social conditions in the communities in which it operates". According to these authors the CSV concept is related to the three approaches: reconceiving products and markets, redefining productivity in the value chain, and creating industrial clusters to support the region in which the enterprise is located (Porter, Kramer, 2011).

It is also worth mentioning that already in 1999, these authors pointed to the need to take into account the economic dimension of corporate activities aimed at helping the public and the environment. This problem is presented in the articles entitled "Philanthropy's New Agenda: Creating Value" (1999), and then in "The Competitive Advantage of Corporate Philanthropy" from 2002, which were also published in the Harvard Business Review. Another work in this field is an article by S.L. Hart and M.B. Milstein in "Creating sustainable value" (2003), focusing on the attempt to combine the concept of sustainable development and value creation theory, in which sustainable value was defined as: "strategies and practices contributing to a more sustainable development of the world, while enhancing shareholder value". References to similar concepts can also be found, among others in:

- Publications of the Roberts Enterprise Development Fund (REDF) from 2000, on the initiative of which the term was created: Social Return On Investment - SROI, which is defined as a method for measuring non-economic values mainly: environmental and social but mostly concerning non-profit entities,
- The work of J. Emerson (2003), who, referring to the concept of "blenden value" he created himself, underlined the need to create value in three dimensions: economic, environmental and social,
- The recent strategic management literature, in which corporate economic and social values were linked as a value for shareholders and stakeholders (Verboven, 2011) or social benefit along with business value (Pfitzer, Bockstette, Stamp, 2013),
- A co-authored work published by: G. Hills, P. Russel, V. Borgonovi, A. Doty, and L. Iyer (2012), who treat CSV as the basis for creating economic value by "better serving existing markets, accessing new ones, or developing innovative products and services that meet social needs",
- In the proposal of M. Scholz and G. De los Reyes (2015), according to which the attractiveness of shared value framework is similar to the "mantra of fundamental compatibility of societal and entrepreneurial interest",

- In the paper published by M. Kramer and M.W. Pfitzer in 2017 - according to them creating a shared value requires cooperation with local communities and other entities, including: non-governmental organizations and government, which together with companies could create an eco-system of shared value.

It is worth indicating that according to Breidbach and Maglio (2016) the shared value has promoted the societal and entrepreneurial strategies for better corporate performance leading to the benefit of the society.

While in the corporate practice, this concept was presented for first time by Nestle, which has been publishing reports related to the application of this concept in corporate management since 2007. It should be also notice that in the literature, it is emphasized in particular that the „shared value" is not "social responsibility, philanthropy, or sustainability". According to Porter and Kramer (2011) it is "a new way for companies to achieve economic success". These authors present this new concept as a management strategy in which the social problems become areas of business opportunities. In the philanthropy and CSR the main effort of corporations is related with minimizing the harm business has on society. While the shared value focuses the companies leaders on maximizing the competitiveness during the solving of social problems, development of talents and finding the new solutions accepted by both sides: society and business.

While in the literature, the enterprises' activity to the pursuit of creating common value seems to be a relatively well described concept, there are no examples of understanding and the possibility of realizing this concept on the macroeconomic grounds, e.g. from the perspective of managing a country or a region. Meanwhile, examples of such activities aimed at creating common value for the state as a superior unit in the sense of, for example, its economy and society are numerous. One can, among others mention: various social programs aimed at supporting the fertility of residents of the European Union countries, which on the one hand are government support for families with children, on the other - their implementation is also considered through the prism of economic values related to, for example, increased internal consumption, a frequent form of support there are also various forms of economic intervention by the governments of countries, for example through access to cheap loans, deleveraging of selected branches of the economy, or organization of public works aimed at stimulating local labor markets.

According to the authors, it is justified to analyze the process of creating a shared value in macroeconomic terms, and so in relation to actions undertaken, for example, by governments of countries whose goal is, among others, financing of programs and projects supporting social, economic and environmental development. What is important is the relationship between the level of development achieved in these areas and the level of financing programs supporting their development, considered both through the prism of expenditure for these purposes and also the proceeds from the development of these areas. It is also worth stressing that such analyzes are also an important area of research within the so-called sustainable finances (Emerson, 2003; Sergi, Fidanoski, Ziolo, Naumovski, 2018), which have only recently become the subject of the first studies and scientific reports.

In Polish literature, some kind of connection with this concept can be found in works (Jabłoński, Jabłoński, 2014) presenting the value of the region as the sum of various types of partial values. According to these authors the value of the region is „...the sum of the various values produced by the region (including the financial, investment, social and human capital) (...), which created the potential of the region, on which its development may be based on...".The shared area of different partial areas is the region value, which can also be considered in relation to smaller and larger spatial units.

In the work this concept, as well as the proposition of Porter and Kramer (2011), were used as a basis for searching for common areas (of development and values) considered in the macroeconomic context. This means searching for those areas of development that in traditional economics can stand in some kind of opposition to each other, e.g. economic development is very often carried out at the expense of the environment, or as in countries such as China at the expense of social security and lack of decent working conditions and life. In graphical terms, this concept was presented as follows (Fig. 1):

However, it should be remembered that only recently have governments in a more systemic way taken actions, the purpose of which is, for example, to provide priorities for financing environment-friendly investments, such as green technologies. Recently, research has also been carried out, the aim of which is to assess the current level of development in the world of countries in the field of so-called "green economy". In the same time the regulations on providing citizens with decent working conditions are the standard in highly developed countries.

Hence, in the work, answers are sought for questions related to identifying countries in which similar social, environmental changes are taking place along with economic development and financial support for this development.

THE DESCRIPTION OF THE STATISTICAL DATA

The basis of analyzes presented in this chapter are the values of indicators describing the competitiveness of the world economies published annually by the World Economic Forum (WEF) in the reports: "The Global Competitiveness Index" (GCI). The authors decided to use this data set because their complexity

Figure 1. Areas creating the shared value of countries
Source: own elaboration

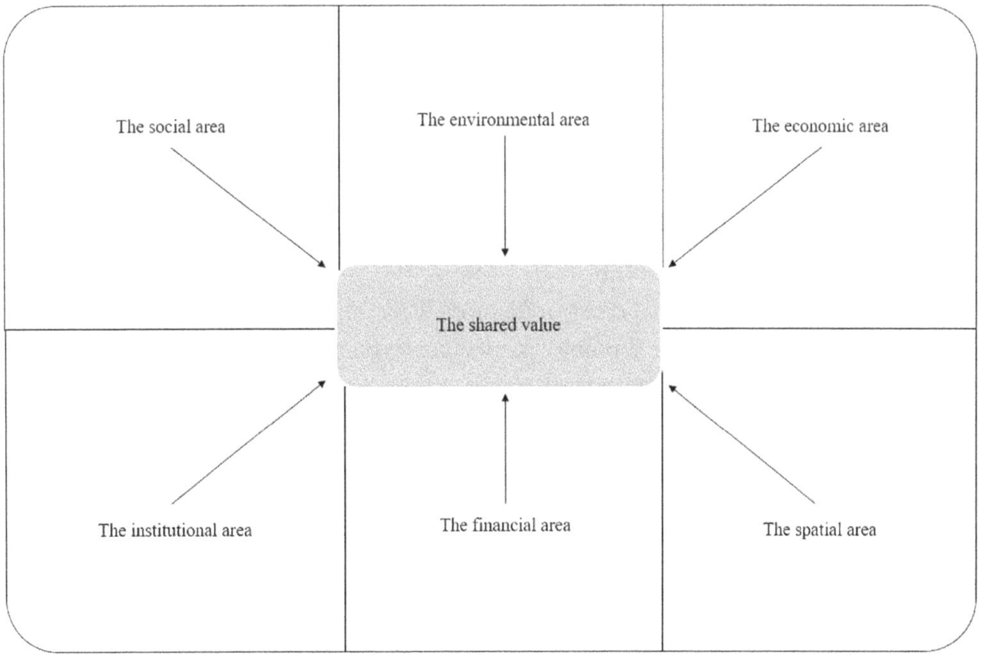

and relation to various areas of development of countries in the world. The WEF database has got only one limitation. It does not take into account activities directly referring to competitiveness considered from the perspective of environmental protection. However, this is a very important direction of research and identifying countries in which the socio-economic development is implemented without harming the natural environment is a very important direction of future analyzes.

In accordance with the methodology for measuring the level of competitiveness of international economies proposed by WEF as the measures of this level, the results obtained by individual countries in the twelve following pillars are assumed: F_1 – institution, F_2 – infrastructure, F_3 – macroeconomic environment, F_4 – health and primary education, F_5 – higher education and training, F_6 – goods market efficiency, F_7 – labor market efficiency, F_8 – financial market development, F_9 – technological readiness, F_{10} – market size, F_{11} – business sophistication, F_{12} – innovation.

In total, the entire database contains information on over 100 indicators describing nearly 150 countries around the world. The results of the last available report from 2017-2018 were used in the work. It was suggested, that due to the purpose of the study, which is related to the search for dependencies between areas describing the sustainable development of countries around the world and indicators describing the financial area of this development, these indicators have been assigned to these areas. It means a completely different arrangement than in the research presented by the WEF and their division into five groups describing the development: social, economic, institutional, spatial and financial. In accordance with the adopted assumptions, the indexes divided in this way were used to:

1. Identification of groups of countries similar due to the level of development achieved in each of the analyzed areas,
2. Indication the relationship between the results of countries achieved in these areas.

The countries belonging to the Organization for Economic Co-operation and Development (OECD) were selected for the study. It is an international organization with an economic profile that brings together 36 highly developed and democratic states of Europe and the world. The literature on the subject indicates that the changes taking place in this group of countries are ahead of the trends of changes taking place in other countries of the world. Therefore, it is important to know the current level of development of OECD countries in areas highlighted for research.

The initial database created a total of 111 indicators, including: 26 indicators describing the social area, 37 - describing the economic area, 12 - spatial area, 21 - institutional area and 14 - financial area. All indicators that created this database were characterized by high spatial variability. The estimates of the coefficients of variation, which are normally used for this purpose, definitely exceeded 10% (V_s> 10%). However, it should be noted that many indicators were very strongly correlated. This concerned mainly the indicators assessed on the 7 point Likert scale (where 7 is the best), which in the study are used to get to know the opinions of respondents (mainly representatives of foreign enterprises operating in the assessed country). The high level of correlation of indicators assessed as part of surveys is in this case the effect of duplication of information and assessments made by respondents who are willing to similarly assess individual areas that make up the assessment of the competitiveness of countries around the world.

The effect is a significant reduction in the number of indicators used in further research, which was also confirmed by the results of the selection obtained on the basis of Hellwig's parametric method. The studies should not include indicators that are strongly correlated because they are the carrier of the same information. Eventually, to the final set of features which are characterized by high spatial variability with low correlation within the selected sets and asymmetric distribution, the following indicators were selected: in the social area only 8 indicators, in the economic area – 7 indicators, in the spatial area – 6 indicators, in the institutional area – only 3 indicators and in the financial area – 6 indicators. The detailed list of these indicators contained Table 1. In this table, the stimulants are numbers whose bigger values indicate a higher level of progress of a given phenomenon, while the destimulants are diagnostic characteristics whose smaller values signify a higher level of development (Bąk, 2010). The indicators chosen for the study represent 10 out of 12 pillars assessed by WEF. There are no indicators describing 12th pillar: Innovation, which were qualified to describe the economic development area of the surveyed countries.

RESEARCH METHOD

In the work to analyze the relationships between the highlighted areas, an analysis of correspondence was used, which is one of the methods for statistical, multiple analysis. The method makes it possible to recognize accurately the coexistence of the categories of variables (or objects) measured on a nominal scale (Gatnar, 2008; Stanimir, 2005). The chapter proposes that the computational algorithm of this

Table 1. The final set of indicators divided into selected area of sustainable development

Area	Indicators
Social	• from the 4th pillar: Health and primary education: X_{11D} – tuberculosis cases/100,000 pop.; X_{12D} – infant mortality, deaths/1,000 live births, • from the 5th pillar: Higher education and training: X_{13S} – secondary education enrollment, gross %; X_{14S} – tertiary education enrollment, gross %; X_{15S} – quality of the education system, 1-7 (best); • from the 7th pillar: Labor market efficiency: X_{16S} – flexibility of wage determination, 1-7 (best); X_{17S} – redundancy costs, weeks of salary; X_{18S} – effect of taxation on incentives to work, 1-7 (best).
Economic	• from the 6th pillar: Goods market efficiency: X_{21S} – effect of taxation on incentives to invest, 1-7 (best); X_{22D} – no. procedures to start a business; X_{23D} – no. days to start a business; X_{24S} – prevalence of foreign ownership, 1-7 (best); X_{25D} – trade tariffs, % duty; • from the 10th pillar: Market size: X_{26S} – domestic market size index, 1–7 (best); • from 11th pillar: Business sophistication: X_{27S} – control of international distribution, 1-7 (best).
Spatial	• from the 2nd pillar: Infrastructure: X_{31S} – quality of overall infrastructure, 1-7 (best); X_{32S} – quality of port infrastructure, 1-7 (best); X_{33S} – available airline seat km/week, millions; X_{34S} – fixed telephone lines/100 pop.; X_{35S} – mobile telephone subscriptions/100 pop., • from the 9th pillar: Technological readiness: X_{36S} – Int'l Internet bandwidth, kb/s per user.
Institutional	• from the 1st pillar: Institutions: X_{41S} – Public trust in politicians, 1-7 (best); X_{42S} – business costs of terrorism, 1-7 (best); X_{43S} – strength of investor protection, 0–10 (best).
Financial	• from the 3rd pillar: Macroeconomic environment: X_{51S} – government budget balance, % GDP; X_{52S} – gross national savings, % GDP; X_{53D} – inflation, annual % change (in this case even to big and to small - "in minus" – value of this indicator is not good, it was the reason way the absolute values were taken into account; X_{54D} – general government debt, % GDP; • from the 8th pillar: Financial market development: X_{55S} – financial services meeting business needs, 1-7 (best); X_{56S} – legal rights index, 0–10 (best).

Source: own elaboration based on WEF data, where every indicator was presented in the form of X_{ij}, where i denotes the considered area and j is the number of indicator, S or D is related to the character of indicator, i.e. S is stimulant and D – destimulant method should be used to search for relationships between highlighted areas, using for this purpose diagnostic features transformed in accordance with the method of zero unification (Kukuła, 2000). It means conducting research including the following 2 stages:

1. 1. Construction of rankings of OECD countries separately for each of the highlighted areas on the basis of diagnostic features selected for the study, transformed as follows:

for stimulant $z_{ij} = \dfrac{x_{ij} - \min_i x_{ij}}{\max_i x_{ij} - \min_i x_{ij}}, \quad \max_i x_{ij} \neq \min_i x_{ij}$ (1)

for destimulant $z_{ij} = \dfrac{\max_i x_{ij} - x_{ij}}{\max_i x_{ij} - \min_i x_{ij}}, \quad \max_i x_{ij} \neq \min_i x_{ij}$ (2)

The features transformed according this way were the basis for the estimation of taxonomic measures of development for each of the fifth areas. For this purpose the following formula was (Nowak, 1990):

$$z_i = \frac{1}{K} \sum_{k=1}^{K} z_{ki} \tag{3}$$

where: z_i – value of a taxonomic measure of development for i-object, z_{ki} – standardized value of k-feature in i-object, K – number of features examined.

Because the arithmetic average of the measure determined in this way equals one, it is possible to conduct the comparisons of the development of objects with multiple features. If the following inequality appears for the object examined: $z_i > 1$, then the object examined reaches a higher level of development than the average in the whole set of objects. In the case when $z_i < 1$, then the object examined reaches a lower level of development than the average in the set of the compared units (Nowak, 1990).

2. The application of the correspondence analysis for identifies the relations between the considered areas according the results obtained in the first stage of the analysis.

The starting point involves creating a complex contingency table (contingent, cross tabulation) which comprises the number of particular categories of variables adopted to specify n objects. In practical issues, the data recording system which is very often applied is the Burt matrix (Greenacre, 1984; Greenacre, 1994; Andersen, 1991; Lebart, Morineau, Warwicka, 1984). In the first step, it is required to create a complex matrix of Z indicators which comprises blocks (submatrices) referring to consecutive variables: $\mathbf{Z}=[\mathbf{Z}_{1,\ldots,}\mathbf{Z}_Q]$, where Q means the number of characteristics. The components of complex indicator matrix take only 0 and 1 values, depending on whether a particular object has the distinguished category of variable or not.

The Burt matrix results from equation: $\boldsymbol{B}=\boldsymbol{Z}^T\boldsymbol{Z}$. Then, we obtain the symmetrical block matrix with diagonal matrices containing the number of categories of characteristics, and outside the diagonal matrix there are contingency tables for each pair of analysed variables. The total number of each submatrix equals the number of analysed n units, and the total number of Burt matrix amounts to $n \bullet Q^2$. Since the Burt matrix is symmetrical ($b_{ij}=b_{ji}$), the boundary number of rows and columns are identical and are computed as follows:

$$\sum_{j=1}^{J} b_{ij} = b_{i\bullet} = b_{\bullet j=Q} = Q \cdot b_{ii} \tag{4}$$

where:

b_{ij} — components of the Burt matrix,
J — total number of categories of all characteristics.

The boundary frequency of rows and columns are equal and amount to:

$$p_{i\bullet} = \frac{Q \cdot b_{ii}}{n \cdot Q^2} \tag{5}$$

The values of $p_{i\bullet}$ are the components of diagonal matrix of boundary frequencies of rows and consequently the columns. At the same time, they are the components of vector of boundary frequencies **r**. The matrix of observed frequencies is computed as:

$$\mathbf{P} = \frac{1}{n \cdot Q^2}\mathbf{B} \tag{6}$$

The matrix B is symmetrical so we can indicate it will decompose but as per own values:

$$\mathbf{A} = \mathbf{D}_{\mathrm{r}}^{-1/2}(\mathbf{P} - \mathbf{r}\mathbf{r}^T)\mathbf{D}_{\mathrm{r}}^{-1/2} = \mathrm{U}“_B^2\mathbf{U}^T \tag{7}$$

where:

U – matrix of eigenvectors of matrix,
$“_B^2$ – diagonal matrix containing squares of singular values $\gamma_{B,k}^2 (k = 1,2,...,K;\ K = \sum_{q=1}^{Q}(J_q - 1)$ of matrix ***A***,
$\mathbf{J}_q$ – number of categories of characteristics q,
D_{r} – diagonal matrix of observed boundary frequencies of rows.

We can provide that $“_B^2 = ›_B$, where $\lambda_{B,k}$, are eigenvalues of matrix A. Therefore, we can observe the decomposition of matrix A as per eigenvalues, and the coordinates of characteristics categories are included in only one:

$$\mathbf{F} = \mathbf{D}_r^{-1/2}\mathbf{U}``_B \tag{8}$$

The dimension of actual space of the coexistence of answers to questions is determined under formula:

$$K = \sum_{q=1}^{Q}(J_q - 1) \tag{9}$$

Under Greenacre's criterion, we choose, as the best, the size of projection of the categories of variables where eigenvalues meet the condition: $\lambda_{B,k} > \frac{1}{Q}$.

To the assumed criterion for selecting the significant eigenvalues ($\lambda_{B,k} > \frac{1}{Q}$) Greenacre provides a manner to „improve" the results of the analysis of variables recorded in the form of Burt matrix (Greenacre, 1984):

$$\tilde{\lambda}_k = \left(\frac{Q}{q-1}\right)^2 \cdot \left(\sqrt{\lambda_{B,k}} - \frac{1}{Q}\right)^2 \tag{10}$$

where:

Q – number of variables,
$\lambda_{B,k}$ – k-th eigenvalue.

The conducted correspondence analysis give the results in graphic form of simultaneous occurrence of the categories of variables (Greenacre, Hastie, 1987; Goodman, 1986). It is possible by indicating points depicting the categories of variables at one-, two- or three-dimensional coordinate system, losing the smallest possible part of information on the actual structure of links between them. Upon interpreting the dispersion of points in graphs we need to consider the following elements: position of point relative to the centre of projection (the origin of coordinates), position of point relative to other points defining the categories of the same variable, position of point relative to the point defining the categories of another variable (Stanimir, 2005). If the point is positioned close to the origin of coordinates, it means that the profile determined for that point is close to average profile. The points positioned far from the centre of projection confirm the hypothesis on characteristics dependency. If two points defining different categories of the same variable are positioned close to each other, their profiles are similar and it is possible to combine the number of two categories into one without significant impact on the results of further research. Upon analysing the position of points defining the categories of two different variables we can confirm that there are relations between categories, if the points are positioned close to each other. However, if the points are positioned on the opposite sides of the centre of projection, it means that the categories fail to occur together and the frequency of both categories at the same time should be close to zero.

If the space larger than three is the best form to present the coexistence of characteristics, then we need to select another method for analysing the results. For such purpose, in the space of both smaller and larger size we can apply the methods of classification (Bąk, 2010). The categories of all analysed characteristics shall be defined as objects and the values of projection coordinates of each category are the variables. The methods of classification are also useful when the number of all options of characteristics is significant and the dispersion of points in the graph makes it impossible to distinguish the classes unambiguously.

STUDY RESULTS: THE RANKING OF THE OECD COUNTRIES

The obtained results of the classification of OECD countries within particular areas analyzed in the work are presented in the Table 2.

The results of classifications are significantly diversified. In the first place in the social area was classified Israel, followed by Belgium and Chile. However, in the last places in this ranking countries such as Mexico, Austria, and Italy were classified. The results of some countries, which are widely considered to be one of the most socially and economically developed countries in the world, are surprising. This applies, for example, to Austria, which in the social area was classified only on the 34th place. The classification of this country in such a remote place is on the one hand the effect of the indicators on the basis of which the ranking was created, on the other it results from the specificity of the group, which included the most developed countries in the world. Therefore, the results obtained by individual countries should not be interpreted too unambiguously.

The country classified in the last place is in this case a country whose result turned out to be the lowest among other highly developed countries. The following characteristics had the greatest impact on the results of the OECD classification in this ranking: X_{11D} – tuberculosis cases/100,000 pop.; X_{15S} – quality of the education system, 1-7 (best). On the other hand, the low position of Austria in the constructed ranking was mainly due to lower results in the case of such indicators as: X_{13S} – secondary education enrollment, gross %; X_{15S} – quality of the education system, 1-7 (best); X_{16S} – flexibility of wage determination, 1-7 (best); X_{17S} – redundancy costs, weeks of salary. To the last typological group (with the lowest results of the taxonomic development measure) were also classified: Hungary, Latvia and the Slovak Republic (Table 2).

On the other hand, the results of the surveyed countries are quite different in the case of the economic area, where the first places were: the Republic of Korea, Switzerland and Canada, and the last ones: Greece, Poland and Slovenia. The high score of Republic of Korea classified in the top three of the best countries in this area was influenced by high ratings of most indicators (except X_{24S} – prevalence of foreign ownership, from 1 to 7, where 7 means the best). For the first (best) typological group in this area also includes: the New Zealand, the Netherlands and the United States.

For the next area describing the spatial dimension of OECD countries' development, the first places were classified as: Luxembourg, the United States and the Netherlands. In the first group, to which countries with the highest values of the taxonomic development indicator are classified, there are also: Japan and Switzerland. In the last group of typologies, the following countries were qualified: Mexico, the Slovak Republic, the Czech Republic, Turkey and Hungary. The following indicators had the great-

Table 2. The results of the ordering of OECD countries according their level of development in each considered areas

Country	Area of development:									
	social		economic		spatial		institutional		financial	
	z_i	rank/ group	z_i	rank/ group	z_i	rank/ group	z_i	rank/ group	z_i	rank/ group
Australia	0,6000	8/II	0,5498	11/II	0,2796	24/III	0,4562	21/III	0,6346	11/II
Austria	0,4089	35/IV	0,3560	31/IV	0,4315	10/II	0,4987	15/III	0,5561	22/III
Belgium	0,6257	2/I	0,5492	12/II	0,3492	18/II	0,3206	32/IV	0,4835	28/III
Canada	0,5688	16/II	0,6051	6/I	0,3077	21/III	0,6142	11/II	0,5651	21/II
Chile	0,6249	3/I	0,4246	24/III	0,2535	29/III	0,3693	30/III	0,4959	27/III
Czech Republic	0,6003	7/II	0,4335	22/III	0,1459	34/IV	0,3762	28/III	0,6452	7/II
Denmark	0,5253	30/III	0,5163	15/II	0,3797	16/II	0,5632	14/II	0,6604	5/II
Estonia	0,6052	6/II	0,4776	21/III	0,4001	12/II	0,4686	18/III	0,6402	8/II
Finland	0,5493	19/III	0,5162	16/II	0,3800	15/II	0,6162	9/II	0,6114	13/II
France	0,5278	28/III	0,5297	13/II	0,4464	7/II	0,3389	31/III	0,4686	30/III
Germany	0,5755	13/II	0,5075	19/II	0,4484	6/II	0,4781	17/III	0,6371	10/II
Greece	0,5694	15/II	0,2753	36/IV	0,2691	27/III	0,3114	33/IV	0,2624	36/IV
Hungary	0,4917	31/IV	0,3668	30/IV	0,1897	32/IV	0,2478	35/IV	0,5989	16/II
Iceland	0,5953	10/II	0,3490	32/IV	0,4444	9/II	0,6360	8/II	0,6875	3/I
Ireland	0,6085	4/I	0,5664	10/II	0,2586	28/III	0,5943	12/II	0,6229	12/II
Israel	0,6353	1/I	0,5125	17/II	0,3364	20/III	0,3875	26/III	0,5958	17/II
Italy	0,4399	34/IV	0,3389	33/IV	0,2823	22/III	0,2598	34/IV	0,3532	35/IV
Japan	0,5407	20/III	0,5256	14/II	0,4940	4/I	0,4357	22/III	0,4298	32/IV
Korea, Rep.	0,5264	29/III	0,5820	7/II	0,4463	8/II	0,3842	27/III	0,6082	14/II
Latvia	0,4867	32/IV	0,3740	29/III	0,2360	31/III	0,3886	25/III	0,6007	15/II
Lithuania	0,5348	25/III	0,3774	28/III	0,2823	23/III	0,3735	29/III	0,5256	24/III
Luxembourg	0,5731	14/II	0,5121	18/II	0,6020	1/I	0,4242	24/III	0,6381	9/II
Mexico	0,3924	36/IV	0,4261	23/III	0,1012	36/IV	0,2126	36/IV	0,5072	25/III
Netherlands	0,5983	9/II	0,6125	5/I	0,5153	3/I	0,4963	16/III	0,5799	20/II
New Zealand	0,5635	17/II	0,6164	4/I	0,3417	19/III	0,8043	4/I	0,7253	2/I
Norway	0,5333	26/III	0,5030	20/II	0,2715	26/III	0,9043	2/I	0,6645	4/II
Poland	0,5373	22/III	0,3127	35/IV	0,2460	30/III	0,5875	13/II	0,5524	23/III
Portugal	0,5352	24/III	0,3870	27/III	0,3779	17/II	0,4263	23/III	0,3664	34/IV
Slovak Republic	0,4804	33/IV	0,3953	26/III	0,1224	35/IV	0,4603	20/III	0,5848	19/II
Slovenia	0,5308	27/III	0,3284	34/IV	0,2753	25/III	0,7705	5/I	0,4761	29/III
Spain	0,6084	5/I	0,4137	25/III	0,3847	14/II	0,6152	10/II	0,4586	31/III
Sweden	0,5545	18/II	0,5718	9/II	0,3930	13/II	0,8204	3/I	0,6525	6/II
Switzerland	0,5933	11/II	0,5764	8/II	0,4745	5/I	0,4649	19/III	0,7407	1/I
Turkey	0,5365	23/III	0,6461	3/I	0,1815	33/IV	0,6719	7/II	0,3698	33/IV

continues on following page

Table 2. Continued

Country	Area of development:									
	social		economic		spatial		institutional		financial	
	z_i	rank/ group	z_i	rank/ group	z_i	rank/ group	z_i	rank/ group	z_i	rank/ group
United Kingdom	0,5823	12/II	0,7207	2/I	0,4298	11/II	0,9307	1/I	0,4988	26/III
United States	0,5381	21/III	0,7782	1/I	0,5864	2/I	0,6907	6/II	0,5951	18/II

Source: own calculation based on WEF data.

est impact on the results of the classification of countries in this area: X_{33S} – available airline seat km/ week, millions and X_{36S} – Int'l Internet bandwidth, kb/s per user. Their combined share in explaining the overall variability of diagnostic features is over 87%.

Within the next area describing the institutional dimension of development of OECD countries, the United Kingdom, Norway and Sweden were classified first. To the first typological group, the New Zealand and Slovenia were also classified. However, the last three places were classified: Mexico, Hungary, and Italy. In addition in this typological group, the following countries with the lowest scores were also included: Greece and Belgium. However, it should be emphasized that after the selection of diagnostic features, this area is described only by 3 indicators, and their share in explaining the overall variability of diagnostic features is comparable.

The results of the classification of OECD countries in the case of the last area describing the financial dimension of development of OECD countries differ from the other analyzed areas. In this case, the first places were classified as New Zealand, Switzerland, and Iceland, and the last ones were Greece, Italy and Turkey. The last typological group also included: Portugal and Japan. The classification of this last country in this typological group was due to lower than in other countries results in such indicators as: X_{51S} – government budget balance, % GDP and X_{54D} – general government debt, % GDP.

The relatively small compatibility of classification results within particular areas is also demonstrated by Tau-Kendall correlation of coefficients (Table 3).

The assessment of correlation coefficients for every areas are low, the lowest for social and institutional areas (0.0730). The observed regularities were also confirmed by previous studies of authors (Bąk, Cheba, 2018) regarding the European Union countries. Research in this area shows that in the case of EU countries, the course of socio-economic development of countries belonging to this group is not consistent with the development of these countries, e.g. in the framework of environmental development. It means that in the field of economic development high ratings are also caused by higher pressure of these countries on the natural environment. In the results of the research cited in this chapter, the lack of conformity of classification results in OECD countries was confirmed.

STUDY RESULTS: THE RELATION BETWEEN THE CONSIDERED AREAS

Deciding to use a multidimensional correspondence analysis to identify the OECD countries' connections due to sustainable development in 2017, it was assumed that the basis of the analysis will be the following variables:

Table 3. The results of the ordering of OECD countries according their level of development in each considered areas

Area	social	economic	spatial	institutional	financial
social	1,0000	0,1714	0,1333	0,0730	0,1302
economic	0,1714	1,0000	0,2698	0,2667	0,1714
spatial	0,1333	0,2698	1,0000	0,1587	0,1206
institutional	0,0730	0,2667	0,1587	1,0000	0,2254
financial	0,1302	0,1714	0,1206	0,2254	1,0000

Source: own calculation based on WEF data

- A synthetic measure for the social order (S),
- A synthetic measure for the financial order (F),
- A synthetic measure for the institutional order (IN),
- Synthetic measure for spatial order (P),
- A synthetic measure for the economic order (G).

The mentioned variables were transformed by replacing their real values with order categories determined using the three means method. The procedure of proceeding in the method of three means to determine four groups of typological objects on the basis of the value of a synthetic measure can be found, inter alia, in the works (Nowak, 1990; Szymkowiak, Młodak, Wawrowski, 2017). Thanks to this method, four categories were obtained for each variable, the first (1) of which is associated with the highest values of the variable, and the fourth - with the lowest. The categories of individual variables are marked with the following symbols:

- A synthetic measure for the social order (S): S1 (the best situation due to the social order), S2, S3, S4 (the worst situation due to the social order),
- A synthetic measure for the financial order (F): F1 (the best situation due to the financial order), F2, F3, F4 (the worst situation due to the financial order),
- A synthetic measure for the institutional order (IN): IN1 (the best situation due to the institutional order), IN2, IN3, IN4 (the worst situation due to the institutional order),
- Synthetic measure for spatial order (P): P1 (the best situation due to the spatial order), P2, P3, P4 (the worst situation due to the spatial order),
- A synthetic measure for the economic order (G): G1 (the best situation due to the economic order), G2, G3, G4 (the worst situation due to the economic order).

In the set of analyzed variables, in addition to the five synthetic variables characterizing individual works, the variable OECD Countries, which has 36 categories, was introduced.

Due to the number of variables ($Q = 6$) and the number of their categories, Burt's matrix, which is the starting point in the analysis of correspondence, was 56x56. However, the dimension of the actual space of co-existence was $K = 50$ and was determined based on the formula:

Table 4. Eigen-values and singular values with the characterizing the distribution of the variables studied the degree of explanation of total inertia in the original and modified versions

K	Eigenvalues γ_k	Singular values λ_k	Percentage of Inertia λ_k/λ	Cumulative Percentage τ_k	Eigenvalues $\tilde{\lambda}_k$	Percentage of Inertia $\tilde{\lambda}_k / \tilde{\lambda}$	Cumulative Percentage $\tilde{\tau}_k$
1	0.8050	0.6480	7.7758	7.7758	0.5867	15.8334	15.8334
2	0.6823	0.4655	5.5860	13.3618	0.3828	10.3312	26.1645
3	0.6593	0.4347	5.2161	18.5779	0.3495	9.4310	35.5956
4	0.6388	0.4081	4.8970	23.4748	0.3210	8.6629	44.2585
5	0.6126	0.3753	4.5031	27.9779	0.2863	7.7271	51.9856
6	0.6011	0.3613	4.3353	32.3132	0.2717	7.3330	59.3186
7	0.5982	0.3578	4.2939	36.6071	0.2681	7.2362	66.5548
8	0.5731	0.3284	3.9414	40.5485	0.2379	6.4194	72.9742
9	0.5398	0.2914	3.4968	44.0453	0.2005	5.4110	78.3853
10	0.5091	0.2592	3.1105	47.1558	0.1689	4.5575	82.9428
11	0.4901	0.2402	2.8819	50.0377	0.1506	4.0643	87.0070
12	0.4821	0.2324	2.7892	52.8269	0.1433	3.8669	90.8740
13	0.4580	0.2097	2.5167	55.3436	0.1222	3.2974	94.1713
14	0.4485	0.2012	2.4140	57.7577	0.1144	3.0871	97.2585
15	0.4323	0.1869	2.2423	60.0000	0.1016	2.7415	100.0000
					$\tilde{\lambda}_k$ =3.7055		

Source: own calculation.

$$K = \sum_{q=1}^{Q} (J_q - 1) \tag{11}$$

where:

J_q – number of feature categories q ($q = 1, 2, \ldots, Q$),
Q – number of features.

In Table 4 for the real space of co-existence, there are eigenvalues (γ_k), singular values (λ_k), the degree of explanation of total inertia (λ)by eigenvalues for k-th dimension ($\lambda_k/\lambda \cdot 100\%$) and the degree of explanation total inertia by eigenvalues in the k-dimensional space ($\tau_k \cdot 100\%$).

In order to check to what extent the eigenvalues of the lower space space explain the total inertia, the Greenacre criterion (Greenacre, Hastie, 1987) was applied. According to this criterion, the main inertia that is greater than $\frac{1}{Q}$. Because the number of variables in the study is 6, the intrinsic values above 0.1677 should be considered significant. The eigenvalues meeting this condition are assigned to k having a value of at most 15 and in a space with such a dimension the explanation of the total inertia is 60.00%. However, in two- and three-dimensional spaces, which are important due to the possibility of graphical presentation of the results of the correspondence analysis, the degree of explanation of the total inertia is 13.36% and 18.58%, respectively.

In order to improve the quality of the mapping of results in the spaces of lower dimensions, the custom values are modified according to the Greenacre proposal (Stanimir, 2005) using the following transformation:

$$\tilde{\lambda}_k = \left(\frac{Q}{q-1}\right)^2 \bullet \left(\sqrt{\lambda_{B,k}} - \frac{1}{Q}\right)^2 \qquad (12)$$

where:

Q – liczba analizowanych zmiennych,

$\lambda_{B,k}$ – k-ta wartość własna ($k = 1, 2, \ldots, K$), $\left(\sqrt{\lambda_{B,k}} = \gamma_{B,k}\right)$,

$\gamma_{B,k}$ – k-ta wartość osobliwa macierzy B (Burta).

For $k \le 15$, after applying Greenacre's modifications, eigenvalues and the degree of explanation of total inertia by eigenvalues for k-th dimension and for k-dimensional space are presented in the previous table.

Table 4 shows that the applied modification significantly improved the quality of the mapping and in the case of three-dimensional space the degree of explanation of total inertia by eigenvalue increased twice, i.e. from 18.58% to 35.60%.

In addition, the eigenvalue diagram was drawn up (Figure 2) and "the elbow" criterion was applied, based on which it was found that the presentation space for the co-occurrence of feature categories should be at most seven-dimensional. "The elbow" criterion as the basis for choosing the number of dimensions of the coexistence of variable categories is discussed in the paper published by Stanimir (2005). Taking into account these dimensions allows to explain over 66% of the total inertia.

Visualization of the results of a multidimensional analysis of correspondence in the seven-dimensional space is not possible. Therefore, in order to make an unambiguous interpretation, the Ward method was used, which made it possible to identify connections between variant variables. The Ward method is one of the agglomeration classification methods. It is used in empirical research both in terms of object and characteristics classification. In this method the distance between groups is defined as the module of the difference between the sums of squares of the distance of points from the means of the groups to which these points belong (Pociecha, Podolec, Sokołowski, Zając, 1988; Malina, 2005; Szymkowiak, Młodak, Wawrowski, 2017).

New (modified) coordinate values in the seven-dimensional space for individual variable categories were determined according to the formula (Stanimir, 2005):

$$\tilde{F} = F^{*} \bullet \Gamma^{-1} \bullet \tilde{\Lambda} \qquad (13)$$

where:

Figure 2. Eigenvalues – the criterion of "elbow"
Source: own elaboration based on Table 4.

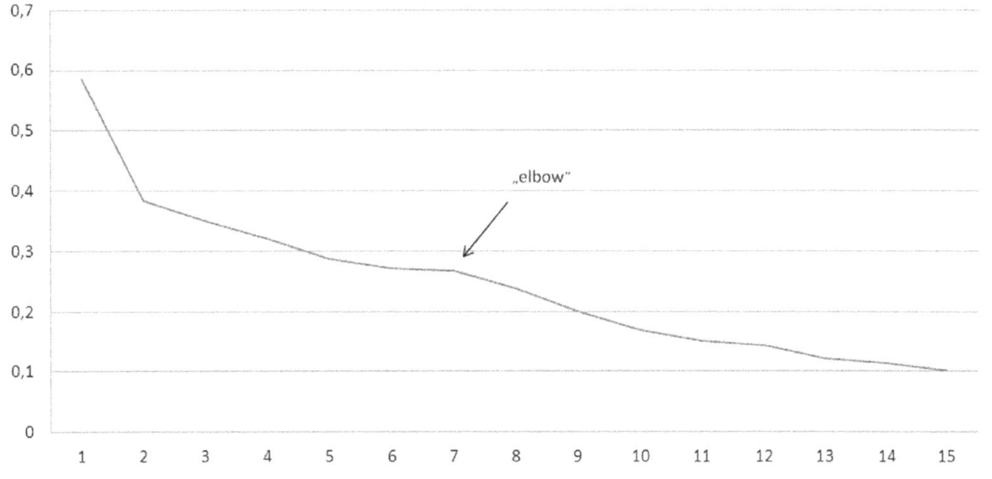

$\tilde{F}$ – matrix of modified values of coordinates for the category of examined variables with the $K\times k$ dimension (in the chapter: 56x7 dimension),

F^* – matrix of original values of coordinates for the category of examined variables with the $K\times k$ dimension (56x7),

Γ^{-1}– diagonal inverse matrix of specific values (γ_k) with the $k\times k$ dimension (in the chapter: 7x7),

γ_k – k specific value which is the square root of the k eigenvalue (λ_k),

$\tilde{\Lambda}$ – diagonal matrix of modified eigenvalues with the $k\times k$ dimension (7x7), K – dimension of the genuine coexistence space.

In Figure 3 showing the joins of categories into classes, the horizontal line was marked, in which the class merger was discontinued. Seven classes were obtained, which gave the name of the countries and the categories of synthetic variables accepted for the study:

Class I: Italy, Greece, G4, IN4, F4;
Class II: Turkey, Mexico, Slovak Republic, Hungary, P4, S4;
Class III: Lithuania, Latvia, Slovenia, Poland, Chile, P3, S3;
Class IV: Spain, France, Korea, Rep., Portugal, Belgium, Finland, Austria, Czech Republic, G3, P2, F3, IN3, F2;
Class V: Norway, Iceland, New Zealand, IN1, S1;
Class VI: Japan, United States, Netherlands, Switzerland, G1, P1;
Class VII: United Kingdom, Denmark, Luxembourg, Germany, Canada, Israel, Ireland, Estonia, Australia, Sweden, IN2, F1, G2, S2.

Figure 3. Connecting category of diagnostic features using the Ward method
Source: own elaboration, the results from STATISTICA.

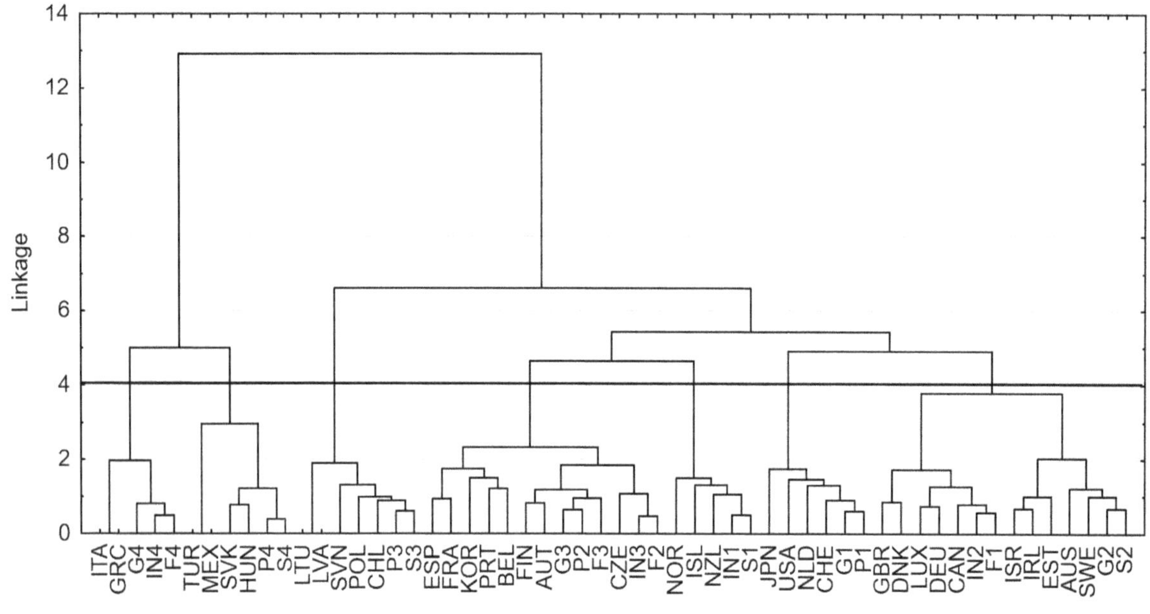

Based on the coexistence of the variable categories in the above-mentioned classes, the following relationships can be observed:

Class I: includes two countries of Southern Europe, in which the worst situation was due to the characteristics characterizing the economy, finances and institutional order,
Class II: also includes the countries of Southern Europe and Mexico, characterized by a difficult situation due to the features characterizing spatial and social order,
Class III: in this group of countries, spatial and social order below the average;
Class IV: countries with good standing due to spatial order, diversified financial situation and below average due to economic and institutional governance;
Class V: the best situation due to institutional and social order;
Class VI: the best economic and spatial situation;
Class VII: the best financial situation and good due to institutional, economic and social order.

The use of correspondence analysis and in particular the use of hierarchical classification based on it, allowed to determine the links between variable categories. This made it possible to group OECD countries due to the identified type of connections between factors taken into account in the study, describing different dimensions of the created common value in macroeconomic terms.

CONCLUSION

In the chapter based on the concept of shared value presented by Porter and Kramer in 2011, the authors tried to indicate the shared value from the macroeconomic perspective between the various areas of traditional notion of sustainable development and a new area jointed to this development related to the financial aspects. The results of the studies confirmed the previous effects of analyses conducted by authors which do not allows to indicate real common areas of the sustainable development. It means that quite good economic development is not still supported by positive changes in the other areas of sustainable development. This constatation a little surprised the authors of this chapter. The same conclusions were made by authors in previous research but they were related to the connection between the economic and environmental development. In this chapter, according to the database utilized for the study, this area was not included. The main conclusion is related with the lack of similar changes in every areas of sustainable development considered in the work. The authors expected that the financial aspects of this development may fall behind the changes in other areas but in the same time the closer connection between the results obtained in different analyzed areas by the most developed countries was expected. The main result of the study is the division into typological groups obtained based on the analysis of correspondence. The OECD countries, according to this method, were classified to the 7 groups with different level of development in economic, social, spatial, institutional and financial level of development. This classification confirmed the considerable diversity even in the case of the group of the most development countries such as OECD countries. The presented results should be treated only as an introduction to the larger analyses including also the changes in the area of environmental development.

Additional conclusion of this study is related to the quality of the WEF database which contains the indicators to much correlated. Because of this correlation many indicators during the statistical verification had to be rejected from the final set of diagnostic features. These kinds of difficulties are very often a side effect of the study in which to many indicators is presented on the order scale (from 1 to 7 or 10). This leads to duplication of the respondents' answers in the survey and thus to too much correlation. In further research in this area this conclusion should be taken into account and a higher quality database should be created.

REFERENCES

Aguilera, R. V., Rupp, D. E., Williams, C. A., & Ganapathi, J. (2007). Putting the S back in corporate social responsibility: A multilevel theory of social change in organizations. *Academy of Management Review*, *32*(3), 836–863. doi:10.5465/amr.2007.25275678

Andersen, E. B. (1991). *The statistical analysis of categorial data*. Berlin: Springer-Verlang. doi:10.1007/978-3-642-97353-6

Bąk, I. (2010). The use of the correspondence analysis in the research of the tourist activity of university students. *Folia Oeconomica Stetinensia*, *8*(1), 7–18.

Bąk, I., & Cheba, K. (2018). An analysis of dynamic changes in selected areas of sustainable development of the European Union countries. *Folia Oeconomica Stetinensia*, *18*(1), 93–107. doi:10.2478/foli-2018-0008

Beschorner, T. (2013). Creating Shared Value: The one-trick pony approach. *Business Ethics Journal Review, 1*(17), 106–112. doi:10.12747/bejr2013.01.17

Bonini, S., & Emerson, J. (2005). *Maximizing Blended Value – Building Beyond the Blended Value Map to Sustainable Investing, Philanthropy and Organizations*. Retrieved from https://pdf-max-blendedvalue.pdf

Bowen, H. R. (1953). *Social Responsibilities of the businessman*. New York: Harper & Row.

Breidbach, C. F., & Maglio, P. P. (2016). Technology-enabled value co-creation: An empirical analysis of actors, resources, and practices. *Industrial Marketing Management, 56*(1), 73–85. doi:10.1016/j.indmarman.2016.03.011

Carroll, A. B. (1991). The pyramid of corporate social responsibility: Toward the moral management of organizational stakeholders. *Business Horizons, 34*(4), 39–48. doi:10.1016/0007-6813(91)90005-G

Carroll, A. B. (2008). A History of Corporate Social Responsibility: Concepts and Practices. *The Oxford handbook of corporate social responsibility*, 19-46. Retrieved from: https://www.academia.edu/860777/A_history_of_corporate_social_responsibility_concepts_and_practices

Carroll, A. B. (2015). Corporate social responsibility: The centerpiece of competing and complementary frameworks. *Organizational Dynamics, 44*(2), 87–96. doi:10.1016/j.orgdyn.2015.02.002

Chapple, W., & Moon, J. (2005). Corporate social responsibility in Asia: A seven country study of CSR website reporting. *Business & Society, 44*, 415–441. doi:10.1177/0007650305281658

Christiansen, N. (2014). 6 steps to create shared value in your company. *Greenbiz*. Retrieved from: http://www.greenbiz.com/blog/2014/06/20/6-stepsimplement-csv-your-company

Crane, A., Palazzo, G., Spence, L. J., & Matten, D. (2014). Contesting the Value of "Creating Shared Value.". *California Management Review, 56*(2), 130–153.

Emerson, J. (2003). The Blended Value Proposition: Integrating social and financial returns. *California Management Review, 45*(4), 36. Retrieved from: https://wuecampus2.uniwuerzburg.de /moodle/pluginfile.php/235946/mod_resource/content/0/Emerson03%20-%20The%20Blended% 20Value%20Proposition%20%20Integrating%20Social%20and%20Financial%20Returns%20(California%20 Management%20Review).pdf

Gatnar, E. (2008). *Multiple-model approach to classification and regression*. Warsaw: PWN.

Goodman, L. A. (1986). Some useful Extensions of the Usual Correspondence Analysis Approach and Usual Log-Linear Models Approach in the analysis of Contingency Tables. *International Statistical Review, 54*(3), 243–309. doi:10.2307/1403053

Greenacre, M. (1984). *Theory Applications of Correspondence Analysis*. London: Academic Press.

Greenacre, M. (1994). Multiple and Joint Correspondence Analysis. In M. Greenacre & J. Blasius (Eds.), *Correspondence Analysis in Social Sciences. Recent Developments and Applications*. San Diego, CA: Academic Press.

Greenacre, M., & Hastie, T. (1987). The geometric Interpretation of Correspondence Analysis. *Journal of the American Statistical Association, 82*(398), 437–447. doi:10.1080/01621459.1987.10478446

Hart, S. L., & Milstein, M. B. (2003). Creating Sustainable Value. *The Academy of Management Executive, 17*(2), 56–69. doi:10.5465/AME.2003.10025194

Jabłoński, A., & Jabłoński, M. (2014). A modern model of strategic management and value management of the region - key issues (translated from Polish). *Samorząd Terytorialny, 11*, 22–31.

Jensen, M. C. (2001). Value maximization, stakeholder theory, and the corporate objective function. *Applied Corporate Finance, 14*(3), 8–21. doi:10.1111/j.1745-6622.2001.tb00434.x

Kramer, M., Kingsbury, T., Mundle, D., & Voûte, J. (2011). Creating Shared Value In Action [PDF Slides]. *FSG*. Retrieved from: https://www.fsg.org/sites/default/files/tools-and-resources/CSV_ Webinar.pdf

Laszlo, C. (2008). Sustainable Value. *Problems of Sustainable Development, 3*(2), 25–29.

Lebart, L., Morineau, A., & Warwick, K. M. (1984). *Multivariate Descriptive Statistical Analysis. Correspondence Analysis and Related Techniques for Large Matrices*. New York: John Wiley & Sons, Inc.

Lindgreen, A., Swaen, V., & Campbell, T. (2009). Corporate Social Responsibility Practices in Developing and Transitional Countries: Botswana and Malawi. *Journal of Business Ethics, 90*(S3), 429–440. doi:10.100710551-010-0415-3

Malina, A. (2005). Research on structural similarities between Poland and EU countries in terms of employment structure. *Argumenta Oeconomica Cracoviensia, 4*, 57–70.

Nestlé. (2014). *Nestlé in society: Creating Shared Value and meeting our commitments 2013*. Retrieved from: http://www.nestle.com

Nowak, E. (1990). *Taxonomic methods in the classification of socio-economic objects (translated from Polish)*. Warsaw: PWE.

Pfitzer, M., Bockstette, V., & Stamp, M. (2013). Innovating for shared value. *Harvard Business Review, 91*, 100–107.

Pociecha, J., Podolec, B., Sokołowski, A., & Zając, K. (1988). *Taxonomic methods in socio-economic research (translated from Polish)*. Warsaw: PWN.

Porter, M. E., & Kramer, M. R. (1999). Philanthropy's new agenda: Creating value. *Harvard Business Review, 77*, 121–131. Retrieved from http://www.fsg.org/publications/philanthropy%E2%80%99s-new-agenda PMID:10662001

Porter, M. E., & Kramer, M. R. (2002). The Competitive Advantage of Corporate Philanthropy. *Harvard Business Review, 80*(12), 56–68. Retrieved from https://hbr.org/2002/12/the-competitive-advantage-of-corporate-philanthropy PMID:12510538

Prahalad, C. K., & Ramaswamy, V. (2004). *The Future of Competition*. Boston: Harvard Business School Press.

Scholz, M., & De los Reyes, G. (2015). Creating Shared Value: Limits and Suggestions for Further Development. *ZeitschriftfürWirtschafts- und Unternehmensethik, 16*(2), 192-201.

Sergi, B., Fidanoski, F., Ziolo, M., & Naumovski, V. (2018). *Regaining Global Stability After The Financial Crisis*. IGI Global. doi:10.4018/978-1-5225-4026-7

Stanimir, A. (2005). *Analysis of correspondence as a tool for studying economic phenomena* (translated from Polish). Wroclaw: Wydawnictwo AE we Wroclawiu.

Szopik-Depczyńska, K., Cheba, K., Bąk, I., Stajniak, M., Simboli, A., & Ioppolo, G. (2018). The study of relationship in a hierarchical structure of EU sustainable development indicators. *Ecological Indicators*, *90*, 120–131. doi:10.1016/j.ecolind.2018.03.002

Szymkowiak, M., Młodak, A., & Wawrowski, Ł. (2017). Mapping poverty at the level of subregions in Poland using indirect estimation. *Statistics in Transition New Series*, *18*(4), 609-635.

Verboven, H. (2011). Communicating CSR and business identity in the chemical industry through mission slogans. *Business Communication Quarterly*, *74*(4), 415–431. doi:10.1177/1080569911424485

ADDITIONAL READING

Bąk, I., & Cheba, K. (2018). Study of spatial uniformity of sustainable development of the European Union before, during and after the economic crisis. *Przegląd Statystyczny*, *65*(2), 222–246.

Bąk, I., & Cheba, K. (2018). An analysis of dynamic changes in selected areas of sustainable development of the European Union countries. *Folia Oeconomica Stetinensia*, *18*(1), 93–107. doi:10.2478/foli-2018-0008

Szopik-Depczyńska, K., Cheba, K., Bąk, I., Kiba-Janiak, M., Saniuk, S., Dembińska, I., & Ioppolo, G. (2017). The application of relative taxonomy to the study of disproportion in the area of sustainable development of the European Union. *Land Use Policy*, *68C*, 481–491. doi:10.1016/j.landusepol.2017.08.013

Szopik-Depczyńska, K., Cheba, K., Bąk, I., Stajniak, M., Simboli, A., & Ioppolo, G. (2018). The study of relationship in a hierarchical structure of EU sustainable development indicators. *Ecological Indicators*, *90*, 120–131. doi:10.1016/j.ecolind.2018.03.002

Chapter 3
Investment Appraisal of Sustainability Projects: An Assortment of Financial Measures

Ria Sinha
TERI School of Advanced Studies, India

Manipadma Datta
TERI School of Advanced Studies, India

ABSTRACT

This chapter is an attempt to review the existing approaches in appraising sustainability projects using the conventional approaches of net present value (NPV) and introduce the modified forms of NPV (i.e., net present sustainable value [NPSV]). The chapter also elucidates on the prominent characteristics of sustainability projects and the inadequacy of traditional financial tools in appraising the same. Consequently, the need to transition from using only time value of money as in payback period approach to include opportunity costs as in NPV and furthering this approach to broaden the capital theory of sustainability by including both the time value of money and the opportunity costs has been strongly advocated. In addition to controlling the time value of money, risk-adjusted NPV measures are effective in evaluating sustainability projects. For assessment of renewable energy projects, real option analysis is suggested as an effective measure.

ORGANIZATION BACKGROUND

The TERI School of Advanced Studies (TERI SAS) was set up as a trust by TERI (The Energy and Resources Institute), a not-for-profit, independent research institute recognized globally for its contribution to scientific and policy research in the realms of energy, environment, and sustainable development since 1998. The different departments at the institution cater to the different research aspects pertaining to sustainable development, climate change, sustainable business and policy.

DOI: 10.4018/978-1-7998-1033-9.ch003

SETTING THE STAGE

Sustainability poses substantial challenges to business in the form of environmental and social risks. If these risks are not accounted for in investment appraisals, it will lead to inaccurate costs and budget cuts, thereby leading to wrong decisions. As argued in the present chapter using traditional and unmodified measures such as NPV in evaluating investments may lead to incorrect assessments. Hence the use of modified measures of NPV by taking into account time value of money, risks and variable discount rates is essential.

CASE DESCRIPTION

The present chapter elucidates upon the necessity for sustainability inclusion in project appraisals. The text is elucidated in a lucid manner for ease of understanding for students, academia, business enterprises, project developers and the policy makers.

INTRODUCTION

Sustainable factors such as environmental, social and governance pose huge risks to business. KPMG (2008) categorises these risks into regulatory, physical, litigation and reputational risks. According to UNEP, extreme weather events, increased GHG emissions, increased exposure to chemical products, decreased water availability, increased water pollution, biodiversity and land conversion might have impacts in the form of market shifts to lower carbon products, operational and supply chain disruptions, higher cost of energy, food, and other commodities increased cost of operations and materials, damage to shared public infrastructure, increased demand for reconstruction services, increased demand for pollution control devices and systems, increased cost of water treatment, increased demand for healthcare services to treat health impacts, new markets for water-efficient products, constraints on growth due to water scarcity, operational and supply chain disruptions, increased market, reputational, and regulatory pressure to reduce biodiversity impacts, reduced opportunity for new product breakthroughs, limitations on access to land, new and growing markets from urban expansion, restricted access to land-based resources, loss of ecosystem services, competition for arable land and increasing pressure to protect critical natural resources (UNEP, 2013). The risks emanating from ESG factors thus affect businesses in a large number of ways, affecting investment decisions, consumer behavior and government policies etc. In fact businesses are likely to suffer in the longer run if they fail to recognize these factors.

Clearly, ESG risks have to be managed and monitored. Businesses are increasingly recognizing the need for managing and monitoring such risks. Though initially recognition to sustainability factors was a consequence to increasing stakeholder pressure, the trend is now led by the fact that hedging of ESG risks makes good business sense. Prior to this, one of the pertinent methods used by businesses involved formulating corporate sustainability or CSR strategies. By obtaining the license to operate and delving into community development businesses manage litigation and reputational risks. According to Epstein and Roy (2003), an increasing number of senior managers across various organisations recognize the importance of formulating sustainability strategies. However in several instances they find it difficult to translate strategy into action. This makes it difficult to set performance standards and accomplish performance objectives. In terms of financial strategies, management and control systems and capital budgeting processes are widely used (Wisner and Fawcett, 1991; Clarke, 1997). The traditional ones include NPV (McSweeney, 2006). Conversely, corporate strategies not only aim for better financial performance but also aim to maximise financial, environment and social performance of companies. According to Moore (2003), sustainability strategies include social and environmental performance as an end to their own and beyond the degree to which they foster corporate financial performance. Hence financial evaluation of sustainability projects with existing tools is inadequate as implementation of sustainability strategies within institutions requires not only efficient allocation of economic capital but also efficient allocation of environmental and social capital (Liesen et al., 2013).

The present chapter attempts to elucidate on the financial evaluation of sustainability projects and the inadequacy of traditional financial tools in appraising the same. Section 2 highlights the conventional financial measures for investment appraisal. The characteristics of sustainability projects and need for modified evaluation measures is elaborated in section 3. Section 4 elucidates upon the different types of financial evaluation techniques for appraising sustainability projects and section 5 provides the concluding remarks..

Financial Tools for Investment Appraisal

Traditional methods of evaluating investment projects can be classified into two categories; viz. (i) Profitability based (ii) Cash Flow based. The profitability based techniques may include return on investment (ROI), accounting rates of return (ARR), return on capital employed (ROCE) to list a few. On the other hand, the cash flow based techniques include payback period, pay back profitability, discounted pay back, discounted cash flows (DCF), net present value (NPV) and internal rate of return (IRR).

NPV is the most common measure used for economic evaluation of investment projects. It is based on discounting all present and future cash flows from a particular project with a discount rate. NPV is commonly expressed in the following manner:

$$NPV = \sum\{(C_t)/(1+i)^t\} - C_0 \quad (1)$$

where C_0 is the initial investment at t=1, i is the discount rate and $C_{t\,is}$ the cash flow in the time period t.

This concept takes into account the time value of money by considering the discount rate i which means that any unit of a particular currency today is more valuable than in the future and hence future cash flows need to be discounted every year. The discount rate reflects the opportunity cost of capital which is also conveniently approximated with the weighted average cost of capital (WACC). Typical discount rates used for projects normally ranges from 10% to 15% depending on the riskiness of the project and can be as high as 25% to 30% (Žižlavský, 2014). Payback period on the other hand evaluates the time taken to breakeven the initial investment cost and hence ignores the time value of money. This apart it also does not take into account the terminal or the final value of the project which can be zero for innovation projects which face obsolescence or negative in the case of innovation projects requiring rehabilitation or recycling as applicable to projects in the energy sector.

Using opportunity costs in investment appraisal is a predominant method used in capital budgeting assessments (Scarlett 2002). However, post the Stern Review on economics of climate change[1], social and environmental resources have gained increased prominence of inclusion in investment appraisal. However, the basic question pertains to the fact whether different kinds of capital can be substituted by one another (Pearce et al., 1989). The capital approach to sustainability has been put forward by economists and financial economists. The genesis of the capital approach to sustainability lies with the launch of the Brundtland Commission Report titled 'Our Common Future'. The report empathised on the need of sustainable usage of resources by the present generation in such a manner that the future generations are also able to avail the resources. As a natural corollary to this statement it emphasized on sustainable use of all capital resources such as economic, environmental and social. This approach is also expanded to include the built environment by Atkinson (2008). He focuses on wealth accounting and indicators of genuine savings. Indicatively, a negative savings rate will mean that current behaviour is eroding the capital on which its own development depends. Though there are several critiques to this approach, one of the initial ones were provided by Stern (2001) in which he questioned on the substitutability of the various capital resources. However, expanding upon the capital approach to sustainability to include opportunity costs which was usually applied only to include financial resources, Figge (2001), Figge and Hahn (2004, 2005) have broadened this concept and stated that sustainable value is created only when the value accrued through economic, social and environmental resources surpasses the opportunity costs of resource use. Liesen et al. (2013) have furthered this approach at the firm level by introducing the concept of NPSV, the details of which are elucidated in section 4.

Characteristics of Sustainability Projects and Need for Modified Evaluation Techniques

Before we delve into the concerns relating to appraisal of sustainability projects, it is necessary to understand the typology of sustainability projects and in what ways they are different from traditional investment projects. In common parlance, sustainability projects can be classified into two categories; viz. environmental and social projects. Environmental projects cover certain factors related to the natural environment. Examples of this include green power, rainwater harvesting, waste management, and recycling to name some of the few. Social projects usually cater to social issues and needs such as corporate social responsibility projects etc. These projects are usually undertaken by individuals or groups of individuals in order to bring some social change that will benefit individuals, communities and societies. The objectives underlying sustainability projects aim to achieve social or environmental outcomes or both (as the case may be) and hence require efficient allocation of economic capital to achieve the sustainability outcomes. As a matter of fact, profit maximisation is not the sole aim of such projects. Rather value maximisation is aimed through efficient allocation of resources towards achieving environmental and social objectives.

The characteristics of sustainability projects vary widely depending on the intended outcomes. An exemplary example of this is an experimental conservation project carried out by two ecologists from Princeton University. Approximately 12000 tonnes of orange peel waste generated by the juice company Del Oro was dumped in a barren pasture in Costa Rica in the mid 1990's. The turnaround took place after 16 years when the barren land developed in a lush green forest with thick loamy soil with enormous ecological benefits[2]. Although, no potential financial benefits were envisaged from this project in the first place, it's surely an indication of involvement of the private sector paving the way for conservation finance.

The critical concerns relating to the use of traditional tools for financial valuation of sustainability projects are as follows:

1. Sustainability factors pose severe risks to business both in the short and long run. As aforementioned, these risks may emanate in the form of physical, regulatory, legal or reputational risks to business. Traditional NPV measures do not accommodate these risks.
2. Traditional financial tools are inadequate to capture sustainable value as efficient allocation of capital is not the only objective in value maximisation but efficient allocation of social and environmental resources also needs to be accommodated in valuation methodologies.
3. Traditional financial tools are incapable of accurately quantifying the non-cash benefits and costs accruing to the organisation and to the society as a whole from any specific investment.
4. The discounting factor and hurdle rate increases with the inclusion of environment and social risks, which is not accommodated by the traditional NPV measures
5. Cash inflows from sustainability projects occur usually in the long term. Hence these projects have long pay back periods. Hence low NPV value in the present term is not an accurate measure to discard the project.
6. Traditional measures do not take into account the fragmented nature of potential benefits accrued from sustainability projects over the long term.
7. Projects in the renewable energy and recycling are staged projects which incorporate modularity. This provides additional flexibility to the investor to assess the viability of the project after completion of a segment and decide whether to proceed with the project or wait till the demand reaches a certain level. Hence in all these cases, the investor does not make the initial investment all at once.
8. Most of the sustainability projects are innovation projects which require technological up-gradation. Hence technology obsolescence may pose a risk factor for such projects.

Non-consideration of these factors can lead to disastrous outcomes such as cuts in budgets, locked in costs, stranded assets and unsustainable development (Global footprint Network, 2015). Thus, the moot question relates to what extent the unmodified traditional financial measures are capable of valuing assets and securities in a carbon constrained world. Consequently, concerns are also related to whether it can support the implementation of corporate sustainability strategies. As a matter of fact, capital budgeting decisions once made are irreversible and hence incorrect evaluation might lead to incur huge costs.

Financial Techniques for Evaluating Sustainability Projects

The traditional techniques used for evaluating sustainable projects include life cycle assessments (LCA), full cost assessments, integrated assessment models, sustainability balanced scorecards, green shareholder value, key performance indicators and sustainability management systems. Financial assessments using cost-benefit analysis and multi-criteria analysis have been used to evaluate investment projects. The idea behind these approaches has been to maximise returns and minimise the sustainability risks in the portfolios. Assuming the fact that sustainability is an overriding concern, cost-benefit analysis is applied to projects by conducting a feasibility analysis in which a discount rate is determined. According to Pelt et al. (1990), economists blame low discount rates for unsustainable development. Discount rates are usually defined depending on the whether the particular project poses a case of strong sustainability or weak sustainability. Although, considering a single discount rate for all types of sustainability projects is questionable, concerns have also been raised as to whether application of different sustainability rates for different sustainability projects are viable and applicable.

Liesen et al. (2013) have defined four criteria which can be used for investment appraisal of sustainability projects.

1. **Strategy Orientation:** The tools for investment appraisal should provide guidance on whether the sustainable resources i.e. economic, environmental and social resources be deployed for a specific investment purpose. Hence the need has to be defined.
2. **Multi-Period Strategy Support:** Whether the tools cover the entire duration of the investment and are forward looking.
3. **Multi-Target Orientation:** The tools for investment appraisal should be able to target an improved financial and sustainability performance in an integrated manner.
4. **Ease of Communication:** The tools for sustainable investment appraisal should be able to communicate results in a manner that is easily comprehendible across the entire organisation.

Using the above mentioned criteria Liesen et al. (2013) finds that the traditional tools for investment appraisal of sustainability projects are not adequately equipped to capture the sustainability aspects

For example, although sustainability management systems are able to resort to multi- target orientation by targeting better sustainability performance, the ease of communication is extremely low as they are usually communicated in physical units which are not clearly understood by mainstream managers. Similarly, sustainability balanced scorecards usually do not fulfil the first three criteria; however, it is being easily understood by managers. This assessment clearly necessitates the use of non-conventional and modern financial tools which can fulfil the above mentioned criteria.

Sustainable Return on Investment

Financial techniques such as sustainable return on investment (SROI) is increasingly used nowadays to take into account the entire scope of pertinent costs and benefits related to sustainability along with a risk analysis of the project life cycle. This has an advantage over the traditional financial return on investment as it incorporates the external cost factors such as environmental pollutants over the internal cost factors including health risks of employees. While the traditional life-cycle cost analysis (LCCA) considers only the project's cash impacts, the SROI considers the cash impacts (capital, operational and maintenance costs) along with internal non-cash benefits such as productivity, health, safety accruing to the organisation and external costs and benefits from greenhouse gas (GHG) emissions, solid waste, air pollution etc. accruing to the society. Hence, SROI provides a comprehensive scenario of cost-benefit analysis, business case analysis, risk assessment, economic impact assessment and a consensus-based decision making for inputs (William and Parkar, 2010).

According to Nicholls et al. (2012) the six steps to SROI calculation include the following:

1. Establishing the scope and identifying key stakeholders
2. Mapping outcomes
3. Evidencing outcomes and giving them a value
4. Establishing impact
5. Calculating SROI
6. Reporting, using and embedding

Figure 1. Six stages of SROI

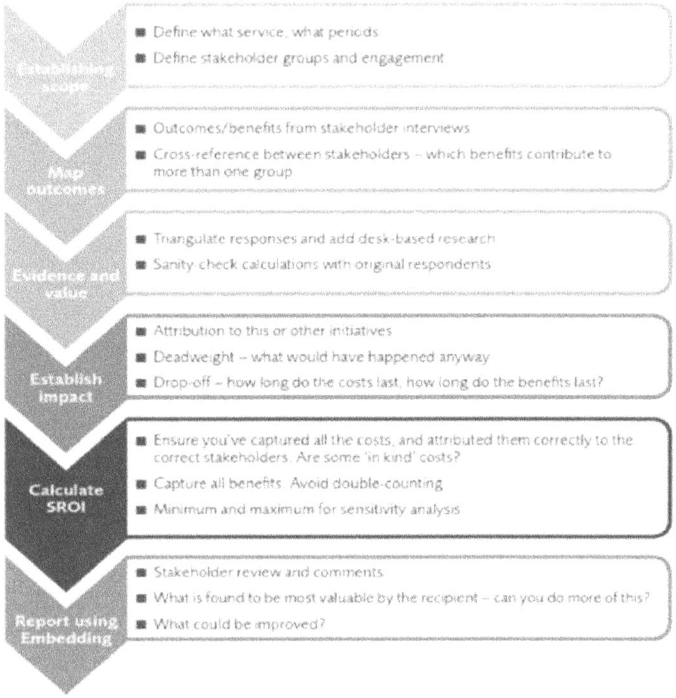

Source: Association for Project Management (2016). A social return on investment: A powerful tool for the realisation of benefits

The steps are illustrated in Figure 1 by defining the sub-indicators.

SROI has been broadly used for financial evaluation purposes. Companies like Siemens, Grupo Botacario, Adidas, AES Brasil have calculated SROI for certain projects which includes reduction of medical wastes, reduction in energy consumption, reverse logistics of products, territorial development, community capacity development, water recycling to list a few.

Net Present Sustainable Value (NPSV)

In contrast to the existing traditional tools of investment appraisal, Liesen et al. (2013) has developed NPSV as a strategic tool for managerial decisions for evaluation of investment projects. These tools not only consider the economic value of resources but also take into account the environmental and social value of resources. It builds on a strong analogy to examine whether the present value of the anticipated future returns from using environmental and social resources are in sync with the targets defined by a company's sustainability strategy. The modified tool for sustainability valuation as a modified version of NPV is defined as NSPV or net present sustainable value. This concept builds on a strong analogy to examine if the present value of the anticipated future returns from use of social and environmental resources is in sync with the company's defined sustainability strategy. In fact the robustness of this particular indicator is measured by its ability to orient towards a particular strategy, forward looking, covering the entire duration of an investment, aiming for a higher sustainability performance and also easily understandable across the implementing organisation. As aforementioned, this concept incorporates the idea of capital approach to sustainability at the firm level by broadening the opportunity cost principle according to which the returns earned from justifiable use of economic, social and environmental resources surpasses the opportunity cost of resource use. NSPV is mathematically expressed as under (Equation 2):

$$NPSV = \frac{1}{n}\sum_{i=1}^{n}\sum_{t=1}^{m}\underbrace{\frac{\left(\frac{R_t}{U_{i,t}} - F_t\,(1+c_i)^t\right)U_{i,t}}{(1+r)^t}}_{\text{Net present value contribution of resource } i}$$

Here n = number of resources considered, $U_{i,t}$ = anticipated amount of resource i used by the investment in period t, c_i = targeted yearly percentage change of the minimum rate of return for resource i, m = the number of periods covered, R_t = anticipated return of the investment in period t, F = the minimum rate of return or the hurdle rate, D_t = the depreciated book value and r the discount rate.

NPSV as an indicator is effective in planning for implementation of economic, social and environmental resources in order to execute the company's sustainability strategy. In this assessment, the minimum rate of return might not be a static one as the company may want to increase its sustainable resource efficiency and thus reduce the consumption of sustainable resources over time. For such cases, the hurdle rate may be a dynamic one. The discount rate r chosen for evaluating NPSV is the same as used in traditional analysis and the social or environmental discount rates are discounted in the same manner as those of the financial resources and depends ultimately on the time value of money.

For controlling the size of projects, the rate of sustainable return (RSR) is used which indicates the percentage by which the anticipated net present return from an investment project exceeds the opportunity cost. It is mathematically expressed as under (Equation 3):

$$RSR = \left(\frac{\sum_{t=1}^{m}\frac{R_t}{(1+r)^t}}{\sum_{t=1}^{m}\frac{R_t}{(1+r)^t} - \text{NPSV}} - 1\right)\cdot 100\%$$

Where the numerator measures the net present value of the future returns (which is also equivalent to the net anticipated returns from deployment of economic, social and environmental resources) and the denominator expresses the net present value of the opportunity costs (the minimum return required to achieve the sustainability targets of the company).

Other Modified Measures of NPV

Modified versions of NPV are used in certain innovation projects. The measures include risk adjusted NPV measures, certainty equivalent NPV and stochastic NPV measures. The use of NPV to evaluate sustainability projects has faced severe criticism owing to the discount rate factor. According to some researchers such as Doctor et al. (2001), the calculation of discount rate for innovation projects should include two factors, (i) a risk free rate (ii) a risk premium rate which includes the perceived financial, technical and commercial risks associated with the project.

Risk adjusted NPV measures take into account the time, costs and risks associated thereby producing realistic estimates. The risk adjusted measure of NPV is proposed by Stewart et al. (2001). In this model, the risk is calculated by multiplying the payoff with a probability which reflects conclusion of the development process and the generation of sales. The associated costs are then subtracted from this. The equation for risk adjusted NPV value is mentioned as under:

$$rV = PR_0 - \sum C_i R_0/R_i \text{ where i ranges from 0 to n} \quad (4)$$

Here rV = risk-adjusted value; P = payoff; R_0 = current risk; C_i = associated costs; R_0/R_i = likelihood of having to pay each cost

Accordingly, the risk adjusted NPV is calculated as follows:

$$rNPV = NPVPR0 - \sum NPVC_i R_0/R_i \text{ where i ranges from 0 to n} \quad (5)$$

where rNPV = NPV of the risk adjusted payoff minus the sum of the NPV of the risk-adjusted costs; $NPVPR_0$ = NPV of the risk-adjusted payoff; R_0 = current risk; $NPVC_i R_0/R_i$ = sum of the risk-adjusted costs (Stewart et al., 2001).

Kaufmann and Ridder (2003) have calculated this value of NPV in terms of cash flows from innovation projects. It is mathematically expressed as under:

$$rNPV = \sum[CF_t R_0/(1+r)^t R_t + R_0 CF_{n+1}/\{(r-g)(1+r)^n\}] \quad (6)$$

where rNPV = risk-adjusted NPV; CF_t = cash flow in period t; R_0 = the present probability of successfully concluding the development process and as a result of making sales; R_t = the probability as considered in period t of successfully taking the product to market maturity ($p_{t,8}$ with t>1); R_0/R_t = the probability as considered today generating the cash flows arising in period t, i.e. of reaching period t or attaining this stage of development (corresponds to $p_{1,k}$); r = discount factor; n = the last period for which costs and revenues are accurately planned; g = growth rate.

Risk based NPV measures can be extremely pertinent and used for different industries in the innovation sector. However, owing to the fact that there are certain shortcomings in this concept as highlighted by Schmeisser (2010), a stochastic NPV has been developed by Kellog and Charnes (2000).

Stochastic NPV further considers each component of cash flows as a stochastic variable with a probability distribution which is usually a normal distribution. As a result, the calculated NPV is a stochastic variable as is expressed in the following manner:

$$E(NPV) = \sum E(NCF_t)/(1+r_f)^t, \text{ where t varies from 0 to n} \quad (7)$$

where E(NPV) = expected NPV; $E(NCF_t)$ = the expected value of the net cash flow in each year t; r_f = the risk-free rate.

A certainty equivalent NPV on the other hand is a certain cash flow which an investor is likely to receive. However, contrary to the traditional measures of adjusting the discount rates, this method adjusts future cash flows by incorporating the risks through introducing α ranging from 0 to 1. The higher the risk anticipated with a given cash flow, the lower is the value of coefficient α. The mathematical expression developed by Chiesa and Frattini (2009) is expressed as under:

$$NPV_{CEQ} = \sum \alpha_t E(NCF_t)/(1+r_f)^t \quad (8)$$

where NPV_{CEQ} = certain equipment NPV; $E(NCF_t)$ = expected value of cash flows in the year t; r_f = risk free rate. This approach is a simple and neat method of calculating NPV and has been mostly used in R&D projects.

These risk adjusted measures of NPV can be applied for sustainability projects owing to the fact that sustainability factors such as social and environmental ones pose considerable risks to business and a-priori anticipation of the risk adjusted cash flows will enable the investor to conduct accurate assessments.

NPV Positive

Very recently, a modified concept of NPV termed as NPV+ has been constructed by the Global Footprint Network (GFN) to construct the economic case for sustainable investments in Maryland. This unique concept expands on the conventional concept of NPV by including the costs and benefits from unpriced factors such as costs incurred from environmental degradation and climate change and the benefits accrued from ecological resilience. It uses scenario analysis to capture possible economic futures and create a more realistic framework for capital decisions. The uniqueness of this approach lies in the fact that instead of taking a constant discount factor, several scenarios are created using different discount factors. A modified life cycle accounting with near complete information is attempted for such an approach (GFN, 2015). The concept of NPV+ has been used to analyse diverse investments in the field of electric vehicles which faces the problem of incremental costs, land conservation, weatherisation and facilities.

Real Options Analysis for Evaluating Renewable Energy Projects

The previous sections have focused on assessing risk adjusted measures of NPV. However, there are certain projects where uncertainty is a critical factor. Examples of this include renewable energy projects. The reasons for uncertainty can be many such as fluctuating prices of fossil fuels, policy uncertainty especially in the environment, uncertain demand, supply related uncertainties, costs over run, obsolete technologies to mention a few. Real options (RO) allow business managers to consider a choice or an opportunity for a particular investment ie expanding, changing or curtailing projects based on changing economic, market or technological conditions. There has been extensive work pertaining to this as stated by Dixit and Pindyck (1994), Trigeorgis (1995, 1996), Venetsanos et al. (2002). The most common types of RO include the following:

1. **Option to Defer Development:** In such cases even though there is possibility of positive NPV, it may be an optimal choice to start project development. Hence the holder of the option has the right to start the project immediately or wait for favourable market conditions.
2. **Option to Abandon:** If the estimated NPV of the project is close to zero, the management has the right to shelve the project.
3. **Time to Build Option:** This is also known as staged investment in which decision to defer or abandon the project can be taken in stages. Accordingly, each stage is considered to be an option on the value of subsequent stages and valued as a compound option. This is more pertinent in renewable energy projects where there is uncertainty.
4. **Option to Alter the Scale of Operations:** This is to take advantage of the scale of operations in which production can be increased more than the planned if market conditions are conducive and similarly decreased if non-conducive. However, increasing the scale of operations beyond what is planned might call for additional costs for installing additional capacity.
5. **Switching Options:** In case of any change in the market conditions, management might change the output mix or continue producing the same product with different inputs thereby allowing for both product and process efficiencies.
6. **Growth Options:** RO allows evaluating whether any particular project has growth options in which case the owner can create subsequent channels of profit creation. NPV approach ignores this possibility.
7. **Multiple Interacting Options:** Real life projects might include multiple options, in which case the combined value of the options may be different from the sum of individual options. However, the RO models mostly consider single value. Hence a more complex model is required to incorporate the interactive effect into its formulation.

Based on the aforementioned RO, Venetsanos et al. (2002) has evaluated the RO's which are applicable for wind energy projects. According to them the options which are applicable for wind energy projects include option to defer, time to build option, option to alter the operating scale, option to abandon and growth options. A comparative assessment of wind energy projects using discounted cash flows and RO approach highlights that although RO creates value it can be expensive. In addition to this, identification of the opportune moment to exercise the option is of utmost importance.

CONCLUDING REMARKS

This chapter is an attempt to explore the different financial measures used to evaluate sustainability projects whose characteristics are widely different from traditional projects. While DCF and NPV have been frequently used in evaluating sustainability projects, concerns have been raised due to the typical characteristics of such projects. Different types of sustainability projects aka social and environmental projects need to be appraised differently given their mandates and objectives. The chapter is indicative of the slow uptake of financial measures from traditional cost-benefit analysis to NPV and subsequently using risk adjusted measures of NPV for project evaluation purposes. Considering the fact that sustainability projects account for varied types of risks, NPV measures are not adequate to evaluate such projects. This shortcoming is overcome by using different types of risk adjusted NPV measures, stochastic NPV and certainty equivalent NPV measures. Other recent studies emphasize on the use of NPSV as a modified version of NPV and new strategic tool for managerial decision making in the context of sustainable investment appraisal. Creating scenarios by using different discount factors and hence different NPV's has also been introduced. Use of real options which are analogous to financial options are increasingly been used to evaluate renewable energy projects. However the main challenges remain not in discounting, but in handling the risks, uncertainties and cashflow estimation. Similarly, in case of return based techniques, challenge lies in ascertaining costs and benefits.

REFERENCES

APM. (2016). *A social return on investment: A powerful tool for the realisation of benefits*. Available at https://www.apm.org.uk/media/2218/sroi-report-2016-web-final.pdf

Atkinson, G. (2008). Sustainability, the capital approach and the built environment. *Building Research and Information*, *36*(3), 241–247. doi:10.1080/09613210801900734

Clark, D. N. (1997). Strategic management tool usage: A comparative study. *Strategic Change*, *6*(7), 417–427. doi:10.1002/(SICI)1099-1697(199711)6:7<417::AID-JSC281>3.0.CO;2-9

Dixit, A., & Pindyck, R. (1994). *Investment Under Uncertainty*. Princeton, NJ: Princeton University Press.

Doctor, R. N., Newton, D. P., & Pearson, A. (2001). Managing uncertainty in research and development. *Technovation*, *21*(2), 79–90. doi:10.1016/S0166-4972(00)00026-2

Epstein, M. J., & Roy, M. J. (2001). Sustainability in Action: Identifying and Measuring the Key Performance Drivers. *Long Range Planning*, *34*(5), 585–604. doi:10.1016/S0024-6301(01)00084-X

Figge, F. (2001). Environmental Value Added: A new measure for measuring eco-efficiency. *Journal of Applied Environmental Research*, *14*(1-4), 184–197.

Figge, F., & Hahn, T. (2004). Value-oriented impact assessment: The economics of a new approach to impact assessment. *Journal of Environmental Planning and Management*, *47*(6), 921–941. doi:10.1080/0964056042000284901

Figge, F., & Hahn, T. (2005). The Cost of Sustainability Capital and the Creation of Sustainable Value. *Journal of Applied Environmental Research*, *14*(1-4), 184–197.

Global Footprint Network (2015). *NPV+: Making the Economic Case for Sustainable Investments in Maryland*. Author.

Kaufmann, L., & Ridder, Ch. (2003). Valuation of biotechnology companies. *Financial Operation*, *7*, 448–456.

Kellogg, D., & Charnes, J. M. (2000). Real option valuation for a biotechnology company. *Financial Analysts Journal*, *56*(3), 76–87. doi:10.2469/faj.v56.n3.2362

KPMG. (2008). *Climate Changes your Business*. Available at http://www.climatebiz.com/sites/default/files/document/Climatechang_riskreport.pdf

Liesen, A., Figge, F., & Hahn, T. (2013). Net Present Sustainable Value: A New Approach to Sustainable Investment Appraisal. *Strategic Change*, *22*(3-4), 175–189. doi:10.1002/jsc.1931

McSweeney, B. (2006). Net present value: The illusion of certainty. *Strategic Change*, *15*(1), 47–51. doi:10.1002/jsc.746

Moore, G. (2003). Hives and horseshoes, Mintzberg and McIntyre: What future for corporate social responsibility? *Business Ethics (Oxford, England)*, *12*(1), 41–53. doi:10.1111/1467-8608.00304

Nicholls, J., et al. (2012), A Guide to Social Return on Investment (SROI). *The SROI Network*, 108.

Pearce, D. W., Markandya, A., & Barbier, E. B. (1989). *Blueprint for a Green Economy*. London: Earthscan.

Pelt, M. J. F., Kuyvenhoven, A., & Nijkamp, P. (1990). Project appraisal and sustainability: Methodological challenges. *Project Appraisal*, *5*(3), 139–158. doi:10.1080/02688867.1990.9726764

Schmeisser, W. (2010). Innovation profitability analysis in the assessment of pharmaceutical R&D projects. In *Innovation performance accounting: financing decisions and risk assessment of innovation processes* (1st ed.). New York: Springer. doi:10.1007/978-3-642-01353-9_4

Stewart, J. J., Allison, P. N., & Johnson, R. S. (2001). Putting a price on biotechnology. *Nature Biotechnology*, *19*(9), 813–817. doi:10.1038/nbt0901-813 PMID:11533634

Trigeorgis, L. (1995). *Real options in capital investments: models, strategies and applications*. Westport, CT: Praeger.

Trigeorgis, L. (1996). *Real options for managerial flexibility and strategy in resource allocation*. Cambridge, MA: MIT Press.

Venetsanos, K., Angelopoulou, P., & Tsoutsos, T. (2002). Renewable energy sources project appraisal under uncertainty: The case of wind energy exploitation within a changing energy market environment. *Energy Policy*, *30*(4), 293–307. doi:10.1016/S0301-4215(01)00096-9

William, J. F., & Parker, J. C. (2010). Measuring the sustainable return on investment (SROI) of waste to energy. *Proceedings of the 18th Annual North American Waste to Energy Conference*. 10.1115/NAWTEC18-3552

Wisner, J. D., & Fawcett, S. E. (1991). Linking Firm Strategy to Operating Decisions through Performance Measurement. *Production and Inventory Management Journal*, *32*(3), 5–11.

Žižlavský, O. (2014). Net present value approach: method for economic assessment of innovation projects. *Proceedings from 19th International Scientific Conference; Economics and Management.*

ENDNOTES

1 Report released for the UK Government by economist Nicholas Stern, chair of the Grantham Research Institute on Climate Change and the Environment at the London School of Economics (LSE).

2 Refer to: https://www.sciencealert.com/how-12-000-tonnes-of-dumped-orange-peel-produced-something-nobody-imagined

Chapter 4
Environmental Issues in Reporting of Public Interest Entities

Anna Spoz
https://orcid.org/0000-0001-5071-0017
The John Paul II Catholic University of Lublin, Poland

Marian Żukowski
The John Paul II Catholic University of Lublin, Poland

ABSTRACT

Public interest entities are socially and economically important elements of the economy. Since 2017 some of them have been obliged to prepare non-financial statements, which should contain among others a description of the policies pursued by the entity with regard to environmental issues. In this chapter, the authors analyzed the scope of environmental matters disclosed with non-financial statement and positively verified the hypothesis according to which the environmental issues in reporting of public interest entities increase the usefulness of the financial statement for stakeholders. Public interest entities fulfil their duties, but the scope and specificity of data contained in the statement on non-financial information differed between entities. Imposing requirement to annually present activities undertaken in environmental matters can make entities more sensitive to these issues and raise efficiently of implementation of the environmental policy. The research methods used in the study are a critical analysis of the literature, description, analysis, and synthesis methods.

INTRODUCTION

Despite criticism expressed by theoreticians and practitioners of accounting, the financial statement is still the main source of information about an enterprise and a tool of its communication with the environment. As a result of changes in business environment and growing expectations of stakeholders, the traditional financial reporting is evolving in the direction of a financial statement which extends the scope of data disclosed with non-financial information.

DOI: 10.4018/978-1-7998-1033-9.ch004

Since 2017 certain entities have been obliged by the legal regulations to prepare non-financial statement. Pursuant to the Directive 2014/95/EU of the European Parliament and of the Council of 22 October 2014 and the amended Accounting Act, large public interest entities became obliged to prepare additional statements which contain at least: a coherent description of the business model of the entity, key non-financial performance indicators related to the entity's operations, a description of the policies pursued by the entity with regard to social, employee-related and environmental issues, respect for human rights, solutions to counteract corruption and bribery, as well as a description of significant risks associated with these issues. (Directive 2014/95/EU, the Act of 29 September 1994).

Nowadays, it is very important for enterprises to be evaluated positively, to be credible, loyal and reliable in performance of actions which will be estimated by others not only from the economic but also social perspective. (Dusiński, 2003, p. 59).

In this chapter, the scope and manner of presentation of the environmental issue in non-financial statement will be presented. The first section of this study describes requirements for non-financial statement of public interest entities. Section two has been focused on verifying the hypothesis according to which the environmental and social issues in reporting of public interest entities increase the usefulness of the financial statement for stakeholders.

NON-FINANCIAL STATEMENT AS A REPORTING REQUIREMENT FOR PUBLIC INTEREST ENTITIES

Nowadays, the financial reporting is evolving in two directions. Micro and small entities can choose simplified forms of financial reporting. Large and important from the social and economic perspective entities extends the scope of disclosed data in financial statement (non-financial statement). According to Prof. A. Kamela-Sowińska, accounting as a system of financial records and reporting may be replaced with the so-called tailor-made accounting during the next 50 years or so. (Kamela-Sowińska, 2016, p. 309 et seq; Kamela-Sowińska, 2014, p. 108-109). The traditional accounting, emphasizing identification, valuation and reporting of information of exclusively financial character, is disappearing. The usefulness of classical financial statements is decreasing (Fijałkowska 2016, p. 30).

On the other hand, the role and value of additional information is growing (Krasadomska J., 2010, s. 46). Perception of an enterprise, its role, credibility and transparency by the broadly understood environment becomes increasingly important. The contemporary users of financial statements expect that the solutions introduced (new reporting models) will enable a more complete description of the enterprise's operations and value. E. Walińska rightly notes that non-financial reporting was developed throughout the years by means of systematic and consistent extension of financial statements with non-financial information. Additional information became included in statements. Management's comments, statements on non-financial information and other reports were introduced (Walińska, 2015, pp. 153-154). Thus, the previous scope of reported data is supplemented with non-financial information.

Extension of the scope of reported information and an increase in transparency of financial statements are grounded in such business theories as: stakeholder theory, legitimation theory, theory of asymmetric information, social responsibility theory etc. Among the reasons for disclosing non-financial information, including the introduction of a duty to prepare a statement on non-financial information, the concept of corporate social responsibility is worthy of note. In the most general sense, corporate social responsibility is the responsibility of an entity towards its stakeholders (Wójcik-Jurkiewicz 2016, p. 142).

Figure 1. Directions of the evolution of financial reporting of enterprises
Source: Compiled by the author

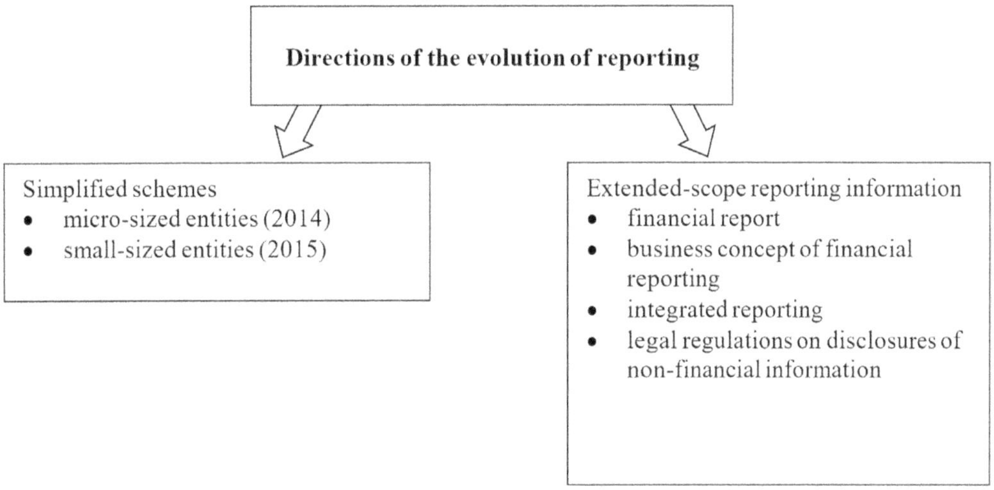

The originator of the corporate social responsibility concept is K. Davis (1975), who strongly emphasized social obligations of the management, putting them on a par with the economic goals of the enterprise (Masztalerz 2014, p.71). It promotes a rational management of the enterprise while respecting the rights of citizens, communities and the principles of social coexistence. It combines the overriding objective of a modern enterprise, which is the increase in its value for the benefit of shareholders, with its responsibility in terms of impact on the natural environment and the broadly understood society.

The CSR concept is based mostly on the "stakeholder theory" discussed by R.E. Friedman in the 2nd half of the 20th c. This theory pertains to the rules of strategic management in an enterprise. According to this theory, each enterprise is functioning in a certain environment where there are a number of entities interested in anything associated with the enterprise's operations. Stakeholders always interact with the enterprise and the enterprise interacts with them, but also with other entities, such as: suppliers, contractors, opinion-forming entities, journalists, employees etc. The stakeholder theory is a way to develop stable, long-term, partner relations between the entities concerned. In general, stakeholders are defined as individuals or groups of people, organizations, institutions or commercial entities which are interested, directly or indirectly, in operations of an enterprise and its pursuance of the goals set, and which can also have an influence on the enterprise or be affected by it (Roszkowska 2011, p. 58).

Studying the relations which can be developed between an enterprise and its stakeholders, we should distinguish the following groups:

1. A group creating the enterprise with their decisions, work and capital. These will be the enterprise owners, shareholders and employees. These entities are located inside the enterprise and hence they are called internal stakeholders.
2. A group associated with the enterprise's operations on the market. These will be clients, contractors, financial institutions and advertising agencies. Since the relations among them typically have the character of a formal contract, they are described as contract stakeholders.
3. The third group comprises the common interest institutions, such as local government and community institutions.

The process of identifying stakeholders is very important when implementing the concept of corporate social responsibility, and thus the ability to understand their needs and the selection of appropriate methods for the presentation of information provided (Costa and Pesci 2016, pp. 113-116).

In the case of some enterprises, the extension of reporting information with non-financial information is independently decided by their management, in line with the trend of integrated reporting and the aforementioned concept of corporate social responsibility. Certain entities were obliged to do so under legal regulations.

The statement on non-financial information can be a part of the entity's operations report or a separate statement compiled along with the operations report. The legislator let the entities decide on the selection of rules of non-financial information reporting. The selection of the reporting standard (national, EU, international or one's own) is an individual decision of the entity's management. However, there is a "comply or explain" rule which means that if an entity does not pursue a policy in a given area (that is, social or employment-related issues, natural environment, respect for human rights or bribery counteracting) the entity is obliged to reveal this fact and give reasons why such policies are nor implemented.

The entity's management board can refrain from disclosing information concerning future events or issues which are currently under negotiation if, in the opinion of the entity's head, members of the supervisory board or other body supervising the entity, disclosure of this information could adversely affect the entity's market position. These should be exceptional situations treated as a deviation from the rule and not as a way to evade binding regulations. In the case an entity makes use of this exception, information about this fact should be included in the report on non-financial data.

Furthermore, capital groups are also obliged to prepare a statement on non-financial information. In this case, two forms of compiling such a statement are acceptable: either each entity prepares a statement independently, or if this obligation is fulfilled by the parent company, then the subsidiary company does not have to prepare such a statement.

The statement is drawn up in the Polish language and currency. Quantitative data can be represented in the Polish zloty or rounded off to thousands PLN on condition that it does not distort the credibility of the entity's image contained in the statement. The deadline for preparing such a report is until the end of the third month from the balance sheet date. It should be signed by the head of the entity – since 1 October 2018 with the trusted or qualified electronic signature. If the report has to be submitted to the National Court Register, the entity has 15 days from approval of the financial statement to submit such a report. If the statement on non-financial information is prepared as a separate report, it should be published on the entity's website within 6 months from the balance sheet date.

ENVIRONMENTAL ISSUES IN REPORTING OF PUBLIC INTEREST ENTITIES

Public interest entities (PIE) are primarily financial sector entities and issuers of securities on the regulated market of EU Member States. They are defined in Article 2 item 9 of the Act of 11.05.2017 on Statutory Auditors, Audit Firms and Public Oversight (The Act on Statutory Auditors, 2017). These are the entities which are socially and economically important due to the scale and complexity of their operations.

The first of research hypothesis supported by authors is:

Hypothesis 1: Public interest entities constitute a significant element of economy.

As at 21.03.2019 there were 1309 public interest entities functioning in Poland. However, apart from the quantitative description, a special feature of these entities should be emphasized, that is their role in economy. The most numerous group among the public interest entities is domestic banks (591). As an economic entity, a bank is characterized by the fact that it undertakes banking activities (colloquially: banking operations). Banking activities can be divided into the activities reserved only for banks (sensu stricto) and the banking activities (sensu largo) treated as such so long as they are undertaken by banks. The latter activities can be pursued also by other entities or natural persons as operations. On the other hand, the right to undertake banking activities sensu stricto is reserved only for banks. This monopoly on performing banking activities by banks results from the special character of their operations: they take very high risks and manage various repayable funds entrusted to them. Therefore, special supervision of their operations by the state is necessary in order to ensure liquidity and security of the funds entrusted to them. Banks need to have the status of a public trust organization, because this enables them to undertake banking activities safely (Iwanicz-Drozdowska, 2017, pp. 16-17). Furthermore, the state's supervision is also supposed to prevent management of entrusted monetary funds by other economic institutions from the sectors of production, trade or services. A considerable part (up to 100,000 EUR) of funds entrusted to banks is guaranteed by the state. Another special institution is security issuers – there are 425 of them in Poland. They obtain funds for investment on the domestic and international markets in exchange for securities offered – shares or bonds. The state has to supervise their activity appropriately so that investors are able to take decisions on entrusting their funds to issuers of securities on the basis of full and reliable knowledge of their operations. Banks and issuers of securities account for over 77% of public interest entities. Their list was prepared on the basis of a qualification criterion that is fulfilment of the conditions for a public interest entity, determined on the basis of financial reports for 2016-2017, and it is published on the website of the Ministry of Finance. In comparison to the list compiled as at 15.12.2017, based on the reports for the financial years 2015-2016, the number of public interest entities rose by 13. The changes pertained mostly to entities operating as investment funds and banks.

The structure of public interest entities in Poland, shown in Figure 2, is dominated by domestic banks (45.1%) and issuers of securities (32.5%). On the other hand, reinsurance institutions and their divisions have the fewest representatives (both are represented only by one entity).

Figure 3 presents the structure of public interest entities with respect to the registered office address, on condition that only the localities with at least 4 public interest entities are included. Unsurprisingly, the largest number of public interest entities has their registered offices in Warsaw (32%), followed by Wrocław, although only 4.58% of public interest entities are located there.

Figure 4 shows that the entities other than large PIE have the highest share (65.70%) when we adopt the conditions for classification of a large entity according to Article 2 item 8 of the Act on Statutory Auditors. A large entity is understood as an entity in the case of which at least two of the following three numbers were exceeded at the end of a given financial year and at the end of the financial year preceding a given financial year (The Act on Statutory Auditors 2017):

1. 85 million PLN – in the case of the sum of balance sheet assets at the end of the financial year,
2. 170 million PLN – in the case of the net revenue from sale of goods and products for the financial year,
3. 250 people – in the case of the average annual employment as expressed in full-time jobs.

Figure 2. Structure of public interest entities in terms of a type of operations (as at 21.03.2019)
Source: compiled by the authors

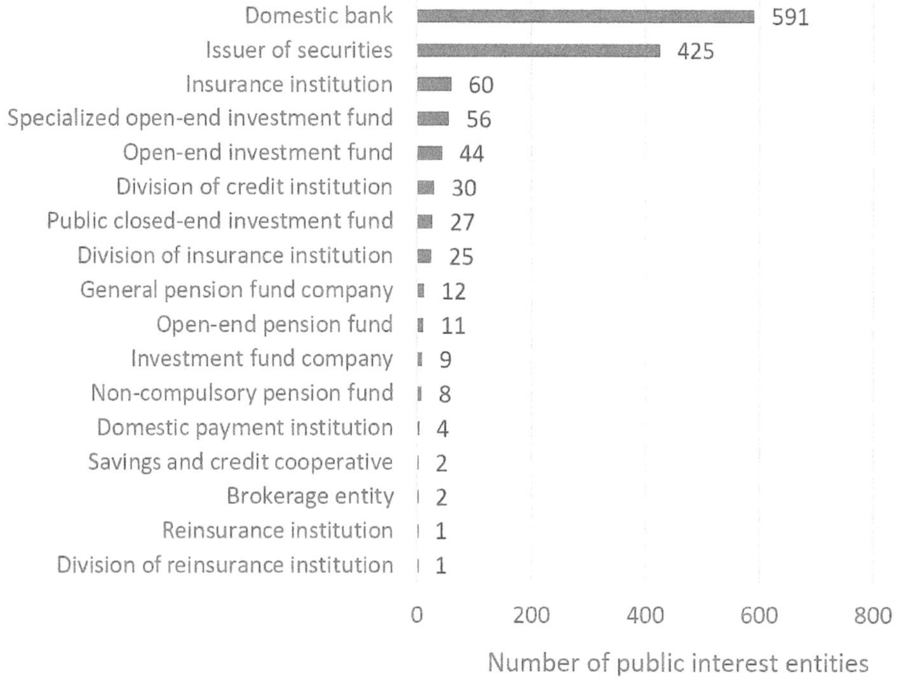

Figure 3. Number of public interest entities with respect to the registered office address
Source: compiled by the authors

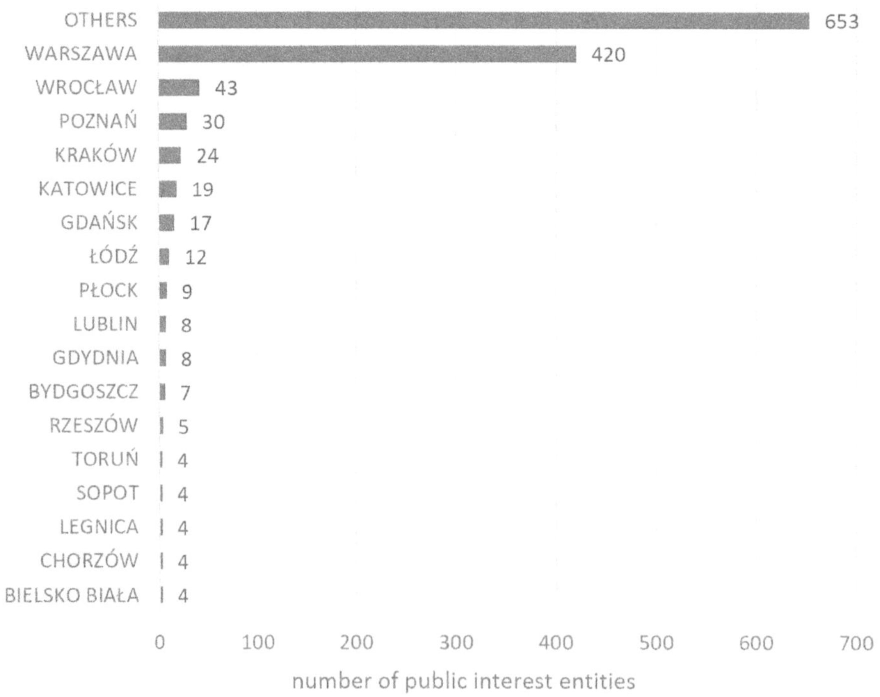

Figure 4. Structure of public interest entities with respect to their size
Source: compiled by the authors

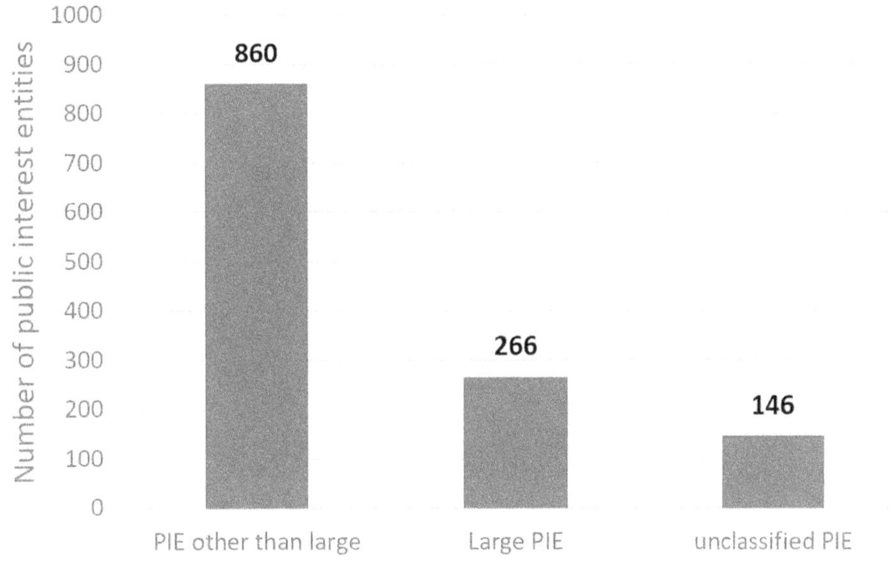

Large entities account for 20% of all public interest entities. The remaining PIE are non-classified entities.

Owing to the scope and character of activity of public interest entities, the consequences of decisions taken by them, even if not reflected in their financial results yet, affect the economic situation of the country as a whole, this is why the reporting of public interest entities gains particular significance, especially in the context of the last financial crisis (Zaleska M., Koleśnik J., 2018, p. 83).

At this point authors suggest another research hypothesis, which are:

Hypothesis 2: Public interest entities obliged to compile a non-financial reporting including environmental issue fulfil their duties.

Hypothesis 3: The environmental issues in reporting of public interest entities increase the usefulness of the financial statement for stakeholders.

In Poland the vast majority of public interest entities obliged to prepare a statement on non-financial information are listed companies. There were 96 issuers of securities obliged to compile a non-financial report for 2017, of which 90 issuers had also a duty resulting from Article 55 section 2b of the Accounting Act (hence, they were consolidated entities). The number of parent companies obliged to report only on the level of the capital group equaled 62.

In the research carried out for the purposes of this study, the statements on non-financial information of 60 entities were analyzed.

In the analyzed group of entities, issuers of securities were the most numerous (82%), followed by banks (18%) (Figure 5). Most of the studied entities were operating in the financial sector (22%), chemical and resources industry (17%), industrial production, construction sector (13%) and hi-tech sectors. Health care entities were the fewest (5%) (Figure 6).

Figure 5. Structure of the analyzed public interest entities with respect to a type of business operations
Source: compiled by the authors

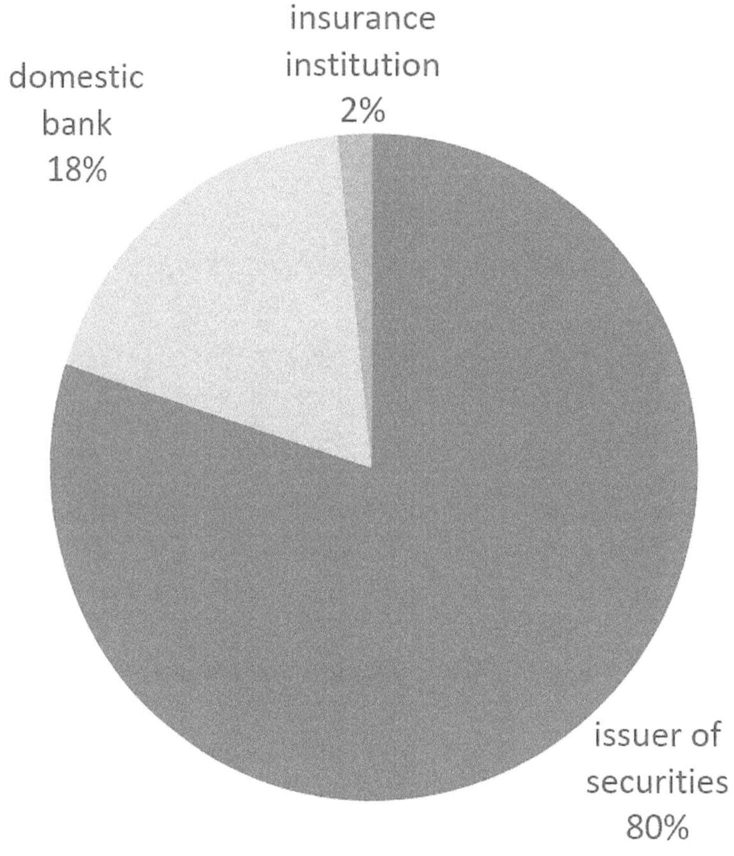

In the vast majority of the analyzed entities, information on environmental and social issues was included in the statement on non-financial data being a part of the Management Board's report on activity. Only a few of the analyzed entities decided to prepare a separate report published on the entity's website, but in the case of some entities the information on environmental and social policy was available on their websites, usually in the section devoted to corporate social responsibility.

Further, study did not demonstrate a clear relationship between the size of the entity, its organizational and legal form and the possession and operation of an environmental responsibility policy. For example, as regards financial institutions, Bank Pekao S.A. and BGŻ BNP Paribas S.A. declared that they had and operated an environmental policy. Bank Handlowy in Warsaw even announced the introduction of a comprehensive Environmental Management Plan in 2017. On the other hand, Bank Pocztowy S.A. stated that due to the territorial distribution of its branches, pro-environmental initiatives were undertaken only in areas of particular importance. Bank BP S.A. adopted a position view that due to the nature of its business operations, its impact on the natural environment was only marginal and negligible. Nevertheless, it announced the commencement of pro-environmental initiatives, such as optimization of printing tasks and reduction of employment. Alior Bank S.A. and Credit Agricole Bank Polska S.A.

Figure 6. Structure of the analyzed public interest entities with respect to a business sector
Source: compiled by the authors

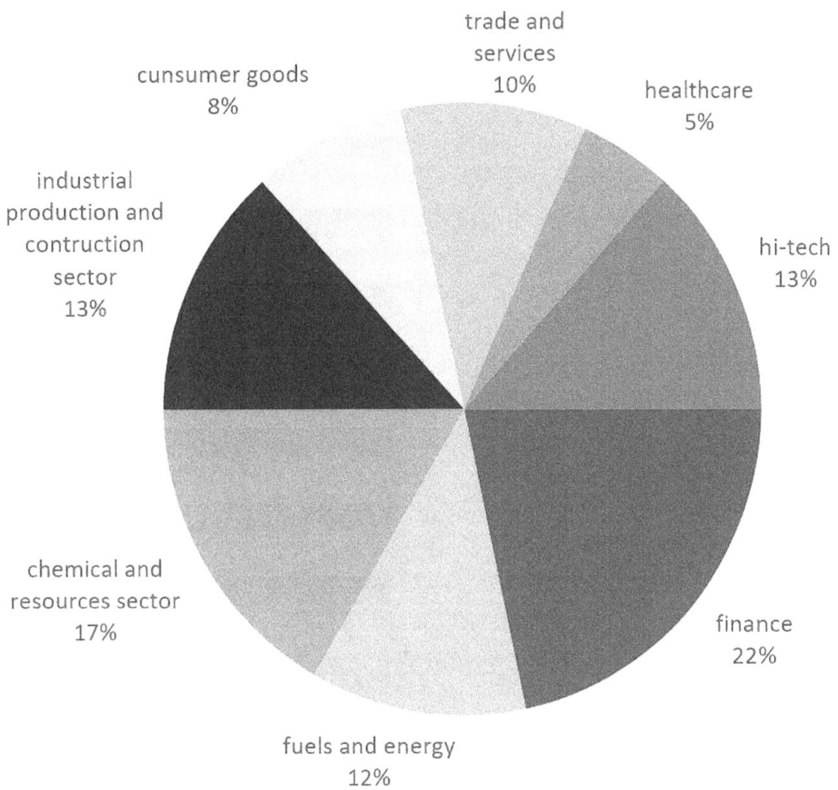

in their statements wrote that they did not have separate Environmental Policies. However, even those entities gave examples of pro-environmental activities, for example promoting pro-ecological attitudes among employees.

The scope and level of details of the information contained in the non-financial statements of individual entities vary, which is undoubtedly due to the fact that the entities prepared such reports for the first time and they had neither clear guidelines nor developed practices yet how such reports should look like. Synthetic lists of environmental policy matters disclosed in the non-financial statements of selected public interest entities in breakdown by industry/sector are given in the Table 1.

On the basis of the research carried out, it can be noticed that statements on non-financial information, particularly concerning environmental issues, of entities operating in such sectors as: chemical and resources, fuels and energy, as well as industrial production sectors, are more thorough and detailed. All entities from these sectors participating in the research declared that they had an environmental policy. Without doubt, it results from the fact that the operation of these entities directly affects the natural environment, as well as health and quality of life of local communities. These entities, even for the sake of their image, are interested in promotion of their initiatives aimed at reduction in adverse influence of a given entity on the environment, e.g. by a decrease in emission of harmful gases into the atmosphere, or modernization and investment in infrastructure in order to limit the damage caused by the production

Figure 7. Public interest entities from various sectors having an environmental policy in the form of an official document
Source: compiled by the authors

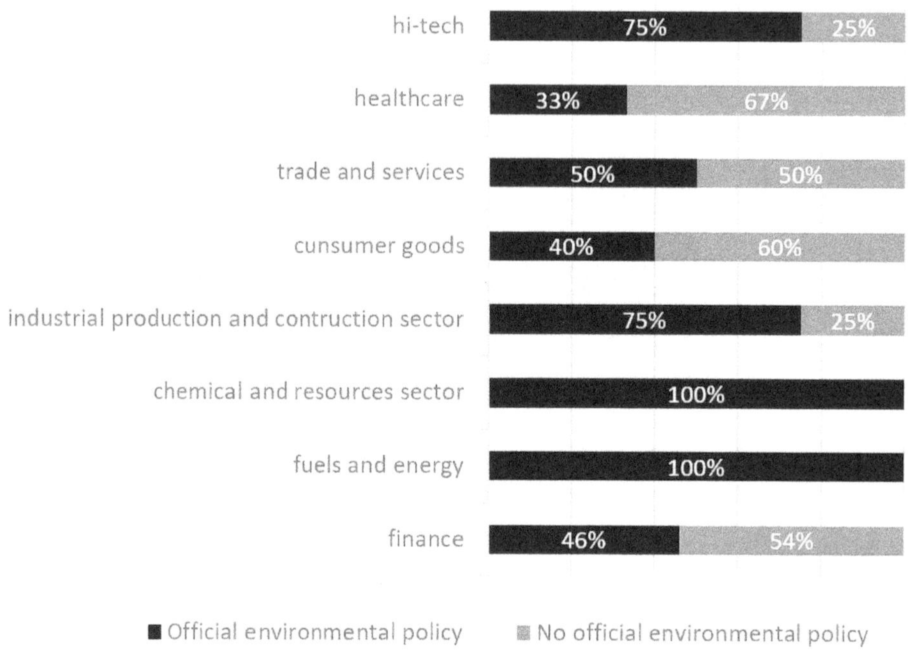

processes implemented. However, only Energa S.A. and PGE Polska Grupa Energetyczna S.A. have environmental declarations complying with the requirements of the EMAS[1] – Eco-Management and Audit Scheme.

However, it should be noted that compared to other policies, i.e. social and employee-related matters, respect for human rights and anti-corruption policies, to publish which public interest entities preparing a non-financial statement are required, information on environmental policies included in the statements is extensive and comprehensive, and often supported by figures. The scope of information provided by individual entities varies, which is due to both the specific nature the entity's operations, its accounting system and the resulting capabilities for data acquisition, the competence of persons responsible for the preparation of non-financial reports and environmental awareness of the company's management. For example, AGORA S.A. in the area devoted to environmental matters presented indicators giving insight into the performance of materials management, consumption of energy, water, materials and resources, and waste management. On the other hand, entities such as Amica S.A., Arctic Paper S.A., RADPOL S.A., and Grupa Kęty S.A. declared the application of ISO 14001 standards in the area of environmental protection. Among the initiatives pursued for environmental protection, the entities covered by the study also listed reductions in the amount of waste, management of waste generated, reductions in consumption of energy and office materials, use of recycled materials, revamps and upgrades of the machinery, care for the technical condition of the enterprise's vehicle fleet.

Table 1. Environmental matters in non-financial statements of enterprises operating in the financial sector

Entity	Environmental matters disclosed in non-financial statements
Bank PEKAO S.A.	In the "Management report on the activities of Bank Pekao SA for 2017", environmental matters are presented in the "Non-financial statement of Bank Pekao SA for 2017". The Bank states that it does not have a single policy that would comprehensively cover environmental protection matters. This area is covered in other policies adopted by the Bank. The key governance document in this respect is the "Policy for optimization of energy consumption at Bank Polska Kasa Opieki Spółka Akcyjna". The Bank reduces the consumption of electricity and paper, among others through the use of energy-efficient equipment and lighting, elimination of unnecessary backup power connections, fax communication in electronic form, scanning and transmission of documents in electronic form. The company engages in activities to protect the natural environment by including ecological matters in the process of credit risk analysis, financing environmentally friendly projects and through financial support to organizations and institutions which operate initiatives related to environmental protection, with particular focus on the protection of the European bison.
Bank PKO Bank Polski S.A.	The Management Board's report on activity of the PKO Bank Polski S.A. Capital Group did not present any environmental matters, which, however, were disclosed in the Annual Report for 2017 in the section on non-financial information. The information was divided into three parts: consumption of natural resources and waste generation, pro-ecological programs, environmental responsibility in lending policy. In the first part, the Bank shows that due to the nature of its business activity, the direct impact of the Bank and the Capital Group on the natural environment is marginal and negligible. The second part presents: - energy optimization program, under which the company plans to perform a feasibility study for the implementation of the system in the organization, including an analysis of its financial viability. – printing optimization and paper consumption reduction program "Process optimization - faster and zero paper", based on the objective to eliminate a part of paper correspondence to the customer, and to replace it with SMS communication; encouraging customers to switch from paper bank statements to electronic documents; combining correspondence with two borrowers in a single envelope (if legally permitted and acceptable business-wise) and combining instructions and confirmations for payment and withdrawal transactions in a single document; reducing printed reports in the process of cash transactions. An extended environmental responsibility of the Capital Group, including the Bank, is mainly covered in the policy of financing the activities of private business and public entities.
Bank Ochrony Środowiska S.A.	Matters related to the natural environment were included in the Management Board's report on activity of BOŚ S.A. in the Non-financial statement. The environmental policy is a separate document adopted by the Bank. In its mission, the Bank declares that it is a Polish ECO Bank - for people, businesses and the environment. It has been combining business and eco-friendliness for the benefit of customers for years. This slogan is pursued in two ways: by minimizing the negative impact on the environment, but above all, by promoting pro-ecological behavior among customers, partners and suppliers. The Bank finances projects that have a real impact in improving the environment and supporting sustainable development of Poland. – promotion of eco-friendly transport among employees – reduction of energy consumption – reduction of water consumption – effective waste segregation

Source: compiled by the author

Table 2. Environmental matters in non-financial statements of enterprises operating in the chemical and resources sector

Entity	Environmental matters disclosed in non-financial statements
Grupa Azoty S.A.	Environmental matters were disclosed in the "Management report on the activities of Grupa Azoty S.A. and the Grupa Azoty Capital Group for the period of 12 months ended on 31 December 2017", in the section "Other significant information and events". Matters such as sustainable development policy, Respect Index, legal requirements, safety, gaseous emissions, water and wastewater management, waste management and pro-ecological investment projects were described in detail. The Parent Entity pursued an extension project for its R&D Centre, tasked with the work, among others, in areas such as: – launching new or improved technologies and pro-ecological products, – reducing energy intensity of existing technologies, – reducing the amount of waste in operated technologies, – developing new technologies to utilize synergies with by-products generated by the Group. Environmental matters were also presented in the "Non-financial statement of the Grupa Azoty Capital Group for 2017". It gives a summary description of the Group's approach to environmental protection, environmental management solutions put in place, and pro-ecological investment projects completed.
Fabryka Farb i Lakierów Śnieżka S.A.	Environmental matters were presented in the "Consolidated statements of the Company and the Group for 2017". Ecological activities in the Parent Company are pursued in accordance with the applicable legal requirements, and the procedures and instructions set out in the Integrated Management System (IMS), which covers: – quality management system according to the PN-EN ISO 9001 standard, – environmental management system PN-EN ISO 14001 operated in the Parent Company. A detailed description of environmental protection indicators was included in the Non-financial statement of the Company and the Group. It also featured a description of the due care policy and procedures applied by the Company in relation to the natural environment. The following environmental aspects are classified as significant in the Parent Company's operations: – emissions of volatile organic compounds and particulate matter; – emissions from the combustion of high-methane natural gas; – generation of hazardous waste; – generation of non-hazardous waste; – generation of non-hazardous packaging waste; – wastewater - rainwater and snowmelt.
CIECH S.A.	Key matters related to environmental protection were disclosed in the "Management report on the activities of the CIECH Group and CIECH S.A. for 2017", in the section concerning Corporate Social Responsibility. In 2016, a uniform Environmental Protection Policy was developed and put in place. The policy imposes an obligation on all Group companies to comply with the applicable environmental laws, reduce emissions to the atmosphere and the amount of waste generated, to optimize the use of natural resources and to counteract climate change by reducing CO_2 emissions. The report also lists some of the investment projects in the soda lye segment that the CIECH Group has completed in recent years as part of atmosphere protection initiatives. The "Non-financial statement of the CIECH Group for 2017" makes a disclosure of the uniform Environmental Policy in force in the Group, which imposes an obligation to all Group companies to: – comply with environmental laws, – reduce emissions to the atmosphere and the amount of waste generated, – optimize the use of natural resources and counteract climate change by reducing CO_2 emissions, – maintain good social relations in the communities in which they operate business, – promote environmentally friendly products and services. Selected companies of the CIECH Group have implemented an environmental management system in accordance with the requirements of ISO14001.

Source: compiled by the author

Table 3. Environmental matters in non-financial statements of enterprises operating in the industrial production and construction sector

Entity	Environmental matters disclosed in non-financial statements
Stalprodukt S.A.	The non-financial statement constitutes a part of the Management Board's report on activity. Environmental matters are described in the environmental area section. The Group does not declare the adoption of a single environmental policy for the entire Group, claiming a diversified profile and specific nature of the companies' operations in support of its position. Environmental management is based on solutions rooted in certified management systems put in place in individual subsidiaries, and the Group declared that all elements of the companies' operations had been identified: - Stalprodukt S.A. operates an Integrated Quality and Environmental Management System compliant with ISO 14001. Initiatives for the protection of the natural environment cover in particular the use of technologies compliant with the best available techniques (BAT), reduction in the consumption of resources, materials and energy, reduction in emissions to the environment, minimization and proper handling of waste generated, compliance with legal and other requirements for environmental matters, raising employees' awareness of the impact of their work on the natural environment and the potential consequences of failure to follow the applicable policies. - ZGH "Bolesław" Group - the environmental policy of these companies focuses on the alignment with the growing environmental protection requirements. The companies pursue proactive initiatives, including measurements of gas and particulate matter emissions, measurements of noise emissions to the environment, and monitoring the consumption of energy utilities and fuels. A register of waste generated is also kept. - Other companies of the Stalprodukt Capital Group - only those companies whose impact can be considered significant are listed, e.g. STP Elbud sp. z o.o. operates an Integrated Management System compliant with ISO 9001, ISO 14001, EN 1090-1, EN 1090-2 and ISO 3834-2. Subsequent sections quote figures for the consumption of resources and materials, consumption of water in individual Group companies, protection of biodiversity, emissions to the atmosphere, waste management and extended environmental responsibility.
Polimex Mostostal S.A.	The Management Board's report on activity of the Group confirms that the non-financial statement of the Polimex-Mostostal Capital Group is part of the Group Management report published on the website of Polimex-Mostostal S.A.; however, one can hardly find the document on the website. When searched via a web browser, the document found provides a separate non-financial statement of the Group. Environmental matters are addressed in a dedicated section of the statement. A disclosure is made in that part that the Polimex-Mostostal Capital Group has put in place the "Environmental management" process, compliant with the PN-EN ISO 14001 standard, operated and followed in all Group companies. The business objective of the Group, which is to minimize its operating costs, is supported by pro-environmental initiatives, such as monitoring energy and energy commodities consumption, reducing industrial waste emissions, reducing the share of unsorted municipal waste generated at construction sites. Other initiatives provide for monitoring of emissions to air, contaminants in sewage, noise, waste, groundwater extraction and use of resources and materials. Subsections show figures for the consumption of materials and resources, energy, biodiversity, emissions, sewage and waste, regulatory compliance and transport, in breakdown by individual Group companies.
ELEKTROBUDOWA S.A.	The non-financial statement forms a part of the Management Board's report on activity of Elektrobudowa S.A. and the Elektrobudowa Capital Group. Environmental matters are disclosed in a separate section comprising the following subsections: resources and materials, fuels and energy, biodiversity, atmospheric emissions and waste. The statement provides that the environmental policy results from the policies of the Integrated Management System compliant with ISO 14001, of which it is an integral part. In its operations, the company follows a preventive approach to environmental protection, i.e. before any new projects are commenced, it identifies, evaluates and registers environmental aspects. It monitors noise levels, emissions to air, waste generation, energy consumption and biodiversity. Relevant figures are given in subsections. The company undertakes activities aimed at eliminating or minimizing the impact of the above-mentioned emission sources on the environment, using, if possible, the best available technologies to maintain clean production, i.e. systematic reduction of pollutant emissions, reduction in of raw materials, energy and water, wastewater treatment and failure prevention. The subsections that follow give a detailed account of activities in these areas.

Source: compiled by the author

Table 4. Environmental matters in non-financial statements of enterprises operating in the hi-tech sector

Entity	Environmental matters disclosed in non-financial statements
Comarch S.A.	As disclosed in the "Non-financial statement of Comarch S.A. and the Comarch Group for 2017", the environmental policy and procedures put in place within the Integrated Management Systems provide for a commitment of Comarch S.A. to take proactive measures with a view to reducing the negative impact on the natural environment. As part of the implemented Environmental Management System compliant with the requirements of the ISO 14001 standard, Comarch identified environmental aspects that it monitors, supervises and influences. The statement gives a detailed account of environmental matters in breakdown by the following areas: use of natural resources, finished products, energy, emissions, water, waste, car fleet. Individual areas feature relevant figures, e.g. CO_2 and other gas emissions, consumption of water, electricity and heat, fuels and gas, the amount of waste generated.
Cyfrowy Polsat S.A.	According to the information contained in the "Non-financial statement of the Cyfrowy Polsat S.A. Capital Group and Cyfrowy Polsat S.A. for the years 2016-2017", the Group's environmental initiatives consist mainly of: – control of resources consumption, – electricity saving projects, – effective waste management, – examinations of the impact of broadcast equipment on the environment.
Netia S.A.	In its "Non-financial statement of Netia S.A. and the Netia S.A. Capital Group for 2017" the company gives information on the establishment and implementation of the Environmental Policy, the content of which meets the requirements of Directive 2014/95/EU and the PN-EN ISO 14001:2015-09 standard. The areas of the Netia Group's environmental impact as disclosed in the statement are as follows: – Emissions of gases or particulate matter into the air – Marketing of packaged products – Waste electrical and electronic equipment – Marketing of batteries or accumulators – Ozone-depleting substances (controlled substances) – Keeping the noise level below or at the maximum permissible level – Waste generation and management.

Source: compiled by the author

Table 5. Environmental matters in non-financial statements of enterprises operating in the fuels and energy sector

Entity	Environmental matters disclosed in non-financial statements
ENEA S.A.	The Management Board's report on activity of the Capital Group gives a holistic account of environmental matters, with a focus on the challenges faced by the Group as a whole and its member companies, e.g. the need to take action to reduce particulate matter and SO2 emissions by PEC Piła and MEC Oborniki as a consequence of the alignment process with the requirements of the MCP Directive. The statement makes a reference to specific corporate documents that present the solutions for environmental policies, procedures and standards implemented by the entity, as listed on pages 121-122 of the statement. The statement presents figures for the Group's results as regards environmental matters (e.g. energy production from renewable energy sources (RES), energy consumption by the Enea Capital Group in 2017, water consumption in 2017 vs. the previous year, carbon dioxide emissions of the Generation Area as related to energy production processes), along with examples of pro-environmental activities undertaken in these areas (e.g. significant initiatives to reduce emissions at Kozienice Power Plant, or measures to reduce emissions of the Heat Segment). Information about pro-environmental activities undertaken in individual Group companies can be found in the part of the statement entitled "Organization and activities of the Enea Group", section "Natural Environment".
ENERGA S.A.	Environmental matters are incorporated in the company's strategy. Environmental policy assumptions are contained in the CSR report, which is published on the website of the entity to which the management refers in its report on the activities. As is clear from the CRS report, the goal of the entity is to constantly strive to improve energy efficiency, reduce emissions and use resources in an optimized manner. The environmental policy lists the following initiatives: - maintaining a high share of RES in electricity production - implementation of the EMAS environmental management system in all Group companies - implementation of the energy management system in accordance with the ISO 50001:2012 standard The Group further declares an optimized use of resources, reduction in emissions to air and in the waste stream, improvement of reliability and safety of energy production and supply. It also monitors activities focused on minimizing the negative impact on the natural environment, promotes initiatives related to environmental protection and undertakes actions aimed at promoting ecological responsibility The report presents figures on direct emissions of greenhouse gases (the list includes all Group companies), emissions of NOx, SOx compounds and other emissions to air, as well as the free allocation of CO_2 emission allowances.
TAURON POLSKA ENERGIA S.A.	In its non-financial statement, the TAURON Capital Group declared that with a view to ensuring compliance with new regulatory requirements in 2017, the Group adopted the TAURON Group Environmental Policy (Environmental Policy), as described in very general terms in further parts of the statement. The statement confirms that the TAURON Capital Group is committed to care for the natural environment and takes responsibility for the consequences of using its resources. Recognizing this as an important social obligation, TAURON has been undertaking a number of initiatives aimed at minimizing the negative impact of its operations on the natural environment. All Group companies have adopted the Environmental Policy defining the approach to environmental management, including the general direction of environmental initiatives of the organization and the principles followed in environmental management. However, activities undertaken in the field of environmental protection are disclosed in another part of the report on the activities, i.e. the corporate social responsibility (CSR) policy, in the section on the impact on the natural environment. The key activities in this respect include: continued construction project of a 910 MW power unit in Jaworzno III Power Plant, to bring a reduction of NOx, SO_2, CO_2 and particulate matter emissions to air, commencement of Jaworzno III Power Plant - II Power Unit sewage treatment revamp with auxiliary chemical treatment module, commencement of upgrading projects for the road tanker unloading station for hydrochloric acid, sodium hydroxide and ferric sulphate at Łaziska Power Plant. The Group minimizes the negative impact by constantly monitoring the main aspects of direct and indirect environmental impact of its operations. The Group also boasted the results of its activities, stating that in 2017 its power units generated emissions considerably lower than the currently applicable emission standards for NOx, SO_2 and particulate matter, and often already close to the future environmental emission limits. As a confirmation, the report discloses annual emission levels of NOx, SO_2, particulate matter and CO_2 for 2017 from fuel combustion in energy generation.

Source: compiled by the author

Table 6. Environmental matters in non-financial statements of enterprises operating in the trade and services sector

Entity	Environmental matters disclosed in non-financial statements
IMPEL S.A.	The non-financial statement is a separate document. Environmental matters are discussed in the "Environmental Aspects" section. The statement announces that in the sense of responsibility for environmental protection matters, the company uses and develops such service delivery technologies and processes that minimize the negative impact on the environment. Pro-environmental activities undertaken are described in breakdown by the types of services provided, i.e. janitorial, laundry, rental and catering, with a focus on matters related to the use of resources and materials, biodiversity, water, waste and sewage, fuels and energy. The statement also describes the effects of BLABO technology on the environment. The matters discussed are supported with figures, such as the amount of consumed clothing, consumption of water and energy, etc., while the company puts an emphasis on the reduction in consumption of the presented items. The statement lists the activities contributing to the pro-ecological portfolio, including: training and motivating the personnel performing the service, raising awareness and promoting appropriate perceptions of synergies between technology and effective methods of reducing harmful substance emissions, optimizing waste generation control processes, efficient collection and disposal of waste, and support to customers in the implementation of their policies and hierarchies of values that promote corporate responsibility for environmental protection.
Inter Cars S.A.	The report on the activities gives information that non-financial statements can be found on the website in the non-financial statements section. The statement is also referred to as "Responsible business in the Inter Cars Group". In the statement, the company declares that its approach to environmental matters is based on the Code of Conduct and Good Market Practices of the Inter Cars Group. The Code also provides examples of desired behaviors, e.g. disposal of waste only into appropriate containers, reducing paper consumption, promoting pro-environmental attitudes among customers and partners. Educated waste management is the foundation of care for the environment, the framework of which is determined by the OSHE Policy of the Group. The company reaches out to include its business partners in these initiatives. The Group is looking for new solutions that will help increase the efficiency of operations and optimize the use of resources (extension of the European Centre for Logistics and Development in Zakroczym). The statement discloses selected figures.
BENEFIT SYSTEM S.A.	Non-financial information as required under the Accounting Act was included in the CRS non-financial statement. A separate section is devoted to environmental matters, which presents the main assumptions of the company's environmental policy. The company, as an entity promoting active lifestyle, supports and undertakes pro-environmental initiatives. It raises employee awareness of environmental matters both in the context of their work and non-professional life (organization of knowledge quizzes and environmental contests). Other activities include the very location of the company's headquarters, provision of infrastructure for bicycle commuters and reducing the amount of paper printouts (by use of electronic invoices). This part of the statement is hardly extensive (2 pages)

Source: compiled by the author

Table 7. Environmental matters in non-financial statements of enterprises operating in the healthcare sector

Entity	Environmental matters disclosed in non-financial statements
CENTRUM MEDYCZNE ENEL MED. S.A.	The non-financial statement is a separate document. The last section of the statement is devoted to environmental matters, with a declaration that the company takes actions aimed at minimizing the negative impact on the environment. Examples of such actions include: minimizing the consumption of electricity through the use of LED lighting systems in new investment projects, disposal of used equipment and waste segregation, and use of an economical and environmentally friendly car fleet. The statement does not present any figures.
MERCATOR MEDICAL S.A.	The non-financial statement is a separate document. The Group has not yet adopted a formal environmental policy, although it undertakes a number of pro-environmental initiatives. The following initiatives are disclosed: using, where possible, raw materials of natural origin, conducting effective and economical management of resources and materials, striving for reduction in energy consumption, emissions of pollutants, carrying out upgrading works for water purification, using recycled packaging, etc. These matters are supported with figures
BIOTON S.A.	The non-financial statement is included in the Management Board's report on activity. The company has put in place an "environmental policy", which defines the framework of the environmental management system, and sets its objectives, including: Managing the optimized consumption of water and electricity, limiting the amount of waste generated (reduction of quantities, segregation and transfer to appropriate disposal companies), raising the level of pro-ecological awareness among employees and subcontractors. All initiatives in this regard are supported with figures.

Source: compiled by the author

SOLUTIONS AND RECOMMENDATIONS

In view of the fact that non-financial information has nowadays a growing impact on the financial results of entities (e.g. loss of reputation), and the share of intangible assets in corporate property is rising, it is difficult to undermine the merits of the decision on introducing the obligation to draw up non-financial statements for public interest entities. With the requirement to annually present activities undertaken in designated areas (environmental matters, social and employee-related matters, anti-corruption), the obligation of non-financial reporting may raise entities' sensitivity to and awareness of those matters. The adoption of a policy in this area in the form of a document will allow entities to structure and systematize the initiatives pursued.

It would be recommended to prepare a good practice document containing guidelines for non-financial reporting for entities obliged to prepare such statements. To establish such a document is important for several reasons, including:

- To ensure that the entity's management does not treat the presented non-financial statement as a form of marketing brand creation but to increase the reliability and transparency of the presented results of the enterprise. Departure from the "hard" and easily verifiable principles of creating financial statements may cause difficulties in the assessment of accuracy and reliability of their preparation. The consequence of subjectivity in the selection of disclosed information (financial and non-financial) may be that users of financial statements will obtain a creation of an enterprise picture devised by those who prepare financial statements, instead of an objective presentation of the assets and financial position and financial result of the entity.
- To determine the scope and level of detail of the information presented in order to ensure comparability of reports between entities obliged to provide non-financial statements.
- To ensure that extending reporting information with non-financial information does not lead to an informational "overload" of financial statements, thereby reducing their transparency and increasing the difficulty in extracting material information. IASB pointed to that problem when introducing amendments to IAS 1 that allow the inclusion in the explanatory notes only of information that is relevant to the users of the statement. It should be stressed, however, that given the number and variety of recipients of financial statements of individual entities, it is extremely difficult to choose the most important items. What adds to that is a problem that has already been raised above, i.e. the subjectivity of the choice of disclosed reporting information.

The extension of the scope of reporting information to non-financial statements increase the usefulness of the financial statement for stakeholders. The potential investors making a decision to buy shares take into an account not only financial parameters but all aspects of the company including the manner and style of governance and its attitude to environmental issues.

FUTURE RESEARCH DIRECTIONS

The objective pursued in this research is to present the scope and details information on environmental issues included in non-financial statements. By answering the research question "How do public interest entities fulfil their duties within the scope of environmental matters as a part of non-financial statement?", this study tries to attribute to both literature and practice. There is not much literature available regarding non-financial statement prepared by Polish public interest entities.

The study showed that public interests entities prepare non-financial statement in accordance with the requirements of the Directive 2014/95/EU of the European Parliament and of the Council of 22 October 2014 and the amended Accounting Act. In the future, research on a non-financial statement should be conducted to prepare a good practice document containing guidelines for non-financial reporting. In this way their scope and details could be unified, and thus non-financial statements of different companies would be comparable.

Some thought should also be given to how the scope of disclosure of non-financial information may affect the competitive position of an entity. The legislator obliged entities to disclose a concise description of the business model in the non-financial statement. In the author's opinion, this is the optimum solution. It gives entities the opportunity to inform stakeholders about the model of the company's operation, without exposing it to the risk of disclosure of trade secrets and thus protecting its competitive position. One should bear in mind that competitors are also the recipients of financial statements, besides business partners and the management.

CONCLUSION

Public interest entities constitute a significant element of economy. Since 2017 the large ones have been obligated to compile non-financial statement including environmental issue. Extension of the scope of financial statement is grounded particularly in social responsibility theory, which is focused on the social, ecological and ethical aspects of business. Nowadays business partners assess the companies not only from the point of view of financial results but also from their attitudes to social and environmental matters. The authors confirmed all the research hypothesis. Public interest entities compile non-financial statements, although their scope of information is different. Undoubtedly, this is due to the fact that in 2017, the entities prepared such reports for the first time. Therefore, in the future the scope and details of non-financial information should be explored to create a good practice guidebook. Introducing the obligation to description of policies with respect to environmental matter should be assessed positively, because the need to create such policy in this area or to provide the reasons for not introducing them may make enterprises more sensitive to these issues and may be the basis for verification of declared activities with the real ones.

The Ministry of Finance noticed the issue and significance of non-financial reporting and in cooperation with the Ministry of Investment and Economic Development prepared a study: "Reporting on extended non-financial information for 2017 in accordance with the Accounting Act – first experiences and best practices." This is the first, greatly needed step towards creation of the catalogue of best practices in this area.

REFERENCES

Costa, E., & Pesci, C. (2016). Social impact measurement: Why do stakeholders matter? *Sustainability Accounting. Management and Policy Journal, 7*(1), 99–124.

Dusiński, A. (2003). Zasady etycznego postępowania w firmie. In W. Gasparski, A. Lewicka-Strzałecka, B. Rok, & G. Szulczewski (Eds.), Europejskie standardy etyki i społecznej odpowiedzialności biznesu (pp. 167-177). Warszawa, Poland: Wydawnictwo Wyższej Szkoły Przedsiębiorczości i Zarządzania im. Leona Koźmińskiego.

Fijałkowska, J. (2016). Raportowanie informacji niefinansowych zgodnie z nową dyrektywą UE 2014/95/UE jako wyzwanie dla przedsiębiorstw. In E. Kożuchowska, (Ed.), Rachunkowość na rzecz zrównoważonego rozwoju. Gospodarka - etyka – środowisko (pp. 30-40). Wrocław, Poland: Wydawnictwo Uniwersytetu Ekonomicznego we Wrocławiu.

Iwanicz-Drozdowska, M., Jaworski, W., Szelągowska, A., & Zawadzka, Z. (2017). *Bankowość- Instytucje, operacje, zarzadzanie*. Warszawa, Poland: Poltext.

Kamela-Sowińska, A. (2014). Od rachunkowości do opisu gospodarczego. *Zeszyty Teoretyczne Rachunkowości, 77*(133), 107–115.

Kamela-Sowińska, A. (2016). Czy rachunkowość to już nauka społeczna? In A. Karmańska (Ed.), *Nauka o rachunkowości na progu gospodarki opartej na wiedzy* (pp. 309–328). Warszawa, Poland: Oficyna Wydawnicza - Szkoła Głowna Handlowa w Warszawie.

Krasodomska, J. (2010). Informacje niefinansowe jako element rocznego raportu spółki. *Zeszyty Naukowe. Uniwersytet Ekonomiczny w Krakowie, 816*, 45–57.

Masztalerz, M. (2014). Wartość dla interesariuszy w zrównoważonym przedsiębiorstwie. *Studia Oeconomica Posnaniensia, 2*(8), 66–77.

Raportowanie rozszerzonych informacji niefinansowych za rok 2017 – pierwsze doświadczenia i dobre praktyki. (n.d.). Retrieved from https://www.gov.pl/documents/1079560/1080340/Raport_MF.PDF/1b41abe7-a7db-60a8-4641-cbbb0fb35764

Roszkowska, P. (2011). *Rewolucja w raportowaniu biznesowym. Interesariusze, konkurencyjność, społeczna odpowiedzialność*. Warszawa, Poland: DIFIN.

29. September 1994 - The Accounting Act (uniform text Dz. U. z 2019 r. poz. 351).

The Act of 11.05.2017 on Statutory Auditors, Audit Firms and Public Oversight (uniform text Dz. U. z 2017 r. poz. 1089).

The Act of The Directive 2014/95/EU of the European Parliament and of the Council of 22 October 2014.

Walińska, E. (2015). Zintegrowany raport - początek końca sprawozdania finansowego? *Zeszyty Teoretyczne Rachunkowości, 82*(138), 151–165.

Wójcik-Jurkiewicz, M. (2016). Idea społecznie odpowiedzialnego biznesu a kształtowanie wyniku finansowego spółki. *Studia Ekonomiczne: Zeszyty Naukowe Uniwersytetu Ekonomicznego w Katowicach, 253*, 140–150.

Wykaz jednostek zainteresowania publicznego. (n.d.). Retrieved from https://www.gov.pl/web/finanse/wykaz-jzp-1

Zaleska, M., & Koleśnik, J. (2018). Zarządzanie sytuacją kryzysową - działania pomocowe i gwarancyjne. In M. Zaleska (Ed.), *Świat bankowości*. Warszawa, Poland: DIFIN.

ENDNOTE

1 Eco-Management and Audit Scheme is the EU system of environmental certification functioning on the basis of the Regulation (EC) No. 1221/2009 of the European Parliament and of the Council of 25 November 2009 on the voluntary participation by organisations in a Community eco-management and audit scheme (EMAS). The requirements of this system provide guidelines and instructions owing to which entities organize their environmental duties, optimize costs and manage energy and resources efficiently. This is also a credible system of reporting on an entity's influence on the environment.

Chapter 5
Sustainable Public Procurement as an Instrument for the Implementation of Sustainable Development in the European Union

Małgorzata Burchard-Dziubińska
University of Lodz, Poland

Tomasz Jakubiec
City Hall of Lodz, Poland

ABSTRACT

The aim of the considerations is to assess the effectiveness of sustainable public procurement (SPP) as a tool for the implementation of sustainable development in the European Union. The chapter discusses the legal bases for the use of sustainable public procurement in the EU, the potential of the public sector in the implementation of sustainable development through public procurement in the EU, functioning of the market for sustainable public procurement, market potential of the public sector of the European Union in the implementation of sustainable development through public procurement, good practices and barriers related to green public procurement (GPP), and socially responsible procurement (SRPP). The chapter ends with conclusions from the research and practical recommendations regarding the use of sustainable public procurement in the European Union.

INTRODUCTION

The paradigm of sustainable development, starting from dilemmas related to responsible management of the environment and its resources, with a rapidly added extension to social issues, shaped in the theory of economics and economic policy the need for integrated treatment of development processes in an intra- and intergenerational approach. The concept of sustainable development, a political priority

DOI: 10.4018/978-1-7998-1033-9.ch005

in the European Community at the turn of the 20th century, triggered the need for conscious action of the authorities at all levels of governing in the implementation of policy creating political and socio-economic progress. These activities are accompanied by the search for new effective tools which enable real implementation of sustainable development. This chapter is devoted to the theoretical and practical aspects of sustainable public procurement in the European Union. Public procurement is a set of rules and procedures governed by specific regulations resulting from the public finance management concept, enabling the implementation of public tasks, for the public good in the broad sense, implemented through territorial and functional structures (public institutions) of the state. (Jakubiec, 2018), (Buying Green, 2016). Such procurements are designed to include the public sector into the implementation of sustainable development. Taking into account the legal aspects of the sector's functioning, it became necessary to develop appropriate regulations and procedures which would make it possible to use environmental and social criteria consistent with the concept of sustainable development in public procurement. It is about using, in the procurement processes, solutions making it possible to include, at each stage of project implementation, clauses relating to the three pillars of sustainable development, i.e. environmental protection, social inclusion and stimulating the economy.

The aim of the considerations is to assess the effectiveness of sustainable public procurement (SPP) as a tool for the implementation of sustainable development in the European Union. The chapter discusses, respectively; the legal bases for the use of SPP in the EU, the potential of the public sector in the implementation of sustainable development through public procurement in the EU; functioning of the market for SPP, market potential of the public sector of the European Union in the implementation of sustainable development through public procurement, good practices and barriers related to green public procurement (GPP) and socially responsible public procurement (SRPP). The chapter ends with conclusions from the research and practical recommendations regarding the use of sustainable public procurement in the European Union.

The chapter uses the results of many years of research on the application of SPP in the practice of EU countries, statistical data and literature studies.

LEGAL ASPECTS OF THE USE OF SUSTAINABLE PUBLIC PROCUREMENT IN THE EUROPEAN UNION

Sustainable public procurement by applying criteria which reduce the negative impact on the environment and affecting attitudes and socially responsible actions, ensuring social inclusion, is aimed at implementing technical and organizational solutions, methods and materials to obtain goods and services or implement investments in a way which guarantees that they will have an impact on the environment and social environment much more favorably than those obtained in a traditional way. In order to successfully achieve the desired environmental and social goals, it is necessary to appropriately implement actions in the legal system, in particular relating to public procurement. In the European Union, this problem was noticed already in 2001, when the Interpretative communication of the Commission on the Community law applicable to public procurement and the possibilities for integrating environmental considerations into public procurement COM (2001) 274, and Interpretative Communication of the Commission on the Community law applicable to public procurement and the possibilities for integrating social considerations into public procurement, COM (2001) 566 were adopted.

In the following years, a whole range of regulations related directly or indirectly to these issues was adopted. The most important were: Communication from the Commission on Integrated Product Policy (IPP) COM (2003) 302, and Communication from the Commission to the European Parliament, the Council, the European Economic and Social Committee and the Committee of the Regions Public procurement for a better environment COM (2008) 400. The aim of the Communication was to harmonize environmental criteria in tender procedures throughout the EU. The priority categories of industries and products were indicated. They include construction, food and catering services, transport and transport services, energy, office computer equipment, clothing, and other textiles, paper and printing services, furniture, cleaning products and services in the field of cleaning and gardening and services in this area. The criteria within each sector have been divided into "basic" and "comprehensive". The Communication introduced the Set of Green Criteria for Public Procurement; the so-called *GPPTool Kit* constantly developed by the European Commission as part of increasing cohesion, popularizing good practices and disseminating GPP standards. The Communication also pointed to the need to build competitiveness, since award criteria, if given a significant weighting, may give an important signal to the market place. Depending on the type of product, the number and importance of the other - non-environmental - award criteria, a weighting of 15% is considered to be "significant" from 2008 onwards.

An important role plays also integrated product policy - an initiative of the European Commission. Its aim is to link the broadly understood product policy with environmental protection by referring to the so-called product life cycle. The European Commission has obliged all Member States to present by the end of 2006 action plans in the field of GPP, i.e., strategic documents indicating the objectives of "greening" public procurement, activity in dissemination of knowledge on GPP, good practices and monitoring progress in implementing this policy.

The core of currently applicable EU regulations on sustainable public procurement consists of three directives adopted and approved by the Council of the European Union: Directive 2014/24/EU of 26 February 2014 on public procurement, Directive 2014/25/EU of 26 February 2014 on procurement by entities operating in the water, energy, transport and postal services sectors, and Directive 2014/23/EU of 26 February 2014 on the award of concession contracts. The deadline for the implementation of directives into the legal orders of EU Member States has been set at 24 months since their entry into force. In connection with the need to update the public procurement system in the European Union and adapt them to the implementation of the Europe 2020 strategy, these directives have replaced the regulations applicable since 2004. In particular, it was about simplifying the regulations, adapting them to the changing political and socio-economic situation and increasing their effectiveness and efficiency (Aspey, 2015).

Under the 2014 directives, significant practical changes have been introduced, including:

- A new principle on the award of public procurement contracts related to ensuring that contractors comply with obligations in the field of environmental law, social and labor law in the implementation of public procurement, applicable primarily in determining the terms of implementing procurement;
- Extension of the scope of entities which can apply for reserved contracts in public reserved procurement and relaxation of requirements regarding the level of employment of people from specific socially marginalized groups;
- Extension of the catalog of crimes (including those against the environment) resulting in obligatory exclusion of contractors from the tender procedure;

- New optional grounds for excluding contractors from the tender procedure; e.g. (those who/which have not paid taxes, fees or social security or health contributions for their employees);
- Environmental, social and employment-related aspects, at the same time taking into account all stages of the life cycle as acceptable conditions of the contract implementation;
- The requirement to draw up technical specifications, taking into account the accessibility criteria for people with disabilities or design for all users;
- An additional regime of reserved orders for specific health, social and cultural services;
- Allowing the possibility of requiring a specific label within technical specifications, award criteria or contract performance conditions;
- Cost criterion as a criterion for awarding the contract and allowing the use of Life Cycle Costing;
- Extension of the admissible criteria for awarding the contract to all aspects and all stages of the life cycle of the subject of the contract.

It can be stated that currently the directives create better opportunities for contracting entities to use public procurement in the field of supporting ecological and social objectives, and to a greater extent include public entities which belong to the so-called social entrepreneurship and social economy into public procurement.

In particular Directive 2014/24/EU on public procurement, repealing the Directive 2004/18/EC with effect from 18 April 2016, significantly expanded the possibilities of applying existing solutions regarding social aspects and introduced new instruments to promote social inclusion through public procurement. The Directive contains new regulations concerning, inter alia, promotion and real use of non-economic objectives of public procurement, including such as social integration. The preamble in item 37 states:

"With a view to an appropriate integration of environmental, social and labor requirements into public procurement procedures it is of particular importance that Member States and contracting authorities take relevant measures to ensure compliance with obligations in the fields of environmental, social and labor law that apply at the place where the works are executed or the services provided and result from laws, regulations, decrees and decisions, at both national and Union level, as well as from collective agreements, provided that such rules, and their application, comply with Union law."

This also includes international agreements listed in Annex X to this Directive. These are ILO conventions 87, 98, 29, 105, 138, 111, 100, 182 regarding labor rights, forced labor and child labor, and conventions related to the protection of the natural environment: Vienna Convention for the protection of the ozone layer and its Montreal Protocol on substances that deplete the ozone layer, Basel Convention on the Control of Transboundary Movements of Hazardous Wastes and their Disposal, Stockholm Convention on Persistent Organic Pollutants, and Convention on the Prior Informed Consent Procedure for Certain Hazardous Chemicals and Pesticides in International Trade (UNEP/FAO) (The PIC Convention) Rotterdam, and its 3 regional Protocols.

In turn, point 40 of this preamble refers to the issue of monitoring compliance with environmental law, social law and labor law. "It should be performed at the relevant stage of the procurement procedure, when applying the general principles governing the choice of participants and award of contracts and when applying the exclusion criteria and applying the provisions concerning abnormally low tenders."

From the point of view of the implementation of socially responsible public procurement, important provisions are included in Article 20 of this directive, which concerns reserved contracts. It states that "Member States may reserve the right to participate in public procurement procedures for sheltered workshops and economic operators whose main aim is the social and professional integration of disabled or disadvantaged persons or may provide for such contracts to be performed in the context of sheltered employment programs, provided that at least 30% of the employees of those workshops, economic operators or programs are disabled or disadvantaged workers."

In addition, Article 43 of the Directive provides for the use of labels confirming that works, supplies or services meet the required environmental or social characteristics.

It is worth noting that the Directive 2014/24/EU also provides grounds for exclusion of tenderers from participation in the procurement procedure if it is determined that a valid judgment has been issued against that tenderer for one of the following acts: Child labor and other forms of trafficking in human beings, as defined in Article 2 of Directive 2011/36/EU of the European Parliament and of the Council, and/or when a person convicted by final judgment is a member of the administrative, management or supervisory body of that economic operator or has powers of representation, decision or control therein. Contractor exclusion also applies to cases of breach of obligations relating to the payment of taxes or social security contributions.

Pursuant to item 39 of Directive 2014/24/EU, the obligations of economic operators in public procurement regarding compliance with labor law and social law should be included in the provisions of the public procurement contract.

It is worth adding that the above regulations included in the framework directives are strengthened by a number of Community regulations imposing on the public entities certain additional obligations in the scope of environmental management, the recognition of ecological and social standards. The more important are: Regulation (EC) No 106/2008 of the European Parliament and of the Council of 15 January 2008 on a Community energy-efficiency labeling program for office equipment; Directive 2010/30/EU of the European Parliament and of the Council of 19 May 2010 on the indication by labeling and standard product information of the consumption of energy and other resources by energy-related products; Directive 2009/33 / EC of the European Parliament and of the Council of 23 April 2009 on the promotion of clean and energy-efficient road transport vehicles; Regulation (EC) No. 66/2010 of the European Parliament and of the Council of 25 November 2009 on the EU Eco-label.

The dissemination of sustainable public procurement is implemented by so-called national action plans for sustainable public procurement. They are developed in all Member States of the European Union. Already in 2003 the European Commission in its Communication on Integrated Product Policy (IPP) encouraged Member States to develop publicly available national action plans (NAPs - *National Action Plans*) for "greening" - making their public procurement more environmentally friendly. National action plans should include an assessment of the current situation and ambitious targets for the next three years, specifying what measures will be taken to achieve them. They are not legally binding, but constitute a political impetus for the implementation process and raise awareness of the use of sustainable public procurement and are a tool for monitoring it. They allow Member States to choose options best suited to their political framework and levels achieved in the practical implementation of sustainable development using the public procurement system.

MARKET POTENTIAL OF THE EUROPEAN UNION PUBLIC SECTOR IN THE IMPLEMENTATION OF SUSTAINABLE DEVELOPMENT THROUGH PUBLIC PROCUREMENT

The market of public procurement which includes environmental and social criteria, may apply to virtually all contracts carried out by public institutions and entities, covering the entire public sector's expenditure. Its potential is determined by its value and quantitative parameters, such as the number of notices of tender procedures. Regarding the area of the European Union, the impact of the common market, which is estimated at around 500 million consumers, needs to be emphasized. In the sectoral cross-section, the most important indicator is the volume of purchasing power represented by the public sector, the largest consumer in the European economy. This is reflected by the nominal values of total public expenditure and their share in the Community GDP (Table 1.). In 2015, the EU public expenditure market for works, supplies and services ordered by classical entities was valued at EUR 2015.3 billion, representing 13.7% of the total GDP of the European Union (Public Procurement Indicators 2015). Classical entities do not include entities operating in strategic departments, so-called sectors; therefore they do not include the so-called utilities and defense orders. The contracts awarded by enterprises operating in the water, energy, transport and postal services sectors, known as sectoral orders are a specific part of the public procurement market. The defense sector is also treated separately. A small group of entities here has a significant share in the total value of the market, and the average value of "sectoral" tenders is clearly higher than the average value of all tenders (Sprawozdanie, 2016). At the same time, according to the estimated value of public tenders published in the Supplement to the Official Journal of the European Union *Tenders Electronic Daily* the so-called TED (excluding utilities tenders) the value of the market was 349.18 billion euros, and with utilities and defense tenders 450.21 billion, with the total number of tenders published in TED for EU28 reaching 154,129 tenders without utilities and defense tenders and 172,888 with utilities and defense orders (Public Procurement Indicators 2015). *Tenders Electronic Daily* is an online version of the "*Supplement to the Official Journal of the European Union*" dedicated to European public procurement. About 460,000 procurement notices are published annually on the TED website, including 175 thousand calls for tenders, with a total value of EUR 420 billion (including media supplies and the defense sector). As to the quantitative structure of public procurement published in the EU's Official Electronic Procurement Journal, it was as follows: The volume of 128,246 (74.18%) tenders was announced by the "old" (EU15) member countries of the Community, and 44,642 (25.82%) by "new" countries. For example, Polish contracting entities published in 2015 - 21,116 procurement notices, which constituted 12.21% of tenders announced in TED by all EU countries. Orders from Poland accounted for 47.3% of tenders announced by the "new" member countries (Sprawozdanie, 2016).

Due to the lack of data on the GPP and SRPP collected cyclically at the Community level, the European Commission derives estimates from studies or analyzes in this area carried out occasionally on representative samples from Member States. Based on the "*The uptake of green public procurement in the EU27*" study it was estimated that the GPP market in 2012 had approx. 38% share in the total value of public procurement and about 26% share in the number of published tenders, without taking into account EU thresholds in the area of public procurement, i.e. outside TED. On the basis of the above-mentioned study, an image of the spatial distribution of the application of environmental criteria by the EU Member States was also obtained, both as regards the percentage share in terms of the number and value of tenders with the GPP criteria. Regarding the number of tenders, the dominance of the Scandi-

Table 1. The size of the public procurement market in the European Union (2012 - 2015)

Category	2012	2013	2014	2015	Mean
Public sector purchasing power estimated by the value of public expenditure on construction works, supplies, services (excluding sectoral expenditure) in EUR billion	1,867.5	1,880.5	1,933.2	2,015.3	1,924.1
Estimated value of public expenditure on construction works, supplies, services (excluding sectoral ones) as % of GDP	13.9	13.9	13.8	13.7	13.8
Estimated value of tenders published in TED (including utilities and defense) in EUR billion	401.72	422.10	421.33	450.21	423.84
Estimated value of tenders published in TED (excluding utilities and defense) in EUR billion	326.69	335.51	319.66	349.18	332.86
Number of tenders published in TED (non-utilities and defense)	149,145	152,663	151,058	154,129	151,749
Number of tenders published in TED (with utilities and defense)	166,216	170,238	169,687	172,888	169,757

Source: Authors' own compilation based on: *Public Procurement Indicators 2015* European Commission, DG GROW G4 - Innovative and e-Procurement, December 19, 2016.

navian and Benelux countries is evident, they account for 60-80% of tenders containing GPP criteria. The "new" EU countries are maturing in this respect, the tenders with environmental criteria account there for 20%. (Renda et al, 2012).

In terms of tenders' value, the situation is slightly different. In this case Finland is in the first place (80%). The high share of tenders with GPP criteria in the range of 40-80% is presented by the Benelux and Baltic States as well as Hungary, Romania and Italy. The low level (below 20%) was observed in 11 countries: Bulgaria, Cyprus, Poland, Greece, Slovakia, France, Estonia, Malta, the United Kingdom, Ireland and Portugal.

However, it should be emphasized that a thorough analysis of green markets and socially-responsible public procurement remains a methodological challenge. It was not possible to obtain comprehensive statistical data. At the same time, the research is expensive and difficult to carry out due to technical and organizational reasons. Inference about the entirety of the market on the basis of fragmentary research on random samples will always be subject to some error. Considering the scale and complexity of the public procurement market, the results published in the *'Strategic use of public procurement in promoting green, social and innovation policies'* developed by PwC in December 2015 can be considered as worth noting. The analysis concerned the use of so-called strategic public procurement, including: green public procurement, socially responsible public procurement and innovative procurement. The substantive value of the study is demonstrated by the methodology based on the use of three objective sources of data acquisition for 2013, i.e. desk research - comparative analyzes based on EU and national publications, including reports to public procurement offices and their counterparts, guidelines and information sheets; TED data analysis based on data from 2013; and in-depth interviews with interested parties in 10 selected EU Member States regarding the value of the GPP market, SRPP and IPP, and the number and type of tender procedures: The following countries were analyzed: Austria; France; Latvia, the Netherlands; Poland, Portugal; Slovakia; Spain; Sweden; and United Kingdom. Based on the analysis of TED data, GPP's share in the public procurement market was estimated at 14% of all published tenders and at 25% of the monetary value of this market. GPP proved to be the most institutionalized and the most frequently used type of strategic tenders. In the case of SRPP it was respectively: 10% of the number of

Table 2. Estimated size of the GPP and SRPP markets by number and value of tenders in 10 selected EU countries in 2013

EU country	Number of GPP procurement procedures and their share in the total number of procurement procedures (%)	Number of SRPP procurement procedures and their share in the total number of procurement procedures (%)	Value of GPP procedures (in millions EUR)	Value of SRPP procedures (in millions EUR)	Total number of procurement procedures per country	Total value of the procedures per country (in millions EUR)
Austria	40 (3%)	42 (3%)	47	49	1,261	2,411
Spain	517 (8%)	89 (1%)	3,518	197	6,115	19,636
France	5,320 (23%)	3,622 (16%)	15,928	13,330	23,312	42,842
Latvia	20%)	0 (0%)	5	-	821	1,633
Netherlands	648 (25%)	486 (19%)	1,788	1,748	2,613	5,531
Poland	820 (4%)	397 (2%)	2,096	1,115	18,584	28,159
Portugal	17 (2%)	3 (%)	24	1	729	7,025
Sweden	96 (3%)	17 (1%)	64	18	3,039	3,025
Slovakia	103 (9%)	105 (9%)	555	107	125	12,506
United Kingdom	1,139 (27%)	1,288 (30%)	40,785	28,180	4,253	141,153
Total	8,702 (14%)	6,049 (10%)	64,810	44,745	61,852	263,921

Source: Authors' own compilation based on: *Social and innovation policies*, European Commission, *op. cit.*, p. 52.

tenders and 17% of the monetary value. Using the keyword search in the tender documents as a research tool, it was found that the most commonly used keywords concern sustainable development, respect for basic human rights and working conditions as well as prototypes and pilot projects (Table 2).

As shown by the data in Table 2 the use of GPP and SRPP varies between EU countries. GPP are definitely more popular. This is evident both in terms of their number and total value. Slovakia was an exception in the surveyed group of countries. It showed a slight quantitative advantage of the SRPP, although in terms of value in this country, GPP prevailed more than five times.

Multilevel governance model is becoming increasingly important in the spending of public funds, which is associated, in accordance with the principle of subsidiarity, with the delegation of powers and tasks by the state to the levels of administration and management, giving the highest efficiency of providing specific services to citizens (Szlachta 2011).

When analyzing the public procurement market in the EU in the field of the awarding administration level (central, local/self-government), it is also important to take into account the large number of contracting entities and their different size and legal formula. The number of awarding entities in the EU is estimated at over 250,000 of which only about 35,000 publish announcements in the Official Journal (*Impact and Effectiveness of EU Public Procurement Legislation 2011*). Disproportions between the number of awarding entities and publishing announcements in accordance with the requirements of the directives result from the adopted political and organizational solutions related to the centralization or decentralization of public procurement (Łapacz, 2015).

CRITERIA FOR THE USE OF SUSTAINABLE PUBLIC PROCUREMENT

It is important that the criteria mentioned in the specification of the essential terms of the tender are clearly defined and related to the subject of the procurement procedure. Greener goods and services can be determined, for example, based on their life cycle or a life-cycle cost analysis. The acceptance of the fact that the criterion of the price of a product is not always a good choice is the basic assumption in the discussed approach. Therefore, if possible, environmentally friendly aspects should be introduced into the tender procedure, which in delivery contracts may:

- Indicate the material from which the device is to be made;
- Ban the use of substances harmful to human health and the environment;
- Specify technical parameters affecting the environment (e.g. emission level);
- Determine noise level, emission level, energy consumption, and water consumption);
- Indicate the minimum percentage share of the recycled component.

In considering the environmental criteria, it is also important that they are voluntary and that their introduction is to disseminate environmentally friendly technologies and models of solutions (in terms of products and services) and bring economic benefits, generate innovation, and affect production and consumption patterns, stimulating the market in line with the objectives of the *Europe 2020* strategy.

The social criteria of public procurement themselves, as defined by the European Commission, mean such contracts that, taking into account the principles of the Treaty on European Union and directives on public procurement, cover at least one of the following social aspects:

- Employment opportunities (including a contract of employment),
- Decent work,
- Compliance with social and labor laws,
- Social inclusion (including people with disabilities),
- Equal opportunities,
- Accessibility design for everyone,
- Protection against violation of human rights and encouraging respect for these rights,
- Supporting ‘social inclusion’ and promoting organizations involved in the social economy,
- Stimulating integration,
- Demonstrating the social sensitivity of the authorities,
- Sustainable development criteria, including ethical trade issues and wider voluntary compliance with the principles of corporate social responsibility (CSR) understood as the conscious need to respect both moral principles and the obligation to account for their actions before the public.

In a broad sense, social clauses are solutions which allow for taking into account important social considerations when implementing procurement procedures, giving the contracting authority the possibility of making the contract conditional upon the contractor fulfilling certain conditions which are important due to the social benefits achieved due to their fulfillment.

Social clauses are understood as derogation from the public procurement rules in accordance with public procurement law, allowing for the application of additional criteria for selection of the contractor due to important social considerations. They are an instrument of social policy. The immediate purpose of their application is primarily to maintain employment and create new jobs for socially excluded people, as well as to support the development of the social economy.

Issues related to the SRPP are not only legal in nature. Ensuring that all employees throughout the supply chain are treated appropriately is a challenge for procurement personnel, especially when the extraction of raw materials and/or the production of goods take place in different countries. This is particularly difficult when some part of the supply chain is implemented outside the EU. It is always required that compliance with all the social criteria specified in the tender, such as the exclusion of goods produced using child labor or the fulfillment of the basic conventions of the International Labor Organization, can be verified in a transparent and reliable manner. Achieving this can be time-consuming and complicated for both suppliers and buyers. Social clauses which testify to public social tenders can take different forms. The social nature of the order is decided by the functionality and a group of beneficiaries to whom the services, products are dedicated. Social clauses may define social requirements related to the implementation of the procurement procedure, e.g. by obliging contractors to hire persons from specific groups when contracting, or by specifying the forms of employment of persons performing specific activities during the procurement procedure. Socially responsible procurement also allows limiting the group of contractors applying for a public contract to entities whose activities include the social and professional integration of people from socially excluded, marginalized groups, including entities of the so-called social economy (de Rosa, 2007).

It should be remembered that the criteria and clauses, including catalogs of references to such issues as: quality, technical value, aesthetic and functional properties, directly environmental aspects, innovation, social clauses, maintenance, life cycle costing shall be used provided that they:

- Concern the subject of the procurement procedure;
- Do not grant the contracting authority unlimited freedom of choice;
- Are clearly identified;
- Were indicated in the tender announcement and documentation;
- Comply with Community law/basic treaty rules (Zielone zamówienia publiczne. Praktyczny podręcznik, 2008).

GOOD PRACTICES FOR APPLYING ENVIRONMENTAL AND SOCIAL CLAUSES IN PUBLIC PROCUREMENT

Despite the initial difficulties and doubts about how to implement the SPP, local governments throughout the EU can boast of significant achievements in this field. Analysis of economic practice proves that green public procurement is used more often than socially responsible orders. This may be due to the fact that many "green" projects lead to measurable financial benefits related in the future to, for example, increased energy efficiency. However, projects with a social responsibility clause are usually not the cheapest and require additional organizational and financial effort related to the control of compliance with the terms of the procurement by suppliers and even their subcontractors. Below are some examples of good practices related to the use of both categories of sustainable public procurement by self-governments and public administration. Their synthetic description is in Table 3.

Table 3. Good practices in the application of GPP and SRPP in selected EU countries

Green Public Procurement	Socially Responsible Public Procurement
Germany, Alte Hansestadt Lemgo, a program of comprehensive energy efficiency improvement in municipal buildings.	Sweden, Municipality of Malmö, Sweden municipalities join forces to monitor compliance with social criteria amongst suppliers.
Italy, Cremona province, modernization of road infrastructure, use of water from sewage treatment plants for irrigation, use of environmentally friendly materials and technologies.	Portugal, Municipalities Association LIPOR, LIPOR'S Approach: From waste management to socially responsible procurement
Poland, the City of Łódź area revitalization with the use of environmentally friendly technologies	Spain, Municipality of San Sebastian, The City of San Sebastian's approach: Work wear & foot wear for employees of San Sebastian City Council, respecting the core ILO Conventions
Poland, Warsaw Ursynów, establishment of a naturalistic EKOpark which combines green and blue infrastructure	Poland, Lower Silesian Social Policy Center in Wrocław, numerous projects implemented as part of the social economy, mainly of an inclusive nature with reference to disadvantaged social groups.

Source: Authors' own compilation

Green Public Procurement

A program which used ecological standards in public procurement was the program implemented in 2012 by the city Alte Hansestadt Lemgo including a comprehensive thermo-modernization, equipment for remote monitoring, automation, ventilation with heat recovery, photovoltaics and features of passive buildings. It has been used in 58 municipal buildings to reduce energy costs by 20%. By investing EUR 30-35 million in 13 schools in the last 15 years the annual costs have been reduced by 2-10% (consumption of heat, electricity, water), generating up to EUR 100,000 of annual savings. The program was supported by the school social project "Saving energy builds a school" and involved students in saving energy and environment-friendly activities. It made it possible to use the funds saved for school development initiatives, additional classes, IT equipment, teaching aids and dissemination of environment-friendly standards of behavior among residents. At the same time, it generated demand for high-quality energy and construction solutions ordered on the market.

In turn, Italian examples of generating benefits from the application of the GPP include, inter alia, the Milanese treatment plant, where 1/3 of treated wastewater is used for irrigation of arable fields and broadly understood horticulture as well as infrastructural investments of the Italian province of Cremona, analyzed in 2012. The investments under which GPP has been applied include road construction from recycled materials and with the use of environmentally friendly technologies, implementation of streetlight control systems and devices for street traffic lights using materials and technologies which generate both environmental and economic benefits.

Environmental clauses, as part of revitalization projects which have been implemented since 2017 in the Polish city of Łódź, relate to functional and utility programs forming part of the tender documentation - giving implementation in the design and build formula. In the case of Łódź projects, the so-called area revitalization, transformations of entire urban spaces and facilities are taken into account through the selection of vegetation which fulfills a specific environmental and functional role. The use of pro-environmental solutions results in this case in ecosystem services. The implemented area revitalization projects are aimed at greening areas in the urbanized center. "The idea of the project is to revitalize existing facilities in order to raise the aesthetic values of buildings and their surroundings, consisting in the redesign of unattractive backyards space into a space with high aesthetic values with the aim of integrating the local environment and improving the comfort of property users. Planting lawns is to introduce biologically active areas into spaces which are currently completely hardened." (The Functional and Utility Program (PFU) of the public procurement contracts). General comments in these procurement procedures include requirements for plant material, structural substrate system and plant irrigation systems, shrubs, species selection and information on how to plant and maintain plants on urban grounds.

It is also a good practice to introduce new solutions in revitalization projects at the interface between the human-material tissue (historic building) - nature, the use of new forms of design (eco-design) and materials (natural materials), by creating solutions for nesting birds - breeding boxes for swifts in architectural details of tenement façade. For example, the Specification of Essential Terms of the Procurement Contract (SIWZ documentation) of the functional and operational program regarding the preparation of documentation for revitalization projects in the center of Łódź provides "(...) In the elements of the reconstructed architectural details, it is necessary to place the boxes for swifts (birds) in accordance with the "Łódź for Swifts, Swifts for Łódź" project. In addition, breeding boxes for other birds should be made - they should not be mounted on the front façade, whereas their installation is possible on the top wall of the outbuilding (partially hidden in the insulation layer) or on the wall of the annex from the side of yard, provided that they will not damage or obscure the existing architectural design."(Świątkowska. 2015)

The comprehensive implementation of the first EKOpark in Warsaw in the post-industrial areas of the Warsaw district of Ursus is another interesting example of the use of a GPP approach. The park, according to the specification, will be naturalistic, with spontaneously growing vegetation. Existing valuable trees are to be preserved, and invasive species of trees and shrubs are to be replaced by native ones. Planting of plants which are food for insects and small animals and the construction of nesting boxes will lead to increased biodiversity. Hedges are to provide nesting conditions for birds. Seventy percent of the EKOpark's surface is to be biologically active. The EKOpark will use innovative technical solutions, including elements from recycling. As part of the order, educational playgrounds for children will be created, promoting ecological awareness. It is planned to develop ecological educational paths with information points on the existing flora and fauna elements in this area. Environmental friendly mineral materials (permeable, consisting of high quality natural stones, grits and ecological binders) will be used to build the surface of transport routes. The elements of small architecture are to be made of the simplest materials, such as wood and galvanized steel, and the lamps used for lighting are to be powered by renewable energy from photovoltaic cells. The park will build a system of bioretention basins for retrieving, collecting and draining rainwater from the park to ensure permanent irrigation of plants (Demiańczuk. 2018).

Socially Responsible Public Procurement

The implementation of SRPP is still less advanced compared to GPP, but despite the obstacles in some areas, significant progress has been made. Public authorities across the EU are seeking to increase the effectiveness of using social criteria in tender procedures. Many municipalities have adopted a resolution regarding observance of ILO conventions in public procurement for products and services. In addition, many public authorities are at different stages of developing and using verification systems to ensure that suppliers comply with the required standards. Public authorities, decide to choose a variety of ways to verify and monitor procurement contracts. This applies to the subject and/or the scope of application of social criteria. For example, requirements for exclusion of child labor, compliance with ILO conventions or other ethical commercial purposes are to be verified through simple declarations of bidders, codes of conduct, labels and certificates, follow-up questionnaires and inspections.

To illustrate how this may look in practice, examples from several European municipalities will be used.

Municipality of Malmö, Sweden, municipalities join forces to monitor compliance with social criteria amongst suppliers. The city started using social criteria in public procurement in 2007 in relation to flowers, tea, coffee, bananas and textiles. Several policy guidelines have been adopted on how to formulate contracts so that low environmental impact and production in a socially responsible manner are the first choice. For certain product categories, the assessment is carried out three times a year to examine the percentage share of goods meeting these criteria. Between March 2011 and February 2012, Malmö bought 37% of goods, including fruit, tea and coffee, dairy products, fish and meat products using environmental criteria, and 54% of tea, coffee and bananas produced in a socially responsible manner. The verification system uses a code of conduct, a follow-up questionnaire and inspections. The main purpose of its development and application was to minimize the negative social effects of Malmö's shopping activities in the supply chain, as well as to use purchasing power to help the strive to improve working conditions. A special working group was also set up to develop a verification system whether the purchases are socially responsible. The risk analysis carried out in 2010 was to identify the product categories in terms of the probability of violation of employee rights set out in the basic ILO conventions. Three product groups were considered as high risk: electronic equipment, furniture and office supplies. The City of Malmö decided that for these three categories a verification system such as the Code of Conduct is needed to ensure that the supplier is genuinely involved in taking into account the social aspects of supply. Ultimately, it was decided that Malmö would use the same design as the Swedish Environmental Management Council. Supplementary questions have been developed to assess whether a given company poses a risk and whether it must make any improvements or provide explanations regarding the current process in use. This concept has been supported by other public authorities in Sweden. Forty four other Swedish municipalities including Gothenburg, Lund and Växjo joined a cooperation agreement in the field of control over suppliers in order to verify whether they comply with the Code of Conduct. Each successful tenderer must complete a follow-up questionnaire based on a code of conduct. This questionnaire is then evaluated using the criteria developed in Malmö. All suppliers who receive a code of conduct undergo an inspection during the contract period. The suppliers whose responses in the questionnaire are considered unsatisfactory undergo a more rigorous control process. Inspections are financed from a fund set up by Malmö and 44 other Swedish municipalities. Due to time and resource constraints, the city does not currently apply the Code of Conduct with suppliers of lower risk product groups. If the audit shows that the social criteria do not meet the requirements of the Code of Conduct, suppliers are asked to improve their system. Malmö does not necessarily terminate contracts with suppliers who do not meet the criteria, but rather works with them to improve the situation in this respect in accordance with the basic ILO Conventions. Numerous municipalities entered into cooperation, which increased the efficiency of operations and reduced the costs borne by individual municipalities. The fact is, however, that activities related to the monitoring of contracts in terms of social responsibility turned out to be difficult and time-consuming, especially since it was not initially clear what issues should be investigated. Since many authorities probably use the same supplier of products and services it is considered beneficial to develop more intensive cooperation between public authorities. Currently, inspections are carried out by inspectors on the basis of ILO criteria not on specific codes of conduct, as these are very different. It is also important that suppliers have not reacted negatively or raised prices in response to the verification system.

Municipalities Association LIPOR, Portugal LIPOR'S approach: From waste management to socially responsible procurement is another initiative related to the application of social criteria in public procurement. Eight Portuguese municipalities: Espinho, Gondomar, Maia, Matosinhos, Porto, Póvoa de Varzim, Valongo and Vila do Conde formed Association of Municipalities in 1982. Since then, they have been implementing the integrated waste management system together by improving infrastructure and running awareness campaigns addressed to members of local communities. Every year, LIPOR processes around 480,000 tonnes of municipal solid waste produced by about 1 million inhabitants. LIPOR employs about 220 people and makes purchases worth about EUR 23 million (2011). The activity in the field of sustainable procurement dates back to 2008, and was confirmed in 2009 by the achievement of the corporate social responsibility (CSR) SA80004 standard. Since 2010 LIPOR has participated in the "Building SPP - building capacity in sustainable public procurement" international project, supported by the LIFE + 5 program. Sustainable procurement procedures are published on the LIPOR's website (www.lipor.pt).

LIPOR has developed its verification system based on the exchange of ideas with other certified companies, auditing team and employees from several departments. It introduced a code of conduct for their suppliers to commit to comply with the main principles of the human rights declaration, the basic ILO conventions and national legislation. The procedures apply to all suppliers with a turnover of 10,000 euros or more. Every year LIPOR invites its suppliers to workshops on social responsibility, during which the patterns and verification criteria in the Code of Conduct are discussed. Suppliers then have the opportunity to present their own observations on the impact of the application of the Code on their activities. LIPOR recommends that suppliers also work with other actors throughout the supply chain to increase socially responsible production. Recent assessments indicate that LIPOR's recommendations are accepted and used by all suppliers.

Municipality of San Sebastian, Spain: The City of San Sebastian's approach: Work wear & foot wear for employees of San Sebastian City Council, respecting the core ILO Conventions.

San Sebastian is a municipality with a population of 180,000, employing about 2,000 people in city administration. The annual expenditure on the purchase of work clothes and footwear by the City Council amounts to EUR 230,000. The city started analyzing the issue of socially responsible public procurement in 2000, and in 2006 a city agreement was concluded on the best practices used for the greening of specifications. The introduction of social criteria in the purchase process was carried out in cooperation with specialists from other cities and the government of the Basque Country, which cooperated with other Basque town councils in similar cases. The purchasing department in San Sebastian also contacted the non-governmental organization Fundación EMAUS, which previously cooperated in the field of public procurement with other NGOs. The first procurement contracts with the use of social criteria were carried out in 2009. Social clauses (ILO criteria and their verification) are included in the technical specifications of the offer, which relate to the subject of the contract, which is: the delivery of work clothing and footwear produced in a socially responsible manner. Tenderers must provide proof of compliance (attestations and certificates) at the time the offer is submitted. If tenderers do not meet the minimum technical specifications, they are excluded from the tendering procedure. Tenderers must provide a signed "Supplier's Ethical Declaration" to ensure that all products have been manufactured respecting the basic ILO conventions. As part of this declaration, suppliers are asked to list all their subcontractors and details of deliveries.

The Lower Silesian Center for Social Policy in Wrocław indicates a wide range of activities related to the application of social clauses which, in accordance with public procurement law, provide derogation from the public procurement rules, allowing for additional criteria for selecting a contractor due to important social considerations. "Provision of catering services" is an example of such a procurement contract for which may apply contractors which employ over 50% of employees who are disabled persons within the meaning of provisions on vocational and social rehabilitation and employment of disabled persons or relevant provisions of EU Member States or the European Economic Area. Another example concerns an open tender for the preparation and service of meals in primary schools, gymnasiums and kindergartens in which the contracting authority, in accordance with Article 29 para. 3a of the Public Procurement Law requires the contractor to employ by the contractor or subcontractor based on a contract of employment the persons performing the following activities in the scope of the contract: a) cook - during the whole period of the contract, b) persons serving meals throughout the contract.

As can be seen from the presented examples, the possibilities of applying sustainable public procurement are very wide. In particular, it is important to develop and apply such procurement contracts in cases of repetitive and, to some extent, routine procedures. Thanks to this, it is not only possible to achieve significant environmental and social benefits, but also increase the social awareness of the existence of needs and possibilities in this area. Of course, the GPP and SRPP clauses and criteria must be applied in relation to other public procurement contracts.

BARRIERS RELATED TO THE USE OF SUSTAINABLE PUBLIC PROCUREMENT

Research conducted among local government units in relation to the use of SPP led to the conclusion that there are still many fears and barriers related to tendering and purchasing procedures. For example, the international GPPinfoNET project implemented in the years 2010/2011 under the LIFE + mechanism, which concerned the delivery and dissemination of knowledge about the "green" approach in tenders and the promotion of green public procurement as an effective instrument for environmental protection and sustainable development of cities and regions, identified the following types of barriers:

- **Mental**: Lack of education system and the need to build awareness of decision-makers and other stakeholders in the scope of SPP;
- **Legal:** Lack of reference indicators in the implementing regulations; lack of implementing regulations for some national regulations, lack of interpretation of regulations, incoherence of regulations, dispersion and frequent amendments to legal acts (information chaos), unenforceable law;
- **Organizational and Technical:** Lack of integral drawing of documentation, lack of good practice bases, and no offer evaluation tools.

Particularly many emotions were raised by the issue of moving away from the lowest price criterion as the main criterion for the evaluation of offers. Concerns were raised about the possibility of corruption charges. Therefore, the introduction at EU level of detailed specifications on the conditions for calling tenders and placing orders should be assessed positively.

Specific problems concern the performance of SRPP. The matter is relatively simple, if the whole supply chain is within the EU, where high standards in the field of labor law and human rights are in force. In this case, it may be more about improving the situation of disadvantaged groups on the labor market. It is much more difficult to implement the SRPP when some subcontractors and sub-suppliers operate in countries outside the EU, which is a common phenomenon in the conditions of globalization.

Difficulties arise from the differences in legal regulations between countries, as well as the possibility to carry out undoubted control over the observance of human rights and workers' rights. For example, it may be difficult to trace the origin of cobalt, a metal increasingly used in connection with the production of batteries for smartphones or electric cars. More than half the world's cobalt mine production comes from the Democratic Republic of the Congo. It is known that forced labor, including child labor, is used for its extraction. However, the market is dominated by Chinese enterprises, so in practice it is almost impossible to trace how a specific cobalt batch was produced. However, this should not mean giving up control in this regard when purchasing electronic equipment or electric cars. In the case of the SRPP, the high costs of controlling provisions regarding compliance with social clauses are an important barrier.

CONCLUSIONS AND RECOMMENDATIONS

Evaluating the effectiveness of sustainable public procurement as a tool for the implementation of sustainable development in the European Union it can be said that it varies between countries. This is evident both in the number and value of these contracts as well as in the percentage share in total public procurement. In comparison with the first years of implementation of the SPP after 2004, when the first directives in this field were adopted, now one can speak about significant progress, which undoubtedly results from the amendment of the regulations. Directives 2014/24/EU and 2014/25/EU of the European Parliament and of the Council create opportunities for contracting authorities to use public procurement to support environmental and social objectives. The barriers, observed especially in the first years after the regulations came into force, slowly become less noticeable. First of all, there is growing knowledge about the possibilities of using GPP and SRPP and the benefits associated with it. In the case of GPP, these are primarily:

- Ecological benefits resulting from lower consumption of raw materials, materials and energy; promoting resource-efficient technologies; lower emission of pollutants, in particular what is important, greenhouse gases responsible for climate change;
- Social benefits resulting from the improvement of the quality of the natural environment, which positively affects the living conditions of the population;
- Economic benefits associated with lower purchase costs of raw materials, materials and energy and operating costs, especially in the long-term.

Advantages and benefits of using social clauses and social aspects in public procurement include:

- The possibility, when awarding a public contract, of simultaneously achieving other results, in particular of solving the problem of employment of people from groups at risk of social exclusion and disadvantaged groups;
- Obtaining a higher return from the public funds spent for the implementation of the contract, for example by reducing social assistance expenses by employing people who receive social assistance benefits;
- Strengthening the ethical basis of decisions made;
- Building the image of the contracting authority by using social clauses as socially responsible clauses;

- Increasing the chances of winning the tender by social enterprises.

Ecological and social clauses allow, at the same time, to achieve many effects, which fully corresponds to the concept of sustainable development.

Despite the progress made in the application of the SPP, much remains to be done to increase the use of these contracts. It is also worth paying attention to the issue of monitoring the use of SPP. So far, information on this subject is collected on a random basis, which does not give a full picture of the SPP market. To disseminate reliable information on ecological and social effects, it is worth considering building an SPP effects indexing system, grouping more perceptible product indicators into aggregated groups of result indicators. It is about demonstrating real effects, benefits which are responsible for building a better quality of life within the adopted model of sustainable development.

The Contribution of The Authors

M. Burchard-Dziubinska (conception, acquisition of data about SRPP, analysis and interpretation of data) 50%.

T. Jakubiec (literature review, acquisition of data about GPP, analysis and interpretation of data) 50%.

REFERENCES

Aspey, E. (2015). The Reform to EU utilities Procurement: Smart, Sustainable and Inclusive? In K. V. Thai (Ed.), *International Public Procurement, Innovation and Knowledge Sharing, Public Administration, Governance and Globalization* (pp. 255–270). Springer International Publishing Switzerland. doi:10.1007/978-3-319-13434-5_13

Buying Green. A Handbook on green public procurement. (2016). (3rd ed.). Publications Office of the European Union.

Buying Social, A Guide to Taking Account of Social Considerations into Public Procurement. (2011). Publications Office of the European Union.

Communication from the Commission. (2020). *EUROPE 2020 A strategy for smart, sustainable and inclusive growth.* Brussels: COM. (Original work published 2010)

Communication from the Commission to the European Parliament. the Council, the European Economic and Social Committee and the Committee of the Regions Renewed social agenda: Opportunities, access and solidarity in 21st century Europe, COM (2008) 412 final, Brussels.

Communication from the Commission to the European Parliament. the Council, the European Economic and Social Committee and the Committee of the Regions. Public procurement for a better environment COM (2008) 400 final, Brussels.

de Rosa, F. (2007). Zamówienia publiczne a partnerstwo publiczno-prywatne [Public Procurement and public-private partnership]. DIESIS.

Demiańczuk, T. (2018). *Powstaje EKOpark w Ursusie*. Retrieved from http://www.um.warszawa.pl/aktualnosci/powstaje-ekopark-w-ursusie

Directive 2004/17/EC of the European Parliament and of the Council of 31 March 2004 coordinating the procurement procedures by entities operating in the water, energy, transport and postal services sectors.

Directive 2004/18/EC of the European Parliament and of the Council of 31 March 2004 on the coordination of procedures for the award of public works contracts, public supply contracts and public service contracts.

Directive 2009/33 / EC of the European Parliament and of the Council of 23 April 2009 on the promotion of clean and energy-efficient road transport vehicles.

Directive 2010/30/EU of the European Parliament and of the Council of 19 May 2010 on the indication by labeling and standard product information of the consumption of energy and other resources by energy-related products.

Directive 2014/23/EU of 26 February 2014 on the award of concession contracts.

Directive 2014/24/EC of the European Parliament and of the Council of 26 February 2014 on public procurement and repealing Directive 2004/18/EC.

Directive 2014/25/EU of 26 February 2014 on procurement by entities operating in the water, energy, transport and postal services sectors.

Evaluation Report "Impact and Effectiveness of EU Public Procurement Legislation". Commission Staff Working Paper, European Commission, DGInternal Market SEC (2011) 853. (n.d.). Functional and Utility Program (PFU) of the public procurement contract. Retrieved from http://zim.lodz.bip-e.pl/zim/zamowienia-publiczne

Guide to the application of the European Union rules on state aid, public procurement and the internal market to services of general economic interest, and in particular to social services of general interest SWD (2013) 53 final/2, European Commission, Brussels.

Interpretative communication of the Commission on the Community law applicable to public procurement and the possibilities for integrating environmental considerations into public procurement. COM (2001) 274 final, Official Journal of the European Communities 28.11.2001.

Interpretative Communication of the Commission on the Community law applicable to public procurement and the possibilities for integrating social considerations into public procurement, COM (2001) 566 final, Official Journal of the European Communities C 333/27, 28.11.2001.

Jakubiec, T. (2018). *Green public procurement as an instrument for the implementation of sustainable development* (PhD Dissertation). University of Lodz, Faculty of Economics and Sociology.

Łapacz, D. (2015). Zamówienia publiczne w Unii Europejskiej – analiza porównawcza procedur w wybranych państwach członkowskich [Public Procurement in the European Union - a comparative analysis of procedures in selected Member States]. In *Biznes międzynarodowy w gospodarce globalnej 2015* [International business in the global economy 2015], No. 34. Instytut Biznesu Międzynarodowego, Uniwersytet Gdański.

Public Procurement Indicators 2015. (2016). European Commission, DG GROW G4 - Innovative and e-Procurement.

Regulation (EC) No. 66/2010 of the European Parliament and of the Council of 25 November 2009 on the EU Eco-label.

Regulation (EC) No 106/2008 of the European Parliament and of the Council of 15 January 2008 on a Community energy-efficiency labeling program for office equipment.

Renda, A., Pelkmans, J., Egenhofer, C., Schrefler, L., Luchetta, G., & Selcuki, C. (2012). *The uptake of green public procurement in the EU27.* Academic Press.

Sprawozdanie Prezesa Urzędu Zamówień Publicznych o funkcjonowaniu systemu zamówień publicznych w 2015 roku. (2016). [Report of the President of the Public Procurement Office on the functioning of the public procurement system in 2015]. Urząd Zamówień Publicznych.

Study on "Strategic use of public procurement in promoting green, social and innovation policies." (2015). Final Report. European Commission, DG GROW, written by PwC.

Świątkowska, S. (2015). *Budki lęgowe dla jerzyków – dokumentacja projektowa.* Retrieved from http://docplayer.pl/9088975-Budki-legowe-dla-jerzykow-dokumentacja-procesu-realizacji-pracy.html

Szlachta, J. (2011). Odniesienia europejskie nowej generacji programowania rozwoju regionalnego w Polsce [European References of the new generation of regional development programming in Poland]. In J. Szlachta & J. Woźniak (Eds.), *Krajowa Strategia Rozwoju Regionalnego do roku 2020 a strategie rozwoju społeczno-gospodarczego województw* [National Strategy of Regional Development until 2020 and strategies for socio-economic development of voivodships]. Polska Akademia Nauk, Komitet Przestrzennego Zagospodarowania Kraju, Warszawa. Retrieved from http://zim.lodz.bip-e.pl/zim/zamowienia-publiczne

Zielone zamówienia publiczne; Praktyczny podręcznik dla beneficjentów funduszy europejskich; Nowe drogi rozwoju, człowiek, natura, infrastruktura. (2008). [Green public procurement; A practical manual for beneficiaries of European funds; New ways of development, man, nature, and infrastructure]. Academic Press.

Chapter 6
Impact of Green Taxes on the Public Financial System:
An Example of European Union Countries

Beata Zofia Filipiak
University of Szczecin, Poland

Dorota Wyszkowska
University of Białystok, Poland

ABSTRACT

The EU has become a promoter of the idea of sustainable development and a defender of the global climate, which in many sectors results in ever higher and more ambitious ecological and efficiency requirements. State wants to protect the environment use various intervention instruments, including environmental taxes: "green taxes." In addition to the fiscal function, they are to stimulate various types of entities to undertake specific actions conducive to reducing pressure on the environment. The aim of the considerations (discussion) is to present changes in the approach to the use of "green taxes," as an important instrument of the public sector environmental policy in the impact on reducing pollution on the environment conducive to sustainable development. The research aims to verify the hypothesis and assumes the impact of environmental taxes on the public system of financing expenditure on environmental protection. The authors will also look for an answer to the question whether the policy of "green taxes" can contribute to the sustainable public financial system.

INTRODUCTION[1]

Historically the financial system has responded to the needs of the time and violent changes in the social and economic environment. A global consensus has arisen that sustainable growth will be one of the greatest challenges of the 21st century — as demonstrated by the United Nations (UN) Sustainable Development Goals (SDGs) adopted as part of its 2030 Agenda for Sustainable Development. As in previous changes caused by crises and structural transformations, the financial system will play a major role in this process: the full potential of the financial system needs to be harnessed to serve as an

DOI: 10.4018/978-1-7998-1033-9.ch006

engine in the global economy's transition toward sustainable development. (A. Adam, 2015; N.Robins, & S. Zadek, 2017). The present problems, both environmental (such as climatic changes, the loss of bio-diversity and depletion of natural resources) and social (mostly associated with steep inequalities in income distribution), present an enormous challenge to social and economic development. When assessing the role of the financial system in the economy, it can be stated that this system plays a key role in the implementation of the sustainable development goals (M. Jeucken, 2001). Effectively operating financial system ensure efficient capital transfer in the economy, reducing financial risk (P. Arestis, 2006). The public pillar of the financial system through appropriate tools and instruments (especially financial) affects market decisions of enterprises and communities, but also shapes consumer awareness and behaviors. The financial instruments and tools evolving towards sustainable finance allows for the inclusion of social and environmental aspects in the general theory of finance, correlating with the pillars of sustainable development (S.T. Fullwiler, 2015).The sustainable development as a very specific economic category requires an effecting funding mechanism that should take into account the three-dimensional (economic, social, environmental), sustainability perspective.

They also influence the stability of the financial system and force the use of appropriate tools and make the right decisions. Changes of this scale and in these three pillars of sustainable development (i.e the environmental pillar, the social pillar and the economic pillar) can only be effected through concerted effort of various economic actors: companies, industry sectors, decision-makers, political powers, consumer groups, socially responsible civil societies, engineers, inventors and scientists. (P.M. Boulanger 2008; R.W. Kates, T.M. Parris, &A.A. Leiserowitz, 2005; T. Kuhlman, J. Farrington, 2010) In effect, the postulated transition should be interpreted as a complex and prolonged process involving a multitude of areas and actors (F. Geels, 2011).

While the relationship between the market financial system and sustainability have a wider context and are examined (especially in the context of the crisis), the relations between the public system and sustainability require a broader contextual discussion.

Earlier theoretical discussions and research were based on a selected aspects of sustainable finance. The research conducted by S.Abu-Bader & A.S. Abu-Qarn (2003) indicated both positive and negative effects of the active role of the public sector in the economy. The relationship between the public finance sector's expenditure and GDP growth has been considered in numerous studies. The impact of government spending on GDP in the context of development factors was examined by M.Q.Dao (2017), M.M.Dandan (2011) and T.Garba& Abdullahi, S.Y. (2013). Additionally, W.D.Nordhaus & J.Tobin's (1973) studies and the subsequent H.E. Daly&J. B. Cobb (2001) studies provided a basis for determining the positive impact of consumer expenditure (N.A. Ashford &R.P Hall, 2011) on the financial system (public financial system).

It should be stressed that the classic approach indicates that it is necessary to balance consumer expenditure by such factors as revenue distribution, costs related to environmental pollution, and other undetectable, intangible costs (A.Alińska, B.Z.Filipiak& A.Kosztowniak, 2018). For the modern citizen, the issues related to environmental protection, actions for sustainable development, and respect of the principles of social responsibility are of particular importance and have often become a priority, as demonstrated by C.Cobb, M.Glickman, & C.Cheslog (1989). Therefore, the public sector, in pursuing its public policy, refers to the protection of the natural environment through the prism of measures for sustainable development (B.Z.Filipiak, 2016, European Commission, 2017).

The models and research failed to search for the relation between public financial system and green tax from the perspective of sustainable development. Our study provides an original approach to sustainable financial system and the factor of determining the possibilities of intervention of public authorities through the public system towards sustainable development. The research aims to verify the hypothesis assumes that, occurs impact of environmental taxes on the public system of financing expenditure on environmental protect. The authors will also look for an answer to the question whether the policy of "green taxes" can contribute to the sustainable public financial system. The study aims to draw attention to the significant gap in the existing research the impact of environmental taxes on the public system of financing expenditure on environmental protection.

BACKGROUND

Sustainable Public Financial System as the Direction of Sustainable Development Policy

The sustainability public finances also referred to as fiscal sustainability, is the ability of a government to sustain its current spending, tax and other policies in the long run without threatening the government's solvency or without defaulting on some of the government's liabilities or promised expenditures. (F. Balassone& D. Franco, 2000; A. Krejdl 2005; European Commission (2017)

The multiplicity of market failures that constitute barriers to sustainable finance require governments to kick-start, sustain, and accelerate its development through the use of fiscal resources and public policy measures. Public authorities (such as: governments, central banks, regulators, supervisors) are taking legislative, policy, regulatory, and supervisory steps to achieve a range of objectives linking sustainability and the financial system, such as (S.J. Miller &M. A. Vela, 2013;N. Robins & S. Zadek, 2017,R. Radula, K. Keel, 2018):

- Mainstreaming environmental factors into financial decision making and correct for market failures (such unpriced environmental externalities);
- Supporting policy frameworks and standards that promote the issuance of green financial products (that is, green bonds and securities), the development of new market platforms (that is, crowdfunding and fintech), or the competitiveness of financial centers promoting transparency and efficiency;
- Strengthening risk management, often by integrating environmental factors into the prudential oversight of financial institutions, supervising financial markets, and providing sector and system-level stress testing;
- Facilitating flows and services, with investment and lending to priority sectors, restrictions or limitations on financing, insurance requirements, or the provision of financial services as a way to promote inclusion and support development;
- Enhancing conduct and behavior, with codes of conduct and guidelines for environmental issues and compacts for sustainable development;
- Creating effective public instruments for influencing the behavior of the society, enterprises, banks and other entities as well as the incentive system.

Therefore, the observance of the European sustainable policy, including the budget: income with green taxes and expenses with proctological expenses) is used to implement the sustainable development policy, and fiscal rules are used. Indeed, the budget (income and expenses) has, at least, three main functions (T. Atkinson & P. Van de Noord, 2001; A. Schick, 2002; J. Diamond, 2003; A. Giosi, S. Testarmata, S. Brunelli & B. Staglianň, 2012):

- Ensure fiscal discipline and close-to-balance trend;
- Allow the allocation of resources (the efficient factor is one of the components of the sustainable development policy
- Ensure an efficient use of public resources (the efficient factor is one of the components of the sustainable development policy).

Modern countries are trying to influence the economic situation, and thus implement a policy of sustainable development, using specific macroeconomic policy tools. Among these tools, the most important are: monetary policy and fiscal policy. In its monetary policy, the central bank uses the financial markets in a sense and also affects the situation on these markets. There is an increasing use of instruments related to the sustainable development policy, such as green securities and the policy of preferring projects that take into account environmental elements. Through the market financial impulses of monetary policy are transferred to the real sphere of the economy. An important element is green taxes, which are associated with fiscal policy. Green tax-based instruments are the smartest candidates for raising own resources for governments. They could greatly enhance European advances in realization of sustainability policy and overcome the deficiencies apparent in the current system of financing the shaping spending for sustainable development. They are a win-win for climate, the environment, a smart and equitable transition to a fossil fuel- and nuclear energy-free society (C. Adolf, K. Röhrig, 2016).

Taxes in the economy of sustainable development are included in the group of economic policy instruments and are intended, among others, to stimulate specific actions for sustainable development. Most often they are associated with ecological taxes and the greening of the fiscal system. The genesis of ecological taxes and the greenalization of the fiscal system goes back to the neoclassical school of the 1920s and the so-called of Pigou (1920), assuming the internalization of environmental costs.

A taxation system and policy of public expenditure allows a country to stabilize the economy, respond promptly to economic shocks, and assure the correct functioning of the goods, service, and labor markets (A. Afonso, W. Erbert, L. Schuknect & M. Thone, 2005; S. Barrios & A. Schaechter, 2008). Therefore, striving for the sustanable public finance includes the public policy evaluation field and encompasses, on one hand, the relationship between public expenditure and economic growth and, on the other, the correlations between fiscal policy and public policy targets.

Many researchers analyzed directions of environment policy within the member states of OECD. W. Lafferty & E. Hovden (2003), C.Knill et al. (2010), respectively K. Holzinger et al. (2011), K.G.Ruffing (2010), (I.Bostan et al., 2016) highlight the importance of the economic leverages used on the level of environment policy, observing that the environment policy directions always follow the direct environment regulations (environment standards, emission standards, design standards, product standards, etc.) and the economic instruments (green taxes and green expenditure, as integrant parts of the environment policy. The economic instruments meant to stimulate the public financial support as an encouragement of the practices in accord with the environment and of the environment financing investments. Recent studies belonging to authors like Haibara (2009), P.O. Do Valle et al. (2012) highlight that, in reality, the environment taxes, as part of the environment policy, only represent redistribution by environment expenditure and subventions (I.Bostan et al., 2016).The public financial system could be a very important factor to promote sustainable development as it could foster economic growth and development, efficient resource allocations, the protection of the environment, and social responsibility. (S.T. Fullwiler 2015; M.G. Andrada, 2015; M.Q. Dao, 2017; A. Alińska, B.Z. Filipiak& A. Kosztowniak 2018.) Actions undertaken as part of the sustainability finance concept could contribute to changing the orientation of finance measures and to strengthening efforts to generate a long-term positive impact on socio-economic development. (G. Van der Waldt, 2016).

Based on this brief overview it is evident that an integrative response to sustainable development is a necessity. Governments need to design integrative strategies for sustainable development, which should combine social, economic, and environmental concerns with financial stability towards sustainability financial system. Decisions taken by governments should ensure that a careful balance is struck between the need for economic growth, social development, and the protection of the environment the use of appropriate instruments and tools, programs and strategies to ensure fiscal governance. The sustainable public finances based on current spending, tax and other policies they strive to achieve a complex ecological goal as an important pillar of sustainable development. At the same time, they constitute a constant stimulus for undertaking such behaviors of enterprises, society, banks and financial institutions in order to trigger an adjustment reaction on the part of producers, consumers and the state in accordance with the needs of environmental protection.

"Green Taxes' as an Instrument of Sustainable Development

Through their activities, various types of entities limit the usefulness of natural factors to perform their production and consumption functions, resulting in the creation of ecological external costs. The entities which are the perpetrators of this cost are most often aware of their creation and infringement by their activity of the interests of other entities. In the absence of establishment of property rights to the natural environment, there is a tendency to pass these costs on to the whole society, i.e. to make them public. In order to prevent this, state intervention is necessary, which through the use of various instruments may undertake actions that force the entities to behave in a predetermined manner. Without government intervention in this respect, there are no market incentives for polluters to take environmental damage into account. Their impact is spread over many entities and has little or no direct cost to the polluter (European Environment Agency, 1996).

The lack of interest of the businesses themselves in actions aimed at reducing the pressure on the environment makes the state intervention in the market necessary in this respect. (S. Smith, 2007). When creating ecological policy tools, the state takes into consideration many diverse criteria, including not only the criterion of economic effectiveness, but also: ecological effectiveness, distributive justice, social and political acceptability, legal and administrative barriers, transaction costs as well as the impact of a pro-innovative instrument (A. Graczyk, 2009). Public authority has at its disposal a fairly broad set of environmental policy tools, namely: regulatory instruments and market instruments (e.g. regulatory instruments, market-based instruments (such as envaironmental taxes, tradable permits), negotiated agreements, subsidies, environmental management systems and information campaigns) (J. Rosiek, 2005).

What is characteristic of economic instruments is that they generate lower costs of reaching a complex environmental goal (higher efficiency). At the same time, they provide a constant incentive to reduce pollution. When deciding on their reduction, companies base their choice on the economic calculation, by choosing such a form of pollution level regulation as to achieve it at the lowest possible costs. However, when assessing them from the point of view of all the criteria indicated above, an objective assessment in relation to the other types of instruments is very difficult. Hence, the authorities' approach to their application was subject to evaluation. In the initial phase of the implementation of the environmental protection policies, the authorities of individual states used mainly instruments based on prohibitions, orders and imposing pollution limits (European Environment Agency, 1996). In recent decades, however, there has been a growing interest in the use of market-based instruments, such as environmental taxes, which allow the internalisation of external costs, meaning the inclusion of the polluter's activities in their economic accounts. Three primary ways of internalising external costs can be found in the literature (A. Graczyk, 2009):

- Introduction of taxes,
- The application of Coase's theorem (R.H. Coase, 1960),
- Treating the perpetrator and the recipient as a single body (joint delivery of goods).

Among these instruments, particularly interesting are environmental taxes which do not generate more revenue themselves, but the resulting incentives can be quite effective from an environmental point of view. Hence, governments are increasingly resorting to this instrument[2]. Revenue gained from environmental taxes can help with fiscal consolidation or contribute to reducing other taxes.

In the economic literature, the environmental taxes are referred to as one of the key instruments for mitigating such environmental problems as pollution or climate change. These taxes are regarded as market-based incentive-driven mechanisms as they provide adequate incentives for economic operators and households to abstain from pollution and contribute to irreversible environmental change. They are identified in the literature as more efficient than so-called regulation and control mechanisms and their acquisition costs are usually low (S.J. Miller & M.A. Vela, 2013).

Therefore, the implementation of the eco-tax system is aimed at triggering adjustment reactions on the market on the part of producers, consumers and the state in accordance with the needs of environmental protection. The purpose of introducing such taxes is not to achieve fiscal objectives, but specific environmental ones (F. Grądalski, 2006). The theoretical basis for a green tax was developed by A.C. Pigou in 1920. Pigou, who proposed to include so-called externalities in the tax concept. The externalities reduce the usable value of the environment (the welfare of a society) and constitute a general social cost. Thus, if the presence of externalities results in disparities between individual (private) and marginal social costs of production, internalisation is bound to lead to its removal. This should lead to the polluter's response to reduce the volume of production of goods and services the manufacturing and/or consumption of which generate external costs. It may also prompt the company responsible for generating external costs to take action to reduce pollution, e.g. by implementing new technologies, eco-innovation, etc. (A. Graczyk, 2009).

In a situation where external costs are generated, the achievement of the Pareto optimum requires a positive price for generating external costs for polluters and a zero price for the consumption of externalities for the affected parties. It cannot therefore be a normal market price which is symmetrical for both parties to a transaction. An optimal solution requires not market prices, but fiscal instruments, which would have asymmetrical features resulting from passing the cost of the external effect on only one party to the transaction (A. Graczyk, 2009). The amount of tax is determined individually for each emitter. According to the theory of externalities, it should be equal to the marginal external costs per unit of product (change of activity) to which these costs are related. In practice, however, this is not possible (M. Kudełko, 2016).

Without the government intervention, it is likely that the polluters would completely ignore these costs of their operation. The application of environmental taxation is intended to internationalise the costs of externalities, i.e. to attribute them to the perpetrator of the cost. This means that the polluters pay for the costs they generate to the society and the environment, and these taxes are therefore used as an instrument to internalise the actual production costs of goods and services (T. Subhanij, S. Banerjee & Z. Jian, 2018). The polluter must then decide whether they will bear the additional costs due to environmental taxation or whether they will decide to switch to a different production technology that reduces environmental pollution.

The practical application of Pigou's theoretical contribution to the practice of taxation is the so-called concept of standard ambient tax (the approximation of Pigouvian taxes (S. Smith, 2007)). The concept was developed by W.J. Baumol and W.E. Oates who adjusted the solutions proposed by Pigou to the market limitations and proposed a concept of indirect and incomplete internationalisation. From this concept the ambient taxes are derived taking the form of emission and energy taxes. In the case of the emission tax, the tax base is the emission of harmful substances (e.g. CO_2), while the energy tax is based on the input of an energy carrier into the production or consumption process (e.g. petrol, coal). Companies liable to pay these taxes, in order to reduce their burdens on this account, have to undertake actions aimed at reducing emissions of pollutants or consumption of energy carriers, thus contributing to the improvement of the natural environment. This is what the regulating authority wants to achieve by applying these taxes. At the same time, it raises funds which can be used to implement measures to improve the state of the environment. Such taxes may also be imposed on products and services, the production of which has a harmful impact on the natural environment (e.g. batteries, artificial fertilisers). Environmental taxes can also be designed to replace other distortionary taxes on labour or capital and shift the tax burden from "economic goods" to "economic losses" without increasing the overall tax burden (T. Subhanij, S. Banerjee & Z. Jian, 2018).

In the literature of the subject one can also find a third type of environmental taxes based on the principle of mutualisation taxes. The main purpose underlying these taxes is to raise funds for strictly defined public expenditures on environmental protection. Individual businesses are not interested in incurring such expenditures, as they serve the general public rather than the interest of a particular company. Examples include expenditure on the construction and maintenance of an air pollution monitoring system.

The implementation of environmental taxes should lead to a reduction of the tax burden on traditional factors of production - labour and capital, as their introduction should be fiscally neutral. It is linked to the achievement of the so-called double dividend. On the one hand, the environmental taxes are related to economic benefits (dividend) and, on the other hand, to environmental benefits (dividend). The literature emphasizes that this double dividend may bring measurable benefits in the economy (M. Tomala, 2018).

Another way to internalize external costs is the approach proposed by Coase, called Coase theorem. According to it, if non-costing negotiations are possible, property rights are well defined, and the redistribution of income does not affect marginal values (Coase, 1960):

1. The allocation of resources will be the same regardless of the allocation of property rights,
2. The allocation will be effective (in the Pareto sense), external effects will not occur.

According to the presented theorem, there is symmetry of property rights to the environment. Therefore, the polluter and the recipient of external costs are responsible for the creation of external costs. It can be assumed that the described theorem was the basis for the introduction of regulations relating to pollution limits and trade in them.

The last way of external costs internationalization described in the literature is to combine objectives and/or entities, one of which is the perpetrator and the other recipient of pollution, which should help reduce the costs of perpetrators and victims of joint actions. It seems that a significant obstacle to the spread of such a method of internalization is the combination of interests (goals) that cause these costs and their recipients. The problem is also the lack of identification of external costs, both by the perpetrators and polluters. It is difficult for them to determine the benefits they could achieve from "joining forces". This type of solution is practically not used in practice.

The practical application of the ecological tax proposed by Pigou and Coase's theorem is subject to numerous limitations, and their application to the internalisation of external costs is not possible in its pure form. Hence, researchers and practitioners are deliberating on the effective tax rate (e.g. I. Parry& J. Small, 2004) or the negative consequences of implementing environmental taxes (e.g. distribution effects, see: M. Wier, K. Birr-Pedersen, H.K. Jacobsen & J. Klok, 2005, S.E. West &R.C. Williams III, 2004). Environmental taxes also involve certain political costs, which further complicates their application.

Despite difficulties and shortcomings accompanying the implementation of environmental taxes, they are increasingly widely recognised and used as instruments to promote the balance between the economic, social and environmental dimensions of sustainable development (T. Subhanij, S. Banerjee & Z. Jian, 2018). Therefore, public authorities apply environmental taxes in pursuit of their environmental policy objectives. In areas such as transport, energy efficiency, air pollution and climate change, this instrument is the most common in OECD countries. Environmental taxes are most often imposed on businesses operating in the transport sector (more than 80%[3] of the EU's GDP).

The number and rates of environmental taxes vary considerably from country to country. Some of them, while implementing environmental protection policy, apply on a large scale relatively high environmental taxes, while the others award subsidies on a similarly large scale. These differences can be clearly seen when comparing revenues from environmental taxes. In 2016, revenues from environmental taxes in OECD countries amounted to USD 742,460 million. The highest revenues from these taxes, almost 17% of all revenues, were recorded in the USA. Total revenues from environmental taxes in the EU countries in 2017 amounted to €364,398 million. The countries with the highest revenues are Germany, Italy, the United Kingdom and France. Their contribution to this type of income in the EU in 2017 reached a little over 61%.

Volume, Dynamics and Structure of Environmental Taxes in European Union Countries[4]

Between 2008 and 2017, there was a steady but marginal increase in environmental tax revenues in the EU countries from €298 billion to €369 billion. Significantly higher growth was observed in earlier years, especially in the early 2000s (annual average of around 3%).

Revenues from environmental taxes vary considerably between the EU countries. However, this is a natural phenomenon, given the existing differences in the size of these countries (their economies). These revenues constitute less than 2.5% of their gross domestic product (GDP) and a little over 6% of their total revenue from taxes and social contributions. These shares remained practically unchanged throughout the analysed period.

Figure 1. Environmental taxes in EU countries [mln euro]
Source: own calculation, https://ec.europa.eu/eurostat/data/database.

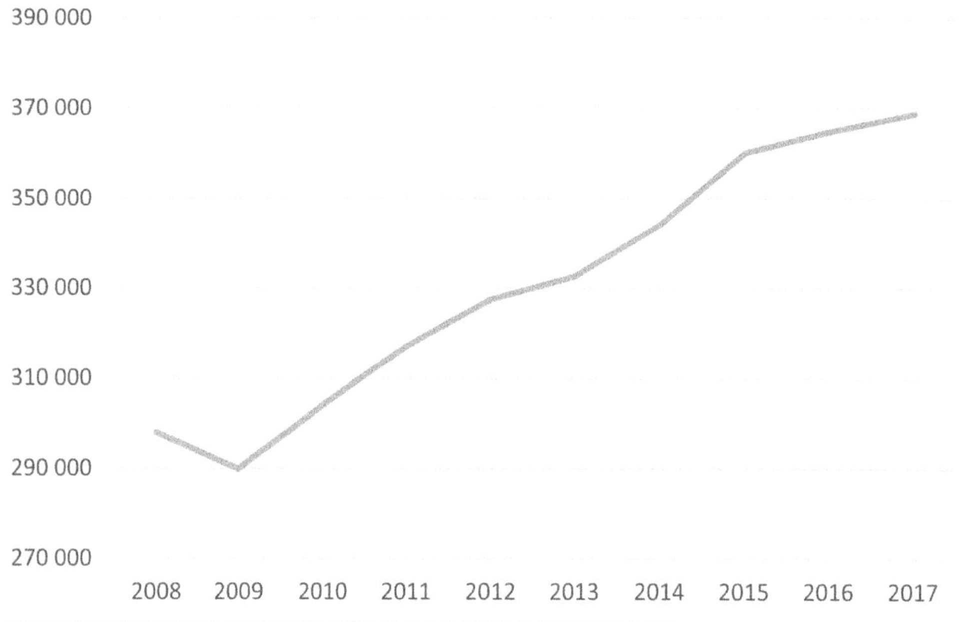

These figures vary considerably from country to country. When we look at the share of environmental taxes in GDP, the minimum value was below 2% (in different countries depending on the year) to about 4%. In all the years covered by the analysis, the highest share was reported in Denmark. In 2016, the average share was 2.6%, while the median - 2.4%. Taking into account the coefficient of variation, it can be concluded that the diversity of this share was moderate (the coefficient was at the level of about 25%).

When analysing the share of environmental taxes as a percentage of total revenue from taxes and social contributions, the minimum value stood at 3.2%, the maximum at 11.7%, while the median and the arithmetic mean were at the same level of 7.4%. The level of differentiation between countries was similar to that of the first analysed indicator (the coefficient of variation was around 25%).

In all the EU countries, revenues from energy taxes are the highest, accounting for 74-76% over the whole period under analysis. Significantly lower incomes were generated by transport taxes (about 20-22%). Revenues from this source showed a downward trend. Taxes on pollution and resources were of marginal importance. Their contribution to the revenues from environmental taxes was at the level of ca. 3%. The structure of environmental taxes in the EU countries is presented in Figure 2.

The structure of environmental taxes varies between EU countries. Although in all countries energy taxes are predominant, their share ranges from less than 51% to 93%. In 2017 the highest proportion of energy taxes in the total of environmental taxes was seen in Lithuania, Luxembourg, Romania and the Czech Republic (more than 90%), while the lowest share was recorded in Malta and Denmark (below 54%). In the latter two countries, transport taxes constituted a significant part of environmental tax revenue (40%), similarly to Norway and Switzerland. The last group of environmental taxes is of rather marginal importance among the revenues generated from this source. Only in the Netherlands, Estonia and Hungary, revenues from pollution and resource taxes accounted for slightly more than 10% of all the environmental taxes (cf. Figure 3).

Figure 2. Environmental taxes in EU countries by type
Source: own calculation, https://ec.europa.eu/eurostat/data/database.

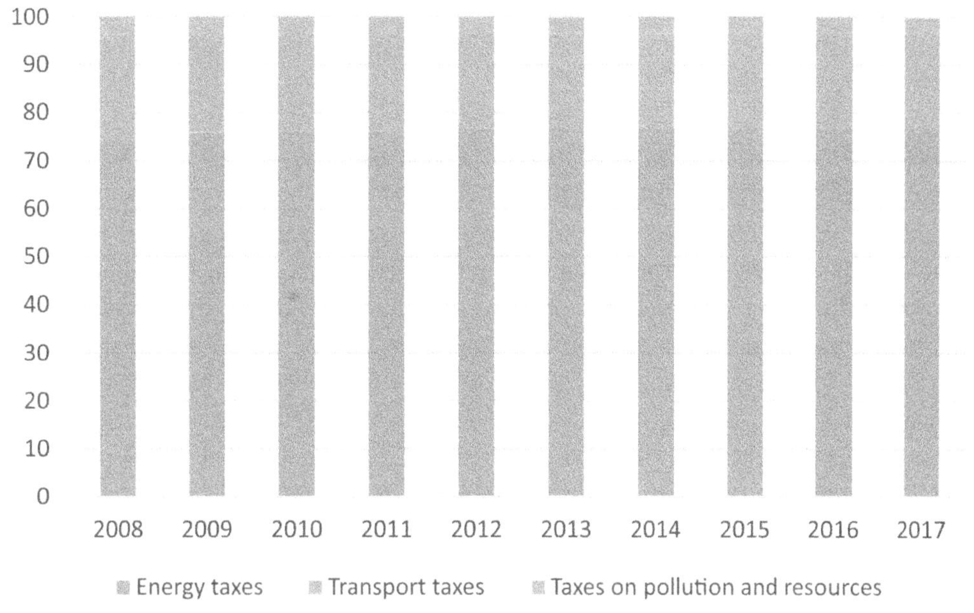

Figure 3. Environmental taxes in EU countries by type in 2016
Source: own, https://ec.europa.eu/eurostat/data/database.

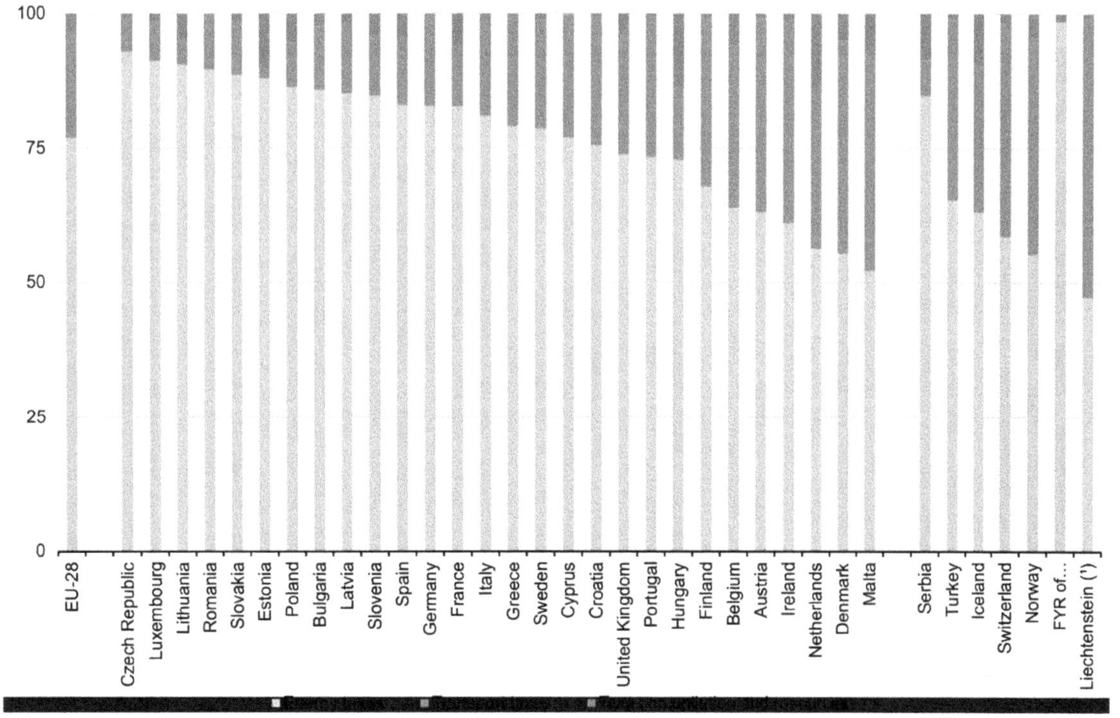

In conclusion, it should be noted that the revenue from environmental taxes does not play a significant fiscal role, whether in relation to GDP or total revenue from taxes and social contributions. In our opinion, however, they have an effect on the public expenditure aimed at environmental protection. Therefore, further in the paper we describe environmental protection expenditures and their relation to revenues from environmental taxes.

Environmental Protection Expenditures: Volume, Dynamics and Structure by Institutional Sector

Various organisations - general government and non-profit institutions serving households, corporations, households, rest of the world - spend funds aimed at limiting the negative impact on the environment, and thus at limiting the payment of environmental taxes. In 2017 national spending on environmental protection in the EU countries amounted to €316 billion. That included current and capital expenditure on environmental protection in each country[5]. The amount of those expenditures in the last analysed year was by nearly 19% higher than in 2008 (on average 2% annually). The development of national environmental protection expenditures in the EU countries in 2008-2017 is presented in figure 4.

The largest annual increases in national expenditure were observed in 2015 and 2011. (by about 3.5%). Those expenditures, as well as the amount of revenues from environmental taxes differed considerably from country to country. Decidedly the highest environmental expenditures were incurred in Germany, France, Italy and the UK.

Figure 4. National expenditure on environmental protection, EU-28
Source: own calculation, https://ec.europa.eu/eurostat/data/database

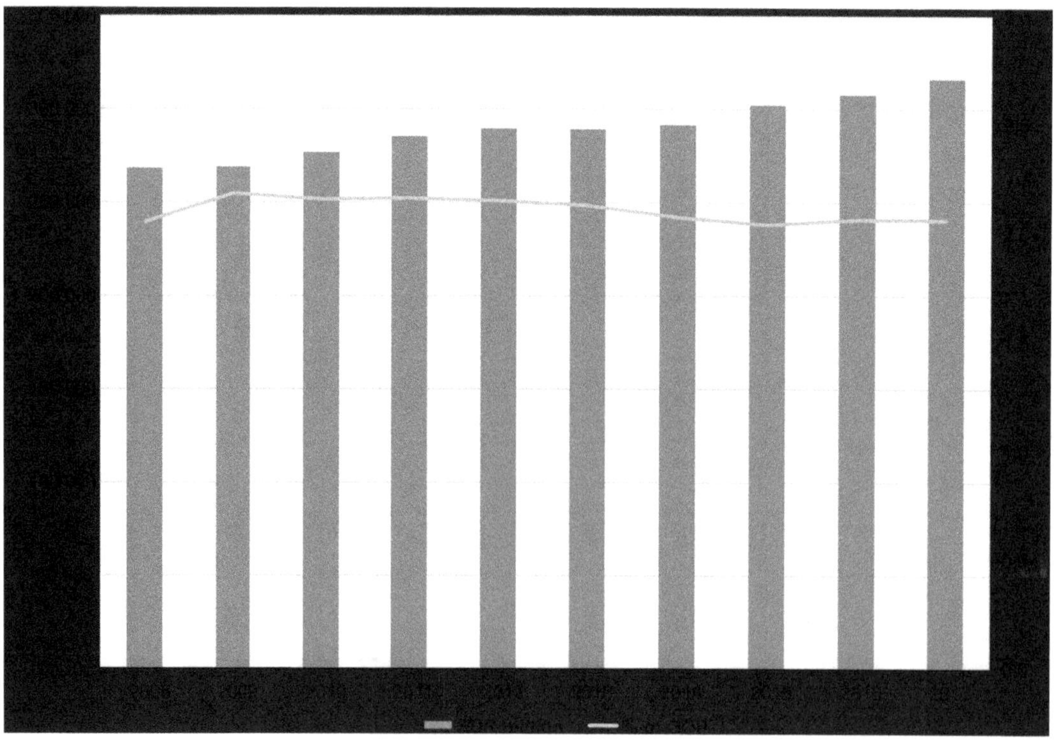

In all analysed years national expenditure on environmental protection in the EU accounted for a little over 2% of GDP. That share was markedly differentiated among the member states. In 2017, the highest share of energy taxes in environmental taxes was recorded in Lithuania, Luxembourg, Romania and the Czech Republic (over 90%), while the lowest proportion was seen in Malta and Denmark (less than 54%). The disparities among the EU countries in terms of the analysed relation are quite large (in 2015 the coefficient of variation amounted to 36%).

Amidst environmental protection expenditures, investment expenditures incurred on infrastructure, especially on water and sanitation, designed to reduce pollutant emissions and to utilise renewable energy sources, as well as on the purchase of land and equipment necessary to provide environmental protection services, is of significant importance. However, the possibility to present them after 2013 was significantly limited due to the change in the Eurostat methodology of calculating and distributing data on environmental protection expenditures, which is discussed in more detail in the Methodology Part of this paper.

In 2017 investment expenditures incurred by the EU national governments, local governments, non-profit institutions serving households and enterprises amounted in total to almost €78 billion. The majority of investments in fixed assets dedicated to the provision of environmental services were made by businesses (63% of their total assets). In 2017 their investment expenditure amounted to €49 billion, while the expenditure incurred by central and local government institutions and non-profit institutions serving households amounted to €29 billion. Between 2006 and 2017, the investment fell by an average of 1.3% per annum (in current prices) for businesses, while it increased by 1.6% in the case of general government and non-profit institutions serving households[6].

In 2017 in the EU, the share of investments in environmental protection in the total amount of investment expenditure incurred by enterprises amounted to 2.5%. Over the entire time of the analysis that share was declining. In the general government and non-profit institutions serving households, the above proportion was much higher and amounted to 7.1% in 2017. What is worth noting is that, similarly to the value of those investments, that share followed an upward trend.

METHODOLOGY AND VARIABLES

When commencing the development of the methodology to analyse environmental taxes and public expenditure on environmental protection, as well as their interrelations, it was necessary, first of all, to specify their definitions and the purpose of the research. At the beginning, we present selected data related to the size and structure of environmental taxes in European Union countries. Then, we outline the volumes and structure of national environmental protection expenditures by institutional sectors. We also present the correlation coefficients between the above-mentioned categories and the results of the analysis of correlations among the variables in the linear regression of a single variable[7].

In the study, data relating to environmental taxes and public sector expenditure (general government) are presented in accordance with the calculation methodology adopted by Eurostat [8]. Data accepted for the analysis - environmental taxes and environmental protection expenditures are expressed in millions of euro (in current prices)[9].

Before presenting the results of linear regression analysis, we show selected quantities that represent both the categories under analysis. This allows us to describe European Union countries in terms of the analysed categories with the help of such measures of descriptive statistics as: the minimum and maximum indicator, the measure of location (median, arithmetic mean) and the measure of variation (coefficient of variation).

When selecting the indicators to assess the level of environmental taxes and expenditures on environmental protection as well as the approach to identify their correlations, we were guided primarily by the availability of comparable aggregated data in a manner enabling their use. The source of the data used in the survey were the resources collected in the Eurostat atabase[10].

Taking into consideration the availability of data (their timeliness and comparability), we decided to analyse environmental taxes and their relation to public expenditure on environmental protection using the Eurostat data (presented for 28 EU countries, Norway, Switzerland and Serbia). However, a significant problem encountered was the lack of data for individual countries, which made it difficult or impossible to conduct dependency analyses for selected years (e.g. in the case of 2013, data on public investment expenditures on environmental protection are available only for a handful of countries). Another problem was the change in the manner of presentation of data relating to environmental protection expenditures in 2014, which is related to the introduction of environmental protection expenditure accounts (EPEA) as an integral part of European Environmental Economic Accounts (E. Broniewicz &W. Domańska, 2016). The change in the way data is presented makes it impossible to conduct a separate analysis of current and investment expenditures on environmental protection from 2014 onwards.

The presented Pearson correlation coefficients are used to study the linear dependence of variables. An increased value of one variable causes proportional changes in the average value of the other variable (increase or decrease depending on the sign - plus/minus). The coefficient of linear correlation of two variables is the quotient of covariance and the product of standard deviations of those variables. It is calculated according to the formula:

$$r_{xy} = \frac{cov\left(x, y\right)}{Sd_x \times Sd_y}$$

where:

$$cov_{(x,y)} = \frac{\Sigma\left(x_i - \overline{x}\right)\left(y_i - \overline{y}\right)}{n}$$

$Cov_{(x,y)}$ – covariance x,y

x_i – variable x

y_i – variable y

$\overline{x}, \overline{y}$ – arithmetic mean of variable x, y

n – number of observations

$Sd_{x,y}$ – standard deviation of variable x,y

The most important element of the study was to determine the relationship between the level of green taxes income and the expenditures on environmental protection that were conducive to limiting the pressure (adverse impact) on them in European Union countries. That enabled us to establish whether environmental taxes actually constituted the determinant of environmental protection expenditures.

Assuming such a goal, we decided to apply the analysis of correlation and interdependence of variables in regression. The regression analysis assumes that the model can be described approximately as a function in the form of h (x,b); where b is a certain parameter vector and h is a given continuous function (a regression function). The aim of the analysis is to find such values of the parameter vector b that the regression model is best suited to the observation. If the h function is linear with respect to parameters b then the regression (and also the model) can be called linear, otherwise it is non-linear. We chose the linear regression model (J. Syska, 2014; N.R. Draper& H. Smith, 1973; M. Rószkiewicz 2011; M. Szaleniec, 2008; D.R. Cox, 1972) to investigate the dependence. Linear regression makes it possible to examine the existence of a relationship between the categories concerned, which is a condition for a causal link between them. This method enables the construction of models of linear relationships between variables. The result is an empirical model in the form of a regression equation that takes the form:

$$y_t = b_0 + b_1 x_{1t} + {}_t$$

where:

y_t – dependent variable at time t,
x_t – independent variable at time t (predictor),
b_0, b_1 – model parameters,
${}_t$ – a random component expressing an impact on a variable dependent by all the factors that are not included in the model.

Linear regression requires the assumption that the relationship between variables is linear. In practice, the validity of such an assumption is almost impossible to prove, but regression procedures are quite resistant to small deviations from this assumption (P. Rydzewski, 2010). Regression coefficients are estimated by the least squares method (LSM), which was introduced at the beginning of the 19th century by A.-M. Legendre and C. F. Gauss (H.L. Seal, 1967; M. Abazid, A. Abdulrahman, & S. Samine 2018) According to LSM, when we have observations (x_i, y_i); i = 1, …, n, we choose b_0 and b_1 so that the value:

$$\sum_{i=1}^{n}(y_i - (b_0 + b_1 x_1))$$

can be the lowest[2].

The basic measure of regression matching is the determination factor R^2, which takes the form:

$$R^2 = \frac{\sum_{i=1}^{n}(b_0 + b_1 x_i - \bar{y})2}{\sum_{i=1}^{n}(y_i - \bar{y})2}$$

It describes the strength of the linear relationship between variables, i.e. the matching of the regression line to the empirical data. The coefficient of determination takes values from [0,1] and indicates which part of the variability of the variable y is explained by the estimated model. The higher the level of the determination factor, the greater part of the variability of the variable explained by the model. Another important parameter used to assess the quality of the regression model is significance, which should not exceed 0.05. The significance of the simple regression model is equivalent to the significance of the factor b1 and is determined by testing the H_0 hypothesis: $b_1 = 0$, the alternative hypothesis H_1: $b_1 \neq 0$. If the significance of the model is less than or equal to 0.05, the H_0 hypothesis must be rejected; if otherwise, there is no basis for rejecting the H_0 hypothesis. In a situation where the H_0 hypothesis is not rejected, it can be concluded that a linear relationship between a dependent variable and an independent variable does not exist.

The calculations were performed with the use of software for statistical data analysis – SPSS (M. Rószkiewicz, 2011).

In the regression analysis we used data from 2016 (as the last year for which data was available) for 30 countries (only for the general government and non-profit sectors). The calculations were repeated for 2015, 2012, 2010 and 2008 with a breakdown by institutional sectors incurring environmental expenditures. In addition, we performed calculations for 2008, 2010 and 2012 for current and investment expenditures. Data for analysis came from Eurostat resources.

SOLUTIONS AND RECOMMENDATIONS: STUDY ON IMPACT OF ENVIRONMENTAL TAXES ON PUBLIC FINANCE SYSTEM

When undertaking the assessment of the impact of environmental taxes on the public system of financing expenditure on environmental protection, the first step was to calculate the correlation coefficients. Their results are presented in Table 1.

Taking into account the values presented in Table, it is clear that there is a very strong positive linear relationship between the analysed categories. This may be interpreted as meaning that the increase in revenues from environmental taxes results in an increased public expenditure on environmental protection. The coefficient of correlation is close to 1, which means that almost all variables meet the assumption (an increase in 1 variable causes an increase in the second variable) - the trend is evident.

Subsequently, in order to establish a correlation between the analysed categories, we constructed simple regression models, in which the dependent variable was public expenditure on environmental protection, while the independent variable was environmental taxes revenues. Separate regression analysis was performed for each year. The results of modelling are presented in Table 2.

Table 1. The relationship between environmental taxes and general government expenditure on environmental protection - Pearson correlation coefficients

2008	2009	2010	2011	2012	2013	2014	2015	2016
0.9349	0.9520	0.9423	0.9383	0.9383	0.9519	0.9528	0.9656	0.9680

Table 2. Simple regression models – results

	2008	2009	2010	2011	2012	2013	2014	2015	2016
coefficient of determination R^2	0.8740	0.9062	0.8885	0.8803	0.8835	0.9096	0.9078	0.9328	0.9375
absolute term b_0	-8.8	-70.83	-100.27	49.04	48.46	-52.13	-12.94	-104.86	-267.39
slope b_1	0.34	0.38	0.37	0.34	0.33	0.34	0.34	0.34	0.33

It should be noted that for all constructed regression models (for individual years) the coefficient of determination (R^2) is high oscillating around 88-94%, which indicates a very high degree of model matching. This may be interpreted as meaning that the revenues from environmental taxes explain to a large extent the variability of public expenditures on environmental protection. Models are statistically significant because their significance is 0.000, which rejects the hypothesis that $b_1 = 0$ (slope).

When analyzing the values of the calculated directional coefficients, we can conclude that the increase in revenues from environmental taxes by PLN 1 million results in the increase in public expenditure at the level of EUR 0.33-0.38 million. It should be remembered that the amount of these expenditures is also affected by other variables that are not included in the models.

In addition to the conducted regression analysis, we also built simple regression models for a specific timeframe, where environmental taxes remained the independent variable, while the dependent variable was public investment expenditures on environmental protection. The modelling results are presented in Table 3.

It should be noted that also in the case of all the constructed regression models (for individual years) the coefficient of determination (R^2) was high, although lower than in previously analysed regression models, which also indicates a high degree of model matching. This may be interpreted as meaning that revenues from environmental taxes explain to a large extent the variability of public investment expenditures on environmental protection. These models are statistically significant because their significance is 0,000, which allows to reject the hypothesis that $b_1 = 0$ (slope).

Assuming that the constructed linear regression models are well matched and explain to a large extent the variability of the independent variable (public environmental investment expenditure), we can conclude that the impact of environmental taxes revenues by EUR 1 million results in an increase of only EUR 0.05 million in public environmental investment expenditure. It can be interpreted that revenue from environmental taxes has a small impact on the growth of public investment expenditures on environmental protection, much lower than on general public expenditures on environmental protection.

Table 3. Simple regression models – results

	2008	2009	2010	2011	2012
coefficient of determination R^2	0.8137	0.8042	0.8118	0.8391	0.8304
absolute term b_0	30.04	67.69	69.02	51.49	28.36
slope b_1	0.05	0.05	0.04	0.05	0.05

DISCUSSION AND CONCLUSION

The application of the environmental taxes, being an environmental protection policy instrument, is to encourage actions aimed at future limiting emissions or ambient concentration of pollutants as well as at reducing the consumption of environmental resources. These activities involve specific capital expenditures, as well as current expenditures for equipment (infrastructure) maintenance in order to reduce the pressure on the environment.

In the existing literature, the authors have dealt with environmental taxation, mainly in the EU countries, in the context of utilising taxes to improve the state of the natural environment, with the use of revenues from environmental taxes. They consider them as an instrument to reduce the distortionary taxes on labour and production (B. Bosquet, 2000). On the other hand, they seek a relationship between environmental taxes (or one-off taxes, e.g. M.S. Andersen, 2007) and economic growth (e.g. A.M. Leiter, A. Parolini, & H. Winner, 2011). In their studies, they state that environmental taxes have a positive but decreasing impact on investment in general. Other studies also confirm the positive impact of environmental policy on economic growth. Ricci (2007) suggests a number of ways to improve environmental performance and economic growth, such as the prospect of a better environment, can encourage savings.

The authors showed that the revenues from environmental taxes explain to a large extent the variability of public expenditures on environmental protection. With high probability we can conclude that the increase in revenues from environmental taxes results in the increase in public expenditure. It should be remembered that the amount of these expenditures is also affected by other variables that are not included in the models. Therefore, the authors see the need for deeper research with respect to other variables. The analysis of the determination coefficient (R^2) in the analyzed regression models, showed that income from environmental taxes explains to a large extent the evolution of investment public expenditure on environmental protection. However, the increase of revenue from environmental taxes does not directly translate into an increase of environmental expenditures, especially if investment expenditures are analyzed.

The conducted research confirms that it is purposeful in the context of the use of taxes to improve the state of the environment, with the use of income from environmental taxes. However, governments' actions should tighten up in other activities, as income, including the use of income from environmental taxes, is not the only base for making expenses to improve the environment. The public finance system's arrangements are an important, but not the only, instrument to influence sustainable development. The discussion as well as the results obtained the impact of environmental taxes on the public system of financing expenditure on environmental protection.

ACKNOWLEDGMENT

Research results presented in this paper are an element of research project implemented by the National Science Center Poland under [the grant OPUS13 no UMO-2017/25/B/HS4/02172].

REFERENCES

Abazid, M., Abdulrahman, A., & Samine, S. (2018). Least Squares Methods to Forecast Sales for Company. *International Journal of Scientific & Engineering Research*, *9*(6), 864–868.

Abu-Bader, S., & Abu-Qarn, A. S. (2003). Government Expenditures, Military Spending and Economic Growth: Causality Evidence from Egypt, Israel, and Syria. *Journal of Policy Modeling*, *25*(6-7), 567–583. doi:10.1016/S0161-8938(03)00057-7

Adam, A. (2015). Challenges of Public Finance Sustainability in the European Union. *Procedia Economics and Finance*, *23*, 298–302. doi:10.1016/S2212-5671(15)00507-9

Adolf, C., & Röhrig, K. (2016). *Communicating Green Own Resources: A New Narrative for the EU Budget*. Brussels: Green Budget Europe.

Afonso, A., Erbert, W., Schuknect, L., & Thone, M. (2005). Quality of Public Finances and Growth. *ECB Working Paper*, *438*, 1-47.

Alińska, A., Filipiak, B. Z., & Kosztowniak, A. (2018). The Importance of the Public Sector in Sustainable Development in Poland. *Sustainability*, *10*(9), 3278. doi:10.3390u10093278

Andersen, M. S. (2007). *Carbon-energy Taxation Contributed to Economic Groth*. National Environmental Research Insitute News.

Andrada, M. G. (2015). Sustainable development and CSR in the financial sector. *Ann. Econ. Ser.*, *1*, 217–221.

Arestis, P. (2006). Financial liberalization and the relationship between finance and growth. In P. Arestis & M. Sawyer (Eds.), *A Handbook of Alternative Monetary Economics* (pp. 346–364). Cheltenham, UK: Edward Elgar Publishing.

Ashford, N. A., & Hall, R. P. (2011). *Technology, Globalization, and Sustainable Development: Transforming the Industrial State*. New Haven, CT: Yale University Press.

Atkinson, T., & van de Noord, P. (2001). *Managing public expenditure: Some emerging policy issues and a framework for analysis*. OECD Economics Department Working Paper, No. 285. Paris: Organisation for Economic Co-operation and Development.

Balassone, F., & Franco, D. (2000). *Assessing Fiscal Sustainability: A Review of Methods with a View to EMU*. Rome: Bank of Italy. doi:10.2139srn.2109377

Barrios, S., & Schaechter, A. (2008). The quality of public finances and economic growth. *Economic Papers*, *337*, 2–49.

Bosquet, B. (2000). Environmental Tax Reform: Does it Work? A Survey of the Empirical Evidence. *Ecological Economics*, *34*(1), 19–32.

Bostan, I., Onofrei, M., Dascălu, E. D., Fîrţescu, B., & Toderaţcu, C. (2016). Impact of Sustainable Environmental Expenditures Policy on Air Pollution Reduction, During European Integration Framework, *Amfiteatru. Economic Journal (London)*, *18*(42), 286–302.

Boulanger, P. M. (2008). Sustainable development indicators: A scientific challenge, a democratic issue. *SAPIENS*, *1*(1), 45–59.

Broniewicz, E., & Domańska, W. (2016). Rachunki wydatków na ochronę środowiska (EPEA) jako moduł Europejskich Rachunków Ekonomicznych Środowiska, Optimum. *Studia Ekonomiczne*, *1*(79), 165–181. doi:10.15290/ose.2016.01.79.11

Coase, R. H. (1960). The Problem of Social Cost. *The Journal of Law & Economics*, *3*, 1–44. doi:10.1086/466560

Cobb, C., Glickman, M., & Cheslog, C. (2001). *The genuine progress indicator 2001 Update*. Edefining Progress Issue Brief. Available online: URL https://www.researchgate.net/profile/Clifford_Cobb/publication/237470296_THE_GENUINE_PROGRESS_INDICATOR_2000_UPDATE/links/56fe2d0a08aee995dde673d1.pdf

Cox, D. R. (1972). Regression Models and Life-tables (with discussion). *Journal of the Royal Statistical Society. Series B. Methodological*, *2*(2), 187–220. doi:10.1111/j.2517-6161.1972.tb00899.x

Daly, H. E., & Cobb, J. B. (1989). *For the Common Good. Redirecting the Economy toward Community, Environment, and a Sustainable Future*. Boston, MA: Beacon Press.

Dandan, M. M. (2011). Government expenditures and economic growth in Jordan. *IPEDR, 4*, 467–471.

Dao, M. Q. (2017). Public Policies, Institutions, and Economic Growth in Low-Income and Lower Middle-Income Countries: Further Empirical Evidence. *Adv. Econ. Bus*, *5*(8), 440–447. doi:10.13189/aeb.2017.050802

Diamond, J. (2003). *Performance-budgeting: Managing the reform proces*. IMF Working Paper, No. 33.

Do Valle, P. O., Pintassilgo, P., Matias, A., & Andre, F. (2012). Tourist Attitudes Towards an Accommodation Tax Earmarked for Environmental Protection: A Survey in the Algarve. *Tourism Management*, *33*(2), 1408–1416. doi:10.1016/j.tourman.2012.01.003

Draper, N. R., & Smith, H. (1973). *Analiza regresji stosowana*. Warszawa: Państwowe Wydawnictwo Naukowe.

European Commission. (2017). Sustainability Of Public Finances. *EU Commission*. Available at: Https://Ec.Europa.Eu/Info/Business-Economy-Euro/Economic-And-Fiscal-Policy-Coordination/Eu-Economic-Governance-Monitoring-Prevention-Correction/European-Semester/Thematic-Factsheets/Fiscal-Stability_pl

European Environment Agency. (1996). *Environmental Taxes. Implementation and Environmental Effectiveness*. Author.

Eurostat. (2017). *Energy, Transport and Environment Indicators*. Luxembourg: Publications Office of the European Union.

Filipiak, B. Z. (2014). Challenges of Sustainable Development in the New Financial Perspective—Financial Approach. In H. Witte (Ed.), *Nachhaltigkeit, ökonomiche Gleichgewichte und Wertschöpfung* (pp. 169–192). Bahia Blanca, Argentina: Edi UNS.

Fullwiler, S. T. (2015). *Sustainable finance: Building a more general theory of finance*. Binzagr Institute for Sustainable Prosperity, Working Paper No. 106.

Garba, T., & Abdullahi, S. Y. (2013). Public Expenditure and Economic Growth: An Application of Cointegration and Granger Causality Tests on Nigeria. *J. Econ. Soc., 15*, 1–30.

Geels, F. (2011). The multi-level perspective on sustainability transitions: Responses to sev-en criticisms. *Environmental Innovation and Societal Transitions, 1*(1), 24–40. doi:10.1016/j.eist.2011.02.002

Giosi, A., Testarmata, S., Brunelli, S., & Staglianň, B. (2012). *Does the Quality of Public Finance Enhance Fiscal Discipline in the European Union? A Cross-Country Analysis*. Milano: McGraw-Hill Education.

Graczyk, A. (2009). Ekonomiczne podstawy ochrony środowiska. *Biuletyn Polskiego Towarzystwa Ekonomicznego, 1*(39), 4–11.

Grądalski, F. (2006). *System podatkowy w świetle teorii optymalnego opodatkowania*. Warszawa: Szkoła Główna Handlowa w Warszawie.

Haibara, T. (2009). Environmental Funds, Public Abatement, and Welfare. *Environmental and Resource Economics, 44*(2), 167–177. doi:10.100710640-009-9276-6

Holzinger, K., Knill, C., & Sommererb, T. (2011). Is there convergence of national environmental policies?An analysis of policy outputs in 24 OECD countries. *Environmental Politics, 20*(1), 20–35. do i:10.1080/09644016.2011.538163

Institute for European Environmental Policy (IEEP). (2014). Environmental Tax Reform in Europe: Opportunities for the Future. Annexes to Final Report. Brussels: IEEP.

International Institute for Labour Studies. (2011). *Green Policies in the EU: a Review*. International Labour Organization. EC-IILS Joint Discussion Paper Series, 14.

Jeucken, M. (2001). *Sustainable finance and banking: The financial sector and the future of the planet*. London: Earthscan Publications Ltd.

Kates, R. W., Parris, T. M., & Leiserowitz, A. A. (2005). What is sustainable development? Goals, indicators, values, and practice. *Environ. Sci. Policy Sustain. Dev., 47*(3), 8–21. doi:10.1080/00139157.2005.10524444

Knill, C., Debus, M., & Heichel, S. (2010). Do parties matter in internationalised policy areas? The impact of political parties on environmental policy outputs in 18 OECD countries, 1970-2000. *European Journal of Political Research, 49*(3), 301–330. doi:10.1111/j.1475-6765.2009.01903.x

Krejdl, A. (2006). *Fiscal Sustainability – Definition, Indicators and Assessment of Czech Public Finance Sustainability*. Working Papers No.3. Czech National Bank, Research Department.

Kudełko, M. (2016). Korygowanie niekorzystnych efektów zewnętrznych – ujęcie teoretyczne i empiryczne. *Jurnal of Management and Finance, 14*(3), 339-351.

Kuhlman, T., & Farrington, J. (2010). What is Sustainability? *Sustainability, 2*(11), 3436–3448. doi:10.3390u2113436

Lafferty, W., & Hovden, E. (2003). Environmental policy integration: Towards an analytical framework. *Environmental Politics*, *12*(3), 1–10. doi:10.1080/09644010412331308254

Leiter, A. M., Parolini, A., & Winner, H. (2011). Environmental Regulation and Investment: Evidence from European Industries. *Ecological Economics*, *70*(4), 759–770. doi:10.1016/j.ecolecon.2010.11.013

Miller, S. J., & Vela, M. A. (2013). *Are Environmentally Related Taxes Effective?* Washington, DC: Inter-American Development Bank. doi:10.2139srn.2367708

Miller, S. J., & Vela, M. A. (2013). *Are Environmentally Related Taxes Effective?* Inter-American Development Bank. doi:10.2139srn.2367708

Nordhaus, W. D., & Tobin, J. (1973). Is Growth Obsolete? The Measurement of Economic and Social Performance. In National Bureau of Economic Research (pp. 509–532). Columbia University Press.

OECD. (2001). *Environmentally Related Taxes in OECD Countries*. Paris: Issues and Strategies.

OECD. (2010). *Taxation*. Paris: Innovation and the Environment.

OECD. (2012). *Environmental Tax and Green Growth*. Southeast Asian Economic Outlook 2011/12.

Parry, I., & Small, K. (2004). *Does Britain or the United States Have the Right Gasoline Tax?* Discussion Paper 0212 rev. Washington, DC: Resources for the Future.

Pigou, A. C. (2010). *Economics of Welfare*. London: Macmillan Publishing.

Radula, R., & Keel, K. (2018). *The Effects of Crises and EU Fiscal Governance Reforms on the Budgetary Institutions of Member States* Paper presented at the ECPR SGEU conference, Paris, France.

Robins, N., & Zadek, S. (Eds.). (2017). *Roadmap for a Sustainable Financial System*. Washington, DC: World Bank and UNEP.

Rosiek, J. (2005). *The Impact of Envirronmental Tax Policy on Sustainable Developmentof the EU Economies. DEA Approach.* 11th International Conference of ASECU. Retrieved from asecu.gr/files/11th_conf_files/18.pdf

Rószkiewicz, M. (2011). *Analiza klienta*. Kraków: Wydawnictwo SPSS Polska.

Ruffing, K. G. (2010). The Role of the Organization for Economic Cooperation and Development. *Environmental Policy Making Review of Environmental Economics and Policy*, *4*(2), 199–210. doi:10.1093/reep/req007

Rydzewski, P. (2010). Metody analizy danych w socjologicznych badaniach rozwodów. *Roczniki Nauk Społecznych, 2*(38).

Schick, A. (2002). Does budgeting have a future? *OECD Journal on Budgeting*, *2*(2), 7–48. doi:10.1787/budget-v2-art8-en

Seal, H. L. (1967). Studies in the History of Probability and Statistics. XV The historical development of the Gauss linear model. *Biometrika*, *54*(1-2), 1–24. doi:10.1093/biomet/54.1-2.1 PMID:4860564

Smith, S. (2007). *Podatki a środowisko naturalne. In Efektywność polityki podatkowej* (pp. 285–344). Warszawa: Wydawnictwo Sejmowe.

Subhanij, T., Banerjee, S., & Jian, Z. (Eds.). (2018). *Tax Policy for Sustainable Development in Asia and the Pacifi*. United Nations.

Syska, J. (2014). *Współczesne metody analizy regresji wspomagane komputerowo*. Uniwersytet Śląski. Retrieved from http://el.us.edu.pl/ekonofizyka/images/b/b6/MetodyDoboruModeli.pdf

Szaleniec, M. (2008) *Sieci neuronowe i regresja wieloraka – czyli jak okiełznać złożoność w badaniach naukowych*. Statsoft Polska. Retrieved from https://media.statsoft.pl/_old_dnn/downloads/sieci%20 neuronowe.pdf

Tomala, M. (2018). Opodatkowanie ekologiczne narzędziem ochrony środowiska państw nordyckich. Bezpieczeństwo. *Teoria i Praktyka*, *1*, 103–115.

Trehan, B., & Walsh, C. (1991). Testing the Intertemporal Budget Constraints: Theory and Applications to U.S. Federal Budget and Current Account Deficits. *Journal of Money, Credit and Banking*, *23*(2), 206–223. doi:10.2307/1992777

United Nations. (2018). *Scaling up Finance for the Sustainable Development Goals: Experimenting with Models of Multilateral Development Banking*. United Nations. Available online: http://unctad.org/en/PublicationsLibrary/gdsecidc2017d4_en.pdf

Van der Waldt, G. (2016). The Role of Government in Sustainable Development. *Towards a Conceptual and Analytical Framework for Scientific Inquiry Administratio Publica*, *24*(2), 49–72.

West, S. E., & Williams, R. C. III. (2004). Estimatesfrom a Consumer Demand System: Implications for the Incidence of Environmental Taxes. *Journal of Environmental Economics and Management*, *47*(3), 535–558. doi:10.1016/j.jeem.2003.11.004

Wier, M., Birr-Pedersen, K., Jacobsen, H. K., & Klok, J. (2005). Are Co_2 Taxes Regressive? Evidence from the Danish Experience. *Ecologocal Economisc*, *52*(2), 239–251. doi:10.1016/j.ecolecon.2004.08.005

Withana, S., Brink, P., Illes, A., Nanni, S., & Watkins, E. (2014). Environmental Tax Reform in Europe: Opportunities for the future. Institute for European Environmental Policy (IEEP) for the Netherlands Ministry of Infrastructure and the Environment.

ADDITIONAL READING

Anger, N., Böhringer, Ch., & Lange, A. (2006). *Differentiation of Green Taxes: A Political-Economy Analysis for Germany*, Centre for European Economic Research, Discussion Paper, 06-003.

Archer, J. H., Eppling, M. P., & Biegel, C. A. (2002). Sustanable Development: Legal Issues and Incentives. Dimensions of Sustainable Development Law. Encyclopedia of Life Support Systems (EOLSS), 1.

Cieślukowski, M. (2017). *Nauka o finansach publicznych w świetle paradygmatu zrównoważonego rozwoju. Finanse*. Czasopismo Komitetu Nauk o Finansach PAN, 1(10), 11-22.

Cieślukwski, M. (2014). *Podatki i system podatkowy w ekonomii zrównoważonego rozwoju. Studia Oeconomica Posnaniensia*, 2, 6 (267), 193-207.

Green Fiscal Commission. (2009). *How Effective Are Green Taxes?* London: Briefing Paper Two.

Hewett, Ch., & Ekins, P. (2014). *Environmental Fiscal Reform in Europe. An overview of policy and politics of implementing environmental fiscal reform in Europe between 1990 and 2013.* Green Budget Europe and the Danish Ecological Council.

Kosonen, K., & Nicodème, G. (2009). *The Role of Fiscal Instruments in Environmental Policy*. Luxemburg: Office for Official Publications of the European Communities. Working Paper, 19.

ENDNOTES

1 EU countries belong to the OECD, except Bulgaria, Croatia, Cyprus, Malta and Romania.

2 Hence, in the literature on the subject, research has been undertaken into the impact of environmental taxation on innovative activities (in a broader sense, into "green growth"). (OECD, 2010). The environmental taxes ensure that markets take account of environmental impacts by including their amount in the prices of goods and services. Environmental prices through taxation leave consumers and economic operators the flexibility to determine how best to reduce their environmental footprint. This requires low-cost solutions or encourages innovation.

3 OECD data retrieved from http://www.oecd.org/environment/indicators-modelling-outlooks/policy-instrument-database.

4 Initially, the authors intended to analyze environmental taxes, environmental protection expenditures and relationships between them in OECD countries, but the unavailability of data at the appropriate level of aggregation or lack of comparability prompted the authors to accept the analysis of the European Union countries.

5 They are defined as the sum of the final and intermediate consumption of environmental products by resident units other than in the case of the environmental producers themselves, of capital raised for environmental protection products, of gross accumulation of other products required for environmental protection activities, of additional (current and capital) specific transfers by resident units not included above, of additional (current and capital) funding provided by transfers to the rest of the world and of minor funding by transfers received from the rest of the world.

6 https://ec.europa.eu/eurostat/statistics-explained/index.php/Environmental_protection_expenditure_Accounts#General_overview.

7 We also considered the analysis of relations between different independent variables and a dependent variable (amount of expenditures on environmental protection) with the use of the multiple regression analysis. However, taking into account the nature of the study and the adopted objective, we finally decided to continue the study of correlation and regression of one variable.

8 https://ec.europa.eu/eurostat/cache/metadata/en/env_ac_tax_esms.htm. https://ec.europa.eu/eurostat/cache/metadata/en/gov_10a_exp_esms.htm.

9 Both categories are expressed in current prices, which does not disturb the possibility of conducting analyzes. The analysis were also carried out for selected years on data including harmonized indices of consumer prices. Obtained results of R^2 coefficient as well as direction coefficients in regression models underwent slight changes. The analysis of these values was not made into fixed prices due to the fact that a part of environmental protection expenditures have investment nature and should be transformed using the price index of investment goods. The official public statistics do not give the analyzed categories at constant prices.

10 https://ec.europa.eu/eurostat/data/database.

Chapter 7
Challenges and Opportunities of the Sustainability in Healthcare:
Multicriteria Assessment of Polish Healthcare Sector

Katarzyna Malgorzata Miszczyńska
University of Lodz, Poland

ABSTRACT

Public health, affecting the operations of the entity and its environment, plays an important role in the concept of sustainable development. Health condition affects the quality of life of the individual thus the condition of the economy. Taking into consideration the complex relationship of public health and the concept of Sustainable Development Goals, the analysis seems to be fully justified. The aim of the analysis is to determine challenges and opportunities of the sustainability of selected United Nations Member States healthcare sectors. Particular emphasis in the analysis was placed on the situation of the Polish sector against the background of the analyzed countries. The analysis was based on the Sustainable Development Goals and was carried out using one of the MCDA method.

INTRODUCTION

The health condition of the population and access to healthcare are fundamental factors determining the people's lives, which are pointed out in the Sustainable Development Goals (SDGs). The multifaceted nature of relations between public health and the concept of sustainable development is manifested in such aspects as improving the quality of life, efficiency and costs of the functioning of the economy or the impact of the environment on society's health. Sustainable socio-economic development is one of the most important challenges of the modern world and that is why it requires evaluating systems and implementing measures along with appropriate budget planning. The aim of the analysis is to determine

DOI: 10.4018/978-1-7998-1033-9.ch007

challenges and opportunities of the sustainability of selected United Nations Member States healthcare sectors. Particular emphasis in the analysis was placed on the situation of the Polish sector against the background of the analyzed countries. The methods of measuring efficiency are an appropriate tool for detecting not only efficiency or lack of it, but also showing good practices, on which inefficient units should model themselves.

BACKGROUND

The health condition of the population and access to health care are fundamental factors determining the quality of life. The primary focus of health care should be put on optimizing patient outcomes (Harris, Green, Ramsey, Allen, & King, 2017), but without due consideration of value for money healthcare systems will not be sustainable (Garner & Littlejohns, 2011; Scott, 2012). There are many challenges of the sustainability of healthcare services presented in the literature (Leeder, 2013; Stuart & Adams, 2007).

All of them threaten the ability to maintain health services at acceptable standards and as a consequence in a sustainable way. Sustainability is defined here as the development that meets the needs of the present without compromising the ability of future generations to meet their own needs (Shah, 2008). The multifaceted nature of this relationship manifests itself in such aspects as the improvement of the quality of life, the efficiency and costs of the functioning of the economy or the impact of the environment on the health of the society. As Sustainable Development Commission underlines the concept of the sustainable development is an approach to development that looks to balance different needs against the awareness of the environmental, social and economic limitations (Sustainable Development Commission, 2011).

Sustainable socio-economic development is one of the most important challenges of the modern world, and by many countries, including Poland, it is considered the Constitutional Principle of the Republic of Poland.

In the global perspective, the overarching organization dealing with sustainable development is the UN. During the work done, at many cyclical conferences, on the idea of sustainable development, the goals of sustainable development have been distinguished. The Sustainable Development Goals were developed to mobilize efforts in all countries to end all forms of poverty, fight inequalities and tackle climate change, while ensuring that no one is left behind. The goals apply universally and are part of the 2030 Agenda for Sustainable Development (EPF, 2019).

As it was mentioned above, health is inextricably linked to the concept of sustainable development. Equitable access to health care for all is undoubtedly a benchmark, recognized in the Millennium Development Goals and its follow-on, the recently announced Sustainable Development Goals (Wong, 2016). The interconnectedness of the SDGs is clear. Hence, the importance of healthy lives and well-being for all (Goal 3) is unquestionable as it is interlinked with ending poverty and hunger (Goals 1 & 2), reducing inequalities (Goal 10), providing clean water and sanitation facilities (Goal 6), protecting the environment (Goals 7, 13, 14, 15), providing decent work (Goal 8), ensuring gender equality (Goal 5) and having access to quality education (Goal 4). (Wong, 2016)

With reference to the idea of Sustainable Development Goals Hertwig and Grune-Yanoff (2017) have underlined in their research that numerous governments and organizations have begun to acknowledge the huge potential of behavioral science in improving the efficiency of public policies. What is more, the behavioral science is being considered to become a powerful policy tool in the great majority of OECD countries. The growing popularity of behavioral science owes the nudge approach, which has been disseminated by Thaler and Sustein (2008). However, "nudges" understood as nonregulatory and nonmonetary interventions that steer people in a particular direction while preserving their freedom of choice (e.g., Alemanno & Sibony, 2015; Halpern, 2015) is not the only tool used in the public policy. As it was underlined by Hertwig and Grune-Yanoff (2017) the scientific study of human behavior also provides support for a distinct kind of interventions called boost. The objective of boosts is to improve people's competence to make their own choices fostering existing competences or instilling new ones. All in all, it should be underlined that nudges and boost have been they are becoming more and more popular in supporting sustainable development policy. Thanks to these tools, institutions and countries influence decisions and behavior of individuals, thus striving to achieve global SD goals. What is more, public policy create various strategies aiming at encouraging and enabling, at the same time, individuals to lead healthier lives (Thaler & Sustein, 2008). In this way, the individuals are becoming 'choice architects'(Quigley, 2013). All this is a good contribution to increasing public awareness and thus to achieving better results in the field of sustainable healthcare.

MEASURING THE SUSTAINABLE DEVELOPMENT: GOALS, TARGETS AND INDICATORS

The UN, as it was already mentioned, holds the main care over the policy of sustainable development in a global perspective. However, it is not the only institution involved in creating and monitoring individual actions in the field of sustainable development and SDGs. In addition to the UN, OECD and the European Union also contribute.

Therefore, to make the picture complete, approaches for measuring sustainable development in health care will be presented in the perspective of all three organizations, i.e. the UN, the OECD and the EU.

Different Approaches in the Measurement of Sustainable Development: OECD's Perspective

The Organization for Economic Co-operation and Development takes an active part in the sustainable development initiatives, including the 2030 Agenda realization. OECD supports its members in SDGs implementation through i.e. .(Statistics Poland, 2019):

- Assistance with domestic resource mobilization
- Policy review and adjustment to specific Goals.

Among the most important OECD's initiatives, both adopted in 2011, are (Statistics Poland, 2019):

1. Better Life Initiative - The initiative engages the political world into actions aimed at fostering well-being, and enhances social engagement.
2. Green growth and Sustainable development - actions towards policy enhancement for economic growth, while preserving natural environment assets and developing environment-friendly infrastructure. OECD's activity in the area of green growth is based on the Green Growth Strategy, adopted in 2011.

Different Approaches in the Measurement of Sustainable Development: EU's Perspective

The course of action for sustainable development in the EU was outlined for the first time in the EU Sustainable Development Strategy, adopted in 2001 and revised in 2006. The EU SDS goals were monitored by a relevant set of sustainable development indicators (SDIs). What is more, joining the global initiative of the 2030 Agenda, the European Commission issued the communication 'Next steps for a sustainable European future' in 2016. The document declared integration of SDGs in EU policy framework and regular reporting of the progress in SDGs implementation. Taking into account that EU development priorities were determined in i.e. Europe 2020 Strategy, 10 Priorities of the European Commission and Circular Economy Package, a special set of 100 indicators was adopted for monitoring the Sustainable Development Goals, different from the UN set of SDG indicators and consistent with challenges faced by EU member states. The set fully relies on the statistical resources of the European Statistical System.(Eurostat, 2019)

The selected set of 100 indicators are divided into 17 groups, whose names are corresponding with officially adopted names of global SGD goals. However, as it was underlined before, it is different from the UN set of SDG indicators.

According to the analysis presented on the Eurostat webpage (Eurostat, 2019) the EU made progress towards almost all of the 17 sustainable development goals over the last 5 years. What is more, under Goal 3, a significant improvement in the value of monitored indicators has been observed. Within 17 monitored goals, the movement away from the sustainable development objectives was also observed however, it did not distort the overall trend within the objective pursued. The Figure 1 below shows a statistical summary of the EU progress towards the 17 SDGs over this period. However, trends for 4 out of 17 goals could not be measured due to lack of time series for more than 25% of the indicators. Goals that could not be measured were: 6. Clean water and sanitation, 13. Climate action, 14. Life below water and 16. Peace, justice and strong institutions.

As it was presented above, on Figure 1, a significant progress was observed in Goal 3 – Good health and well-being. In terms of this goal a set of 11 indicators are being monitored. Table 1presents the set of indicators in question. Detailed information along with the definitions of individual indicators are available on the Eurostat website (Eurostat, 2019).

Details regarding the development of indicators under Goal 3 are presented in Table 2 according to which a moderate progress towards SD objective was observed in terms of life expectancy at birth. On the other hand, a moderate movement away from SD objective has been noted in terms of self-perceived health and people killed in road accidents. In all other indicators a significant progress towards SD objectives was observed.

The indicator for which significant progress towards SD objectives was recorded was the death rate due to tuberculosis, HIV and hepatitis (see Table 2). The value of this indicator has decreased in almost all countries presented in Figure 3. The exceptions were: Hungary, Latvia, Cyprus and Czech Republic. The biggest decrease in the size of this indicator was recorded in Lithuania.

Figure 1. Statistical summary of the EU progress in the context of SDGs in the past 5 year period
Source: own elaboration on the basis of Eurostat database (Eurostat, 2019)

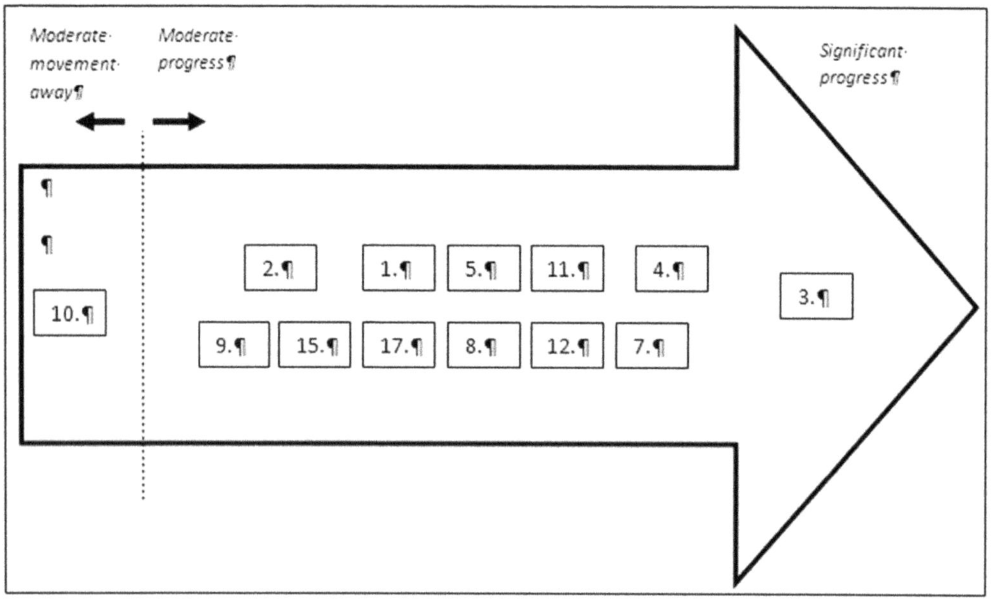

Table 1. The list of indicators, related to health protection, used in monitoring sustainable development in the European Union area

Goal 3 - good health and well-being			
Healthy lives: • Self-perceived health. • Life expectancy at birth.	**Health determinants:** • Obesity rate. •Smoking prevalence. •Population living in households considering that they suffer from noise. •Exposure to air pollution by particulate matter.	**Causes of death:** • Death rate due to chronic diseases. • Death rate due to tuberculosis, HIV and hepatitis. • People killed in accidents at work. • People killed in road accidents.	**Access to healthcare:** • Self-reported unmet need for medical examination and care.

Source: own elaboration based on Sustainable development indicators (Eurostat, 2019)

Table 2. The overview of the progress of SD Goal 3. Good health and well- being and its subindicators

Significant progress towards SD objectives	Moderate progress towards SD objectives	Moderate movement away from SD objectives
Smoking prevalence. Population living in households considering that they suffer from noise. Exposure to air pollution by particulate matter. Death rate due to chronic diseases. Death rate due to tuberculosis, HIV and hepatitis. People killed in accidents at work. Self-reported unmet need for medical care.	Life expectancy at birth.	Self-perceived health. People killed in road accidents.

Source: own elaboration on the basis of Eurostat webpage (Eurostat, 2019)

Figure 2. Death rate due to tuberculosis, HIV and hepatitis, the EU countries
Source: elaboration based on Eurostat database (Eurostat, 2019)

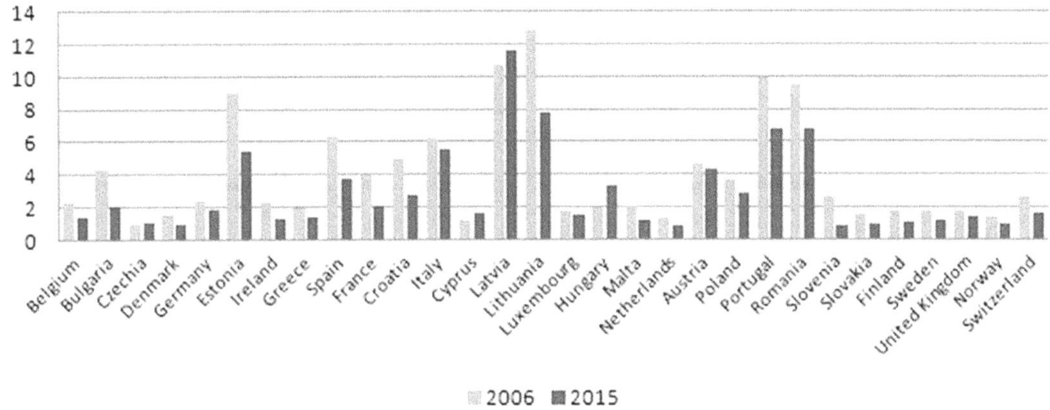

A moderate progress towards SD objectives was observed in terms of life expectancy at birth, defined as the mean number of years that a new-born child can expect to live if subjected throughout his life to the current mortality conditions, an increase was observed in all countries. This trend, presented on Figure 3, shows a positive tendency and is stimulated for example by an increasingly well-functioning sector of health protection, living conditions of residents etc.

Moderate movement away from SD objectives was noted in the case of two indicators. One of them was self-perceived health; a measure on how people judge their health in general on a scale from "very good" to "very bad". It is expressed as the share of the population aged 16 or over perceiving itself to be in "good" or "very good" health (Eurostat, 2019). According to this indicator in the group of countries in which the highest percentage of people perceiving their health as good or very good were: Ireland, Italy, Cyprus, the Netherlands, Sweden and Norway. Poland, together with Lithuania, Latvia, Estonia, Portugal and Serbia, found itself in a group of countries with the lowest percentage of people perceiving their health as good or very good.

Different Approaches in the Measurement of Sustainable Development: United Nation's Perspective

The global indicator framework was developed by the Inter-Agency and Expert Group on SDG Indicators (IAEG-SDGs) and agreed to, as a practical starting point at the 47th session of the UN Statistical Commission held in March 2016. The report of the Commission, which included the global indicator framework, was then taken note of by ECOSOC at its 70th session in June 2016. This framework includes 232 indicators, of which 26 indicators refer to health protection (Goal 3 - Ensure healthy lives and promote well-being for all at all ages). These indicators are divided into 13 groups, with targets assigned to each group. Below, individual objectives will be presented along with the analysis of indicators monitoring the progress of countries in given areas.

Target 3.1. *By 2030, reduce the global maternal mortality ratio to less than 70 per 100,000 live births*

Figure 3. Life expectancy at birth
Source: own elaboration based on Eurostat database (Eurostat, 2019)

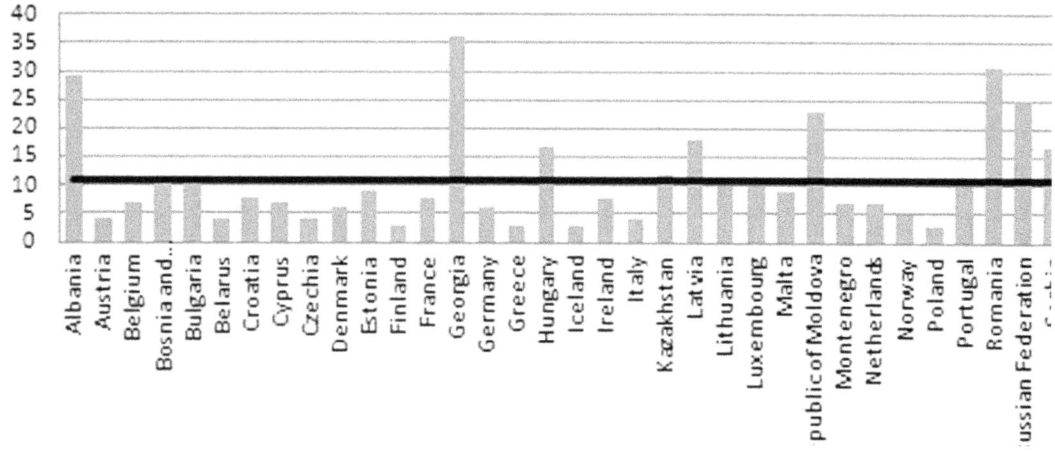

The achievement of target 3.1 is monitored by means of two measures: maternal mortality ratio and proportion of births attended by skilled health personnel.

Maternal mortality ratio, presented in Figure 4, is defined as the number of maternal deaths per 100 thousand live births. As the WHO underlines, it depicts the risk of maternal death relative to the number of live births and essentially captures the risk of death in a single pregnancy or a single live birth (World Health Organization, 2018a). None of analyzed UN countries recorded the value of this indicator higher than 36 cases per 100,000 births. The average value in 2015 was around 11, which was a decrease of about 12 percent compared to the year 2010. The lowest percentage of this indicator is recorded in Finland and Greece, and the highest in Georgia and the Republic of Moldova. Poland was in the group of countries with the lowest percentage of maternal mortality ratio.

Figure 4. Maternal mortality ratio per 100 000 live birth (%)
Source: own elaboration on the basis of Eurostat database (Eurostat, 2019)

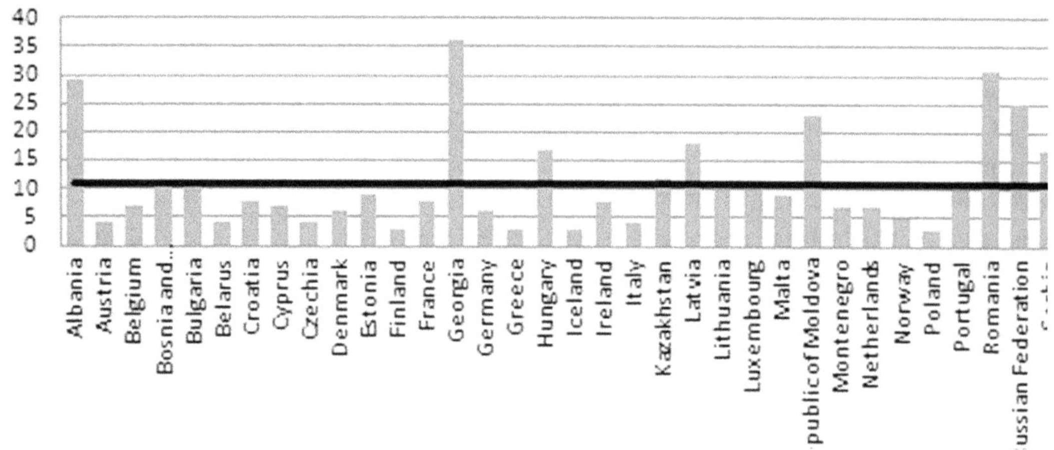

The percentage of births attended by skilled health personnel (generally doctors, nurses or midwives) is the second indicator that is being monitored as a part of this target. It is the percentage of deliveries attended by health personnel trained in providing lifesaving obstetric care, including giving the necessary supervision, care and advice to women during pregnancy, labor and the post-partum period, conducting deliveries on their own, and caring for newborns (World Health Organization, 2016).

As WHO underlines, having a skilled attendant at the time of delivery is an important lifesaving intervention for both mothers and babies. Not having access to this key assistance is detrimental to women's health and gender empowerment because it could cause the death of the mother or long lasting disability, especially in marginalized settings. (World Health Organization, 2016)

In 19 out of 30 countries the proportion of births attended by skilled health personnel exceeded the average level of 99,04%. The lowest rate, as the Figure 5 shows, was recorded in Denmark. However, it should be emphasized that over the years, the value of this indicator has been oscillating to a relatively stable level (97% - 99.9%). Poland found itself in a group of countries with one of the highest proportion of births attended by skilled health personnel. In the majority of analyzed countries, a constant increase in the value of this indicator was observed. The exception was Denmark, where the opposite trend was noticed.

Target 3.2 *By 2030, end preventable deaths of newborns and children under 5 years of age, with all countries aiming to reduce neonatal mortality to at least as low as 12 per 1,000 live births and under-5 mortality to at least as low as 25 per 1,000 live births*

This target is being monitored by: under-five mortality rate and neonatal mortality rate. Mortality rates among young children are a key output indicator for both, child health and well-being, and, social and economic development. It is closely watched public health indicator as it reflects the access of children and communities to basic health interventions (United Nations, 2018).

Figure 5. Proportion of births attended by skilled health personnel
Source: own elaboration on the basis of Eurostat database (Eurostat, 2019)

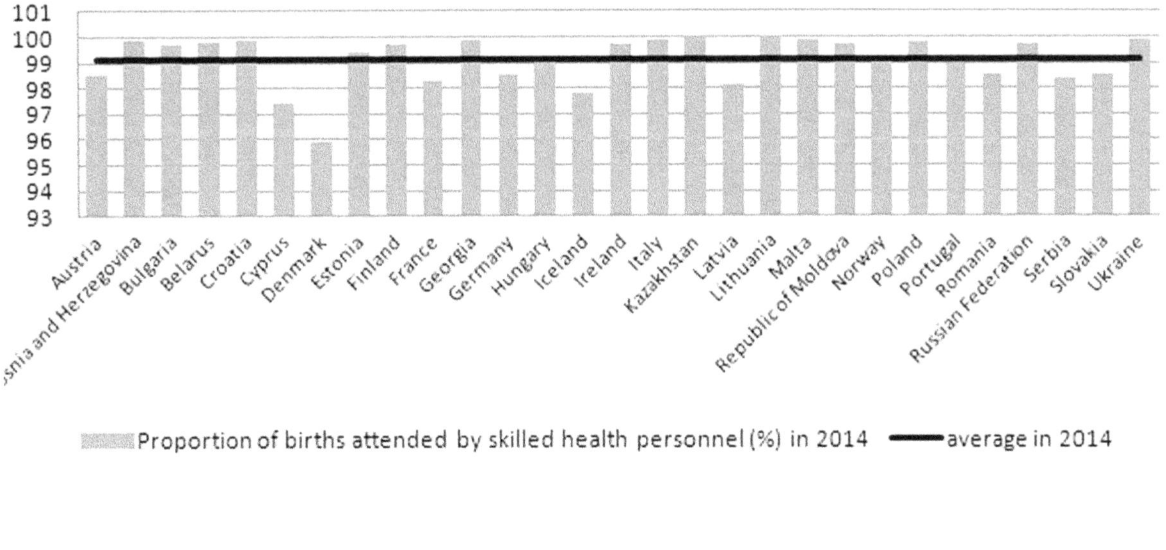

The under-five mortality rate, presented in Figure 6, refers to mortality of children under the age of 5, if subject to the age-specific mortality rates of that period, expressed per 1,000 live births. Less than 6 out of 1000 people under the age of 5 die in the analyzed countries. In almost 81% of the countries, also in Poland, this indicator was below average. Only in 29% of countries the average value was exceeded, of which the highest percentage was recorded in Moldova. Five children under the age of five die for every 1000 live births in Poland, which is below the average for this year.

The second observed ratio was the neonatal mortality rate. It is the probability that a child born in a specific year or period will die during the first 28 completed days of life if subject to age-specific mortality rates of that period, expressed per 1000 live births. (World Health Organization, 2018c)

The value of this indicator has dropped between years 2010 and 2016 in almost all analyzed countries. This trend was shown in the Figure 7. The highest drop was observed in Kazakhstan and Georgia. The lowest neonatal mortality rate was observed in San Marino and Iceland, and the highest in Republic of Moldova. In 12 out of 45 countries the neonatal mortality rate was under the average level (3,19). Poland, in both years, was characterized by the neonatal mortality rate above the average level. In Poland, a decline in the value of the indicator has been noted over the analyzed years, however, it is still above the average.

Target 3.3. *By 2030, end the epidemics of AIDS, tuberculosis, malaria and neglected tropical diseases and combat hepatitis, water-borne diseases and other communicable diseases*

Figure 6. Under-five mortality rate (deaths per 1,000 live births)
Source: own elaboration on the basis of Eurostat database (Eurostat, 2019)

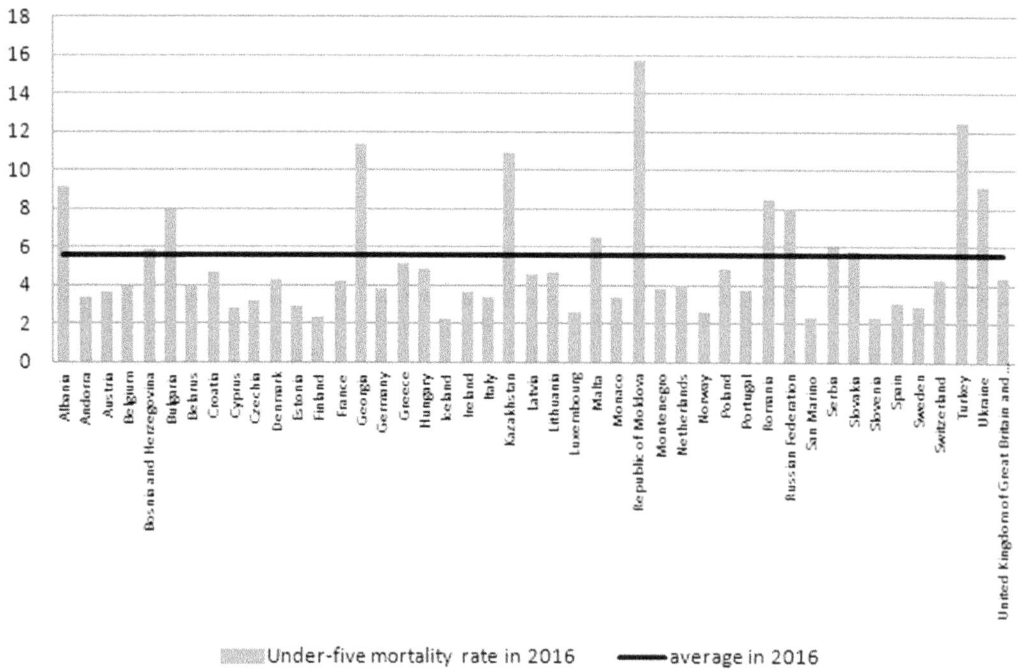

Figure 7. Neonatal mortality rate
Source: own elaboration on the basis of Eurostat database (Eurostat, 2019)

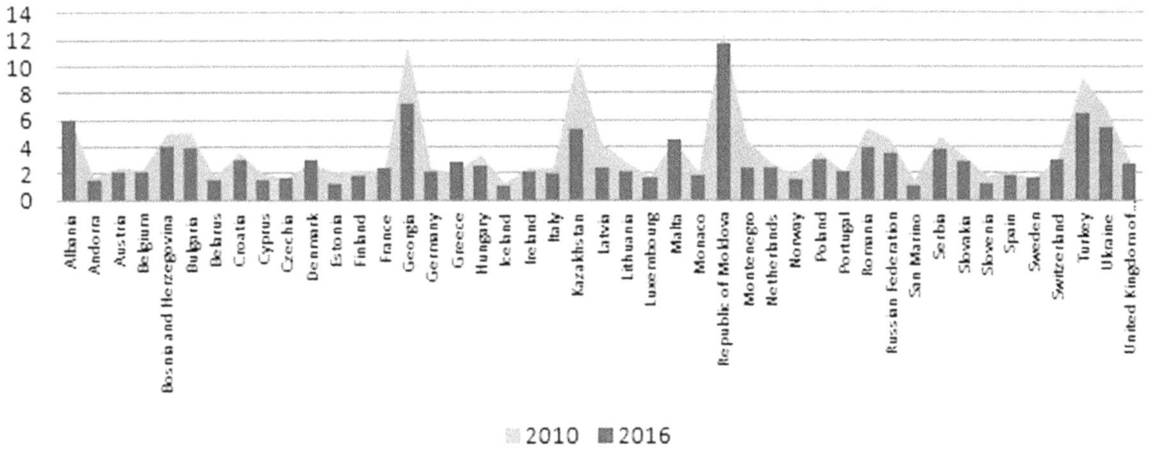

The achievement of target 3.3 is being monitored by five different indicators:

- Number of new HIV infections per 1,000 uninfected population
- Tuberculosis incidence per 1,000 population
- Malaria incidence per 1,000 population
- Hepatitis B incidence per 100,000 population
- Number of people requiring interventions against neglected tropical diseases

Due to the significant limitation of data availability on the trends shaping the values of indicators for monitoring the target 3.3, the tuberculosis incidence indicator is the most complete source of information.

In 2014, after two years of consultations, a new post-2015 global tuberculosis strategy was endorsed by the World Health Assembly. The overall goal, set up in the period 2016-2035, is to "End the global tuberculosis epidemic", and correspondingly ambitious targets for reductions in tuberculosis deaths and cases are set for 2030 (80% reduction in incidence rate compared with the level of 2015) and 2035 (90% reduction in incidence rate), in the context of the SDGs (World Health Organization, 2018d).

The average incidence of tuberculosis, shown in Figure 8, decreased in 2016 compared to 2010 it decrease by 21%. This means that in 2016, it fell by an average of 6.6 per 100 000 population less than in 2010. Moreover, over the analyzed years, in 24% of countries (i.e. in 11 out of 45 countries) this percentage was above average. Moldova, Georgia and Ukraine were the most prevalent countries. In 2016, the most rare cases were recorded in the following countries: Iceland (2.1 per 100 000 population), Greece (4.4 per 100 000 population) and Finland (4.7 per 1000 cases). In addition, no cases have been reported in Monaco and San Marino. Poland is in the group of countries with an increased rate of disease, which on the one hand does not exceed the average value (23 per 100 000 population), but exceeds median (9.9 cases per 100 000 population).

Figure 8. Tuberculosis incidence (per 100,000 population)
Source: own elaboration on the basis of Eurostat database (Eurostat, 2019)

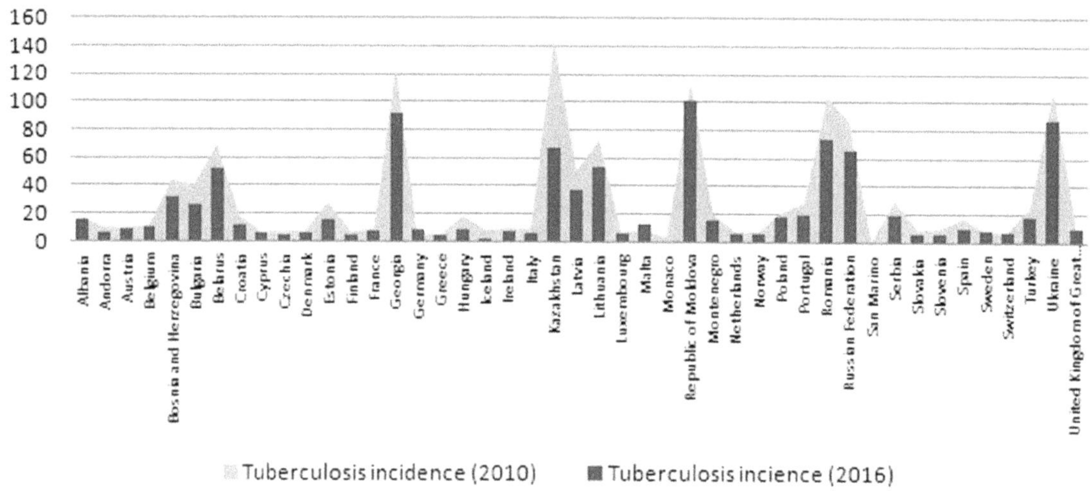

Target 3.4 *By 2030, reduce by one third premature mortality from non-communicable diseases through prevention and treatment and promote mental health and well-being*

This target is being monitored by: mortality rate attributed to cardiovascular disease, cancer, diabetes or chronic respiratory disease and suicide mortality rate.

According to WHO, disease burden from non-communicable diseases among adults is rapidly increasing in developing countries due to ageing. Diseases monitored in target 3.4 are the four main causes of non-communicable diseases burden. Measuring the risk of dying from them is important to assess the extent of burden from premature mortality. (World Health Organization, 2017)

The probability of dying between the ages of 30 and 70 years from cardiovascular diseases, cancer, diabetes or chronic respiratory diseases, defined as the per cent of 30-year-old-people who would die before their 70th birthday from cardiovascular disease, cancer, diabetes, or chronic respiratory disease, assuming that s/he would experience current mortality rates at every age and s/he would not die from any other cause of death was the highest in 2016 in Kazakhstan, Georgia and Ukraine (World Health Organization, 2017). In almost all observed countries the value of this indicator has dropped in 2016 in comparison to the year 2010. The lowest probability rate, showed in Figure 9, was recorded in Iceland and Sweden. In Poland, the value of the indicator was below the average, both in 2010 and in 2016.

Mental disorders occur in all regions and cultures of the world. Depression plays a very important role among them, because it often lead to suicide. According to WHO data, in 2012, suicide was the second leading cause of deaths among young adults aged 15–29 years, after road traffic injuries (World Health Organization, 2018e). Almost in all countries, apart from Germany and Switzerland, a decline in the value of this indicator was recorded between 2010 and 2016. As it is showed in the Figure 10, in more than 45% of countries, the suicide rate was higher than the average (i.e. 14.6 cases per 100,000 inhabitants). In half of the countries, the value of this indicator was 13.6 or less (median). The highest percentage was recorded in Russia, and the lowest in Greece (5 per 100,000 inhabitants). In Poland, the percentage of suicides was both greater than the average and median (13.6).

Figure 9. Mortality rate attributed to cardiovascular disease, cancer, diabetes or chronic respiratory disease
Source: own elaboration on the basis of Eurostat database (Eurostat, 2019)

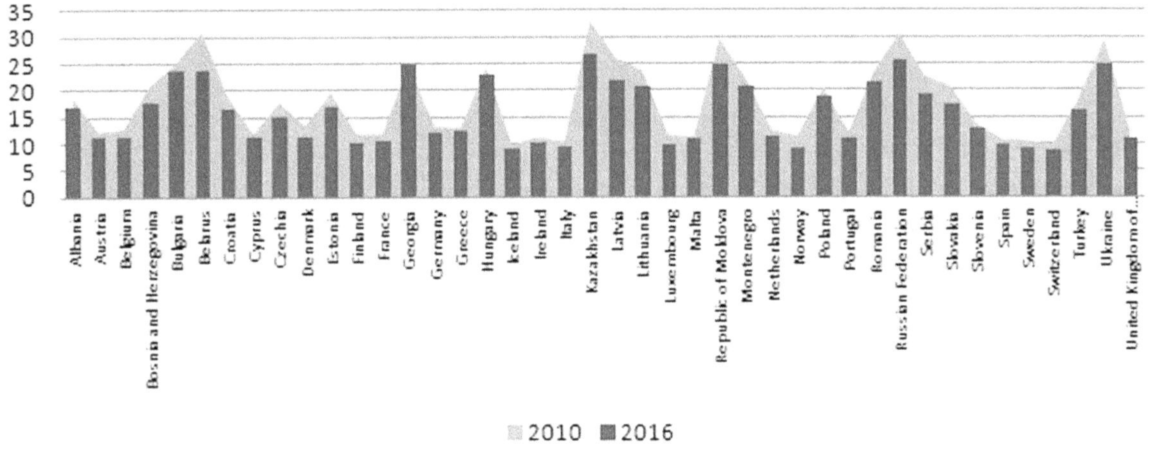

Figure 10. Suicide mortality rate (deaths per 100,000 population)
Source: own elaboration on the basis of Eurostat database (Eurostat, 2019)

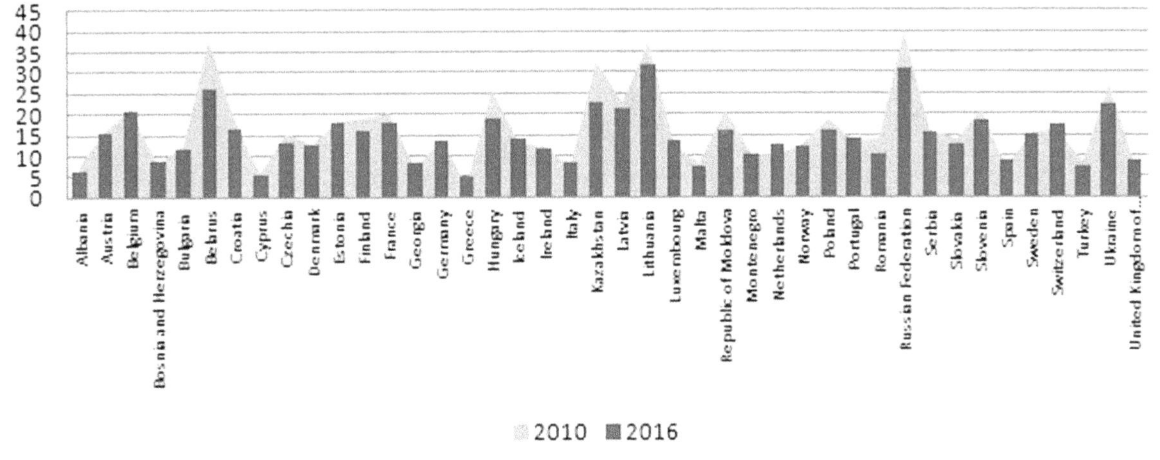

Target 3.5 *Strengthen the prevention and treatment of substance abuse, including narcotic drug abuse and harmful use of alcohol*

This target is being monitored by two different indicators:

- Coverage of treatment interventions (pharmacological, psychosocial and rehabilitation and after-care services) for substance use disorders.

- Harmful use of alcohol, defined according to the national context as alcohol per capita consumption (aged 15 years and older) within a calendar year in liters of pure alcohol.

As for the first indicator it should be underlined that, according to the United Nations Statistics no data for this indicator is currently available and its methodology is still under development.

The spectrum of alcohol's impact on human life and health is enormous. It can have impact not only on the incidence of diseases or injuries, but also on the course of disorders and their outcomes in individuals. Alcohol consumption has been identified as a component cause for more than 200 diseases, injuries and other health conditions. In 14 out of 43 observed countries, this indicator increased in 2016 in comparison to 2010. In slightly over 60% of countries in 2016, more than 10.7 l of pure alcohol per capita was consumed. As it is presented in Figure 11, half of the countries consumed 11.3 liters and more of pure alcohol. The most alcohol was consumed in Moldova, Lithuania and the Czech Republic. Poland has found itself in a group of countries where 11.6 liters of alcohol per capita is consumed annually, which is both above average and median.

Target 3.6 *By 2020, halve the number of global deaths and injuries from road traffic accidents*

Figure 11. Alcohol consumption per capita (aged 15 years and older) within a calendar year (liters of pure alcohol)
Source: own elaboration on the basis of Eurostat database (Eurostat, 2019)

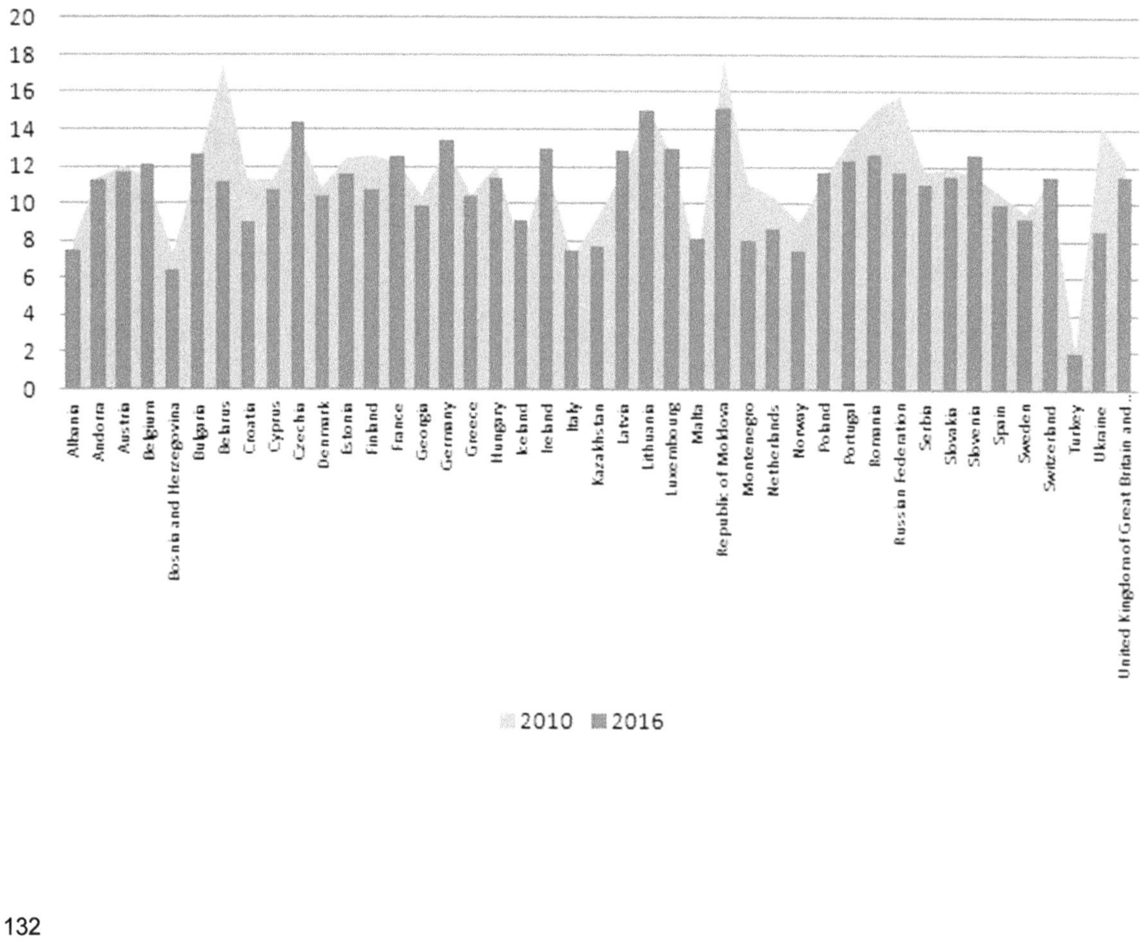

This target is being monitored by death rate due to road traffic injuries. In just over 30% of countries in 2013, death rate due to road traffic injuries amounted to more than 8.48 people per 100,000 population (see Figure 12). In half of the countries, this ratio was 6.7 and more cases. Most people died in Russia and Kazakhstan. Poland has found itself in a group of countries, 10.3 people per 100,000 population per year are lost, which is both above average and median.

Target 3.7 *By 2030, ensure universal access to sexual and reproductive health-care services, including for family planning, information and education, and the integration of reproductive health into national strategies and programs*

Two different indicators are being monitored in this target. These include:

- Proportion of women of reproductive age (aged 15-49 years) who have their need for family planning satisfied with modern methods.
- Adolescent birth rate (aged 15-19 years) per 1,000 women in that age group.

Unfortunately, statistics on the first indicator do not allow making comparisons between countries. However, in terms of the second indicator, in 33.3% of countries, the index was characterized by values higher than 13,28 per 1,000 women aged 15-19. The largest number of women aged 15-19 gave birth to a child in Georgia, Bulgaria and Romania. The lowest value of this indicator was observed in Denmark. In half of the countries, this percentage was 9,12 and more. In Poland, the figure was 12,31 per 1000 women, which was below the average. In almost all countries the level of this indicator dropped. The exceptions are shown in the Figure 13.

Figure 12. Death rate due to road traffic injuries (per 100,000 population)
Source: own elaboration on the basis of Eurostat database (Eurostat, 2019)

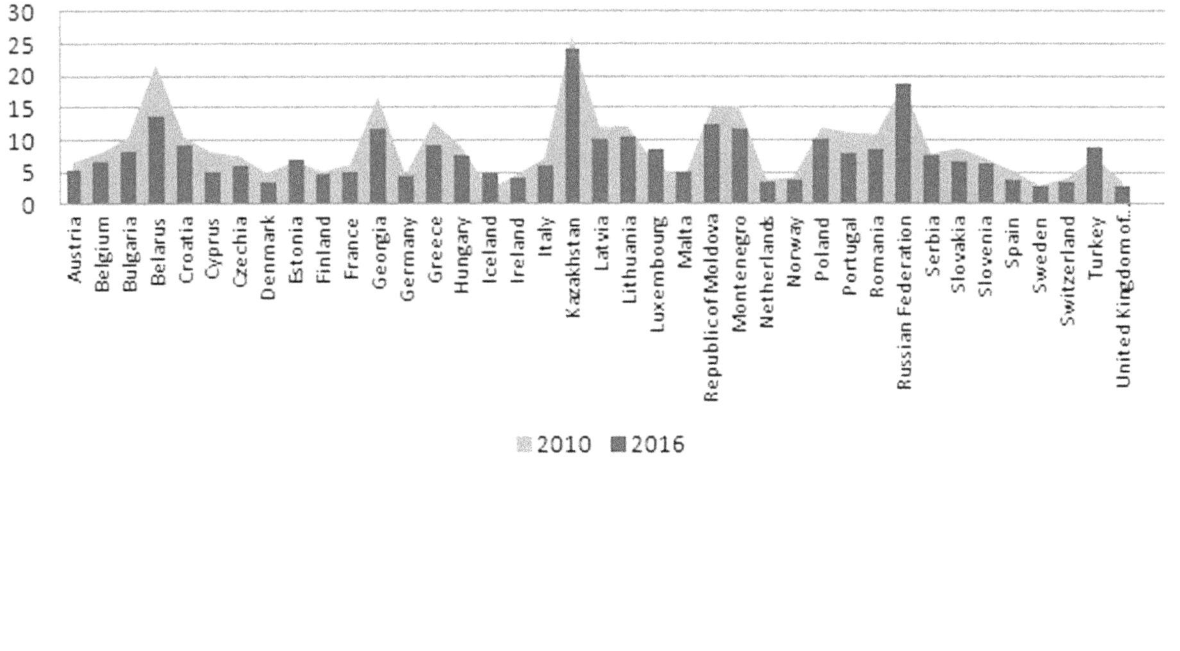

Figure 13. Adolescent birth rate (per 1,000 women aged 15-19 years)
Source: own elaboration on the basis of Eurostat database (Eurostat, 2019)

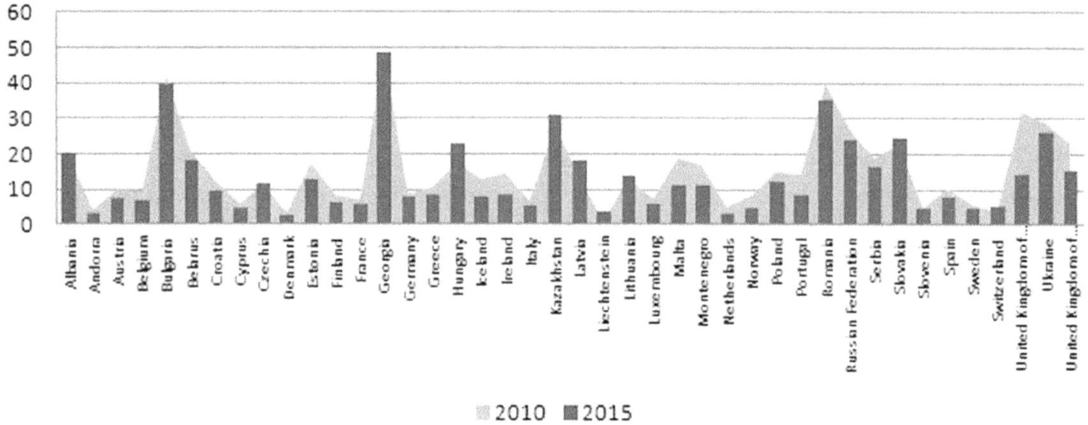

Target 3.8 *Achieve universal health coverage, including financial risk protection, access to quality essential health-care services and access to safe, effective, quality and affordable essential medicines and vaccines for all*

This target was treated as a priority in the implementation of Sustainable Development Goals in 2015. According to the WHO, universal health coverage enables everyone to access the services that address the most significant causes of disease and death. It also ensures that the quality of those services is good enough to improve the health of the people who receive them. (WHO, 2019)

The emphasis put on UHC was due to the fact that if the country makes progress under the universal health coverage, this progress will have a positive effect on other health-related targets. To make it more specific, Good health allows children to learn and adults to earn, helps people escape from poverty, and provides the basis for long-term economic development (WHO, 2019).

WHO underlines that the target connected with universal coverage is genuinely important as protecting people from the financial consequences of paying for health services out of their own pockets reduces the risk that people will be pushed into poverty. In other words, people will not be forced, due to unexpected illness, to use up their life savings, sell assets, or borrow – destroying their futures and often those of their children. (WHO, 2019)

According to the latest statement of WHO monitoring progress towards UHC should focus on 2 things:

- The proportion of a population that can access essential quality health services.
- The proportion of the population that spends a large amount of household income on health.

The first indicator is an index reported on a unitless scale of 0 to 100, which is computed as the geometric mean of 14 tracer indicators of health service coverage. According to the most recent data (year 2015) UK, Sweden, Switzerland, Portugal, Norway, Netherlands, Luxembourg, Denmark and Belgium, Italy, Iceland gather more than 80 points. The smallest number of points was collected by Bosnia and Herzegovina and Montenegro. Poland collected 75 points and was in the group chasing the leaders.

The most complete data regarding the second indicator refers to the year 2010. The average proportion of population with large household expenditures on health recognized as a share of total household expenditure/income was 8,56% in this year (see Figure 14). In 2010, around 56% of countries were characterized by the values of this indicator at the level above the established average. Proportion of population with large household expenditures on health is the biggest in Georgia and the smallest in the United Kingdom. Poland has found itself in a group of countries in which proportion of population with large household expenditures is greater than the average level of 8,56%.

Target 3.9 *By 2030, substantially reduce the number of deaths and illnesses from hazardous chemicals and air, water and soil pollution and contamination*

This target is being monitored by three indicators such as:

- Mortality rate attributed to household and ambient air pollution.
- Mortality rate attributed to unsafe water, unsafe sanitation and lack of hygiene.
- Mortality rate attributed to unintentional poisoning.

In order to adequately depict the situation monitored in this market, the author decided to present trends in the value of mortality rate attributed to unsafe water, unsafe sanitation and lack of hygiene. The indicator expresses the number of deaths from inadequate water, sanitation and hygiene which could be prevented by improving those services and practices (World Health Organization, 2018f). The largest mortality rate within this interpretation, presented as a share of total household expenditure or income, was recorded in 2016 in Serbia. The country with the second largest value of this indicator was Germany. As it is presented in the Figure 15, in Estonia, Finland, Luxembourg, Greece, Latvia, Malta, Montenegro, Slovakia and Slovenia no cases of death caused by unsafe water/sanitation or lack of hygiene were recorded. Poland was in the group of countries where the value of this indicator was definitely lower than the average value.

Figure 14. Proportion of population with large household expenditures on health (greater than 10%) as a share of total household expenditure/income (%)
Source: own elaboration on the basis of Eurostat database (Eurostat, 2019)

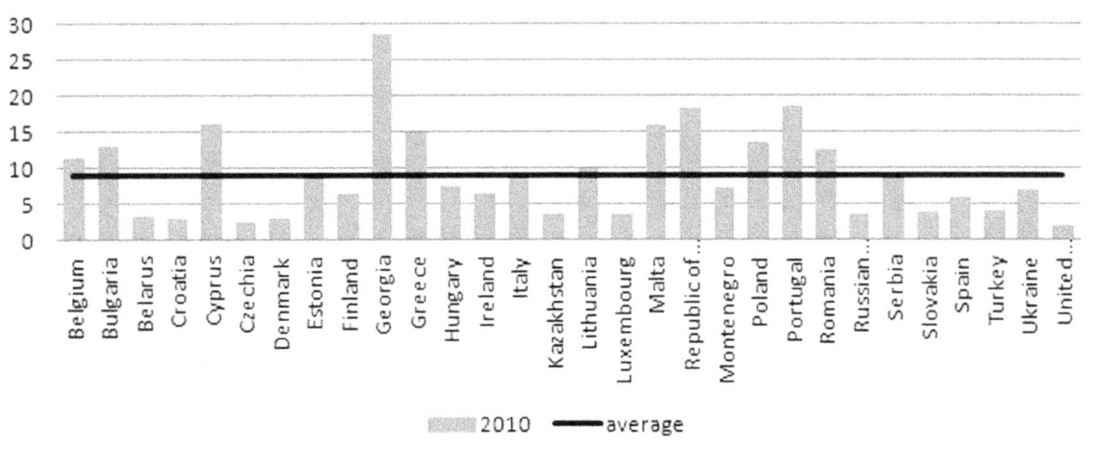

Figure 15. Mortality rate attributed to unsafe water, unsafe sanitation and lack of hygiene in 2016
Source: own elaboration on the basis of Eurostat database (Eurostat, 2019)

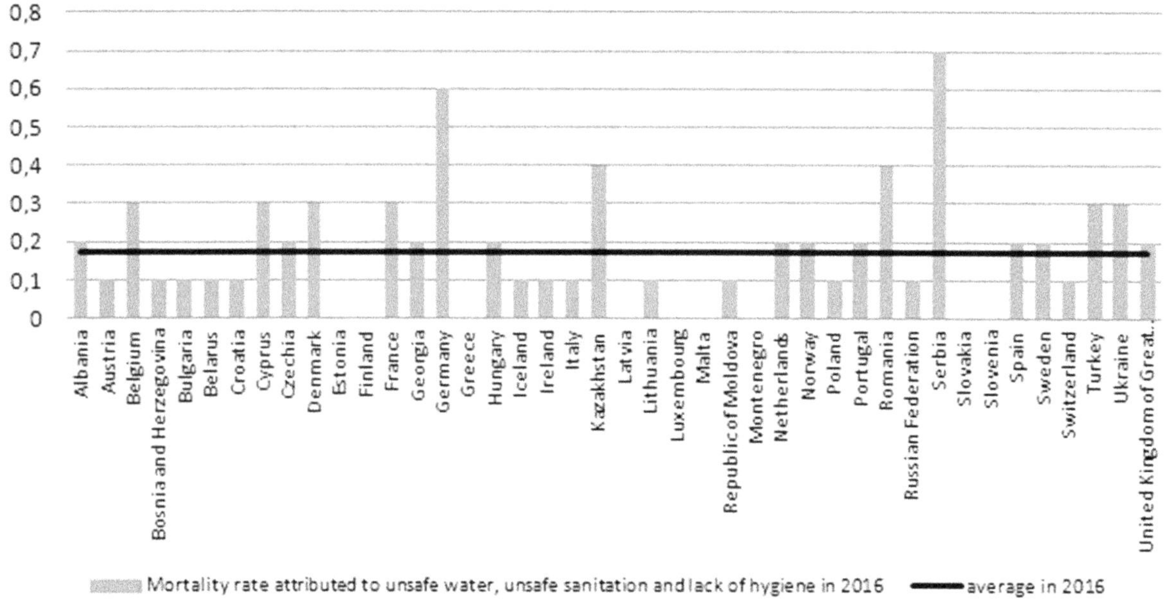

Target 3.a *Strengthen the implementation of the World Health Organization Framework Convention on Tobacco Control in all countries*

Target 3.a is being assessed by the age-standardized prevalence of current tobacco use among persons aged 15 years and older. According to WHO, this indicator is defined as the percentage of the population aged 15 years and over who currently use any tobacco product (smoked and/or smokeless tobacco) on a daily or non-daily basis (World Health Organization, 2018g).

An average value of this indicator was in 2015 slightly above the 28-year limit in the analyzed countries (see Figure 16). In less than half of the countries, the standardized age of cigarette spread among people aged 15 and older is above average. The highest rate was recorded in Greece, Latvia and Ukraine, and the lowest in Moldova and Kazakhstan. Poland, with a value of 28.6, is on an average level.

Target 3.b *Support the research and development of vaccines and medicines for the communicable and non-communicable diseases that primarily affect developing countries, provide access to affordable essential medicines and vaccines, in accordance with the Doha Declaration on the TRIPS Agreement and Public Health, which affirms the right of developing countries to use to the full the provisions in the Agreement on Trade-Related Aspects of Intellectual Property Rights regarding flexibilities to protect public health, and, in particular, provide access to medicines for all*

This target is being monitored by:

- Proportion of the target population covered by all vaccines included in their national program.
- Total net official development assistance to medical research and basic health sectors.

Figure 16. Age-standardized prevalence of current tobacco use among persons aged 15 years and older
Source: own elaboration on the basis of Eurostat database (Eurostat, 2019)

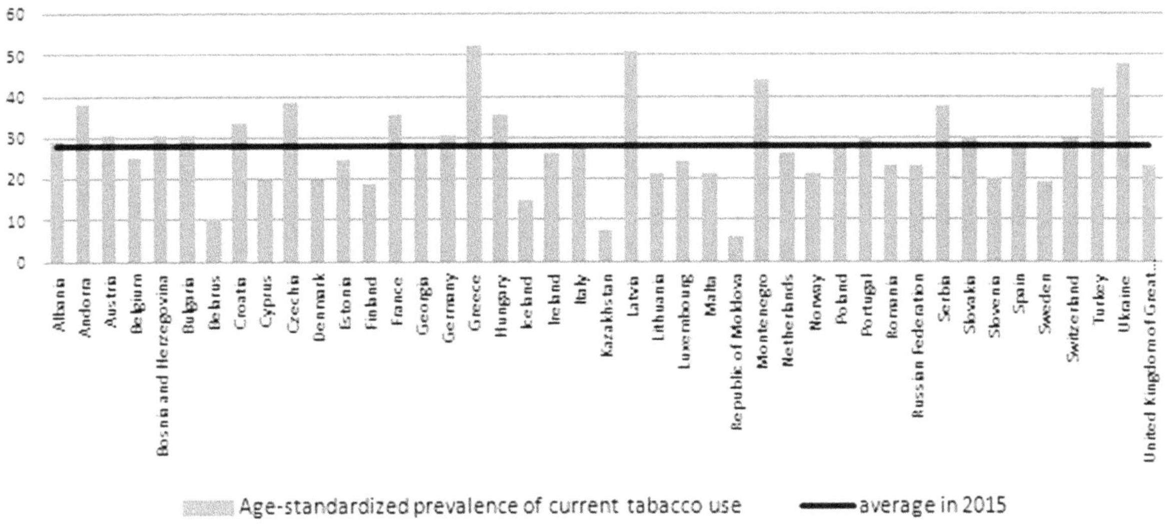

- Proportion of health facilities that have a core set of relevant essential medicines available and affordable on a sustainable basis.

As in a few cases, the availability of current data is somewhat difficult. Countries do not undertake current reporting. Therefore, it is possible to show the trend of shaping the value of only the first indicator. It will be presented on the example of national vaccination programs on DTP. As can be seen in Figure 17, most countries, except Ukraine and San Marino, have index values close to the average. The majority of countries are characterized by those at the level of approx. 90%. Poland is also in this group of countries. Over the years 2010 - 2016, almost all countries have improved the value of this indicator. The exceptions were: San Marino, Bosnia and Herzegovina, Kazakhstan and Ukraine.

Target 3.c *Substantially increase health financing and the recruitment, development, training and retention of the health workforce in developing countries, especially in least developed countries and small island developing*

Within this target the indicator concerning health worker density and distribution is being monitored. Statistics are conducted in terms of the number of physicians, nurses, dentists and pharmacists.

According to the WHO statistics, the density of medical doctors is defined as the number of medical doctors, including generalists and specialist medical practitioners per 10,000 population in the given national and/or subnational area. (World Health Organization, 2018h)

Unfortunately, statistics are not updated on an ongoing basis by all member states, hence the comparative analysis in this sphere seems to be very difficult. As an example, the situation regarding the physicians will be presented in Figure 18.

The highest density of physicians in 2015 was observed in Austria and Norway. The lowest value of this indicator was denoted in Poland.

Figure 17. Proportion of the target population with access to 3 doses of diphtheria-tetanus-pertussis (DTP3) (%)
Source: own elaboration on the basis of Eurostat database (Eurostat, 2019)

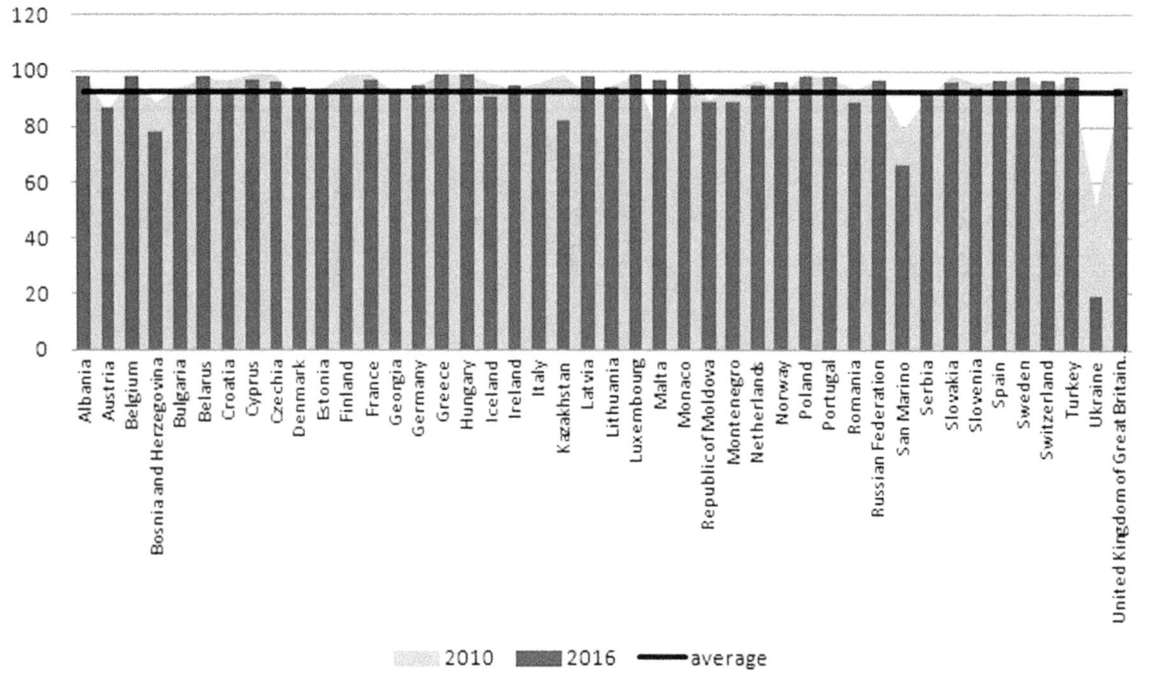

Figure 18. Health worker density (physicians per 1,000 population)
Source: own elaboration on the basis of Eurostat database (Eurostat, 2019)

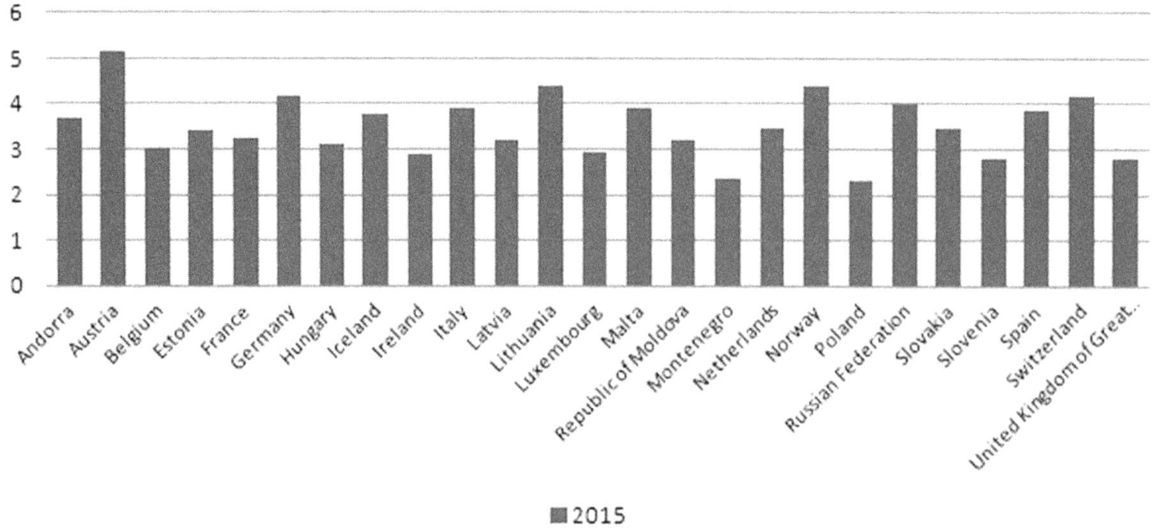

Target 3.d *Strengthen the capacity of all countries, in particular developing countries, for early warning, risk reduction and management of national and global health risks*

This target is being monitored by one indicator - International Health Regulations (IHR) capacity and health emergency preparedness. This indicator denotes the percentage of attributes of 13 core capacities that have been attained at a specific point in time (World Health Organization, 2018i). Those core capacities are: National legislation, policy and financing, Coordination and National Focal Point communications, Surveillance, Response, Preparedness, Risk communication, Human resources, Laboratory, Points of entry, Zoonotic events, Food safety, Chemical events and Radio nuclear emergencies.

In most cases, an increase in the value of the analyzed ratio was observed (see Figure 19). In 2016, the average value of this indicator was around 82%. 12 out of 33 countries had values below the average. The lowest percentage was recorded in Serbia in 2016.

SOLUTIONS AND RECOMMENDATIONS

Efficiency Measurement of Sustainable Development in Healthcare in Selected United Nations Member States

Data Envelopment Analysis in the Process of Efficiency Measurement

The Data Envelopment Analysis is of a non-parametric linear programming method (Charnes, Cooper, Lewin, 1994). It derived from the concept of productivity defined as the ratio of individual output to a single input (Birman, Pirondi, 2003). DEA computes a comparative ratio of weighted inputs for every unit. It is called the relative efficiency score. The efficiency score is presented as a percentage or value between 0 and 1. For example, if a decision-making unit reaches the score less than 1 it is perceived as inefficient in relation to the others. (Avkiran, 2003)

Figure 19. Average of 13 International Health Regulations (IHR) core capacities
Source: own elaboration on the basis of Eurostat database (Eurostat, 2019)

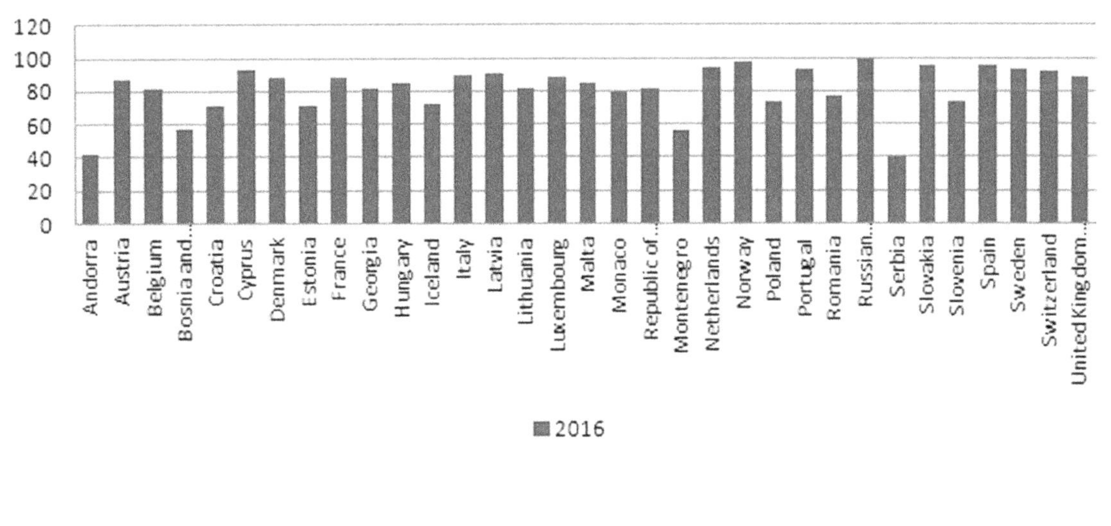

The formal denotation of output-oriented CCR model with the assumption of constant economies of scale states that for a given set of n DMUs each one consumes m inputs $(x_{1r}, x_{2r}, \ldots, x_{sr})$ to produce s outputs $(y_{1r}, y_{2r}, \ldots, y_{sr})$. The output oriented efficiency of o unit (θo) is given by the solution of the above linear programming problem:

$$\max,_{o} = \sum_{r=1}^{s} \text{¼}_{ro} y_{ro}$$

$$\sum_{i=1}^{m} v_{io} x_{io} = 1$$

$$\sum_{r=1}^{s} \text{¼}_{ro} y_{rj} - \sum_{i=1}^{m} v_{io} x_{ij} \leq 0 \quad \text{for } j = 1,\ldots,n$$

$$v_{io}, \text{¼}_{ro} \geq \mu > 0$$

where, ε - non-Archimedean infinitesimal value entered into the model with computational reasons to ensure non-zero multipliers.

Data and Results of the Analysis

According to the non-parametric nature of DEA method the appropriate variable selection plays a fundamental role. The choice of variables was dictated by the purpose of the study and the availability of data. The author's intention was to show the efficiency in terms of sustainable development in the year 2016. However, due to the considerable data limitation, in some cases the most recent and available year was taken into the analysis.

The overarching goal of the study was to show the efficiency of the policy of the analyzed countries in achieving the Millennium Sustainable Development Goals in Objective 3, that is to ensure a healthy lives and promote well-being for all ages at all ages. The summary overview of variables along with brief definitions is given in Table 3.

The analysis of the efficiency of sustainable development in terms of Objective 3 in UN Member States was carried out by means of the DEA method. The analysis has been divided into several parts. First of all, the output – oriented CCR model based on the assumption of constant economies of scale has been conducted. The assumption was related to the nature of inputs and outputs used in the study in conjunction with the specificity of DMUs (countries). The results of the analysis was presented in the Table 4. In the process of determining the effectiveness of the studied countries, 4 countries were eliminated. Partial results obtained in the course of the conducted procedure indicated a significant heterogeneity of the test sample resulting from the analyzed indicators. Therefore, Ukraine, Turkey, Iceland and Greece were eliminated from the study.

Table 3. Specification of DEA model variables

Output {O} / Input {I}	Variable	Definition	Last available year	SDG code
Input variables				
{I}1*	Age-standardized prevalence of current tobacco use among people over 15 years	The percentage of the population over 15 years who currently use any tobacco product on a daily or non-daily basis	2015	3.a.1
{I}2	Proportion of the target population with access to 3 doses of diphtheria-tetanus-pertussis	Percentage of surviving infants who received the 3 doses of diphtheria and tetanus toxoid with pertussis containing vaccine in a given year	2016	3.b.1
{I}3	Health worker density and distribution	The number of physicians, including generalists and specialist medical practitioners per 10,000 population in the given area	2013-2016	3.c.1
{I}4	International Health Regulations (IHR) capacity and health emergency preparedness	Percentage of attributes of 13 core capacities that have been attained at a specific point in time	2016	3.d.1
Output variables*				
{O}1	Maternal mortality ratio (per 100,000 live births).	The number of maternal deaths during a given time period.	2015	3.1.1
{O}2	Under-five mortality rate (per 100,000 live births).	Probability of a child born in a specific year or period dying before reaching the age of 5 years, if subject to the age-specific mortality rates of that period.	2016	3.2.1
{O}3	Tuberculosis incidence (per 100,000 population).	The estimated number of new and relapse TB cases (all forms of TB, including cases in people living with HIV) arising in a given year	2016	3.3.2
{O}4	Mortality rate attributed to cardiovascular disease, cancer, diabetes or chronic respiratory disease.	Probability of dying between the ages of 30 - 70 years from particular diseases.	2016	3.4.1
{O}5	Suicide mortality rate.	The number of suicide deaths in a year, divided by the population, and multiplied by 100 000.	2016	3.4.2
{O}6	Alcohol consumption (liters of pure alcohol) per capita (aged: over 15) within a calendar year.	Alcohol consumption defined as alcohol per capita consumption (aged 15 years and older) within a calendar year in liters of pure alcohol.	2016	3.5.2
{O}7	Death rate due to road traffic injuries.	The number of road traffic fatal injury deaths per 100,000 population.	2013	3.6.1
{O}8	Adolescent birth rate (aged 10-14 years; aged 15-19 years) per 1,000.	Annual number of births to females aged 15-19 years per 1,000 females in the respective age group.	2015	3.7.2
{O}9	Mortality rate attributed to unsafe water, unsafe sanitation and lack of hygiene.	The number of deaths from causes in question per year, divided by the population, and multiplied by 100,000.	2016	3.9.2

Legend * One of the assumptions of the DEA method is a single direction preferences. This means that output must be defined so that its growth is evaluated positively in terms of the evaluation of the examined units' activities (a stimulant). In the case of all outputs and {I}, it is not, because it should be minimized. Therefore, in order to transform destimulants in stimulants the following transformation was used: 1/Z, where Z-size of an output (Guzik, 2009).

Source: Author's preparation on the basis of Sustainable Development Goals, United Nations (Statistics Poland, 2019)

Table 4. CCR output oriented DEA model (constant economies of scale)

Country	Score	Country	Score
Albania	100%	Latvia	100%
Austria	100%	Lithuania	78%
Belgium	92%	Luxembourg	100%
Bosnia and Herzegovina	100%	Malta	100%
Bulgaria	76%	Republic of Moldova	50%
Belarus	80%	Montenegro	100%
Croatia	84%	Netherlands	100%
Cyprus	100%	Norway	100%
Czechia	100%	Poland	100%
Denmark	100%	Portugal	92%
Estonia	100%	Romania	68%
Finland	100%	Russian Federation	48%
France	100%	Serbia	100%
Georgia	90%	Slovakia	100%
Germany	93%	Slovenia	100%
Hungary	83%	Spain	100%
Ireland	100%	Sweden	100%
Italy	100%	Switzerland	100%
Kazakhstan	81%	UK	100%

Source: Author's preparation on the basis of EMS program

According to the results presented below, all countries with the score 100% tends to be efficient in terms of sustainable development. The worst results in terms of the effectiveness index were achieved by: Russia, Moldova and Romania. 34% of the analyzed countries were inefficient.

In the second part of the study, the author analyzed selected countries for the separation of economies of scale in individual countries as part of the analyzed problem. For this purpose, the BCC-I (expenditure-driven) model has been chosen, which allows to isolate the global technical efficiency (TE) from pure technical efficiency (PTE) and scale efficiency (Scale) (Ziębicki, 2014). The purpose of such procedure was to determine whether economies of scale have any impact on the country's efficiency. The analyzed country (Domagała, 2009):

- Is characterized by pure technical efficiency and is in an optimum the area of economies of scale, i.e. in the area of constant economies of scale.
- Is efficiently technically clean, but it does not work in the optimal area of benefits scale.
- Is inefficient both technically and respect to the scale.

According to the results presented below in Table 5 all countries inefficient in terms of pure technical efficiency (calculated by BCC input oriented model) were also inefficient in terms of economies of scale. Similarly, all efficient countries were also efficient in terms of economies of scale.

Table 5. Pure technical efficiency and scale efficiency in UN Member Countries

Country	PTE	Scale	Country	PTE	Scale
Albania	100%	100%	Latvia	100%	100%
Austria	100%	100%	Lithuania	93%	84%
Belgium	95%	97%	Luxembourg	100%	100%
Bosnia and Herzegovina	100%	100%	Malta	100%	100%
Bulgaria	93%	81%	Republic of Moldova	89%	57%
Belarus	90%	90%	Montenegro	100%	100%
Croatia	93%	90%	Netherlands	100%	100%
Cyprus	100%	100%	Norway	100%	100%
Czechia	100%	100%	Poland	100%	100%
Denmark	100%	100%	Portugal	94%	98%
Estonia	100%	100%	Romania	91%	74%
Finland	100%	100%	Russian Federation	80%	60%
France	100%	100%	Serbia	100%	100%
Georgia	93%	96%	Slovakia	100%	100%
Germany	99%	94%	Slovenia	100%	100%
Hungary	92%	90%	Spain	100%	100%
Ireland	100%	100%	Sweden	100%	100%
Italy	100%	100%	Switzerland	100%	100%
Kazakhstan	95%	85%	UK	100%	100%

Source: Author's preparation on the basis of EMS program

To make the analysis complete, one should answer the question which of the efficient countries were the most efficient, and thus constitute the benchmark for inefficient countries. To answer this question, DEA analysis was carried out according to the SE-CCR model, assuming constant economies of scale. According to the results presented in Table 6 the most efficient countries, in terms of chosen inputs and outputs, were Cyprus, Montenegro, Albania, Finland and Czechia. The most inefficient countries were Russian Federation, Republic of Moldova, Romania and Bulgaria. Poland was also efficient and located in the group of 10 the most efficient units.

The SE-CCR model made it possible to conduct a benchmarking analysis. The results of the conducted procedure showed which countries constitute a benchmark for other, inefficient countries. Table 7 presents details for 5 of the most inefficient countries. Thus, Bulgaria should follow its technology in Cyprus, Denmark, Switzerland, Finland, Ireland and Italy. Poland was also detected as benchmark country for Belarus. The other inefficient countries can be characterized in a similar way.

Table 6. Results of the DEA SE_CCR model

Country	Score	Country	Score
Cyprus	186%	Spain	112%
Montenegro	180%	Norway	111%
Albania	175%	Ireland	110%
Finland	168%	France	110%
Czechia	162%	Austria	104%
Bosnia and Herzegovina	155%	Estonia	101%
Poland	146%	Germany	93%
Denmark	146%	Belgium	92%
UK	144%	Portugal	92%
Slovenia	137%	Georgia	90%
Italy	126%	Croatia	84%
Latvia	124%	Hungary	83%
Serbia	124%	Kazakhstan	81%
Netherlands	122%	Belarus	80%
Sweden	121%	Lithuania	78%
Malta	121%	Bulgaria	76%
Switzerland	121%	Romania	68%
Slovakia	120%	Republic of Moldova	50%
Luxembourg	119%	Russian Federation	48%

Source: Author's preparation on the basis of EMS program

Table 7. Benchmarks in DEA SE_CCR model

Country	Benchmark
Belgium	Cyprus (0,16) Denmark (0,06) Finland (0,01) Ireland (0,53) Italy (0,18) Switzerland (0,04)
Bulgaria	Albania (0,02) Cyprus (0,22) Montenegro (0,45) Serbia (0,11) UK (0,19)
Lithuania	Denmark (0,70) Montenegro (0,11) Slovenia (0,19)
Republic of Moldova	Bosnia and Herzegovina (0,41) Cyprus (0,25) Italy (0,07) Malta (0,00) Netherlands (0,13) Norway (0,14)
Romania	Albania (0,00) Bosnia and Herzegovina (0,39) Cyprus (0,38) Serbia (0,01) UK (0,21)
Russian Federation	Bosnia and Herzegovina (0,88) Finland (0,00) Italy (0,05) Norway (0,24)

Source: Author's preparation on the basis of EMS program

FUTURE RESEARCH DIRECTIONS

Future research will focus on a more detailed analysis of the implementation of sustainable development principles in individual countries. The plans include not only an analysis of the implementation of the sustainable development policy at the national level, but also its analysis in specific units providing health care services.

CONCLUSION

This chapter deals with the monitoring of progress in one of the objectives of sustainable development, which is objective 3, that is to ensure a healthy lives and promote well-being for all ages at all ages. The chapter presents different approaches in monitoring sustainable development in the field of objective 3 and states the need to monitor it. The analysis carried out in the chapter also emphasizes that the importance of health and well-being for all (Goal 3) is unquestionable as it is interlinked with ending poverty and hunger (Goals 1 & 2) inequalities (Goal 10), providing clean water and sanitation facilities (Goal 6), protecting the environment (Goals 7, 13, 14, 15), providing decent work (Goal 8), ensuring gender equality (Goal 5) and having access to quality education (Goal 4). In other words, the implementation of the objectives contained in objective 3 determines the improvement of the quality of life and functionalization of both citizens and the whole country. This improvement is visible in the other monitored SDGs.

The chapter presents a number of indicators presented to monitor progress in sustainable health used not only by United Nations methodology but also by OECD and the EU countries. What is more, it has been pointed out that monitored indicators used in the EU and OECD methodology for monitoring Sustainable Development Goals are derived from the approach used by the UN.

In reference to the methodology used to monitor the SDGs by the UN, a comparative analysis of the countries was carried out with regard to the majority of indicators used to monitor targets separated under Goal 3. It should be emphasized that in the majority of analyzed indicators their improvement was in line with the UN guidelines.

Poland, along with Finland, Greece and Iceland, was in the group of countries with the lowest percentage of maternal mortality ratio. In 19 out of 30 countries the proportion of births attended by skilled health personnel exceeded the average level of 99,04%. On the whole, in the majority of analyzed countries, a constant increase in the value of this indicator was observed. . Poland, together with for instance Italy, Malta and Lithuania, found itself in a group of countries with one of the highest proportion of births attended by skilled health personnel. In terms of under-five mortality rate in almost 81% of countries, along with Poland, this indicator was below the average and is constantly decreasing. The mortality rate attributed to cardiovascular disease, cancer, diabetes or chronic respiratory disease was also decreasing in Poland between years 2010-2016. The lowest probability rate was recorded in Iceland and Sweden., however in Poland, the value of the indicator was below the average, both in 2010 and in 2016. The problem of a relatively high percentage of suicides should also be taken in Poland, as the percentage of suicides in Poland was greater than the average of UN countries. The mortality rate attributed to unsafe water, unsafe sanitation and lack of hygiene in 2016 was also decreasing between 2010-2016, and Poland was in the group of countries where the value of this indicator was definitely lower than the average value. The prevalence of current tobacco use among people older than 15 years is on an average level of 28 years. Over the years 2010 - 2016, almost all countries have improved the value of the proportion of the target population with access to 3 doses of diphtheria-tetanus-pertussis. The proportion in Poland was about 90%. According to the International Health Regulations adopted y analyzed countries, in most cases, an increase in the value of the analyzed ratio was observed. In 2016, the average value of this indicator was around 82%. 12 out of 33 countries had values below the average.

As for the challenges of Polish healthcare, some action should be undertaken to improve values of the infant mortality rate. Over the years 2010 – 2016 the neonatal mortality rate was above the average level. In Poland, a decline in the value of the indicator has been noted over the analyzed years, however, it is still above the average. Due attention should also be given to tuberculosis incidence. Poland was in the group of countries with an increased rate of disease, which on the one hand does not exceed the average value (23 per 100 000 population), but exceeds median (9.9 cases per 100 000 population). Alcohol consumption is also a challenge in the field of sustainable health in Poland. Poland has found itself in a group of countries where 11.6 liters of alcohol per capita is consumed annually, which is both above average value. The number of deaths and injuries from road traffic accidents has declined in Poland in 2016 in comparison to the year 2016. However, it is still above the average value. Unfortunately, Poland is characterized by low intensity of doctors per 1,000 inhabitants. The problem of insufficient number of doctors is repeatedly raised on the national arena.

The main goal of the study was to show the efficiency of the policy of the analyzed countries in achieving the Sustainable Development Goals in Objective 3. For this purpose, one of the MCDA methods – Data Envelopment Analysis was applied. This non-parametric linear programming method derived from the concept of productivity is nowadays commonly used to compare the efficiency of different units (companies, countries etc.).

The analysis was set up to compare UN countries in terms of sustainable development in health care. Unfortunately, due to the fact that not many countries provided values of indicators monitoring the progress in the field of Objective 3, 43 countries were analyzed in 2016. Four outlays and nine effects were isolated for the analysis. Dealing with the DEA method revealed that over 68% of the surveyed countries turned out to be effective in the field of Objective 3. The ineffective countries included, among others, Russia, Romania, Portugal, Lithuania, Moldova. Poland turned out to be an effective country from the point of view of effectiveness presented in the study.

The procedure carried out under the DEA method also showed the absence of any impact of economies of scale on the results achieved in DEA models.

What's more, the conducted analysis also allowed to show which of the most effective countries are effective. For this purpose, the SE-CCR model was used, targeting permanent scale effects. The results revealed that the best-functioning countries were: Cyprus, Montenegro, Albania and the Czech Republic. Poland was also in the group of the 10 most effective countries.

All in all, it should be underlined that Poland apart from some areas monitored within Goal 3 tend to function well. The majority of monitored indicators shows positive tendencies in the value development over time. The analysis carried out by the DEA method indicated the effectiveness of Poland's functioning, compared to the analyzed countries, in the field of sustainable health. Of course, this situation should be assessed positively, however, one should not forget to pay special attention to the aspects that showed discrepancies in the policy presented and suggested by the UN.

REFERENCES

Alemanno, A., & Sibony, A. (2015). *Nudge and the law: A European perspective*. Oxford, UK: Hart. doi:10.5040/ 9781474203463

Avkiran, N. K., & Rowlands, T. (2003). How better identify the true managerial performance: State of art using DEA. *Omega International Journal of Management Science*, *36*(2), 317–324. doi:10.1016/j.omega.2006.01.002

Birman, S. V., Pirondi, E. R. E., & Rodin, E. Y. (2003). Application of DEA to Medical Clinics. *Mathematical and Computer Modelling*, *37*(9-10), 923–936. doi:10.1016/S0895-7177(03)00108-0

Charnes, A., Cooper, W., & Lewin, A. Y. S. L. (1994). Data Envelopment Analysis – theory, methodology and applications. London: Kluwer Academic Publishers.

Domagała, A. (2009). *Zastosowanie metody Data Envelopment Analysis do badania efektywności europejskich giełd papierów wartościowych*. Uniwersytet Ekonomiczny w Poznaniu.

EPF. (2019). *Sustainable Development Goals*. Retrieved April 10, 2019, from http://www.eu-patient.eu/campaign/access-to-healthcare/sustainable-development-goals/

Eurostat. (2019). *Sustainable development indicators*. Retrieved April 9, 2019, from https://ec.europa.eu/eurostat/web/sdi/main-tables

Garner, S., & Littlejohns, P. (2011). Disinvestment from low value clinical interventions: NICEly done? *BMJ (Clinical Research Ed.)*, *343*(jul27 2), d4519. doi:10.1136/bmj.d4519 PMID:21795239

Guzik, B. (2009). *Podstawowe modele DEA w badaniu efektywności gospodarczej i społecznej*. Wydawnictwo Uniwersytetu Ekonomicznego w Poznaniu.

Halpern, D. (2015). *Inside the nudge unit: How small changes can make a big difference*. New York, NY: Random House.

Harris, C., Green, S., Ramsey, W., Allen, K., & King, R. (2017). Sustainability in Health care by allocating resources effectively (SHARE) 1: Introducing a series of papers reporting an investigation of disinvestment in a local healthcare setting. *BMC Health Services Research*, *17*(1), 1–13. doi:10.118612913-017-2210-7 PMID:28472962

Hartwig, R., & Till Grüne-Yanoff, T. (2017). Nudging and Boosting: Steering or Empowering Good Decisions. *Perspectives on Psychological Science*, *12*(6), 1–14. doi:10.1177/1745691617702496 PMID:28792862

Leeder, S. (2013). Australia's leadership in developing goals for sustainable global health. *The Medical Journal of Australia*, *199*(6), 377. doi:10.5694/mja13.c0916 PMID:24033193

Quigley, M. (2013). Nudging for health: On public policy and designing choice architecture. *Medical Law Review*, *21*(4), 588–621. doi:10.1093/medlaw/fwt022 PMID:24081425

Scott, I. A. (2012). Looking for value in health care. *The Medical Journal of Australia*, *197*(10), 538–539. doi:10.5694/mja12.11497 PMID:23163667

Shah, M. M. (2008). Sustainable Development. Encyclopedia of Ecology.

Statistics Poland. (2019). *Sustainable Development Goals*. Retrieved March 31, 2019, from http://sdg.gov.pl/

Stuart, N., & Adams, J. (2007). The Sustainability of Canada's Healthcare System: A Framework for Advancing the Debate. *Healthcare Quarterly*, *10*(2), 96–103. doi:10.12927/hcq.2007.18839 PMID:18271106

Sustainable development Commission. (2011). *What is sustainable development?* Retrieved from http://www.sd-commission.org.uk/pages/what-is-sustainable-development.html

Thaler, R., & Sunstein, C. R. (2008). *Nudge: Improving decisions about health, wealth and happiness*. New York, NY: Simon & Schuster.

WHO. (2019). *Universal health coverage (UHC)*. Retrieved April 9, 2019, from https://www.who.int/en/news-room/fact-sheets/detail/universal-health-coverage-(uhc)

Wong Y., A. P., & R. D. (2016). Sustainable development goals, universal health coverage and equity in health systems: The Orang Asli commons approach. *Glob Health Epidemiol Genom, 1*.

World Health Organization. (2016). *Metadata SDG indicator 3.1.2*. Retrieved from https://unstats.un.org/sdgs/metadata

World Health Organization. (2017). *Metadata SDG indicator 3.4.1*. Retrieved from https://unstats.un.org/sdgs/metadata/files/Metadata-03-04-01.pdf

World Health Organization. (2018a). *Metadata SDG indicator 3.1.1*. Author.

World Health Organization. (2018b). *Metadata SDG indicator 3.2.1*. Author.

World Health Organization. (2018c). *Metadata SDG indicator 3.2.2*. Author.

World Health Organization. (2018d). *Metadata SDG indicator 3.3.2*. Author.

World Health Organization. (2018e). *Metadata SDG indicator 3.4.2*. Author.

World Health Organization. (2018f). *Metadata SDG indicator 3.9.2*. Author.

World Health Organization. (2018g). *Metadata SDG indicator 3.a.1*. Author.

World Health Organization. (2018h). *Metadata SDG indicator 3.c.1*. Author.

World Health Organization. (2018i). *Metadata SDG indicator 3.d.1*. Author.

Zięcbicki, B. (2014). *Efektywność organizacyjna podmiotów sektora publicznego*. Kraków: UEK.

ADDITIONAL READING

Avkiran, N. K., & Rowlands, T. (2003). How better identify the true managerial performance: State of art using DEA. *Omega International Journal of Management Science*, *36*(2), 317–324. doi:10.1016/j.omega.2006.01.002

Birman, S. V., Pirondi, E. R. E., & Rodin, E. Y. (2003). Application of DEA to Medical Clinics. *Mathematical and Computer Modelling*, *37*(9-10), 923–936. doi:10.1016/S0895-7177(03)00108-0

Leeder, S. (2013). Australia's leadership in developing goals for sustainable global health. *The Medical Journal of Australia*, *199*(6), 377. doi:10.5694/mja13.c0916 PMID:24033193

Quigley, M. (2013). Nudging for health: On public policy and designing choice architecture. *Medical Law Review*, *21*(4), 588–621. doi:10.1093/medlaw/fwt022 PMID:24081425

Scott, I. A. (2012). Looking for value in health care. *The Medical Journal of Australia*, *197*(10), 538–539. doi:10.5694/mja12.11497 PMID:23163667

Stuart, N., & Adams, J. (2007). The Sustainability of Canada's Healthcare System: A Framework for Advancing the Debate. *Healthcare Quarterly*, *10*(2), 96–103. doi:10.12927/hcq.2007.18839 PMID:18271106

Sustainable development Commission. (2011). What is sustainable development? Retrieved from http://www.sd-commission.org.uk/pages/what-is-sustainable-development.html

WHO. (2019). Universal health coverage (UHC). Retrieved April 9, 2019, from 2019 website: https://www.who.int/en/news-room/fact-sheets/detail/universal-health-coverage-(uhc)

Wong Y., A. P. and R. D. (2016). Sustainable development goals, universal health coverage and equity in health systems: the Orang Asli commons approach. *Glob Health Epidemiol Genom, 1*.

KEY TERMS AND DEFINITIONS

Maternal Deaths: The number of female deaths, calculated on annual basis, from any causes related to pregnancy during pregnancy, childbirth or within 42 days of termination of pregnancy, irrespective of the duration and site of the pregnancy, expressed per 100,000 live births.

Universal Health Coverage: The population receives healthcare services according to their needs without suffering financial hardship. Healthcare services are understood as actions connected with health promotion, prevention, treatment, rehabilitation, and palliative care.

Chapter 8
Shock Theory:
Financial Mechanisms of Economic System Destabilization

Zoya Andreevna Pilipenko
Bank of Russia, Russia

ABSTRACT

The purpose of this chapter is connected with the rationale for the approach to understanding shock as an economic phenomenon in terms of its nature and forms of manifestation, the conditions of aging and the factors of realization, the mechanism of self-development, and the consequences for the sustainability of the national financial and economic systems. The author's interest is initially aimed at identifying the circumstances in which the system loses its ability to restore sustained structural relationships and to preserve integrity in the sphere of national finance and economy. An approach allowing the identification of the transmission mechanisms connected with market exchange that can generate marginal states of economic structural links as necessary and sufficient conditions for the destructive shocks impact on them is identified. Based on the obtained theoretical conclusions, it becomes possible to model the marginal states of different structural relationships and evaluate their impact on the sustainable state of economic systems as a whole on the base of shock theory.

INTRODUCTION

This chapter is aimed at identifying shocks as an economic phenomenon, which allows not only to anticipate the formation of necessary and sufficient conditions for its destructive impact, but also to use it for the purpose of a qualitative restructuring of the economic system, for example, in the context of expanding the potential of its growth. The synergistic effect of the shocks' theory is great, because it allows to get closer to understanding the self-development of economic systems, the role of financial intermediaries in it, the mechanisms for the emergence of the financial bubbles at the national level and their ability to influence other countries of the world, the role of impulse, called shocks as a trigger of the above phenomenon. This approach is aimed at understanding economic and financial crises by shifting

DOI: 10.4018/978-1-7998-1033-9.ch008

the emphasis on research into the causes, mechanisms and significance of price shocks in implementing the laws of self-development of economic integrity at various local levels. The latter makes it possible to substantiate theoretically the effective practical actions of national mega-regulators in the context of the financial bubbles aging and the price shocks' emergence.

The continuing urgency of all the problems mentioned above is confirmed by the words of experts expressed both during the global financial crisis (2007-2008) and ten years later. The studies of the following authors serve as a very important base for preparing this chapter: C. Perez (2009); C. M. Reinhart, and K. S. Rogoff (2009); Jaromír Beneš, İnci Ötker-Robe, and David Vávra (2009); Staff Team from the Fiscal Affairs Department IMF (2009*);* Jan Hatzius, and et al. (2010) as well as many others. The results of a decade researches since the last global financial crisis devoted to the self-development of national and global economies, to the role of financial intermediaries, including the nature and forms of manifestation of financial shocks, can be summed up in the words of Valerie Cerra (2018, P. 4), Assistant Director in the IMF's Institute for Capacity Development: "….During the past decade, a lot of good work has been done to incorporate financial frictions into our economic models. … Some economists also underestimated the role of the financial sector before the crisis."

In other words, ten years after the last global financial crisis, not all the questions about it have been answered. According to V. Cerra (2018, P. 4): "We still don't understand very well why transitory shocks from the financial sector or elsewhere can lead to a persistent fall in productivity, employment, and investment." This conclusion is confirmed by other researchers: M. Schularick, and A. Taylor, A. (2012); R. Sahay, and et al., (2015); O'Sullivan, and et al. (Eds.) (2015); Cerra, Valeria, and Sweta C. Saxena, (2017); B. Sergi, F. Fidanoski, M. Zioło, and V. Naumovski (Eds.), (2018); and etc.

As a result it should be stated that it is about ten years since the onset of the global financial crisis, but some fundamental questions connected with it remain open. A misunderstanding of some aspects related to the global financial crisis of 2007–2008 and of subsequent slowdown of the global economic growth forced the author to focus on the study of the nature of financial shock, which served as a trigger in multiplying the phenomenon of the breakdown of the structural transnational relations in the late 2000s. The need for a systemic interpretation of the phenomenon of shock (impulse) in the context of the self-development laws of national economies was generated by ideas that remained outside the attention of theorists for many decades. Back in 1933, Ragnar Frisch (1933) in his famous work "Propagation Problems and Impulse Problems in Dynamic Economics" substantiated the "impulsive-propagation" approach to modeling the macroeconomic business cycle. In addition, at the beginning of the last century, such coryphaeus of Russian science as N.D. Kondratiev (1984), E.E. Slutsky (2010) and other representatives of the famous Kondratyev's Conjuncture Institute, linked economic shocks with the most important areas of research. So, in particular, E.E. Slutsky (1937) was one of the first to question the acceptability of deterministic models for explaining economic cycles. He substantiated the hypothesis that it was precisely random effects - "impulses" (or shocks – as they are called today) on the economic system - that serve as the beginning of a cyclical model of its reaction to external influence. In the late 50s of the last century Irma and Frank Adelman (1959) tested the impulse-propagation approach in the empirical studies of economic fluctuations. It turned out that the amplitude and duration of economic cycles caused by simulated external impulses, surprisingly exactly repeated those that actually took place in the United States.

In addition, we should mention the authors and their scientific publications well-known in the world devoted to some aspects of the above problems: Ch. Kindleberger (1996); H. P. Minsky (2008); Garry J. Schinasi (2006); Iikka Korhonen (2007*).*

In a sense all these papers deal with the fundamental problems of the mechanism of the economic systems' cyclic development in the long run of 50-60 years ("Kondratyev's big cycles"). Based on all the above results this chapter is devoted to the fundamentals of the theoretical concept of shocks, using a dialectic approach and including all the elements necessary for the scientific theoretical construction: the essence and forms of shocks, their causes, the mechanism of their impact on economic systems and the multiplication of their influence on structural relationships and the possible consequences. The special attention is paid to the definition of the financial mechanism of destabilization of national economic systems. The dialectical approach allowed the author to single out the financial segment of the national economy, which is associated with the emergence, development and implementation of modern price shocks as a trigger in structuring the stages of the national economic dynamics. The moment of realization of the price shock is modelled taking into account R. Frisch's hypothesis (1933) about the acceleration effect at the moment of "continuity" break, taking place when the system jumps from the stage of accumulation of quantitative changes to the stage of denial of its own denial.

BACKGROUND

The impetus to the growth of scientific interest in the phenomenon of shocks as impulses, initiating a "continuity break" in the dynamics of economic systems, was due to the frequent mention of price shocks, currency shocks, government debt shocks, liquidity shocks and etc. in connection with the last global financial crises. The search for theoretical interpretations of shocks gave nothing: having become a widespread term in the economic and financial literature, it acquired a certain importance due to the frequency of its references, especially in connection with the global economic crisis of 2007-2008 (Korhonen, 2007; Reinhart, and Rogoff, 2009; Krugman, 2009; Kindleberger, 1996).

For a holistic view of the phenomenon of shock the author was forced to justify his own approaches to the interpretation of this phenomenon. Certain results which became the basis of the theory of shocks were obtained only after their interpretation from the standpoint of the general theory of systems and the dialectic laws of their self-development. It is in this connection that the methodological aspects of this chapter are connected with the system concepts of the national economy, structured on the basis of the scientific conclusions obtained by representatives of the general systems theory of (A.A. Bogdanov, 1934; H. Hacken, 1977, and etc.), of catastrophe theory (V.I. Arnold, 1975, 1979; J. Guckenheimer, 1973; E.C. Zeeman, 1977; R. Thom, 1969; 1974; and etc.). At the same time, the author tried to interpret the phenomenon of shocks not by itself, but from the point of view of its functions in the self-development of economic integrities. And this became possible due to the dialectical interpretation of the self-development laws by such outstanding but long forgotten philosophers as G.W.F Hegel, 1967; K. Marx, 1995; Vladimir I. Vernadsky, 1967; and etc.

A significant place in the chapter is given to the rethinking of the dialectical approach of K. Marx (1995) to the research of the phenomenon of shocks with a shift of emphasis from the priority of production according to Marx to the sphere of exchange. It allowed the author to highlight the essential, elementary structural relationships in the economic system, with exchange relations in the sense that John R. Commons (1934) represented the transaction with its participants as the smallest unit of measure of institutional economics. Defining the structure of economic integrity, this relationship dialectically connects at least two participants, predetermining their unity and struggle as opposites as sellers and buyers. The rupture of these structural relationships with the accumulation of certain quantitative changes destroys the integrity of the economic system, giving it a new quality. It turned out that the phenomenon of shocks manifests itself at the stage of implementation of the dialectic law of negation of negation in the economic systems development. As a result, it was the philosophy and the dialectical approach that served as the starting point in shaping the shocks' theory fundamentals.

Significant place in the chapter is devoted to adaptation of scientific results of Garry J. Schinasi (2006), who interpreted financial stability through the prism of understanding the dialectics of partner relations in the financial market. The presence of interconnections between its participants, and, consequently, of interactions, brought the author to the idea of their dialectical unity, contradictory in itself. This allowed to single out the financial relations and the financial subsystem of the national economy as a sphere that is somehow connected with the maturation, development and realization of shocks. Thus, it became possible to identify a mechanism that constantly carries the threat of destabilization of the economic system. In this regard, mention should be made of the hypothesis H.P. Minsky (2008) on the immanent instability of a market economy due to its financial segment, which allowed the author to define the functions of shocks accompanying the build-up of financial imbalances and implementing the law of negation of negation in the development of the economic system. So the author identifies transmission mechanisms connected with financial markets that become capable to generate marginal states of economic structural links as necessary and sufficient conditions for the shocks' impact on them.

The empirical part of the work is based on the interpretation of statistical data in the framework of the shocks-propagation model through the increasing gap between the market and the base price. At the same time, R. Frisch's hypothesis (1933) became extremely useful in the process of modelling the acceleration effect of shock's "continuity break" of the economic system' development due to the marginal state (Arnold, 1975) of its structural relations.

The above logic allowed the author to form the fundamentals of the shocks theory, including shocks characteristics, forms of manifestation, as well as mechanisms for transferring shocks of break "continuity" through the structural (financial) interrelations in the economic system. In conclusion, the author raised a number of questions that are not solved and require new multidisciplinary approaches to understanding shocks phenomenon.

METHODOLOGY

Shocks: The Case of "Unexplained" Phenomenon in Economic Theory

In numerous publications of foreign and Russian authors on crisis issues in economics and finance, "shocks" have become common words, the essence of which is supposed to be intuitively clear, to which they add as a definition: price, currency, public debt, liquidity, and etc. (Hatzius, and et al., 2010; Easterly, and et al., 2000; Boz, and et al., 2019). In educational literature on macroeconomics, "shocks" are traditionally interpreted in conjunction with their causes — non-price determinants, which cause both demand and supply shocks, which shift aggregate demand and aggregate supply curves to new points of macroeconomic equilibrium (for example, McConnell, and et al., 2008; Brue, and et al., 2013; Sachs, and et al., 1993). However, the first global financial shock in the recent history destroyed the idea of the automatic restoration of macroeconomic equilibrium in the post-shock period, being the "starting button" in the mechanism of multiplication of financial and economic imbalances in interconnected national economic systems. As a result, the author sets herself the goal of substantiating the methodological approaches necessary to form a holistic theory of shocks, from a unified position satisfactorily interpreting essential characteristics, forms of manifestation and mechanisms of transfer of shock effects through the structural relationships of the economic system.

The relevance of the theory of shocks has increased due to the numerous problems of the theoretical and applied plan, which are put by the global financial crisis of the late 2000s. The former BIS chief economist W. White (2009, PP. 15-18) argues that the global crises should prompt a rethinking of macroeconomic theory, that will likely not be sufficient to avoid future crises. There are many dead ends from which to escape, but there are also many promising strands of thought to be pursued. These words can be fully attributed to rethinking the place of shocks in the cyclical self-development of economic systems. Indeed, the multifunctional deepening of interconnections and strengthening of interdependencies of national economies have caused a number of negative consequences, first of all, connected with the mechanism of maturation and realization of financial shocks. At first they appeared in individual countries and regions in the form of temporary local violations of the activities of financial intermediaries of various nationalities. At the same time, along with other factors, shocks caused a sharp price adjustment in the US stock markets in 1987 («black Monday») and in 1997; increased fluctuations in bond markets in the countries of the G10 in 1994 and in the United States in 1996; generated currency crises in Mexico in 1994–1995, in Asia – in 1997 and in Russia – in 1998, when hedge fund «Long-Term Capital Management» suffered a financial collapse (1998); increased volatility on global stock exchanges in 2000 – 2001. But in 2008, the price shock in the market of unsecured mortgage loans in the US not only generated crisis phenomena in other segments of the American financial sector, but also extended shock damage to banking systems and stock markets all over the globe. In 2009, the leading world economies lost up to 5% of GDP, and by the end of 2010, according to the calculations of the BIS, the global losses from bad debts and securitized assets reached US$4.1 trillion (Bunde, and et al., 2011). Assessing its destructive power, it became associated with the Great Depression of 1929-1933.

Thus, the rethinking of many economic and financial realities in connection with the last global economic crisis also concerns the formation of the fundamentals of the theory of shocks, which makes it possible to treat the category "shock" not as a "thing in itself".

Dialectical Laws of Economic Systems' Self-Development: Maturation and Realization of Shocks

The search for theoretical developments of the phenomenon of "impulse" (or "shock" in the modern interpretation) led the author to the researches of N. D. Kondratiev (1984), E.E. Slutsky (1937), A.A. Bogdanov (1934), Ragnar A. Frisch (1933). However, the above studies' continuation was hampered by the lack of systemic ideas about the phenomenon of "impulses -shocks" in the context of the self-development laws of economic integrity. Using the dialectical logic and the results of the general theory of systems, synergetics, of the catastrophe theory, and etc., the author developed a systematic approach to interpreting shocks in the context of the self-development mechanism of economic integrity.

So, any national economy is considered as a self-developing systemic organization characterized with the quality of integrity. It is expressed in the fact that the internal connections of the elements and the system as a whole become stronger and more stable than their interactions with the external environment. In accordance with K. Marx (1995), the elements of the system are combined in such a way that the absolute (separate, independent) existence of them becomes impossible due to the appearance of their new quality - integrity. This means that, having become organizational integrity, the system and elements become interconnected dialectically and begin to develop dialectically interacting according to the law of unity and struggle of opposites. As for shocks, their generation, maturation and realization in economic systems can only be understood in connection with the dialectical laws of their self-development: of unity and struggle of opposites, of the transition of quantitative changes to a new quality and of the negation of negation. (G.W.F. Hegel, 1967).

The author has structured the stages of self-development of economic systems as follows. At the initial stage, their dynamics are determined by the law of the unity and struggle of opposites that ensures the self-development of economic integrity. This is due to the fact that the *dialectical interrelations* of the system and of its elements necessarily necessitate the *interaction* of interconnected participants, which, in fact, is always *contradictory*. As the interaction between opposites (for example, between sellers and buyers on the market) deepens, the differences of participants in dialectical pairs gradually begin to dominate, disrupting the harmony of their originally coordinated behavior. In the process of enhancing contradictions of dialectically interconnected elements, the system moves to a new stage of its self-development, which is dominated by the law of transition of quantitative changes to qualitative ones.

In accordance with the findings of R. Frisch (1933) and E.E. Slutsky (2010) the author highlights the quality of "shocks" ("impulses") to influence the economic system, destroying the "continuity" in its development. Then it is logical to assume that a shock effect on system integrity can occur only in the process of its moving from one stage to another in the process of its self-development under the influence of the above three dialectical laws. In principle, the rupture of the "continuous" dynamics in the development of a system or the violation (suspension, change of quantitative or qualitative characteristics) of the mechanism of its self-development can happen precisely in connection with increasing contradictions that cannot be resolved. In fact, this tendency begins at the end of the first stage (unity and struggle of opposites) of self-development of organizational integrity and increases as quantitative changes become qualitative ones in its second stage. In this case, the system reaches a certain marginal state (Arnold, 1979), which is characterized by the dominance of contradictions between dialectically interrelated elements and the system. It is the law of transition of quantitative changes into qualitative ones that brings the system to its margin state, when it is ready for the break of the previous dialectically interrelated connections, contradictory in essence. It is at this (second) stage of self-development of the system that the necessary quantitative changes accumulate and predetermine its new quality.

At the same time, a mechanism is being formed that can force the system to move to a new stage of its self-development is dominated by the law of negation of negation. It is this mechanism that the author connects with "shock", the essence of which is in mediating the action of the law of negation of negation in the self-development of the economic system. As for the variety of realization forms of this shock mechanism, it depends on the specific sphere of economic activity (or rather, of the exchange of its results or market segments) where the shock breaks the "continuity" of development. This, apparently, determines a wide range of definitions of shocks in the literature: oil shocks, tulip shocks, government bonds shocks, as well as the credit ones, shocks of demand and supply, and etc. However, the essence of shocks as a mechanism of breaking the development "continuity" of the economic integrity does not change.

Thus, internal communications of the system reach their ultimate state in the process of transition of its quantitative changes to a new quality, and external communications of the system and elements with the external environment, developing according to the same scenario, also become extremely fragile. In this case, it deals with the formation of the necessary and sufficient conditions for a shock violation of the "continuity" in the system's self-development (*according to the type of resonant coherent oscillations*).

The Structure of the Economic System and the Exchange of Its Results: Manifestation of Shocks as Price Phenomenon

Using the dialectic approach "from the general to the particular" in the study of the phenomenon of shocks, the author needs to identify a certain component of the economic system, which will allow understanding the functions of shocks in terms of breaking the "continuity" of its dynamics. The philosophical interpretation of the laws of self-development of systemic integrity always connects them with structural relationships. It is their constant internal changes, caused by the interaction of dialectic pairs of conflicting elements that have the effect of preserving system integrity. It is logical to assume that shocks can break the "continuity" in the development of self-organizing systems only if they destroy their internal structural relationships mediated by the participants of dialectical pairs. It is the structure that implements the internal interconnection of elements within the framework of system integrity.

As for the economic system, its structure or "internal moment" of self-movement is associated with the exchange of economic activity and/or of its results, which mediates the relationship of coexisting economic activities in society. Moreover, the emergence of exchange objectively (with necessity) is predetermined by the specialization (division, disintegration) of coexisting economic activities, but its cooperation (association, integration), according to A.A. Bogdanov (1934), genetically and functionally contains the exchange in itself. It follows that a shock break of "continuity" in the self- development of an economic system can only be realized by destroying its structural links, predetermined by the exchange of economic activity and / or of its results. Specialization and cooperation of economic activity are the forms of its existence (of economic system's organization), and the exchange of its results embodies the quality of the structure of system integrity. From a philosophical point of view, the form of manifestation of any economic system is always labile, plastic, quickly responding to minor quantitative changes of elements due to the external environment' influence and as a result of the development of interrelations with it. The system is the first to respond to external factors. As for the structure of the economic system, it represents a way of internal interrelationships of elements, capable of maintaining the system unchanged until a certain moment, when it reaches its marginal state.

As a result, the relative independence of the disintegration (division) and integration (cooperation) of economic activity as forms of economic systems' organization predetermines its mobility and at the same time the response of the qualitatively preserved integrity to external influences. And the exchange of economic activity and of its results acts as an internal aspect of the above-mentioned forms of economic organization it is distinguished by its stability and conservatism with respect to changing the elements of the system at certain stages of its self-development. Disintegration (division) and integration (cooperation) of economic activity cannot be carried out otherwise than through exchange, at the same time acting as its starting points. Thus, the exchange becomes a necessary condition for the disintegration (division) and integration (cooperation), since the unification of its existing species is impossible without communication with each other. Karl Marx (1995) believed that exchange does not create differences between economic spheres, but establishes connections of sectors, already separated, and turns them into segments of the national economy more or less dependent on each other. Being forms and structures of economic activity, its division, cooperation and exchange of its results perform relatively independent functions in the national economy, and also have their own laws of development. According to A.A. Bogdanov (1934), at any time, the latter, thus, mutually condition each other, which can be called the abscissa and ordinate of the economic curve.

As for shocks their break of “continuity” in the self-development of the economic integrity is realized only if they can destroy the structure of the system, i.e. relations of participants in the exchange of economic activity and / or of its results. In other words, the impact of shocks on the organizational forms of economic systems does not interrupt their development. Only if shocks destroy the structural connection of the system, only then the effect of breaking the “continuity” in its self-development is realized. It is not by chance that Ludwig von Bertalanffy (1968) considers the development of systems as the realization of the dialectical principle of universal communication and interdependence, which necessarily implies the existence of differentiation and integration of system integrity. A.A. Bogdanov (1934) singles out at all levels of the organization of systems a universal tectological law, which coordinates the processes of an ever greater system specialization and of forming as a result the additional connections, and predetermines the systemic integrity' self-development. Ludwig von Bertalanffy (1968) considers this consistent pattern as a dialectical unity of the stability and mobility of the system under the condition that the latter dominates. Then, in his opinion, the structure of system integrity demonstrates a slow process of changes of a great duration over time, and the forms of its manifestation predetermine a fast process of short duration.

So, shocks, mediating the leap of the system from the stage of new quality' accumulation to the stage of denial of denial, break the “continuity” in the self-development of the system by destroying its structural connections. The latter arise between the participants of the dialectic pairs involved in the exchange of goods, services, and any other assets as their sellers and buyers. Exchange as a structure of the economic system resolves the dialectical contradiction of economic agents by realizing the desire of one to sell his utility (traded asset), and of the other one to buy it. Exchange as a set of structural relationships arising between sellers and buyers of goods, representing a dialectical pair of economic agents, itself contains a contradiction. According to Karl Marx (1995), this is due to the fact that the good in exchange (any tradable asset) itself is at the same time as a utility (diverse as to quality and incommensurable as to quantity) and as a value (homogeneous as to quality and commensurable as to quantity). Being a dialectical unity of contradictions, a commodity predetermines the need for an exchange to resolve them. Participants of the exchange of goods, which dialectically combines their incomparable qualities, are objectively carriers of the dialectical contradiction inherent in the exchanged commodities. It is this double contradiction that makes the exchange as the structure of the economic system so difficult to change, to destroy, etc. Consequently, the shock' break of the “continuity” of the self-development of the economic system should manifest itself precisely in the destruction of goods exchange (purchase and sale acts), which resolves all dialectical contradictions of structural relations, represented by goods as objects of exchange and mediated by sellers and buyers as its subjects.

The resulting dialectical contradictions in the exchange are resolved by the market assessment of this transaction by setting the market price. In other words, price as a market valuation of an exchange transaction regulates the demand and supply of a particular good, allowing one to single out that dialectical pair of exchange participants who consider it equivalent. The final settlement of the relations of sellers and buyers is carried out by means of exchange of good (as utility) for money (as equivalent from the point of view of participants of sales and purchases acts). As such, the exchange mediated by the monetary equivalent forms the integrity of the economic system, ensuring the constant transformation of goods created in society into money and money into goods. The latter means the formation of a constant circulation of goods produced in money and vice versa, which ensures commodity-money circulation in society and the integrity of the whole economic system.

Shocks realize their essence in the rupture of structural relations that arise in the exchange between dialectically interconnected economic agents who sell and buy the desired utility. If shocks break the structural ties that are formed in the exchange of economic activity and of its results, this means that the price parameters of the goods being exchanged in the market are unacceptable for some reason for the participants in dialectic pairs. In this case, the seller may estimate the market price as too low, and the buyer as too high. All other things being equal, it turns out that the shock's break of the structural ties that realize the exchange resolves the irreconcilable contradiction between the sellers and the buyers, destroying the price relationship between them in the market due to the mismatch of their interests. In other words, any shock, manifesting its essence in breaking the structural connections of the economic system, takes the form of a price shock, since it is accompanied either by a sharp fall or a sharp rise in prices, which violates price harmony. At the same time, the forms of price shocks are diverse depending on the market segment and the asset traded on it.

The possibility of shock to destroy price interdependencies in the market for a tradable good is necessarily realized when these connections are ready to be destroyed. In other words, market structural links should achieve a certain quality by the imbalance of sellers and buyers interdependencies about the exchange of certain utilities, in which they can be easily destroyed. And, the essence of this imbalance can be identified with irreconcilable contradictions between the participants of the market exchange, but as for the forms of their manifestation, they are realized in the form of price jumps on the traded assets to their maximum level (maximum or minimum) compared to its base value.

The failure of structural links (in exchange between sellers and buyers) to restore dynamic equilibrium in the form of negotiating the prices of sellers and buyers, which allows them to freely exchange a traded asset, creates the necessary conditions for a shock breakdown of dialectical relations in market exchange. As a result, they are blocked, sellers no longer interact with buyers, goods accumulate at one pole, and cash equivalents at the other, i.e. structural connections are destroyed, the system must change in order to develop further but at a qualitatively different level. Thus, the shock destruction of the structural relationships of the economic system is realized only if they reach the marginal state in the form of the maximum separation of the asset's market price from its base value (Arnold, 1979). In this case, it should be noted that the shock gap of "continuity" in the self-development of economic systems is realized as a repetition effect of shock destruction, which takes the form of price spikes around the base value of assets traded in structurally interrelated market segments. And the peculiarity of this destruction is in the fact that it generates other disruptions of market relations according to the type of the "house of cards" effect. This is explained by the fact that market relations in the economic system are interdependent, and diverse, and as such they form its structure. As a result, the shock destruction effect on the structural links of one market exchange segment is extended through cooperation relationships to its other segments that are dialectically interconnected with the first, and so on along a chain of cooperative dialectic interactions. This effect of the shock impact multiplication is explained by the fact that any economic system represents a dialectical unity that integrates all the diversity of its many elements and structural levels. The above describes the mechanism of destruction of interrelated structural relations of the system under the influence of their shock gap in one of its market segments. As a result, this shock causes a shift in the economic system from the stage of increasing qualitative changes to the stage of denying denial. The extent of shock destruction depends on the degree of integration of economic integrity by the stages of deployment of organization processes.

Financial Markets and Price Shocks: The Mechanism of National Economic Systems' Destabilization

The exchange of economic activity and of its results has its own stages of development, associated both with changes in the objects of exchange and in its subjects. Complication of the exchange occurs along the line of changing the already existing structural links between its participants in the dialectic pairs, of eliminating the outdated ones, and of forming new dialectic pairs. In other words, market exchange mediates the formation of structural links of the economic system and develops according to the laws of its self-organization. At the same time, the dialectic of the market exchange development is understandable only when it is considered as the process of continuous formation of its new properties due to the changing relations of the subjects of exchange, the emergence of its new objects and the structural interdependencies of various segments of market exchange and of their interacting levels.

However, as for shocks, their new quality associated with the destructive ability is predetermined by the emergence of the financial market and its many segments that mediate the acts of buying and selling money and their many substitutes, credit resources, securities and various financial instruments, including modern financial innovations such as bit-coins and crypto-currencies. Initially, the financial markets served the exchange of goods, services and other tangible assets in the situation when acts of sale and purchase did not coincide in time and space. As the demand for money in the means of payment function was constantly growing, the scale of financial markets functionally designed to serve this demand was also expanding. The scale of financial operations gradually increased, the number of players aimed at speculative operations with financial assets increased. As a result, a dialectic leap took place in the development of the financial market and its new quality was formed. This was expressed in the dialectical separation of the financial market from the markets of goods and services that originally generated it, and in turning the financial market into the dominant of the development of the entire market exchange.

In modern economies all the stages of market exchange processes are uniquely related to money. Being separated in time and space, acts of purchase and sale involve elements of participant's trust. Financial markets, mediating the relations of participants in the exchange of assets, are actually built on the relationship of the trust of participants in the sale and purchase under conditions of growing uncertainty that is difficult to adequately evaluate to the participants of the transactions. In other words they are designed to ensure the fulfillment of obligations by the partners according to financial transactions and to eliminate their opportunistic behavior. In this sense the main uncertainty factor is connected with the problem whether an economic exchange of full contracted value actually occurs (Schinasi, 2006). In essence, financial market is mediating the temporary exchange of the finality-of-payment services of fiat money for a promise that involves uncertainty about human trust (Schinasi, (2006) P. 33; Kindleberger, (1993) P. 21). So human trust plays an essential role in financial market as the latter offers the superior store-of-value services compared with the fiat money facilitating inter-temporal exchange. So financial market operates with trust as a fragile human emotion and as a result becomes subject to instability under certain conditions when according to G.J. Schinasi (2006, P. 40) "too much finance is created on too little trust". This situation is realized when the market price of an asset deviates as much as possible from its base price. This increases uncertainty and risks, which generates conditions for a potential shock break of dialectical relations in the financial market and its interrelated segments. And this mechanism of shocks realization acquires behavioral content, i.e. becomes subjective in the essence.

According to G.J. Schinasi (2006, p. 82), the macroeconomic sustainability takes place if all the financial market's segments are capable, at first, to efficiently and smoothly facilitate the inter-temporal allocation of resources from savers to investors as well as economic resources in general; secondly, to reasonably assess price and to relatively well manage forward looking financial risks; and, thirdly, to comfortably absorb financial and real economic surprises and shocks. If any of these key functions is not been properly executed, the economic system as integrity becomes less and less stable down to its shock destruction. The core of concept of the gradual instability reintroduction in financial markets is connected with the inter-temporal contracts that voluntarily and gradually reintroduce uncertainty and risks about human trust. Financial markets can create potentially superior near-fiat-money substitutes as stores of value (in the form of bank credit, for example), but do it successfully only to the extent that uncertainty about trust can be properly priced and risk-managed.

In the mid of the last century H.P. Minsky (1957) revealed the unbearable propensity of a market economy and financial markets to instability. It was he who described the paradoxical situation in which economic stability could be destabilizing, i.e. market players of developed economies independently generate forces leading to their destabilization. According to I. Rozmainsky, 2015), Minsky's main idea could be reduced to the following three main points: (1) to decision-making under uncertainty; (2) to the cyclical nature of the capitalist production process; and (3) to the financial relations of a developed market economy (Minsky, 1985). From view point of H.P. Minsky (1985), a market economy is based on private ownership of production assets and functions largely due to the peculiarities of investing in these assets. Lack of reserves to meet the firms' investment demand (Keynes, 1937; 1939) was satisfied by banking institutions with the help of financial innovations (Minsky,1985), such as repurchase agreements, certificates of deposit, euro-dollar loans, securitization, "off-balance sheet activities" (for example, the provision of credit lines). With the increase of debt investment, the risks grow, which limits the amount of capital investment. So the financial instability hypothesis of H.P. Minsky is based on the ability of a market economy to endogenously generate a financial structure that is predisposed to shocks' break of "continuity" in the self-development. According to the first theorem of the financial instability hypothesis of Minsky H.P., different financing regimes of the market economy makes it stable or unstable. The second theorem of the financial instability hypothesis of Minsky H.P. proves that periods of long-term prosperity make the economic system move from stable financial relations to unstable ones (Minsky, (1992), PP.7-8).

To structure all of the above in the context of the theory of shocks it is necessary to build the following logical reasoning. The state of structural (financial) relations of the participants of dialectical pairs will be stable until the price fluctuations of the traded asset overcome their marginal level. This happens through the agitated behavior of one group of participants of dialectical relations which turn to become a dominant of market relations and demonstrate the irrational behavior of partners of a transaction, either on the side of demand for an asset or on the side of its supply. As a result the amplitude of fluctuations of asset prices around its base value increases, regardless of the exchange object or the specifics of speculation with them. Exactly the aggressive behavior of one group of participants on the market (either on the demand-side or on the supply-side) determines the assets' price jump over its marginal level (the whole society could not afford to pay for the good at such a speculative price). This phenomenon is confirmed by G. Akerlof and R. Shiller (2004) introducing "the confidence' multiplier" that works because of the existence of several rounds of the expenditure' circle.

The marginal states of commodity markets as well as the markets of other assets, can be characterized from the view point of their increasing fragility, when, under the influence of external factors, they lose the ability to restore their integrity (stability) (Pilipenko, 2012; Pilipenko, and et al., 2018). It means that the price shocks destroy the contacts of the dialectically interconnected pairs of market "players" that form the structural relations. Their breakdown leads to the violation of the integrity and sustainability of the financial market as well as the of the whole market economy.

Results and Discussion

The financial crisis of the late 2000s took a special place among the diverse crises of the past and present, as it became global in coverage of countries and damage propagating at each stage of the complicated process in which a risky home loan was originated, then became an asset-backed security that then formed part of a collateralized debt obligation (CDO) that was rated and sold to investors. Specifically, banks are estimated to have $740 billion of net subprime exposure, mostly held by U.S. banks (53 percent), with the remainder held by European (41 percent), Asian (5 percent), and Canadian (1 percent) banks (see International Monetary Fund, April 2008). In terms of composition, U.S. banks (together with government-sponsored enterprises) hold a greater proportion of overall exposure to the subprime market through unsecuritized subprime loans and asset-backed securities (ABS) collateralized debt obligations (CDOs) compared with European banks. On the other hand, European banks hold a greater proportion of their exposure to the subprime market via ABS. Banks are assumed to hold the most senior tranches.

Based on average loss estimates of 15 percent for unsecuritized mortgage loans, 30 percent on ABS, and 60 percent on ABS CDOs as described above, potential losses of U.S. banks ($144 billion) are likely to be similar to those borne by European banks ($121 billion) (Table 1). Losses of Asian banks are likely to be less than one-tenth of losses in Europe. More than half of the aggregate subprime-related loss would likely come from exposure to CDOs, while the remainder is expected to come from ABS, unsecuritized subprime loans, and losses on off-balance-sheet liquidity lines. In particular, potential losses on off-balance-sheet conduit and structured investment vehicles (SIV) liquidity lines could result in $40 billion of losses globally ($27 billion for European banks and $13 billion of losses for U.S. banks). These estimates are based on the assumption of an average loss of 5 percent on liquidity lines to off-balance-sheet conduits and SIVs. The 5 percent loss assumption is based on losses on a typical asset composition for conduits and SIVs. Losses on conduit assets are assumed to pass directly to the liquidity line, but losses on SIV assets are assumed to be mostly absorbed by the junior notes, given their funding structures (see International Monetary Fund, April 2008).

Conduits and SIVs are weighted by their market proportions — 90 percent and 10 percent of the total, respectively — and it is assumed that all liquidity lines eventually get called (Table 1). One of the important questions emerged from the above, was, according to R. Dodd, and Paul Mills (2008), how these losses could spread to other parts of the global financial system like an epidemic of an invisible virus infecting many people and communities. Really the financial crisis spread the losses to intermediaries in one nontransparent market but the last raised concerns about liquidity and solvency elsewhere (Dodd, et al., 2008).

This phenomenon is quite understandable on the basis of the shocks' theory foundations. The dialectic of the concept of markets in general, including financial markets, conditions their interpretation through the prism of the constant, simultaneously process of self-organization, which is realized through the interaction of trends towards integration and disintegration. Moreover, the emergence of new segments

Table 1. Global bank losses as of March 2008 (in billion U.S. dollars)

Country/Region	Total Reported Losses	Estimated Losses on U.S. Subprime/Alt-A Loans	Estimated Losses on ABS	Estimated Losses on CDOs	Estimated Losses on Conduits/SIVs	Total Estimated Subprime-Related Losses	Remaining Subprime-Related Losses Expected
Europe	80	16	27	53	27	123	43
Of which:							
United Kingdom	19	16	1	12	11	40	22
Switzerland	23	0	7	15	1	23	0
Scandinavia	0	0	0	0	1	1	1
Euro area	33	0	10	20	15	45	12
Unallocated	5	0	9	6	0	14	9
United States	95	29	12	90	13	144	49
Asia excluding Japan	1	0	3	0	0	4	3
Of which: China	1	0	3	0	0	3	2
Japan	10	0	5	5	0	10	0
Asia	11	0	9	5	0	13	3
Canada	7	0	2	5	0	7	0
Gulf Cooperation Council	1	0	1	1	0	1	0
Total	193	44	50	153	40	288	95

Sources: Goldman Sachs; UBS; IMF staff estimates, IMF (April, 2008)

Note: Bank allocation to asset-backed securities (ABS) in Table 1includes estimated losses on ABS and conduits/SIVs. CDO = collateralized debt obligation; SIV = structured investment vehicles.

of the financial market as a result is identical to the formation of a new quality of exchange as a set of dialectical interconnections and interdependencies between participants in financial transactions. The exchange problems arising between them are resolved by the emergence of new financial products, new markets, dialectical pairs of participants in transactions that contribute to the development of financial markets. These processes are very clearly illustrated by the example of the development of structured finance that contributed fundamentally to the duration and depth of the last financial crisis, namely, the valuation and disclosure of structured finance products. Structured finance normally entails aggregating multiple underlying risks (such as market and credit risks) by pooling instruments subject to those risks (for example, bonds, loans, or mortgage-backed securities) and then dividing the resulting cash flows into "tranches," or slices, paid to different holders (Laura Kodres, 2008). Payouts from the pool are paid to the holders of these tranches in a specific order, starting with the "senior" tranches (least risky) and working down through various levels to the "equity" tranche (most risky) (Fig.1).

If some of the expected cash flows into the pool are not forthcoming (for instance, because some loans default), then, after a cash flow buffer is depleted, the equity tranche holders are the first to absorb payment shortfalls. If payments in the pool are reduced further, the next set of tranche holders (the "mezzanine" tranche) does not receive full payment. Typically, the super senior tranches and the senior tranches at the top of the capital structure are constructed so that they qualify for AAA credit ratings, meaning there should be a very low probability of their not receiving promised payments. Until July 2007, when the financial crisis hit, the growth in structured credit finance products had been exponential. For example, issuance of selected structured credit products in the United States and Europe grew from $500 billion in 2000 to $2.6 trillion in 2007.

Figure 1. The formation of highly complex structured credit products: adequate reflection of the dialectics of the emergence of new segments of the financial market, of its new participants and of new tradable financial products
Source: Laura Kodres (2008).

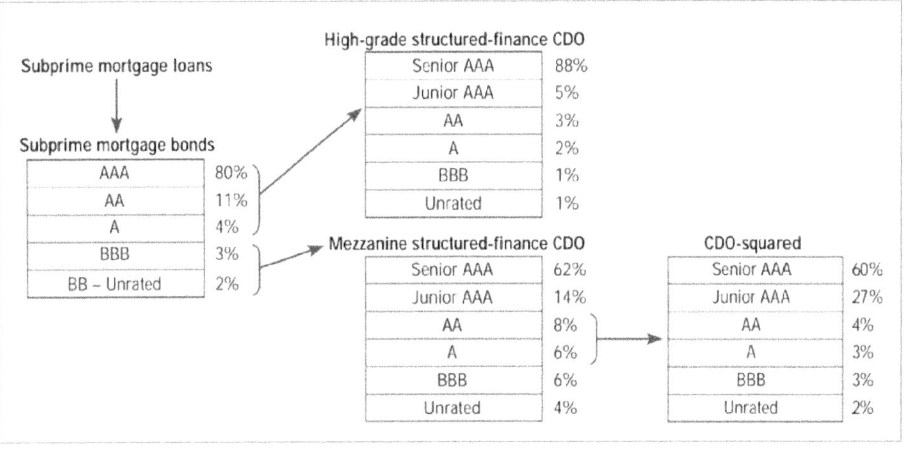

In fact, it was precisely the price shock on the US subprime unsecured mortgage loan market that triggered a global financial crisis, which, in essence, was a break in the "continuity" in the development of related segments of the financial market. Moreover, outwardly, that took the form of a shock violation of confidence between participants of dialectical couples who exchange highly complex structured financial instruments (Fig. 2) for monetary liquidity. Low nominal interest rates, ample liquidity, low financial market volatility, and a general feeling of complacency encouraged many types of investors to take on more risk. The lengthy period of benign financial market conditions was expected to continue, global growth had been robust, and the previous excesses of the dot-com bubble seemed in the distant past. In short, many believed in a new paradigm for financial markets. The resulting situation clearly demonstrated the overlapping of the trends of increasing demand for complexly structured financial instruments, supported by the concentration of the necessary financial resources for their payment, and an increase in the supply of the required exchange objects.

All that testified to the approach of these markets to their marginal state, which manifested itself in the maximum gap of the market price of the tradable asset - financial instruments and subprime mortgages loans - from its base value. And in accordance with the theory of shocks, the ultimate state of market relations means the formation of necessary and sufficient conditions for a shock break in the "continuity" of self-development of economic integrity. In the above case, it was about the market of unsecured mortgage loans, which was difficult and multivariately integrated into the system of interrelated and interdependent segments of diverse markets.

As a result when confidence deteriorated, many holders of shorter-term asset-backed commercial paper (ABCP) that was backed by illiquid structured credit products cashed out of their holdings shortened the maturity they were willing to accept, or demanded higher yields. That tendency had been exacerbated as suspicions had become increasing that credit products held were based on unsecured subprime mortgages. As banks became unsure of their own liquidity needs, they hoarded liquidity, further exacerbating interbank market illiquidity.

Figure 2. Self-organization of the financial market: the growth of trade of highly complex structured financial instruments
Source: Inside MBS & ABS; JPMorgan Chase & Co.; and European Securitization Forum, Laura Kodres (2008). Note: CDOs = collateralized debt obligations; ABSs = asset-backed securities, including auto, credit card, etc., and excluding MBSs; and MBSs = mortgage-backed securities, excluding U.S. agency MBSs.

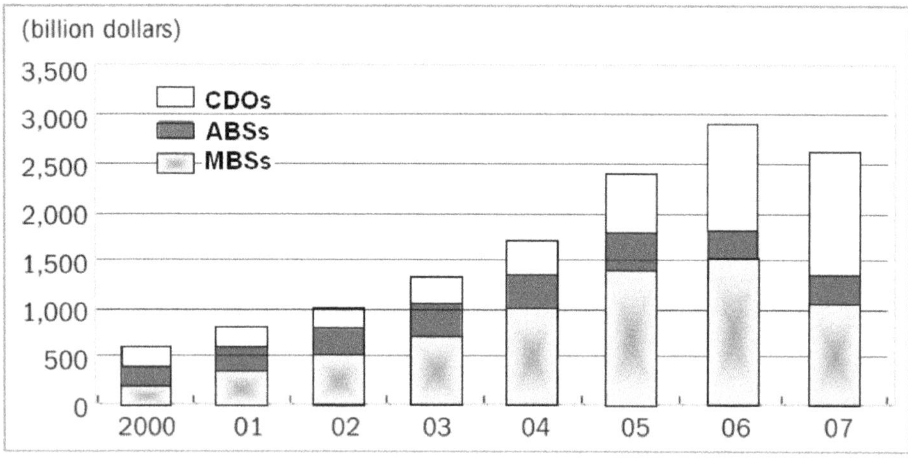

All of the above confirms Minsky's hypothesis about financial instability mechanisms embedded in an economic system that enhances its actions during periods of apparent stability. At the same time, it is implemented through the behavior of participants in the financial market, who are capable of feverishly (in shock reproduction) bring it down. So the change in the confidence will lead to the changes in incomes and confidence in the next round of the expenditure' circle and it will be the same in all the subsequent rounds. This confidence multiplier leads either to increase or to decrease of demand (in direct proportion to the trust) for a particular asset. Finally, the initial increase in demand, pushing the market to a certain marginal state, finishes causing the shocks' collapse of all the market operations with tradable goods. In this very process, the bifurcation effect takes place as the increasing gap between the market price and the base price of the tradable asset (its actual cost).

But the basis for such a collapsing chain disruption of interrelations in the interacting segments of the financial market is the marginal levels of insecurity of financial transactions, such as, for example, in the case of exchange of structured financial products for unsecured loans received from banks. Such a dual nonequivalence of exchange, with the participation of representatives of a dialectical couple in the segment of structured financial products of the financial market, in fact explains the phenomenon of the constant presence of mechanisms that can unbalance any economic system. Nevertheless, the financial shocks on a global scale, including countries and numerous market segments, have so far left many unanswered questions about global financial stability, minimization of the likelihood of recurring financial shocks of this kind and, of course, mechanisms to eliminate possible causes of the future financial shocks (or rather price shocks in financial markets) (Dodd, and et al., 2008; Raghuram, 2010).

Empirical Evidence

Financial markets are complex organizations with their own economic and institutional structures that play a critical role in determining how prices are established, or "discovered." These factors also shape markets are complex organizations with - the stability and orderliness of the marketplace. The architecture of over the counter (OTC) markets helps explain why CDOs (which divide the risk of the underlying assets into several slices, each of which is sold separately) and other structured securities faced problems during the last crisis. Credit derivatives, commercial paper, municipal bonds, and securitized student loans were traded on OTC markets, which were liquid and functioned well during normal times (Dodd, et al., 2008). But they failed to demonstrate resilience to market disturbances and had become illiquid and dysfunctional. That led to two serious complications: the inability to value one's holdings and the inability to trade them. More problems occurred when the securities were distributed and traded.

The vulnerability of leveraged, or thinly capitalized, investment positions and the illiquidity of many structured credit markets were exposed when trading was disrupted in a host of other markets—subprime-linked MBSs, CDOs, asset-backed commercial paper (ABCP), and credit derivatives (Dodd, 2007). High degrees of leverage, in which investors borrowed heavily or used derivatives to increase returns to capital, made investment strategies vulnerable to large market price movements. Mortgage originators, broker-dealers, hedge funds, and the structured investment vehicles (SIVs) banks maintained off their balance sheets were highly leveraged. The principal risk management strategy was to plan to trade rapidly out of a loss-making position. But such a strategy, which relies on markets remaining liquid, failed when markets rapidly became illiquid. It is a challenge to any financial market when trading becomes one-sided—with everyone trying to sell or to buy. But some markets have proved to be more reliably liquid than others.

Below there is the author's model of presenting the situation of the formation of a price shock in the financial market, when the market price of an asset maximally detaches from its base price, forming the marginal gap between them. Let the market price of the financial instrument being traded be - $Price_{Market}$, and its base price - $Value_{Base}$. For greater clarity of the graphic image of this dependence, it is advisable to assume that the base prices are a linear function of time with an angular coefficient k

$$Value_{Base}(t) = k \times Value_{Base} t ,$$

or more compact equation

$$V_B(t) = kV_B t . \tag{1}$$

Market prices will be interpreted as a non-linear function of the base price

$$\Pr ice_{Market} = f\left(Value_{Base}(t)\right),$$

or in a compact form

$$\mathrm{P}_M = f\left(V_B(t)\right). \tag{2}$$

As a non-harmonic oscillator that generates fluctuations (spread or separation) of market prices near the base price, it has been chosen the second-order differential equation of Euler (Leonhard Euler) in the form

$$\frac{d^2P_M}{dV_B^2} + b_1\frac{dP_M}{dV_B} + b_0P_M = 0. \tag{3}$$

Relations (1) and (3) specify the model being developed:

$$\left.\begin{array}{l}\dfrac{d^2P_M}{dV_B^2} + b_1\dfrac{dP_M}{dV_B} + b_0P_M = 0\\ V_B(t) = kV_Bt\end{array}\right\}. \tag{4}$$

To construct the corresponding graphs, it should be obtained an analytical solution of the Euler' equation, i.e. to identify consistent pattern (2).

The general solution of the differential equation (3) is conveniently represented as:

$$_M(V_B) = CV^\rho \sin\left[q\ln(V_B) + A\right], \tag{5}$$

where A, C = const, ρ and q non-harmonic parameters.

In the oscillatory process (5) the constant C – is the amplitude at zero value of the parameter ρ ($\rho = 0$). In general, the parameter ρ does not accept a zero value. In this case, the multiplier V^ρ essentially plays the role of a non-linear multiplier of the process of dispersion of market prices. The constant A can be considered as the initial phase of the oscillations. The multiplier $qln(V_B)$ represents a phase of oscillation that changes non-linearly with time.

For simplicity and clarity of calculations, it is advisable to assume that $C = 2$; $A = 0$; $\rho = 1/2$; $q = 5$. The results of the relevant calculations are presented in Figure 3.

Here, for more informative and comparative elements of the model (4), two dependencies are combined: (1) $V_B(t) = kV_Bt$, where $k = 0.5$, in the axes tOV_B; and in the axes V_BOP_M solution (5) is presented taking into account the accepted numerical values of parameters $_M(V_B) = 2V^{\frac{1}{2}}\sin\left[5\ln(V_B)\right]$. To match the elements of the two graphs, data labels are also applied – coordinates of some points.

As it is known, real market price fluctuations are far from harmonious. As far as the author knows, modifications of the Euler' differential equation have not been considered as non-harmonic oscillator of price modeling in the financial market. As it turned out, the results obtained in the framework of model (4) adequately describe the dynamics of market prices in the direction of maturing price shocks.

Hence, if the economic agents on the markets begin increasing purchases or sales of tradable assets regardless of their real cost, it is possible to prove that upon reaching the bifurcation point (marginal

Figure 3. Model idea of the mechanism of maturing price shocks in the financial market based on Euler' differential equation
Source: developed by the author

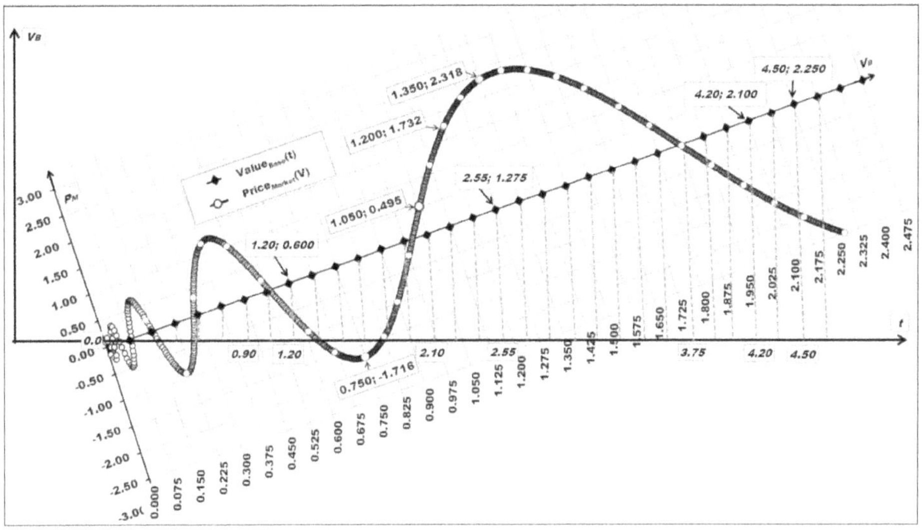

divergence of market prices of assets and their real value) any economic system loses its stability because of the breakdown of its structural connections (Pilipenko, and et al., 2018). The confidence multiplier leads either to increase or to decrease of demand (in direct proportion to the trust) for a particular asset. Finally, the initial increase in demand, pushing the market to a certain margin, finishes causing the shocks' break of "continuity" in all the market operations with tradable goods.

So, such a rapid spread of the price shock, first in the US market of unsecured mortgage loans, and then in other segments of the global financial market can theoretically be explained by the fact that there has been a shock break of dialectical relations in the interacting segments of the financial market. In 2007 the shock's discontinuity in the development of the US unsecured mortgage loans market was due to the combination of unsecured obligations from both the seller and the buyer of complex structured financial instruments. On the one hand, issuers of structured financial instruments had come a long way to deprive their market analogs of material security, but at the same time to achieve a high level of leverage and of capital gains. On this thorny path, the number of participants grew, starting with organizations that originally issued mortgage loans, broker-dealers, and ending with hedge funds and companies that traded structured investments that were not registered in banks' balance sheets. On the other hand, the buyers of these complexly structured financial instruments presented an increasing demand for them, paying cash based on loans, less and less secured by tangible assets. Such a build-up of debts in the process of issuing unsecured loans is associated with the Ponzi-crediting model described by H. Minsky (2008).

If these arguments include the subjective aspect of a shock discontinuity, considered in the author's theory of shocks, then a picture of the "financial bubble" is built. Moreover, it arose as a result of the material insecurity of the structured asset offered by the seller, as well as due to the material insecurity of the loans that provided cash to their buyers. In fact, this exchange was based on "trust" (Garry J. Schinasi, 2006) of sellers and buyers of complexly structured financial instruments that were not provided with tangible assets. In this situation, the real separation of market prices from their base value in this market was mediated by the mutual exchange of unsecured tangible assets. Thus, the Ponzi-relations (according to H. Minsky, 2008) have developed for both participants of the dialectical couple in exchange on the financial market. And while trust was multiplied (according to Shiller R., 2004) in the market, sales transactions were carried out. But as soon as the confidence of the exchange participants (sellers and buyers) was replaced by mutual distrust, a shock break became inevitable. This is understandable, since the principal risk management strategy in such transactions was to trade rapidly out of a loss-making position. As soon as there were signs of illiquid market, the number of sales increased, which meant the beginning of the end.

More than 10 years have passed since the crisis of 2007–2008 in the global financial markets, which was initiated by a price shock in the US market of unsecured mortgage loans. And 2019 marks the formation of new segments of macroeconomic instability, that are linked to the global financial debt market, including sovereigns (Tabarraei, and et al., 2019), firms, nonbank financial institutions and households. For example, the level of corporate debt has been rising around the world, and there is a weak tail of companies with high leverage and weak earnings prospects. There are growing signs that this credit cycle may be maturing, and risks of an economic slowdown are rising. The most highly indebted companies could be vulnerable to such a shock.

As to emerging markets their fundamentals are stronger and policy frameworks generally more resilient than in the past, some countries have low reserves, high leverage, or high foreign currency exposures that could make them more vulnerable to capital flow pressures. Furthermore, in Europe, fiscal challenges in some countries have reignited worries about the sovereign bank nexus as a potentially powerful amplification mechanism in economies with more indebted sovereigns. Finally, housing markets in many advanced and emerging markets are at risk (International Monetary Fund. April, 2019).

In sum, these rising financial vulnerabilities point to elevated medium-term risks to financial stability. Yet there is more debt than ever in the global financial system (Fig. 4).

The combined global debt of governments, nonfinancial corporations, and households has grown by US$72 trillion since the end of 2007 (Fig. 4) (Raghuram, 2010). The increase is smaller but still pronounced when measured relative to GDP. From 2008 to mid-2017, global government debt more than doubled, reaching US$60 trillion. Among Organisation for Economic Co-operation and Development countries, government debt now exceeds annual GDP in Japan, Greece, Italy, Portugal, Belgium, France, Spain, and the United Kingdom (McKinsey Global Institute, 2017; World Economic Outlook, October, 2018). High levels of government debt have set the stage for pitched battles over spending priorities well into the future. Public debt across all emerging economies is more modest, at 46 percent of GDP on average compared with 105 percent in advanced economies.

As to corporate indebtedness, an extended period of historically low interest rates has enabled companies around the world to take on cheap debt. Global nonfinancial corporate debt, including bonds and loans, has more than doubled over the past decade to hit US$66 trillion in mid-2017. This nearly matches the increase in government debt over the same period. In a departure from the past, two-thirds of the growth in corporate debt has come from developing countries. This poses a potential risk, particularly when that debt is in foreign currencies (International Monetary Fund, April, 2019). The growth of corporate debt in developing countries poses a risk, particularly as interest rates rise and when that debt is denominated in foreign currencies. If the local currency depreciates, companies might be caught in a vicious cycle that makes repaying or refinancing their debt difficult. Over the next five years, a record amount of corporate bonds worldwide will come due, and annual refinancing needs will hit US$1.6

Figure 4. Global debt has continued to swell since the crises but has remained stable relative to world GDP since 2014
Source: Bank for International Settlements (BIS); McKinsey Country Debt Database; McKinsey Global Institute (2018). Note: Total debt outstanding in US$ trillion, constant H1 2017 exchange rate, includes household, nonfinancial corporate, and government debt; excludes debt of the financial sector. Estimated bottom up using data for 43 countries from Bank for International Settlements (BIS) and data for eight countries from McKinsey's Country Debt Database. Figures may not sum to 100% because of rounding.

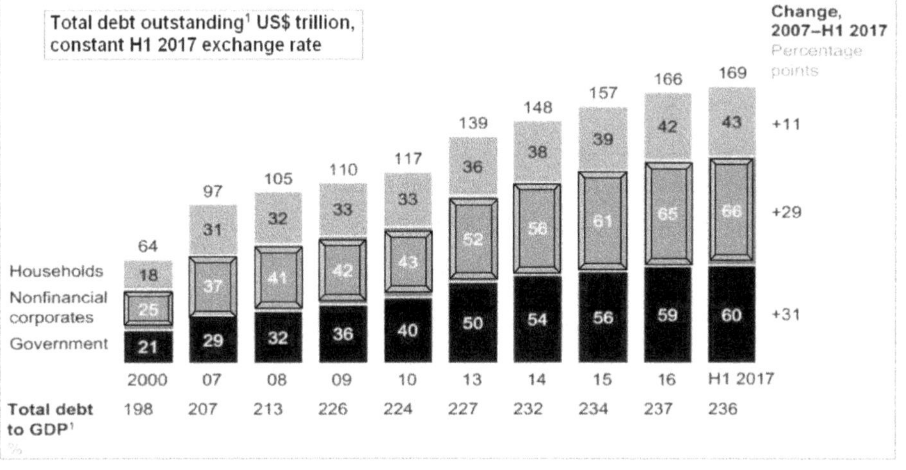

trillion to US$2.1 trillion (McKinsey Global Institute, June 2018). Given that interest rates are rising and some borrowers already have shaky finances, it is reasonable to expect probability of price shocks in the years ahead.

Unsustainable household debt in advanced economies was at the core of the 2008 financial crisis. It also made the subsequent recession deeper, since households were forced to reduce consumption to pay down debt. Ben Bernanke pointed to the "global savings glut" generated by China and other countries with large current account surpluses as a factor driving interest rates lower and fueling the real-estate bubble. (Ben S. Bernanke, (2005). Because much of this capital surplus was invested in US Treasuries and other government bonds, it put downward pressure on interest rates. This led to portfolio reallocation and, ultimately, a credit bubble. Today, this pressure has subsided—and with it, the risk that countries will be hit with shock if foreign capital suddenly pulls out.

The above is a possible scenario for creating conditions for a price shock in the global financial debt market. A necessary and sufficient condition for a shocks' break of "continuity" will be the threat of illiquidity in one of the segments of this market and the multiplication of distrust of sellers and buyers of financial instruments. And an objective condition for the realization of price shocks can be marginal levels of material insecurity of market transactions for the sales of debts in the global financial market.

The world is full of other unknowns. High-speed trading by algorithms can cause "flash shocks." Over the past decade, investors have poured almost US$3 trillion into passive exchange-traded products. But their outsized popularity might create volatility and make capital markets less efficient, as there are fewer investors examining the fundamentals of companies and industries. Crypto-currencies are growing in popularity, reaching bubble-like conditions in the case of Bit-coin, and their implications for monetary policy and financial stability is unclear. And looming over everything are heightened geopolitical tensions, with potential flash points now spanning the globe and nationalist movements questioning institutions, long-standing relationships, and the concept of free trade (International Monetary Fund, April, 2019). All the above confirms the hypothesis of H.P. Minsky (2008) on the immanent instability of a market economy, predetermined by the state of its financial segments, which in every moment create the conditions for the shocks' break of "continuity" in macroeconomic development.

CONCLUSION

The presentation by the author of the material in the chapter is subordinated to dialectical logic when developing the foundations of the theory of shocks from the point of view of determining the essence of shocks, describing the forms of their manifestation and structuring mechanisms of transferring shocks through the structural links of the financial (national economic) systems.

The explanation of this phenomenon is as follows: there are dialectically connected properties of the tradable goods (any asset on the market). From one side the sellers supply them, and at the same time, the buyers demand them. The contradictions and the harmony between supply and demand (as well as between sellers and buyers) relating to the exchange of an asset take the form of market price fluctuations around its base value. If the market faces the irrationally increasing demand or supply, the market price of an asset can jump smoothly up or fall down compared to its base value ("bifurcation effect"). Therefore any shock's impulse realizes as a price shock, causing the effect of bifurcation in the form of the increasing gap between the market price and the base price of the tradable asset. So a phenomenon of price shock is connected with the gap between market price and the real value of any tradable asset and is capable to destroy the structure of any economic system causing the bifurcation process in its development. Very many historically known shocks are concentrated in the sphere of circulation of goods, factors of production, services and other assets. All the price shocks appear in the form of assets market prices volatility around their real (base) cost (value). Marginal jump or drop of the market price is accompanied by the speculative behavior of the participants of the market transactions. It could generate the problem of economic instability. The theoretical studies obtained by the author allow her to interpret the events of the last global financial crisis from the point of view of the fundamentals of the theory of shocks.

The epicenter of the global financial crisis was really the housing market. Households were borrowing more than they could afford. Banks were giving out loans at very low interest rates and increasingly having enticing features like interest rates that were very low but then ballooned after a year or two. This meant that households could borrow more than they could really afford to borrow and to buy a bigger house. At the same time, all of this was fueling housing-price increases. These houses are worth a lot, so they have an asset. But the problem started when housing prices stopped growing and instead started declining. And suddenly a lot of households found that they had a lot of debt (McKinsey Global Institute, 2018).

But what made the 2008 financial crisis so globally devastating was that there were a lot of complex, opaque derivative securities that had been built on top of these underlying mortgage assets. So the subprime mortgage market in the US was pretty small. It was not more than maybe 10 percent of all US mortgages. Yet banks had taken these mortgages, pulled them together, and created something called asset-backed securities. Then they took those and pooled them together again. And so they built trillions and trillions of dollars of financial instruments whose value was riding on those mortgages being repaid. When a few households started defaulting on mortgages, the pain went far beyond those households and the banks that originated them to all these investors around the world.

Moreover, it arose as a result of the material insecurity of the structured asset offered by the seller, as well as due to the material insecurity of the loans that provided cash to their buyers. In fact, this exchange was based on "trust" (Garry J. Schinasi, 2006) of sellers and buyers of complexly structured financial instruments that were not provided with tangible assets. In this situation, the real separation of market prices from their base value in this market was mediated by the mutual exchange of unsecured tangible assets. Thus, the Ponzi-relations (according to H. Minsky, 2008) have developed for both participants of the dialectical couple in exchange on the financial market. But as soon as the confidence of the exchange participants (sellers and buyers) is replaced by mutual distrust, a shock break is inevitable. This is understandable, since the principal risk management strategy in such transactions is to trade rapidly out of a loss-making position. As soon as there are signs of illiquid market, the number of sales increases, which means the beginning of the end.

Theoretical results' comparison with the statistical data for the period from the last global financial crisis up to now let the author affirm that it is possible to identify the macroeconomic cycle' beginning as the economic integrities' reaction on shock influences of external impulses. In any case, it confirms authenticity of the impulse transmission character of the macroeconomic cyclical development hypothesis, but requires further theoretical research.

REFERENCES

Adelman & Adelman. (1959, October). The dynamic properties of the Klein-Goldberger model. *Econometrica.*

Arnold, V. I. (1975). Critical points of smooth functions. *Proc. of International Congress of Mathematicians*, 19-40.

Arnold, V.I. (1979). Catastrophe theory. *Nature*, (10), 54-63.

Beneš, J., Ötker-Robe, İ., & Vávra, D. (2009). *Modeling with macro-financial linkages: credit and policy shocks in emerging markets.* IMF Working Paper, WP/09/123.

Bernanke, B. S. (2005). The *global savings glue and the US current account deficit.* Remarks at the Sandridge Lecture. Virginia Association of Economists.

Bertalanffy, L. (1968). *The General System Theory. Foundation, Development, Applications.* New York: George Braziller.

Bogdanov, A. A. (1934). Tectology or General Organizational Science. Moscow: Academic Press.

Boz & Tesar. (2019). The global financial cycle. *IMF Economic Review, 67*, 1–3. doi:10.105741308-019-00076-2

Brue, S. L., McConnell, C. R., & Flynn, S. M. (2013). Essentials of Economics (3rd ed.). New York: McGraw-Hill.

Bunde, A., & Kantelhardt, J. (2011). *Diffusion and Conduction in Percolation. Diffusion in Condensed Matters*. Berlin: Springer.

Cerra, V. (2018). The global financial crises: 10 years on, why many still feel the pain. IMF Research Perspectives, 19(1).

Cerra, V., & Saxena, S. C. (2017). *Booms, crises, and recoveries: a new paradigm of the business cycle and its policy implications.* IMF Working Paper, WP/17/250.

Commons, J. R. (1934). *Institutional Economics. Its Place in Political Economy*. New Brunswick, NJ: Transactions Publishers.

Dodd, R. (2007). Subprime: tentacles of a crisis, *Finance & Development, 44,* 15–19.

Easterly, W., Islam, R., & Stiglitz, J. E. (2000). Shaken and stirred: explaining growth volatility. In *Macroeconomic Paradigms for Less Developed Countries.* The World Bank. Retrieved from: http://www.worldbank.org/research/growth/growth%20volatility%20jan%202000.html

Frisch, R. (1933). Propagation Problems and Impulse Problems in Dynamic Economics. In *Economic Essays in Honour of Gustav Cassel*. London: Allen and Urwin.

Guckenheimer, J. (1973). Bifurcation and catastrophe', Proc. International Sympos. In M. Peixoto (Ed.), *Dynamical Systems*. New York: Academic Press.

Haken, H. (1977). *Synergetics. An Introduction*. Berlin: Springer - Verlag.

Hatzius, J., Hooper, P., Mishkin, F., Schoenholtz, K. L., & Watson, M. W. (2010). *Financial conditions indexes: a fresh look after the financial crisis.* NBER Working Paper Series, 16150. Retrieved from: http://www.nber.org/papers/w16150

Hegel, G. W. F. (1967). *Hegel's Philosophy of Right* (B. T. M. Knox, Trans.). Oxford, UK: Oxford University Press.

International Monetary Fund. (2008). *Global Financial Stability Report: Containing Systemic Risks and Restoring Financial Soundness*. Washington, DC: IMF.

International Monetary Fund. (2019). *Global Financial Stability Report: Vulnerabilities in a Maturing Credit Cycle*. Washington, DC: IMF.

Keynes, J. M. (1937). The "ex ante" theory of the rate of interest. *Economic Journal (London)*, *46*(186), 241. doi:10.2307/2225525

Keynes, J. M. (1939). The process of capital formation. *Economic Journal (London)*, *49*(195).

Kindleberger, C. (1993). *A Financial History of Western Europe*. Oxford, UK: Oxford University Press.

Kindleberger, C. P. (1996). *Manias, Panics and Crashes. A History of Financial Crises*. New York: John Willey&Sons, Inc.

Kondratiev, N. D. (1984). The Long Wave Cycle (G. Daniels, Trans.). New York: Richardson and Snyder.

Korhonen, L. (2007). *Economic shocks in large emerging market countries.* Bank of Finland, BOFIT.

Krugman, P. (2009, April 19). How did economists get it so wrong? *The New York Times.*

Laura, K. (2008). Crises of confidence…and a lot more. Finance & Development, 45(2), 9-13.

Marx, K. (1995). *Capital: A New Abridgement.* Oxford, UK: Oxford University Press.

McConnell, C., & Brue, S. (2008). *Economics* (17th ed.). New York: McGraw-Hill.

McKinsey Global Institute. (2015). *Debt and (Not Much) Deleveraging.* McKinsey Global Institute.

McKinsey Global Institute. (2017). *The New Dynamics of Financial Globalization.* McKinsey Global Institute.

McKinsey Global Institute. (2018). *A decade after the global financial crisis: what has (and hasn't) changed?* Briefing Note. McKinsey Global Institute.

McKinsey Global Institute. (2018a). *Rising corporate debt: peril or promise*? Discussion Paper. McKinsey Global Institute.

McKinsey Global Institute. (2018b). How secure is the global financial system a decade after the crisis? *McKinsey Podcast.*

Minski, H. P. (1957). Central banking and monetary market changes. *The Quarterly Journal of Economics, 71*(2).

Minsky, H. P. (1985). The financial instability hypothesis: a restatement. In P. Arestis & T. Skouras (Eds.), *Post-Keynesian Economic Theory: A Challenge Neoclassical Economics.* Brighton, UK: Wheatsheaf.

Minsky, H. P. (1992). Profits, deficits and instability: A policy discussion. In D. B. Paradimitriou (Ed.), *Profits, Deficits and Instability.* London: Macmillan. doi:10.1007/978-1-349-11786-4_2

Minsky, H. P. (2008). *Stabilizing an Unstable Economy.* New York: McGraw-Hill.

O'Sullivan, P., Allington, N. F. B., & Esposito, M. (Eds.). (2015). *The Philosophy, Politics and Economics of Finance in the 21st Century. From Hubris to Disgrace* (1st ed.). Cambridge, UK: University of Cambridge. doi:10.4324/9780203797723

Perez, C. (2009). The double bubble at the turn of the century: technological roots and structural implications. *Cambridge Journal of Economics, 33*(4), 779–805.

Pilipenko, A., & Pilipenko, Z. (2018). Shocks in global economy: Impulse model of macroeconomic cycle. In B. S. Sergi, F. Fidanoski, M. Ziołо, & V. Naumovski (Eds.), *Regaining Global Stability After the Financial Crisis. A volume in the Advances in Finance, Accounting, and Economics (AFAE) Book Series* (pp. 238–256). Hershey, PA: IGI Global. doi:10.4018/978-1-5225-4026-7.ch012

Pilipenko, Z. A. (2012). *Global Financial Shocks' Impact on the World Economy.* Abstract of the Doctoral Thesis in Economics. Moscow: M.V. Lomonosov' Moscow State University Press.

Rajan, R. G. (2010). *Fault Lines: How Hidden Fractures Still Threaten the World Economy.* Princeton, NJ: Princeton University Press.

Randall, D., & Mills, P. (2008). Outbreak: U.S. subprime contagion. Finance & Development, 45(2), 14-18.

Reinhart, C. M., & Rogoff, K. S. (2009). *This Time is Different. Eight Centuries of Financial Folly*. Princeton, NJ: Princeton University Press. doi:10.2307/j.ctvcm4gqx

Rozmainsky, I. V. (2015). Investor myopia and persistence of the global crisis: A Post-Keynesian view. *Montenegrin Journal of Economics*, *11*(1), 107–116.

Sachs, J. D., & Larrain, F. B. (1993). *Macroeconomics in the Global Economy*. Englewood Cliffs, NJ: Prentice Hall.

Sahay, R., Cihak, M., N'Diaye, P., Barajas, A., Bi, R., Ayala, D., … Yousefi, S. R. (2015). *Rethinking financial deepening: stability and growth in emerging markets*. IMF Staff Discussion Note, SDN/15/08.

Schinasi, G. J. (2006). *Safeguarding Financial Stability: Theory and Practice*. Washington, DC: IMF.

Schularick, M., & Taylor, A. (2012). Credit booms gone bust: monetary policy, leverage cycles, and financial crises, 1870–2008. *American Economic Review*, *102*.

Sergi, B. S., Fidanoski, F., Ziolo, M., & Naumovski, V. (Eds.). (2018). *Regaining Global Stability After the Financial Crisis*. Hershey, PA: IGI Global.

Shiller, R. (2004). *Irrational Exuberance* (2nd ed.). Princeton, NJ: Princeton University Press.

Shubik, M. (1999). *Theory of Money and Financial Institutions*. Cambridge, MA: MIT Press.

Slutsky, E.E. (1937, April). The summation of random causes as the source of cyclic process. *Econometrica*.

Slutsky, E. E. (2010). *Economic and Statistical Works: Favorites*. Moscow: Eksmo.

Staff Team from the Fiscal Affairs Department IMF. (2009). *Fiscal Implications of the Global Economic and Financial Crisis*. Washington, DC: IMF.

Tabarraei, H. R., Rouabah, A., & Pierrard, O. (2019). *Sovereigns and financial intermediaries spillovers*. IMF Working Paper, February, WP/19/43.

Thom, R. (1969). Topological models in biology. *Topology*, *8*, 313-36.

Thom, R. (1974). Catastrophe theory: its present state and future perspectives. In Dynamical Systems (pp. 1-75). Berlin: Springer-Verlag.

Vernadsky, V. I. (1967). The Biosphere and the Noösphere. Moscow: Publishing House "Mysl"

White, W. (2009). Modern macroeconomics is on the wrong track. Finance & Development, 46(4).

World Economic Outlook. (2018). *Challenges to Steady Growth*. October. Washington, DC: IMF.

Zeeman, E. C. (1977). *Catastrophe Theory: Selected papers, 1972-1977*. Reading, MA: Addison-Wesley.

Chapter 9
Mysteries of Unsustainable Public Finance and of Low Economic Growth:
Trap of Low Efficiency of the State

Olga Ivanovna Pilipenko
The Russian Presidential Academy of National Economy and Public Administration, Russia

Andrey Igorevich Pilipenko
The Russian Presidential Academy of National Economy and Public Administration, Russia

ABSTRACT

The authors structure the main functions of the state in the economic system as the "famous triad" of R. Musgrave. They are connected with allocating resources, redistributing income (equality in income distribution), and stabilizing economy (economic efficiency). The aim is to find the causes of their low efficient implementation by the state. This is manifested in the fact that society itself does not have the ability to adequately control the current activities of the state created and put over it in order to protect its interests; in the contradictory essence of the state itself, which is the regulator, which forms the rules of behavior of economic agents and at the same time acts as the economic agent participating in market transactions. To model the options for the effective resolution of the problems of the "magic triangle," the authors formulated the Musgrave uncertainty principle by analogy with the Heisenberg uncertainty principle in physics. This makes it possible to assess the budget expenditures of the state in order to get out of its low efficiency trap.

INTRODUCTION

In economic theory, one of the most important remains the problem of increasing the efficiency of the state in the national economy and identifying the factors that contribute to this. The understanding of these problems can be expressed with the words of the Russian philosopher N. Berdyaev: "The state does not exist to transform earthly life into paradise, but in order to prevent it from turning into hell"

DOI: 10.4018/978-1-7998-1033-9.ch009

(V. Tanzi, (2011), P. 19). This interpretation of the role of the state allows the authors to consider the effectiveness of its activities in the marginal categories: how far it can move society to the border with paradise. Unfortunately, many years of research have made it possible to pass a verdict on the inefficiency of the state (Tanzi, and Schuknecht, 1997, 2000; Angelopoupos, Philippopoulos, and Tsionas, 2008). In the new century specific forms of this phenomenon' manifestation have become (1) national states' inability to foresee the global crises emergence such as the latest one of 2007-2008, and to block quickly their devastating impact; (2) national governments inefficiency to change radically the modern slow down trend of economic dynamics and of aggregate factor productivity growth; (3) inadequate state performance of its function of an equitable income distribution in society, which has increased the income polarization of the richest and the poorest members of society; (4) and, finally, the helplessness of the state to compensate financial losses from the global economy's disintegration by activating the factors of inclusive development of its countries. Given the significant share of GDP redistributed by the state all over the world through budget channels (the taxation system and government expenditures), it should be recognized to a large extent responsible for the economic problems of all the countries. This determines the paramount importance of an adequate theoretical understanding of the essence of the state as a phenomenon that is contradictory in its essence and has ample opportunities to influence the national economic system.

In 2009 R.P. Bootle (Bootle, 2009a; 2009b) noted, that the boundaries between government and the markets are now back in the melting pot. Really throughout the post-war years until the 1980s Keynesian view of the macro-relationships between markets and government were widespread in most Western countries. According to J.M. Keynes (1936) the state is the only agent in society capable of working for the collective interest on a sufficient scale. Moreover, this is its duty—first to try to prevent a depression and then, if it occurs, to get the society out of it. As to financial markets huge uncertainty and long time horizons make them subject to wild swings of sentiment and herd behaviour. Because of the importance of the financial markets for real economic activity, they cannot be left to their own devices. They require intervention, management, regulation, and restriction. After1980s the driving force became Milton Friedman (1962), who argued fervently that markets were rational and effective. From his viewpoint governments, by contrast, were inefficient and often irrational and could fall prey to corruption or be captured by group interests. As a result the Keynesian explanation for the Great Depression was that the last derived from a collapse of the confidence of investors, interacting with the peculiarities of a monetary economy. Friedman's explanation was based on policy failure. The Federal Reserve made many mistakes, and the most important of them was related to the introduction of restrictions on the money supply.

But, as usual, the truth is somewhere in the middle: the society needs more of the markets to do what they are good at — incentivizing, signalling, and encouraging the best use of scarce resources, especially now in the fields of environmental protection, climate change, and road usage. However, this increases the need to adjust the rules for the functioning of financial markets, which means, in various respects, a greater role for the government. But countries do not need more government, they need to adjust the market economy as a whole. It is necessary to agree with R.P. Bootle (2009a) that it is not the wrong regulation of a particular market, it is necessary to eliminate the practice of mismanaging the entire economy. The state should improve the quality and efficiency of its management in the sphere of economics and finance as a whole without expanding the scale of its impact on the market economy.

Despite significant progress in researching the factors that predetermine macroeconomic dynamics, many aspects of this fundamental scientific problem, especially in the context of the state's influence on the laws of its self-development, are far from understanding (Helpman, 2004). To make some aspects of these two problems clear the authors aim at investigating the interconnection of the government as a mega-regulator and its activities as the main factors capable to influence on the economic dynamics of any national society.

BACKGROUND

Increasing the effectiveness of the state remains the most burning issue for all countries in the world. All researchers of this problem are united in the opinion that the effective state formation is predetermined by the peculiarities of national economic systems and national communities (Pigou, 1924; Musgrave, 1959; Bator, 1960). However, the resolution of these particular problems must be preceded by an understanding of the fundamental problem related to the effective state functions and their positioning relative to the whole society preferences. The concept, proposed by authors, is based on the dialectical approach to the interpretation of the state as one of the components of its dialectical unity with society. In this interpretation, the state itself does not mean anything and is not able to create, provide or realize nothing. Being dialectically connected with society, the state assumes the existence of the latter and makes sense only if it exists. Such a dialectical unity can exist and develop only being dialectically contradictory, and all the contradictions should be resolved dialectically, i.e. subject to the coordination of the interests of both the society itself and the state. Otherwise, this dialectic unity simply ceases to exist, and as a result, the very foundations of the institutional structure of the modern national community are destroyed. As a result the state denial of the public opinion and the state behavior as the main partner in the dialectical unity is the main delusion of policy makers which violates the dialectical status of the interconnection of the society and of the state. And this hinders the dialectical resolution of contradictions, taking into account the dialectical laws unity and struggle of opposites, of the transition of quantity to quality; of negation of negations. In modern conditions, an example of the non-dialectical behavior of the state in relation to society is the implementation of pension reform in a number of countries with an emphasis on the retirement age and budgetary arithmetic with state funds. However, these issues are consistent with society under the new social contract. And it is between the future and current retirees, on the one hand, and the state, on the other. Only a preliminary public approval of government steps in relation to its interests will ensure the effectiveness of the state in this area as well as the dialectical social unity with the state. However, the theoretical interpretation of the interaction of the state and society as a dialectical unity, as well as the reasons for the ineffectiveness of the state defined on this theoretical platform has not yet been presented.

The theoretical emphasis on the state's ability to compensate for the market's "failures" has showed that in their majority they focus on the state' function related to the adequate allocation (allocation) of resources. However, the history of national economies development shows that the modern state fulfills significantly more obligations to society. J.M. Keynes (1936) substantiated that the state should implement stabilization policy in the national economy, ensuring the equilibrium of savings and investments in order to safeguard "full employment" in the economic system. That approach served as a theoretical basis for substantiating the state importance growth without focusing on the effectiveness of its activities. This apparently explains the fact that for a long time none of the known economic theories has considered the role of the state in reducing income inequality, in poverty combating or in protecting citizens from economic and financial risks. Today, with the growth of the importance of inclusive development factors of national societies, the social aspects of state activity could serve as adequate parameters for assessing the effectiveness of the government in the context of dialectical unity with society. It is not by chance that a number of philosophers and economists have seen great importance in the state's activities aimed at allocating budget expenditures for the purpose of implementing equity in the society income distribution (Hochman, and Rogers, 1969; Rawls, 1971; Sen, 1979).

R. Musgrave (1959) assigned an important role to the "redistributive function" of the state. He was sure that the redistribution of national incomes, allocation of resources and stabilization of the economy exhaustively determined all the key functions of the state. The national society redistributes part of GDP to the budget, and the state, in turn, spends it to financing its own functions. At the same time, there is no evaluation of the effectiveness of public spending, at least in the parameters of macroeconomic dynamics. This can explain a number of phenomena that arise with the mediation of the state as in the example of the Piketty's effect (Piketty, et al., 2016). Thus, there have been fundamental changes in the functions of modern national states, the quantitative and qualitative parameters of which are still not well understood (Ritter, 1996; Tanzi, and Schuknecht, 2000).

In the second half of the 21st century the state turned into a giant insurance company and an intermediary for all its citizens. Theoretically, this is due to the state functions expansion, which should be covered by increasing share of GDP redistributed through budgetary channels in favor of the state. It is during this period that phenomenal growth of public expenditures takes place all over the world. As a result the citizens are obliged to pay taxes (price), and in return receive public goods and services (benefits) (De Viti de Marko, 1936; Myrdal, 1954). For most citizens, the relationship between paid taxes and received benefits is not entirely obvious. This has led to the fact that in recent years the problems of fairness and efficiency have become a threat to the legitimacy of the dialectic integrity of the society and the state, which, apparently, underlies the non-effectiveness of the modern state (Solow, 1957; King, and Rebelo, 1993). As time passes the problem of the government activities effectiveness has only worsened (Solow, 1957; King, and Rebelo, 1993). The fact of a significant proportion of GDP used by any national state makes it possible to assess negatively its impact on the economic development in its country. And this means inadequate performance by the state of its function to stabilize the economy. The results show the evidence that investigation of the state as a key element of the dialectical unity with the national society is very important for understanding the real causes of the state activities' inefficiency as to the contemporary national economic slowdown.

The chapter is structured as follows. The methodology section presents a review of the investigations dealing with the specific features of the state as a reflection of the public interests, the formation of its fundamental functions, and several dialectical contradictions connected both with the essence of the state phenomenon itself and with the simultaneous fulfillment of the functions entrusted to it. Further author's idea is presented about the effectiveness of the activity of the state itself in the realization of its basic functions. Particular attention is paid to the functions implementation effectiveness.

Analytical part of the chapter is devoted to the modeling of structural connections' changes in national economy taking into account the dialectical unity of the state and society. The authors evaluate the dynamics of growth rates of GDP, budget revenues and budget expenditures in order to single out a tool for redistributing GDP in favor of the state, which has a dominant influence on the national dynamics. As a result the central object of analysis becomes the magical triangle of the state functions structured by R. Musgrave that can be concretized as its main budget expenditures. Here for the first time it has been implemented the uncertainty principle of Musgrave called so by the authors, as analogous of the Heisenberg uncertainty principle in physics. As a result, a certain constant has been obtained reflecting the impact of the human factor or informal institutions, which in many ways predetermines the discrepancies between the planned and executed macroeconomic parameters of the country's development. This is the essence of the dialectical contradiction within the framework of the integrity of the state and society, which is realized in the form of state activities inefficiency. The concretization of this model is connected with the identification of the main areas of budget expenditures that affect the macroeconomics dynamics.

The authors' calculations confirm their hypothesis that the state should perform its functions, structured as the triangle dilemma of Musgrave, only in dialectical interaction with society. The last means the interrelation of the parameters of the state activities' efficiency and minimization of the subjective adjustment of the planned budget indicators within the budget period.

The final part of the chapter shows the conclusions.

METHODOLOGY

Scientific Researches Covering State Phenomenon Topics

In economic theory, two basic approaches to understanding the state' phenomenon prevailed: in accordance with the exploitation theory and on the basis of the social contract theory. The exploitation theories, including the theory of Karl Marx (Marx, 1995), view the state as an instrument of the predominance groups or classes. As such, the state performs the function of "redistribution" of the income of the rest of society in favor of the predominance groups or classes. D. North (1981, P. 22) wrote that the exploiting state would establish a structure of property rights that would maximize the income of the group in power regardless of how that would affect the welfare of society as a whole. The contractual theory emphasizes the fact that the state provides benefits to all members of the society as participants of the original treaty. In accordance with the theory of the social contract, the appearance of a state is viewed as an initial contract that recognizes the individual's rights to certain resources compared with the rights of other parties to the treaty in exchange for their refusal to claim other resources and the consent to respect other people's rights to them. Such interpretation determines the emergence of the state and its function of the arbitration party, which is designed to guarantee compliance with the terms of the original social contract. In fact, it is about the fundamental function of the state to form a system of formal institutions that provide the necessary rules for the behavior of participants in market transactions, incentive mechanisms and penalties for their violations.

Taking into account all the above, the authors' research concept is based on the dialectics of the state formation, the dialectical laws of its interaction with society which could help to understand the phenomenon of low efficiency of its activity and its negative impact on economic growth. A systematic approach to the interpretation of the state allows the authors to consider it as the central element of any national economic system, since it embodies the structural (organizing) beginning of the last. Acting this role, the state arose and developed, performing only those functions that were necessary for society to preserve its integrity. The last was formed objectively in the process of expanding non-personalized exchange of goods and other assets in the markets. Indeed, as the dense network of stable personified communications was destroyed, the state was forced to specialize in forming an institutional environment as the set of formal institutions necessary to implement non-personalized transactions of economic agents. D. North (1990) argued, that the formation of non-personalized rules and contractual relations means the formation of the state. In other words, the state created formal institutions that provided for non-personalized exchange in the market, as society needed it, thereby replacing informal institutions and expanding its own sphere of influence through formal institutionalization of market transactions (Hodgson, 1988). Thus, without resorting to dialectical rhetoric, the theorists of institutionalism established the dialectical nature of the interrelations between the state and society.

With the development and expansion of the diversity of forms of society manifestation, the quantitative parameters of the state's activity are objectively increasing and its quality varies depending on social needs. Only an understanding of the dialectic principals determining the mutual influence of society and the state within their dialectical integrity makes it possible to identify the cause-effect relationship between the low efficiency of state activity and slowing the growth of national economies. It is this approach that has become the basis for further interpreting the problems identified in the title of this chapter.

Fundamental Reason of the State' Ineffectiveness: Its Contradictory Internal Essence

So, the evolutionary development of countries is accompanied by significant changes in the state, which, in turn, is predetermined by qualitative changes in society. So the development of non-personalized market exchange accelerated the growth of transaction costs of its participants. The latter were forced to insure risks of uncertainty in sales transactions, which objectively predetermined the state intervention in their institutional support for the purpose of costs minimization of the sellers and the buyers. For this reason, the fundamental function, initially imputed to the state by the national society, was the formation of an adequate institutional environment that ensures the smooth functioning of market exchanges. However, the effective implementation of this function is hampered by the contradictory nature of the state itself as a phenomenon that manifests itself simultaneously in two of its hypostases: on the one hand, the state as the creator of formal institutions (mega-regulator) acts as a subject of management (creating the rules of the game and watching for their strict implementation by economic agents); and on the other hand, the state simultaneously participates in the market transactions as the seller and / or the buyer of goods and services, the owner of real estate and of financial assets (the object of management). Combining these mutually exclusive qualities, the state falls in the crosshairs of conflicting interests, simultaneously acting as both a subject and an object of management. Often, being an object of control, it behaves opportunistically, thereby performing itself as an object of control to a conflict with itself as a subject of control. As a mega-regulator the state' behavior is motivated by the goal of maximizing social welfare, because this function is imputed to the state and is financially provided by the society. But in the case of the state as an economic agent, its behavior should be determined by the goal of maximizing income (profit or other usefulness), which is absolutely far from ensuring public welfare.

It is difficult to assess the effectiveness of the state in serving the interests of the national community in comparison, for example, with the parameters of maximizing profits or minimizing costs, as in the case of the goal aimed by the firm. As a result, the inefficiency of the state is predetermined by the contradictory essence of the state itself, which can behave as a subject, as well as an object of management. Such a contradictory nature of the state leads to contradictions of its interests and of society, reducing their coincidence. And this, in turn, has a negative impact on the effectiveness of their joint activities: if the state behaves opportunistically, the society ceases to trust it and the effectiveness of economic activity in the national system as a whole falls. Such an interpretation of state' efficiency allows the author to approach the understanding of the phenomenon of inclusive development of the economic system, which bases on the trust of society to the state, continuity of generations in terms of, for example, law-abiding, households' choice of strategies for development or survival, on their propensity to current spending or savings, preferences of formal and informal employment and etc. It does not take much time to cause public distrust of the state, that is, to destroy its dialectical unity with society, but to restore their consent often takes much more time than the life of one generation of citizens (Guillemette, and Turner, 2018).

R. Musgrave's "Dilemma of Triangle": Impossibility of Basic State Functions' Simultaneous Fulfillment

Initially, R. Musgrave (1959) united the whole variety of specific responsibilities of the state to society in three main groups of functions: (1) allocation of resources; (2) economic stabilization (subject to cost-effectiveness) and (3) (fair) redistribution of income. All the activities of the state are subordinated to the goal of institutionalizing these basic functions. From the point of view of R. Musgrave (1998), they can be structured in the form of a contradictory set that predetermines the phenomenon, which is called the "dilemma of the triangle". Its theoretical paradox is that the state in principle cannot optimize the performance of all three basic functions simultaneously, not to mention their implementation efficiently. This is due to the fact that it is objectively impossible at the same time to reach the three above mentioned conflicting goals structured as the "dilemma of the triangle". In practice only two of these three groups could be effectively realized at the same time. (The mathematical description of this paradox is given in the empirical evidence of this chapter.)

In any case, by performing any two groups of functions out of three possible, the state ensures the priority of public interests. This is manifested in each specific case by the institutional provision of economic agents as representatives of the society with the opportunities to minimize transaction costs and maximize revenues (profits, utility). In this case, R.A. Posner (2009) argues that the effectiveness of state actions is determined by how adequately the institutional conditions created by them for the success of economic agents duplicate the market principles of management. At the same time, the state, interacting dialectically with societies, is obliged first of all to form an institutional system that effectively specifies the structure of property rights of economic entities (D. North, 1990). Only under these conditions the goal of stabilizing economic growth could be achieved, and ensuring the multiplier effect in improving the welfare of the whole society. Negative or even zero GDP growth will not be enough. That is why the researchers of public finance believe that the principle of efficiency realized with institutional provision of resources allocation, economic stability and fair distribution of incomes should be objectively integrated into the state activities goals. But in practice, the modern state faces a slowing pace of economic growth and this exacerbates the problem of social inequality, which cannot be resolved in the conditions of economic stagnation. Thus, the dialectical integrity of the state and society is at risk because of the insoluble fundamental contradictions inherent in the state itself, created by society, and in its functions, designed to maximize social welfare.

Public Finance: Mechanism for Non-Equivalent Redistribution of GDP

The state's obligations to the society structured into three groups of specific functions are performed in the form of budget expenditures. Since any expenditure must be financed, in the case of public expenditures they are realized at the expense of national income. The corresponding share of GDP and national income is redistributed through the mechanism of public finances in favor of the state, through which its functions are paid by the society. This mechanism allows to generate budget revenues of the state with the help of taxes, and to finance its budget expenditures in the process of fulfilling the functions defined by society. In his original model of the state D. North (1981) described this mechanism in the categories of mediation in exchange, when the state performs its functions to ensure, for example, "defense and justice", and society finances them by paying taxes to the budget incomes. As a result, the society as a whole wins, as these services are implemented by a specialized agency, whose functions are performed by the state. Such a delegation of functions for the public goods and services production to the state is predetermined by considerable economies of scale (Arrow, 1970). In this case, the state is charged with the function of a discriminating monopolist. It differentiates the population that pays taxes, into groups, and for each group it specifies property rights so as to maximize tax revenues of the state budget. As a result, the tasks assigned to the state are contradictory: the second task assumes a fully effective set of property rights in order to maximize the aggregate product of society. In this case, the first task leads to attempts to specify a set of fundamental rules that would allow the state to maximize his income (or maximize the monopoly rents of a group or class whose agent the state acts) (Alchian, (1984), P.6). Thus A. Alchian (1984) formulated the contradictoriness of state interests, caused by the contradictoriness of the state' essence as a subject and as an object of management. This quality is also manifested by the mechanism the GDP redistribution between the society and the state. It's about public finances that replace money in the exchange of public goods and services, real estate, financial assets between the state and society. Specificity of finance in general, replacing money as a mechanism for mediating sales transactions, is associated with deferred payment for transactions in time and space (Schinasi, 2006; Pilipenko, et al., 2019). To ensure such transactions the state is obliged to create rules for behavior of the participants and penalties for their non-compliance with transaction contract. In other words, when the finance replaces money in payments with deferred maturity, the state as a subject of management creates formal institutions, dictating the rules of conduct that are binding on participants, encouraging their conscientious behavior and punishing them for their opportunism towards each other. At the same time, becoming an economic partner of market transactions, the state must itself strictly abide by these requirements. When confidence in the trust underlying economic and financial transactions breaks down, so too can the ability of markets and financial institutions perform their basic pricing, allocative and intermediary functions (Schinasi, (2006), P. 43).

As for evaluation of the equivalence of a deferred payment transaction mediated by finance, then it is equivalent, because suits both the seller and the buyer, since the partners agree to it, although in terms of money it is unequal. In the case of a state's partnership in transactions with conventional economic agents, it is not only a party to the market exchange, but also a management institution creating formal rules to ensure these transactions. Acting as a state, it promises to produce and to offer public goods and services, getting for this part of the national income of the society. This is realized through public finances, which form the revenues and expenditures of the state budget. In essence, public finances reproduce the key feature of finance in general, as a mechanism for mediating transactions, which are characterized by a mismatch in time of acts of buying (receiving) and selling (paying) in the case of private or public goods. Public finance relates to the trust that, instead of the taxes listed in the budget revenues, the taxpayer will someday receive his taxes' equivalent in the form of public goods and services (norms of free health care, education, pension and social security). If in the conditions of private finance the equivalence of a transaction can be estimated from the position of two equivalent partners that justify it in a market contract, then the profitability of exchange with the state should be evaluated by society as a whole. At the same time, the state is contradictory in its essence, and the society is differentiated both in terms of share in budget revenues and in the number of public goods received from the state.

As a result, the public finance system a priori mediates unequal transactions of exchange between the state and society. In the event of violation of the terms of the contract, the state as one of the parties to the transaction reports only to itself as a subject of management. The state's partner in the transaction is doomed to fail in the event of a judicial showdown with its partner, represented by the state. This situation is not critical, because at the national level, there is at least minimal growth in real GDP, which could allow at least one citizen to improve his position thanks to an increase in the supply of public goods by the state. In this case, Pareto efficiency is manifested in the actions of the state.

But public finance obviously unequally redistributes national income in terms of generating tax revenues and spending them, for example, on social functions. And this also suits the society as a whole. By paying taxes, taxpayers agree on the disparity of the transaction with the state, since public goods and services received in return do not necessarily have to be the equivalent of those tax payments that taxpayers have listed in the state budget revenues. This kind of disparity justifies the existence of the state, since public goods in any society are designed for large families, disabled, people in need, retired people, for those, who have lost their jobs, sick, crippled, etc., for those unable to solve his own problems without the help of the state. It is in their favor that the tax payments and received public goods of wealthy citizens of the society are unequal. From the theoretical point of view, this is the essence of public finances aimed at providing special categories of citizens with public goods based on the non-equivalent redistribution of GDP (national income) in favor of low-income members of society at the expense of citizens with high incomes.

But if taxes increase for all, and the situation of the bulk of citizens worsens, the middle class is eroding and the share of wealth grows against the backdrop of economic stagnation, then the inefficiency of the state and the inadequacy of its functions are evident, which is naturally conditioned by the fundamental contradictoriness of the very essence of the state. As a result, the share of national income redistributed through public finances is reduced (at best) and increases (in the worst case), the state cannot count on the growth of budget revenues, its budget deficit increases, and budget expenditures remain unchanged or reduced, which even more limits the state's ability to solve society's problems. Without restoring dialectical unity with society, the state is not able to effectively realize its activity, because society will interfere with it in every possible way. So the subjective factor - the trust - implemented by public finances as a mechanism for mediating relations between the state and society can reveal the contradictions inherent in the state itself.

Inefficiency of the National State: Budget Deficit and GDP' Growth Slowdown

High growth rates of the world economy and its leading groups of countries are in the past. In recent decades, the tendency has been rooted in slowing economic growth in all segments of the global economy (Fig.1-3). In 1970-1985 developed economies demonstrated an average 3% GDP growth per year; countries with average incomes and emerging markets – (+4%) and (+6%) respectively; and the annual growth rates for developing countries with low incomes were slightly higher than 4% in 2005-2010. The International Monetary Fund experts predict the economic development rates' decay all over the world in the perspective until 2020. The same opinion is shared by the World Bank experts.

As to OECD (Guillemette, and Turner, 2018) baseline scenario with no institutional or policy changes, world trend real GDP growth declines from about 3½ per cent now to 2% in 2060, mainly due to a deceleration of large emerging economies as these continue to account for the bulk of world growth. India and China take up a rising share of world output as the world's economic centre of gravity shifts toward Asia.

Figure 1. Real GDP per capita growth: Advanced Economies, 1970–2020 (Percent)
Source: Based on the IMF. Fiscal Monitor (April 2018), P. 24. Note: The dashed lines represent trends based on a Hodrick-Prescott filter.

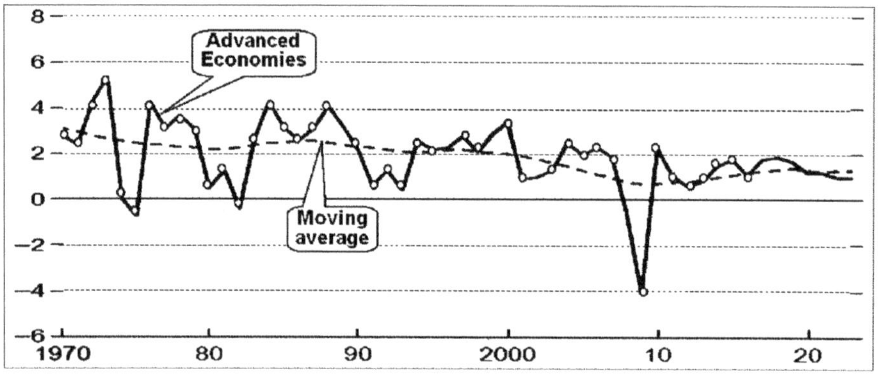

Figure 2. Real GDP per capita growth: Emerging Market and Middle-Income Economies, 1970–2020 (Percent)
Source: Based on the IMF. Fiscal Monitor (April 2018), P. 24. Note: The dashed lines represent trends based on a Hodrick-Prescott filter.

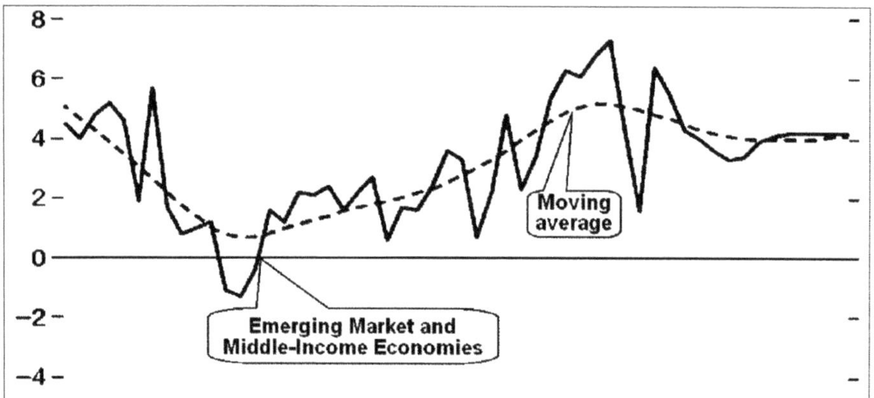

The summary of the problems of global development retardation can be summed up in the words of El. Helpman (2004), a specialist in economic growth issues. In his opinion, until now it has not been possible to understand the patterns of such a sustained downward dynamic, although it was possible to single out the forms of manifestation of inhibition processes of the global economy development and to describe these tendencies using statistical indicators. It was confirmed that the accumulation of physical and human capital remained the most important factor determining the rate of economic growth of the countries all over the world. However, now this only partially explains the deviations in per capita income and the rate of GDP growth (Aghion, and Kharroubi, 2013). As for the institutional factors, they have an even more serious impact on the rate of accumulation of the main factors of production,

Figure 3. Real GDP per capita growth: Low-Income Developing Countries, 1970–2020 (Percent)
Source: Based on the IMF. Fiscal Monitor (April 2018), P. 24. Note: The dashed lines represent trends based on a Hodrick-Prescott filter.

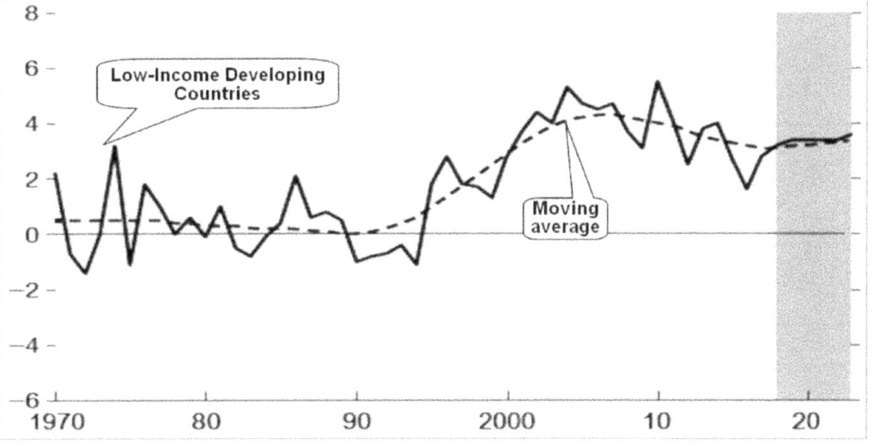

and, consequently, on the economic dynamics, but their study has not been brought to an understanding of the laws of inhibition of the economic dynamics of modern communities (Helpman, (2004), P. 10).

In this connection, the question of the role of the state and public finance in these mechanisms of inhibition remains open. To answer this question, it is advisable to analyze statistical data, which allows to judge about the importance of the share of GDP that is redistributed by the state through the mechanism of public finances. First of all, it should be analyzed the dynamics of state budget revenues on the example of developed countries (Table 1).

The authors will proceed from the fact that the developed countries of the world are somewhat ahead of the future of all other countries and show a long-term or medium-term outlook for the low-income developing countries, as well as for middle-income and for emerging markets. Over the period of 2010-2020, as to the average parameters for the world and for the developed countries of the G20, the share of the national governments revenues varies steadily around 34% of their national GDP: in 2010 that share averaged about 34%, and in 2020 it is projected at the level of 35.5% of GDP. In other words, the states in the developed countries redistribute through taxes 1/3 of their national GDPs, and this third they predetermine its downward dynamics. At the same time, for 10 years period, the governments revenues' share of GDP has gradually been increasing in all countries except Denmark (in 2010 it was 54%, and in 2020 it would be 50.6% of GDP). Even in the USA, with the focus of fiscal policy on the priority of market principles, the corresponding share has increased, albeit slightly: from 29.1% of GDP to 30.8% accordingly. The budgets revenues of such countries as Austria, Belgium, Denmark, France, Italy are approaching to 50% of GDP. So judging by the share of budget revenues in GDP, the states play a crucial role in adjusting the dynamics of its countries' GDP in the long term.

Other, no less effective instruments of public finance, which have a serious impact on macroeconomic dynamics, are government expenditures (Garcia-Escribano, and Liu, 2017). According to the data of Table 2, the national states redistribute an average in the globe of 40% of GDP by means of budgetary expenditures: in 2010 this figure was 42.6% of GDP, which was comparable to the average for the developed countries of the world - 42%.

Table 1. Advanced Economies: General Government Revenue, 2010–2020 (Percent of GDP)

Years	2010	2015	2018	2019	2020
Countries					
Australia	32.0	34.6	35.1	35.2	35.5
Austria	48.4	49.9	48.9	48.9	48.9
Belgium	49.3	51.3	50.4	50.1	49.9
Canada	38.4	39,8	39.4	39.5	39.5
Denmark	54.0	53,3	51.3	50.8	50.6
France	49.6	53,1	53,5	52,2	51.7
Germany	43.0	44.5	45.4	45.5	45.5
Italy	45.6	47,7	46.7	47.5	47.5
United Kingdom	35.3	35.6	36.7	36.7	36.6
United States	29.1	31.6	30.7	30.4	30.8
Global Average	34.9	36.5	36.3	36.1	36.4
G20 Advanced	33.7	35.7	35.4	35.3	35.5

Source: Composed by the authors on the base of official data of IMF. Fiscal Monitor (October, 2018)*; IMF. Fiscal Monitor (*April 2018), P. 111.

As for the budget expenditures of the advanced economies that ensure the state fulfilment of its obligations to the society, the trend of their changes has the opposite direction in 2010 - 2020 compared to the above described (Table 2). For the same period the share of government spending in GDPs of the advances economies is decreasing: in Denmark - from 56.7 to 50.9%; in France - from 56.4 to 50.9%, in the USA - from 40.0 to 37.9% of GDP respectively.

Table 2. Advanced Economies: General Government Expenditure, 2010–2020 (Percent of GDP)

Years	2010	2015	2018	2019	2020
Countries					
Australia	37.1	37.4	36.8	36.3	35.7
Austria	52.8	51.0	49.2	49.0	49.1
Belgium	53.3	53.8	51.7	51.4	51.1
Canada	43.2	39,9	40.3	40.3	40.2
Denmark	56.7	54.8	52.1	51.3	50.9
France	56.4	56.7	55.9	55.3	53.7
Germany	47.3	43.9	44.0	43.8	43.8
Italy	49.9	50.3	48.2	48.4	47.8
United Kingdom	44.7	39.8	38.5	38.3	37.9
United States	40.0	35.2	36.0	36.3	37.9
Global Average	42.6	39.1	39.0	38.9	38.8
G20 Advanced	42.0	38.5	38.6	38.6	38.5

Source: Composed by authors on the base of official data of IMF. Fiscal Monitor (April, 2018), P. 112.

Over 10 years, this indicator fell slightly, changing from 2010 an average of 38.8% to 38.5% of Global Average GDP to 2020. Following the logic of the previous arguments, this allows the authors to assess the contribution of the state to the downward economic dynamics of the countries of the world at a level of about 40% in terms of the state budgets expenditures' share of GDP. And in countries such as Austria, Belgium, Denmark, France, Italy, the share of the state's budget expenditures fluctuates around 50% of GDP, declining slightly for the period of 2010-2020. In the rest of the countries, this share is expected to decrease somewhat by the end of the analyzed period, remaining above 35% of GDP in the case of Australia and below 44% in Germany. In other words, if we consider the role of the state in the life of society on the developed countries' example, then their governments manage about a third of their countries' GDP through budget revenues and about 40% - in the process of performing their budgets expenditures.

In addition, states have the opportunity to influence the economic dynamics of their countries, financing the sustainable deficits of their budgets. External and / or domestic loans for current budgets deficit' financing reduce gross investments in the economy and increase the debts of future generations (Fig. 4, Table 3) (Checherita-Westphal, and Rother, 2012). Thus, public finances mediate an additional channel for the redistribution of GDP in favor of the state. Judging from the data of Table 3 in 2010-2020 practically all the advanced countries (with the only exception of Germany), will maintain a negative balance of the consolidated budgets of their states. In other words, on average, for this group of countries, government spending consistently exceeded state budget revenues throughout the period under review. This trend has not changed even during periods of significant reduction in the growth rates of GDP in these countries (for example, see 2009 and 2015 on Fig.4).

This raises the need to divert an increasing proportion of the national budgets expenditures for servicing the public debt, which means an additional redistribution of GDP in favor of the state and ineffective spending of budget funds, which negatively affects the dynamics of the national economies. The OECD

Figure 4. Advanced Economies: General Government Revenue (average, share of GDP (%); General Government Expenditure (average, share of GDP(%); GDP Growth Rate (%, yearly)
Source: The authors' estimations on the base of official data of IMF. Fiscal Monitor(October,2018)

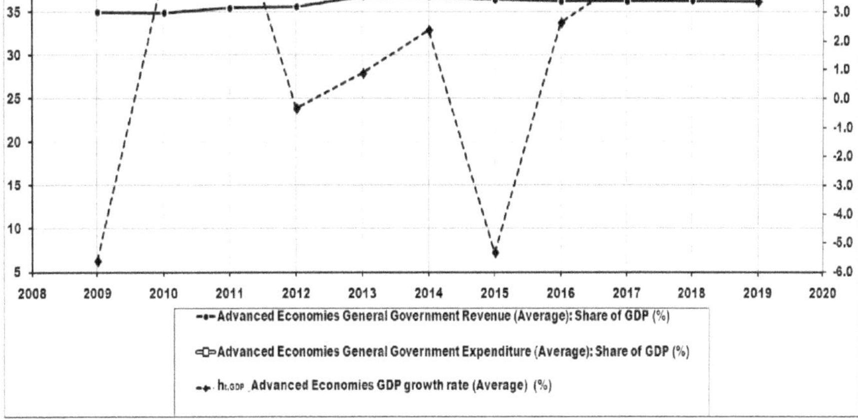

Table 3. Advanced Economies: General Government Gross Debt, 2010–2020 (Percent of GDP)

Years	2010	2015	2018	2019	2020
Countries					
Australia	20.5	37.8	40.7	41.1	40.6
Austria	82.4	84.4	74.2	71.2	68.4
Belgium	99.7	106.5	101.4	99.6	98.1
Canada	81.3	91.3	90.6	88.0	84.7
Denmark	42.6	39.8	34.3	33.6	32.9
France	85.3	95.6	98.6	99.2	98.7
Germany	81.0	70.8	59.8	56.9	53.8
Italy	115.4	131.6	132.1	133.4	134.1
United Kingdom	75.2	87.9	86.9	85.7	84.4
United States	95.4	104.7	105.8	106.7	107.5
Global Average	98.2	104.2	103.6	104.0	103.7
G20 Advanced	105.9	110.8	111.2	111.8	111.8

Source: Composed by authors on the base of official data of IMF. Fiscal Monitor (April, 2019).

aggregate underlying primary deficit went from 4½ per cent of potential GDP in 2010 to ¼ per cent in 2016, and that of the Euro Area went from 1¾ to a 1½ per cent surplus over the same period. Public debt levels have nevertheless generally continued to increase over this period, rising by about 15 percentage points of GDP in both the OECD and Euro Area, and are now high by historical standards (Guillemette, and Turner, (2018), P. 37). Thus, the multidirectional trends in changes of government revenues and expenditures relative to GDP in the developed countries make evident the problem of the inefficiency of the state's activities both in terms of the current fulfilment of obligations and the parameters of accumulated public debt relative to GDP (Tables 1-3).

But with interest rates having fallen to historically low levels, debt servicing has remained affordable. Experts suggest that the precise confluence of factors behind this trend continues to be debated, but one hypothesis is that desired saving has been relatively stronger than desired investment, leading to a global saving glut (Bernanke, 2005; 2015). The decline in investment as of the early 2020s is driven largely by slowing employment and labour efficiency growth, so less capital investment is required to maintain a given capital-to-output ratio. But more fiscal space for cyclical increases in the government debt-to-GDP ratio could support larger fiscal stimulus in future recessions (Blanchard, and Summers, 2017).

Reducing debt ratios would necessitate greater increases in fiscal burdens in the near term, although not in the long run as a lower debt ratio can be maintained with a lower primary balance. In an alternative scenario targeting gross debt ratios of 60% of GDP in European countries, with fiscal consolidation limited to 1% of GDP per annum, primary revenue in Italy and Portugal needs to be about 8 percentage points of GDP higher than in the baseline scenario at the peak in the mid-2020s, but can be about 2 percentage points lower by 2060. Similarly, lowering the gross debt ratio to 170% of GDP in Japan (implying reducing net debt to the current OECD average) requires the fiscal burden to rise by an extra 5¼ percentage points of GDP in the near term relative to baseline, but alleviates it by 1¼ percentage points in the long run. While fiscally demanding in the short run, public debt reduction can thus help alleviate fiscal burdens in the long run and in so doing make room for the fiscal costs associated with population ageing. By 2020 only Denmark (16.1% of GDP); Australia (17.3% of GDP) and Canada (25.7% of GDP) differed in modest shares of GDP, in which state debts were assessed in the overall results of the annual activity of the entire national society. According to IMF experts, on average, this indicator for all developed countries is projected at 80% of GDP, including, for example, 114.1% of GDP - for Italy; 85.8% - for France; 76.2% - for the United States (McKinsey Global Institute, 2015; IMF. October, 2018; International Monetary Fund, April, 2019).

Since a greater or less imbalance in the public finance system is typical for all countries of the world, it is possible to raise the universal question of the inefficiency of the modern state, at least in terms of the chronic deficit of its budget. However, in the modern economy this problem should be analyzed in the context of the universal trend of slowing growth rates of the entire global economy, including the developed countries of the world (Cottarelli, and Jaramillo, 2013). As a hypothesis, we can construct the following interdependent deductions. The state is called upon to perform the functions that society imposes on it a duty, as efficiently as possible in terms of public welfare. The most common indicator of the latter is GDP, from a third to half of which is redistributed to the state budget and is intended to finance public needs in almost all countries of the world. Theoretically, the higher the growth rate of GDP, the sooner social welfare grows, all other things being equal. If growth rates are low and are gradually declining on a global scale, then the state can be blamed and its contribution to this negative trend (Table 4, Fig. 5). This is due to the inefficient use of a significant proportion of GDP, due to which the company finances state functions. The persistent inefficiency of public finances is externally manifested in the chronic excess of state budget expenditures over their revenues. At the same time, as noted above, the resulting budget deficit increases in current prices and is not reduced relative to GDP, regardless of the dynamics of the latter.

As an adequate indicator to analyze the effectiveness of public finances in connection with the macroeconomic dynamics of the countries of the world, the authors select the elasticity coefficient of the consolidated state budge expenditure according to GDP. Moreover, the scatter of countries is arbitrary and, along with developed countries, there are included countries with transition economies. It turned out that from 2010 to 2023 for countries such as the United States, France and Germany, there is a typical trend of outpacing growth in expenditures of the state budget of similar indicators for GDP. In other words, if the elasticity of government spending according to GDP is more than one, then the state redistributes with the help of public finance a large share of the GDP increase that is produces by the society for a year. There is nothing reprehensible if it were not for the important BUT. With effective use of the growing share of GDP increase the state is able to stimulate the acceleration of GDP growth with its actions. However, the state not only does not change macroeconomic trends for the better, but also increases the cost of its maintenance by increasing public debt (Table 3).

Logically, the budget gap (the current state budget deficit) is covered by market sources of funding. This allows the authors to consider the size of the budget deficit as a current indicator of the inefficiency of public finances. And the aggregate public debt relative to national GDP can be considered as a cumulative (integral) indicator of public finance' inefficiency since it is associated with the expenses of future generations to pay for the results of inefficient state work in previous periods.

In the UK, Latvia and Russia, the situation is no better, but in each case there are specificities. Their analysis make it possible to confirm the above conclusion about the inefficiency of the modern state in the context of the growing cost of maintaining the state for society and its negative contribution to the macroeconomic dynamics of the countries of the world.

Table 4. The United States of America, (USA), the United Kingdom, France, Germany, Latvia, the Russian Federation: Government Expenditures Elasticity of GDP, 2010-2023

Year	Expenditures elasticity of GDP (USA)	Expenditures elasticity of GDP (UK)	Expenditures elasticity of GDP (France)	Expenditures elasticity of GDP (Germany)	Expenditures elasticity of GDP (Latvia)	Expenditures elasticity of GDP (Russian Federation)
2010	1.6352	2.6383	0.9797	32.4693	0.7919	0.9389
2011	1.2826	1.2236	1.4306	1.6959	1.7500	1.3661
2012	1.0025	0.9579	0.7413	-0.6117	-5.6663	0.9132
2013	3.0683	1.3811	1.3874	0.9680	0.1371	0.2626
2014	0.8997	0.7253	2.5052	0.5162	-2.4634	0.9011
2015	1.1320	0.8340	0.9199	1.0281	2.6869	1.1178
2016	0.5366	0.8448	3.7134	0.7644	-1.5081	0.5456
2017	0.8814	-0.2181	1.2668	1.4280	2.5110	1.0952
2018	1.0713	0.9889	1.1367	1.7467	0.4966	-98.6819
2019	1.0903	8.0157	1.2171	1.2466	1.0799	1.0201
2020	1.4202	0.9177	1.0490	1.5611	0.0368	0.1245
2021	1.0756	0.7785	0.8955	0.9749	0.1035	0.2927
2022	1.2924	1.0471	1.0091	1.2021	0.2252	0.6369
2023	1.3015	1.0453	1.0463	1.1049	0.4536	0.7600

Source: The authors' estimations on the base of official data of IMF, Fiscal Monitor, October 2018.

RESULTS AND DISCUSSION

The theoretical explanation of the phenomenon of the built-in mechanism of the inefficient functioning of public finances lies in the fundamental contradiction inherent in the state phenomenon: between the state in the role of a management entity (as a mega-regulator and creator of formal institutions) and at the same time in the role of the object of management (as an economic entity). Moreover, both in the first and in the second cases, the activity of the state is motivated by the goal of maximizing social welfare, which should be implemented by the government. But personal goals of the government representatives are predetermined by individual motives of behavior. This is one of the fundamental factors contributing to the macroeconomic in-sustainability as the phenomenon of the public finance inefficiency. But one should not forget that the basis of public finance is GDP produced by the whole society and by the society only (and not by officials!!!!).

The second fundamental reason for the constant imbalance of public finances is the impracticability at the same time of all without exception of the functions of the state, built according to the "dilemma of triangle" of R. Musgrave. In his investigations R.E. Wagner (Wagner, 1976) singled out the "redistribution" as a significant category, which allowed R. Musgrave (1998) to link it with the functions of the state and to structure them into three main groups according to the number of angles in its magic triangle. These are functions such as, (1) allocation of resources, (2) redistribution of income (implied to ensure equity in society) and (3) economic stabilization (in the context of economic efficiency). This triad does not specifically include the state functions of economic development and economic growth, although

Figure 5. The United States of America, (the USA), the United Kingdom (UK), France, Latvia: Government Expenditures Elasticity of GDP, 2010-2023
Source: The authors' estimations on the base of official data of IMF, Fiscal Monitor, October 2018.

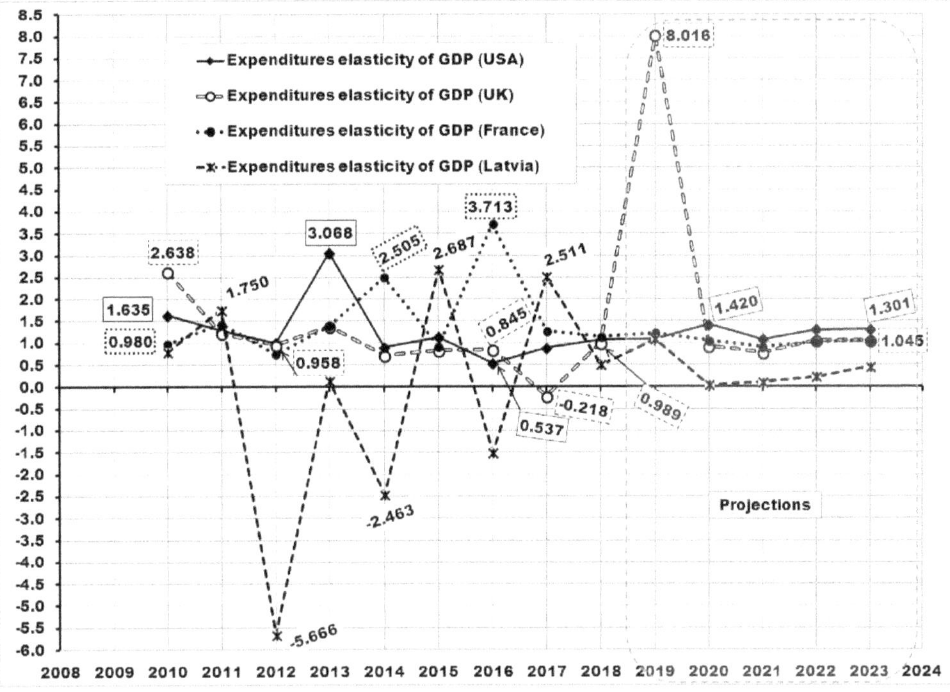

many modern governments increasingly declare them in the list of goals of their policies. (Tanzi, (2011), PP. 159, 169). The first and third functions of the state, mentioned above, do not contradict each other and theoretically more or less successfully can be realized in its activity. However, the second function, related to the institutional maintenance of equity in the distribution of income in national societies, in principle cannot be successfully implemented simultaneously with the other two.

In many ways this problem, as well as the inconsistency of the state itself as a phenomenon predetermine the formation of a "low efficiency trap". At present, the importance of this issue is increasing due to the fact that the inefficiency of public finances largely determines unstable economic growth, causing a chain transfer of their negative mutual influence in the national economy. So far this problem has not been solved theoretically or practically. As for the "insolvability" of the "dilemma of triangle" of Musgrave (1998), the authors propose their approach based on a comparison of budget elasticity ratios associated with the three basic functions of the state, relative to GDP, and on method of cyclic permutations of combined pairs of groups of functions of the three possible ones for the purpose of consistently multi-step improvement in the macroeconomic return on public finances.

Table 5. "Dilemma of Triangle" of Musgrave as to the state basic functions

State basic functions (possible combinations of two functions from three)	***Explanation of the impossibility of simultaneously performing the third excluded function***
Ensuring (***C***) *macroeconomic stability* by reducing horizontal inequality. Improving (***B***) *social equality (justice)* by reducing horizontal inequality.	The state can realize both (***C*** and ***B***) functions only on condition of fiscal consolidation in the context of strengthening its tax base (due to the centralization of tax flows). However, the latter will lead to a decrease in revenues of lower budgets and will not allow for *allocative efficiency* (***A***).
Ensuring (***A***) *allocative efficiency* on the basis of strengthening the revenue autonomy of local budgets. Achieving (***C***) *macroeconomic stability* by reducing the vertical imbalance of the budget system.	Achieving (***A***) *allocative efficiency* on the basis of revenue autonomy will cause increasing (***B***) *social inequality* due to the horizontal inequality in the budget system. As a result, when (***C***) *macroeconomic stability* is achieved, (***B***) *social injustice* will increase.
Ensuring (***A***) *allocative efficiency* could be achieved by strengthening the revenue autonomy of local budgets. The same fiscal policy measures let the local governments ensure (***B***) *social justice*.	However, the implementation of these two functions ((1) *allocative efficiency and (**B**) social equality (justice)*) could be carried out by the state only if (***C***) *macroeconomic stability* is reduced.

Source: Composed by authors on the base of R. A. Musgrave's results (1959)

EMPIRICAL EVIDENCE

So the "dilemma of triangle" of R. Musgrave (1998) is based on the fact that conditionally all the basic functions of a state can be structured into three groups: (***A***) *allocative efficiency*, (***B***) *social equality (justice)*, (***C***) *macroeconomic stability* (Table 5). The simultaneous effective performance by the state of all these functions is in principle impossible. Below, the authors presented their version of the contradictory relationship of these state obligations.

On practice ***A*** and ***C*** of the above-mentioned groups of functions of the state from the "dilemma of triangle" of R. Musgrave do not contradict each other and can theoretically more or less successfully be implemented almost simultaneously. As for the function of ensuring an equitable distribution of income (*social equality (justice)*) in national societies, it is difficult to implement simultaneously with the other two. And, moreover, it, as a rule, is implemented according to the residual principle in conditions of unfavourable macroeconomic dynamics and in the implementation of fiscal consolidation by national governments. Meanwhile, in the conditions of slowing economic growth in all countries of the world, social expenditures as the implementation of the state's function to ensure a fair distribution of income in society are directly related to the quality of human capital development (Cingano, 2014). And, the last one, according to the recognition of the leading theorists-economists in the conditions of fading rates of economic dynamics, can become a real productive force of society.

Taking into account all the above, the authors tried to give a mathematical solution of the "dilemma of triangle" of R. Musgrave. They proceed from the following considerations. The statistical nature of economic phenomena is ensured by the presence of a large number of dynamic links between elements of the economic system. Accumulating these dynamic relationships lead to statistical relationships in economic systems. One of the most important manifestations of such statistical laws is the phenomenologically announced Musgrave's position that it is impossible to simultaneously achieve the effectiveness of the three main groups of state functions (Musgrave, 1959). This phenomenon, by the way, is confirmed by the fundamental dilemma "*macroeconomic stability - social equality (justice)*", expressed by A.M. Okun (Okun, 2015). It is about the futility of the state's desire to combine implementation of all the following functions: (***A***) *allocative efficiency*, (***B***) *social equality (justice)*, and (***C***) *macroeconomic stability*. It is the incompatibility of these functions of the state and the results of their implementation that explains the emergence of c (Fig. 6).

Analytically visual content of the "dilemma of triangle" phenomenon, discovered by R.A. Musgrave (1959), adequately reflects the principle (ratio) of uncertainty proposed by the authors

$$\Delta A \times \Delta B \times \Delta C \geq M , \tag{1}$$

where ***A, B*** and ***C*** represent the conjugate values, respectively, of the following groups of functions: (***A***) *allocative efficiency*, (***B***) *social equality (justice)*, and (***C***) *macroeconomic stability*. These values are subject to constraints, which, as R.A. Musgrave discovered, contain inevitable uncertainties. $\boldsymbol{\Delta A}$, $\boldsymbol{\Delta B}$ and $\boldsymbol{\Delta C}$ at their joint consideration, the scale of which is associated with the constant ***M***. For these purposes, a certain constant is introduced by analogy with the Planck constant in physics to estimate the Heisenberg uncertainty. The last parameter in the theory of state and public finance was named by the authors as the "Musgrave uncertainty principle" in connection with the recognition of his merits in studying the problems of effective state performance of state functions and the introduction of the "triangle dilemma" paradox. In this regard, the authors consider it very appropriate to call the proposed relation (1) the "Musgrave uncertainty principle", and the constant ***M*** - the "Musgrave constant"[1]

Following the Musgrave uncertainty principle, the fullest realization of the function group A and the function group B, means reducing (minimizing) the uncertainty (spread) of the values of $\boldsymbol{\Delta A}$ and $\boldsymbol{\Delta B}$ (i.e. $\boldsymbol{\Delta A} \to 0$ и $\boldsymbol{\Delta B} \to 0$). But in this case, in terms of the "dilemma of triangle", the group of functions ***C*** practically cannot be realized: $\boldsymbol{\Delta C} \to \infty$. In other words, the choice of the most complete (best) intersection $\boldsymbol{A \cap B}$, introduces a significant and uncertain variation in values of $\boldsymbol{\Delta C}$ (i.e. $\boldsymbol{\Delta C} \to \infty$)

Figure 6. "Dilemma of triangle" of Musgrave as for the three basic functions of the state
Source: Composed by authors on the base of R. A. Musgrave's results (1959)

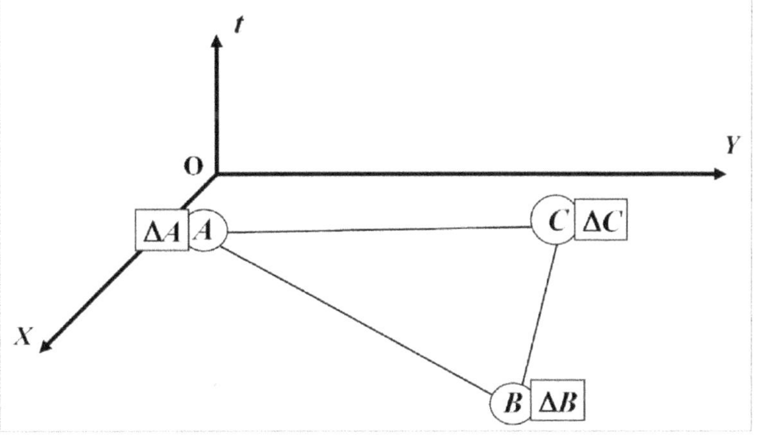

Within the framework of relation (1), the case of small inaccuracies of $\boldsymbol{\Delta A}$ and $\boldsymbol{\Delta B}$, i.e. at $\boldsymbol{\Delta A} \rightarrow 0$ and $\boldsymbol{\Delta B} \rightarrow 0$, in calculations of characteristics of ***A*** and ***B*** leads to complete uncertainty in calculating characteristic of ***C:***

$$\Delta C \geq \left. \frac{M}{\Delta A \times \Delta B} \right|_{\substack{\Delta A \to 0 \\ \Delta B \to 0}} \rightarrow \infty \qquad (2)$$

Analytically visual content of the phenomenon of the triangle dilemma, it is advisable to compare the corresponding graphic images. As mentioned above, figure 7 shows the graphical display of the Musgrave "triangle dilemma" phenomenon. Figure 7 illustrates the graphical image of the authors' vision of the practical resolution of the triangle dilemma.

For an adequate resolution of the "triangle dilemma" (the effective implementation by the state of its basic functions), the authors propose a cyclic change in the combined groups of functions at certain intervals of time. Obviously, this also cyclically changes the corresponding groups of functions, characterized by complete uncertainty.

In the XOY coordinate plane at the vertices of the Musgrave triangle, the conjugate groups of functions of ***(A)*** *allocative efficiency*, ***(B)*** *social equality (justice)*, and ***(C)*** *macroeconomic stability* are placed, which inevitably are subject to constraints in the form of uncertainties of $\boldsymbol{\Delta A}$, $\boldsymbol{\Delta B}$ and $\boldsymbol{\Delta C}$. The time axis **O*t*** is introduced for further consideration of modifications of triangles in the process of sequential resolution of the dilemma at different fixed points in time ***t***.

To achieve a balanced use of all groups of functions ***A, B,*** and ***C***, the authors propose the following scheme for resolving "the triangles dilemma" of Musgrave.

In the first stage (***t* = 1**) whenever possible, a complete realization of the group of functions ***A*** and the group of functions ***B*** is carried out, that is shown in Fig. 5 with double arrow between ***A*** and ***B***. Choosing the most complete intersection $\boldsymbol{A \cap B}$ introduces significant uncertainty values of $\boldsymbol{\Delta C} \rightarrow \infty$. In Fig. 8 this circumstance is represented by the symbol ***C*** in a black circle in combination with the symbol

Figure 7. Resolving "The Triangle Dilemma" of Musgrave as for the state basic functions
Source: Composed by authors

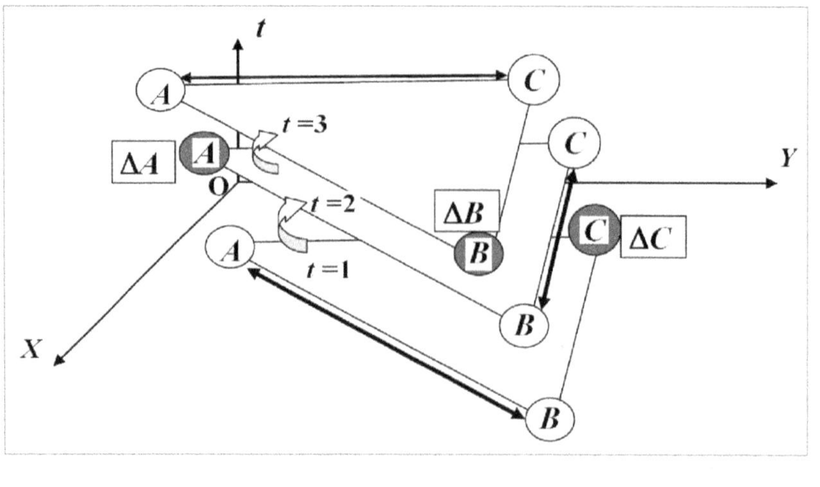

Δ*C*. When achieving acceptable results in the first stage, the transition to the second stage (***t* = 2**). This transition is indicated by an arrow from ***t* = 1** to ***t* = 2**. At the second stage, a cyclic transition from a pair combination of groups of functions ***A*** and ***B*** to the selection of a new pair of groups of functions ***B*** and ***C*** is performed. In Fig. 8 this selection is indicated by the corresponding arrow. In this case, the uncertainty of **Δ*C*** is removed, but instead, the uncertainty of **Δ*A*** appears, which is indicated in the same way as was done for the uncertainty of **Δ*C*** at the first stage. When a sufficiently complete realization of the combination of function group ***B*** and function group ***C*** is reached (due to the intersection of ***B*∩*C***), a new cyclic transition to the third stage (***t* = 3**) from the pair combination of function groups ***B*** and ***C*** to the choice of a new pair of function groups ***C*** and ***A*** (shown in Fig. 7 by a double arrow between ***C*** and ***A***). At this stage, the **Δ*A*** uncertainty is removed, but the uncertainty ***ΔB*** appears instead. Achieving an acceptable result at this stage means the possibility of a cyclical transition to a new stage, etc. The beginning and duration of the stages are fixed on the time axis **O*t***. The duration of the resolution of the "dilemma of triangle" of Musgrave could be significantly reduced if it was possible to start the multipliers' mechanism.

Thus, the comparison of the vectors of changes in the elasticity of GDP by income and by expenditure could be used to highlight those specific directions for spending budgets that give a real macroeconomic effect, that is, the fiscal multiplier in their case gives a value greater than zero. If, however, the item of budget expenditures is estimated by the fiscal multiplier at a level much greater than zero, then this direction of spending budget funds should increase. And its growth should be compensated by the reduction of inefficient expenditures from the point of view of macroeconomic returns. The conclusions confirm the results obtained by S. A. Vlasov, and E. B Deryugina (2018) in connection with fiscal multipliers and with the factors that determine their estimates. This could help to obtain the assessment of the degree of effectiveness of the state activity (implementation of state basic functions groups) in terms of safeguarding the public finance stability as well as the national economic growth as an indispensable condition for 'triangle dilemma' solution. In general, the overall effect of the budgetary measures implemented in the globe can be realized in providing 0.81% of the growth of the global economy with different contributions of tax and expenditure instruments: the fiscal multipliers used by the IMF for this estimate were 0.30.6 for state revenues, 0.51.8 for public investments, and 0.31.0 for other public expenditures (Spilimbergo, and et al., 2009).

In the course of recent research (Berg, et al., 2012; Berg, and Ostry, 2011a) it was found that, if the economic growth is considered in the long term, the dilemma between economic efficiency and social equality may disappear. In other words, ensuring sustainable growth lets the state to gradually solve the problem of social equality (justice). But these two goals, contradictory in their essence, which the state should pursue, at a certain ratio, can mutually ensure the achievement of each of them. According to the authors, the problem of the simultaneous impracticability of the three basic functions of the state could not be solved only in a short period.

Moreover, the effectiveness of the state in carrying out its function of equitable distribution of incomes is the most important determinant of the duration of economic growth. It has been empirically proven that income inequality (*social inequality (injustice)*) is distinguished by the strength of its connection with the duration of the economic growth periods: a 10-percentile decrease in inequality (represented by a change in the Gini coefficient from 40 to 37) increases the expected duration of the growth periods by 50 percent (Berg, and Ostry, 2011b). Moreover, each direction of social expenditures should be calculated from the point of view of (1) the economic effect of scale and (2) a delay in the implementation of this effect. As a result, it will be possible to differentiate the increase in budget expenditures for the three groups of basic functions of the state, based on the need to obtain faster or the possibility of waiting for a delayed (time-postponed) economic effect. This is a short-term alternative choice between the impact of the state on economic growth and income distribution. In this case, the author's approach allows using the Musgrave's "uncertainty" method to determine how to proceed. As a result, in the long run, this choice of combined pairs of basic state functions can harmonize the goals of reducing inequality and of sustainable growth as two sides of a single coin.

So, the problem of the public finance efficiency growth, due to the dual nature of the state which manifests itself in the contradiction of the state as a subject of management and at the same time as its object requires further research. And as the efficient public finance largely determines national sustainable economic growth the importance of this problem' solution is increasing due to their mutual influence. This is the author's vision of the destruction of the "inefficiency / low inefficiency trap".

CONCLUSION

So, the problem of slowing economic growth in the global space is predetermined by very many causes of external and internal origin, including in part the inefficiency of the public finance in the hand of the national state. This is proved by the conclusions obtained by the authors of empirical studies (Panizza and Presbitero, 2012, 2013; Presbitero, 2012; Egert, 2012, 2015). It has become central to this study due to its complexity and the presence of many unresolved issues related to the activities of the state in modern national economies. In recent years, the share of GDP redistributed by the state through the channels of public expenditure, income and servicing of public debt has increased significantly. As a result, the already significant scale of state influence on the dynamics of national economies has been constantly increasing in recent times. Consequently, the state and public finances bear a certain share of responsibility for the declining rates of economic development of their countries.

What is wrong with the state? The state is connected with society by its functions (budget expenditures), which were imputed to it for the purpose of maximizing utility for members of society. In order for them to be executed, the society redistributes part of the national income (GDP) in the form of tax payments to the state budget revenues. Since the share of revenues and expenditures of the budgets of national states vary from 20 to over 50% of GDP, from 1/5 to 1/2 of the responsibility for reducing the growth rate of macroeconomics, the state should assume. In other words, either GDP is ineffectively redistributed in the form of taxes to state budgets, or the government makes inefficient use of them in the form of expenditures on the needs of society.

The answers to these questions are based on a theoretical platform that interprets the essence of the state and its functions. Firstly, the state, being created as a megaregulator in society, initially contained a fundamental contradiction, which essentially predetermines its inefficiency. But originally it is designed to maximize social welfare. However, functionaries from the state will not objectively maximize it, since it is deprived of personal motivation. And this factor of inefficiency is most clearly manifested in the contradiction of the state, which, on the one hand, acts as a subject of management (mega-regulator), and, on the other hand, it functions as an object of management (economic agent). Externally, the form of expression of this fundamental contradiction of the state, which predetermines the inefficiency of public finances at its disposal, manifests itself in the phenomenon of corruption, informal (shadow) economics, and etc. Secondly, the three groups of conditionally distributed functions imputed to the state cannot, in principle, be simultaneously and effectively implemented. This was noticed by R. Musgrave (1998) describing this incompatibility in the triangle dilemma. In modern conditions, such inconsistency does not allow the state and society to realize itself as a self-organizing dialectical unity, which they essentially are, which negatively affects the macroeconomic dynamics.

The lessons of the crisis of 2007–2008 are concluded that the state should not expand the scope of its regulation, it should improve it. This is due to the fact that the crisis in the management of the economy as a whole as a result of the over-dependence of the economy on credit; assumptions and even the adoption of inflated (unrealistically high) housing prices, and in the case of the USA, Great Britain, Spain and a significant part of Eastern Europe - in excessive dependence on foreign capital, which allowed them to have huge deficits in the current account. To be effective, at least from the point of view of stimulating economic stability, a state must minimize its money requirements in the market and maintain the ratio of public debt to GDP at a low level. However, in almost all countries of the world, the state is clearly unable to cope with this, predetermining to a large extent the reduction in the rate of economic growth in the global space.

The study found that the negative impact of the state on macroeconomic dynamics through the inadequate use of a significant proportion of GDP, redistributed by society in favor of the state, and accompanying processes of concentration of current income and wealth of society in the hands of a few members to the detriment of low-income citizens, predetermined by fundamental duality (duality) of the state itself. Taking into account this objective reality, the state should be oriented in its activity towards indicators of the elasticity of public expenditures (functions of the state secured by public finances) according to GDP. This means that in order to get out of the inefficiency trap, public finances must adjust their scale in accordance with macroeconomic dynamics. In addition, in structuring their expenses, the state should bear in mind their different macroeconomic effects, both in terms of size and in time of receipt. And taking into account fiscal multipliers, the state, even being ineffective in its contradictory essence, can quite efficiently manage its public finances in order to ensure sustainable economic growth of its countries.

REFERENCES

Aghion, P., & Kharroubi, E. (2013). *Cyclical macroeconomic policy, financial regulation and economic growth.* BIS Working Paper, 434. Basel, Switzerland: Bank for International Settlements.

Alchian, A. A. (1984). Specifity, specialization, and coalitions. *Journal of Institutional and Theoretical Economics*, *140*(1), 6.

Angelopoupos, Philippopoulos, & Tsionas. (2008). Does public sector efficiency matter? Revisiting the relation between fiscal size and economic growth in world sample, *Public Choice, 137*(1-2), 245-278.

Arrow, K. J. (1970). Political and economic evaluation of social effects and externalities. In J. Margolis (Ed.), *The Analysis of Public Output*. New York: Columbia University Press.

Bastiat, F. (1864). *Oeuvres Completes* (Vols. 1–7). Paris: Guillaumin.

Bator, F. M. (1960). *The Question of Government Spending: Public Needs and Private Wants.* New York: Harper and Brothers.

Berg, A., Ostry, J. D., & Zettelmeyer, J. (2012). What makes growth sustained? *Journal of Development Economics*, *98*(2), 149–166. doi:10.1016/j.jdeveco.2011.08.002

Berg, A.G., & Ostry, J.D. (2011a). *Inequality and unsustainable growth: two sides of the same coin?* IMF Staff Discussion Note, No. 11/08.

Berg, A. G., & Ostry, J. D. (2011b). Equality and efficiency: Is there a trade-off between the two or do they go hand by hand. IMF. Finance & Development, 48(3), 12-15.

Bernanke, B. (2005). *The Global Savings Glut and the U.S. Current Account Deficit.* Remarks at the Homer Jones Lecture.

Bernanke, B. (2015). *Why Are Interest Rates So Low, Part 3: The Global Savings Glut.* Ben Bernanke's Blog.

Blanchard, O., & Summers, L. (2017). *Rethinking stabilization policy. Back to the future. Prepared for the "Rethinking macroeconomic policy" Conference.* Washington, DC: Peterson Institute for International Economics.

Bootle, R. P. (2009a). Redrawing. Rethinking the role of the state and markets. Finance & Development, 46(1), 34-35.

Bootle, R. P. (2009b). *The Trouble with Markets: Saving Capitalism from Itself.* London: Nicholas Brealey Publishing.

Checherita-Westphal, C., & Rother, P. (2012). The impact of high government debt on economic growth and its channels: An empirical investigation for the Euro Area. *European Economic Review*, *56*(7), 1392–1405. doi:10.1016/j.euroecorev.2012.06.007

Cingano, F. (2014). *Trends in income inequality and its impact on economic growth.* OECD Social, Employment and Migration Working Papers, No. 163. Retrieved from http: // www.oecd-ilibrary.org/docserver/download/5jxrjncwxv6j.pdf?expires=1439464823&id=id&accname=guest&checksum=EA020172B6EE209A3A7A70E3D3FC5D1F.

Cottarelli, C., & Jaramillo, L. (2013). Walking hand in hand: Fiscal policy and growth in advanced economies. *Review of Economics and Institutions*, *4*(2), 1–25. doi:10.5202/rei.v4i2.113

De Viti de Marko, A. (1936). First Principles of Public Finance. London: Jonathan Cape.

Égert, B. (2012). *Public debt, economic growth and nonlinear effects: myth or reality?* OECD Economics Department Working Papers, 993, October. OECD Publishing.

Égert, B. (2015). Public debt, economic growth and nonlinear effects: Myth or reality? *Journal of Macroeconomics*, *43*, 226–238. doi:10.1016/j.jmacro.2014.11.006

IMF Fiscal Monitor, (2018a, October). *Managing Public Wealth.* Washington, DC: IMF.

IMF Fiscal Monitor. (2018b, April). *Capitalizing on Good Times.* Washington, DC: IMF.

IMF Fiscal Monitor. (2019). *Curbing Corruption.* Washington, DC: IMF.

Friedman, M. (1962). *Capitalism and Freedom.* Chicago: Chicago University Press.

Garcia-Escribano, M., & Liu, C. Y. (2017). *Expenditure assessment tool (EAT). Fiscal Affairs Department Technical Notes and Manuals, 17/06*. Washington, DC: International Monetary Fund.

Guillemette, Y., & Turner, D. (2018). *The long view: scenarios for the world economy to 2060. OECD. Economic Policy Paper, May, No. 22*. Paris: OECD Publishing.

Hausmann, R., Pritchett, L., & Rodrik, D. (2005). Growth accelerations. *Journal of Economic Growth, 10*(4), 303–29.

Helpman, El. (2004). *The Mystery of Economic Growth*. Harvard University Press.

Hochman & Rodgers. (1969). Pareto optimal redistribution. *American Economic Review, 59*, 542-557.

Hodgson, G. M. (1988). *Economics and Institutions. A Manifesto for a Modern Institutional Economics*. Philadelphia, PA: University of Pennsylvania Press, Polity Press. doi:10.9783/9781512816952

International Monetary Fund (2019). *Global Financial Stability Report: Vulnerabilities in a Maturing Credit Cycle*. Washington, DC: IMF.

Keynes, J. M. (1936). *The General Theory of Employment, Interest and Money*. London: McMillan.

King & Rebelo. (1993). Transitional dynamics and economic growth in the neoclassical model. *American Economic Review, 83*, 908-931.

Marx, K. (1995). *Capital: A New Abridgement*. Oxford, UK: Oxford University Press.

McKinsey Global Institute. (2015). *Debt and (Not Much) Deleveraging*. February, McKinsey Global Institute.

Musgrave, R. (1959). *The Theory of Public Finance*. New York: McGrow-Hill.

Musgrave, R. (1998). The role of the state in the fiscal theory. In P. B. Sorensen (Ed.), *Public Finance in a Changing World* (pp. 35–50). London: Macmillan. PP. doi:10.1007/978-1-349-14336-8_2

Myrdal, G. (1954). *The Political Element in the Development of Economic Theory*. Cambridge, MA: Harvard University Press.

North, D. C. (1981). *Structure and Change in Economic History*. New York: W. W. Norton & Co.

North, D. C. (1990). *Institutions, Institutional Change and Economic Performance*. Cambridge, UK: Cambridge University Press. doi:10.1017/CBO9780511808678

Okun, A. M. (2015). *Equality and Efficiency: The Big Tradeoff*. Washington, DC: Brooking Institution Press.

Orsetta, C., Vindics, A., & Akgun, O. (2018). *An empirical investigation on the drivers of income redistribution across OECD countries*. OECD Economics Department Working Papers, No. 1488.

Panizza, U., & Presbitero, A. F. (2012). *Public debt and economic growth: is there a causal effect?* Mo.Fi.R. Working Papers, 65.

Panizza, U., & Presbitero, A. F. (2013). Public debt and economic growth in advanced economies: A survey. *Swiss Society of Economics and Statistics, 149*(2), 175–204. doi:10.1007/BF03399388

Pigou, A. (1924). *The Economics of Welfare* (2nd ed.). London: McMillan.

Piketty, T., Saez, E., & Zucman, G. (2016). *Distributional national accounts: methods and estimates for the United States.* NBER Working Paper Series, No. 22945.

Pilipenko, A., Dikhtiar, V., Baranova, N., & Pilipenko, Z. (2019). Financial stability: modeling the Russian budgetary and tax policy with fiscal multipliers' attraction. In S. S. Bruno (Ed.), *Modeling Economic Growth in Contemporary Russia* (pp. 63–92). London: Emerald Publishing Limited. doi:10.1108/978-1-78973-265-820191003

Posner, R. A. (2009). *A Failure of Capitalism.* Cambridge, MA: Harvard University Press.

Presbitero, A. F. (2012). Total public debt and growth in developing countries. *European Journal of Development Research, 24*(4), 606–626. doi:10.1057/ejdr.2011.62

Rawls, J. (1971). *A Theory of Justice.* Cambridge, MA: Belknap Press of Harvard University Press.

Ritter, G. (1996). Storia dello Stato Sociale. Rome: Laterza.

Schinasi, G. J. (2006). *Safeguarding Financial Stability: Theory and Practice.* Washington, DC: IMF.

Sen, A. (1979). Personal utilities and public judgments; or what is wrong with welfare economics? *Economic Journal, 89*, 537-589.

Solow, R. M. (1957). Technical change and the aggregate production function. *Review of Economics and Statistics, 39*, 312-320.

Spilimbergo, A., Symansky, S., & Schindler, M. (2009). *Fiscal multipliers.* IMF Staff Position Note, No. 11. Retrieved from http://www.imf.org/external/pubs/ft/spn/ 2009/spn0911.pdf

Tanzi & Schuknecht. (1997). Reconsidering the fiscal role of government: the international perspective. *American Economic Review, 87*, 164-168.

Tanzi & Schuknecht. (2000). *Public Spending in the 20th Century.* Cambridge, UK: Syndicate of the Press of the University of Cambridge.

Tanzi, V. (2011). *Government versus Markets: The Changing Economic Role of the State.* Cambridge, UK: Syndicate of the Press of the University of Cambridge.

Vlasov, S. A., & Deryugina, E. B. (2018). Fiscal multipliers in Russia. *Journal of the New Economic Association, 38*(2), 104-119.

Wagner, R.E. (1976). Revenue structure: fiscal illusion and budgetary choice. *Public Choice, 25*, 45-61.

ENDNOTE

1. Relation (1) echoes Werner Heisenberg's uncertainty principle, which resolves the dialectical contradiction of wave-particle duality in physics.

Chapter 10
Trade-Off Between Intergenerational Equity and Economic Growth:
Social and Financial Stability Puzzle

Nataliya Sergeevna Makarova
Russian State University Named After A. N. Kosygin, Russia

ABSTRACT

The global financial crisis of 2007-2008 posed the problems of the slowing world economy growth rates that predetermined the necessity to investigate a national economy's structural characteristics associated not so much with the objective, easily modeled factors of its development as with the subjective ones, difficult to be understood but increasing in importance. The latter is connected with inequity in the simultaneously living generations' perception, which is fueled by the trends of accelerated income polarization of the population, the middle-class reduction, and decreasing possibilities of achieving higher living standards for the socially vulnerable groups. All the above predetermines the behavior of economic agents in society and ultimately the prospects for the long-run economic growth in the country. The author conducted a model experiment with the dynamics of intergenerational equity and economic growth on the basis of the sub-martingale. The results show the growing importance of the human factor in ensuring the stable growth of the global economy.

1. INTRODUCTION

Society has always faced the problem of social choice between priorities related to ensuring equality of generations or economic growth (Okun, 2015). However, in modern conditions, it has become particularly acute with the slowdown in economic growth throughout the global space, increasing the life expectancy of people of retirement age, as well as increasing polarization of society due to faster growth of incomes of a few very rich members of society, on the one hand, and reducing the share both of the poor and the middle class in gross domestic product (GDP), on the other hand. Theoretically, there are three pos-

DOI: 10.4018/978-1-7998-1033-9.ch010

sible solutions to this problem: (1) an orientation towards stimulating economic growth by ignoring the "costs" of social justice, including intergenerational equity; (2) emphasis on ensuring intergenerational equity to the detriment of accelerated economic growth; and (3) the simultaneous combination of these priorities in varying proportions (Musgrave, 1998). However, in such dilemmas there can be no simple choice, since the main driver of economic acceleration in the future definitely becomes human capital represented by individuals. This means that without taking into account the motivational component of the latter, society cannot count on macroeconomic success. At the same time, the main factors determining the economic behavior of a person in society should include his individual assessment of social justice, related to the participation of society in the provision of older people pensions, in the upbringing and education of children, in social security of poor members of society, in the provision of health services, in helping the unemployed, and etc. And the importance of this social aspect in the context of forming a driver for future economic growth cannot be overestimated, since modern labor force feels the need to serve or not serve society through the prism of the prospects for its future old age and the ability to plan for the birth and upbringing of children in current conditions. So, in order to achieve stable economic growth and financial stability, it is necessary that all generations feel like a fair attitude of society (and the state) to themselves from birth to pension provision.

However, in the modern world, the number of problems in the relationship between society and individuals is increasing. Unemployment rates have declined in many parts of the world from post-financial crisis highs. But this macro improvement hides a worrying trend of persistent youth unemployment and underemployment in many parts of the world (WEF, 2018). Many of the opportunities that do exist lie in the "gig economy," offering flexible, short-term but largely unstable employment. Youth unemployment differs structurally from unemployment at more advanced ages. "Lost wages, lost savings, can be extremely difficult to recover later in life," said Christine Lagarde, Managing Director of the International Monetary Fund (WEF, 2018).

In any case, the understanding of justice from viewspoint of different generations is changing. However, the fact that current retirement benefits of old people is an example of the future for working youth remains unchanged. This predetermines the motivation of the behavior of the generations "Y" and "Z", the specifics of their social contract with the state, and, consequently, social, economic and financial stability or instability. It turns out that inequalities are different, and it is necessary to exclude their forms that destroy the economic and financial stability of society.

Unfortunately, in the modern world, there becomes evident such negative manifestation of injustice as polarization of income between the very rich and the very poor as well as the squeezed middle class (OECD, 2019). And the last is felt and interpreted the same way by all simultaneously living generations. Current findings reveal that the top 10% in the income distribution holds almost half of the total wealth. While the bottom 40% accounts for only 3%. The OECD (2019) has also documented that the natural result of such an "unfair" income polarization is the fact that economic insecurity concerns a large group of population: more than one in three people are economically vulnerable, meaning that they lack the liquid financial assets needed to maintain a living standard at the poverty level for at least three months.

The experts of the World Economic Forum (World Economic Forum, 2018) created the most promising indicator called Inclusive Development Index (IDI). It relates to the evaluation of the intergenerational equity in a country in connection with national economic growth sustainability. It deals, in particular, with national existing pension system' quality, which directly links the elderly and young family members and predetermines informal institutions' quality, regulating the economic agents behavior in the society. The OECD report (OECD, 20I8a) makes a key contribution to the OECD's Inclusive Growth initiative and its effort to develop a "people-centred inclusive growth model"' in which well-being is the metric of success: where everyone has an equal opportunity to prosper; and where equity considerations are important in defining effective economic policies. In this mixture of the problems of personal reflecting justice in society, the place of the middle class becomes the central determining the individual behavior. The investment of the middle class in education, health, and housing, their support for good quality public services, their intolerance of corruption, and their trust in others and in democratic institutions, are the very foundations of sustainable economic growth. A strong middle class is also essential to properly fund social protection and lift millions of families out of poverty. The most promising in this regard is the institutional aspect associated with the interaction of formal and informal institutions (Hodgson, 1988). It is their causal interrelationship that predetermines both the intergenerational equity and economic growth (EBRD, 2018). Now there is the stage of the scientific investigation of the subjective factors of the contemporary economies' growth in connection with the informal institutions, which are evaluated with the help of indicators of intergenerational equity and macroeconomic growth sustainability. In this connection, the published works of the following authors are of great interest: J. Gruber, K. Milligan, and D.A. Wise (2009); T.M. Maleva (2014); J.W. Buckholtz, and R. Marois (2012); C.-Y. Chiu, M. J. Gelfand, T. Yamagishi, G. Shteynberg, and C. Wan (2010).

For some time now, it has begun appearing assessments of the intergenerational equity as a major factor of the economic stability and financial sustainability of countries (OECD, 2008; Berg, et al., 2011). It should be emphasized that this is not just about growth, which can be short-term and not giving a real long-term macroeconomic effect. And long-term growth is ensured by more than one generation, therefore, for sustainable long-term economic development, awareness of justice in the context of the continuity of generations takes on particular importance. In this regard, public finance and the effectiveness of their redistributive function come out on top. As a result, the central problem is not economic growth per se, but the efficiency of the distribution of GDP and national income through public finance channels. It is an adequate redistribution of GDP from the point of view of ensuring a sense of justice between generations that can ensure the stability of economic development and the sustainability of national finances in the long term.

The aim of the study is to formulate an author's approach to the interpretation of the value orientations of individuals as the main motivational aspects in the process of turning human capital into the main driver of stable economic growth in the future. The author's hypothesis of solving the "social and financial stability puzzle" is based on the idea that the growth of social budget expenditures can only keep the level of poverty unchanged, but not necessarily ensure the stability of economic development But the sense of justice, most clearly manifested in the assessment of equality between generations by the people themselves, gives a long-term economic return. The latter can be achieved through the adequate institutionalization by the state of formal and informal relations in society.

But a number of recent OECD reports have highlighted structural inequalities that persist in social and economic outcomes in various domains. The evidence suggests that income inequality has increased in three quarters of the OECD countries over the past three decades and remains even higher in most emerging economics, albeit declining in some (OECD, 2011). High and persistent income inequalities have negative consequences not only for social cohesion in our societies but also for economic growth to the extent they undermine the opportunities to access quality education and health services as well as good jobs. Many middle-income households race a considerable risk of sliding down into the lower-income class: one-in-seven households in the middle 60% of the income distribution and one-in-five of those living in the second-lowest income quintile slide into the bottom 20% over a four-year period.

These risks have increased over the past two decades in main OECD countries (OECD, 2018b). Three decades ago, the aggregate income of all middle-income households was four times the aggregate income of upper income households, i.e. those with incomes above two times the national median: today, this ratio is less than three (Saez, 2018). Therefore, the economic influence of the middle class and its role as "centre of economic gravity" has weakened. In this interpretation the problem of the sustainable economic growth is strictly connected with the interdependence of formal and informal institutions. And sustainability of macroeconomic growth will be ensured only under the condition that informal institutions, in fact, determining the continuity of generations in the understanding of justice, will ensure high public confidence in the state and its social policy.

The chapter is organised as follows. Section 1 represents Introduction. In Section 2 – methodology – it has been presented a revision of the investigations dealing with the public choice between the intergenerational equity and economic growth that let the author reduce this issue to interrelated problems: the theoretical description of manifestation forms of inequality and injustice from the viewpoint of different generations from the view point of institutional approach; the description of the interdependence of reducing the middle class and limiting the social lifting possibilities: objectification of an individual idea of injustice in society. After the assessment of interdependencies of intergenerational equity and economic growth there are discussed the preferences of institutional support or budget spending in connection with the relationship of social and financial stability. As a result, it was justified that only taking into account the new scientific research, it is advisable to develop and implement socio-economic policies as an effective set of informal and formal institutions that can ensure the sustainability of macroeconomic growth at the national level in the long term, given the priority of state activities aimed at implementing the principles of equality and equity (including intergenerational).

Analytical part of the chapter is devoted to the modeling of structural interdependences of categories of intergenerational equity and macroeconomic growth including the public finance sustainability. It deals, in particular, with national existing pension system' quality, which directly links the elderly and young family members and predetermined informal institutions' quality, regulating the economic agents behavior in the society. Based on the random walk hypothesis (Brownian motion), a sub-martingale model was constructed to describe and compare the indicators of the dynamics of intergenerational equity and of sustainable macroeconomic growth. The corresponding model experiment with random changes in the dynamics of intergenerational equity and macroeconomic growth sustainability showed that, within the limits of acceptable variation of the Gini coefficient, steady growth of GDP could be achieved.

The last part of the chapter shows the conclusions.

METHODOLOGY

Scientific Researches Covering the Public Choice: Intergenerational Equity or Economic Growth

To prove the validity of the author's hypothesis, it is necessary to understand whether there is a relationship between social aspects that predetermine the behavior of individuals and economic dynamics. Back in 1975, Artur M. Okun (Okun, 2015) posed the problem of equality and efficiency as a dilemma. He argued that both a more even income distribution reduces incentives for more efficient work and investment, and the actions of the state in connection with taxation and wage regulation violate the sustainability of the economy and public finances. As a result, he determined the need for public choice: either in favor of efficient production through the equitable distribution of wealth and income, or vice versa.

The opinion that inequality favorably affects economic growth has been dominant until recently. The main reason for this was that for a long time it was investments and physical capital that played a dominant role in stable economic growth. Really, the economic growth matters because it measures an important component of social progress—namely, economic welfare, or how much benefit members of society get from the way resources are used and allocated. A look at GDP per capita over the long haul tells the story of innovation and escape from the Malthusian trap of improvement in living standards that is inevitably limited by population growth (Coyle, 2017). Until the mid-1980s the income distribution in most OECD countries did not change much and ignoring this issue mattered very little (Zhang, 2017).

However, after the crisis of 2007-2008, much has changed. As global economic growth slowed down, the inadequacy of the GDP indicator for the purposes of assessing the real socio-economic progress of society became apparent. GDP growth is instrumentally important as well. It is closely correlated with the availability of jobs and income, which are in themselves vital to people's standard of living and underpin their ability to achieve the kind of life they value (Sen, 1999). GDP measures the monetary value of final goods and services—that is, those that are bought by the final user—produced and consumed in a country in a given period of time. The limit of GDP as a measure of economic welfare is that it records, largely, monetary transactions at their market prices. This is why economists and statisticians have been working to introduce estimates of natural capital and its rate of loss (World Bank, 2016). When they do, it will be clear that sustainable GDP growth (that enables future generations to consume at least as much as people today) is lower than GDP growth recorded over many years.

Charles I. Jones and Peter J. Klenow (2016) have proposed a single measure incorporating consumption, leisure, mortality, and inequality. Their calculations show that this approach closes much of the apparent gap in living standards between the United States and other OECD countries when this is assessed on the basis of GDP per capita (Jones, and Klenow, 2016). These measures, extending the standard national accounts approach in a way that at least takes inequality into account, address some of the challenges to gauging GDP, but not all.

At present, the most important shifts in the structure of factors of stable economic growth have become obvious. They are predetermined by the specifics of technological changes, which the farther, the more demand will be placed on human capital as the main driver of economic acceleration in the future. This could not but determine the growing importance of such social aspects related to the carriers of human capital, as their understanding of "equality" and "equity" (justice) (Rawls, 1971). A number of researchers have paid attention to the fact that the replacement of physical capital by human capital accumulation turns the last into a prime engine of growth along the process of development (Galor, and Moav, 2004). And in this regard, the behavioral aspect of the individual is decisive for the social stability of society as a reflection of his perception of society and the assessment of his attitude to himself. As a result, the notions of equality and justice from the point of view of different generations living at the same time become the key factor that will allow them to be included as a driving force of economic and financial stability in the long term, provided that the state creates corresponding formal institutions. It is in this context that it becomes possible to understand the phenomenon of the transformation of individual ideas about equality and justice (equity) in society into a real factor of ensuring high rates of economic growth in the future. Hypothetically, it can be assumed that the differences between countries with rapid development over many years or even decades and many others that have not been able to keep bursts of growth are determined by the level of inequality in society. If the hypothesis is correct, then equity in distribution of income should take a crucial place among the key determinants of sustained economic growth and financial stability of the society.

Thomas Piketty (2013) became one of the first to attract attention to the investigation of the process of growing income gap between very rich and very poor strata of the population all over the world. Thanks to his publication or to the populist movements springing up in many countries nobody has been ignoring distributional questions anymore. Besides the tendencies of the global economic stagnation has become stable and this situation makes the scientists and policy-makers rethink the factors of future development. Taking into account the disintegration attempts in the globe the scientific interest to the inclusive long term sustainable development of the country becomes clear. It is not surprising that the Report 2018, prepared by the World Economic Forum' staff (WEF, 2018), has raised a set of difficult and increasingly urgent questions of whether a secular correction is required in the existing economic model in order to counteract economic stagnation in the parameters of chronic low growth and rising inequality. Over the past several years governments, business, and other leaders from every region all over the world have come to consensus on the need for a more sustainable economic development model by increasing the importance of the human factor, given its motivational component. And the latter is associated with a sense of fairness in the relationship between generations and the state representing the whole society. But now sustainable inclusive growth of a national economy remains more a discussion topic than an action agenda (WEF, 2018). And this is due to the fact that the transformation into a real action is connected with the activities of the state and the implementation of its social obligations through the redistribution of GDP created by society.

Manifestation Forms of Inequality and Injustice from the Viewpoint of Different Generations

Deepening into the problems of social aspects of human behavior forced the author to identify specific forms of injustice in the understanding of different generations of young people. Addressing the category of intergenerational equity today is all the more important in light of the prospect of less favorable global economic conditions. In the face of new technological challenges sustainable economic growth is associated with a more equitable sharing of the benefits of increased prosperity, decent-paying jobs, equal employment and education opportunities, and improved access to and provision of health care and financial services. As a result, compared with the developed economy, emerging markets experience a large difference in incomes and higher poverty access to key social services, such as health care and finance. This significantly limits these countries in terms of using human capital as a driver for sustainable economic growth in future. Everything must be done to create a sense of justice (equality and equity) in people not only because it is the morally right thing to do, but also because it is critical for achieving sustainable strong growth.

But the events of recent years testify to the strengthening of inequality processes in national communities. Current findings of the OECD team (OECD, 2019) reveal that the top 10% in the world income distribution holds almost half of the total wealth, while the bottom 40% accounts for only 3%. As a result economic insecurity concerns a large group of the population: more than one in three people are economically vulnerable, meaning they lack the liquid financial assets needed to maintain a living standard at the poverty level for at least three months. It follows that one of the three representatives of society feels a sense of injustice in relation to itself, which really excludes them from the potential of drivers of stable economic growth. Growing inequality in society entails significant social and political costs. However, everything is much more serious, since growing inequality causes great economic problems both for the poor themselves and for the sustainability of the entire national economy and public finance. Moreover, these trends are compounded. The last crisis period also saw a marked rise in income poverty in OECD countries especially when measured in terms of "anchored" poverty compared to the established real minimum level of profitability before crisis. This leads to the idea of absolute changes in the living standards of the poor than the more commonly used "relative" measure of poverty, because the benchmark also changes. Generally between 2007 and 2011, the OECD anchored poverty rate rose by just over one percentage point to 9.4% (Figure 1).

Over the past three decades cyclical factors have played a role as well, as steep drops in income during downturns lead to scarring and longer-term disadvantage when social policies are insufficiently counter-cyclical (OECD, 2014a). In the 1980s, the richest 10% of the population earned seven times more than the poorest 10%; today they earn almost ten times more. In broad terms, this long-term trend has been driven by two main movements: at the top end, and especially among the top 1%, a surge in incomes; at the bottom end, much slower income growth during good times and often a fall in incomes in bad times, especially during and after the Great Recession. The Gini coefficient of income inequality stood at 0.29, on average, across OECD countries in the mid-1980s.

But by 2013, it had increased by about ten percent or 3 points to 0.32, rising in 17 of the 22 OECD countries for which long-time series are available1 (Figure 2) (OECD, 2015). Trends differed by age groups and the working-age population often bore the brunt of inequality increases.

Figure 1. Income inequality varies greatly across OECD countries and emerging economies. Level of income inequality (Gini coefficient), 2013 or latest available year

Source: OECD Income Distribution Database (IDD), www.oecd.org/social/income-distribution-atabase.htm, for OECD countries, Latvia, Russian Federation and Colombia. World Bank, Poverty and Inequality Database for India. Statistics Indonesia (Susenas) for Indonesia. SEDLAC database for Argentina and Brazil. National Bureau of Statistics of China for China. National Income Dynamics Survey (NIDS) from Finn, and Leibbrandt, 2013; OECD, 2015. Note: Data refer to 2014 for China, 2013 for Finland, Hungary, Netherlands and the United States and India, 2011 for Canada, Chile, Israel, Turkey and Brazil, 2010 for Indonesia, 2009 for Japan, and 2012 for the other countries. Data from secondary data sources are not strictly comparable and should be interpreted with caution. Gini coefficients are based on equivalised incomes for OECD countries, Colombia, Latvia and the Russian Federation; per-capita incomes for other countries; and per-capita consumption for India and Indonesia.

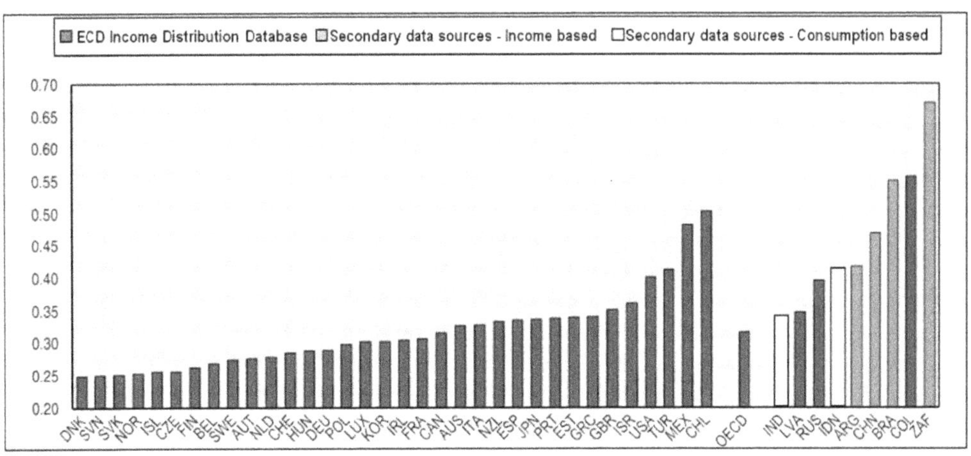

Gender disparities persist worldwide and are still particularly large in some regions. When indicators of disparities of opportunity with respect to education, health, financial access, and legal rights are taken into account, Europe appears to be the most gender-equal region, the Asia and Pacific region and the Western Hemisphere follow, and sub-Saharan Africa and the Middle East remain the regions with the highest gender inequality (Figure 3).

These various dimensions of gender-based inequality have major macroeconomic implications. For example, gender equality is positively associated with a country's per capita GDP and its level of competitiveness (World Economic Forum, 2014, Duflo, 2012). Gender gaps in economic participation restrict the pool of talent in the labor market and can thus result in total factor productivity losses (Cuberes, and Teignier, 2016; Esteve-Volart, 2004). Wider gender gaps also go hand-in-hand with broader inequality of income. C. Gonzales and others (2017) document the strong association between gender-based economic inequalities and a more unequal overall income distribution. They find that for advanced economies—with more equal economic opportunities across sexes—income inequality arises mainly through gender gaps in economic participation. In emerging market and low-income countries, inequality of opportunity, in particular, gender gaps in education, political empowerment, and health, appears to pose the main obstacle to a more equal income distribution.

It is this problem that scientists and practitioners have fixed, investigating the phenomenon of polarization of national communities as to concentration of current incomes and accumulated wealth. It is these consequences of the decline in GDP growth rates in the world recorded by Filip Novokmet and his co-authors (Novokmet, et al., 2017) (Figure 4) and began being used in publications as evidence of the ineffectiveness of the state's activities to ensure high social standards of public life.

In the current context, the gap between rich and poor in the most OECD countries has reached its highest level for the past 30 years. In the modern world, 10% of the richest citizens of the OECD countries earn 9.5 times more than 10% of the poorest segments of the population. Inequality has been growing

Figure 2. Income inequality increased in most OECD countries. Gini coefficients of income inequality, mid-1980s and 2013, or latest available year

Source: OECD Income Distribution Database (IDD), available at: www.oecd.org/social/income-distribution-database.htm; OECD, 2015. Note: "Little change" in inequality refers to changes of less than 1.5 percentage points. Data year for 2013 (or latest year): see Figure 1. These values differ slightly from those in Figure 1. for some countries as they have been adjusted to be comparable with 1985 values.

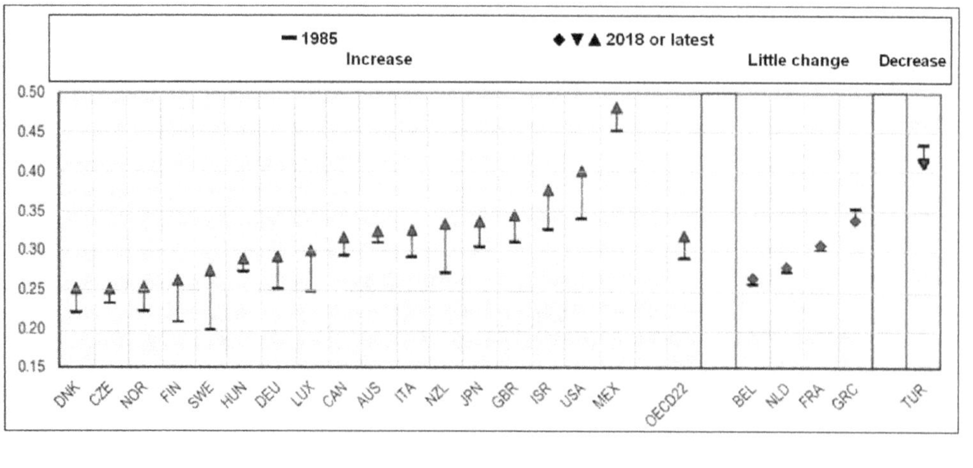

Figure 3. Gender Inequality Measures, 2015
Source: IMF staff calculations; IMF, 2017; Jain-Chandra, et al., 2017.

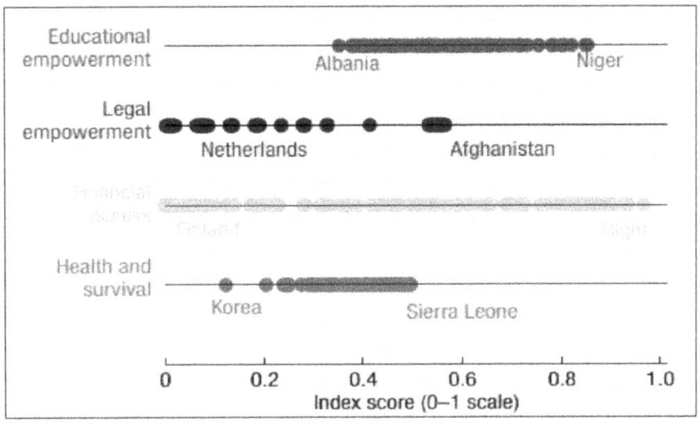

steadily since 1980, when this ratio was 7:1. However, the increase in general income inequality is not only related to the growth of incomes of the richest citizens. More often, incomes of low-income segments of the population grew significantly slower in the years of economic prosperity and decreased much more rapidly during crisis, thus actualizing the problem of relative (and in some countries and absolute) poverty. Moreover, this tendency directly concerns the state and its fulfillment of the function of ensuring social justice (Cingano, 2014). This problem is most acute in emerging markets. Thus, over the 20 years from 1995 to 2015, top 10% wealth share' changes in USA, France were more or less smooth in nature, varying within the range of 5-8% changes. As for Russia, these changes are characterized by considerable volatility: so, only for 5 years from 1995 to 1999 top 10% wealth share grew from about 53% to 66%. And this despite the severe crisis in Russia in 1998, which, judging by the Figure 4, was used to redistribute the national wealth and concentrate it at the disposal of a few. As compared with 1995 the growth of top 10% wealth share in 2015 amounts to almost 20%. It should be noted that since the post-crisis 2009, the top 10% wealth share has grown steadily, which has led to an increase of 10% by 2015 to 72%. And in 2015 parameters of top 10% wealth share in USA and Russia almost equalized and amounted to 73 and 72% accordingly.

As a whole, over the past 30 years, median incomes increased a third less than the average income of the richest 10%. Moreover, in some countries the share of incomes at the very top has surged: in the United States, for example, the share of top 1% on total income has almost doubled from about 11% to 20% over the past three decades and almost half of all income growth over this period accrued to this group (Förster, et al., 2014; Saez, 2018). Three decades ago, the aggregate income of all middle-income households was four times the aggregate income of upper income households, i.e. those with incomes above two times the national median: today, this ratio is less than three (Saez, 2018). Thus, the increasing tendency of unequal income distribution in national societies and of the concentration of wealth in the hands of a few of its representatives led to a phenomenal change in the functions of the middle class. Therefore, the economic influence of the middle class and its role as "centre of economic gravity" has weakened.

Figure 4. Top 10% wealth share' changes in USA, France, China and Russia in 1995-2015
Source: Novokmet, and et al. (2017, Table 12c) Note: Distribution of personal wealth among adults. Estimates obtained by combining Forbes billionaire data for Russia, generalized Pareto interpolation techniques and normalized WID. World wealth distributions.

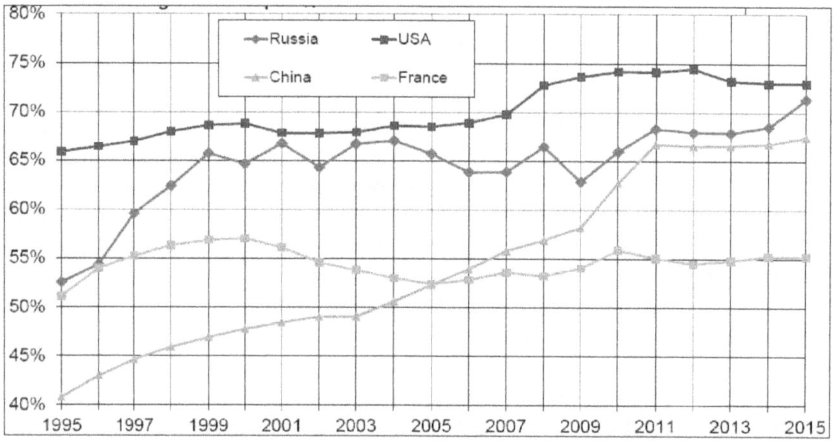

Reducing the Middle Class and Limiting the Social Lifting Possibilities: Objectification of an Individual Idea of Injustice in Society

The result of the study of the problem of injustice among the generations of X, Y, Z became a modeling description of social ladder that takes form of reaching the standard of living of the middle class. It is advisable to single out the main social stratum, which began to squeeze as a result of the increasing polarization of the incomes of the rich and the poor. This will allow objectifying the phenomenon of injustice in people's assessments. It turned out that over the past 30 years, the increasing trend of increasing concentration of income in the hands of a few was due to stagnation or braking income growth of the middle-income households. Thus, it becomes precisely the middle class that has objectified the assessment of the injustice of the socio-economic system. And these estimates are based on a comparison of the middle class benefits from economic growth and its contribution to the provision of the latter. A clear disproportion between the last indicators in the case of the middle class is manifested in the deterioration of its position in society. And this, in turn, objectifies evaluations of injustice as they are subjectivized by representatives of the middle class.

Since the mid-1980s, middle incomes have grown significantly less than higher incomes, and the global financial crisis exacerbated this trend further. Between 2007 and 2016 the annual growth rate of real median incomes was 0.3% on average across OECD countries, compared to 1% between the mid-1980s and mid-1990s, and 1.6% between the mid-1990s and mid-2000s - a period when income growth was strongest among all income groups (OECD, 2019). Households with 20 to 40% of the median income fared even worse, especially since the early 2000s (Figure 5).

Across the OECD area, except for a few countries, middle incomes are barely higher today than they were ten years ago. Furthermore, the cost of living has become increasingly *expensive* for the middle class, as the cost of core services and goods such as housing have risen faster than income. Traditional middle-class opportunities for social mobility have also withered as labour market prospects become

Figure 5. Median incomes grew more slowly than top incomes. Real disposable income growth by income position, average for 17 OECD countries, 1985-2016(1985 -100%)
Source: OECD (2019). Under Pressure: The Squeezed middle Class. Paris: OECD Publishing. Note: Unweighted average for I7 countries for which long-term data are available: Canada, Germany, Denmark, Finland, France, United Kingdom, Greece, Israel, Italy, Japan, Luxembourg, Mexico, Netherlands, Norway, New Zealand, Sweden and United States. Incomes are disposable incomes, corrected for household size.

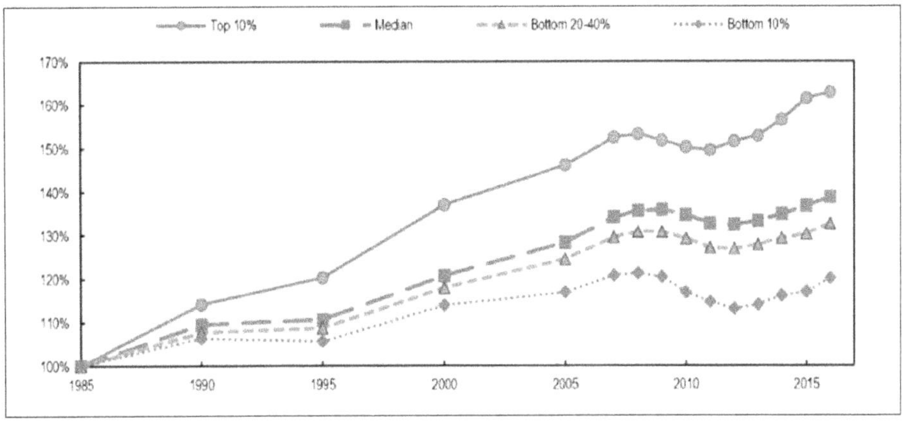

increasingly uncertain: one in six middle-income workers is in jobs that are at high risk of automation. Uncertain of its prospects, the middle class is also concerned about those of their children; the current generation is one of the most educated, and yet has lower chances of achieving the same standard of living as its parents. Moreover, the standard of living of the middle class predetermines a model of life success and achievable opportunities for low and middle-income families. The latter used to be an aspiration. For many generations it meant the assurance of living in a comfortable house and affording a rewarding lifestyle, thanks to a stable job with career opportunities. This is about their employment, consumption, wealth and debt, as well as perceptions and social attitudes. It is also a basis from which families aspire to an even better future for their children. It gives energy to their representatives to move up the social ladder. But opportunities for low and middle-income families to move up the ladder became limited over the past decades. Moreover, many middle-class families faced a growing risk of falling down to a lower income or a lower status: the share of people in the middle income group has declined over time, especially among the new generations, and that the cost of a middle class lifestyle is rising faster than middle incomes. Under these conditions, the reduction of the middle class indicates the impossibility for the lower social groups to realize the possibilities of social upgrade and makes sustainable the feeling of inequality and injustice in society.

Meanwhile the investment of the middle class in education, health, and housing, their support for good quality public services, their intolerance of corruption, and their trust in others and in democratic institutions, are the very foundations of inclusive growth. A strong middle class is also essential to support sustained productivity growth and to properly fund social protection and lift millions of families out of poverty. As a result, in the modern world, a sense of injustice is being intensified by all simultaneously living generations (Novokmet, et al., 2017). Making the rich richer, while incomes of the bottom 40% remain flat, could be seen as sensible from an economic perspective – after all, some are better off, and none are worse off. However, policies which lead to this outcome may not be even economically sensible if wider inequality reduces the capacity of the bottom 40% to improve their position and that of their children in the future

Research inside and outside the IMF has shown that high levels of inequality tend to reduce the pace and durability of growth. In this connection policymakers should not be afraid to adopt measures that ensure shared prosperity, including ones that redistribute wealth (OECD, 2008, 2011; T. Zhang, 2017). So it will be important for the state to ensure that growth's benefits are shared equitably. Failure to do so risks increasing political and social instability, stifling investment in human and physical capital, and eroding support for structural reforms—which would impede the sustained growth that emerging markets need to achieve high-income status. High and persistent income inequalities have negative consequences not only for social cohesion in our societies but also for economic growth to the extent they undermine the opportunities to access quality education and health services as well as good jobs.

Intergenerational Equity and Economic Growth: Assessment of Interdependencies

The above 3 stages of development of the author's hypothesis make it possible to determine the relationship between intergenerational equity and economic growth. Fundamentally, rising uncertainty stems from fewer opportunities to climb up the ladder for middle-class people and their children than in the past and higher risks to slide down. Social mobility at different stages of life is limited: education attainments, occupational status, earnings, and even health status are very persistent across generations. Two fifths of the earnings differences between fathers carry over to the next generation (OECD, 2018b). Many middle-income households face a considerable *risk of sliding down* into the lower-income class: one-in-seven households in the middle 60% of the income distribution and one-in-five of those living in the second lowest income quintile slide into the bottom 20% over a four-year period (OECD, 2019). These risks have increased over the past two decades in many OECD countries. At the same time, more affluent middle-income households have somewhat lower risks today. This indicates a rising chance of fracturing among the middle-income class (OECD, 2018b), which will negatively affect long-term economic prospects.

A.M. Okun (2015) would recognize that stagnation in middle-class incomes is a central issue for democracies. He would emphasize the importance of a constructive supply-side agenda that embraces the development of human capital, scientific knowledge, public infrastructure, and business investment. Not by chance the OECD team makes a key contribution to the OECD's Inclusive Growth initiative aiming at developing a "people-centred inclusive growth model" in which well-being is the metric of success: where everyone has an equal opportunity to prosper; and where equity considerations are important in defining effective economic policies (OECD. 20I8a). In fact, this study confirms the idea that it should not be considered as an alternative (irreconcilable) public choice in favor of ensuring a fair distribution of wealth and income in society, on the one hand, or in favor of generating economic growth, on the other. A number of researchers (Berg, Ostry, and Zettelmeyer, 2011; Berg and Ostry, 2011, Ostry, 2011) argue that, provided economic growth in the long term, dilemmas of efficiency and equality may not exist. In other words, equality should be seen as an important component of supporting long-term economic growth (Berg, and Ostry, 2011).

On the theoretical side, many channels through which inequality affects growth in opposite ways are presented by Gustavo A. Marrero and Juan G. Rodríguez (2016). There are several routes through which inequality might have a negative effect on growth:

1. The rich have a higher marginal propensity to save but they make many unproductive investments (Mason 1988);
2. The poor people consume more local goods, so their declining demand hinders the national economic growth (Marshall 1988);
3. High levels of inequality provoke large distortionary taxes and, therefore, less private investments and growth (Alesina, and Rodrik 1994; Alesina, and Perotti 1994; Persson, and Tabellini 1994);
4. Political instability and violence are typically fed by high levels of inequality, which harms growth (Gupta 1990);
5. Rent-seeking activities generate a clear miss-allocation of resources and thus inequality of opportunity (because certain profitable activities are not developed by the most talented individuals but those with better social contacts), which deters future growth (Stiglitz, 2012).

Besides inequality in the presence of credit market imperfections would have a negative impact on growth through the investment in human capital channel (Galor, and Zeira, 1993) and the entrepreneurial channel (Banerjee, and Newman, 1993). Voitchovsky (2005) estimates inequality among the poor (the 50/10 ratio) and finds that inequality among the poor deters growth because of the existence of constraints in the credit market and political instability.

As shown in Cingano, F. (2014) the Solow model implies that the growth of GDP depends on (increases with) its distance from the steady state, to which it converges at a constant rate (the speed of convergence). The steady state of GDP is in turn a function of underlying determinants including human and physical capital and, in the current application, inequality. According to his estimates (Cingano, 2014), a 1 Gini point reduction in inequality would raise average growth by slightly more than 0.1 percentage points per year, with a cumulative gain in GDP at the end of the period of around 3%. Figure 6 shows the estimated impact on the 1990-2010 growth rate of GDP of changes in inequality occurred between 1985 and 2005 (the most recent inequality trends are not taken into account as they affect future growth patterns).

For each country, it also reports the actual rate of growth and a counterfactual figure, obtained subtracting the estimated impact of inequality from actual growth. All the above is to be interpreted as the growth rate that would have been observed in the country had inequality not changed (and holding all other variables constant). Rising inequality is estimated to have knocked more than 10 percentage points off growth in Mexico and New Zealand. In the United States, the United Kingdom, Sweden, Finland and Norway, the growth rate would have been more than one fifth higher had income disparities not widened (Berg, and Ostry, 2011). On the other hand, greater equality helped increase GDP per capita in Spain, France and Ireland prior to the crisis.

There are many scientific researches, describing the negative influence of inequality on the economic performance (growth, employment, allocation). G.A. Marrero, and J.G. Rodriguez, (2010, 2012, 2013, 2015, 2016) found robust evidence of the hypothesis that the impact of overall inequality on economic performance is ambiguous because the two main components of inequality may have opposite effects on economic growth: inequality of opportunity (IO) - negative and inequality of effort (IE) - positive (Marrero, and Rodríguez, 2013). According to their estimations, increasing IE by one standard deviation could raise decade growth between 2.3 and 4.1 percentage points depending on the method (the average decade growth in the 1970–2000 period was 20.2 percent), and between 209 and 834 real U.S. dollars per person (the average income in the 1970–2000 period was 14,363 U.S. dollars per person). Meanwhile, decreasing IO by one standard deviation could raise growth between 1.1 and 1.7 percentage points and steady-state income between 124 and 229 real U.S. dollars per person (Marrero, and Rodríguez, 2015).

Figure 6. Estimated consequences of changes in inequality on cumulative per capita GDP growth (1990-2010). (Growth rate, in percentages)

Source: Cingano, F. (2014). 'Trends in income inequality and its impact on economic growth.' OECD Social, Employment, and Migration Working Papers, No. 163. Note: There are the estimated consequences of changes in inequality (observed in 1985-2005) on the cumulative growth rate of GDP per capita over the period 1990-2010. GDP per capita is computed relative to the population aged 25-64. "Actual" is the actual growth rate; "Impact of inequality" is obtained based on the observed changes in inequality across OECD countries (in 1985-2005) and the impact of inequality on growth estimated in the analysis; "Counterfactual" the difference "Actual - Impact of inequality". Actual growth in Germany is computed starting in 1991; the changes in inequality are limited to the period 1985-2000 in the case of Austria, Belgium, Spain and Ireland.

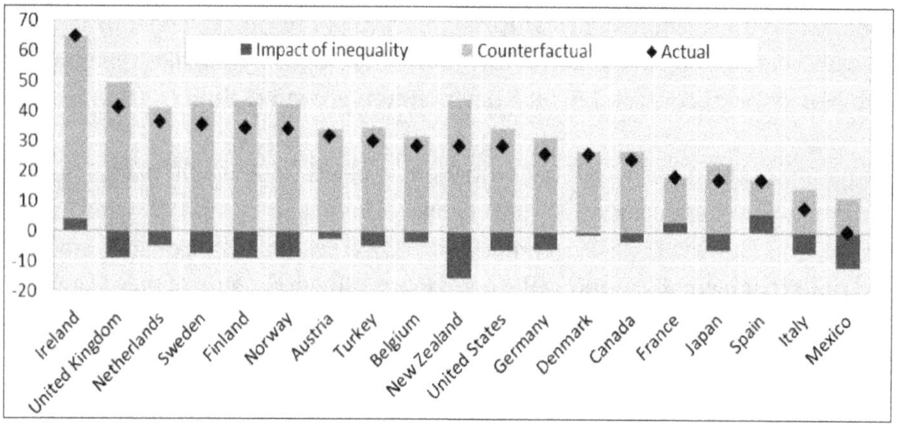

For illustrative purposes, Gustavo A. Marrero and Juan G. Rodríguez (2013) show the main intuition of the results (Figure 7) for the case of the United States.

The Figure 7 shows the relationship of inequality of opportunity and the growth, which is clearly negative. As a result Marrero, Gustavo A., and Juan G. Rodríguez (2016) prove that the impact of overall inequality on economic performance is ambiguous because the two main components of inequality have opposite effects on growth: IO (inequality of opportunity) negative and IE (inequality of effort) positive.

A variety of different channels via which inequality could affect growth have been suggested over the years. An aging population and slower labor force growth affect economies in many ways—the growth of GDP slows, working-age people pay more to support the elderly and public budgets strain under the burden of the higher total cost of health and retirement programs for old people. Yet an aging population may raise the amount of capital per worker, which would boost wages and output per hour worked (productivity) and reduce interest rates as higher wages lower the return on capital (Lee, and Mason, 2017). But individual well-being depends not on aggregate, but on per capita, growth. Standard growth models predict that slower population growth also leads to rising output and wages per worker.

The underlying question is whether this higher output per worker will translate into higher per capita income. That will depend on how much, as the population ages, increased productivity offsets the rise in the number of dependents (old and young) per worker (Lee, and Mason, 2011; United Nations, 2013). The former US Treasury Secretary Lawrence Summers argued that over the past decade and a half, economic development has been hampered by "a significant increase in the propensity to save and a substantial decrease in the propensity to spend and invest" - these factors kept equilibrium interest rates and economic growth at a low level. From his viewpoint to warn egalitarians that redistribution of a rapidly growing pie would be much easier than redistribution of a pie that was not growing. He also

Figure 7. Growth and inequality of opportunity (IO) worldwide 1990-2010 (long-run cross-country analysis – 20 years' interval)
Source: Marrero, Gustavo A., and Juan G. Rodríguez, (2016). 'Inequality ... of opportunity and economic performance.' In: Economic Mobility: Research & Ideas on Strengthening Families, Communities & the Economy, USA: Federal Reserve Bank of St. Louis and the Board of Governors of the Federal Reserve System, pp. 385-420. Note: Variables in the axes are OLS adjusted by initial log of per capita GDP, time dummies, and regional dummies.

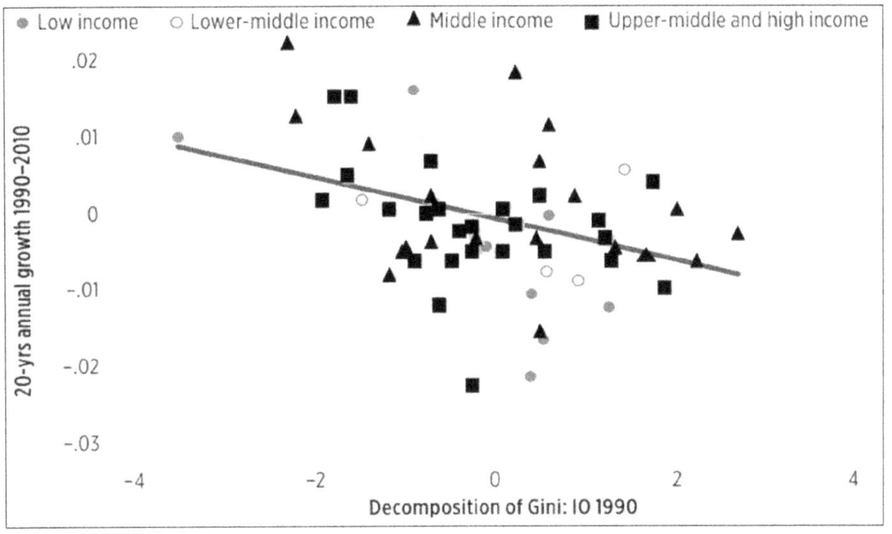

would warn that the level and growth of GDP were far from sufficient statistics for gauging economic success, as issues of distribution of income are central. In other words, the central problem, in fact, is not so much economic growth as its duration, which, in turn, depends on the ideas of human capital carriers about justice and equality in society.

The Relationship of Social and Financial Stability: Preferences of Institutional Support or Budget Spending

Now it becomes possible to theoretically describe all the basic interrelations that underlie the author's hypothesis of solving the "social and financial stability puzzle" and thereby ensuring economic development. After the 2008-2009 global financial crises leaders of national governments and other stakeholder institutions faced the puzzle of rising in-country inequality, fiscal space limited, interest rates near zero and chronic low economic growth. And increasingly urgent question is raised: what way should be chosen to turn the current cycle of stagnation and dispersion into another one in which greater social inclusion and stronger and more sustainable growth reinforce each other? The author's conceptual approach supports among others the view points of G.A. Marrero, and J.G. Rodriguez (2010); D. Acemoglu, S. Naidu, P. Restrepo, and J.A. Robinson (2015), who consider bad quality of institutions as the main cause of all the latter problems.

These changes have created opportunities, but the challenges cannot be overlooked. Services such as education and health care—key inputs to the accumulation of productive human capital—are becoming more expensive, and equal access to good-quality services is becoming an issue. Risk-sharing arrangements via targeted assistance or more general insurance have limitations. This uneven playing field generates inequality traps: without mobility and flexibility, technology and globalization-driven opportunities become elusive, some groups are left behind, and distributional tensions arise. Curbing the trends—stopping trade or rejecting technologies—as well as passively compensating the losers have not worked in the past, and these measures will not work in the future. But inaction is not an option. The way societies adjust to distributional tensions and maintain social cohesion can make a big difference, not just in terms of equity but also in terms of future prosperity

In this connection the formal institutions are becoming of great importance especially in connection with the relationship between intergenerational equity and macroeconomic growth sustainability accompanied by institutions.

The institutions are called upon to introduce an element of stability in the interconnection of individual and society and can be meaningfully defined as ways of their cooperative solutions (North, 1996). Formal institutions are a restrictive framework created by the state (acting on behalf of society) and predetermining the structure of incentives for people's behavior. At the same time the institutions act as the opportunities for individuals. So the most important function of institutions is to solve the problems of cooperation in any sphere of socio-economic life (Coase, 1960). In accordance with the above problems, the state and the formal institutions created by it are acquiring growing importance. In this context both growing inequality and inequity, from one side, and the economic growth inhibition, from another, are predetermined by the state and its inefficient formal institutions. Accordingly, governments must be aware of implementing general redistribution policies. These policies might affect total inequality but without knowing which type of inequality is being affected. This finding is in line with Jonathan D. Ostry, Andrew Berg, and Charalambos G. Tsangarides (2014), who find that some redistribution can reduce inequality and is good for growth (maybe because it reduces IO), but too much redistribution is growth deterring (maybe because, too much redistribution ends up reducing IE). The bottom line for policymakers is clear, they should focus on reducing IO while improving incentives to effort, which reduces unfair inequality and promotes growth (Figure 8).

At the same time, in the late 70s of the last century, A.M. Okun (Okun, 2015) singled out two basic functions of the state, which he outlined as the fundamental dilemma "*macroeconomic stability - social equality (justice)*". At the end of the second decade of the 21st century, the importance of effectively implementing this fundamental dilemma by the state increased many times amid a global slowdown in economic growth and an increase in the polarization of the world's population in terms of income and wealth (Boarini, et al., 2018). To the extent that the system succeeds, it generates an efficient economy. But that pursuit of efficiency necessarily creates inequalities. And hence society faces a tradeoff between equality and efficiency (Okun, 2015).

From the theoretical point of view, this is the essence of public finances aimed at providing special categories of citizens with public goods based on the non-equivalent redistribution of GDP (national income) in favor of low-income members of society at the expense of citizens with high incomes. Thus, the functions of the state are realized in the context of ensuring equality and equity in society through government spending. But public finance obviously unequally redistributes national income in terms of generating tax revenues and spending them, for example, on social functions. And this also suits the society as a whole. By paying taxes, taxpayers agree on the disparity of the transaction with the state, since public goods and services received in return do not necessarily have to be the equivalent of those tax payments that taxpayers have listed in the state budget revenues. This kind of disparity justifies the existence of the state, since public goods in any society are designed for large families, disabled, people in need, retired people, for those, who have lost their jobs, sick, crippled, etc., for those unable to solve his own problems without the help of the state. It is in their favor that the tax payments and received public goods of wealthy citizens of the society are unequal. A dialectical unity of the state and society is formed on this basis, ensuring the succession of generations in terms of replicating trust in the state, demonstrating support to families, on the one hand, in financing the maintenance of children, and, on the other hand, in decent provision of the elderly. Violation of this chain is fraught with the state's loss of public confidence, a reduction in the range of intersection of interests with the latter and the loss of the growing part of the national income in the informal ("shadow") segment of the economy. Public finance represents the bulk of GDP created in society and redistributed through the government budget mechanism. And in the social contract between the state and the society, non-equivalence is implicitly provided for, as some pay more taxes, but receive less public goods, while others, on the contrary, pay less taxes, and receive more public goods.

Figure 8. Interrelationships between inequality, redistribution, and growth
Source: Ostry, Jonathan D., Andrew Berg, and Charalambos G. Tsangarides, (2014). 'Redistribution, inequality, and growth.' IMF Staff Discussion Note, February, SDN/14/02. Note: This picture shows the main channels of interrelationships between inequality, redistribution, and growth. The direct effects of redistribution are marked with line D and net inequality – with line E, in each case in effect holding the value of the other variable constant. Ostry, Jonathan D., Andrew Berg, and Charalambos G. Tsangarides, (2014) also calculate the "total effect" of redistribution on growth. The latter does not affect market inequality, so redistribution affects net inequality one-for-one. The total effect is thus the sum of the estimated direct effect (line D) and the indirect effect, which is a combination of the effect of redistribution on net inequality (line C) and the estimated direct effect of net inequality on growth (line E).

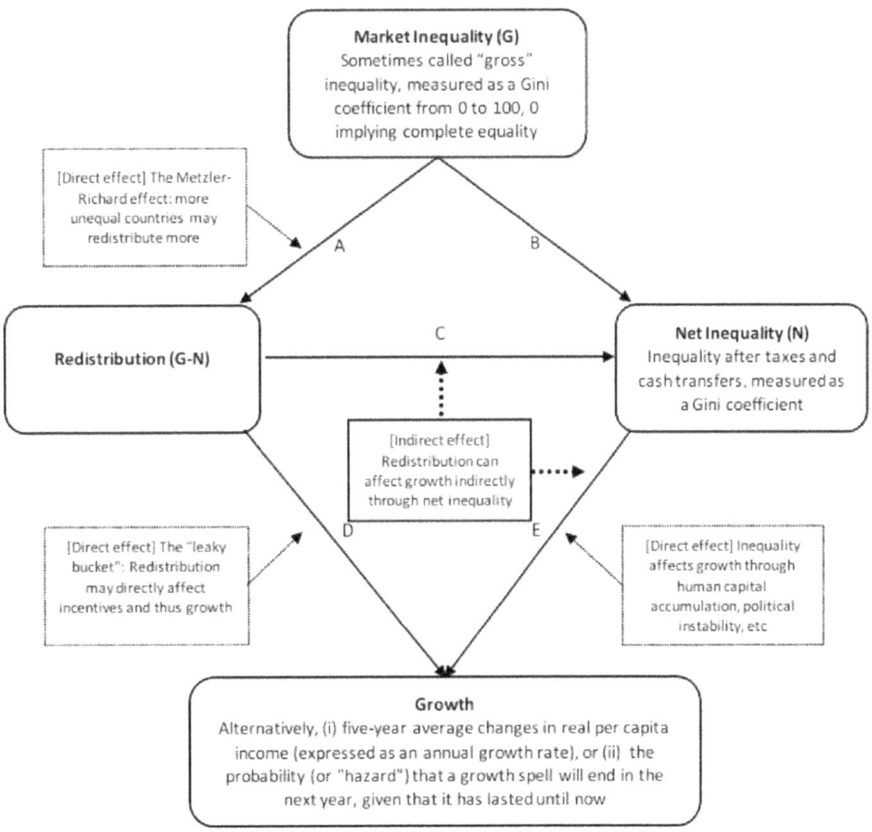

So the presence of a trade-off between efficiency and equality does not mean that everything that is good for one is necessarily bad for the other (Okun, 2015). In short, formal institutions, for example, with respect to securing property rights, can be regarded as inefficient, since they exclude prices that promote savings. However, institutions that provide a comparative advantage, certain incentives trigger an increase in socially productive efforts. If the state finds a way, with the same inputs, to turn out more of some products (and no less of the others), it has scored an increase in efficiency. As a result the quality of economic and political institutions plays a major role when it comes to explaining growth performance, as do the development of equity markets and demographic variables.

Considering the effect of such major factors of growing inequality in developed economies, such as technical progress, institutional shifts, changes in social norms and globalization, the state can and should hinder the processes of increasing inequity in society. Moreover, it is difficult to assess the magnitude of the levelling effect obtained from the growth of government spending on supporting socially vulnerable people or from improving the quality of formal institutions that provide intergenerational equity in the relationship between individuals and society. In any case, their combination in terms of extending social security to a wider range of people (outside the public sector), the introduction of unemployment benefits due to technological challenges, and perhaps even job security for certain categories of workers is among the most important areas for optimizing the institutional and financial measures of the state towards equity and justice. Moreover, such a direction of state activity can resolve the dilemma of economic growth vs equity in the long term (Berg, Ostry, and Zettelmeyer, 2011; and Berg, and Ostry, 2011). Recent research by Andrew Berg, et al. (2011) has shown that strengthening equality can help improve efficiency in the context of ensuring sustainable long-term economic growth of a country. Back in 2000, Lant Pritchett (2000) concluded that economic growth must be interpreted, given its turning points. He focused on such a problem as the ability of countries to maintain growth for a long time, and the inability of others to do so. It was later substantiated the conclusion that it is much easier to cause growth than to sustain it in the long run (Hausmann, Pritchett, and Rodrick, 2005). A number of researchers (Acemoglu, Johnson, and Robinson, 2005; Berg, and Ostry, 2011) found that it is the quality of economic institutions and their orientation towards ensuring equity (justice) as the basis of social contract in society are among the most important determinants of long-term economic growth. To this it can be added the most serious problems of IO and IE, inadequate retirement insurance for the elderly generation and reduction of social lifting opportunities due to the decrease of the middle class and the need to develop human capital that meets the requirements of future technological challenges.

According to IMF estimates, with the increase in incomes of the richest sections of the population and the decline in the poorest by 1%, the economy is slowing by 0.08 pp, and with the growth of incomes of the poorest - is accelerating by 0.38 pp. The OECD also leads to similar assessments: the increase in the Gini coefficient (the indicator of the stratification of society by income level) by 3 points reduces the economic growth by 0.35 percentage points per year.

RESULTS AND DISCUSSION

So, the optimization of the relationship between society and the individual belongs to the eternal problems. Within its framework, the priority of society represented by the state or of the person is constantly changing. The last stage of technological development predetermined physical capital and owners of considerable wealth as drivers of economic growth. Under these conditions, priority in state actions remained on the side of economic growth to the detriment of such value orientations of representatives of different generations as equality and justice. Back in 1975 Arthur M. Okun fundamentally presented the predetermination of this choice as a trade-off between intergenerational equity and economic growth. However, after the global economic crisis of 2007-2008 a tendency to slow the pace of economic growth began to appear more persistently. At the same time, despite all the efforts of national governments to change the vector of its direction, the economies of the developed countries of the world gradually slowed down.

Researchers of the laws of social and economic development were forced to expand their studies, including the problems of motivating individual carriers of human capital. It was they who raised the question of a qualitatively different driver of global economic growth in the face of new technological challenges of the future. It turned out that even the wealth accumulated by a few representatives of society, which makes it possible to finance the new technological breakthrough of humanity, cannot achieve it without adequate human capital. Moreover, new technologies and robotics are not able to replace the human in man. Studies of the value component of individual human capital allowed to identify two types of inequality - inequality of attitudes and inequality of efforts - which have a significant, but opposite effects on economic growth. The literature on equality of opportunity affirms that overall inequality is actually a composite measure of inequality of opportunity and inequality of effort. Thus, the outcome of an individual (income, education, or occupation) is in fact the result of, at least, two main sets of factors. First, the factors beyond the individual's control (taken as given at birth), called circumstances, are related with parental background (including parental income, education, social position, etc.), and also with gender, race, ethnicity, religion, or macroeconomic conditions of the individual's birth place, such as the level of corruption or democracy. Second, it is the set of factors related with free-will action to exert effort and take risks in entrepreneurship activities, or with an individual's ability or talent. The former set of factors determines the level of IO, while the second defines the extent of IE. The hypothesis defended in this paper is that the impact of overall inequality on economic performance is ambiguous because the two main components of inequality have opposite effects on growth: IO negative and IE positive (Marrero, Gustavo A., and Juan G. Rodríguez, 2016; EBRD, 2018).

Thus, for the first time, the value ideas of a person took the first place in assessing the quality of a new driver of economic growth in the future. As a consequence, the balance in the priority functions of the state began to lean toward the institutional support of the individual's ideas of justice, which society demonstrates in relation to him. And it became obvious that the effectiveness of the state should be judged not by the growth of government spending on social needs in general, but by its ability to ensure the fair inclusion of a person in the life of this society. This is due to the fact that a person who assesses how unjust the society in which he lives (or his relatives and friends live) will behave opportunistically towards it. Such a person does not want to become the driving force of the economic development of such an unjust society. These separate ideas about inequality and injustice are compounded by a real increase in the polarization of the population into the rich and the poor due to the erosion of the middle class. This was a real demonstration of reduced opportunities for the social ladder as a mechanism for achieving higher standards of living for the poor and poorest. Under these conditions, the question of the material and the spiritual in man, of their significance for him in the context of his motivation for creative inspiration and life success sounded with new force. Without answering these questions, neither a technological breakthrough nor a new round of the economic spiral for all of humanity could be possible. Hence, another eternal question connected with the functions of the state, with the effectiveness of its activities in the context of orientation towards the welfare of society or the individual, social justice or economic growth, short-term or long-term goals, etc., became actualized. Moreover, judging by the results of some researchers, it is the social orientation of the formal institutions of the state that can provide not just a short-term growth of the national economy, but support it in the long term.

So the global financial crisis of 2008-2009 posed the problems of the world economy' growth rates slowing in the sector of developed countries, that predetermined the necessity to investigate a national economy' structural characteristics associated not so much with the objective, easily modeled factors of its development, as with the subjective ones, difficult to be understood, but increasing in importance. The most promising indicator included into the Inclusive Development Index (World Economic Forum, 2018) relates to the evaluation of the intergenerational equity in a country in connection with its growth sustainability. It deals, in particular, with national existing pension system' quality, which directly links the elderly and young family members and predetermined informal institutions' quality, regulating the economic agents behavior in the society. The formalized evaluation of the interdependence of indicators of intergenerational equity and macroeconomic growth sustainability is very promising for the government leaders and other stakeholders' institutions relating to the purpose of the development and adoption of optimal government decisions.

One way to strengthen equity in society is equalizing opportunity by increasing public spending on the education of children from disadvantaged backgrounds or by promoting cash transfers conditional on school attendance. Empirical findings for Europe show that reducing high school dropout rates is an effective way of increasing opportunities (Marrero, and Rodríguez, 2012). Other policy interventions may include reducing long-term unemployment and improving access to childcare. By curbing inequality of opportunity, these policies may promote not only social justice but plausibly also economic growth. It is unclear, however, where the push for such inclusive growth policies will be coming from, when those in power stand to gain the least from such changes (Marrero, et al., 2017). Recent studies have proved that in the above cases inequality act as a negative factor. One strand of this literature appeals to the Meltzer-Richard median voter hypothesis (Alesina, and Rodrik, 1994; Persson, and Tabellini, 1994). These works argue that high inequality prompts a relatively poor median voter to vote for high tax rates, which in turn reduce incentives for investment and cause low growth. However, a poor median voter could choose redistributive policies that are not necessarily bad for growth, such as investments in public education, for example, emphasise credit market imperfections, namely the inability of the poor to get loans to finance their education and to become entrepreneurs (Saint Paul, and Verdier, 1996; Galor, and Zeira, 1993; Banerjee, and Newman, 1993). More unequal societies may then be more prone to wasting human resources, which would lead to lower growth. According to Oded Galor, et al. (2006), the key to fast growth in modern societies is not capital accumulation but improvements in human capital, i.e. strengthening the institutional environment with a focus on the principles of equality and equity in the distribution and redistribution of GDP.

Today any society will have to think about who benefits from its social protection system, which is a mechanism for sharing risks between a citizen and society, as well as the social insurance of their citizens from failures in the choice of life opportunities. Each society will also have to make a choice regarding the division of responsibilities between the family, the society, the market and the state. This is essential because the welfare state is also a mechanism to ensure the equal status of all citizens so that they can fully participate in public life and in the process of economic growth stimulating. But fundamental questions, connected with the public choice between intergenerational equity and economic growth, remain unanswered. These questions, according to IMF experts, can be formulated as below. Whom do citizens consider it expedient to share the risks and care for their loved ones with? What responsibilities go along with those obligations? How much do obligations extend beyond families to communities or other organizations? Are the society obliged to leave future generations at least an equivalent endowment of physical, social, and natural capital as they were given in due time?

EMPIRICAL EVIDENCE

Marrero and Rodríguez (2012, 2013) decompose total inequality into an inequality of opportunity component (defined as the inequality that is due to circumstances outside the person's control such as parental education, race and country of origin) and a residual inequality component that is assumed to be due to effort and luck. These researchers find that inequality of opportunity is negatively correlated with growth while the residual ("good inequality") tends to help growth. The rationale is that inequality of opportunity may harm economic growth because it favors human capital accumulation by individuals with better social origins, rather than by those with more talent. Perceptions of unequal opportunities, by affecting individual aspirations, may also reduce investments in human capital. Other empirical studies have obtained similar results. C. Hsieh, E. Hurst, C. I. Jones, and P. J. Klenow (2013) exploit data from the US between 1960 and 2008 to show that occupational barriers faced by minorities are bad for growth. K. Bradbury, and R. Triest (2016) used measures of absolute and relative inter-generational mobility as proxies for equality of opportunity and found that mobility had a positive effect on future economic growth. It has proven harder to reproduce the negative relationship between inequality of opportunity and growth using cross-country data (Ferreira, et. al., 2014), either because the relationship does not hold true in all countries, or because the data are not strictly comparable across countries.

Future research will hopefully shed light on how inequality of opportunity affects a person's income success. It is conceivable that inequality of opportunity proxies unequal access to good schooling or discrimination in the labor market, to name two candidate channels. Both of these mechanisms would suggest that inefficiencies disproportionally affect the economic growth prospects of the disadvantaged. For example, the comparison of the 1% share of welfare in Russia, the USA, China and France is given on the Figure 9. From 1997 to 2015, the concentration of wealth in the hands of 1% of the richest part of the entire population was the highest in Russia. Only the United States in 2008-2014 were ahead of Russia on this indicator. And if in 1995, in the hands of the richest population in Russia, a little more than 20% of the total wealth of the country was concentrated, then in 2015 this figure has doubled.

However, since 2002, the increased wealth polarization of the population in Russia negatively correlates with GDP growth rates in the country. Even a superficial view allows us to conclude that the concentration of wealth (as well as current income) in the hands of some due to the reduction in the hands of another part population is unfair, as evidenced by the stagnation of economic activity in Russia (Figure 10).

And the most surprising is that throughout 2002-2017 budgetary parameters of the Russian government exceeded the growth rate of GDP either due to revenues or to expenditures. It means the sustainable public finance imbalance. And if the deficit can somehow be linked with the desire of the state to reduce injustice (inequality) in society, then the budget surplus in the conditions of high polarization of the population in the country is difficult to explain.

As to model's dependencies between the income and wealth polarization of the population all over the world, on the one hand, and economic growth rates in the Globe, on the other, then they can be represented as follows (Figure 11-12).

Figure 9. Top 1% wealth share: Russia vs other countries in 1995-2015
Sources: F. Novokmet, Th. Piketty, G. Zucman (2017). From Soviets to Oligarchs: Inequality and Property in Russia, 1905-2016 // National Bureau of Economic Research. Working Paper 23712. August 2017. http://www.nber.org/papers/w23712

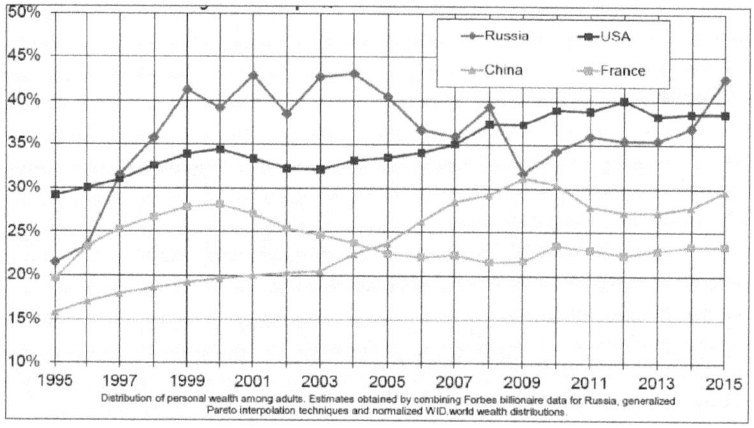

Figure 10. Negative dynamics of growth rates of GDP, federal budget's revenues and expenditures in Russia for the period of 2002-2017 (%%)
Sources: the author's estimations on the base of official data of Rosstat

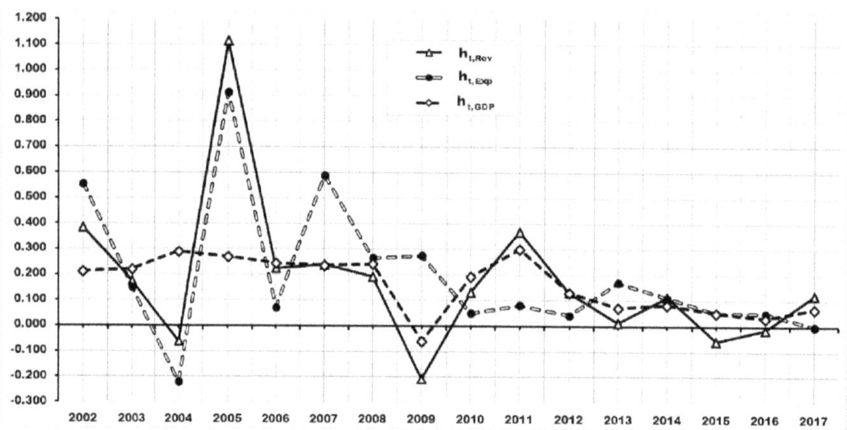

Modeling the oscillations of Gini coefficients on average throughout the world as a first approximation is advisable to associate with modeling the oscillations of inequality (Gini coefficient). As in the mathematical description of any complex system the author will abstract away from the numerous significant and not very significant connections, assuming that the whole variety of factors leads to a real change in the Gini coefficient (inequality) in each period. In this case, in order to simplify the reasoning, it is advisable to proceed from the fact that the random variable change in inequality:

$$\varepsilon_t = Gini_t - Gini_{t-1} \tag{1}$$

for each $t = 1, 2, \ldots, n$ obeys the normal distribution law with zero expectation and variance σ_t^2, $N(0, \sigma_t^2)$.

Figure 11. Modeling the World Gini coefficients (average) for the sequence of years (from 1 to 80)

Sources: the author's estimations according to $Gini_t = \varepsilon_t + \delta_\varepsilon \sigma_\varepsilon + Gini_{t-1}$. *Notes: the sequence of years from the moment 1 to the moment 80*

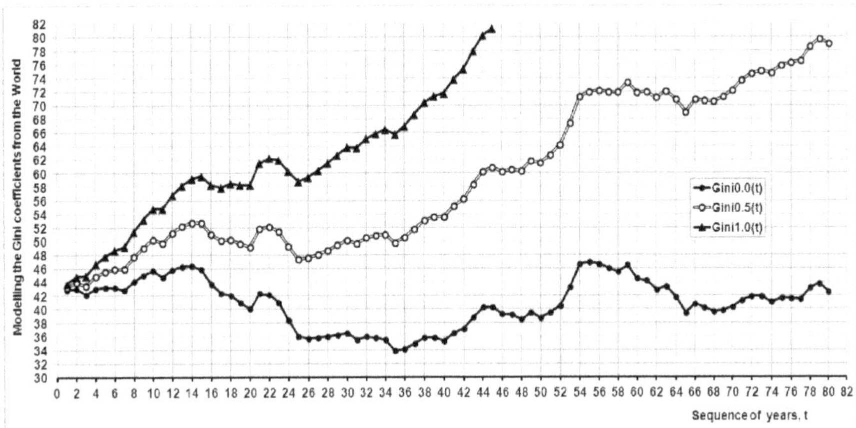

Assuming random walk of inequality, it is easy to obtain that over *n* periods the change in the Gini coefficient will be:

$$Gini_n - Gini_1 = \sum_{t=1}^{n} \varepsilon_t, \tag{2}$$

and the mathematical expectation of this value is zero:

$$E(Gini_n - Gini_1) = E\left(\sum_{t=1}^{n} \varepsilon_t\right) = \sum_{t=1}^{n} \left(E(\varepsilon_t)\right) = 0. \tag{3}$$

Since the distributions of random variables ε_t are independent, the dispersion σ_Σ^2 of sums of random variables (1) can be represented as

$$\sigma_\Sigma^2 = \sum_{t=1}^{n} \sigma_t^2 = n\sigma_\varepsilon^2, \tag{4}$$

where it is taken into account that due to the identity of the distribution laws for each of the random variables ε_t all the dispersions σ_t^2 are the same, i.e. $\sigma_t^2 = \sigma_\varepsilon^2$.

From the simulated wanderings ε_t it becomes possible to obtain the Brownian (economic) wandering of the random value of the Gini coefficient:

$$Gini_t = \varepsilon_t + Gini_{t-1}. \tag{5}$$

Obviously, in order to calculate the value of $Gini_1$, using formula (5), it is necessary to have the value of the Gini coefficient at time 0 ($Gini_0$), i.e. at the beginning of the first period.

As the initial value of the Gini coefficient, it is advisable to take a real value, for example, the characteristic (average) for the global picture of social inequalities. In model calculations, it is advisable to assume $Gini_0 = 45$.

Note that the standard deviation σ_ε can be interpreted as a measure of restoring a more or less acceptable level of inequality $Gini_t$ if, instead of ε_t a random variable with a probability of approximately 0.68 takes the value $\varepsilon_t + \sigma_\varepsilon$.

Therefore, it is logical to add to each value of ε_t the necessary ... (infusion) $\delta_\varepsilon \sigma_\varepsilon$:

$$Gini_t = \varepsilon_t + \delta_\varepsilon \sigma_\varepsilon + Gini_{t-1}\,. \tag{6}$$

In other words, in the first approximation, real changes in social inequality (the Gini coefficient $Gini_t$) correspond to random wanderings with a positive shift $\delta_\varepsilon \sigma_\varepsilon$, i.e. actually represent sub-martingale.

Figure 11 graphically presents the results of the corresponding model calculations of the dynamics of the Gini coefficients by the formula (6) for the cases: $\delta_\varepsilon = 0$; $\delta_\varepsilon = 0.5$; $\delta_\varepsilon = 1.0$

Based on the developed concepts (1) - (6), a model experiment has been performed for the GDP dynamics values corresponding to the obtained model dynamics of the Gini coefficients (Figure 12).

Here the formula (6) takes the form:

$$Modeling\ World\ GDP_t = \varepsilon_t + \delta_\varepsilon \sigma_\varepsilon + Modeling\ World\ GDP_{t-1} \tag{7}$$

As a baseline of *Modeling World* GDP_0 it has been accepted World GDP in current prices (Billions of U.S. dollars) related to 1989 (IMF, 2019):

Modeling World $GDP_0 = 19974.026$ Billion of U.S. dollars

Figure 12. Modeling the World GDP_t (current prices in Billions of US dollars) for the sequence of years (from 1 to 80) for Gini 0.0(t); Gini 0.5(t); Gini 1.0(t)
Sources: the author's estimations. Notes: the sequence of years from the moment 1 to the moment 80

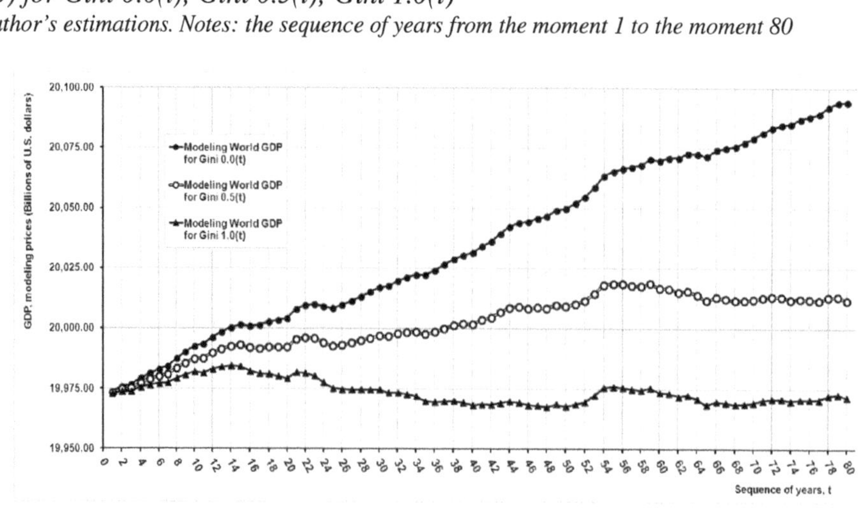

Figure 13. Comparison of the results of a model experiment with the Gini coefficient for $\delta_\varepsilon = 0$ and with indicators of sustainable growth of World GDP_t (in current prices in Billions of US dollars) subject to acceptable dynamics of the Gini coefficient

Sources: the author's estimations on the base of the IMF data (IMF, 2019). Notes: the sequence of years from the moment 1 to the moment 80

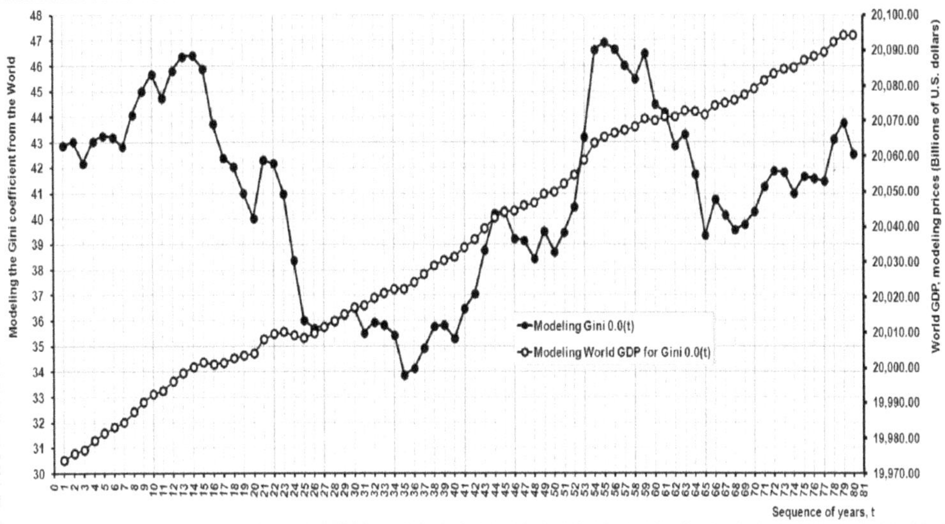

Figure 13 shows a comparison of the model of sustainable GDP growth under the condition of acceptable dynamics of the Gini coefficient.

Judging by the above Figures (11-13), there are no linear relationships between the dynamics of intergenerational equity indicators (represented by the Gini coefficient) and the stable GDP growth rates in the contemporary world. However, the above model experiments make it possible to judge that ensuring the Gini coefficient values within certain limits (below 47) probably contribute to stable growth of GDP. But the Gini coefficient values beyond the designated limits unambiguously suppress the rate of economic growth of the countries all over the world. It is precisely on the basis of these results that it could safely be concluded that the human factor and its own assessments of the equality and equity in society are already becoming one of the most important factor of economic stability. And in the conditions of the new technological platform of the future economy and finance, it is human capital that will determine the vector and stability of economic growth in the Globe.

CONCLUSION

The global financial crisis of 2007–2008 posed the fundamental problem of a steady slowdown in the global economy. This made it imperative to identify the real causes of this phenomenon and the formation of an effective mechanism for a radical change in those negative trends. The study of the dynamics of development of national economies made it possible to state the fact of fundamental changes in the national economy' structural characteristics. Now they are associated not so much with the objective, easily modeled factors of its development, as with the subjective ones, difficult to be understood, but increasing in importance. The latter, in particular, deals with national existing pension system' quality, which directly links the elderly and young family members and predetermined informal institutions' quality, regulating the economic agents behavior in the society. These attributes are inherent in carriers of human capital, the formation of which as a key factor in the development of society can provide an adequate response to the technological challenges of the future. In other words, with the transformation of human capital into the leading driver of the new cycle of the economic spiral, subjective value judgments of equality and equity (including intergenerational one) predetermined by the attitude of society (represented by the state) to the citizen come out. This is due to the fact that human capital can serve the good of society voluntarily, realizing that this society suits it according to the parameters of equity and justice. Such fundamental changes in the structure of economic growth factors on a new technological base have returned both the state and society and citizens to the dilemma of preferences declared by A.M. Okun (2015): either social justice or economic growth. As a rule, the modern idea of social justice is connected with the state budget expenditures for the social needs of society, including the pension system, the health care system and the social protection of the disadvantaged. And hence the chronic government budget deficit, the rising cost of public debt and the greater problems of its financing in the context of falling economic growth rates. It seems that there is no alternative choice of the priority of state policy oriented to economic growth. Only the latter will make it possible to largely solve the problems of state financing of the social needs of society.

However, it becomes clear that the result is not so easy. In modern conditions, the choice in favor of ensuring economic growth to the detriment of maintaining intergenerational equity in a society can really provide an economic surge with its fast fading. Only a systematic improvement of the institutional environment by the state in order for citizens to feel a fair attitude of society towards them can stabilize long-term economic growth in the new conditions of the technological revolution. In this case, the state should make all its best to form and renew a new social contract with the citizens with a focus on the implementation of the principle of justice. It is about a fair pension system, social protection of citizens in conditions of economic and financial instability, a reduction in income polarization of the population, an increase of the middle class in the society, as well as about the equality of opportunities, and etc. The methodology for analyzing the factors of development of economic systems showed a stable relationship between sustainable macroeconomic growth and the implementation of conditions ensuring the equality of generations. This conclusion is well supported by the model experiment with the dynamics of intergenerational equity and economic growth on the basis of the sub-martingale. It becomes of great importance due to the need of managing national economy's long term development with the ultimate purpose to maintain the sustainable GDP growth rates on the base of proper institutionalization of the intergenerational equity conditions. The same conclusion is confirmed by the results obtained by researchers in deep empirical studies of recent years.

REFERENCES

Acemoglu, D., Johnson, S., & Robinson, J. A. (2005). Institutions as the fundamental cause of long-run growth. In P. Aghion & S. Durlauf (Eds.), *Handbook of Economic Growth*. Elsevier.

Acemoglu, D., Naidu, S., Restrepo, P., & Robinson, J. A. (2015). Democracy, redistribution and inequality. In A. Atkinson & F. Bourguignon (Eds.), *Handbook of Income Distribution* (Vol. 2). Elsevier.

Alesina, A., & Perotti, R. (1994). The political economy of growth: A critical survey of the recent literature. *The World Bank Economic Review*, *8*(3), 350–371. doi:10.1093/wber/8.3.351

Alesina, A., & Rodrik, D. (1994). Distributive politics and economic growth. *The Quarterly Journal of Economics*, *109*(2), 465–490. doi:10.2307/2118470

Banerjee, A. V., & Newman, A. F. (1993). Occupational choice and the process of development. *Journal of Political Economy*, *101*(2), 274–298. doi:10.1086/261876

Basel World Bank. (2016). *Natural Capital Accounting. Brief.* Washington, DC: The World Bank Group.

Berg & Ostry, (2011a). *Inequality and unsustainable growth: two sides of the same coin?* IMF Staff Discussion Note, 11/08.

Berg & Ostry, (2011b). Equality and efficiency. Is there a trade-off between the two or do they go hand by hand? *Finance & Development, 48*(3), 12-15.

Berg, A., Ostry, J. D., & Zettelmeyer, J. (2011). *What makes growth sustained?* EBRD Working Paper, No. 133.

Boarini, R., Causa, O., Fleurbaey, M., Grimalda, G., & Woolard, I. (2018). Reducing inequalities and strengthening social cohesion through inclusive growth: a roadmap for action. *Economics. Discussion Papers*. Available at: http://www.economics-ejournal.org/economics/journalarticles/2018-63

Boyd, R., & Richerson, P. J. (1985). *Culture and the evolutionary process*. Chicago, IL: University of Chicago Press.

Bradbury, K., & Triest, R. (2016). Inequality of opportunity and aggregate economic performance. *Russell Sage Foundation Journal of the Social Sciences*, *2*(2), 178–201. doi:10.7758/rsf.2016.2.2.08

Buckholtz J. W., Marois, R. (2012). The roots of modern justice: cognitive and neural foundations of social norms and their enforcement. *Nature Neuroscience*, *15*(5), 655—661.

Chiu, C.-Y., Gelfand, M. J., Yamagishi, T., Shteynberg, G., & Wan, C. (2010). Intersubjective culture: the role of intersubjective perceptions in cross-cultural research. Perspectives on Psychological Science, 5(4), 482—493 doi:10.1177/1745691610375562

Cingano, F. (2014). *Trends in income inequality and its impact on economic growth.* OECD Social, Employment, and Migration Working Papers, No. 163.

Coase, R. H. (1960). The problem of social cost. *The Journal of Law & Economics*, *3*(3), 1–44. doi:10.1086/466560

Coyle, D. (2017). Rethinking GDP. *Finance & Development, 54*(1), 16.

Crafts, N. (2017). Whither economic growth? Finance & Development, 54(1).

Cuberes & Teignier. (2016). Aggregate effects of gender gaps in the labor market: a quantitative estimate. *Journal of Human Capital, 10*(1), 1–32.

Duflo, E. (2012). Women empowerment and economic development. *Journal of Economic Literature*, *50*(4), 1051–1079. doi:10.1257/jel.50.4.1051

EBRD. (2018). *Transition Report 2017-2018: Sustaining Growth*. EBRD.

Esteve-Volart, B. (2004). *Gender discrimination and growth: Theory and evidence from India. Development Economics Paper, 42*. Suntory Centre, Suntory and Toyota International Centres for Economics and Related Disciplines, London School of Economics and Political Science.

Ferreira, L. Lugo, & Ozler. (2014). *Inequality of opportunity and economic growth: a cross-country analysis*. World Bank Policy Research Working Paper, 6915.

Finn, A., & Leibbrandt, M. (2013). *Mobility and inequality in the first three waves of NIDS*. SALDRU Working Paper, No. 120, and NIDS Discussion Paper, No. 2013/2. SALDRU, University of Cape Town.

Förster, M., Llena-Nozal, A., & Nafilyan, V. (2014). *Trends in top incomes and their taxation in OECD countries*. OECD Social, Employment and Migration Working Papers, No. 159. doi:10.1787/5jz43jhlz87f-en

Galor, Moav, & Vollrath. (2006). *Inequality in land ownership, the emergence of human capital promoting institutions, and the great divergence*. SSRN-id670883.

Galor, O., & Moav, O. (2004). From physical to human capital accumulation: Inequality and the process of development. *The Review of Economic Studies*, *71*(4), 1001–1026. doi:10.1111/0034-6527.00312

Galor, O., & Zeira, J. (1993). Income distribution and macroeconomics. *The Review of Economic Studies*, *60*(1), 35–52. doi:10.2307/2297811

Gonzales, C., Jain-Chandra, S., Kochhar, K., Newiak, M., & Zeinullayev, T. (2017). Tackling income inequality. In K. Kochhar, S. Jain-Chandra, & M. Newiak (Eds.), *Women, Work, and Economic Growth: Leveling the Playing Field* (pp. 49–72). Washington, DC: International Monetary Fund.

Gruber, J., Milligan, K., & Wise, D. A. (2009). *Social security programs and retirement around the world: the relationship to youth employment, introduction and summary.* NBER Working Paper, No. 14647

Gupta, D. K. (1990). *The Economics of Political Violence. The Effect of Political Instability on Economic Growth*. New York: Praeger.

Hausmann, R., Pritchett, L., & Rodrik, D. (2005). Growth accelerations. *Journal of Economic Growth*, *10*(4), 303–329. doi:10.100710887-005-4712-0

Hodgson, G. M. (1988). *Economics and Institutions. A Manifesto for a Modern Institutional Economics*. Polity Press. doi:10.9783/9781512816952

Hsieh, C., Hurst, E., Jones, C. I., & Klenow, P. J. (2013). *The allocation of talent and US economic growth.* NBER Working Paper, No. 18693.

IMF. (2017). *Fiscal Monitor: Tackling Inequality*. Washington, DC: International Monetary Fund.

IMF. (2019). *Fiscal Monitor. Curbing Corruption*. Washington, DC: IMF.

Jain-Chandra, S., Kochhar, K., Newiak, M., Zeinullayev, T., & Zhuang, L. (2016). Gender inequality around the world. In K. Kochhar, S. Jain-Chandra, & M. Newiak (Eds.), *Women, Work and Economic Growth: Leveling the Playing Field* (pp. 13–30). Washington, DC: International Monetary Fund.

Jones, Ch. I., & Klenow, P. J. (2016). Beyond GDP? Welfare across countries and time. *The American Economic Review, 106*(9), 2426–2457. doi:10.1257/aer.20110236

Lee, R., & Mason, A. (2017). Cost of aging. Finance & Development, 54(1).

Maleva, T. M. (2014). *The man in the pay-as-you-go pension system*. Paper presented at the Annual Conference. Association of Russian Economic Think-Tanks, Moscow, Russia.

Marrero & Rodríguez. (2015). *Inequality of opportunity and economic performance*. Economic Mobility Conference. Federal Reserve System Community Development Research.

Marrero, G. A., & Rodríguez, J. G. (2010). *Inequality of opportunity and growth.* ECINEQ. Society for the Study of Economic Inequality. Working Paper Series. ECINEQ WP 2010-154.

Marrero, G. A., & Rodríguez, J. G. (2012). Inequality of opportunity in Europe. *Review of Income and Wealth, 58*(4), 597–621. doi:10.1111/j.1475-4991.2012.00496.x

Marrero, G. A., & Rodríguez, J. G. (2013). Inequality of opportunity and growth. *Journal of Development Economics, 104*, 107–122. doi:10.1016/j.jdeveco.2013.05.004

Marrero, G. A., & Rodríguez, J. G. (2016). Inequality … of opportunity and economic performance. In *Economic Mobility: Research & Ideas on Strengthening Families, Communities & the Economy* (pp. 385–420). Federal Reserve Bank of St. Louis and the Board of Governors of the Federal Reserve System.

Marshall, A. (1988). Income distribution, the domestic market and growth in Argentina. *Labour and Society, 13*(1), 79–103.

Mason, A. (1988). 'Savings, economic growth and demographic change. *Population and Development Review, 14*(1), 113–144. doi:10.2307/1972502

Musgrave, R. (1998). The role of the state in the fiscal theory. In P. B. Sorensen (Ed.), *Public Finance in a Changing World* (pp. 35–50). London: Macmillan. doi:10.1007/978-1-349-14336-8_2

North, D. (1996). *Institutions, Institutional Change and Economic Performance*. Cambridge, UK: Cambridge University Press.

Novokmet, F., Piketty, T., & Zucman, G. (2017). *From Soviets to oligarchs: inequality and property in Russia, 1905-2016.* WID. World Working Paper Series, No. 2017/09.

OECD. (2008). *Growing Unequal? Income Distribution and Poverty in OECD Countries*. Paris: OECD Publishing.

OECD. (2011). *Divided We Stand: Why Inequality Keeps Rising OECD*. OECD Publishing. Retrieved from: http://www.oecd.org/els/soc/dividedwestandwhyinequalitykeepsrising.htm

OECD. (2015). *In It Together: Why Less Inequality Benefits All.* Paris: OECD Publishing; doi:10.1787/9789264235120-

OECD. (2018b). *A Broken Social Elevator? How to Promote Social Mobility*. Paris: OECD Publishing. doi:10.1787/9789264301085-

OECD. (2019). *Under Pressure: The Squeezed middle Class*. Paris: OECD Publishing.

OECD. (2018a). *The Framework for Policy Action on Inclusive Growth*. Paris: OECD Publishing. Available at: http://www.oecd.org/mcm/documents/C-MIN-2018-5-EN.pdf

Okun, A. M. (2015). *Equality and Efficiency: The Big Tradeoff*. Washington, DC: Brookings Institution Press.

Persson, T., & Tabellini, G. (1994). Is inequality harmful for growth? Theory and evidence. *The American Economic Review*, *84*, 600–621.

Piketty, Th. (2013). *Le Capital au XXI[e] Siecle*. Editions de Seuil.

Pritchett, L. (2000). Understanding patterns of economic growth: Searching for hills among plateaus, mountains, and plains. *The World Bank Economic Review*, *14*(2), 221–250. doi:10.1093/wber/14.2.221

Rawls, J. (1971). *Theory of Justice. Harvard*. Harvard University Press.

Saez, E. (2018). *Striking it Richer: the Evolution of Top Incomes in the United States*. Berkeley, CA: UC Berkeley. doi:10.4324/9780429494468-9

Saint Paul, G., & Verdier, T. (1996). Inequality, redistribution and growth: A challenge to the conventional political economy approach. *European Economic Review*, *40*(3-5), 719–728. doi:10.1016/0014-2921(95)00083-6

Schwab, K. (2015, December 12). The fourth industrial revolution: What It Means and How to Respond. *Foreign Affairs. Science and Technology.*

Sen, A. (1999). *Development as Freedom*. Oxford, UK: Oxford University Press.

Stiglitz, J. E. (2012). *The Price of Inequality: How Today's Divided Society Endangers Our Future*. New York: W.W. Norton and Company.

United Nations. (2013). *National Transfer Accounts Manual: Measuring and Analyzing the Generational Economy*. New York: ONU Department of Economic and Social Affairs, Population Division.

US Congressional Budget Office. (2016). *An Update to the Budget and Economic Outlook, 2016 to 2026*. Available at: www.cbo.gov/publication/51908

Voitchovsky, S. (2005). Does the profile of income inequality matter for economic growth? Distinguishing between the effects of inequality in different parts of the income distribution. *Journal of Economic Growth*, *10*(3), 273–296. doi:10.100710887-005-3535-3

WEF. (2018). Creating a Shared Future in a Fractured World. Annual Meeting, 2018. World Economic Forum.

World Economic Forum. (2014). *The Global Gender Gap Report 2014*. Insight Report. Author.

World Economic Forum. (2018). *The Inclusive Development Index 2018. Summary and Data Highlights.* World Economic Forum.

Zhang, T. (2017). Toward inclusive growth. Finance & Development, 54(1), 26.

Chapter 11
Education and Theory of Psychological and Cognitive Barriers:
Human Capital as Driver of Stable Economic Growth

Andrey Igorevich Pilipenko
The Russian Presidential Academy of National Economy and Public Administration, Russia

ABSTRACT

The author identifies the psychological and cognitive barriers (PCBs) in the students' consciousness in schooling as the very important factor of the contemporary education system crisis. Focusing on the unresolved "how to learn" problem, the author reveals the essence of PCBs, their causes, and models for overcoming them. At the same time, the main attention is paid to the social aspect of insurmountable PCBs at school. It is about the education failure of schoolchildren, which predetermines their life and professional failure. And this, in turn, predetermines their negative value orientation in social exchange. As a result, the society receives a low-quality educational component of human capital, which is less and less in demand on the labor market due to the technological challenges of the future. The PCBs overcoming creates conditions for the success of schoolchildren as future carriers of high-quality human capital, able to ensure stable economic growth thanks to the activities of highly educated and intellectually autonomous professionals.

INTRODUCTION

The stable growth of modern national economies is usually associated with a certain quality of human capital as its driver. This is due to the fact that only an appropriately formed human capital is able to realize a new stage of technological progress. According to the author, this scenario can be realized only if there is adequate institutional support for an individual vital activity, in particular, in the process of his education and further implementation of his learning output in the profession. The theory of basic

DOI: 10.4018/978-1-7998-1033-9.ch011

values of S. H. Schwartz (Schwartz, 1994), as well as the developments of his followers (Magun, et al., 2015a) allow the author to link the fact that an individual forms his human capital with confessing certain values as desired cross-situational goals as guiding principles in his life (Schwartz, et al., 2012).

To understand the value orientations of carriers of human capital, one should use the oppositely related pairs of value categories identified by S. Schwarz (1994) at the first level as follows: Saving vs Openness to changes; Self-affirmation vs Caring for people and nature. V. Magun, M. Rudnev and P. Schmidt (Magun, et al., 2015b) add to this structure the additional two pairs of broader second-level value categories: Individualistic orientation vs Social orientation and Self-defense vs Growth. As a result, it becomes possible to arrange the carriers of human capital on each of the above value axes, depending on their individual preferences. Then the latter can be estimated using the differences in the values of the corresponding value categories. While taking the "Individualistic Orientation - Social Orientation" value axis, then, according to V. Magun, M. Rudnev and P. Schmidt (2015b), each of the opposing values has a dual nature, which can be interpreted using the principle of social exchange (Homans, 1961; Gouldner, 1960). Then the formation and use of the human capital capable to become a driver of the social and economic progress under certain conditions is associated with the value orientations of its carriers as participants in social exchange.

Unfortunately, experts estimate the current state of education of individuals as future carriers of human capital as a crisis (WDR, 2018). Out of the variety of factors that predetermine this result, the author distinguishes the feeling of "failure" of students, caused by the poor learning of the material in the process of schooling, its unsatisfactory reproduction and the lack of necessary skills. And, meanwhile, it is education that serves as a factor in the formation of high-quality human capital. This process builds the foundation for the value orientation of the individuals, which predetermines the specifics of social exchange with the society. And the phenomenon of the "unsuccessfulness" of the schooler becomes an external manifestation of the modern education crisis, which has fundamental reasons due to the laws of development of the learning process itself. They can be determined on the basis of the last century work of A.A. Pinsky (1978), who formulated his triad related to schooling: what to teach? – how to teach? - how to learn? (how to learn to learn?). The "unsuccessfulness" of the student as an external sign of the crisis of modern education, and the essential cause of the latter, has the same objective nature. It is due to the unresolved nature of the last component of the Pinsky triad - how to teach a student to learn. Abstraction from the problems faced by the student himself in the schooling process, insurmountable barriers in the students' consciousness predetermine the essence of the modern education system crisis. And this, in turn, largely explains the educational "unsuccessfulness" of students in schooling and their future unwillingness to devote their human capital to serving the community.

The author has developed approaches to solving the "how to learn" problem based on the psychological and cognitive barriers'(PCB) theory (Pilipenko, 1997; Pilipenko, et al., 2019). It is focused on identifying the objective obstacles of a schooler in acquiring educational output and on methods and mechanisms for PCBs overcoming. This makes it possible to raise the level of students learning, which will determine their "success" in school as well as in professional activities. In fact, the modern educational system result should associate with the graduates' learning as "intellectually autonomous" individuals able to fully realize their human capital potential in an uncertain external environment and innovative digital future (WEF, 2015).

However, along with the success of graduates of educational structures who are able to use their human capital as a driver of sustainable economic growth, they must achieve vital "success" in order to realize this value orientation. In practice, this scenario is realized when well-educated (and successful) graduates are demanded by society, which proves their importance by providing them with the required standard of living inherent in the middle class. Unfortunately, all the countries are faced with the problem of the middle class reducing, and, consequently, with the fundamental problem of the social lifting possibilities collapse. As a result, the economic influence of the middle class and its role as a centre of "economic gravity" has also weakened (OECD, 2019b). Ignoring this problem, the state will not be able to ensure the sustainable economic development of the country. It is necessary to take into account the quality of the conservativeness of the institutional environment, due to the effect of "path dependence" (Boston Consulting Group, 2017). The meaning of the latter lies in the fact that social exchange, inadequately institutionalized by the state, instead of replicating the "young einsteins", can reproduce in mass the negative "effect of Perelman". This is about the outstanding Russian young mathematics - G.Ya. Perelmane, who brilliantly proved the Poincaré conjecture, which was not solved for 100 years and refused all public confessions and active professional activities for the benefit of society due to considerations of a subjective nature.

BACKGROUND

The steady growth of modern economies is increasingly associated with the transformation of human capital into its main factor. P. Romer, for example, considers the education as the most important component of human capital capable to make it an endogenous factor of long-term economic growth (Romer, 1986). According to the World Bank experts (World Bank, 2018), of the three main components included in the Human Capital Index (HCI), education is among the most important. It is education that can increase the economic potential of a society, regardless of the HCI other two components: survival and health. This is due to the growing contribution of human capital to economic growth as its quality increases, due to the impact of education. However, it is this aspect that causes a lot of problems and disputes connected with their successful solution. This happens as the labor market makes an increasing demand for workers with a different structure of knowledge, skills, attitudes and values than schoolchildren receive in the learning process. Such a discrepancy between demand and supply of labor with a certain level of education gives rise to the problem of the mismatch of the *schooling and of the learning* in education (WDR, 2018).

From the author's point of view, all manifestations of the crisis of modern education are predetermined by the unresolved "how to learn" problem, which has its solutions on the platform of the author's theory of psychological and cognitive barriers (Pilipenko, 1997). The implementation of the PCB theory provisions will reduce the mismatch between schooling and learning in education and deepen the understanding of the changing the educational component quality in the human capital as the real factor of the long-term economic growth of the global community. As for the social aspect of the modern education crisis overcoming, it should be linked with the learner's value orientation. Being unsuccessful in education due to the unresolved PCBs in his consciousness, the graduate will be unfriendly towards society because he understands that, without the necessary quality of education, he will not be able to engage in high-paying professional activities. As a result the sense of success of the human capital carrier is transformed into a real increase of the per capita GDP.

The chapter is structured as follows. The methodology section presents a revision of the investigations dealing with human capital and education as its most important component; with the students "failure" in the learning process as the social manifestation of the modern education crisis. The remaining part of the methodological section of the chapter is reduced to the PCB theory application to the problem of the schooling and learning mismatch and to the social consequences of its solution.

Empirical part of the chapter is devoted to the main characteristics of future knowledge-based economy as a whole and of the model with high educated human capital and with their successful carriers, which is accompanied by estimates of raising the learning level of the "generation Z" in the process of learning as the PCBs overcoming. Some estimates are given about the economic results obtained from the contribution of successful highly educated professionals whose psychological and cognitive barriers were eliminated in the process of schooling. Theoretical results' comparison on the base of the statistical data let the author affirm that it is possible to identify the main problem areas of the contemporary education system, mainly affecting the level of students' learning and to form the necessary conditions as well as the sufficient ones in order to use the human capital as the driver of sustainable development of the future knowledge-based economy.

Finally, the last part of the chapter shows the main conclusions.

METHODOLOGY

Human Capital: Education as its Most Important Component

Knowledge, skills, and health largely determine the quality of human capital, that people accumulate over their lives, enabling them to realize their potential as productive members of society (World Bank. 2018; WDR, 2019). By improving their human capital with the skills, knowledge, and etc., people can be more productive, flexible, and innovative that provides benefits to the whole society. Investments in human capital have become more and more important as the nature of the work has evolved in response to rapid technological change (Kim, Jim Yong, 2018). As it is highlighted in the 2019 *World Development Report* (WDR, (2019), markets are increasingly demanding workers with higher levels of human capital, especially advanced cognitive and sociobehavioral skills. High qualitative human capital adds up to large benefits for national economies because they become richer accumulating more human capital. As a result, between 10 and 30 percent of per capita gross domestic product (GDP) differences is attributable to cross-country differences in human capital (Hsieh, and Klenow, 2010). This percentage could be even higher when considering the quality of education or the interactions between workers with different skills. For the purpose of this chapter it is important to estimate the contribution of education to worker productivity of the country (Table 1).

The World Bank (2018) team measures the HCI in terms of the productivity of the next generation of workers relative to the benchmark of complete education and full health. According to their methodology the units of the index have a natural interpretation: a value of x for a country means that the productivity as a future worker of a child born in a given year in that country is only a fraction x of what it could be under the benchmark (Table 1). Usually, survival, education and health are considered to be the most important components of the Human Capital Index (HCI), based on their contribution to worker productivity (World Bank, 2018). A country in which a child born today can expect to achieve both full health (no stunting and 100 percent adult survival) and full education potential (14 years of high-quality school by age 18) will score a value of 1 on the HCI (it ranges between 0 and 1 (García, et al., 2016).

Table 1. Measuring the productivity as a future worker of a child born in 2018 Maximum productivity = 1

			A country in the	
		25th percentile	**50th percentile**	**75th percentile**
	Component	*for component X has a value of...*		
	Component 1: survival			
1	Probability of survival to age 5	0.95	0.98	0.99
A	*Contribution to productivity*	*0.95*	*0.98*	*0.99*
	Component 2: school			
	Expected years of school	9.5	11.8	13.1
	Test score (out of approx. 600)	375	424	503
2	Quality-adjusted years of school	5.7	8.0	10.5
B	*Contribution to productivity*	*0.51*	*0.62*	*0.76*
	Component 3: health			
3	Fraction of children not stunted	0.68	0.78	0.89
4	Adult survival rate	0.79	0.86	0.91
C	*Contribution to productivity*[a]	*0.88*	*0.92*	*0.95*
	Overall Human Capital Index[b]	**0.43**	**0.56**	**0.72**

Source: WDR 2019 team (World Bank, 2018, WDR, 2019).

Note: "Contribution to productivity" measures how much each component of the index, as well as the overall index, contributes to the expected future productivity as a worker of a child born in 2018 relative to the benchmark of a complete education and full health. A value of x means that productivity is only a fraction x of what it would be under the benchmark of a complete education and full health. Estimates of productivity contributions are anchored in micro-econometric evidence on the returns to education and health. "Quality-adjusted years of school" equals the country's test score relative to the global best test score multiplied by the country's expected years of school. a. C is calculated as the geometric average of the contributions of numbers 3 and 4 to productivity. b. A × B × C.

Therefore, for example, a score of 0.70 signals that the productivity as a future worker for a child born today is 30 percent below what could have been achieved with complete education and full health. If a country has a score of 0.50, then the gross domestic product (GDP) per worker could be twice as high if the country reached the benchmark of potentially complete education and full health (Table 2).

The most important in this regard is due to the fact that this HCI is measured in terms of the productivity of the next generation of workers. In this case, modern education is an essential part of shaping the human capital of the future, since it will have a serious impact on the labor effectiveness of the next generation of workers. In a country at around the 25th percentile of the distribution of each of the human capital' components, a child born in 2018 will be only 43 percent as productive as that child would be under the benchmark of complete education and full health (World Bank, 2018).

Education should be considered critical to ensuring that people are able to fully realize their human capital potential (Altinok, et al., 2018). This is due to the fact that of the three analyzed components of HCI, only education can increase the "leverage" of impact on economic development. The latter is explained by the fact that only education can increase the economic potential of a society, provided there are constant survival rates and health care. It becomes possible on the basis of high quality education, which is associated with the the ability of the individuals to generate and master innovations of the next stage of technological progress of society. Judging by Table 2, no country in the world reaches 1 - the maximum value of HCI.

Table 2. The Human Capital Index (HCI), 2018

Rank	Economy	Lower bound	Value	Upper bound
157	Chad	0.28	**0.29**	0.31
156	South Sudan	0.27	**0.30**	0.33
155	Niger	0.30	**0.32**	0.33
154	Mali	0.29	**0.32**	0.34
153	Liberia	0.31	**0.32**	0.33
152	Nigeria	0.32	**0.34**	0.36
151	Sierra Leone	0.33	**0.35**	0.37
150	Mauritania	0.32	**0.35**	0.38
149	Côte d'Ivoire	0.33	**0.35**	0.37
148	Mozambique	0.34	**0.36**	0.38
147	Angola	0.33	**0.36**	0.39
146	Congo, Dem. Rep.	0.35	**0.37**	0.39
145	Yemen, Rep.	0.35	**0.37**	0.38
144	Burkina Faso	0.35	**0.37**	0.38
143	Lesotho	0.35	**0.37**	0.39
142	Rwanda	0.36	**0.37**	0.39
141	Guinea	0.35	**0.37**	0.39
140	Madagascar	0.35	**0.37**	0.39
139	Sudan	0.37	**0.38**	0.39
138	Burundi	0.36	**0.38**	0.40
137	Uganda	0.37	**0.38**	0.39
136	Papua New Guinea	0.36	**0.38**	0.40
135	Ethiopia	0.37	**0.38**	0.40
134	Pakistan	0.37	**0.39**	0.40
133	Afghanistan	0.38	**0.39**	0.40
132	Cameroon	0.37	**0.39**	0.42
131	Zambia	0.37	**0.40**	0.42
130	Gambia, The	0.37	**0.40**	0.42
129	Iraq	0.38	**0.40**	0.41
128	Tanzania	0.39	**0.40**	0.41
127	Benin	0.38	**0.41**	0.43
126	South Africa	0.40	**0.41**	0.42
125	Malawi	0.39	**0.41**	0.42
124	eSwatini	0.38	**0.41**	0.43
123	Comoros	0.36	**0.41**	0.44
122	Togo	0.39	**0.41**	0.43
121	Senegal	0.40	**0.42**	0.43
120	Congo, Rep.	0.39	**0.42**	0.44
119	Botswana	0.40	**0.42**	0.44
118	Timor-Leste	0.41	**0.43**	0.45
117	Namibia	0.41	**0.43**	0.45
116	Ghana	0.42	**0.44**	0.45
115	India	0.43	**0.44**	0.45
114	Zimbabwe	0.42	**0.44**	0.46
113	Solomon Islands	0.43	**0.44**	0.45
112	Haiti	0.42	**0.45**	0.47
111	Lao PDR	0.43	**0.45**	0.47
110	Gabon	0.43	**0.45**	0.48
109	Guatemala	0.44	**0.46**	0.47
108	Vanuatu	0.45	**0.47**	0.48
107	Myanmar	0.46	**0.47**	0.49
106	Bangladesh	0.47	**0.48**	0.49
105	Kiribati	0.45	**0.48**	0.50
104	Egypt, Arab Rep.	0.47	**0.49**	0.50

Rank	Economy	Lower bound	Value	Upper bound
103	Honduras	0.47	**0.49**	0.50
102	Nepal	0.48	**0.49**	0.50
101	Dominican Republic	0.48	**0.49**	0.51
100	Cambodia	0.47	**0.49**	0.51
99	Guyana	0.48	**0.49**	0.51
98	Morocco	0.49	**0.50**	0.51
97	El Salvador	0.49	**0.50**	0.51
96	Tunisia	0.50	**0.51**	0.52
95	Tonga	0.50	**0.51**	0.53
94	Kenya	0.50	**0.52**	0.53
93	Algeria	0.51	**0.52**	0.53
92	Nicaragua	0.51	**0.53**	0.54
91	Panama	0.52	**0.53**	0.54
90	Paraguay	0.51	**0.53**	0.55
89	Tajikistan	0.51	**0.53**	0.55
88	Macedonia, FYR	0.53	**0.53**	0.54
87	Indonesia	0.52	**0.53**	0.55
86	Lebanon	0.52	**0.54**	0.55
85	Jamaica	0.53	**0.54**	0.56
84	Philippines	0.53	**0.55**	0.56
83	Tuvalu	0.53	**0.55**	0.57
82	West Bank and Gaza	0.54	**0.55**	0.56
81	Brazil	0.55	**0.56**	0.57
80	Kosovo	0.55	**0.56**	0.57
79	Jordan	0.54	**0.56**	0.58
78	Armenia	0.56	**0.57**	0.58
77	Kuwait	0.56	**0.58**	0.59
76	Kyrgyz Republic	0.57	**0.58**	0.59
75	Moldova	0.57	**0.58**	0.59
74	Sri Lanka	0.57	**0.58**	0.59
73	Saudi Arabia	0.57	**0.58**	0.60
72	Peru	0.57	**0.59**	0.60
71	Iran, Islamic Rep.	0.57	**0.59**	0.61
70	Colombia	0.58	**0.59**	0.61
69	Azerbaijan	0.58	**0.60**	0.62
68	Uruguay	0.59	**0.60**	0.61
67	Romania	0.59	**0.60**	0.62
66	Ecuador	0.59	**0.60**	0.61
65	Thailand	0.59	**0.60**	0.62
64	Mexico	0.60	**0.61**	0.61
63	Argentina	0.60	**0.61**	0.62
62	Trinidad and Tobago	0.59	**0.61**	0.63
61	Georgia	0.60	**0.61**	0.63
60	Qatar	0.60	**0.61**	0.63
59	Montenegro	0.61	**0.62**	0.62
58	Bosnia and Herzegovina	0.61	**0.62**	0.63
57	Costa Rica	0.61	**0.62**	0.63
56	Albania	0.61	**0.62**	0.63
55	Malaysia	0.61	**0.62**	0.63
54	Oman	0.61	**0.62**	0.63
53	Turkey	0.61	**0.63**	0.64
52	Mauritius	0.60	**0.63**	0.65
51	Mongolia	0.60	**0.63**	0.65

Rank	Economy	Lower bound	Value	Upper bound
50	Ukraine	0.61	**0.65**	0.68
49	United Arab Emirates	0.64	**0.66**	0.67
48	Vietnam	0.65	**0.67**	0.68
47	Bahrain	0.65	**0.67**	0.68
46	China	0.66	**0.67**	0.68
45	Chile	0.66	**0.67**	0.69
44	Bulgaria	0.65	**0.68**	0.70
43	Seychelles	0.65	**0.68**	0.71
42	Greece	0.67	**0.68**	0.69
41	Luxembourg	0.68	**0.69**	0.70
40	Slovak Republic	0.68	**0.69**	0.71
39	Malta	0.69	**0.70**	0.71
38	Hungary	0.69	**0.70**	0.72
37	Lithuania	0.70	**0.71**	0.73
36	Croatia	0.71	**0.72**	0.74
35	Latvia	0.71	**0.72**	0.74
34	Russian Federation	0.68	**0.73**	0.77
33	Iceland	0.73	**0.74**	0.75
32	Spain	0.74	**0.74**	0.75
31	Kazakhstan	0.72	**0.75**	0.77
30	Poland	0.73	**0.75**	0.76
29	Estonia	0.73	**0.75**	0.76
28	Cyprus	0.74	**0.75**	0.76
27	Serbia	0.74	**0.76**	0.77
26	Belgium	0.75	**0.76**	0.77
25	Macao SAR, China	0.75	**0.76**	0.76
24	United States	0.75	**0.76**	0.77
23	Israel	0.75	**0.76**	0.78
22	France	0.76	**0.76**	0.77
21	New Zealand	0.76	**0.77**	0.78
20	Switzerland	0.75	**0.77**	0.78
19	Italy	0.76	**0.77**	0.78
18	Norway	0.76	**0.77**	0.78
17	Denmark	0.76	**0.77**	0.79
16	Portugal	0.77	**0.78**	0.79
15	United Kingdom	0.77	**0.78**	0.79
14	Czech Republic	0.77	**0.78**	0.79
13	Slovenia	0.78	**0.79**	0.80
12	Austria	0.78	**0.79**	0.80
11	Germany	0.78	**0.79**	0.81
10	Canada	0.79	**0.80**	0.81
9	Netherlands	0.79	**0.80**	0.81
8	Sweden	0.79	**0.80**	0.81
7	Australia	0.79	**0.80**	0.81
6	Ireland	0.79	**0.81**	0.82
5	Finland	0.80	**0.81**	0.82
4	Hong Kong SAR, China	0.81	**0.82**	0.83
3	Japan	0.83	**0.84**	0.85
2	Korea, Rep.	0.83	**0.84**	0.86
1	Singapore	0.87	**0.88**	0.90

HCI < 0.40 | 0.40 ≤ HCI < 0.50 | 0.50 ≤ HCI < 0.60 | 0.60 ≤ HCI < 0.70 | 0.70 ≤ HCI < 0.80 | 0.80 ≤ HCI

Source: World Bank, (2018). *The Human Capital Project.* Washington D.C.: The World Bank Group

Note: The Human Capital Index ranges between 0 and 1. The index is measured in terms of the productivity of the next generation of workers relative to the benchmark of complete education and full health. An economy in which a child born today can expect to achieve complete education and full health will score a value of 1 on the index. Lower and upper bounds indicate the range of uncertainty around the value of the HCI for each economy.

At the same time, there is a significant discrepancy in the labor force structure between what the modern labor market requires and what the modern education system can offer (Fig. 1).

Artificial intelligence and self-teaching computer programs that replicate human skills are combining with other technologies, such as sensors, to produce self-driving cars and trucks. Such innovations usually require a parallel transformation in workers' skills to implement the new technology and business models. David H. Autor and his co-authors (Autor, and Dorn, 2013; Autor, et al., 2016) find that the demand for higher-order cognitive skills—including numeracy, literacy, and problem solving in technology-rich environments—increases with an economy's technological sophistication. A closer look at employment trends in science, technology, engineering, and math (STEM) occupations in the United States confirms that there is a premium associated with the higher-order skills needed in a knowledge-based economy. STEM employment growth has outpaced that of non-STEM occupations over the past decade, at 24 percent and 4 percent, respectively. This trend is expected to continue, with STEM occupations projected to grow 9 percent between 2014 and 2024 compared with about 6 percent for other jobs (Riad, 2017). To illustrate this point, it is advisable to use the model of learning-adjusted years of school, proposed by the World Bank team (Fig. 2). They are calculated by multiplying expected years of school by the ratio of test scores in a country to a benchmark score of 625, which corresponds to the TIMSS standard of advanced achievement (Filmer et al. (2018). This methodology was introduced by the World Bank (2018) and is elaborated by Filmer, Deon, Halsey Rogers, Noam Angrist, and Shwetlena Sabarwal (2018). It provides details on the rationale for this conversion from test scores into equivalent years of school. As a result, all other things being equal, education becomes the decisive factor in ensuring stable economic growth of its national communities (Rychen, and Salganik (eds.), 2003; Rychen, et al., 2003; Rychen, and Salganik (eds.), 2001; Salganik, et al., 1999).

Figure 1. Out of the ordinary: Demand for non-routine analytical and interpersonal skills continues to rise in the US labor market, while that for manual and routine tasks falls or stagnates
Source: Autor, David, and Brendan Price. 2013. "The Changing task composition of the US labor market: An update of Autor, Levy and Murnane." MIT Working Paper, Massachusetts Institute of Technology, Cambridge, MA; Nagwa Riad, 2017.

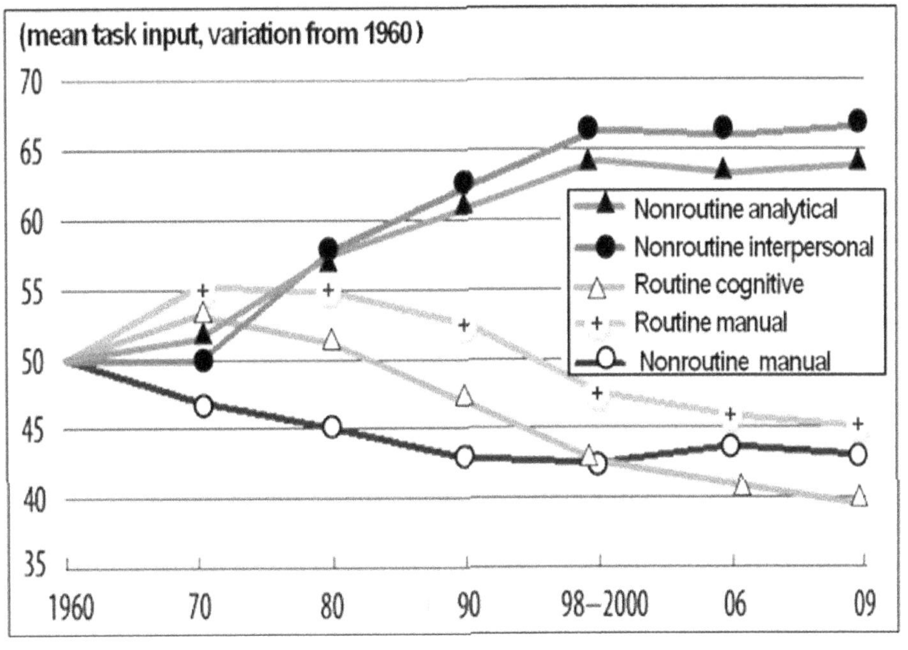

Human capital is important because there is now a higher premium on adaptability (World Bank, 2019). To thrive in today's innovation-driven economy workers need a different mix of skills than in the past. In addition to foundational skills like literacy and numeracy, they need competencies like collaboration, creativity and problem-solving and character qualities like persistence, curiosity and initiative. The shift in skill demand has exposed a problem in skill supply: more than a third of global companies reported difficulties filling open positions in 2014, owing to shortages of people with key skills (Manpower Group, 2014).

Although it is difficult to quantify the contributions of education to economic growth, C. Goldin and L. Katz (2008) emphasize that they are bound to have been quite large. As for the relationship between human capital and technological progress - the creation and adoption of new technologies - it is useful to note that it operates at least through three channels (Acemoglu, and Autor, 2012). *First*, the human capital and access to education of the most talented individuals in society is probably the most important factor underpinning technological progress. *Second*, the human capital of the individuals may influence the pace of technological change both because of human capital externalities and because it changes the incentives for overall technological progress (as many technologies may not be profitable without the requisite skills from the workforce). *Third,* relatedly, the educational level of human capital of the professionals potentially affects the direction of technological progress (Acemoglu, 1998). As a result the most significant investments that stakeholders can make in the sustainable economic growth are in enhancing human capital.

Figure 2. Education: harmonized test scores and learning-adjusted years of school vs log real GDP per capita

Source: See "HCI data notes" section at the end of this appendix, World Bank, (2018.). Note: GDP = gross domestic product; PPP = purchasing power parity. Test scores are used to convert expected years of school into learning adjusted years of school (panel c and d). Learning-adjusted years of school are obtained by multiplying expected years of school by the ratio of test scores to 625, corresponding to the TIMSS benchmark of advanced achievement. For example, if expected years of school in a country is 10 and the average test score is 400, then the country has 10 × (400/625) = 6.4 learning-adjusted years of school. The distance between 10 and 6.4 represents a learning gap equivalent to 3.6 years of school.

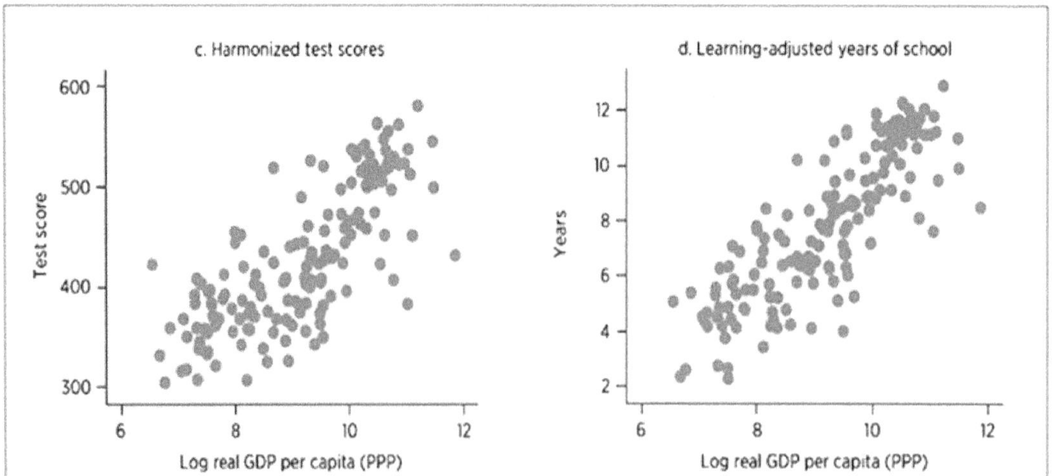

Modern Educational Crisis: The Students "Failure" in the Learning Process

However, modern education cannot be used as a lever of a positive impact on economic growth, since the number of highly educated graduates as carriers of human capital is decreasing. The difference between schooling and learning is dramatic. Country-level average test scores range from around 600 in the best-performing countries to around 300 in the worst-performing according to a benchmark of minimum proficiency set by the Programme for International Student Assessment (PISA), the largest international testing program. Less than half of students in developing countries meet this standard, compared with 86 percent in advanced economies (World Bank, 2018). In Singapore, 98 percent of students reach the international benchmark for basic proficiency in secondary school; in South Africa, only 26 percent of students meet that standard. Essentially, then, all of Singapore's secondary school students are prepared for a postsecondary education and the world of work, while almost three-quarters of South Africa's young people are not (World Bank, 2018). The World Development Report 2018 (WDR, 2018) determines the current position of the education system in the world as the real learning crisis. This is reflected in the fact that learning outcomes are poor because of low levels, high inequality, slow progress (Pritchett, 2013). As a whole schoolers learn very little in many education systems and after several years in school, millions of students lack basic literacy and numeracy skills. Many high-performing students in middle-income countries who have risen to the top quarter of their cohorts—would rank in the bottom quarter in a wealthier country.

The World Bank's experts express four determinants (Fig. 3) of the learning crisis (Hanushek, 1979): learner preparation, teacher skills and motivation, the availability of relevant inputs, and the school management and governance that bring all these elements together. Based on the fundamentals of the theory of PCB, the author justifies the main reason, which predetermines all four components of the learning crisis. This also applies to the inability of epy students to fully understand the curriculum and acquire knowledge, skills, attitudes and values.

Figure 3. Four determinants of the learning crisis
Source: composed on the materials of World Bank (WDR, 2018).

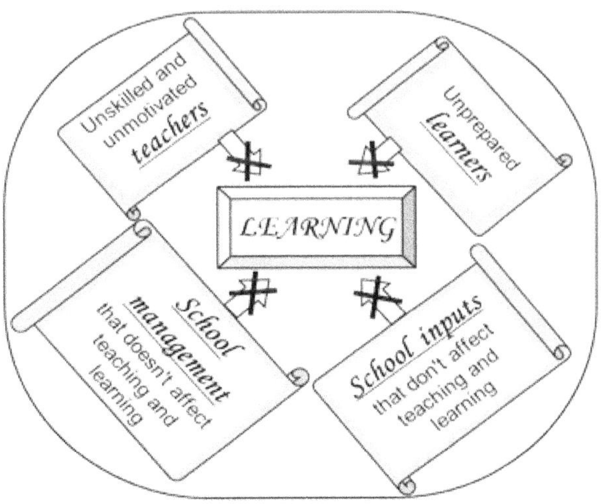

It is about ignoring in each of the four components in Fig. 3, describing the learning process, the presence of PCBs in all its determinants (Pilipenko, at al., 2019). The existence of this phenomenon is proved by the figures below (Fig. 4-5). Thanks to the growing availability of the large-scale student assessments, it becomes possible to explore how learning mediates the relationship from schooling to economic growth (Barro, 2001, 2013).

While the relationship between test scores and growth is strong even after controlling for the years of schooling completed, years of schooling do not predict growth once test scores are taken into account or they become only marginally significant (Barro (2013) (Fig. 4). In other words, what matters is less the years of education completed than the knowledge that students acquire while in school. In other words, if the knowledge gained during the adjusted schooling (test scores) is positively correlated with the GDP per capita growth (Fig. 4a), then there is no correlation between years of unadjusted schooling and economic growth (Fig. 4b). In exactly the same way, there becomes evident the weak link between education spending and learning (Fig. 5).

The link between spending and learning differs enormously, even among countries at similar levels of economic development. (Lavinas and Veiga (2013). As to public spending on education, cross-country correlations between the latter and learning levels are weak and statistically insignificant after controlling for income per capita (Budzier and Flyvbjerg, 2012). Learning shortfalls during the school years eventually show up as weak skills in the workforce. Work skill shortages are often discussed in a way that is disconnected from the debate on learning, but the two are parts of the same problem. Governments have built classrooms and recruited teachers at unprecedented levels. But these efforts do not give tangible results in terms of the quality of knowledge and skills (WDR, 2018). The crisis state of modern education is not related to the absence of one or several of the four key components of the school level for learning: prepared learners, effective teaching, learning focused inputs, and the skilled management and governance that pulls them all together. The main reason for the lack of effect of improving the quality of

Figure 4. Learning and economic growth (Annual average per capita growth in GDP, 1970–2015, conditional on test scores, years of schooling completed, and initial GDP per capita
Source: WDR 2018 team, using data on test scores from Hanushek, Eric A., and Ludger Woessmann (2012) and data on years of schooling and GDP from the World Bank's World Development Indicators (database), 2017. Available at http://bit.do/WDR2018-Fig_1-5.

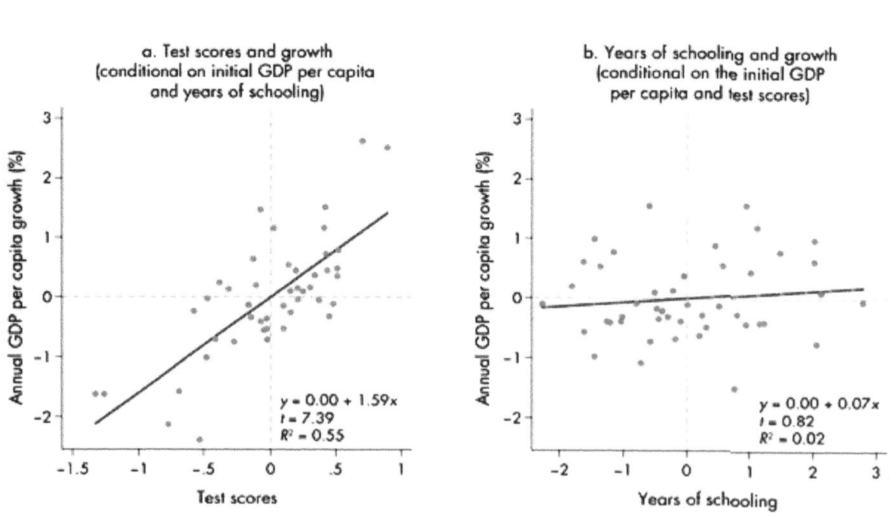

education due to the improvement of the four key components of the learning process is associated with the disregard by all participants of this process of the PCB problem of students. And if this problem is not put at the forefront of all four key components of school learning, then all the mechanisms for their improvement, including the growth of funding for the education system, will not produce results (Fig. 4-5).

Without overcoming the students' PCBs in the learning process, it is impossible to provide them with a high level of knowledge and skills necessary for the modern labor market. But according to the last investigations the channel by which schooling accelerates economic growth appears to be through boosting learning and skills (Glewwe, et al., 2014; Hanushek and Woessmann, 2008, 2012). The PCB phenomenon is complex in its essence and in forms of its manifestation. Unsatisfied students PCBs in the process of acquiring knowledge hinder his successful mastering of skills. As a result, the student cannot independently develop approaches to solving problems outside the school curriculum. All the above predetermines individual sense of dissatisfaction (lack of success, failure) in education and prevents the acquisition of socially oriented attitudes and values.

This influences the value peculiarities of social exchange, when the carrier of low educational quality human capital understands that he cannot claim life success. As a result, the lack of success in education as a result of insurmountable PCBs leads to failure in professional activities and in the appropriate processes of re-skilling and up-skilling. This is how the chain reaction of the unsurpassed PCBs in education is formed, which results in a divergence of the demand for labor force and of its supply. As a result, human capital, having a low educational component, cannot perform the role of a driver of economic growth in the future, dooming the national communities to the stagnation. And the most important thing is that the educational and life failure of an individual as the owner of human capital predetermines his life strategy of behavior, oriented not so much on growth as on survival. For society, it results in an increase in the social stratum below the middle class, which does not generate either the economic growth of society or its social stability.

Figure 5. Simple associations between education spending and learning are weak
Source: WDR, 2018. P. 173; using data from OECD (2016); UIS (2017); World Bank (2017a). Data available at: http://bit.do/WDR2018-Fig_9-2. Note: AUS = Australia; BGR = Bulgaria; BRA = Brazil; COL = Colombia; CZE = Czech Republic; GBR = United Kingdom; HUN = Hungary; IDN = Indonesia; KOR = Republic of Korea; LTU = Lithuania; PER = Peru; POL = Poland; SVK = Slovak Republic. GNI = gross national income; PISA = Programme for International Student Assessment; PPP = purchasing power parity U.S. dollars.

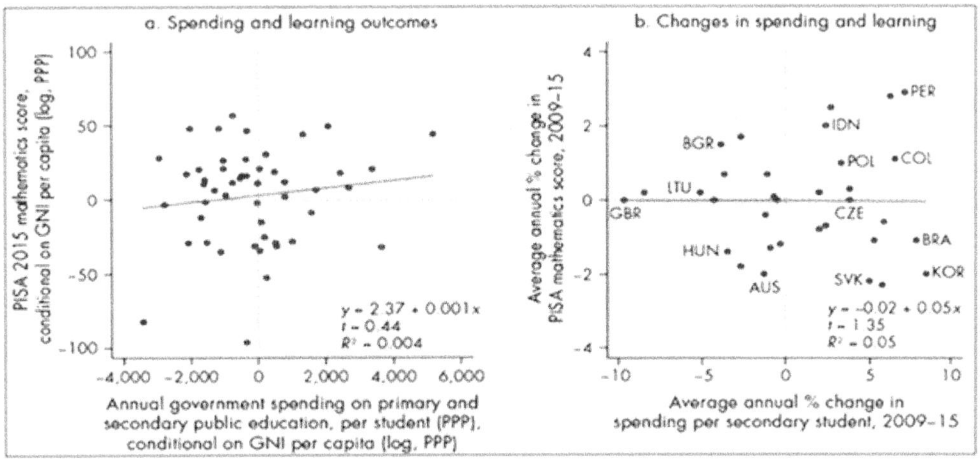

PCB Theory and the Problems of Learning and the Students' "Unsuccessfulness" in Schooling

As mentioned above, the PCB theory makes it possible to select the "how to learn (*learning to learn*)" problem (Pinsky, 1978) as the issue of the great importance in the schooling. This is due to the fact that the identification of the psychology and cognitive barriers in the students' consciousness (as well as of all persons engaged in education), of the reasons for their appearance and the mechanisms for their overcoming will eliminate crisis phenomena from the educational process. The first thing that will allow to partially or completely unlock the process of learning and improving its quality is the overcoming PCBs in the consciousness of both teachers and learners. The remaining two factors (Fig. 3) - school management and school inputs, affecting the quality of schooling can enhance this effect, eliminating the consequences of crisis in learning. If, however, the problem associated with students' psychological and cognitive barriers is not solved (Fig.6), the remaining factors for improving the education system will not lead to an increase in the level of learning.

Given all the investments countries have made in education, these shortfalls in learning are discouraging. Acting effectively requires first understanding how schools are failing learners and how systems are failing schools (World Bank, 2018). As evidence of the learning crisis has grown, so has understanding of what produces learning. Cognitive neuroscience has evolved dramatically, with brain imaging revealing new insights into how children learn (De Smedt, 2014; Insel, and Landis, 2013; Kuhl, 2010). Comprehensive and multidisciplinary analysis of the phenomenon of PCB, presupposing historical and philosophical, psycholinguistic, psychological, categorical, and subject aspects allow lining up the

Figure 6. The model of real cognitive consciousness of students as a form of PCB manifestation
Source: The author's development

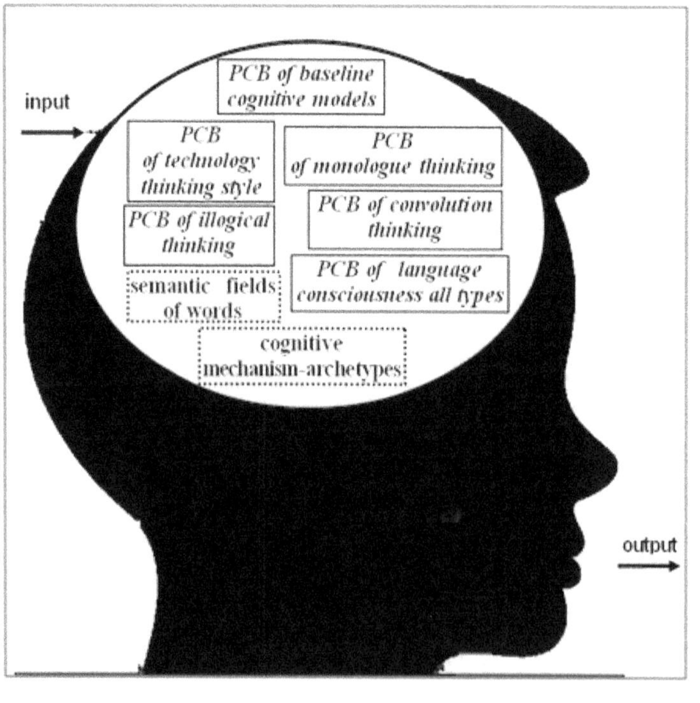

model of real cognitive consciousness of students (Fig. 6). It is this typology that can become in the teachers' hands an effective means of diagnosing various difficulties (PCBs) of students, as well as a real mechanism for optimizing the educational process as a whole.

Consider the probabilistic model proposed by the author, which allows to quantify the results of students' independent educational work, taking into account the level of a certain PCB group overcoming. It should be noted that the educational information that the student processes during the study of school disciplines is naturally distorted by the PCB system, misinterpreted, scattered and simply lost. This negative process can be characterized in two ways.

On the one hand, by modeling the probabilities of manifestation and non-manifestation of one or another PCB groups in the processing a given schooling material, it can be possible to obtain an appropriate set of estimates for different numbers of barriers (difficulties). For example, in the entire volume $\boldsymbol{V}$ of information processed by the student, probabilities $\boldsymbol{P_V(m)}$ are considered that difficulties (the triggering of a certain group of PCB) are encountered $\boldsymbol{m}$ times, where $\boldsymbol{m}$ takes values 0, 1, 2, … . The maximum value of $\boldsymbol{m}$ is chosen so that the sum of the probabilities is close to one:

$$P_V\left(0\right)+P_V\left(1\right)+\ldots+P_V\left(m\right)=\sum_{k=0}^{m}P_V\left(k\right)\approx 1. \tag{1}$$

In other words, a complete system of incompatible events is considered: PCBs occur in the students' consciousness a different numbers of times. On the other hand, with the probabilities $\boldsymbol{P_V(k)}$, it becomes possible to estimate the corresponding entropy' values $\boldsymbol{H_k}$.

$$H_k=-P_V\left(k\right)\log_2\left[P_V\left(k\right)\right] \tag{2}$$

Here, this assessment acts as a measure of the uncertainty of learning outcomes and of the actual teaching itself. It is provided with the mechanism of PCBs functioning in the consciousness of students. In this sense, entropy is associated with the dispersion of educational information processed by a student because of the system of such traps of consciousness, as PCB:

$$H=\sum_{k=0}^{m}H_k=\sum_{k=0}^{m}P_V\left(k\right)\log_2\left[P_V\left(k\right)\right] \tag{3}$$

Given the above, it should be emphasized that even the very high level of formal education of the workers does not develop the skills demanded by the modern labor market. There is a growing skills gap as students progress through the education system, which widens further as they enter the labor market (Fig. 7). The modern education system is facing challenges in teaching students both high-order cognitive skills and the non-cognitive social skills that innovative firms in particular need. This scheme, proposed for the case of the crisis of education in Russia (World Bank, 2016), is very convenient to illustrate the phenomenon of the multiplication of insurmountable PCBs in the educational process when harmonizing knowledge and skills (in the Fig. 7 this is presented as mismatch between the skills supplied and demanded).

Figure 7. The widening skills gap as the manifestation of the mismatch between the supplied and demanded skills
Source: World Bank, (2016). The Russian Federation Systematic Country Diagnostic. Pathways to Inclusive Growth. Paris: World Bank Group.

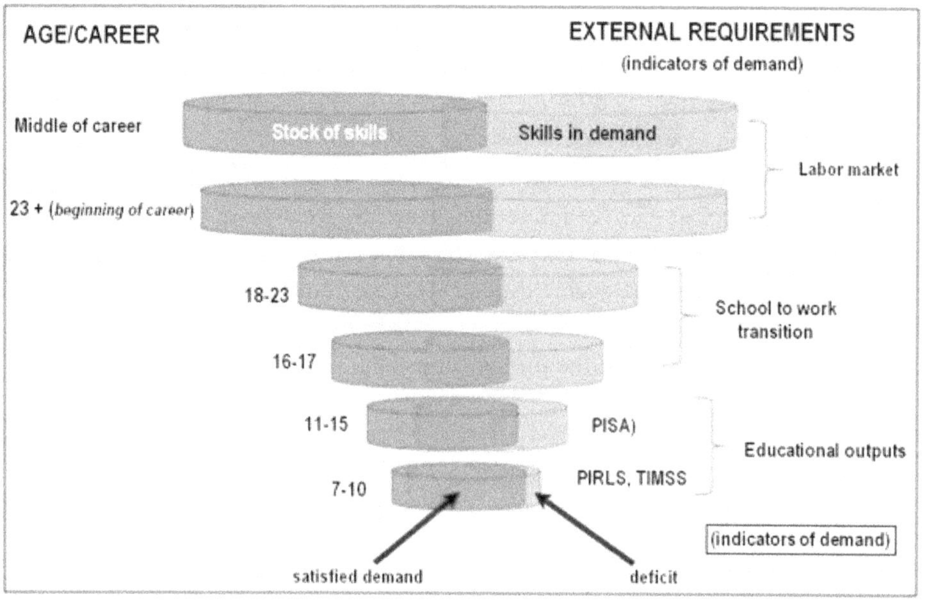

This scheme is remarkable in the sense that its authors demonstrate PCBs, the meaning of which is to allow knowledge without skills, and skills without knowledge. In any case, it becomes impossible to coincide schooling and learning as a manifestation of the educational crisis, and even more so, to solve it. From viewpoint of A.C. Grayling of Britain's New College of the Humanities (The Economist Intelligence Unit Limited, 2017): "If a school teaches how to code, for instance, the important thing the students learn is not the specific computer language, but the understanding of how to manipulate computer software. The really crucial thing now is *how* to learn." A modern graduate and his human capital must possess the qualities of "intellectual autonomy", which allows the future professional to skillfully build a strategy of his behavior that is not focused on survival (while maintaining his family's living positions and that of his own), but on growth (improving the living standards of his relatives as well as of his own). Fig. 7 shows the insurmountable PCBs of schoolers in the form of divergence of skills without knowledge and skills based on knowledge from their age of 11-15 years. The discrepancy between the knowledge and skills of graduates (as PCBs acquired in school) is fixed in their consciousness when they reach the age of 18-23. In the future, this predetermines the formation of an outdated structure of human capital, which is less and less in demand in the modern labor market. Such is the model of formation of the student's failure in education, which predetermines his failure both in his profession and in his life.

The PCBs Overcoming: The Formation of Intellectually Autonomous Carriers of the Future Human Capital

If the teacher is not able to help the student to identify specific PCBs (Fig. 6) and to overcome it, then the student will multiply the process of misunderstanding of the subjects taught. And the more there will be these barriers in the student's consciousness and they will not be overcome, the more the *schooling* (the school attendance) and the learning processes will not coincide. Research on the educational outcomes has become aiming at reflecting the distinction between schooling and learning.

As a result the focus on learning has grown, and some studies confirm that learning and skills matter (Glewwe, Maiga, and Zheng, 2014; Hanushek, and Woessmann, 2008, 2012; Hanushek, Lavy, and Hitomi, 2008; Hanushek, Eric A., and Ludger Woessmann, 2008). This has its explanation associated with the new requirements of technological progress. Its main specificity is connected with the growing uncertainty for the professional activity of the future school graduates, and, therefore, the skills and rules tested by previous generations and taught in the schooling become ineffective in new conditions. Moreover, the previous generations of graduates could be successful even acquiring skills without understanding its knowledgeable base. But the modern schoolchildren should acquire knowledge on the basis of which skills are formed. This predetermines the formation of the intellectual autonomy of the individual. As such, in future he will be able to independently find the new knowledge that will allow him to develop skills effective for professional activities in an uncertain external environment. Moreover, such a result will be achieved only under the condition of elimination of the PCBs in the student's consciousness due to the "schizophrenic" division in acquiring knowledge and skills in schooling.

It is necessary to propose a universal model of the sequence of actions in the learning process, which will allow to eliminate the most stable PCBs in the pupil's consciousness. Only this will make it possible to form human capital that can meet the requirements of the future technological progress and serve as a powerful driver of socio-economic development.

The tendencies of development of the global educational space show a phenomenologically distinct essential difference (common barrier or gap) between the formed and real cognitive representations of students. The psycho-pedagogical cause of this mass phenomenon can be explained at a strict scientific level and corrected only within the framework of the PCB theory in schooling. The present complexity of this reflection is explained very simply. The problem is that PCB as a learning phenomenon remains out of sight and of the activity of the teacher. Only the teacher's acquaintance with the PCB theory foundations will make it possible to discern the fact of mass difficulties and typical errors in the psychological mechanisms of these negative phenomena and to identify the types of psychological and cognitive barriers. Actually the problem of massive real cognitive difficulties begins at school. The psychological and cognitive barriers are spontaneously forming in the schoolchildren' consciousness and are not overcome. The problem of the real cognitive representations that is not adequate to the real environment starts forming at school. The last serves as the basis for significant difficulties of students in learning at secondary and high schools. In order to effectively shape the creative potential of future specialists, secondary school and university teachers should know which barriers inhibit the intellectual development of students.

In this regard, the author's theory of PCB introduces a number of new didactic teaching principles. The most important of them are the two following: a) the principle of systematic and purposeful PCBs overcoming in schooling, and б) the principle of two-level reflection: of students' reflection of the scientific knowledge genesis and of self-reflection of one's own mental difficulties (psychological and cognitive barriers of various types). These principles and the proposed model of the student's cognitive barriers (Fig. 6) are disclosed in the system of the main provisions of the PCBs overcoming methodology in schooling. This approach implements the mandatory correction and prevention of typical difficulties and mistakes in students' learning and thinking activities, subject to their obligatory co-participation in learning and self-reflection of the knowledge components and self-reflection of the cognitive methods themselves. By fixing possible or actual difficulties, mistakes of students, the teacher "breaks" the learning process that proceeds "automatically" at the level of everyday thinking. This is aimed at analyzing, together with the students, the reasons for the failures, explaining the essence of the PCBs, and revealing the gap between knowledge and delusion, incomprehension. As a result, the student learns to find the causes of the current misunderstanding and moves to a higher level of reflection, trying to overcome the resulting PCBs. In other words, the teacher should demonstrate to the student the logic of theoretical knowledge development "near" the error (organizing the knowledge component reflection, expressed as "I know that") and the cause of the error itself as a violation of this logic, a defect in reasoning (organizing the self-reflection, expressed as "I know it and I know how I know it"). Thus, in order to overcome PCBs, the teacher breaks off the natural, proceeding within the customary framework of the everyday consciousness of students, vicious process of the formation of formal knowledge. To do this, he interrupts the learning process and fixes two streams in the student's consciousness - of the scientific information and of his own thoughts. This allows the student to realize the operational-effective structure of new concepts, definitions, theorems, economic and physical laws, the kinetics of chemical reactions, etc. At the same time, the widespread use of elements of entertaining, the theory of solving inventive problems, counterexamples, sophisms, paradoxes, and excursions into the history of mathematical, statistical, economic, physical, and other discoveries is welcomed, as this revives the educational dialogue and stimulates the cognitive activity of students.

However, the teacher-specialist should acquire approaches that enable him to identify PCBs in students' consciousness as well as their reasons and to develop methods to overcome them. In a sense, the school teacher of future intellectually autonomous professionals must himself acquire these qualities, but today.

Education and Living Standard of the Middle Class: Necessary and Sufficient Conditions for the Human Capital Formation as a Driver of Sustainable Economic Growth

Education can be called a genetic code that allows you to save and transfer knowledge, skills and attitudes and values accumulated in society and acquired in the process of learning from past to future generations. This is due to the fact that there is always a significant time lag, for example, between the babies' birth today and the inclusion of their human capital as factors of social development in 18-23 years. In this sense, knowledge, skills, attitudes and values, obtained in the learning in present, are their projection on the future development of society. It is in this sense that human capital is associated with social capital, which in one or another combination integrates the individual-oriented and socially-oriented values of individuals. And in this context, the society, at the stage of learning of individuals, should create the necessary conditions for the formation, both in the current and in the future, of socially oriented values in the form of attitudes and values.

Following the logic of the material presentation in Fig.8, it is advisable to divide the entire path from school as the starting point of an individual's movement along the long way of human capital formation to his professional activity conditionally into three stages.

As for the possibility of using human capital of successful young individuals, provided that they are highly educated, the sufficient conditions are connected with the formation of the corresponding competences in the second stage of the long way to professional success. The latter are interpreted by the author through a prism of *mobilisation of knowledge, skills, attitudes and values, obtained in the education system, to meet complex demands of the society* (Rychen, and Salganik, 2003). In other words,

Figure 8. The OECD Learning Framework 2030: Work-in-progress
Source: OECD, 2018. (OECD, (2018). The Future of Education and Skills:Education 2030. Paris: OECD).

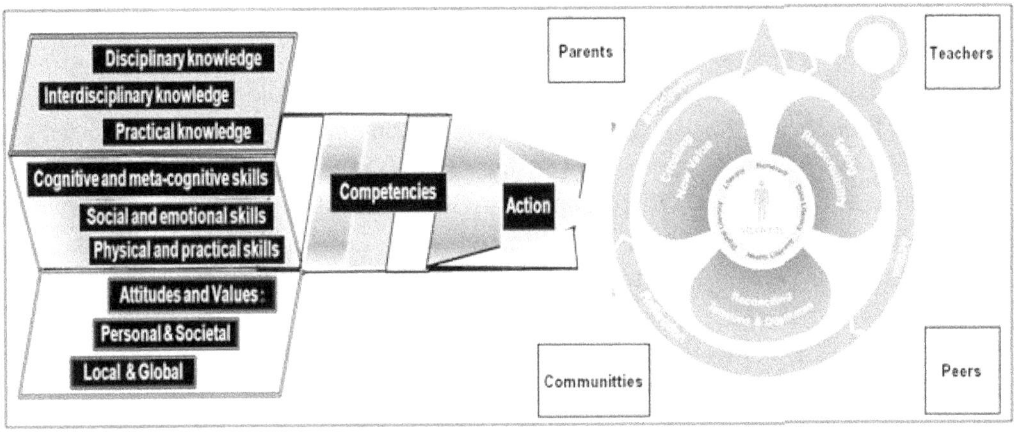

having overcome the PCBs (or rather, knowing about them and having learned to overcome them) in schooling, the individual, as the carrier of human capital, chooses the most acceptable model of adaptation to the requirements of society (Rychen, et al., 2003; Rychen, and Salganik, 2001, Saladnil, et al., 1999). To do this, the individual must be able to transform the learning outcomes into "transformative competencies" (OECD, 2018), allowing him: (1) Creating new value; (2) Reconciling tensions and dilemmas; (3) Taking responsibility.

But this ability to develop competencies is itself something to be learned using a sequenced process of reflection, anticipation and action. Equally, creativity and problemsolving require the capacity to consider the future consequences of one's actions, to evaluate risk and reward, and to accept accountability for the products of one's work. This suggests a sense of responsibility, and moral and intellectual maturity, with which a person can reflect upon and evaluate his or her actions in light of his or her experiences, and personal and societal goals, what they have been taught and told, and what is right or wrong. Central to this competency is the concept of self-regulation, which involves self-control, self-efficacy, responsibility, problem solving and adaptability. And in this case, at the second stage of the beginning of his professional activity, the individual begins to use the formed human capital. If he is successful in education, then, having passed such a difficult way in becoming himself as a high-class specialist, he can become socially oriented in his values. At the same time, the society must ensure the necessary demand for its human capital and offer in return the corresponding material, moral and social status. As a rule, for a successful individual's life, a sufficient condition for such a consensus with society is the living standard of the middle class.

Current trends indicate a reduction in this stratum all over the world, and it serves as an additional barrier created by society towards the full-fledged inclusion of successful individuals with a high level of human capital in the socio-economic development of society (OECD, 2019a, 2019b). On average across OECD countries, the share of people in middle-income households, defined as households earning between 75% and 200% of the median national income, fell from 64% to 61% between the mid-1980s and mid-2010s (OECD, 2019b). The aggregate income of all middle-income households was four times the aggregate income of high-income households three decades ago; today, this ratio is less than three. The middle-income group has grown smaller with each successive generation: 70% of the baby boomers were part of the middle class in their twenties, compared with 60% of the millennial. Overall, over the past 30 years, median incomes increased a third less than the average income of the richest 10%. In parallel, the cost of essential parts of the middle-class lifestyle have increased faster than inflation; house prices have been growing three times faster than household median income over the last two decades. It showed that in many OECD countries, opportunities for low and middle-income families to move up the ladder became limited over the past decades. Moreover, many middle-class families faced a growing risk of falling down to a lower income or a lower status (OECD, 2019b).

The analyses found that in many OECD countries (OECD, 20I8) opportunities for low and middle-income families to move up the ladder became limited as the steps became larger. At the same time, many families witness a growing risk to fall down to lower income or a lower status. In particular, middle classes generally invest heavily in their own education and that of their children, thus increasing current and future stock of human capital (Brown and Hunter, 2004;_Pressman, 2007; Bassanini, and Scarpetta, 2002).

The third stage is connected with the human capital accumulation in the process of the professional growth of the individuals, of their re-skilling and up-skilling. Thus, an increase in the share of the population with secondary and higher education makes it possible to form a strong middle class. And in general, its representatives can consistently ensure the welfare and growth of GDP per capita (Brueckner, et al.. 2017; OECD, 2003). In this context, representatives of the middle class as carriers of human capital create the social capital of society. Moreover, the main result of the integration of necessary and sufficient conditions for the formation of high-quality human capital is the expansion of the social ladder along which the lower social strata of society can see their happy advance upward, thanks to the success in education.

RESULTS AND DISCUSSION

Thus, the quality of human capital education in the future is tested by the market demand and supply of professionals able to meet the technological challenges of the emerging paradigm of human development after 2020 (Ausan, 2017).

According to the approach of J. Rasmussen (Rasmussen, 1983), all employed in the economy can be divided into three categories: in the "skill" group, half of all workers activities are based on repeated typical tasks of mainly physical labor; in the "rule" group, more than half of all tasks are implemented in technical routine work on the basis of prescribed rules and instructions; and in the "knowledge" group, half of all tasks can be performed only in the process of analytical work, improvisation, and creativity under conditions of uncertainty. The specificity of the last group of professionals is connected with their high educational level, broad outlook and ability to create in the conditions of intellectual autonomy. With the increasing penetration of algorithms and computer solutions, today it is already obvious the reorientation of the demand of the labor market towards "human in a human being".

Application of the PCB theory in schooling will allow to achieve the following. Having learned to analyze the PCBs causes in the schooling and to successfully overcome them, school graduates acquire the ability to independently identify obstacles (based on the new knowledge) in their professional activities, to understand their reasons (based on the new knowledge), and to model options for obstacles overcoming, forming new skills by themselves. All the above suggests that countries could innovate to improve learning, drawing on more systematic knowledge than ever available before about what can work at the micro level—the level of learners, classrooms, and schools. But reorientation of schooling to identifying the PCBs in the students' consciousness and their successful overcoming will result in substantial gains in learning. The promising approaches based on the PCB theory make possible to improve learning outcomes. And it gives hope (Evans, and Yuan, 2017).

The PCB theory let understand the causes of the distinction between schooling and learning. In the past, most empirical research equated education with schooling—whether measured by school enrollment, number of years of schooling, or degrees acquired—in part because of lack of other good measures of education. But as the focus on learning has grown, some studies have explored the effects of the skills that students acquire. The results confirm that the contemporary education crisis manifests in the form of the absence of the knowledge-based skills. In other words, what matters is less the years of education completed than the knowledge that students acquire while in school. Some investigations show that providing all students with basic cognitive skills could massively boost economic outcomes, especially in developing countries (Hanushek, and Woessmann, 2015; OECD, 2010).

Without any doubt, education has a much great role to play than simply equipping people with knowledge and skills for the professional activity of the future. Education is what breaks down cycles of poverty and oppression and let the carrier of the human capital climb up the social ladder (WEF, 2018). At times the effectiveness of an apparently similar intervention can vary even within a country, depending on how the innovative educational programs are implemented (Bold, et al., 2016; Kerwin, and Thornton, 2015). The main point is that a concrete adaptation of the possibilities of the PCB theory application should be carried out taking into account the national specifics of the country's education system.

EMPIRICAL EVIDENCE

As an application of the model (1) - (3), it is reasonable to consider the process of students' studying of educational and scientific material as a Poisson stream of events like "manifestation of PCBs ***k*** times" in a student's learning activity. Let, for definiteness, the volume ***V*** of the material being studied by a student is 125 pages of a rather complex text. Obviously, it can be argued that ***V*** = 125 independent tests are carried out, according to which a series of probability distribution of PCBs manifestations is estimated.

To correctly use the Poisson distribution, the number of additional notation should be introduced. It is reasonable to characterize the events "manifestation of PCB ***k*** times" in the process of the student's work with educational material with a constant probability $\boldsymbol{p = \alpha}$ for him.

The author introduces a constant $\lambda = Vp$ as a distribution parameter in the Poisson law.

Now the terms of formula (1) can be represented as follows:

$$\sum_{k=0}^{m} P_{125}\left(k\right) = \sum_{k=0}^{m} \frac{\lambda^{k} e^{-\lambda}}{k!}, \tag{4}$$

and the corresponding entropy values (2) in the formula below

$$H = \sum_{k=0}^{m} H_{k} = \sum_{k=0}^{m} \frac{\lambda^{k} e^{-\lambda}}{k!} \log_{2}\left(\frac{\lambda^{k} e^{-\lambda}}{k!}\right). \tag{5}$$

Table 3. The set of probabilities of the distribution series of the random variable **k** *as the number of possible manifestations of a specific PCB group and the corresponding series of entropy values in the framework of the author's probabilistic model of learning outcomes*

k	**0**	**1**	**2**	**…**	m
$P_V(k)$	$e^{-\lambda}$	$\frac{\lambda^1 e^{-\lambda}}{1!}$	$\frac{\lambda^2 e^{-\lambda}}{2!}$	…	$\frac{\lambda^m e^{-\lambda}}{m!}$
H_k	$-e^{-\lambda}\log_2(e^{-\lambda})$	$-\frac{\lambda^1 e^{-\lambda}}{1!}\log_2\left(\frac{\lambda^1 e^{-\lambda}}{1!}\right)$	…	…	$-\frac{\lambda^m e^{-\lambda}}{m!}\log_2\left(\frac{\lambda^m e^{-\lambda}}{m!}\right)$

Source: The author's development

Based on the formulas (4) and (5), it is possible to construct a series of probability distributions. They quantitatively characterize the features of the manifestation of cognitive difficulties (PCBs) in the student's consciousness including the processing of the information offered to him and the corresponding number of dispersion of the processed educational information within the model of real cognitive consciousness of students (Fig. 6, Table 3).

It is possible to simulate the independent work of four students, assuming that for the first of them (the least successful) $\boldsymbol{\alpha}$ = 0,078; for the second one $\boldsymbol{\alpha}$ = 0,015; for the third one $\boldsymbol{\alpha}$ = 0,010; and for the fourth one (the most successful), $\boldsymbol{\alpha}$ = 0,004. (Obviously, such small values of probabilities indicate a fairly systematic work of the teacher in overcoming the massive cognitive barriers (PCBs) of students).

In the model experiment with the first student, the Poisson distribution parameter $\boldsymbol{\lambda}$ is $\boldsymbol{\lambda} = 125\times0.078 = 9.75$, and the maximum value of $\boldsymbol{m}$ is chosen to be 17, i.e. $\boldsymbol{m} = 17$. In this case, the formula (1) takes the following form:

$$P_{125}(0) + P_{125}(1) + \ldots + P_{125}(17) = e^{-9.75} + \frac{9.75^1 e^{-9.75}}{1!} + \frac{9.75^2 e^{-9.75}}{2!} + \ldots + \frac{9.75^{17} e^{-9.75}}{17!} = 0.989$$

Similarly, model experiments are performed with the second, the third, and the fourth students with the parameters $\boldsymbol{\lambda}$ of the Poisson distribution, with the following values: 1.875; 1.25 and 0.5. The results of the corresponding calculations in MS Excel using the statistical function **POISSON(value; mean; FALSE)**, i.e. **POISSON (k; λ; 0)** are presented in the Table 4.

The Table 4 shows when students work with educational and scientific text as the probability of an event "manifestation of PCB $\boldsymbol{k}$ times" decreases from $\boldsymbol{p} = 0{,}078$ till $\boldsymbol{p} = 0{,}004$:

1) the maximum value of $\boldsymbol{k}$ decreases from $\boldsymbol{m} = 17$ till $\boldsymbol{m} = 5$;
2) the total entropy as a measure of the uncertainty of the results of processing students' learning information decreases from 3.2516 till 1.3361;
3) the volume of the Poisson series of the probability distribution of the random variable $\boldsymbol{k}$ decreases as the number of possible manifestations of a certain PCB group;

4) the highest value of entropy falls on the most probable values of the random variable ***k*** - possible manifestations of a certain PCB group;
5) when $p = 0.004$, the learning activity is most successful: the amount of knowledge gained is adequately implemented in the largest amount of skills (on 125 pages of new learning information there is a minimum number of PCBs).

It should be noted that the result deteriorates dramatically if, when a student works with educational material, the characteristic constant probability ***p*** of the event "manifestation of the PCB ***k*** times" is not less than 0.5 ($p \geq 0.5$). In this case, the Poisson probability distribution, while remaining discrete, is close in shape to the Gauss distribution.

The figures below (Fig. 9-10) show a graphical interpretation of the developed model ideas about the results of the learning activities of each of the four students in the framework of the PCB theory (Fig. 6).

The Fig. 9 clearly shows the probabilities of some of the frequently manifested PCBs in the consciousness of the first student. It is quite obvious that the entropy in these cases is maximal.

Table 4. Calculation of the Poisson series of the probability distribution of PCBs functioning in the students' consciousness and the corresponding values of entropy

k	$P_{125}(k)$ p = 0.078 λ = 9.750	Entropy	$P_{125}(k)$ p = 0.015 λ = 1.875	Entropy	$P_{125}(k)$ p = 0.010 λ = 1.250	Entropy	$P_{125}(k)$ p = 0.004 λ = 0.500	Entropy
0	0.000058	0.000820	0.153355	0.414833	0.286505	0.516674	0.606531	0.437519
1	0.000568	0.006128	0.287541	0.517045	0.358131	0.530550	0.303265	0.522025
2	0.002771	0.023539	0.269569	0.509829	0.223832	0.483368	0.075816	0.282139
3	0.009005	0.061190	0.168481	0.432885	0.093263	0.319198	0.012636	0.079687
4	0.021950	0.120937	0.078975	0.289244	0.029145	0.148656	0.001580	0.014699
5	0.042803	0.194588	0.029616	0.150374	0.007286	0.051736		
6	0.069554	0.267486	0.009255	0.062522				
7	0.096879	0.326257	0.002479	0.021458				
8	0.118072	0.363928						
9	0.127911	0.379485						
10	0.124713	0.374553						
11	0.110541	0.351227						
12	0.089815	0.312277						
13	0.067361	0.262165						
14	0.046912	0.207065						
15	0.030493	0.153543						
16	0.018582	0.106844						
17	0.010657	0.069826						
Sum	**0.988645**	**3.251645**	**0.999271**	**2.398190**	**0.998162**	**2.050182**	**0.999828**	**1.336070**

Source: The author's development

Figure 9. The Poisson series of the probability distribution of PCBs functioning in the consciousness of the first student and the corresponding entropy of the learning information under the study
Source: The author's development

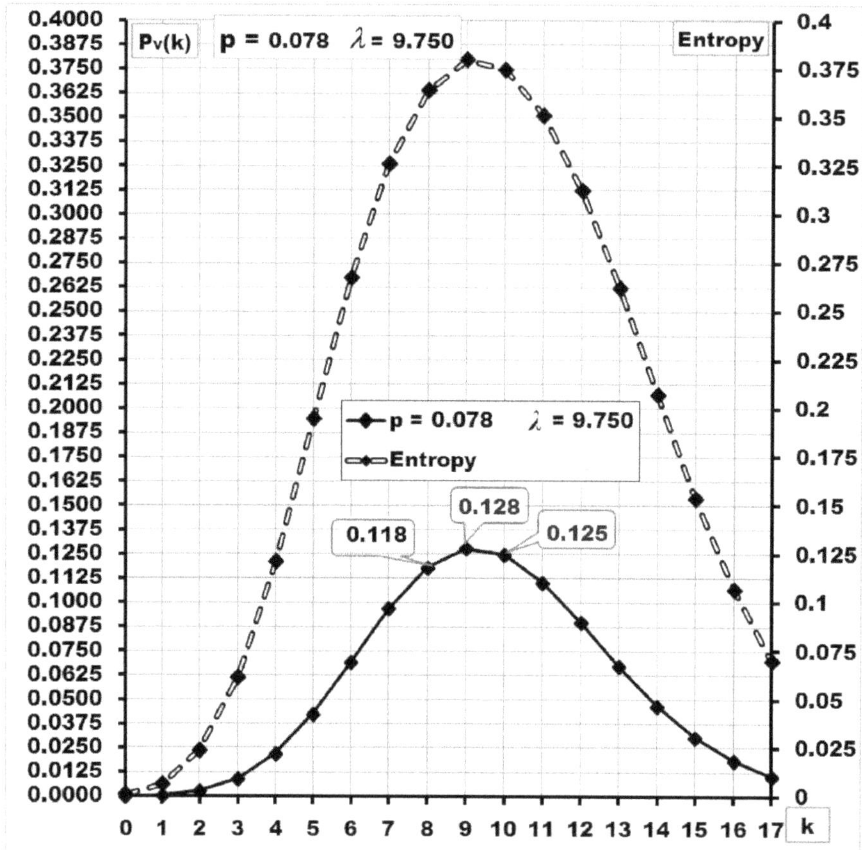

The Fig. 10 clearly demonstrates the following results, which are very important for understanding the necessity of overcoming PCBs in educational consciousness. In particular, the independent work of the second student with educational information with a characteristic constant probability $p = 0.015$ for the realization of the event "manifestation of the PCBs k times" is such that cases of $k = 1$ with a probability of 0.29 and $k = 2$ with a probability of 0.27 are most likely.

As for the third student, within the framework of the developed appraisal model, he will most likely encounter a group of barriers in studying 125 pages of educational text 1 time with a probability of 0.36. Moreover, the characteristic constant probability for it, $p = 0.010$, differs from that of the second student by only 0.5%.

And finally, it becomes the fourth student. His characteristic constant probability $p = 0.004$ for the realization of the event "PCBs manifestation k times" is such that the most likely outcome is the value of $k = 0$ with the Poisson probability $P_{125}(0) = 0.61$.

In other words, the cognitive difficulties will not occur, since the PCBs of a certain group have been overcome. In this situation, the entropy is equal to 0.44, which is significantly less than the probability $P_{125}(0) = 0.61$. Obviously, with this ratio of Poisson probability and entropy, it can be argued that the

Figure 10. The Poisson series of the probability distribution of the functioning of the PCBs in the consciousness of the second, third and fourth students and the corresponding entropy of the learning information for the second and fourth students
Source: The author' development

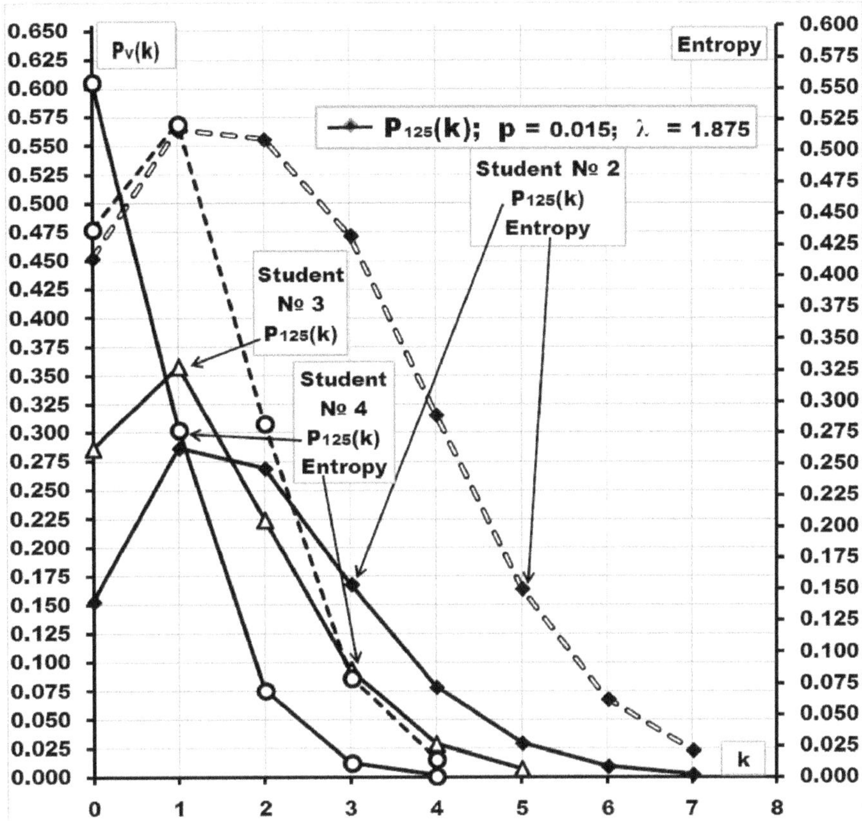

subject knowledge does not cause the student cognitive difficulties (there are no PCBs). Therefore, the ability to work with educational material is adequate to the formed knowledge base. Thus, carriers of human capital whose PCBs have been completely overcome at school, are able to achieve high qualifications in their professional activities and become successful and serve the goals of developing a society subject to certain attitudes and values.

Human capital complements physical capital in the production process and is an important input to technological innovation and long-run growth. As a result, between 10 and 30 percent of per capita gross domestic product (GDP) differences is attributable to cross-country differences in human capital (Hsieh, and Klenow, 2010) This percentage could be even higher when considering the quality of education or the interactions between workers with different skills. The channel by which schooling accelerates economic growth appears to be through boosting learning and skills (Glewwe, Maiga, and Zheng, 2014; Hanushek, and Woessmann, 2008, 2012). Thanks to the growing availability of large-scale student assessments, it is now possible to explore how learning mediates the relationship from schooling to economic growth (Barro, 2001, 2013). It should be emphasized that both objective and subjective forms of manifestation of the modern education crisis have a well-defined economic assessment. It is associated with the slowdown of the economic growth of the countries of the world as a result of the inadequate educational structure of human capital, which as such cannot meet the technological challenges of the future and ensure sustainable socio-economic progress of the global community.

CONCLUSION

The theory of PCB in education focuses on intelligent teacher and student problem comes from the fact that the success of educational activity cannot be carried out without focused and systematic prevention and overcoming the psychological and cognitive barriers of various types, objectively inherent in the student's academic consciousness. Obviously, the idea of learning (especially learning remotely) is not realized strictly through the uniquely designed program teacher, even if it has been laid feedback. Definitely authentic failures of the learning are generated in the process while the educational information is passing through the schoolchildren consciousness between the input and output of the 'potential psychological boxes' (Pilipenko, et al., 2019). What is not sensitive to any particular mechanism of formation of PCB passes smoothly, but falls to the other 'traps of thought'. If the student is not trained, and have not learned by himself to overcome these psychological-cognitive barriers then there is beginning the process of educational scientific information distortion. The adequacy of educational material at the "entrance" and the "exit" of individual consciousness can only be achieved as a result of the student's ability to identify barriers to understanding the subject matter and to eliminate them in the educational process. Moreover, PCBs and the patterns of their appearance are objectively present in the relationship between the teacher and the student in the schooling process. It can be said that the students' PCBs overcoming with the help of a teacher at school allows to eliminate mismatch between the schooling and learning and to approach the solution of the problem of modern education crisis. If not many become unemployed or stuck in low-wage, unstable, informal-sector jobs that offer them few opportunities to strengthen their skills. But the same can happen even to secondary school graduates, if they cannot fulfill labor market needs. Whether an education input is a physical item, such as a tablet or textbook, or a process, such as school management and leadership, it will improve learning only if it directly improves the quality of teacher-learner interactions.

Failure to tackle these PCB constraints can trap countries in a low-learning, low accountability, high-inequality equilibrium. When different parts of a system fail to work together, education outcomes will fall far short of what is possible. Without that, more inputs will pile onto an ineffective process and fail to have the desired impact on the economic development (WDR, 2018). But with the strategic use of the PCB theory, it could be possible to organize effective work with prepared students and knowledgeable, motivated teachers to overcome many PCBs and ensure a high level of learning. The formation of the necessary and sufficient conditions for the corresponding motivation of individuals and society could aim their behavior at the socio-economic progress acceleration. But all the parts of an education system should work together and it becomes as important as ensuring alignment toward learning. If a country adopts a new curriculum that places greater emphasis on creative thinking and PCBs overcoming, the curriculum alone will not change much. Teachers themselves need training so that they can identify PCBs in the students' consciousness and skillfully use adequate methods to overcome them. At the same time, they should exercise sufficient caution to successfully implement these changes, given that the implementation of the new curriculum is much more laborious than the old one, which has allowed them to just memorize something.

REFERENCES

Acemoglu & Autor. (2012). What does human capital do? A review of Goldin and Katz's *The Race between Education and Technology. Journal of Economic Literature, 50*(2), 426–463.

Acemoglu, D. (1998). Why do new technologies complement skills? Directed technical change and wage inequality. *Quarterly Journal of Economics, 113*(4), 1055–89.

Acemoglu, D., & Autor, D. (2011). Skills, tasks and technologies: implications for employment and earnings. In Handbook of Labor Economics (vol. 4). Amsterdam: Elsevier. doi:10.1016/S0169-7218(11)02410-5

Acemoglu, D., & Verdier, T. (1998). Property rights, corruption and the allocation of talent: A general equilibrium approach. *Economic Journal (London), 108*(450), 1381–1403. doi:10.1111/1468-0297.00347

Akgun, O., Cournède, B., & Fournier, J. (2017). *The effects of the tax mix on inequality and growth.* OECD Economics Department Working Papers, No. 1447. OECD Publishing. doi:10.1787/c57eaa14-en

Altinok, N., Angrist, N., & Patrinos, H. A. (2018). *Global data set on education quality (1965–2015).* Policy Research Working Paper, 8314. Washington, DC: The World Bank Group.

Ausan, A. A. (2017). Introduction. In *Russia 2025: From Workforce to Talents.* Moscow: Boston Consulting Group, October.

Autor, D., & Dorn, D. (2013). The growth of low-skill service jobs and the polarization of the US labor market. *The American Economic Review, 103*(5), 1553–1597. doi:10.1257/aer.103.5.1553

Autor, D. H., Figlio, D. N., Karbownik, K., Roth, J., & Wasserman, M. (2016). School quality and the gender gap in educational achievement. *The American Economic Review, 106*(5), 289–295. doi:10.1257/aer.p20161074

Bakija, Cole, & Heim. (2012). *Jobs and Income Growth of Top Earners and the Causes of Changing Income Inequality: Evidence from US Tax Return Data.* Williams College, US Department of Treasury and Indiana University.

Barro, R. J. (2001). Human capital and growth. *The American Economic Review, 91*(2), 12–17. doi:10.1257/aer.91.2.12

Barro, R. J. (2013). Education and economic growth. *Annals of Economics and Finance, 14*(2), 301–328.

Bassanini & Scarpetta. (2002). Does human capital matter for growth in OECD countries? A pooled mean-group approach. *Economics Letters, 74*(3), 399-405. doi:10.10160165-1765(01)00569-9

Bold, T., Kimenyi, M., Mwabu, G., Ng'ang'a, A., & Sandefur, J. (2016). *Experimental evidence on scaling up education reforms in Kenya.* Economic Development and Institutions Project Working Paper. Stockholm: Institute for International Economic Studies, Stockholm University.

Boushey, H., & Weller, C. (2008). Has growing inequality contributed to rising household economic distress? *Review of Political Economy, 20*(1), 1–22. doi:10.1080/09538250701661764

Brown & Hunter. (2004). Democracy and human capital formation. *Comparative Political Studies, 37*(7), 842-864. doi:10.1177/0010414004266870

Brueckner, M., Dabla-Norris, E., Gradstein, M., & Lederman, D. (2017). *The Rise of the Middle Class and Economic Growth in ASEAN*. Washington, DC: The World Bank; doi:10.1596/1813-9450-8068

Budzier, A., & Flyvbjerg, B. (2012). Overspend? Late? Failure? What the data says about IT project risk in the public sector. In Commonwealth Governance Handbook 2012/13: Democracy, Development, and Public Administration (pp. 145–47). London: Commonwealth Secretariat.

Card & Di Nardo. (2002). Skill-biased technological change and rising wage inequality: some problems and puzzles. *Journal of Labour Economics*, *2002*(4).

Cournède, Denk, & Hoeller. (2015). *Finance and inclusive growth*. OECD Economic Policy Papers. No. 14.

De Smedt, B. (2014). Advances in the use of neuroscience methods in research on learning and instruction. *Frontline Learning Research*, 2(4), 7–14.

Evans, D. K., & Yuan, F. (2017). Economic returns to interventions that increase learning. In *World Development Report 2018, Background paper*. Washington, DC: The World Bank Group.

Filmer, D., Rogers, H., Angrist, N., & Sabarwal, S. (2018). *Learning-adjusted years of schooling (LAYS): Defining a new macro measure of education*. Policy Research Working Paper, 8591. Washington, DC: World Bank.

García, J. L., Heckman, J. J., Leaf, D. E., & Prados, M. J. (2016). *The Life-Cycle Benefits of an Influential Early Childhood Program*. NBER Working Paper 22993. National Bureau of Economic Research.

Glewwe, P. W., Maiga, E., & Zheng, H. (2014). The Contribution of Education to Economic Growth: A Review of the Evidence, with Special Attention and an Application to Sub-Saharan Africa. *World Development*, *59*, 379–393. doi:10.1016/j.worlddev.2014.01.021

Goldin, C., & Katz, L. (2008). *The Race between Education and Technology*. Belknap Press for Harvard University Press.

Gouldner, A. (1960). The norm of reciprocity: A preliminary statement. *American Sociological Review*, *25*(2), 161–178. doi:10.2307/2092623

Hanushek, E., & Woessmann, L. (2010). Education and economic growth. In D. J. Brewer & P. J. McEwan (Eds.), *Economics of Education*. Amsterdam: Elsevier.

Hanushek, E. A. (1979). Conceptual and empirical issues in the estimation of educational production functions. *Journal of Human Resources, 14*(3), 351–88.

Hanushek, E. A., Lavy, V., & Hitomi, K. (2008). Do students care about school quality? Determinants of dropout behavior in developing countries. *Journal of Human Capital*, *2*(1), 69–105. doi:10.1086/529446

Hanushek, E. A., & Woessmann, L. (2008). The role of cognitive skills in economic development. *Journal of Economic Literature*, *46*(3), 607–668. doi:10.1257/jel.46.3.607

Hanushek, E. A., & Woessmann, L. (2012). Do better schools lead to more growth? Cognitive skills, economic outcomes, and causation. *Journal of Economic Growth*, *17*(4), 267–321. doi:10.100710887-012-9081-x

Hanushek, E. A., & Woessmann, L. (2015). *The Knowledge Capital of Nations: Education and the Economics of Growth.* Cambridge, MA: MIT Press. doi:10.7551/mitpress/9780262029179.001.0001

Homans, G. (1961). *Social Behavior: Its Elementary Forms.* New York: Harcourt Brace Jovanovich.

Hsieh, C.-T., & Klenow, P. J. (2010). Development accounting. *American Economic Journal. Macroeconomics, 2*(1), 207–223. doi:10.1257/mac.2.1.207

Imbs, J., & Méjean, I. (2015). Elasticity optimism. American Economic Journal: Macroeconomics, 7(3), 43-83. doi:10.1257/mac.20130231

IMF. (2017). *Fiscal Monitor: Tackling Inequality.* Washington DC: IMF.

IMF. (2018). *Inequality and poverty across generations in the European Union.* IMF Discussion Note SDN/18/01.

Immervoll, H., & Richardson, L. (2011). *Redistribution policy and inequality reduction in OECD countries: what has changed in two decades?* OECD Social, Employment and Migration Working Papers, No. 122. Paris: OECD Publishing. doi:10.1787/5kg5dlkhjq0x-en

Insel, T. R., & Landis, S. C. (2013). Twenty-five years of progress: The view from Nimh and Ninds. *Neuron, 80*(3), 561–567. doi:10.1016/j.neuron.2013.09.041 PMID:24183009

Joumard, I., Pisu, M., & Bloch, D. (2012). Tackling Income Inequality: The Role of Taxes and Transfers. *OECD Journal: Economic Studies, 2012*(1). doi:10.1787/eco_studies-2012-5k95xd6l65lt

Kenworthy, L., & Pontusson, H. J. (2005). Rising inequality and the politics of redistribution in affluent countries. Perspectives on Politics, 3(3), 449-471. doi:10.1017/S1537592705050292

Kerwin, J. T., & Thornton, R. L. (2015). Making the grade: Understanding what works for teaching literacy in rural Uganda. PSC Research Report, 15-842. Population Studies Center, Institute for Social Research, University of Michigan.

Kim, J. Y. (2018). The Human Capital Gap: Getting Governments to Invest in People. *Foreign Affairs.* Available at: https://www.foreignaffairs.com/articles /2018-06-14/human-capital-gap

Krueger & Lindahl. (2001). Education for growth: why and for whom? *Journal of Economic Literature, 39*(1), 1011-1136.

Kuhl, P. K. (2010). Brain mechanisms in early language acquisition. *Neuron, 67*(5), 713–727. doi:10.1016/j.neuron.2010.08.038 PMID:20826304

Lavinas, L., & Veiga, A. (2013). Brazil's one laptop per child program: Impact evaluation and implementation assessment. *Cadernos de Pesquisa, 43*(149).

Lindert, P. (2004). *Growing Public Social Spending and Economic Growth since the Eighteenth Century.* Cambridge, UK: Cambridge University Press.

Lupu, N., & Pontusson, J. (2011). The structure of inequality and the politics of redistribution. American Political Science Review, 105(2), 316-336. doi:10.1017/S0003055411000128

Lutz, W., Butz, W., & Samir, K. C. (2014). *World Population and Human Capital in the Twenty-First Century*. London: Oxford University Press. doi:10.1093/acprof:oso/9780198703167.001.0001

Magun, Rudnev, & Schmidt. (2015b). Russian basic human values through the lens of the European value types. *The Russian Public Opinion Herald Data. Analysis. Discussions. Quarterly, 3-4*(121), 74-93.

Magun, V., & Rudnev, M. (2015). Basic human values of the Russians: both different from and similar to other Europeans. In *Culture Matters in Russia and Everywhere: Backdrop for the Russia-Ukraine Conflict*. London: Lexington Books.

Magun, V., Rudnev, M., & Schmidt, P. (2015a). 'Within-and between-country value diversity in Europe: A typological approach'. *European Sociological Review*. Available at http://esr.oxfordjournals.org/content/early/2015/08/20/esr.jcv080.full

Manpower Group. (2014). *The Talent Shortage Continues: How the Ever Changing Role of HR Can Bridge the Gap*. Manpower Group.

Milanovic, B. (2012). *Global income by the numbers in history and now.* World Bank, Working Paper, No. 6259.

Morrisson & Murtin. (2010). The Kuznets curve of human capital inequality: 1870–2010. *The Journal of Economic Inequality, 11*(3), 283-301.

Mourougane, A., Botev, J., Fournier, J.-M., Pain, N., & Rusticelli, E. (2016). *Can an increase in public investment sustainably lift economic growth?* OECD Economics Department Working Papers, No. 1351. Paris: OECD. doi:10.1787/a25a7723-en

OECD. (2003). *The Sources of Economic Growth in OECD Countries*. Paris: OECD Publishing. Available at: https://www.oecd.org

OECD. (2010). *PISA 2009. Results, What Students Know and Can Do: Student Performance in Reading, Mathematics, and Science* (Vol. 1). Paris: OECD.

OECD. (2011). *Divided We Stand: Why Inequality Keeps Rising*. Paris: OECD Publishing; doi:10.1787/9789264119536-

OECD. (2017). *Bridging the Gap: Inclusive Growth 2017. Update Report*. Paris: OECD. Available at: http://www.oecd.org/inclusive-growth/Bridging_the_Gap.pdf

OECD. (2018). *A Broken Social Elevator? The framework of policy action on inclusive growth*. Paris: OECD Publishing. Retrieved from: https://www.oecd.org/mcm/documents/C-MIN-2018-5-EN.pdf

OECD. (2018). *The Future of Education and Skills: Education 2030*. Paris: OECD Publishing.

OECD. (2019a). *Job polarization and the work profile of the middle class*. Cope Policy Brief, April. Available at: http://oe.cd/middle-class-2019

OECD. (2019b). *Under Pressure: The Squeezed Middle Class*. Paris: OECD Publishing. Available at: http://oe.cd/middle-class-2019

OECD Skills Outlook. (2013). *First Results from the Survey of Adult Skills*. Programme for the International Assessment of Adult Competencies (PIAAC). Organisation for Economic Co-operation and Development. Available at: http://www.oecd.org/site/piaac/surveyofadultskills.htm

Okun, A. (1975). Equality and Efficiency: The Big Tradeoff. Washington, DC: Brookings.

Ortiz, I., & Cummins, M. (2013). The Age of Austerity: A Review of Public Expenditures and Adjustment Measures in 181 Countries. New York: Academic Press.

Pilipenko, A. I. (1997). *Cognitive barriers in teaching physics and methodological principles for overcoming them.* The Dissertation Abstract for a Scientific Degree of Doctor of Pedagogics. Moscow: Russian Academy of Education Publisher.

Pilipenko, A. I., Morosova, E. A., Pilipenko, O. I., & Savenkova, E. V. (2015). *Innovative Models of Education: The Aspect of Psychological and Cognitive Barriers*. Available at SSRN: http://ssrn.com/abstract=2597968

Pilipenko, A. I., Pilipenko, O. I., & Pilipenko, Z. A. (2019). Education and Inclusive Development: Puzzle of Low-learning Equilibrium. In B. S. Sergi (Ed.), *Modeling Economic Growth in Contemporary Russia* (pp. 163–198). London: Emerald Publishing Limited. doi:10.1108/978-1-78973-265-820191006

Pinsky, A. A. (1978). Methodology as a science. *Soviet Pedagogy*, 12.

Pressman, S. (2007). The decline of the middle class: an international perspective. *Journal of Economic Issues*, *41*, 181-200. doi:10.2307/25511161

Pritchett, L. (2013). *The Rebirth of Education: Schooling Ain't Learning*. Baltimore, MD: Brookings Institution Press.

Rasmussen, J. (1983). Skills, rules, and knowledge; signals, signs, and symbols, and other distinctions in human performance models. IEEE Transactions on Systems, Man, and Cybernetics, 13(3), 257-266. doi:10.1109/TSMC.1983.6313160

Riad, N. (2017). Education for life: Llabor markets are changing, and millennials must prepare and adjust. *Finance & Development*, *54*(2), 16-19.

Romer, P. M. (1986). Increasing returns and long-run growth. *The Journal of Political Economy*, *94*(5), 1002-1037.

Rychen, D. S., & Salganik, L. H. (Eds.). (2001). Defining and Selecting Key Competencies. Paris: OECD DeSeCo Project.

Rychen, D. S., & Salganik, L. H. (Eds.). (2003). Key Competencies for a Successful Llife and a Well-functioning Society. Paris: OECD DeSeCo Project.

Rychen, D. S., Salganik, L. H., & McLaughlin, M. E. (Eds.). (2003). *Contributions to the Second DeSeCo Symposium*. Paris: OECD DeSeCo Project.

Salganik, Rychen, Moser, & Konstant. (1999). *Projects on Competencies in the OECD Context: Analysis of Theoretical and Conceptual Foundations*. Paris: OECD DeSeCo Project.

Schwartz, S. H. (1994). Are there universal aspects in the content and structure of values? *The Journal of Social Issues*, 50.

Schwartz, S. H., Cieciuch, J., Vecchione, M., Davidov, E., Fischer, R., Beierlein, C., ... Konty, M. (2012). 'Refining the theory of basic individual values'. *Journal of Personality and Social Psychology*, *103*(4), 663–688. doi:10.1037/a0029393 PMID:22823292

Stevens, P., & Weale, M. (2004). Education and economic growth. In G. Johnes & J. Johnes (Eds.), *International Handbook on the Economics of Education*. Cheltenham, UK: Edward Elgar.

The Economist Intelligence Unit Limited. (2017). *The Worldwide Educating for the Future Index: A Benchmark for the Skills of Tomorrow*. London: The Economist Intelligence Unit Limited.

WDR. (2019). *World Development Report 2019: The Changing Nature of Work*. Washington, DC: The World Bank Group.

WDR. (2018). *World Development Report 2018: Learning to Realize Education's Promise*. Washington, DC: World Bank.

WEF. (2015). New Vision for Education: Unlocking the Potential of Technology. World Economic Forum.

WEF. (2018). *Towards a Reskilling Revolution: A Future of Jobs for All.* World Economic Forum

World Bank. (2018). *The Human Capital Project*. Washington, DC: The World Bank Group.

World Bank. (2019). *World Development Report 2019: The Changing Nature of Work*. Washington, DC: World Bank.

Chapter 12
Public-Private Partnership and Financing the Development of National Infrastructure:
Safeguarding Public Finance Sustainability

Irina Yurievna Vaslavskaya
Kazan Federal University, Russia

ABSTRACT

The chapter contains a methodology for formalized evaluation of the model of replacement of budget funds by private investment in the public infrastructure PPP projects for the purpose to ensure public finance sustainability. It can manifest itself only if the state could create appropriate conditions for private investors, including institutional players as its partners. The latter means primarily the stable formal institutional conditions for private investors, low transactional costs, attractive financial parameters, that could bring the ratio of budget and private financing of public infrastructure PPP projects to more than 1 to 1. It has become evident that accelerated development of many public infrastructure PPP projects is hampered by two factors: (1) inadequate institutional support for the design process itself and (2) absence of state-prepared acceptable financial models of public infrastructure PPP projects regarding the division of risks of infrastructure projects and delegating the proprietary rights of the state to private investors.

INTRODUCTION

In contemporary world the importance of new approaches to the adequate institutionalization of a mutually beneficial partnership between the state and private business is increasing as the pace of economic development of almost all countries over the Globe slows down and national governments show the inability to reverse this trend. This is largely due to the fact that lately there have been both quantitative and qualitative changes in the economic functions of modern states that have not received a satisfactory theoretical explanation (Ritter, 1996; Tanzi and Schuknecht, 2000).

DOI: 10.4018/978-1-7998-1033-9.ch012

According to the participants of the World Economic Forum (WEF, 2017) one of the effective mechanisms for ensuring sustainable economic growth in the Globe becomes the development of various forms of public-private partnership. Politicians, scientists and practitioners agreed that by 2030, it would only be possible to achieve sustainable development goals (SDGs) in the global economy if the great potential of various forms of business cooperation between the state and private business could be realized. In fact, there was emphasized the theoretical and practical significance of the search for new and of the expansion of already existing models of cooperation between the public and private sectors in the implementation of transactions with public goods. The fundamental meaning of this partnership is to combine the advantages of organizing transactions by the state and private business in order to minimize the economic and financial losses that are typical for each of them separately.

To assess the potential of PPPs in the context of the necessity to safeguard economic and financial sustainability there turned out to be of extreme significance the scientific developments of the institutional theory, theory of transactional costs, economic theory of law and others, based on the publications of the following authors: G.M. Hodgson (1988); R. Coase (1993); O. Williamson (1996); D. North (2003); C. Menard (2003); as well as the analytical papers of the Global Infrastructure Outlook (2017, 2018), World Economic Forum (2017), McKinsey Global Institute (2017) and etc. This fundamental theoretical basis allowed the author to identify three basic forms of PPP organization (Vaslavskiy, et al., 2019) – quasi-market, hierarchical and hybrid ones. According to the author, the most promising PPP forms are hybrid organizations of partnership between the state and private business in the implementation of infrastructure projects because of their potential to accelerate economic development and to ensure the sustainability of public finance. This is due to the fact that the state is always limited in budget expenditures for capital projects, but private investors could be attracted to invest into them under the conditions favourable for the private partners under the patronage of the state. Taking into account the contribution of infrastructure to economic growth, the hybrid forms of infrastructure PPP projects can be confidently attributed to the most promising in modern conditions of fiscal consolidation and of economic growth slowdown in the Globe. The literature on the above problems presents a wide range of estimates for fiscal multipliers that could be applied to the infrastructure PPP-projects (Spilimbergo, et al., 2009; Christiano, et al., 2011; Batini, et al., 2014; Auerbach, and Gorodnichenko, 2012; Vlasov, and Deryugina, 2018), but the findings are not all certain. The author proposes a model approach to the problem of financial design of the development of the public infrastructure PPP-projects allowing to justify new financial instruments and financial institutions to ensure the national economies' growth rates in the perspective to 2020.

To reinforce the findings, some results associated with other theoretical investigations and analytical researches are presented.

BACKGROUND

The history of PPP development in national economies is not so long, so there are many unresolved issues, both theoretical and practical: what factors predetermine the diversity of PPP forms, what principles should be considered as major ones in organizing partnerships, what determines the effectiveness of PPP funding mechanisms in different areas of the public sector, how could be possible to optimize the interests of public and private partners in diverse PPP models, including their hybrid forms, and etc. The lack of models of best national PPP practices explain the limited use of the potential of various forms of public-private partnerships in the global economy and the lack of a common understanding of their role in stabilizing public finance and ensuring high growth rates of the global economy (Vaslavskiy, et al., 2019). In this regard, there is an obvious necessity for the theoretical interpretation of the diversity factors of the organizational structures of partnerships (cooperation) of the public and private sectors in the economic sphere, as well as highlighting the advantages of each of their "institutional matrices" in relation to different areas of state responsibility and taking into account the factor of efficient use of state budget funds. Besides, this is directly related to the problem of the entire global economy connected with its high growth rates ensuring in the long term.

It is from these positions that it should be assessed the author's contribution to modelling the diversity of potential forms of organizing PPPs for the purpose of accelerating the integration of private business into the implementation of state functions and ensuring the sustainability of public finances. The project approach to the organization of hybrid PPP agreements proves to be the most effective in implementing capital-intensive, long-term socially significant infrastructure projects. Well-designed and efficiently implemented investments in infrastructure can promote economic development and improve the population access to basic services that boost quality of life.

The need for infrastructure investment far exceeds its financing available from traditional sources, including budget funds. The problem is connected with the fact that the public sector has traditionally been providing the bulk of infrastructure investment, given the inherent public-goods nature of infrastructure projects. But now the public resources are strained in developed, emerging markets and developing economies, as governments are faced with rising fiscal vulnerabilities as a result of budget deficits, higher debt-to-GDP ratios, a high-interest-rate environment, depreciating currency and increasing the burden of external debt. At the same time, funding from development institutions and donor agencies is unlikely to fill the infrastructure gap. Although the private sector is often being looked at as an infrastructure "white knight," total private investments in infrastructure in developing countries only over 1990-2016 totalled barely US$1.6 trillion across the transport, energy and water sectors (World Bank, 2017). This is a drop in the ocean compared to the infrastructure-investment needs of more than US$0.8 trillion annually (Ruiz-Nunez, et al., 2015; 2016).

Successful forms of PPP in the modern world can eliminate the temporary cash gaps of national governments, which exacerbate their problems of budget deficit in the context of a general slowdown in economic growth. For these purposes the national governments should use budget funds not so much to finance infrastructure projects but to create appropriate conditions for private investors, including institutional players. These problems are being developed in this chapter for the purpose to manage national economy's stable development using the winning moments of the state and of the private investors in the sphere of public infrastructure as well as of their organization form of cooperation - PPP - in the conditions of forced fiscal constraints and when public infrastructure could be the fundamental long run factor of national economy's development.

The chapter contains a methodology for formalized evaluation of the model of replacement of budget funds by private investment in the public infrastructure projects organized in the hybrid form of PPP contracts. As a result, it has been assessed the positive impact of the public finances consolidation on the growth rate of the national economy.The logic of the presentation of material in the chapter assumes consideration of: (1) the specifics of the state as a private business partner in transactions with public goods; (2) the factor of minimizing transaction costs as the basis for reconciling the interests of the state and private business when choosing forms of PPPs; (3) the exchange of proprietary rights as a function of changing the transaction costs of public and private PPP participants; (4) basic forms of institutional organization of public-private partnerships. It is this goal of the partners that necessitates the demand for the institutional support of their relations regarding the implementation of transactions. With this interpretation, PPP in market exchange becomes a form of realization of public-private cooperation.

So from the view point of the public finance stability it becomes obvious to use the hybrid forms of infrastructure PPP-projects to solve the grave problem of growing budget deficit and increasing cost of public debt servicing all over the world. As a result the government should use budget funds to create appropriate conditions for private investors, including institutional players in order to expand their participation in social projects of the state. The latter means primarily the stable formal institutional conditions for private investors, low transactional costs, attractive financial parameters, that could bring the ratio of budget and private financing of infrastructure PPP-projects to more than 1 to 1. Analytical part of the chapter is devoted to the modeling the structure of national governments' budget expenditures for the purpose of assessing their effectiveness in the sphere of national infrastructure. The base of evaluation is data variation of budget and private investments as well as international and national statistics of PPP' infrastructure projects all over the world.

Finally, the last part of the chapter shows the conclusions.

METHODOLOGY

PPP: A State as a Partner of Private Business in Transactions with Public Goods

Partnership of economic entities in the market is due to the dialectic of their interconnections regarding the implementation of transactions. In fact, partners enter the acts of purchase and sale, being dialectically interrelated as buyers and sellers, while assuming the necessity of each other and denying each other at the same time. Such interdependence of the partnership relations provides every participant of the dialectical couple with the opportunity to maximize their utility, and the society - to stabilize the GDP reproduction and to ensure the sustainability of the national economy as a whole. Such a dialectic market partnership becomes of fundamental importance for understanding the necessity and sufficiency as conditions for its successful development. This is an objective need to coordinate the actions of participants in transactions in the market exchange, their cooperation in solving mutually important problems. Only dialectically interconnected economic entities are forced to coordinate the individual behaviour for the goal of organizing market transactions on partnership terms, since this will bring an economic gain for each of them due to minimizing transaction costs.

However, the partnership of private business in the market and the partnership of the state with private business in the implementation of transactions have significant differences. Private companies as partners in the market objectively have equal rights and obligations with all other things being equal. As for the state, it originally was created by society for the implementation of functions that are charged to it by the society itself. By realizing them, the state is called upon to "personify" the given society, acting as its leading subject and regulating the system of economic relations within its framework. In this case, the author is referring to the creation of a system of formal institutions that are designed to predetermine the basic norms of the economic agents' behavior, the incentives for their cooperative activity and the punishment mechanisms in the case of opportunism of partners. Institutionalizing the market environment, the state generates effective demand, determines the set of rules for competitive interaction, including the conditions of its partnership with private business.

As the personalized exchange was crowded out the institutional function of the state became very important for the participants realizing the market transactions. D. North (1997) wrote that the emergence of non-personalized exchange and contractual relations meant the formation of the state. As a result, the reduction of the sphere of informal restrictions dominance in the conditions of personalized exchange was compensated for by the expansion of the influence of the formal institutions being created by the state in the process of the non-personalized exchange increase. A special place in the institutional system was assigned to formal institutions specifying the property rights of partners. This was due to the fact that in the market exchange, it was not so much goods that were bought and sold, but the rights of ownership to them. As a result, the state has acquired a certain duality, since, on the one hand, it acted as a subject of management, and on the other, as an economic agent (object of management), becoming a partner of private business in transactions. This contradiction predetermines the specifics of PPP, which is manifested in the fact that the state always acts as the dominant party in relations with private investors, dictating their own terms of partnership to them.

The sphere of the PPP is determined by the scale of public goods which production is imputed to the state by the society and which are financed at the expanse of the significant part of the national income. Public goods have characteristics such as the universal utility (non-exclusivity of any member of society from their consumption) and their zero marginal utility (no restrictions on the access of people to their consumption). Actually, these moments define the content of the category of PPP and predetermine the dominant role of the state itself in it.

Considering all the above, public-private partnership can be represented as a cooperation of the state and private business connected with the transactions with public goods at the expense of budget funds with the involvement of private financial resources. In this case, the PPP allows the state to more efficiently use the financial resources allocated by the society (budget expenditures) in terms of the quantity and quality of satisfied social needs. In this case, social gain is realized due to the growth of the welfare of society and the accelerated development of the national economy. As for private business, transactions with the state and on its terms allow companies to stabilize profit (income), reduce the risks of financial losses, as well as decrease transaction costs.

Transaction Costs' Minimization and the Coincidence of the State and Private Business Interests When Choosing PPP Forms

Partnerships between the state and private firms in transactions with public goods and services can be organized in different ways. At the same time, any form of PPP mediates an objective desire of the state and private business to minimize transaction costs. As a result, both the state and private business achieve this aim, having diametrically opposite final goals. As for the state, it is intended to ensure socio-economic efficiency for the whole society. Private business seeks to maximize its own profits by reducing transaction costs. The contribution of the modern state to the slowdown of the national economies' growth is largely related to the problem of chronic budget deficits at all levels of the national government. At the same time, a simple budget expenditure' cuts is unacceptable to solve the problem of restoring the balance of public finance. This is due to the fact that such budget cuts will adversely affect the obligations of the state to provide the national community with public goods that are planned and to be implemented in the current fiscal year.

From the theoretical viewpoint, the functions of the state, imputed to it and paid for by the society, consist of its obligation to perform them at any cost. This means that any current state budget deficit must be financed by raising additional funds. There are market and non-market ways to restore the current balance of the state budget. However, perhaps the most optimal way for society (and, therefore, for the state) to cover the budget deficit is to attract private investment to co-finance public goods based on PPP. As a rule, in practice this is a partnership in capital-intensive socially significant projects that the state is obliged to implement in the current fiscal year, but does not have the necessary financial resources for them.

In this case, the private partner has the opportunity to use PPP as a way to reduce transaction costs due to the patronage of the state and its official institutions. Acting as a centre in a complex system of specialized and integrated non-personalized exchange, the state is able to stabilize the external environment of economic activity and, thus, reduce (theoretically this should be so) the risks of financial losses for its partners in transactions. In other words, private economic agents agree to a partnership with the state, since the formal institutions created by it guarantee the stability of their business, allowing them to minimize transaction costs and generate a steady income.

The structure of transaction costs is constantly changing: their existing list is being expanded their new groups and subgroups are being added. Modern transaction costs are traditionally divided into five main groups: the costs of finding information, the costs of negotiating the costs of measurement, of specification and of the protection of property rights, the costs connected with the opportunistic behaviour (Alchian, and Demsetz, 1972). In other words, as the list of transaction costs expands, so do the options for organizing transactions within PPPs (their institutional matrices) aimed at minimizing the costs of their realization.

PPP: Property Rights Exchange as a Function of the Transaction Costs Dynamics

In addition to transaction costs, the property relationship becomes a significant factor of the development of a partnership between the state and private business in transactions with public goods. According to D. North (1997, PP. 73-74), it is changes in the economic costs and benefits of partners in transactions that predetermine the set of ownership powers to be exchanged and the system of formal institutions ensuring them. Moreover, transaction costs as the most important factor, which objectively determines the desire of the state and private business for partnership, cannot be minimized without the exchange of the respective powers of property. That idea was also expressed by Eugen R. von Boehm Bawerk (1898) in the 19th century. The fact is that for partners it is not so much important a resource in itself, but a "bundle" or a share of property rights connected with the exchanged resource usage (Demsetz, (1967), P. 17). Consequently, only those who manage the set of powers of ownership of the resource being exchanged can be partners in transactions. In the case of PPPs, the state determines the conditions for delegating certain powers of ownership to a private partner in the process of organizing transactions with public goods in order to minimize transaction costs.

Such a dialectic interdependence connected with transaction costs manifests itself only in the case of clearly specified property rights. The last means that formal institutions effectively exclude access to the property of any other individual (who is not the authorized owner of these rights) and ensure the protection of the property rights of the owner (North, (1981), P. 21). In other words, the individual possibility of obtaining utility from the economic good is institutionalized by the state ensuring the system of property rights (North, (1997), P. 68). Only in this case, economic agents have an interest in using resources efficiently, as well as in increasing output and labour productivity.

R. Kapelyushnikov (1990) convincingly substantiated the central place of the principle of "exclusivity" in the property institutionalization, since it serves as the basis for the infinite variety of specific powers of property included in its system. Theoretically, the principle of exclusivity of property rights is constantly changing in the range from 1 to 0. In this case, 1 means open access for only one person (with individual private ownership), and zero means open access to resources for all members of society (with state public ownership) (Kleiner, 2004). Diverse ownership systems, varying the principle of exclusion from access to resources owned by society, contain all the diverse ways of potentially possible relationships between economic agents in relation to their specific use. Representatives of the neo-institutional theory added the principle of divisibility as one of the fundamental characteristics of property relations. This is due to the fact that every partial right of ownership out of the whole its system (of the common "bundle") has a value, since it allows extracting utility from the good. As a result, transaction partners may sell and buy property rights as ordinary goods. At the same time, their quantitative set varies depending on the "narrow" or "broad" interpretation of the category of property. Eggertsson Th. (1990, PP. 34-35) included in the category of ownership in the "narrow" interpretation the "bundle" of the following powers: (a) the owner's rights to use the benefit when extracting its beneficial properties; (b) the right of the owner to derive income from the good; (c) the rights of the owner of the good to alienate him by sale, donation, transfer in inheritance, use as a share, etc.; (d) prohibiting the owner of the good to use it to the detriment of others.

The classic definition of property rights (in the "broad" interpretation) was developed by the English lawyer A.M. Honore (1961), P. 112-128) and included "... 11 elements: 1) the right of ownership, i.e. exceptional physical control over the thing; 2) the right to use, i.e. personal use of things; 3) the right to control, i.e. deciding how and by whom the thing can be used; 4) the right to income, i.e. for benefits arising from the prior personal use of the thing or from allowing others to use it (in other words, the right to assign); 5) the right to "capital value" of a thing, implying the right to alienate, consume, waste, change or destroy a thing; 6) the right to security, i.e. immunity from expropriation; 7) the right to transfer things by inheritance or by will; 8) termlessness; 9) the prohibition of harmful use, that is, the obligation to refrain from using things in a way harmful to others; 10) liability in the form of recovery, i.e. the possibility of selecting things in payment of debt; 11) residual character, i.e. waiting for a "natural" return transferred to someone powers upon the expiration of the transfer or in case of loss of its force for any other reason."

Considering everything said above, the founder of the economics of law G.S. Becker (1976; Becker, et al., 1988) wrote about an infinite number of forms for the institutionalization of transactions in exchange: "...... the number of meaningful combinations (powers, transaction costs and organizational structures) is equal to 1.5 thousand, and if we take into account their variation by subjects and objects of law, then the diversity of ownership forms (and of institutional matrices) becomes truly "intimidating".

The above provisions, along with the variety of transaction costs, predetermine a variety of different forms of PPP organization.

Basic Forms of Institutional Organization of Public-Private Partnership

In the modern market economy there simultaneously coexist many diverse forms of transactions organization between private companies, between private business and the state, between the state and private business, between the state structures themselves. However, the specificity of PPP is attached to the fact that all its forms mediate transactions with public goods financed at the expanse of the government budget. It is the domination of the state as a special economic agent that manifests itself in all known forms of the institutionalization of its transactions with private companies. Moreover, each of them is aimed at minimizing a certain type of transaction costs. And this, in turn, forces the PPP participants to agree on the most appropriate way to exchange property rights in connection with a transaction with public goods. The faster new transaction costs appear, the more the range of alternative ways of combining them with the exchange of property rights in the process of PPPs institutionalization expands. As a result, numerous pairs of mutually interdependent transaction costs and property rights predetermine specific forms of organization of transactions with public goods.

O. Williamson (1996) and his followers argued that the entire aggregate of market exchange is mediated by numerous forms of alternative organizations of market transactions. In their opinion, all of them differ in "management structures" that can be represented as "institutional matrices" in which transactions are being implemented as a whole (Williamson, (1996), P. 378). According to the author, this approach allows in the future to use matrix modeling in relation to PPP-based transaction organization forms. In addition, the author specifys the basic forms of PPP organization as given below.

The first basic form of the transactions organization of the exchange of private goods is represented by a *market organization*. The conditions for the exchange of public goods and services on the basis of PPP are formed by the state itself, which only imitates the ordinary market. In this case, it is about quasi-market forms of organization (Koritsev, (2009), p. 147), which mediate the transactions of the state and private business regarding public goods. These quasi-market relations are provided by formal institutions, which ensure the "competitive" interaction of PPP participants (Shishkin, (2000), PP. 208-209). Private partners are forced to adapt to the principles of quasi-market organization of transactions and build their behaviour in accordance with them (Hodgson, 2003). In such conditions, private firms compete with each other for the right to provide consumers with public goods and services financed at the expense of the government budget funds.

The second basic form of institutionalization of transactions for the purchase and sale of private goods is represented by their hierarchical organization *(within firms)*. In the case of transactions of the state and private business, this form of organization has certain specific features. This is due to the fact that as a partner of private business in PPP, there are hierarchies represented by state enterprises (in Russa, for example, they are state and municipal unitary enterprises resulting from nationalization), as well as by state joint-stock companies (including modern Russian open joint-stock companies - PJSC) and by non-public companies with varying degrees of state participation in their capital.

The third most changeable basic form of private companies' cooperation in market transactions is represented by *hybrid organizations*. At the same time, hybrid forms of organizing transactions with public goods arbitrarily combine certain elements and mechanisms of the first (quasi-market) and the second (hierarchical) basic forms of PPP. It is hybrid transactions that are of the most interest in the context of modeling institutional matrices for organizing transactions based on PPPs.

In practice only a limited options for hybrid organizations of transactions with public goods have become widespread. As a rule, these are concessions, agreements for the lease and use of state property. Moreover, of the whole variety of forms of transactions organization on the basis of PPP, they are realized with only a few specific partnership models that are most in demand in modern market. They, as a rule, have typical characteristics and do not take into account the possibility of their variability in the context of adaptation to specific characteristics of transactions and to specific participants with options for the exchange of ownership powers. Such a narrow use of organizational forms of PPP, depending on the established practice, blocks the realization of the full potential of PPP in solving various economic problems of the state and private business.

Such a theoretical approach of the author to the identification of PPP's basic forms is aimed at the involving all basic types of organization (quasi-market, hierarchical and hybrid) in the practice of market transactions, as well as their numerous modifications. The above interpretation of PPP can be taken as its "broad" interpretation (Public-Private Partnerships, 2014). As for the individual basic forms of PPP organization (which can be represented in the form of their institutional matrices (Menard, 1997)), they contain, as in a matryoshka (Russian doll), many potential sub-variants of their realization. Moreover, it can be considered justified to refer each of them separately to PPP in a "narrow" interpretation.

In the case of PPPs, all basic types (and their subspecies) of organization are mediated by transactions related to the exchange of public goods and services financed (fully or partially) by the government budget. The PPP's effectiveness depends on how optimally the state has managed to share the risks and burden of spending with a private partner, create mutually beneficial "rules of the game" for partners, and encourage expansion of the implementation practice of long-term capital-intensive projects. The result will be to ensure the necessary rates of economic growth, stabilization of state finances and an increase in public welfare.

Hybrid Forms of Infrastructure PPP's Projects vs. Growing Government Budget Deficit and Slowing Economic Growth

The market' and hierarchical "institutional matrices" have been more or less investigated within the framework of the institutional theory. The problems of their implementation have corresponding solutions. As for the hybrid organization of public-private transactions, it has a number of unresolved problems. Besides, hybrid public-private agreements have obvious peculiarities, connected with the partnership' formalization at the pre-sale stage of the transaction, when, for example, a consortium as a joint stock company is being formed by all the participants, responsible for project's financing and implementation (Eganyan, 2015). Hybrid types of PPP organization have shown its effectiveness in the realization of large-scale long-term infrastructure projects. As a rule they mediate transactions between the public and private sectors when implementing such forms of partnership organization as concessions; management and lease contracts; rehabilitate, operate and transfer's contracts; build, rehabilitate, operate and transfer's contracts; "green field" projects' contracts and etc. (World Bank, 2014).

Traditionally, the financing of public infrastructure projects organized on the base of PPP is carried out at the expense of the national government budget. This is because the provision of the necessary quantity and quality of public infrastructure services is originally imposed on the state. However, as the volume of public goods and services is growing in all countries of the world, the problems of the chronic deficit of the government budgets and of the public debt' build-up aggravate. The limits of state borrowing in the financial market are usually limited at the national legislative levels. This situation forces governments to look for ways to reduce current budget spending without sacrificing public goods and services and limiting domestic or foreign borrowing to finance their deficits. In the conditions of economic dynamics' slowdown in the Globe (Fig. 1), the expansion of the scale of PPP implementation could be considered as a necessary panacea for all the above problems (Alesina, et al., 2017).

According to the World Bank experts, global growth is projected to moderate from a downwardly revised 3 percent in 2018 to 2.9 percent in 2019 and 2.8 percent in 2020-2021 (World Bank, 2019).

These trends have a major impact on macroeconomic stability, as well as on the sustainability of public finances. Till 2040 the global population is planned to increase by 25%, i.e. for 2 billion people (Global Infrastructure Outlook, 2017). As a result the global population density will rise from 49 people per square kilometre to 61 that will force governments to develop infrastructure networks to engage human capital in the inclusive development of their countrys. In other words in the face of declining global growth the public infrastructure becomes the main driver of economic development of the national economies. More over in the context of chronic state budget deficits, the solution of this problem is directly related to the large-scale involvement of hybrid forms of PPP for accelerated development of capital-intensive long-term projects in the sphere of public infrastructure. As a result, this will have a significant positive effect on the strengthening of public finances.

The importance of public infrastructure as a factor of the national economic growth is confirmed by the calculations of specialists of the World Bank (May, 2018, P. 39). From their view point the increasing efficiency of transport infrastructure only (in terms of labour, capital and energy consumption) by 10% generates national GDP growth by 0.8%. This is all the more important that the modern national governments have started realizing a policy of fiscal consolidation for the purpose of reducing the accumulated public debt to 2030.

Against the background of this trend in the developed countries on average around 15-16% of budget expenses are invested in fixed assets annually. The record low figure is in Germany -10.6%, but much higher than the average level, for example, is invested in less developed Latvia - 19.2% (Fig. 2). As to this parameter Russia falls in a general trend, but as a whole it lags behind countries like France, the United States and Great Britain on the development of infrastructure. The choice of these countries is dictated by the need to demonstrate the universality of problems discussed for countries with different levels of development.

Figure 1. Global growth (annual percentage change)
Source: World Bank, (2019). Global Economic Prospects: Darkening Skies. January, Washington, DC: The World Bank Group, P. 5. Note: EMDEs - emerging market and developing economies

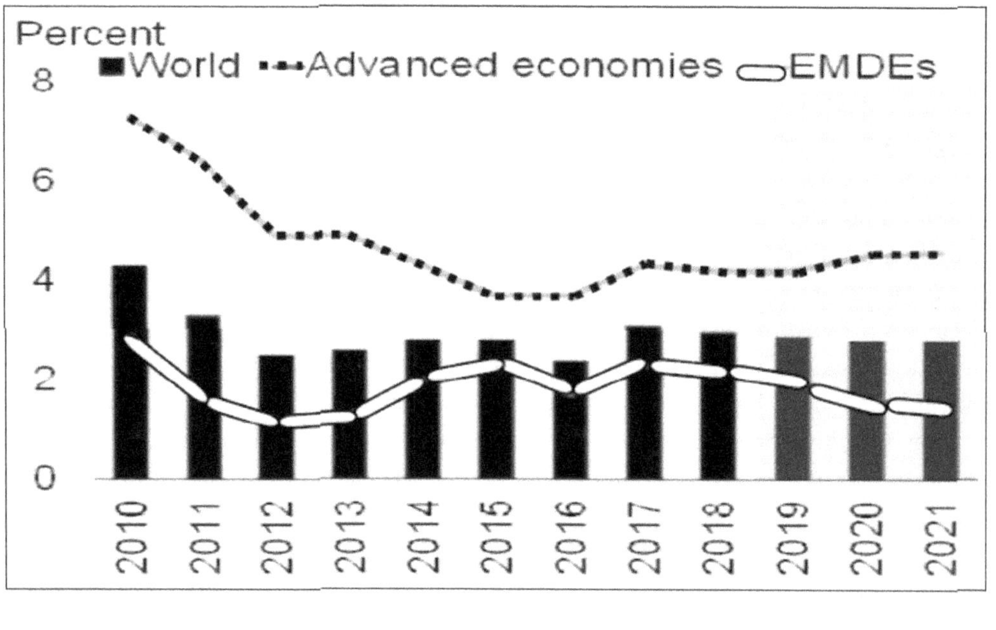

Figure 2. Budget expenditure of some national governments on infrastructure, % of total fixed assets
Sources: Based on the data of EU Open Data Portal, World Bank, InfraONE

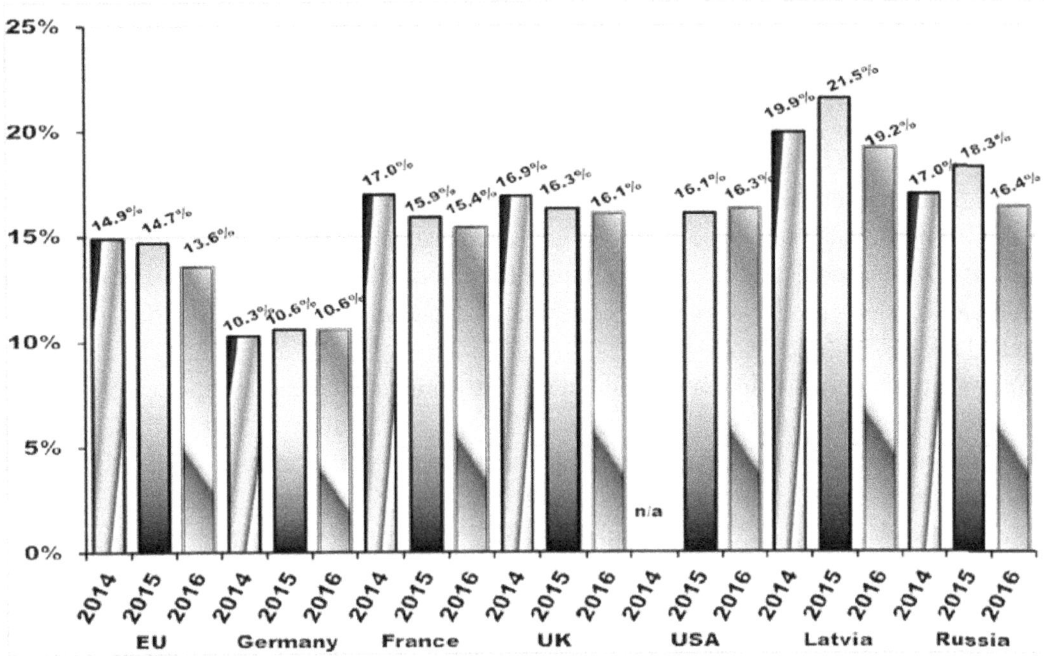

According to the EBRD data (EBRD, 2018) investment in infrastructure of the EBRD region accounts for around 40 per cent of all its capital needs. And this is happening against the background of the trend of the reduction of budget investments in infrastructure projects in most countries of the world in recent years.

In the short-term period, the assessment of the results of the consolidation programs for the transition to the budget balance trajectory is associated with great difficulties. Fiscal consolidation turns around the world with an unsatisfactory or poorly functioning infrastructure that creates serious economic and social problems both for the government itself and for households and businesses. As a result, the need to invest more in infrastructure usually arises at a time when national governments are faced with a budget deficit and significant government debt. And in this case, the effect of investing in infrastructure projects should be evaluated, provided that they are cleverly packaged by the government in one or another form of hybrid PPP. First, the public infrastructure — from transport systems to power grids and water mains — allows for the expansion and realization of economic growth potential. Secondly, this turns into an acceleration of GDP growth and state budget revenues increase, reducing the budget deficit. And, thirdly, it demonstrates the effectiveness of a state that adequately performs its functions in favour of society.

Besides, it should be emphasized that prior to 2008 the economic growth all over the world was driven predominantly by rising productivity of labor. But in recent years the main contribution to this growth has come from the accumulation of fixed capital. According to the EBRD experts, the region's overall infrastructure needs are estimated at €1.9 trillion over the period 2018-2020 (EBRD, 2018) (Fig. 3), which is the equivalent of spending 9 per cent of the region's GDP each year. It could help to support economic growth and help their income levels to converge with those of advanced economies. But the most countries in the EBRD region require either major investment with a view to expanding their infrastructure networks or investment in maintaining and upgrading existing infrastructure (ADB, 2017; Dinkelman, 2011; Jensen, 2007).

The World Bank Report (2018) concluded that the developing world would need to invest US$836.0 billion per year, or 6.1 percent of current GDP, from 2014 to 2020 to meet the new infrastructure demand and maintain the service level of existing assets. Emerging and developing economies would have to double their spending to US$452.0 billion per year (Ruiz-Núñez, and et al., 2015).

The EBRD region continues to lag behind advanced economies in terms of the overall quality of infrastructure, despite comparable access rates in certain sectors. The perceived quality of the EBRD region's transport, electricity and communications infrastructure is very close to the global average, but substantially lower than the levels observed in advanced economies such as Japan, the United States of America and the EU-15 (EBRD, 2018).

In most countries, infrastructure investment needs are dominated by either replacement and maintenance or catch-up investment (Fig. 4). The cases of Poland and Morocco illustrate these two different profiles. Both countries have total estimated infrastructure needs in the order of €100 billion. However, just 1 per cent of Poland's infrastructure needs are accounted for by catch-up investment, compared with 82 per cent in Morocco. In Belarus, Bulgaria and Turkey, however, investment needs are divided almost equally between catch-up investment and the sum of support for future growth and replacement and maintenance. Countries in the same sub-region tend to have similar profiles in terms of their infrastructure investment needs, albeit there are a number of exceptions in this regard (Fig 4).

Central Asia, the SEMED region and parts of the EEC region stand out as needing particularly large amounts of catch-up investment. In contrast, in the CEB and SEE regions – and, to a lesser extent, Russia – replacement and maintenance costs make a much larger contribution to total investment needs, with support for future growth also accounting for a sizeable percentage. At sector level, transport infrastruc-

Figure 3. Global Competitiveness Index – infrastructure
Source: World Economic Forum and EBRD experts' calculations. Note: Scores are on a scale of one to seven, where higher numbers correspond to better infrastructure. Belarus, Kosovo, Turkmenistan and Uzbekistan are not included owing to insufficient data. Annual growth rate (per cent). CEB - Central Europe and the Baltic states; EEC - Russia, Central Asia, and eastern Europe and the Caucasus; SEE - countries in central Europe, south-eastern Europe; SEMED - the southern and eastern Mediterranean countries.

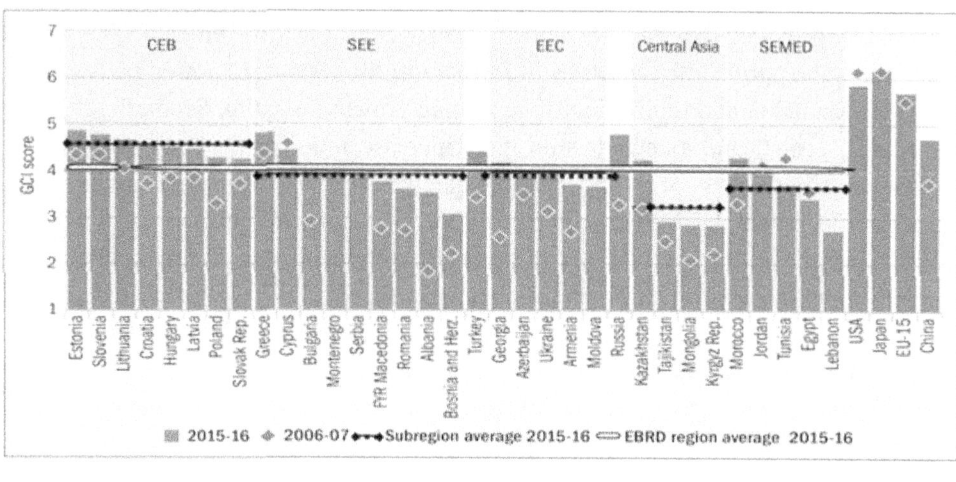

Figure 4. Total investment needs for the period 2018-22, as a percentage of all the infrastructure expenditure needs
Source: WDI, IMF, US Energy Information Administration (EIA), Nunn, and Puga (2012) and the EBRD experts' calculations (EBRD, 2018). Note: Data are not available for Kosovo or Uzbekistan. CEB - Central Europe and the Baltic states; EEC - Russia, Central Asia, and eastern Europe and the Caucasus; SEE - countries in central Europe, south-eastern Europe; SEMED - the southern and eastern Mediterranean countries.

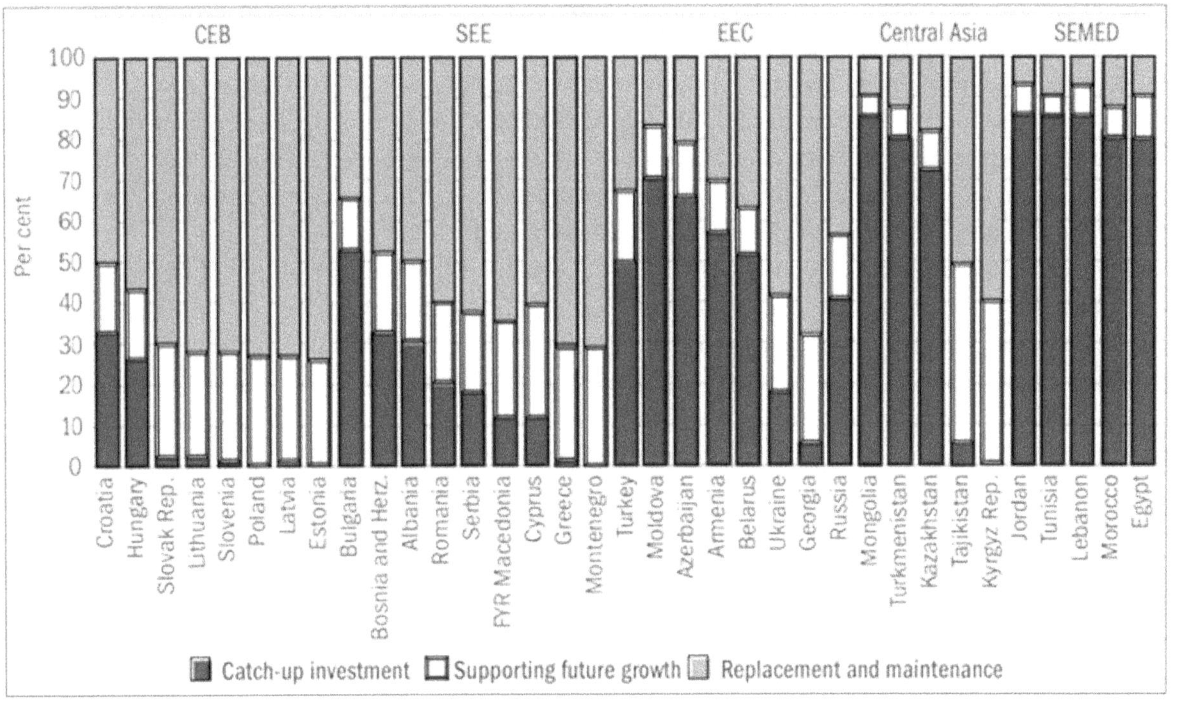

ture makes up an average of 64 per cent of total investment needs, followed by electricity (29 per cent), ICT (5 per cent), and water and sanitation (2 per cent). For example, bridging the gap over a five-year period will involve expenditure totalling approximately 9% of the EBRD region's GDP in each of those five years. The cost of catching up with the levels expected on the basis of the experiences of advanced comparator economies accounts for 52% of that total, while improving infrastructure to support future growth in GDP and population figures over the next five years, accounts for 15%. The remaining 33% relates to infrastructure replacement and maintenance requirements over that same time period. According to the World Bank (2017), only to maintain the current level of global GDP, national governments need to spend at least 3.5% of global GDP ($ 3.2 trillion) per year on infrastructure.

According to the creators of the Global Infrastructure Outlook (2017), the global infrastructure investment needs will be going to reach US$94 trillion by 2040 in order to close infrastructure gaps because of great economic and demographic changes. The McKinsey Global Institute estimates US $57 trillion in infrastructure investment will be required between now and 2030—simply to keep up with projected global GDP growth. This figure includes the infrastructure investment required for transport (road, rail, ports, and airports), power, water and telecommunications. It is, admittedly, a rough estimate, but its scale is significant—nearly 60 percent more than the $36 trillion spent globally on infrastructure over the past 18 years.

China, India and Japan in Asia will have the greatest infrastructure need in the Globe. China alone is expected to need $28 trillion in infrastructure investment, which is more than half of Asia's total needs and 30% of global needs. Under current trends, the Global Infrastructure Outlook (2017) forecast a global infrastructure investment gap (excess demand for investment compared to their supply) of about US$15 trillion – equal to a 16% infrastructure investment deficit – by 2040. Closing the gap will require additional 0.5% increase in annual infrastructure investment from the current level of 3.0% of global GDP.

While European countries in general perform well in meeting their infrastructure needs, there are exceptions. Russia has the fourth largest infrastructure gap in the world, with a forecast investment shortfall of 41% of its total investment needs. Outlook finds that five countries account for 55% of the global infrastructure investment gap. Although China's investment need is more than double that of the US, its investment gap of $1.9 trillion is just 7% of its investment need. This is compared with the investment gap of the US, at $3.8 trillion it is 31% of its investment need.

Further the Global Infrastructure Outlook (2017) estimates that the cost of providing infrastructure to support global economic growth and to start closing infrastructure gaps will be US$94.0 trillion by 2040. This is 19 percent higher than would be delivered under current trends, and is an average of $3.7 trillion per year. To meet this investment necessity, the world will need to increase the proportion of GDP dedicated to infrastructure (Global Infrastructure Outlook, 2017). So the 'investment gap' represents the difference between a country's investment need, and what would be spent under current trends. It seems that if current trends continue, global infrastructure investment will reach $3.8 trillion in 2040, an increase of 67 percent over the 2015 value, in real terms.

However, if countries wish to raise their game to match their best performing peers in terms of the resources they dedicate to infrastructure, the forecast value of infrastructure investment need rises to $4.6 trillion in 2040. That is, by 2040 there could be a gap of $820 billion between what would be spent if current trends continue and what could be spent if all countries matched their best performing peers.

On this background public resources are likely to fall a long way short of what is required in order to meet countries' investment needs in the area of infrastructure. The author links alternative of financing of infrastructure projects at the expense of budget funds with involving private investments into them through the organization of hybrid forms of PPP. Hybrid PPP contracts can attract private investors by using incentives such as, for example, preferential taxation, stable business conditions for the entire duration of an infrastructure PPP project, a predetermined rate of return on investment. In other words, it is not connected with the growth of budget financing, but with the implementation of the state's function to effectively institutionalize the external environment of the economic activities of private partners of PPP hybrid projects. Skillful use of such a mechanism would double the scale of mixed investments in infrastructure projects of PPPs, if a dollar of budget funds could attract a dollar of private investment. At the same time, it is possible to achieve an increase in the economic effect in accordance with an arithmetic progression with an increase in the inflow of private investments attracted with the help of budget funds. Thus, hybrid forms of PPP organization can improve the efficiency of capital expenditures of the state budget and accelerate the development of public infrastructure as a driving force for economic development in the near future. Moreover, judging by the results of recent studies (Arezki, et al., 2017; Eganyan, 2015), almost all countries have a huge potential of private investments that could be attracted for financing long-term infrastructure PPP projects subject to an adequate profit rate from the point of view of a private partner..

RESULTS AND DISCUSSION

The current stage of economic development is characterized by low average rates of development of the world economy. Capital-intensive, long-term infrastructure PPP-projects could largely provide an infrastructure breakthrough as the driver of inclusive development of the countries of the world. That is why it is very important to safeguard the necessary amount of capital flow into the infrastructure projects. Governments of different countries are developing incentives to attract investors and find a reasonable balance between risk and profitability of infrastructure projects.

The solution of the problem of large-scale construction and reorganization of the public infrastructure in the country is possible only within the framework of complementary long-term financing of a system, including the resources of the power structures, institutional and private investors. In other words, subject to the consolidation of budget funds, the state should change the structure of the financial market by institutionalizing the emergence of a debt financing segment focused exclusively on financing public infrastructure PPP projects. The latter means institutionalization of appropriate instruments, for example, infrastructure bonds, intended to attract partners to the hybrid forms of PPP projects.

As a result, it is possible to substantiate the dialectic state of the problem of developing infrastructure projects of PPPs in the countries of the world: it exists and does not exist at the same time. The demand for professionally prepared infrastructure projects is considerable, including potential investors. The potential of infrastructure projects supply is virtually unlimited, taking into account the unsatisfactory state of the public infrastructure. But large-scale development of infrastructure projects in the form of hybrid PPPs does not happen. The main reason is the lack of national public agencies able to offer the private investors highly profitable infrastructure projects in the form of hybrid PPPs, which allow them to reduce their transaction costs and to decrease the uncertainty and risks of financial losses. In other words, the last demonstrates inadequate performance of the state as a mega-regulator and provider of public goods and services including effective PPPs in the public infrastructure projects development. This situation could be radically changed only after realizing the new fundamental mission of the state in the development of public infrastructure: not to increase budget funds to finance hybrid PPP for infrastructure projects realization but attract private investment with the help of fiscal instruments.

Public resources are likely to fall a long way short of what is required in order to meet countries' investment needs in the area of infrastructure. However, recent studies indicate the presence of a huge stock of private savings in the national economies that can be attracted to the implementation of long-term investment PPP projects in the field of public infrastructure. (Arezki, et al, 2017). At present, in the countries of the world it is typical the following ratio of sources of financing the infrastructure PPP - projects: 2/3 of the projects' cost is financed by the state budget, and a third one – at the expense of extra-budgetary funds. But the capacity of national financial markets for PPP infrastructure projects can increase by almost a quarter per year. As a result, the potential of national financial markets in terms of investment sources for infrastructure PPP projects seems to be inexhaustible.

Now the main problem is to find the possibility to attract private capital into the infrastructure for the purposes of substitution of budgetary investment with private capitals. This problem is not insoluble, because there is a demand for large-scale infrastructure projects, there is a potential for their supply. The universal problem is connected with the lack of an adequate institutional strengthening of the market for institutional projects. And in this respect, it is the state that should create the necessary institutional support for infrastructure PPP projects. Only under these conditions the accelerated development of the national public infrastructure can turn into a real factor ensuring stable GDP growth in the future.

The size of the infrastructure gap and concerns about how to find the money to fill it are the linchpins of current debate on this issue. But this focus of discussion veils those problems that could be solved by national governments in the nearest future without additional budgetary expenses: it is about improving planning at the state level, about the conditions for the effective implementation of infrastructure projects and high-quality operation of an already functioning infrastructure. In other words, what any state can do today is to get more quality infrastructure for less money and increase the productivity of using its existing networks. Moreover, institutional measures that should be developed and implemented by countries of the world are the primary cause of success on the path of the optimal combination of budgetary and extra-budgetary funds necessary to launch long-term capital-intensive PPP projects in the field of infrastructure.

Empirical Evidence

The scale of the infrastructure "gap" and the serious problems associated with finding financial sources to overcome it are related to the dominant topics of political and public debate. But all these problems can be reduced to the only one: how to ensure large scale, better quality of infrastructure networks at a lower cost. The author focuses on rethinking how governments together with the private sector could choose, design, implement and manage infrastructure projects, as well as provide more economic benefits from the already existing networks. Experts are sure that only the introduction of PPPs provides a remarkable opportunity to significantly increase the productivity of infrastructure investments.

As mentioned above, the investment in infrastructure accounts for around 40 per cent of all capital needs in the EBRD region (EBRD, 2018). Moreover, in recent years, it has been strengthening the tendency to reduce budget investments in infrastructure projects in most countries of the world. The need for fiscal consolidation at the national level in the context of stagnant GDP growth raises the problem for governments to choose an alternative to implementing fiscal policy in the context of low tax revenues to the budget: either increase tax revenues or cut budget expenditures (Alesina, et al., 2017). If institutional investors were to increase their allocations for infrastructure financing to the above mentioned target levels, this would result in an additional $2.5 trillion in infrastructure investment capital through 2030.

High-quality infrastructure connects people and markets, facilitating the efficient allocation of resources, while inadequate infrastructure hinders productivity. Most of the countries all over the world have basic infrastructure, but there is still room for improvement in terms of sanitation and the supply of energy in poorer countries, and most of the region is lagging behind in terms of access to broadband internet (Fig. 5). Specific infrastructure projects should be decided on within the context of each country's economic environment and needs, taking account of any spill-over effects for other sectors. The cost of expanding networks varies from sector to sector, as does the time required for construction, so the order and composition of upgrades could have an impact on the delivery of benefits in the short term (McKinsey Global Institute, 2013). Moreover, judging by the experience of emerging market countries, there is the lack of institutional structure of the financial market, adequate for institutional projects. And in this respect, it is the state that should create the necessary institutional support for hybrid infrastructure PPP projects in national economies. Only under such conditions it would be possible to accelerate development of public infrastructure and to safeguard growing GDP growth and public finance stability in the upcoming medium-term period.

Figure 5. Total Infrastructure Investment Needs for the Period 2018-2022, as a percentage of GDP per year
Source: Composed on the materials of WDI, IMF, US Energy Information Administration (EIA), Nunn, and Puga (2012), EBRD (2018) and the author's calculations. Note: Data are expressed as a percentage of 2015 GDP figures, in 2010 prices. Estimates for Montenegro exclude the railway sector owing to insufficient data. Data are not available for Kosovo or Uzbekistan.

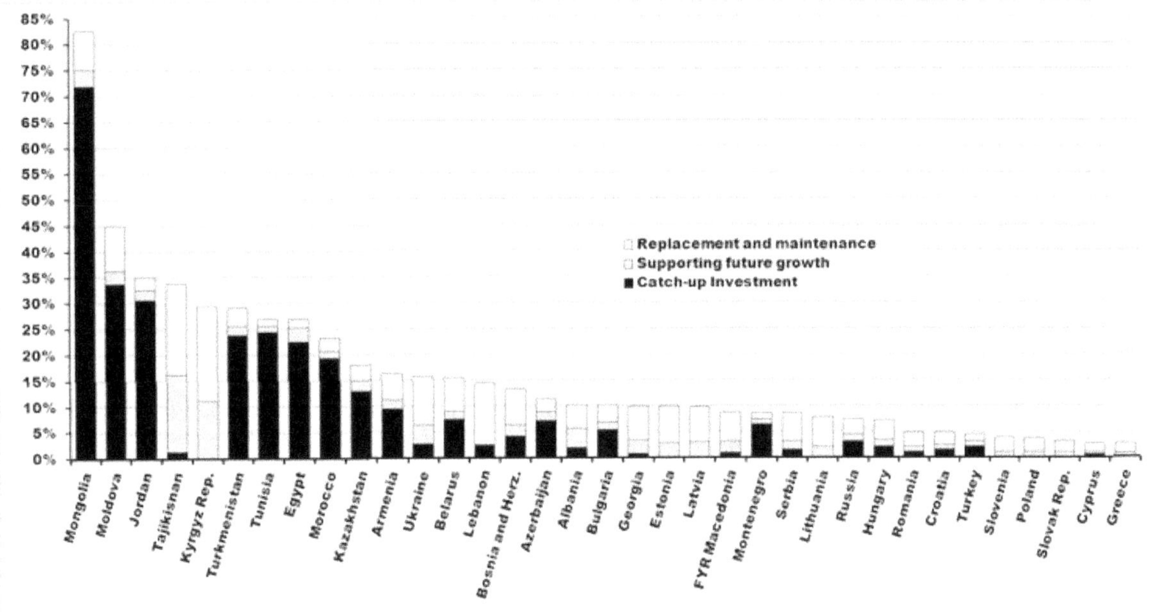

Against the background of a steady decline in budget expenditures on infrastructure, the behaviour of financial market leaders is slowly changing. If three or four years ago all private investors were waiting for state support and the axiom was pessimistic and defined by words: «no government's money - no projects», now, the qualified, rather significant part of the financial market' players understands, that subsidies are not required at all. There are other quite affordable ways to get extra-budgetary funding for an infrastructure projects. Now there are potential projects that can be fully implemented under the current conditions without any direct financial involvement of the budget funds.

As a consequence of private players' entry into the market, preferences of state capital will slowly decline. It means that the situation when investments come only from one class of investors is changing towards long-term equilibrium in the financial market. All these changes eliminate distortions in projects and affect the value of money in the best way. However, in the end, the sentiments of PPP projects partners depend on the sustainability of macroeconomic trends - to accelerate or to slow down GDP growth. Below is an assessment of the macroeconomic trends of a number of countries.

In Fig. 6 there are represented the polynomial trends, approximating empirical curves, where $t = 1, 2, \ldots, 16$ – years are marked with serial numbers:

$$\begin{aligned} Tr(t)_{RF} &= 0.0396257t^6 - 2.147657t^5 + 44.86542t^4 \\ &\quad -449.71162t^3 + 2180.3801t^2 - 4496.8725t + 4512.7013 \end{aligned} \tag{1}$$

$$Tr(t)_{U.K.} = -0.09293t^5 - 4.2213t^4 \\ -69.6518t^3 + 505.5687t^2 - 1505.47225t + 3965.81066 \tag{2}$$

$$Tr(t)_{Germany} = 11.368t^2 \text{ - } 109.95t + 3799.3 \tag{3}$$

Polynomial trends (1) - (3) indicate a high volatility of the GDP dynamics of Russia (1) (the sixth degree polynomial), a very low volatility of the GDP dynamics of Germany (3) (the second degree polynomial). As for the volatility of the GDP dynamics of the UK (2), it is higher than the one in Germany and lower than that of Russia (the fifth degree polynomial). These trends indicate a different degree of uncertainty regarding the macroeconomic dynamics of the above noted countries. In such conditions, in the next three years, the dynamics of capital expenditures on infrastructure projects of the advanced economies will not change much: by 2020 their share in GDP is projected to decline to 0.55% compared to 0.88% in 2014 (IMF Fiscal Monitor, April, 2018).

So emphasizing the idea that the federal budget is the main mechanism for the GDP redistribution in favor of the state for the purposes of financing public goods and services supply it should be stressed that it is the state that is responsible for the inefficiency of budget expenditures. But having such important

Figure 6. Annual dynamics of GDP of United Kingdom, Germany and Russian Federation for the period of 2008-2023 (in billion U.S. dollars)
Source: The author's calculations based on the official data of IMF. Fiscal Monitor (October 2018).

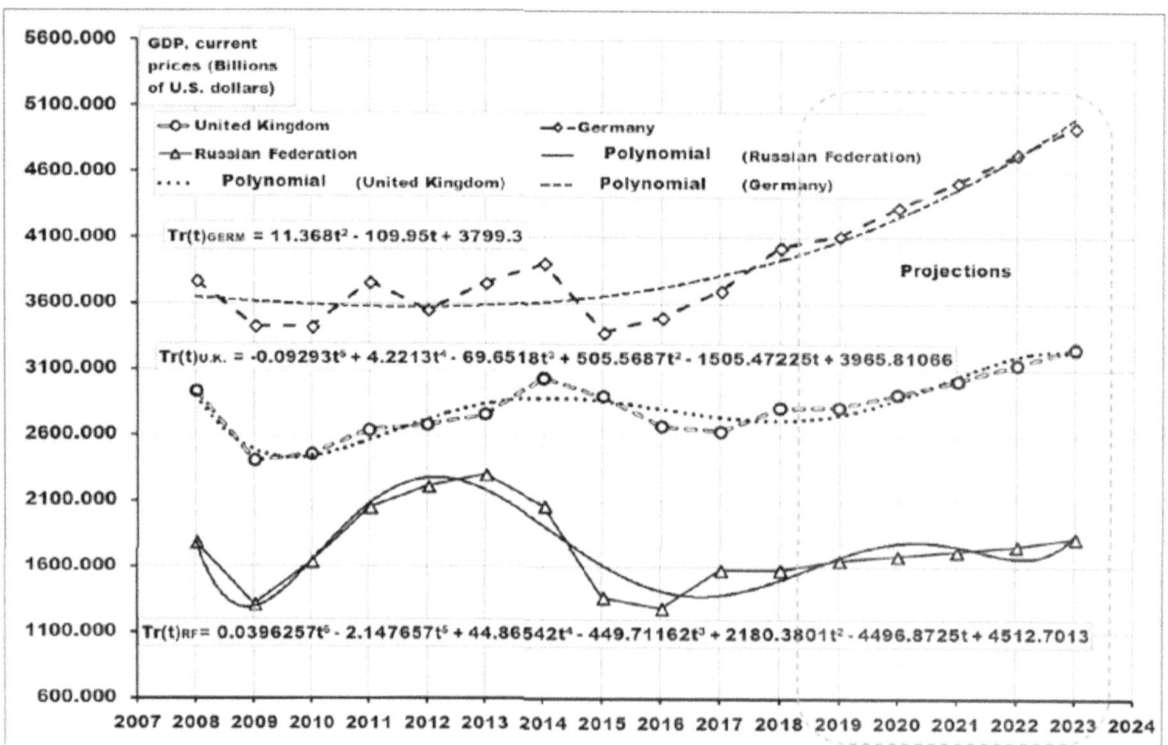

instruments of fiscal impact on macroeconomics, the state meets the opportunity to get a significant return on capital expenditures' scale of the government budget with the help of organizational factors of PPP projects in infrastructure, capable to increase greatly their efficiency.

Looking more closely at the network infrastructure necessary to safeguard sustainable economies—railways, roads, airports, ports, water, power, and telecoms—the Globe needs to invest an average of $3.7 trillion in these assets every year through 2035 (McKinsey Global Institute, June 2016). This need could increase further by up to $1 trillion annually in order to meet the United Nations' sustainable development goals. As a result there will appear a $5.5 trillion spending gap globally between 2017 and 2035, with regional variations. Fifty-four percent of the world's need will be in Asia, the bulk of this in the world's two fastest-growing and most populous countries. China will account for 34 percent of global need and India 8 percent. Investment will continue to shift to emerging markets; nearly two-thirds of global infrastructure investment in the period to 2035 is required in emerging economies (McKinsey Global Institute, June 2016; October 2016; February 2017; July 2017; September 2017).

The world's infrastructure investment has fallen short of investment needs, but the size of the gap varies considerably among different groups of countries. Unless these countries unlock new funding and increase their spending, they will feel the impact of underinvestment most acutely. Closing the infrastructure investment gap will not be easy—but it is both necessary and possible. Private-sector players can ramp up spending while also making better use of investment. Improving productivity in the construction sector alone could unleash an additional $1.6 trillion in value, not to mention the search for new sources of financing infrastructure and for capital projects. Model ideas about the potential for attracting non-state funds in different groups of countries to finance public infrastructure are shown in Figures 7-12 (the choice of countries is determined before Fig. 2).

The results obtained are impressive and allow to raise the question of national and collective global efforts to channel abundant liquidity into much-needed public infrastructure. The above model calculations estimate the growth of investment opportunities of a number of countries with different levels of development, provided that their governments can offer private investors appropriate PPP projects and thus attract an additional 1, 2 or 3 extra-budgetary dollars for each budget dollar.

According to the calculations of InfraONE experts (InfraONE, 2018), if budget funds could be "packaged" in a model of project financing on the base of hybrid PPP (concessions, or any other hybrid PPP model) then the total amount of funds attracted to projects would increase no less than three times.

Consequently, the main problem, oddly enough, is the lack of the necessary proposals from the state of professionally prepared investment projects based on hybrid forms of PPP, which have appropriate institutional support, provide low transaction costs and minimize the risks of financial losses for private investors. In modern conditions, the role of the state should change from a direct investor in public infrastructure to a patron, under the protection of which private investors will direct their capital to long-term capital infrastructure projects that are organized in the form of hybrid PPP' agreements. So the government should create formal institutions capable to ensure favourable conditions for private investors in terms of preferential taxation, insurance of risks, reduction of rates of bank lending, and etc. The above calculations prove the exceptional effectiveness of PPPs as a hybrid form of the state and private business cooperation in the implementation of public infrastructure projects. The state should redirect its efforts to the development of national infrastructure from the desire to increase budget spending on infrastructure PPP projects to the goal to develop adequate financial instruments to attract private investment.

This approach provides a chance for national states to solve the problem of accelerating the growth of their countries' GDP by 2021 without increasing the deficit of state budgets. An example of an integrated

Figure 7. The United States of America: dynamics of economies of scale derived from private investment in addition to the state budget expenditures on infrastructure projects at current prices (in billion US dollars)
Source: The author's estimations on the base of the data of IMF.

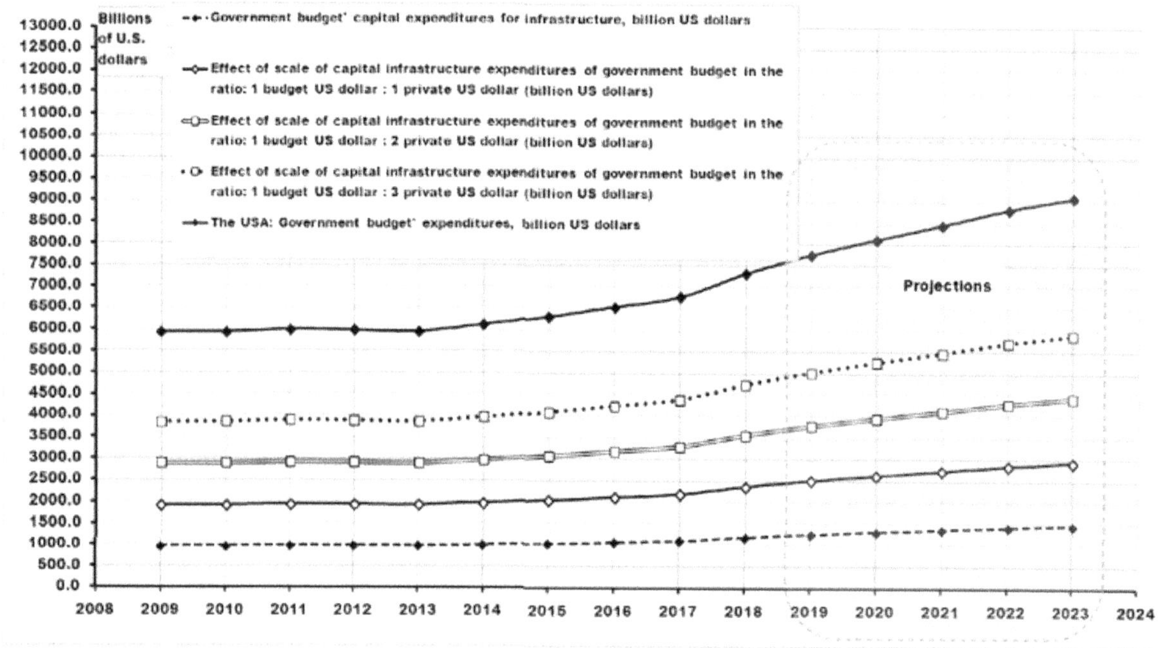

Figure 8. The United Kingdome: dynamics of economies of scale derived from private investment in addition to the state budget expenditures on infrastructure projects at current prices (in billion US dollars)
Source: The author's estimations on the base of the data of IMF.

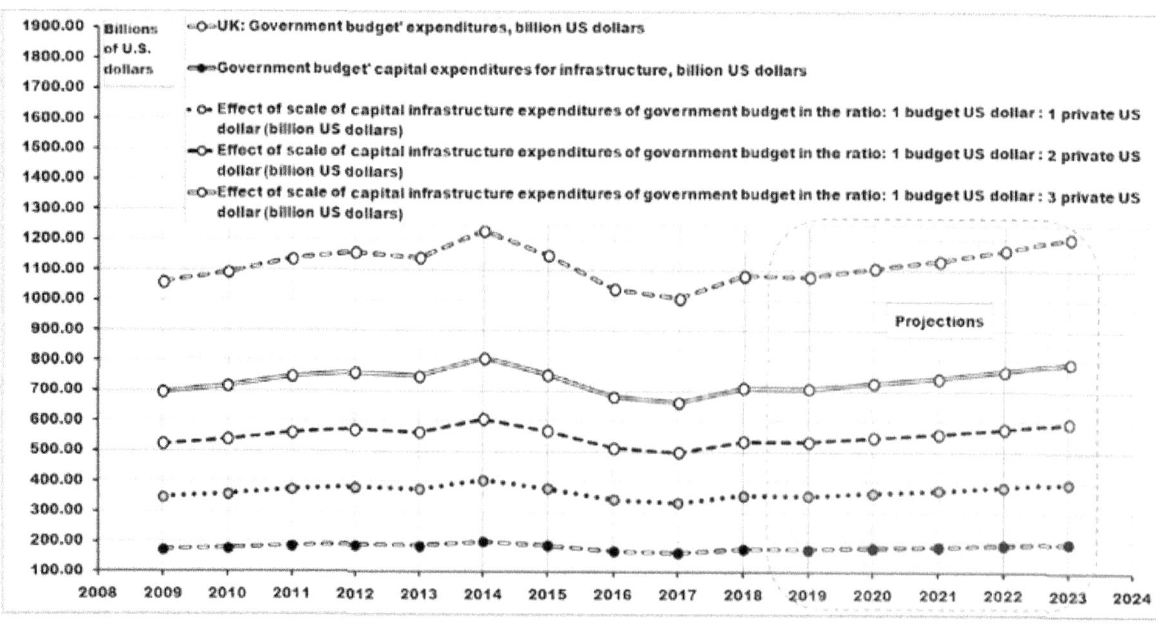

Figure 9. France: dynamics of economies of scale derived from private investment in addition to the state budget expenditures on infrastructure projects at current prices (in billion US dollars)
Source: The author's estimations on the base of the data of IMF.

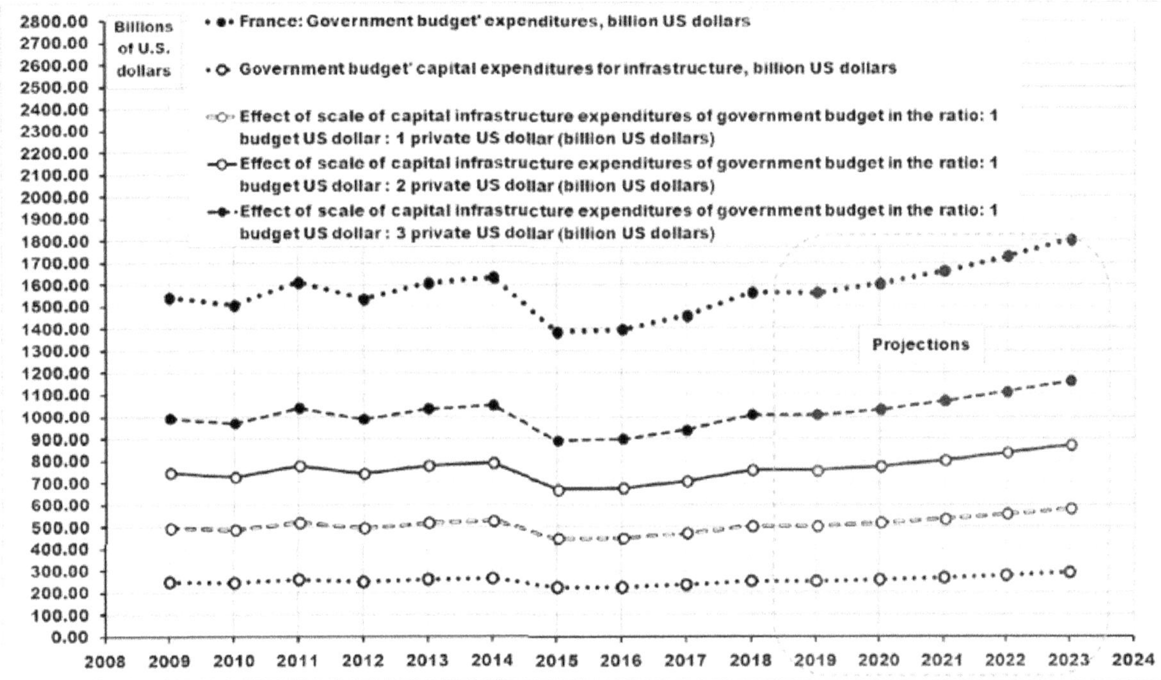

Figure 10. Germany: dynamics of economies of scale derived from private investment in addition to the state budget expenditures on infrastructure projects at current prices (in billion US dollars)
Source: The author's estimations on the base of the data of IMF.

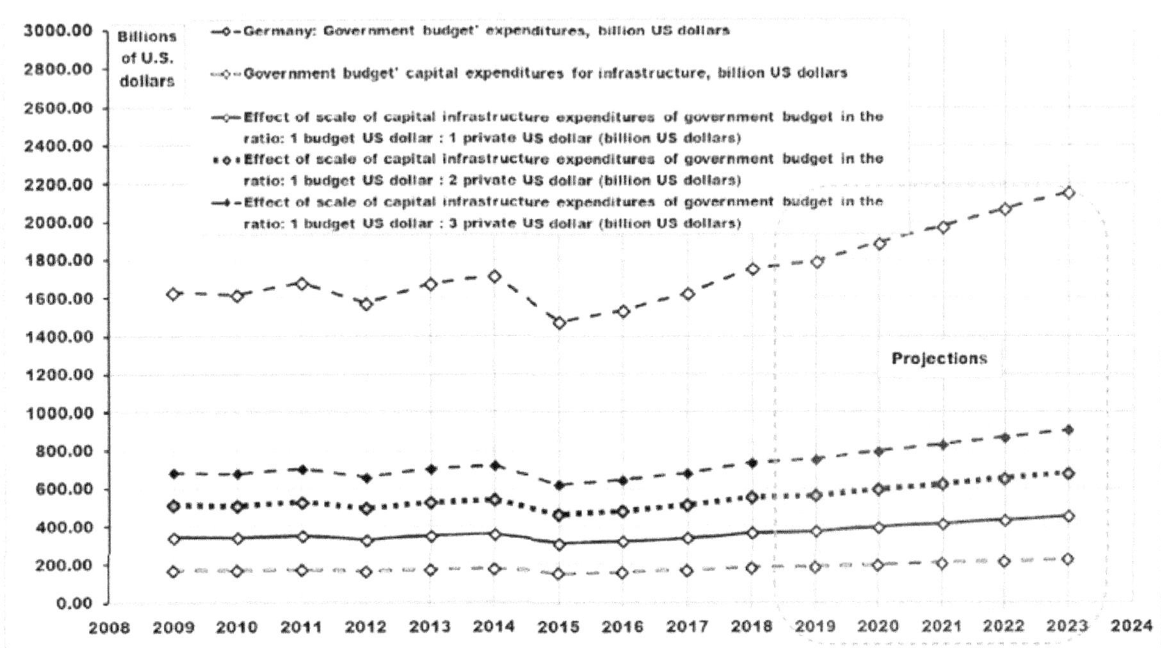

Figure 11. Latvia: dynamics of economies of scale derived from private investment in addition to the state budget expenditures on infrastructure projects at current prices (in billion US dollars)
Source: The author's estimations on the base of the data of IMF.

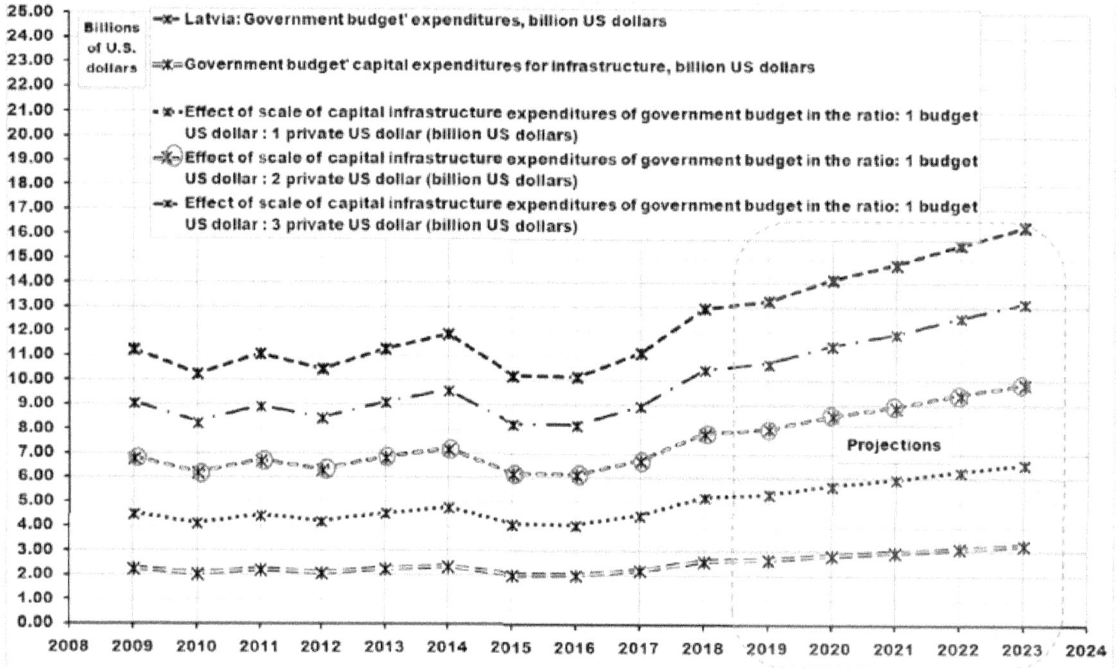

Figure 12. Russia: dynamics of economies of scale derived from private investment in addition to the state budget expenditures on infrastructure projects at current prices (in billion US dollars)
Source: The author's estimations on the base of the data of IMF.

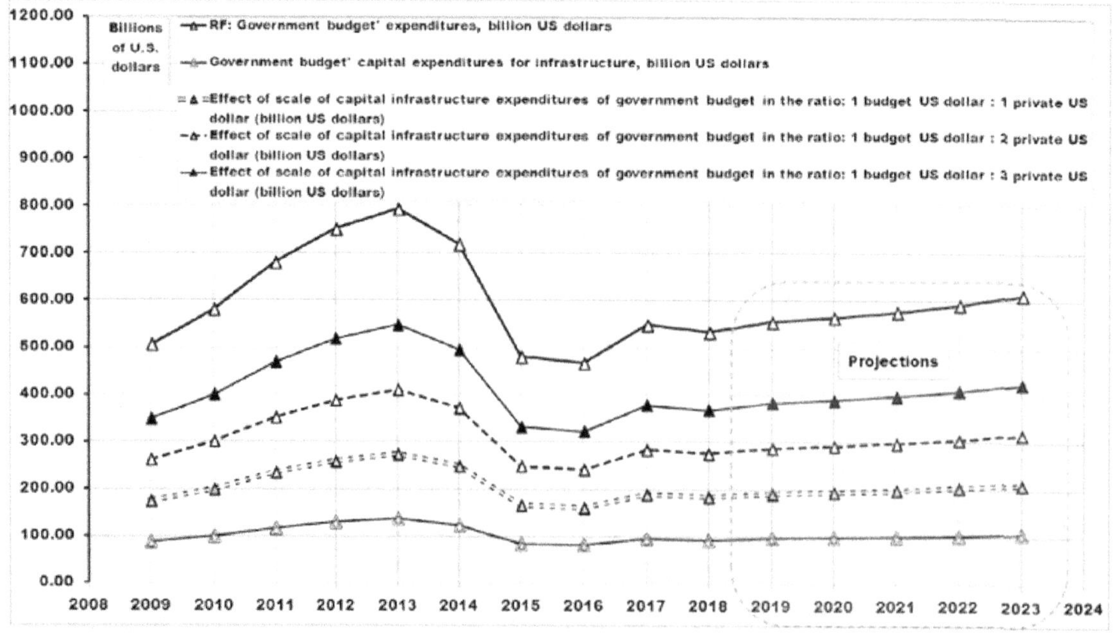

approach to solving the problem of accelerated development of hybrid forms of PPP for the implementation of long-term capital-intensive projects in the field of public infrastructure is given below (Fig. 13).

World-level experts have presented how to link the tools, standards and best practices following the traditional investment cycle that runs from infrastructure planning and prioritisation to transaction support and contract management (Fig. 13). All the above means that specific infrastructure projects should be decided on within the context of each country's economic environment and needs, taking account of any spill-over effects for other sectors. The cost of expanding networks varies from sector to sector, as does the time required for construction, so the order and composition of upgrades could have an impact on the delivery of benefits in the short term. Coordinating investment across sectors and regions can be important in terms of optimising the impact of upgrades.

All these illustrations prove the exceptional efficiency of hybrid forms of PPP organization in the implementation of long-term socially significant capital-intensive PPP projects in the field of public infrastructure. And in the context of the government's orientation towards fiscal consolidation, the development of both basic forms of PPP organization and their various potentially feasible hybrid options can actually solve the problem of stabilizing the growth rates of national economies and stabilizing their public finances.

Figure 13. Tools, guides, rankings, principles & best practices mapped along the infrastructure investment
Source: G20/OECD/WB, (2018), P. 19

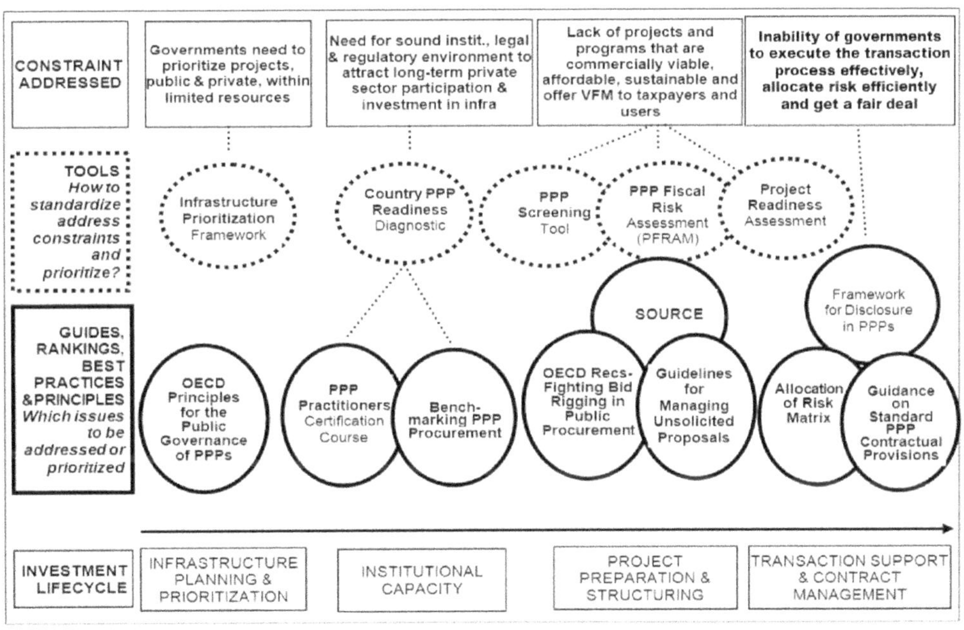

CONCLUSION

Poor governance of infrastructure remains a key stumbling block to achieving the Sustainable Development Goals (SDGs) (World Economic Forum, 2017). As the backbone of countries' economic productivity and connectivity, infrastructure facilitates many actions necessary for development (PPIAF Annual Report, 2018; WEF, 2017). While governance weak spots differ by country and political economy context, many countries need to improve project planning, better assess affordability, and strengthen the rules of the game in their infrastructure PPP' regulations. Otherwise, poor governance and weak capacity could lead to project failure or projects taking too long to materialize—meaning either that infrastructure does not get built or the host government bears significant extra costs due to project delay.

Sustainable infrastructure should also be "inclusive," meaning that it should account for the voices of all citizens—rich, poor, male, and female—and ensure that it meets their needs, is affordable, and complies with design specifications. By 2050, close to 75 percent of the globe's population will live in cities, a development that has big implications for infrastructure. Many countries are increasingly moving infrastructure development, maintenance, and financing responsibilities to state and local governments. This means sub-national institutions must develop the governance and planning capacities—and consequently creditworthiness—to attract finance for much-needed infrastructure.

Modeling the resultant of substitution of budget funds by private investment in public infrastructure PPP projects lets the author evaluate the negative and positive impacts of the budget consolidation on the economic systems' dynamic characteristics. These problems are being developed in this chapter for the purpose to manage national budget fund efficiency using the preferences of the government and of the private investors in the sphere of public infrastructure as well as of their organization form of PPP in the conditions of forced fiscal constraints. Under certain conditions, public infrastructure could be the fundamental long-run factor of national economic development. In other words, the problem of slowing down the rate of economic growth is universal, typical for all countries of the world.

The analyses have proved that public infrastructure building and restructuring on the base of hybrid PPP contracts could become the fundamental factor of national economies' accelerated growth. It has become evident that accelerated development of many hybrid public infrastructure PPP-projects is hampered by two factors: (1) inadequate institutional support for the design process itself and (2) absence of state-prepared acceptable financial models of public infrastructure PPP-projects regarding the division of risks of infrastructure projects and delegating the proprietary rights of the state to private investors.

And often a paradoxical situation arises, related, on the one hand, to a significant shortage of well-structured publicly prepared infrastructure PPP projects, and on the other hand, to the necessary amount of private investment resources that are potentially ready to finance such projects. The proposed model approach to the problem of replacing government budget funds with private investments in public infrastructure PPP projects gives an idea of the new approach of the state, which allows not only to safeguard the public finance sustainability, but also to stabilize the national economy' growth in the future 5-10 years.

REFERENCES

G20/OECD/WB. (2018). *Stocktake of tools and instruments related to infrastructure as an asset class.* G20/OECD/WB. Background Report.

Adamchuk, O., & Papchenkova, M. (2017, November 12). Officials figured out how to “weigh” investors. *Vedomosty*.

ADB. (2017). Transcending the middle-income challenge. *Asian Development Outlook 2017*, Part 2.

Alchian, A. A., & Demsetz, H. (1972). Production, information costs, and economic organization. *The American Economic Review*, *62*(5), 777-795. Retrieved from: http://www.jstor.org/stable/1815199

Alesina, A., Omar, B., Favero, C., Giavazzi, F., & Paradisi, M. (2017). *The effects of fiscal consolidations: theory and evidence.* NBER Working Paper No. 23385.

Alesina, A., & Passalacqua, A. (2015). The political economy of government debt. In Handbook of Macroeconomics (vol. 2A). North Holland. doi:10.3386/w21821

PPIAF Annual Report. (2018). *Public-Private Infrastructure Advisory Facility.* PPIAF Annual Report.

Arezki, R., Bolton, P., Peters, S., Samama, F., & Stiglitz, J. (2017). From global savings glut to financing infrastructure. Economic Policy, 32(90), 221-261.

Auerbach, A. J., & Gorodnichenko, Y. (2012). Measuring the output responses to fiscal policy. *American Economic Journal. Economic Policy*, *4*(2), 1–27. doi:10.1257/pol.4.2.1

Batini, N., Eyraud, L., Forni, L., & Weber, A. (2014). Fiscal multipliers: size, determinants, and use in macroeconomic projections. *IMF. Technical Notes and Manuals*, 4.

Bawerk & Eugen. (1898). *Karl Marx and the Close of His System: A Criticism* (A. M. Macdonald, Trans.). London: T. Fisher Unwin.

Becker, G. S. (1976). Economic analysis and human behavior. In L. Green & J. Kagel (Eds.), *Advances in Behavioral Sciences* (Vol. 1, pp. 3–17). Chicago: University of Chicago Press, PP.

Becker, G. S., & Murphy, K. M. (1988). A theory of rational addiction. The Journal of Political Economy, 96(4), 675–700.

Cheung, S. N. S. (1978). *The Myth of Social Costs. A Critique of Welfare, Economics and the Implications for Public Policy*. London: Institute of Economic Affairs.

Christiano, L., Eichenbaum, M., & Rebelo, S. (2011). When is the government spending multiplier large? *Journal of Political Economy*, *119*(1), 78–121.

Coase, R. H. (1937). The nature of the firm. Economica, 4(16), 368-405. doi:10.1111/j.1468-0335.1937.tb00002.x

Coase, R. H. (1972). Industrial organization: a proposal for research. In V. Fuchs (Ed.), *Policy Issues and Research Opportunities in Industrial Organization* (Vol. 3, pp. 59–73). Cambridge, MA: NBER.

Coase, R. H. (1993). *The Firm, the Market and the Law*. Chicago: University of Chicago Press.

Commons, J. (1931). Institutional economics. American Economic Review, 21(4), 607-619.

Demsetz, H. (1967). Toward a theory of property rights. American Economic Review, 57(2), 347-359.

Dinkelman, T. (2011). The effects of rural electrification on employment: New evidence from South Africa. *The American Economic Review*, *101*(7), 3078–3108. doi:10.1257/aer.101.7.3078

EBRD. (2018). *Transition Report 2017-2018: Sustaining Growth.* EBRD. Retrieved from http://www.tr-ebrd.com

Eganyan, A. (2015). *Investment in Infrastructure: Money, Projects, Motivation. PPP, Concessions, Project Financing*. Moscow: Alpina Publisher Inc.

Eggertsson, Th. (1990). *Economic Behavior and Institutions: Principles of Neo-institutional Economics*. Cambridge, UK: Cambridge University Press. doi:10.1017/CBO9780511609404

IMF Fiscal Monitor. (2018a, October). *Managing Public Wealth.* Washington, DC: IMF.

IMF Fiscal Monitor. (2018b, April). *Capitalizing on Good Times.* Washington, DC: IMF.

Global Infrastructure Outlook. (2017). *Infrastructure Investment Needs: 50 countries, 7 sectors to 2040. July, A G20 Initiative*. Sydney: Global Infrastructure Hub.

Global Infrastructure Outlook. (2018). *Infrastructure Investment Need in the Compact with Africa countries. Prepared by Oxford Economics for Global Infrastructure Hub. A G20 Initiative*. Sydney: Global Infrastructure Hub.

Hodgson, G. M. (1988). *Economics and Institutions. A Manifesto for a Modern Institutional Economics*. Philadelphia, PA: University of Pennsylvania Press, Polity Press. doi:10.9783/9781512816952

Hodgson, G. M. (2003). The mystery of the routine. The Darwinian destiny of an evolutionary theory of economic change. Revue Économique, 54(2), 355-384. doi:10.2307/3503007

Honore, A. M. (1961). Ownership. In A. G. Guest (Ed.), *Oxford Essays in Jurisprudence*. Oxford, UK: Oxford University Press.

InfraONE. (2018). Infrastructure investment: 2018. Analytical Review. Moscow: InfraONE: First Infrastructure Company.

Jensen, R. (2007). The digital provide: information (technology), market performance, and welfare in the South Indian fisheries sector. *The Quarterly Journal of Economics*, *122*, 879-924.

Kapelyushnikov, R. I. (1990). Economic Theory of Property Rights (methodology, basic concepts, range of problems). Moscow: Publishing House of Institute of World Economics and International Relations, the USSR Academy of Science.

Kleiner, G. B. (2004). Evolution of Institutional Systems. Moscow: Russian Academy of Science. Central Economics and Mathematics Institute, Publishing House "Nauka".

Koritsev, M. A. (2009). Institutional Structure and Mechanisms of the Quasi-markets Functioning in the Public Sector. Rostov on Don: Publishing House "Assistance - XXI century."

Le Grand, J., & Bartlett, W. (1993). *Quasi-Markets and Social Policy*. London: Macmillan Press. doi:10.1007/978-1-349-22873-7

McKinsey Global Institute. (2013). *Infrastructure productivity: how to save $1 trillion a year. McKinsey Infrastructure Practice*. Washington, DC: McKinsey & Company.

McKinsey Global Institute. (2016a, June). *Bridging Global Infrastructure Gaps*. McKinsey Global Institute in collaboration with McKinsey's Capital Projects and Infrastructure Practice.

McKinsey Global Institute. (2016b, October). *A Tool Kit to Close California's Housing Gap: 3.5 Million Homes by 2025*. McKinsey Global Institute.

McKinsey Global Institute. (2017a, February). *Reinventing Construction: A Route to Higher Productivity*. McKinsey Global Institute in collaboration with McKinsey's Capital Projects and Infrastructure Practice.

McKinsey Global Institute. (2017b, July). *Improving Construction Productivity*. McKinsey's Capital Projects and Infrastructure Practice.

McKinsey Global Institute. (2017c, September). *Navigating risks in project finance. Interview*. McKinsey's Capital Projects and Infrastructure Practice.

McKinsey Global Institute. (2017d). *Bridging infrastructure gaps. Has the world made progress?* Discussion Paper in Collaboration with McKinsey's Capital Projects and Infrastructure Practice. Washington, DC: McKinsey & Company.

Ménard, C. (1997). Le pilotâge des formes organisationnelles hybrids. *Revue Economique*, *48*(2), 741-751.

Ménard, C. (2003). The economics of hybrid organizations. *Journal of Institutional and Theoretical Economics*.

North, D. (1981). *Structure and Change in Economic History*. W.W. Norton & Co.

North, D. (1997). *The process of economic change*. Research Paper 128. World Institute for Development Economics Research.

North, D. (2003). *Understanding the Process of Economic Change*. Princeton, NJ: Princeton University Press.

Nunn, N., & Puga, D. (2012). Ruggedness: the blessing of bad geography in Africa. The Review of Economics and Statistics, 94, 20-36.

Pejovich, S. (1981). *Fundamentals of Economics: A Property Rights Approach*. Academic Press.

Posner, R.A. (1998). *Economic Analysis of Law*. Austin, TX: A Division of Aspen Publishers, Inc., A Wolters Kluwer Company.

Public-Private Partnerships. (2014). *Reference Guide. Version 2.0*. International Bank for Reconstruction and Development/The World Bank, Asian Development Bank, and Inter-American Development Bank.

Ritter, G. (1996). Storia dello Stato Sociale. Rome: Laterza.

Ruiz-Nunez, F., & Wei, Z. (2015). *Infrastructure investment demands in emerging markets and developing economies*. Policy Research Working Paper, No. 7414. Washington, DC: World Bank.

Ruiz-Nunez, F., & Wei, Z. (2016). *From global savings glut to financing infrastructure: the advent of investment platforms.* IMF Working Paper, WP/16/18.

Shishkin, S. (2000). *Reform of the Russian Health Care Financing*. Moscow: Publishing House of Gaidar Institute for Economic Policy.

Spilimbergo, A., Symansky, S., & Schindler, M. (2009). *Fiscal multipliers.* IMF Staff Position Note, No. 11. Retrieved from http://www.imf.org/external/pubs/ft/spn/2009/spn0911.pdf

Tanzi, V., & Schuknecht, L. (2000). *Public Spending in the 20th Century: A Global Perspective*. Cambridge, UK: Cambridge University Press. doi:10.1017/CBO9780511625800

Vaslavskiy, Y., & Vaslavskaya, I. (2019). Infrastructure Public-Private Partnership projects: budget consolidation policy in Russia and government expenditures' efficiency increase. In B. S. Sergi (Ed.), *Modeling Economic Growth in Contemporary Russia* (pp. 199–228). London: Emerald Publishing Limited. doi:10.1108/978-1-78973-265-820191007

Vlasov, S. A., & Deryugina, E. B. (2018). Fiscal multipliers in Russia. *Journal of the New Economic Association, 38*(2), 104-119.

WEF. (2017). *Sustainable Development Impact Summit*. Geneva: WEF.

Williamson, O. (1996). *The Mechanisms of Governance*. Oxford, UK: Oxford University Press.

World Bank. (2014). *IEG's World Bank Group Support to Public-Private Partnerships. Lessons from Experience in Client Countries, FY02–12 and World Bank Group draft Management Response*. Washington, DC: World Bank.

World Bank. (2017). *Contribution of Institutional Investors. Private Investment in Infrastructure. 2011-H1 2017. World Bank Report. World Bank Group Public-Private Partnerships*. Washington, DC: World Bank.

World Bank. (2018). *Rolling Back Russia's Spatial Disparities: Re-assembling the Soviet Jigsaw under a Market Economy*. Washington, DC: The World Bank Group.

World Bank. (2019). *Global Economic Prospects, January 2019: Darkening Skies*. Washington, DC: World Bank.

World Economic Forum. (2017). *The Inclusive Growth and Development Report, 2017*. Geneva: WEF.

Chapter 13
General Overview to Enterprise Risk Management With Its Key Components and Determinants From the Management Perspectives

H. Ebru Oydag
https://orcid.org/0000-0001-8801-8800
Yeditepe University, Turkey

Ozlem Senvar
Department of Industrial Engineering, Marmara University, Turkey

ABSTRACT

Enterprise Risk Management (ERM) is a comprehensive and holistic approach to risk management, requiring the determination, assessment and management of risks in an integrated and systematic manner. ERM has been considered as a financial, and accounting-based tool used to assess and manage the risks an organisation faces and to meet the compliance requirements of creditors, rating agencies, regulators and stock exchanges. Although ERM is widely examined by internal audit and finance scholars, ERM researches from management and strategy perspectives are limited in the literature. The purpose of this chapter is to provide a comprehensive overview of ERM including ERM concepts and definition of the risks and categorisation of risks surrounding the organisations. Moreover, the chapter handles how the risk management evolved into ERM. The distinguishing components of ERM (pillars) and the leading factors and motivation for ERM adoption (determinants) are presented.

DOI: 10.4018/978-1-7998-1033-9.ch013

INTRODUCTION

A lot of the new tools and techniques carry with them the institutional elements forced by the corporate environment including regulators, competitors, industrial or professional organisations, business publications, and industry leaders. This influence can be mimetic, normative, and coersive (DiMaggio & Powell, 1983). One such newly popular technique is Enterprise Risk Management (ERM), which is the comprehensive and improved version of the traditional risk management for organisations. Some organisations implement ERM, following the leader or other successful organisations in the industry, some other are exposed to it through the consultants or their employees, who used it elsewhere, and some implement ERM due to the rules, regulations and guidelines of the stock exchanges, rating agencies, financial institutions or other governmental or professional bodies. There are organisations, which invest for its inherent merits, as well. This makes ERM an interesting area to explore not only from corporate governance, but also from other angles, such as strategy, management, finance and accounting. ERM can even be addressed from the organisational behaviour and cognitive processes, since it includes perception and evaluation of risk individually and collectively in a social setting. Therefore, ERM is an area where scholars from finance, accounting, internal audit, management, strategy, and behavioural disciplines can and should work together.

It is possible to say that researches are immature on ERM, but they are emerging. Hence, more empirical studies are required to understand ERM practices by creating value for the organisation and its shareholders (Beasley, Branson, Pagach, 2015a; Khan, Hussain, & Mehmood, 2016).

The purpose of this chapter is to provide an overview for ERM from management perspectives. In this regard, comprehensive literature review is presented. This chapter emphasizes the links between strategy and ERM. The chapter involves discussions and recommendations for further directions.

FROM RISK MANAGEMENT TO ENTERPRISE RISK MANAGEMENT

The term risk management came into use in the early 1950s, but no article on risk management was, then, issued in the Journal of Risk and Insurance (JRI), or in its previous titles before 1956. Insurance Institute of America made efforts for the promotion of risk management in the 1960s (Crockford, 1982). First risk management thoughts came from Robert Mehr and Bob Hedges, who mentioned the topic in *Risk Management and the Business Enterprise* in 1963, and they suggested a process for managing risks: “Identify loss exposures, measure those exposures, evaluate possible responses, choose one, and monitor the results” (Mehr & Hedges, 1963). They also provided a general approach to handling risks: “risk assumption, risk transfer, and risk reduction” (Lam, 2017). In the 1970s, both academic and practitioner interest increased for risk management. Management Centre Europe introduced risk management subject in their annual insurance conference in 1971 (Crockford, 1982). The two areas of risk management under focus were insurance risks and financial risks. In the 1970s, financial risk management started as a formal system, and financial derivatives products began to be developed to manage interest rate and foreign exchange risks (Dickinson, 2001).

Fisher Black and Myron Scholes introduced Black–Scholes Model of Option pricing in 1973. This is a revolutionary model of option pricing, and also the most widely used one, which brought the Nobel prize to Black and Scholes in 1997 (Henderson, 2014).

During the 1980s and 1990s, several crises, bankcruptcies, corporate scandals and man-made environmental disasters took place. Some examples are Black Monday in 1987, which was a world-wide stock market crash; Texaco-Pennzoil, which resulted in high costs including loss for shareholders related to Texaco-Pennzoil lawsuit and bankruptcy of Texaco (Cutler & Summers, 1987); Lincoln Savings and Loan Association scandal, which according to some authors involved external audit failure along with management fraud (Erickson, Mayhew, & Felix, 2000); and Exxon Valdez Oil spill resulted in immediate death of sea animals and long-term adverse environmental impact (Peterson et al., 2003). Exxon incurred more than 2 billion dollars on oil spill case and for its restoration (Carson et al., 2003). In addition, there have been several fraudulent financial reporting cases; such as Sunbeam in 1996–1997, Xerox in 1997–2000, and WorldCom/MCI in 2002. Enron scandal in 2002 included a bundle of ethical issues from fraudulent financial reporting, and bribery of government officials to the manipulation of markets (Rockness & Rockness, 2005).

It is witnessed that unmanaged risks resulted in crises, which impacted the public interest both financially and ecologically. As experienced in the 2007-2008 credit crisis, risks can have macro-economic and societal consequences (Simkins & Ramirez, 2008).

As a reaction to the corporate scandals, fraud cases and corporate disasters, governmental bodies, stock exchanges, and professional organisations issued several governance and risk management codes, legislations, and guidance. The underlying reason behind these were the protection of shareholders, financial markets and the public interest via transparency, increased accountability, reporting and information sharing.

Increased corporate governance pressure and awareness via guidelines, rules and regulations from Governments, Stock Exchanges and Rating agencies as a response to financial crises, bankcruptcies and fraud cases played an major role in the evolution of traditional risk management to a more organised-comprehensive structure. Organization for Economic Cooperation and Development (OECD) states that "explicit legal requirements or recommendations on risk management have grown since the financial crisis" (OECD, 2017). The development towards a more comprehensive risk management was also necessitated by the increased uncertainty driven by the speed, technology, and innovation, consolidation of the industries, and the globalisation movement bringing scale, but also new challenges to the organisations. In the mean time, technologies and available softwares were advanced, and statistical tools and models were developed further. All these factors led the traditional risk management understanding to evolve into ERM (Gatzert & Martin, 2013).

ERM OVERVIEW

ERM Definition

One of the difficulties in understanding, conceptualising and understanding the ERM and its benefits is due to its vague and intangible nature. Despite the presence of several frameworks, what exactly ERM is remains as an important question. Table 1 summarises some of the key ERM definitions in the literature.

According to Lundqvist (2015), an integrated approach to risk management is achieved through the addition of risk governance to the traditional risk management process. Risk governance includes formality, centralisation, structure, rules, and procedures.

Table 1. ERM definitions

Author	Definition
International Standards Organisation (ISO, n.d.)	Risk management is the coordinated activities to direct and control an organization with regard to risk
Committee of Sponsoring Organisations of the Treadway Commission (COSO, 2004)	A process, effected by an entity's board of directors, management and other personnel, applied in strategy setting and across the enterprise, designed to identify potential events that may affect the entity, and manage risk to be within its risk appetite, to provide reasonable assurance regarding the achievement of entity objectives
Casualty Actuarial Society (2003)	Discipline by which an organization in any industry assesses, controls, exploits, finances, and monitors risks from all sources for the purpose of increasing the organization's short- and long-term value to its stakeholders
Risk Management Society (RIMS)	A strategic business discipline that supports the achievement of an organization's objectives by addressing the full spectrum of its risks and managing the combined impact of those risks as an interrelated risk portfolio
Liebenberg and Hoyt (2003)	Unlike the traditional "silobased" approach to corporate risk management, ERM enables firms to benefit from an integrated approach to managing risk that shifts the focus of the risk management function from primarily defensive to increasingly offensive and strategic
Beasley, Pagah, and Warr (2008)	ERM is the process of analyzing the portfolio of risks facing the enterprise to ensure that the combined effect of such risks is within an acceptable tolerance
Mikes and Kaplan (2013)	Enterprise risk management consists of active and intrusive processes that (1) are capable of challenging existing assumptions about the world within and outside the organization; (2) communicate risk information with the use of distinct tools (such as risk maps, stress tests, and scenarios); (3) collectively address gaps in the control of risks that other control functions (such as internal audit and other boundary controls) leave unaddressed; and, in doing so, (4) complement—but do not displace—existing management control practices.
Florea and Florea (2016)	ERM is a structured, consistent and continuous process across the whole organization for identifying, assessing, deciding on responses to and reporting on opportunities and threats that affect the achievement of its objectives

ERM is the integrated holistic management of risks an organisation faces with a portfolio management mindset in a systematic and continuous manner.

Conceptual operationalisation of ERM by academics concentrate on the below key features of ERM:

- Total, wide-array, collective risks: (Dickinson, 2001; Harrington, Niehaus and Risko, 2002; Meulbroek, 2002; Liebenberg & Hoyt, 2003; Sobel & Reding, 2004; Nocco & Stulz, 2006; Lam 2017)
- Integrated approach, meaning through different functions and across hiearchical levels (Dickinson, 2001; Meulbroek, 2002; Barton, Shenkir & Walker, 2002; Liebenberg & Hoyt, 2003; Sobel & Reding, 2004; Lam, 2017)
- Corporate wide, not silo-based or fragmented approach: (Harrington et al., 2002; Barton et al., 2002; Liebenberg and Hoyt, 2003; Kleffner, Lee and MacGannon, 2003; Grace et al, 2015)
- Continuous, and ongoing (Barton et al., 2002; Lam, 2017)

Pillars of ERM

In order to conclude if ERM is in use from a researcher perspective, studying the pillars is of high importance.

Table 2. Pillar groups of ERM

General Internal Environment and Objective Setting	General Control Activities and Information and Communication	Holistic Organisation of Risk Management	Specific Risk Identification and Risk Assessment Activities

Source: Lundqvist, 2014

According to Smallman (1996), risk management philosophy contains three factors: Structure (organisational risk infrastructure), Strategy (techniques used); and Culture in organisations.

Lam (2017) states that the components of ERM are "governance and policy" (including risk appetite), "risk analytics", risk management, and monitoring and reporting. Together they form an integrated framework for ERM.

The components of risk management that Standard and Poor (S&P) takes into account when determining the risk management rating for insurers are also important, and they constitute a good summary for the pillars of risk management: risk management culture (tone at the top, commitment of the organisation by involving risk management in decision making concerning all the areas across the entity, communicating the risk management philosophy across the organisation, if the budgeting and management compensation are influenced by risk management); risk control processes to identify and analyse the risks and to keep them within the defined and agreed risk tolerance limit; management of emerging risks (scanning and analysing environment to foresee the risks and to prepare); the presence and effectiveness of risk models; and strategic risk management (McShane, Nair, and Rustambekov, 2011).

There is no consensus about what the principal components of ERM are in the literature. As a proxy to understand the presence of ERM, some studies have used Chief Risk Officer (CRO) existence, although ERM can be implemented by another function, such as finance. In order to overcome the obstacles as to what ERM is like, some researchers developed ERM dimensions. For example, Desender (2007) developed constructs based on COSO ERM framework. As an attempt to determine the integral components of ERM (pillars), Lundqvist (2014) conducted an exploratory study on 151 firms with headquarters based in a Nordic country and which are listed on NASDAQ OMX or Oslo Börsen. The pillars of ERM from this study can be summarised as below:

Lundqvist (2014) suggests that all these four component (pillar) groups should be present and functioning in the right manner at one time in order to conclude that ERM is in place in an organisation.

Beasley et al. (2015a) conducted a study with 645 online surveys targeting the members of American Institute of Certified Public Accountants to understand the factors influencing the ERM maturity measured by current stage of ERM development, current stage of ERM implementation, and the maturity level of risk oversight in the organisation. The independent variables are grouped into four:

1. **Board Engagement Variables:** If one of the board committees has the responsibility for monitoring the risk assessment and risk management processes of management; if the management provides a report on the most important risk exposures to the board; if the top risk exposures are discussed in a separate meeting by the board; the extent of the board's request from senior executives to involve in risk oversight, the extent of risk appetite or risk tolerance in the strategic planning context.
2. **Management Engagement Variables:** CRO presence; presence of a risk committee; presence of a formal policy statement with respect to the risk management approach covering all enterprise;

presence of explicit guidelines on how to assess the impact of risk event; to what level the risk management activities are tied to compensation; to what extent the managers have received formal training; frequency for updating the risk inventory.

3. **Risk Environment Variables:** Level of increase in the volume and complexity of risks for the organisation in the last 5 years; degree of significant operational surprise faced by the organisation in the last 5 years; and the evaluation of the risk management culture (strongly risk seeking, risk seeking, risk neutral, risk averse and strongly risk averse) in the organisation.
4. **Firm Characteristics:** Company size (measured in terms of revenue); whether the organisation is public or private; and if the organisation is U.S. based or not were control variables.

Of these, the extent of the board and senior management engagement influences the ERM maturity positively. Also revenue (firm size) and being a U.S. based firm influence ERM maturity positively and significantly.

Determinants of ERM

Studying the determinants of ERM is important in order to understand the motivations behind ERM implementation, to find out if there is a difference amongst the organisations adopting ERM, and which type of companies see ERM as a value enhancing framework.

The motivation as to why organisations implement ERM is driven by laws, regulations and governance codes, such as banking regulations and stock exchange requirements (Kleffner et al., 2003). The main roles of the audit committee, as stated in the EU Directive (2006/43/EC), include the presense of risk management systems. Another motivation is created by the Rating agencies. Some rating agencies, such as S&P and Moody's, have started to include ERM in their rating evaluation criteria. Gearing level of the organisations (leverage) is a factor that can trigger ERM usage. The position, or even the prospect of financial distress can have costly consequences for organisations (Meulbroek, 2002). Liebenberg & Hoyt (2003) conducted an analysis on the US companies that announced CRO appointment between the years 1997 and 2001, using CRO announcements as ain indicator of ERM implementation. The authors found that the more highly leveraged the firms, the more they adopt ERM. This is a way of showing their commitment to managing the risks, hence attempting to reduce the agency costs. Other factors are the size, growth plans and board composition of organisations.

According to a survey conducted by AON 2017 Global Risk Management survey, organisations with higher revenue are more likely to have a formal risk management department.

According to the quantitative research in French CAC-40 companies by Khan, Hussain, and Mehmood (2016), organisations with high financial distress (operationalised with leverage, opacity and cash ratio), poor earnings performance, and available growth opportunities (operationalised by the ratio of research and development costs to total assets, and the ratio of market value to book value of ordinary equity) are motivated to adopt ERM. In this study, ERM adoption is closely related to six independent variables: Financial leverage, cash ratio, stock volatility, market to book ratio, earnings volatility and the board independence considering the significance levels.

Encouragement from the board and the concern for directors' and officers' liability are important reasons for ERM adoption (Kleffner et al., 2003). Desender (2007) finds that the separation of CEO and Chairman influences the adoption of ERM positively. Although board indepence (operationalised as the percentage of the board of directors considered to be independent) on its own is not a significant factor, board independence together with the separation of CEO and Chairman play an important role in ERM adoption. However, in a more recent study in 2016, a positive influence of the board of directors including more independent members on ERM adoption is noted (Khan et al., 2016).

Another study conducted in 528 Public companies in Malaysia tested the size, profitability, leverage, ownership, international diversification, CRO, and turnover as the determinants, and found that high turnover, hiring CRO and not being diversified internationally have significant influence on ERM adoption. Size (based on assets) is not significant, although Turnover is significant. The ERM awareness of Malaysian companies is low, despite their size and the authors comment that higher sales is a sign of profitability to be able to support ERM programmes. Leverage is not significant, nor is ROA (Razali, Yazid, & Tahir, 2011).

Cescon, Costantini, and Rossi (2013) conducted a study amongst the large Italian manufacturing companies and found "significant relationship between listed firms, and non-probabilistic risk assessment techniques", indicating the importance of the use of sophisticated risk assessment techniques by listed firms vis-a-vis non-listed ones.

Henschel's study involving questionnaires and interviews with German SMEs finds that the company size is a significant factor and industrial sector is a limited factor to differentiate the quality of risk management systems (Henschel, 2010).

Table 3 summarises the selected studies on determinants of ERM. Most analysed determinants in the literature are firm size, financial leverage, volatility in earnings, volatility in share prices, asset opacity, growth opportunities, diversification (industry and/or international), institutional ownership, board independence, separation of CEO and chairman, and the impact of auditors and rating agencies. Some industry specific elements have been taken as independent variables to explain the existence of ERM and/or level of implementation (maturity). Some studies have used secondary data, whilst some others have preferred surveys. Some studies use existence of CRO as a proxy for ERM, some others refer to key-word search for CRO, ERM, and integrated risk management in databases or publicly available reports. The studies are in various markets, including US, Germany, France, Malaysia and Turkey. The industry composition in the surveys are also various. Whilst some studies concentrate on financial sector organisations, some others include organisations from various industries (financial and/or non financial). In terms of time dimension, some studies are longitudinal, and some are cross-sectional. When the results are analysed, the variations in results can be due to different research methodologies employed, due to different industry representations in the selected samples, due to the different (appointment) dates of CROs assuming the start of risk management, and due to cross-sectional versus longitudinal nature of studies. There is a probability that ERM adoption may not explain the variations in secondary data, as it may be influenced by reasons other than ERM. Also the operationalisation of certain independent variables like growth opportunities may be revised and re-considered with other alternatives than Research and Development percentage or Market Value/Book Value of ordinary equity.

More comprehensive longitudinal studies can be conducted for organisations in selected industries and in selected markets. This could add value to the understanding as to which type of companies adopt ERM and why. The data gathering can be based on surveys and as well as secondary data to check consistency of findings, and they can be accompanied by interviews with companies to assess the root-causes of the findings.

An alternative method can be the usage of case studies on selected industries from various markets to understand the determinants thoroughly.

Table 3. Determinants of ERM – summary of the selected empirical studies

[illegible]	[illegible]	[illegible]	[illegible]	[illegible]	[illegible]	[illegible]	[illegible]	[illegible]	[illegible]	[illegible]	[illegible]	[illegible]	[illegible]	[illegible]	[illegible]	[illegible]	[illegible]	[illegible]	[illegible]	[illegible]	[illegible]
[illegible]	[illegible]	[illegible]	[illegible]	[illegible]	√	√					√	√		√							
[illegible]	[illegible]	[illegible]	[illegible]	[illegible]	√	√											√	√			√
[illegible]	[illegible]	[illegible]	[illegible]	[illegible]	√					√					√				√		
[illegible]	[illegible]	[illegible]	[illegible]	[illegible]	√	√		√													
[illegible]	[illegible]	[illegible]	[illegible]	[illegible]		√	√				√	√	√	√	√	√					
[illegible]	[illegible]	[illegible]	[illegible]	[illegible]	√	√			√	√			√				√	√	√	√	
[illegible]	[illegible]	[illegible]	[illegible]	[illegible]	√	√			√									√			√

DV: Dependent Variable

Characteristics of ERM

Characteristics of ERM can be summarised as follows:

1. Risk Management shall be integrated to company strategic management and planning processes. The determination and management of risks are part of the strategic thinking, planning, and management.
2. Common purposes of risk management shall be identified on an enterprise-wide basis and with the participation of the whole staff. Hence ERM is not an exercise undertaken by the top executives behind closed doors.
3. Risk Management should provide reliable and accurate results. In this regard, data collection, organisation, and analyses should be performed in a systematical manner.
4. Main subject that the Risk Management focuses is to limit the risk hunger in an objective way that firms are subject to or undertake.
5. Everyone inside the firm is responsible for the risk management. Enterprise risk management is a team work, and a process that interests and that needs the contributions of the entire staff.
6. It is an obligation that inside the firm, every manager's and staff's duties, authorisations, and the language of risk management shall be determined and outlined. Responsibilities shall be defined in detail. A common generation of risk management consciousness and common language with a risk management policy shall be formed and risk management training shall be embedded with practice. The involvement of the whole organisation may require a culture change triggered by training and continuous feedback and communication. The risks should be informed by all levels, and the actions should be owned and performed again by all levels (as necessary) in the organisation.
7. The key to successful application of risk management is through the consciousness of the top managements for risk management functions, and benefits of application. A powerful risk organisation shall be founded.

ERM, especially ERM understanding which combines the strategic management, optimises the risks by determining risks in a systematic manner, and also developing tailor made risk management solutions. This is also supported by the advance in statistical modelling and available risk management softwares. ERM is an organised process of planning, monitoring and learning and requires Top-Down role modeling and ownership of the organisation. As demonstrated in the above sections, a mature ERM implementation can increase the financial performance and add value, in addition to the protection of the existing value of the business.

In traditional risk management concept, functional structure for superior management is dominant as a controlling tool. While risk is defined as a negative state, it is mostly financial control based, and reduces the risks and protects the enterprise value. Actual risk perspective imposes that enterprise is considered as a whole and used by managers as a tool of management. Table 4 presents differences between Traditional Risk Management and ERM.

ERM Penetration

ERM has become popular, and is widely used especially in certain industries, especially in financial services (banking and insurance) due to the legislations, and also due to the complexity of risks managed.

As stated in the OECD Corporate Governance Factbook – 2017, the number of jurisdictions requiring or recommending the implementation of an enterprise-wide internal control and risk management system is 37 representing 79% of total. In 38 jurisdictions, board responsibilities for risk management is determined via a code, rule and/or regulation.

According to the Trends in Risk Integration and Aggregation report, there is a greater emphasis on the integrated firm-wide risk management and mathematical models are used to aggregate risks based on a survey of a survey of 31 financial institutions in 12 countries (Basel, 2003). According to the RIMS 2017 Enterprise Risk Management Benchmark Survey, percentage of Financial Sector organisations that integrate an ERM programme (fully or partially) increases from more than half in 2013 to 92% in 2017. Amongst the total respondents from 14 industries, organisations that integrate an ERM programme (fully or partially) is 73% of the total respondents, up from 63% in 2013 (RIMS, 2017).

Benefits of ERM and Results of Empirical Studies

In 1952, Harry Markowitz introduced the Portfolio Selection Theory, which states that an investor can reduce his/her risk by investing in a broad portfolio of stocks, so that the idiosyncratic risks could be avoided through offsets. According to this model, since the investors are capable of minimising or diversifying risk this way, then risk management destroys value rather than creating value (Markowitz, 1952). Markowitz's theory has certain assumptions. Totally eliminating the risks can be via stock choices with a correlation of -1, which is not very feasible in reality. On the other hand, managing risks has certainly its costs: It may require investment on software, the organisation may receive consulting from risk management experts, pay insurance premiums, or incur transaction costs for hedging the risks, the organisation may set up teams, and organise training programmes to create a risk culture. Therefore,

Table 4. Risk management: traditional approach versus the modern approach

Traditional Approach	Modern Approach (ERM)
It is mostly financial control	It is mostly strategic
Risk reduction is provided	Risk optimisation is provided
Risk limits exist	Risk strategy exist
Risk measurement is unplanned or partly planned	Risk measurement and monitoring are planned
Risk management is silo-based (limited to some functions/departments)	Risk management is enterprise-wide
To save the Enterprise value is essential	To add value and protection is essential

incurring such costs can be value-destroying from an investor's point of view. However, Stulz (1996) states that the value can be created from risk management by reducing or totally eliminating the real costs with high variability. These real costs are bankcruptcy costs, higher expected payments to corporate stakeholders (e.g. employees, investors, customers) and higher expected tax payments. Bankcruptcy costs can be direct, such as the legal expenses, or indirect such as the potential reduction in firm value. Bankcruptcy costs are part of the costs of financial distress. Financial distress costs include the higher costs the company will face due to weakened financial position, and the "underinvestment problem": the investment opportunities forgone due to high costs of outside funding – if available. Organisations can use risk management to reduce the present value of bankruptcy costs, costs of financial distress and taxes paid. Meulbroek (2012) adds the reduction in external monitoring costs, arising from better performance evaluation to the risk management benefits. ERM approach brings the advantage of managing total risks versus the previous risk management approach, as the total risks would create synergies, and natural hedges amongst them. ERM's benefits for organisations can be the resilience, viability and extended lifecycle of the business, hence protecting the shareholders', investors' and public's interests. COSO posits that ERM can enhance enterprise resilience in the long run (COSO, 2017). Another benefit could be sending signals to investors and creditors for strong governance, and meeting the compliance requirements of regulators.

COSO lists the benefits of ERM as identification of opportunities; enabling the identification and management of risks with an entity-wide approach; increasing positive performance results by decreasing losses and negative surprises; decreasing variability of performance; improving resource deployment via better prioritisation and resource allocation; enhancing enterprise resilience (COSO, 2017).

According to the research by Beasley, Pagach, and Warr (2008), firm-specific characteristics influence benefits of ERM across firms, and hence the benefits of ERM are not equal. Some of the mostly cited studies are by Hoyt and Liebenberg (2008; 2011) measuring the impact of ERM on firm value, with Tobin's Q for U.S. insurers. The results demonstrate a positive impact of ERM on firm value. ERM explains up to 17% of the firm value in the 2008 study, and the ERM premium is roughly 20 percent in the 2011 study.

The empirical study by Gordon, Loeb, and Tseng (2009) based on 112 US firms tests impact of the match of ERM, and the five contingency variables (environmental uncertainty, industry competition, firm size, firm complexity, and board of directors' monitoring) on the relationship between ERM and the performance of the firm. The study confirms the contingency of the ERM-firm performance on these variables. McShane et al. (2011) used (S&P) rating as a different measure of the extent of ERM implementation. The "risk management culture", emerging risks management, risk control processes, systems, risk and economic capital models, and strategic risk management are taken into account in S&P risk management rating. The rating classifies the insurers in five groups as "weak, adequate, adequate with a positive trend, strong and excellent" (as coded from 1 to 5 in this sequence by the authors). The ratings of 1-3 correspond to Total Risk Management (TRM), and 4-5 represent the ERM in authors' opinion. The authors studied 152 insurer groups and found a positive impact of TRM on firm value, but no difference for ERM. Baxter, Bedard, Hoitash, and Yezegel (2013) checked if ERM increases operational performance and if it is value adding. According to this study also, firm performance measured by accounting returns, and market valuation measured by Tobin's Q, are higher for firms with higher quality ERM. A study by Al-Amri and Davydov (2016) aims to test the effectiveness of ERM with respect to operational risk. The sample is based on 2,531 observations from 1992 to 2010 collected from Compustat and CRSP databases, and filtered for ERM using proxy statements. They find evidence for the decrease in both the frequency and severity of operational losses for organisations who have ERM experience. So, firms who have used ERM tend to incur lower and less frequent losses according to this study. The authors estimate a 63% reduction in operational risk frequency, and up to 35% operational loss reduction on the average for the organisations having ERM. Farrell and Gallagher (2014) conducted an analysis to test the impact of ERM maturity on firm value. The sample consisted of companies for which the data was gathered via an online survey developed and collated by RIMS. The researchers filtered the data for publicly listed companies to calculate Tobin's Q as a proxy of firm value. Results show that ERM maturity is related to higher firm value. Top-down executive engagement, and the cascading of ERM culture are the significant elements of maturity. These finding are supported by Florio and Leoni (2017) in their study using a sample of non-financial Italian listed companies. Organisations with advanced ERM implementation enjoy higher performance, both in terms of accounting performance and also market evaluation. Lechner and Gatzert (2018) tested the effect of ERM on shareholder value using a sample of 160 companies listed in the German stock indices. This study also supports the value relevance of ERM with a significant positive impact on Tobin's Q (shareholder value). As a result, it was found that companies using ERM are higher valued for the German data, as well.

ERM FRAMEWORK AND LINKS WITH STRATEGY

Sustainability of Risk Management Process requires a continuous loop and the integration of strategy to risk management process.

According to Maia and Chaves (2016), most of the severe losses in the market value of the large, global, public companies are due to the event of strategic risk. Therefore strategic risks are "most consequential to the organization's ability to execute its strategies and achieve its business objectives" (Frigo and Anderson, 2011). The ERM frameworks also suggest the integration of strategic planning and implementation with the ERM. For example, COSO suggests the inclusion of ERM capabilities in the strategic planning process in the 2017 Enterprise Risk Management - Integrating with Strategy and Performance framework. ERM should be utilised to understand how risks can impact the strategy; to check if the strategy aligns with the mission and vision of the organisation and organisation's risk appetite; and to test the implications from the chosen strategy (COSO, 2017).

These stated benefits are partially seen in practice. Gates (2006) found that out of respondents only 16% integrate their ERM with strategic planning and again 16% with annual budget process. According to 2015 Global Insurance ERM Survey Report by Towers Watson, the satisfaction from ERM amongst insurers, that participated in the survey is higher when ERM is linked to the business goals and the organisations which are most satisfied view the risk function as a business strategy partner. Beasley, Branson, and Hancock (2015b) report that 48% of the respondents believe that the existing risk exposures are considered when evaluating new strategic initiatives. But, 36% of the respondents do not perform formal assessments of emerging strategic, market, or industry risks. Boards in the 27% of the organisations, "mostly" or "extensively" review the top risk exposures for the organisation during the strategic plan discussions. Viscelli, Hermanson, and Beasley (2017) study the ERM-strategy linkage in practice based on 14 organisations. Despite many interviewees seeing ERM process a part of the strategic planning process, the connection is not as strong as expected yet, and also ERM is not that helpful in identifying new strategies. During the identification of risks, they do not use a strategic lens. Also the ERM leaders are mostly from operational or compliance related functions, not from a strategic background. This may accommodate the lack of understanding or practice with respect to strategic management. These findings may be due to the immaturity of ERM implementations in organisations as they are mostly implemented in mid 2000s. Other reasons are culture, structure of ERM leadership and management of key risks.

A study by Beasley, Branson, and Pagach (2015) tested if the perception of ERM as a strategic tool is influenced by the elements of a mature ERM. The authors found that ERM suggests some strategic value especially for larger organisations. In this study, the presence of a risk committee at managerial levels, provision of training and guidance to senior managers, and executive compensation are strongly associated with the strategic value perception of ERM, and there is a weak evidence on the impact of frequent updating of risk inventories in strategic value adding aspect of ERM. Arnold, Benford, Canada, and Sutton (2015) conduct a study on a sample consisting of 155 Chief Audit Executives, and find support that strategic ERM positively promotes both strategic flexibility and supply chain performance.

As it can be seen in Figure 1, when the ERM and strategy are integrated, risks are defined based on the corporate, business and operational strategies, plans and the related programmes. They are assessed with the various quantitative and qualitative techniques and the related risk acceptance/reduction/elimination or transfer decisions are undertaken according to the risk acceptance and tolerance of the firm. Then the risks and related actions are monitored, learnings are taken and communicated to the related parties to ensure learning and improvement take place. The results are also embedded to the strategy process as inputs and the process continues from then on for the next period on hand.

Figure 1. Strategy and ERM process framework

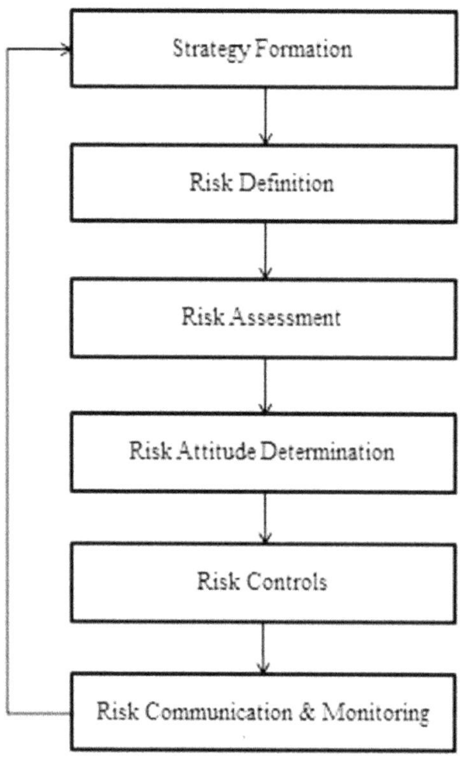

CONCLUSION

ERM is a holistic, integrated, comprehensive and systematic risk management approach. ERM gained popularity together with the increased governance trend, following the corporate failures and scandals that have evolved into crises at macro level as seen in 2008. With the increasing pressure from the regulators, guidance from the professional bodies, due to increased competition in the markets, and the availability of better tools and models supported by technology, risk management evolved into ERM over time. Whilst some organisations still use it as a compliance exercise, it is empirically proven that there are benefits from ERM in terms of value creation both in accounting and market value terms. Empirical studies have some conflicting results, which may probably be driven by the differences in industries tested, variety of research methods, and operationalisation issues. The difficulty with ERM research is that it is not very straight forward to understand the existence, and extent and coverage of risk management practices in the organisations using the publicly available data. Companies do not necessarily disclose the details and coverage of their ERM practices publicly. Therefore some empirical studies refer to the existence of CRO, or use keyword search such as ERM, risk management, or integrated risk management with reference to the publicly available data to understand if ERM exists. Some researchers develop scales and conduct surveys to test the quality, and maturity of ERM practices. More studies with respect to the determinants and pillars of ERM can contribute to a better understanding of the motivation of organisations to implement ERM, as well as to an understanding of the key characteristics of ERM that lead to value creation. Especially the latter will contribute to the preference of ERM. These studies can be conducted with longitudinal data with thorough operationalisation of ERM, using the wide array of findings from previous research literature preferably on specific industries. Some authors like Mikes and Kaplan (2013) suggest company specific case studies to understand the determinants, pillars and benefits of ERM. As stated in the literature, ERM accommodates contingencies, and is a company-specific and tailor-made process, rather than being a one-size fits all process due to size, needs, various risks the organisations are exposed to both internally and externally. Risks vary for different firms and industries despite some general locational PESTEL commonalities present in the context. In addition, the cognitive aspects, organisational culture dimension, ownership, and rolemodelling from top management, and change management aspects require contingent treatment and implementation, whilst the general ERM principles are similar across organisations. Having said that, it would be still interesting to see if there are any task environments, and industry specific commonalities between ERM designs as to the risks prioritised, and how they are managed. Likewise, what the perceived and realised benefits have been after implementation is worth testing in different contexts, but preferably with similar methods. How the companies manage the biases, politics and bounded rationality issues when determining and managing their risks is also another area for future research. These aspects make ERM a new and interesting area not only for finance, accounting and risk scholars, but also for management and strategy scholars.

With respect to the ERM implementation in practice, there are various frameworks and guidelines issued by professional organisations. However, it is not clear-cut and easy for practitioners to take a framework and apply it in the organisation. Therefore, a suggestion for practitioners can be to set the basics first and start with a high level prioritisation of risk areas in line with, but not only limited to corporate and business strategy. General risks, such as risks for natural disasters, compliance risks, macro risks, as well as operational risks need to be taken into account together with the strategic risks. After the base is formed, through the continuous top management ownership, and emphasis, through the continuous communication of risk management philosophy, and promoting the learning, and enabling and encouraging wide participation at all levels, ERM can be implemented, embedded and progressed. The quality of results would progressively increase with the maturity of ERM. In order to be able to achieve the orchestration and smooth progress, the presence of a CRO and risk function may be needed based on the size and resources of the organisation, and the scope of current risk management practices. All in all, ERM has the potential to be an investment with a positive pay-out when implemented in a holistic and carefully designed manner in line with the organisation's needs, size and resource base.

REFERENCES

Al-Amri, K., & Davydov, Y. (2016). Testing the effectiveness of ERM: Evidence from operational losses. *Journal of Economics and Business*, *87*, 70–82. doi:10.1016/j.jeconbus.2016.07.002

Arnold, V., Benford, T., Canada, J., & Sutton, S. G. (2015). Leveraging integrated information systems to enhance strategic flexibility and performance: The enabling role of enterprise risk management. *International Journal of Accounting Information Systems*, *19*, 1–16. doi:10.1016/j.accinf.2015.10.001

Barton, T. L., Shenkir, W. G., & Walker, P. L. (2002). *Making enterprise risk management pay off.* Upper Saddle River, NJ: Financial Times/Prentice Hall.

Basel Committee on Banking Supervision (Basel). (2003). *Trends in risk integration and aggregation.* Retrieved on 5/6/2018 from https://www.bis.org/publ/joint07.pdf

Baxter, R., Bedard, J.C., Hoitash, R., & Yezegel, A. (2013). Enterprise Risk Management Program Quality: Determinants, Value Relevance, and the Financial Crisis. *Contemporary Accounting Research*, *30*(4), 1264–1295. doi:10.1111/j.1911-3846.2012.01194.x

Beasley, M. S., Branson, B., & Pagach, D. (2015a). An analysis of the maturity and strategic impact of investments in ERM. *Journal of Accounting and Public Policy*, *34*(3), 219–243. doi:10.1016/j.jaccpubpol.2015.01.001

Beasley, M. S., Branson, B. C., & Hancock, B. V. (2015b). *2015 Report on the Current State of Enterprise Risk Oversight: Update on Trends and Opportunities.* Retrieved on 13/6/2018 from https://www.aicpa.org/interestareas/businessindustryandgovernment/resources/erm/downloadabledocuments/aicpa_erm_research_study_2015.pdf

Beasley, M. S., Pagach, D., & Warr, R. (2008). Information Conveyed in Hiring Announcements of Senior Executives Overseeing Enterprise-Wide Risk Management Processes. *Journal of Accounting, Auditing & Finance*, *23*(3), 311–332. doi:10.1177/0148558X0802300303

Carson, R. T., Mitchell, R. C., Hanemann, M., Kopp, R. J., Presser, S., & Ruud, P. A. (2003). Contingent Valuation and Lost Passive Use: Damages from the Exxon Valdez Oil Spill. *Environmental and Resource Economics*, *25*(3), 257–286. doi:10.1023/A:1024486702104

Casualty Actuarial Society Enterprise Risk Management Committee (CAS). (2003). *Overview of Enterprise Risk Management.* Retrieved on 4/6/2018 from https://www.casact.org/pubs/forum/03sforum/03sf099.pdf

Cescon, F., Costantini, A., & Rossi, G. (2013). *The influence of Business strategy and Ownership on Management accounting innovations and Risk management techniques: An empirical analysis in large manufacturing companies in Italy*. Retrieved on 20/05/2019 from https://www.uniud.it/it/ateneo-uniud/ateneo-uniud-organizzazione/dipartimenti/dies/ricerca/allegati_wp/wp_2013/wp02_2013.pdf

Committee of the Sponsoring Organizations (COSO). (2004). *Enterprise Risk Management, Integrated Framework (Executive Summary Framework)*. Retrived on 11/6/2018 from https://www.coso.org/Documents/COSO-ERM-Executive-Summary.pdf

Committee of the Sponsoring Organizations (COSO). (2017). *Enterprise Risk Management - Integrating with Strategy and Performance Executive Summary*. Retrieved on 11/6/2018 from https://www.coso.org/Documents/2017-COSO-ERM-Integrating-with-Strategy-and-Performance-Executive-Summary.pdf

Crockford, G. N. (1982). The bibliography and history of risk management: Some preliminary observations. *Geneva Papers on Risk & Insurance*, *7*(2), 169–179. doi:10.1057/gpp.1982.10

Cutler, D. M., & Summers, L. H. (1987). *The Costs of Conflict Resolution and Financial Distress: Evidence from the Texaco-Pennzoil Litigation*. NBER Working Paper No. 2418 (Also Reprint No. r1231). Retrieved on 5/6/2018 from http://www.nber.org/papers/w2418

Deloitte. (2013). *Exploring Strategic Risk*. Retrieved on 2/6/2018 from https://www2.deloitte.com/content/dam/Deloitte/global/Documents/Governance-Risk-Compliance/dttl-grc-exploring-strategic-risk.pdf

Desender, K. (2007). On the Determinants of Enterprise Risk Management Implementation. *Managing Worldwide Operations & Communications with Information Technology, 2007 IRMA International Conference*, 115-118.

Dickinson, G. (2001). Enterprise Risk Management: Its Origins and Conceptual Foundation. *The Geneva Papers on Risk and Insurance. Issues and Practice*, *26*(3), 360–366. doi:10.1111/1468-0440.00121

DiMaggio, P. J., & Powell, W. W. (1983). The iron cage revisited: Institutional isomorphism and collective rationality in organizational fields. *American Sociological Review*, *48*(2), 147–160. doi:10.2307/2095101

Erickson, M., Mayhew, B. W., & Felix, W. L. Jr. (2000). Why Do Audits Fail? Evidence from Lincoln Savings and Loan. *Journal of Accounting Research*, *38*(1), 165–194. doi:10.2307/2672927

Farrell, M., & Gallagher, R. (2014). The Valuation Implications of Enterprise Risk Management Maturity. *The Journal of Risk and Insurance*, *82*(3), 625–657. doi:10.1111/jori.12035

Florea, R., & Florea, R. (2016). Internal Audit and Risk Management. ISO 31000 and ERM Approaches. *Economy Transdisciplinarity Cognition*, *19*(1), 72–77.

Florio, C., & Leoni, G. (2017). Enterprise risk management and firm performance: The Italian case. *The British Accounting Review*, *49*(1), 56–74. doi:10.1016/j.bar.2016.08.003

Fraser, J. R. S., & Simkins, B. J. (2016). The Challenges of and solutions for implementing enterprise risk management. *Business Horizons*, *59*(6), 689–698. doi:10.1016/j.bushor.2016.06.007

Frigo, M. L., & Anderson, R. J. (2011). Strategic Risk Management: A Foundation for Improving Enterprise Risk Management and Governance. *Journal of Corporate Accounting & Finance*, *22*, 81–88. doi:10.1002/jcaf.20677

Gates, S. (2006). Incorporating strategic risk into enterprise risk management: A survey of current corporate practice. *Journal of Applied Corporate Finance*, *18*(4), 81–90. doi:10.1111/j.1745-6622.2006.00114.x

Gatzert, N., & Martin, M. (2013). *Determinants and Value of Enterprise Risk Management: Empirical Evidence from the Literature*. Working Paper. Department for Insurance Economics and Risk Management, Friedrich-Alexander-University (FAU) of Erlangen-Nürnberg. Retrieved on 5/6/2018 from http://citeseerx.ist.psu.edu/viewdoc/download?doi=10.1.1.888.6403&rep=rep1&type=pdf

Gordon, L. A., Loeb, M. P., & Tseng, C. (2009). Enterprise risk management and firm performance: A contingency perspective. *Journal of Accounting and Public Policy*, *28*(4), 301–327. doi:10.1016/j.jaccpubpol.2009.06.006

Grace, M. F., Leverty, J. T., Phillips, R. D., & Shimpi, P. (2015). The Value of Investing in Enterprise Risk Management. *The Journal of Risk and Insurance*, *82*(2), 289–316. doi:10.1111/jori.12022

Harrington, S. E., Niehaus, G., & Risko, K. J. (2002). Enterprise Risk Management: The Case Of United Grain Growers. *Journal of Applied Corporate Finance*, *14*(4), 71–81. doi:10.1111/j.1745-6622.2002.tb00450.x

Henderson, V. (2014). *Black–Scholes Model*. Wiley. doi:10.1002/9781118445112.stat04690

Henschel, T. (2010). Typology of risk management practices: An empirical investigation into German SMEs. *International Journal of Entrepreneurship and Small Business*, *9*(3), 264–294. doi:10.1504/IJESB.2010.031922

Hillson, D. (2003). *Effective Opportunity Management for Projects: Exploiting Positive Risk*. Monticello, NY: Marcel Dekker, Inc. doi:10.1201/9780203913246

Hoyt, R. E., & Liebenberg, A. P. (2008). *The Value of Enterprise Risk Management: Evidence from the U.S. Insurance Industry*. Society of Actuaries, ERM Monograph Paper. Retrieved on 4/6/2018 from http://citeseerx.ist.psu.edu/viewdoc/download?doi=10.1.1.514.6423&rep=rep1&type=pdf

Hoyt, R. E., & Liebenberg, A. P. (2011). The Value of Enterprise Risk Management. *The Journal of Risk and Insurance*, *78*(4), 795–822. doi:10.1111/j.1539-6975.2011.01413.x

Khan, M. J., Hussain, D., & Mehmood, W. (2016). Why do firms adopt enterprise risk management (ERM)? Empirical evidence from France. *Management Decision*, *54*(8), 1886–1907. doi:10.1108/MD-09-2015-0400

Kleffner, A. E., Lee, R. B., & McGannon, B. (2003). The Effect of Corporate Governance on the Use of Enterprise Risk Management: Evidence From Canada. *Risk Management & Insurance Review*, *6*(1), 1098–1616. doi:10.1111/1098-1616.00020

Lam, J. (2017). *Implementing Enterprise Risk Management – From Methods to Applications*. Hoboken, NJ: John Wiley & Sons, Inc. doi:10.1002/9781118922415

Lechner, P., & Gatzert, N. (2018). Determinants and value of enterprise risk management: Empirical evidence from Germany. *European Journal of Finance*, *24*(10), 867–887. doi:10.1080/1351847X.2017.1347100

Liebenberg, A.P. & Hoyt, R.E. (2003). The Determinants of Enterprise Risk Management: Evidence From the Appointment of Chief Risk Officers. *Risk Management and Insurance Review*, *6*(1), 37-52. doi:10.1111/1098-1616.00019

Lundqvist, S. A. (2014). An Exploratory Study of Enterprise Risk Management: Pillars of ERM. *Journal of Accounting, Auditing & Finance*, *29*(3), 393–429. doi:10.1177/0148558X14535780

Lundqvist, S. A. (2015). Why firms implement risk governance – Stepping beyond traditional risk management to enterprise risk management. *Journal of Accounting and Public Policy*, *34*(5), 441–466. doi:10.1016/j.jaccpubpol.2015.05.002

Maia, I. R. D., & Chaves, G. M. M. (2016). Integration of Risk Management into Strategic Planning: A New Comprehensive Approach. *2016 Enterprise Risk Management Symposium*.

Markowitz, H. (1952). Portfolio Selection. *The Journal of Finance*, *7*(1), 77–91.

McShane, M. K., Nair, A., & Rustambekov, E. (2011). Does Enterprise Risk Management Increase Firm Value? *Journal of Accounting, Auditing & Finance*, *26*(4), 641–658. doi:10.1177/0148558X11409160

Mehr, R. I., & Hedges, B. A. (1963). *Risk Management and the Business Enterprise*. Homewood, IL: Irwin.

Meulbroek, L. K. (2002). *Integrated Risk Management for the Firm: A Senior Manager's Guide*. Retrieved from https://ssrn.com/abstract=301331

Mikes, A., & Kaplan, R. S. (2013). *Towards a Contingency Theory of Enterprise Risk Management*. AAA 2014 Management Accounting Section (MAS) Meeting Paper. Retrieved from https://papers.ssrn.com/sol3/papers.cfm?abstract_id=2311293

Nocco, B. W., & Stulz, R. M. (2006). Enterprise Risk Management: Theory and Practice. *Journal of Applied Corporate Finance*, *18*(4), 8–20. doi:10.1111/j.1745-6622.2006.00106.x

Organization for Economic Cooperation and Development. (2017). *OECD Corporate Governance Factbook – 2017*. Retrieved from http://www.oecd.org/daf/ca/Corporate-Governance-Factbook.pdf

Peterson, C., Rice, S., Short, J., Esler, D., Bodkin, J., Ballachey, B., & Irons, D. (2003). Long-Term Ecosystem Response to the Exxon Valdez Oil Spill. *Science*, *302*(5653), 2082–2086. doi:10.1126cience.1084282 PMID:14684812

Razali, A. R., Yazid, A. S., & Tahir, I. M. (2011). The Determinants of Enterprise Risk Management (ERM) Practices in Malaysian Public Listed Companies. *Journal of Social and Development Sciences*, *1*(5), 202–207.

Risk Management Institute (RIMS). (2017). *ERM Benchmarks*. Retrieved on 28/5/2019 from http://www.rmmagazine.com/2017/12/01/erm-benchmarks/

Risk Management Institute (RIMS). (n.d.). Retrieved on https://www.rims.org/resources/ERM/Pages/WhatisERM.aspx

Rockness, H., & Rockness, J. (2005). Legislated Ethics: From Enron to Sarbanes-Oxley, the Impact on Corporate America. *Journal of Business Ethics*, *57*(1), 31–54. doi:10.100710551-004-3819-0

Simkins, B., & Ramirez, S. A. (2008). Enterprise-Wide Risk Management and Corporate Governance. *Loyola University of Chicago Law Journal. Loyola University of Chicago. School of Law*, *39*, 571–594.

Smallman, C. (1996). Risk and organizational behaviour: A research model. *Disaster Prevention and Management: An International Journal*, *5*(2), 12–26. doi:10.1108/09653569610112880

Sobel, P. J., & Reding, K. F. (2004). Aligning Corporate Governance with Enterprise Risk Management. *Management Accounting Quarterly*, *5*(2), 29-37.

Stulz, R. M. (1996). Rethinking Risk Management. *Journal of Applied Corporate Finance*, *9*(3), 8–24. doi:10.1111/j.1745-6622.1996.tb00295.x

The International Organization for Standardization (ISO). (n.d.). *ISO/Guide 73:2009(en)*. Retrieved on 9/6/2018 from https://www.iso.org/obp/ui/#iso:std:iso:guide:73:ed-1:v1:en

Viscelli, T. R., Hermanson, D. R., & Beasley, M. S. (2017). The Integration of ERM and Strategy: Implications for Corporate Governance. *Accounting Horizons*, *31*(2), 69–82. doi:10.2308/acch-51692

Chapter 14
Strategic Corporate Decision Making With Market and Liquidity Risk Management

Mazin A. M. Al Janabi
https://orcid.org/0000-0002-2249-932X
EGADE Business School, Tecnologico de Monterrey, Mexico

ABSTRACT

This chapter examines a practical methodology for the assessment and control of market and liquidity risk exposures for financial trading portfolios that consist of certain equity assets. The applied technique is based on the contemporary concept of liquidity-adjusted value at risk (LVaR) along with the application of optimization risk-engine algorithms. This chapter proposes a broad market and liquidity risk management model that can concurrently perform LVaR estimation under regular and stressed market scenarios. It takes into account the effects of illiquidity of traded equity assets. In order to demonstrate the appropriate application of LVaR and stress-testing techniques, real-world case analysis of trading risk management are presented for the Gulf Cooperation Council (GCC) stock markets. To this end, a number of optimization case studies are examined with the aim of developing a novel technique of trading risk measurement as well as the implementation of a risk optimization process for the computation of the maximum permitted LVaR limits.

INTRODUCTION AND LITERATURE REVIEW

To quantify the risks involved in their trading operations, major financial institutions are increasingly exploiting Value at Risk (VaR) models. Since financial institutions differ in their individual characteristics, a tailor-made internal risk models are more appropriate. Fortunately, and in accordance with the latest Basel capital accord, financial institutions are permitted to develop their own internal risk models for the purposes of providing for adequate risk measures. Furthermore, internal risk models can be used in the determination of economic capital that banks must hold to endorse their trading of securities.

DOI: 10.4018/978-1-7998-1033-9.ch014

The advantage of such an approach is that it takes into account the relationship between various asset types and can accurately assess the overall risk, including liquidity risk and firm-specific factors, for a whole combination of trading assets. As such, the notion of an internal risk model is the fact that the regulators allow financial institutions to develop their own risk models and use their own parameters instead of using models and parameters mandated by the regulatory bodies. The key benefits of internal risk models are convenience for the financial institutions, the ability of the financial entities to account for firm-specific factors, and lower regulatory costs.

Risk management has become of paramount importance in the financial industry and a major endeavor by academics, practitioners, and regulators, and a cornerstone of recent interest is a class of models called Value at Risk (VaR) techniques. The concepts of VaR and other advanced risk management techniques are not new and are based—with some modifications—on modern portfolio theory. Albeit VaR is one of many—both quantitative and qualitative—factors that should be integrated into a cohesive risk management approach, it is remarkably a vital one. In fact, VaR is not the maximum loss that will occur, but rather a loss level threshold that will be pierced some percentage of the time. The actual loss that occurs could be much higher than the VaR estimates. As such, VaR should be used in conjunction with other risk measures such as stress-testing, scenario analysis, and other asset/business specific risk measures. The most common VaR models estimate variance/covariance matrices of asset returns using historical time series, under the assumption that asset returns are normally distributed and that portfolio risk is a function of the risk of each asset and the correlation factors among the returns of all trading assets within the portfolio. The VaR is then calculated from the standard deviation of the portfolio, given the appropriate investment/liquidation horizon, and the specified confidence interval.

In the 1950s Markowitz (1959) described the theoretical framework for modern portfolio theory and the creation of efficient portfolios. Markowitz's mean-variance portfolio optimization methodology is a landmark in the development of modern portfolio theory. The solution to the Markowitz theoretical models revolves around the portfolio weights, or the percentage of asset allocated to be invested in each instrument. Sharpe (1963), developed the single-index model, which relates returns on each security to the returns on a common index—abroad market index of common stock returns such as S&P 500 is generally used for this purpose.

Despite many criticisms and limitations of the VaR method, it has proven to be a very useful measure of market risk, and is widely used in financial and non-financial markets. The *RiskMetrics™* techniques, developed and popularized by J. P. Morgan (Morgan Guaranty Trust Company, 1994), has provided a tremendous impetus to the growth in the use of VaR concept and other modern risk management techniques and procedures. Since then the VaR concept is well-known and scores of specific applications are adapted to credit risk management and mutual funds investments. The general recognition and use of large scale VaR models has initiated a considerable literature including statistical descriptions of VaR and assessments of different modeling techniques. For a comprehensive survey, and the different VaR analysis and techniques, one can refer to Jorion (2001).

In their paper Berkowitz and O'Brien (2001) question how accurate VaR models are at commercial banks. Due to the fact that trading accounts at large commercial banks have considerably grown and become increasingly diverse and complex, the authors presented statistics on the trading revenues from such activities and on the associated VaR forecasts internally estimated by banks. Several other authors have attempted to tackle the issues of extreme events and fat tails phenomena in the distribution of returns. Nonetheless, most of their approaches and techniques are good exercises for academic purposes they do lack evidence of real-world applications with actual market portfolios.

On another front, Garcia et al. (2007) tackle a specific issue within the VaR and that is the subadditivity property required for the VaR to be a coherent measure of risk. The authors argue that, in the context of decentralized portfolio management, central management possesses only a fraction of information that belongs to each specialist (trader). In such a context, a distribution appears always thicker to the central unit than to the specialist. Therefore, because of a lack of information, VaR may appear fallaciously nonsubadditive to the central management unit. Despite evidence to the contrary, the authors show that decentralized portfolio management with a VaR allocation to each specialist will work, and furthermore VaR remains subadditive in many situations of practical interest.

In his research papers, Al Janabi (2005 and 2007a) establishes a practical framework for the measurement, management and control of trading risk. The effects of illiquid assets, that are dominant characteristics of emerging markets, are also incorporated in his models. The established models and the general framework of risk calculations are mainly based on matrix-algebra techniques. A rigorous analytical risk management study of the Mexican Stock Market (BMV) is performed by Al Janabi (2007b). The parameters of a practical framework for the management of market risk are illustrated and a case study is carried out on 11 well-known Mexican stocks in addition to a number of sectors indices and main market indicators. Moreover, in his research paper, Al Janabi (2008), the robust quantitative measurements and procedures of market risk are applied to emerging markets' equity trading portfolios that are combined with foreign exchange trading portfolios. Market risk management models, which are implemented in his latest work, are applied to both, the Mexican foreign exchange and stock markets[1].

Set against this background, the objective of this review chapter is to provide practical and robust guidelines, procedures and measurement of market/liquidity risk for equity trading portfolios (frequently it can be called, trading, investment or price risk). As such, the aim is to create a pragmatic approach to assist in the establishment of sound risk management practices (for equity portfolios that contain both long and short trading positions) and within a prudential framework of rules and policies. To this end, the parameters required for the construction of appropriate and simplified VaR and stress-testing methods are reviewed from previous works and refined to the specific applications of these methods to equity trading portfolios of the six GCC stock markets. Moreover, a robust modeling algorithm for the incorporation of illiquid assets is defined and is appropriately integrated into VaR and stress-testing models.

The remainder of the chapter is organized as follows. The following section lays out all the mathematical/quantitative infrastructures of LVaR method, and its limitations, and a robust modeling algorithm that incorporates the effects of illiquid assets in daily market risk management. The results of empirical tests and optimization of the maximum LVaR limits are drawn in section 3. Section 4 concludes the chapter and provides certain recommendations.

CLOSED–FORM PARAMETRIC TECHNIQUE FOR THE ESTIMATION OF LIQUIDITY-ADJUSTED VALUE AT RISK (LVAR) USING AL JANABI MODEL

A simplified calculation process of the estimation of VaR risk factors (using a closed-form parametric method) for a single and multiple assets' positions is illustrated (Al Janabi, 2005 and 2007a) as follows:

From elementary statistics, it is well known that for a normal distribution, 68% of the observations will lie within 1σ (standard deviation) from the expected value, 95% within 2σ and 99% within 3σ from the expected value, thus the absolute value of VaR of a single asset in monetary terms is:

$$\mathrm{VaR}_i = |(\mu_i - \alpha * \sigma_i)\ (\textit{Mark-to-Market Value of Asset}_i * Fx_i)| \tag{1}$$

where α is the confidence level (or in other words, the standard normal variant at confidence level α) and σ_i is the standard deviation (volatility) of the security that constitutes the single position. The "*Mark-to-Market Value*" is the amount of market value investment in $Asset_i$.

Trading risk in the presence of multiple risk factors is determined by the combined effect of individual risks. A magnitude of the total risk is determined not only by the magnitudes of the individual risks but also by their correlations. Portfolio effects are crucial in risk management not only for large diversified portfolios but also for individual instruments that depends on several risk factors. For multiple assets or portfolio of assets, VaR is a function of each individual security's risk and the correlation factor $[\rho_{i,j}]$ between the returns on the individual securities, detailed as follows:

$$VaR_P = \sqrt{\sum_{i=1}^{n}\sum_{j=1}^{n} VaR_i\, VaR_j\, \rho} = \sqrt{\left[VaR\right]^T \left[\rho\right]\ \left[VaR\right]} \tag{2}$$

This formula is a general one for the calculation of VaR for any portfolio regardless of the number of securities. It should be noted that the second term of this formula is presented in terms of matrix-algebra—a useful form to avoid mathematical complexity, as more and more securities are added. This approach can simplify the programming process and permits easy incorporation of short positions in market risk management process.

Illiquid securities such as foreign exchange rates and equities are very common in emerging markets. Customarily these securities are traded infrequently (at very low volume). Their quoted prices should not be regarded as a representative of the traders' consensus vis-à-vis their real value but rather as the transaction price that arrived at by two counterparties under particular illiquid market conditions. This of course represents a real dilemma to anybody who seeks to measure the market risk of these securities with a methodology which is based on volatilities and correlation matrices. The main problem arises when the historical price series are not available for some securities or, when they are available, they are not fully reliable due to the lack of liquidity.

In fact, if returns are independent and they can have any elliptical multivariate distribution, then it is possible to convert the VaR horizon parameter from daily to any t–day horizon. The variance of a t–day return should be t times the variance of a 1–day return or $\sigma^2 = f(t)$. Thus, in terms of standard deviation (or volatility), $\sigma = f(\sqrt{t}\,)$ and the daily VaR number [*VaR (1-day)*] can be adjusted for any t horizon as:

$$LVaR\ (t - day) = VaR\ (1 - day)\sqrt{t} \tag{3}$$

The above formula was proposed and used by *J.P. Morgan* in their earlier *RiskMetrics™* techniques (Morgan Guaranty Trust Company, 1994). This methodology implicitly assumes that liquidation occurs in one block sale at the end of the holding period and that there is one holding period for all assets, regardless of their inherent trading liquidity structure. Unfortunately, the latter approach does not consider real-life-trading situations, where traders can liquidate (or re-balance) small portions of their trading portfolios on a daily basis. Moreover, this could generate unreliable risk assessments and can lead to considerable overestimates of VaR figures, especially for the purposes of economic capital allocation between trading and/or investment units.

The assumption of a given holding period for orderly liquidation inevitably implies that assets' liquidation occurs during the holding period. Accordingly, scaling the holding period to account for orderly liquidation can be justified if one allows the assets to be liquidated throughout the holding period. In order to perform the calculation of VaR under more realistic illiquid market conditions, we can define the following[2]:

$$LVaR_{adj} = VaR\sqrt{\frac{(2t+1)(t+1)}{6t}} \tag{4}$$

where t is the number of liquidation days (*t–day* to liquidate the entire asset fully), *VaR* is Value at Risk under liquid market conditions and $LVaR_{adj}$ is Value at Risk under illiquid market settings. A linear liquidation procedure of assets is assumed in the above formula, i.e. selling equal parts of each asset every day until the last trading day (t), where the entire asset is sold. The above model is more appropriate for daily trading circumstances where traders can unwind part of their positions on a daily basis.

QUANTIFYING AND MONITORING OF MARKET AND LIQUIDITY RISK EXPOSURE—CASE STUDY OF EMERGING GCC STOCK MARKETS

In the research study, databases of daily price returns of the six GCC stock markets' main indicators (indices) are gathered, filtered and adequately adapted for the creation of relevant inputs for the calculation of all risk factors. The total numbers of indices that are considered in this work are nine indices; seven local indices for the six GCC stock markets (including two indices for the UAE markets) and two benchmark indices, detailed as follows:

1. DFM General Index (Dubai Financial Market General Index, United Arab Emirates)
2. ADSM Index (Abu Dhabi Stock Market Index, United Arab Emirates)
3. BA All Share Index (All Share Stock Market Index, Bahrain)
4. KSE General Index (Stock Exchange General Index, Kuwait)
5. MSM30 Index (Muscat Stock Market Index, Oman)
6. DSM20 Index (Doha Stock Market General Index, Qatar)
7. SE All Share Index (All Share Stock Market Index, Saudi Arabia)
8. Shuaa GCC Index (GCC Stock Markets Benchmark Index, Shuaa Capital)
9. Shuaa Arab Index (Arab Stock Markets Benchmark Index, Shuaa Capital)

For this particular study we have chosen a confidence interval of 95% (or 97.5% with "one-tailed" loss side) and several liquidation time horizons to compute VaR. Historical database of daily closing index levels, for the period 17/10/2004-22/05/2009, are used for the construction of market and liquidity risk management parameters and permitted risk limits (or risk-budgeting constraints). The dataset falls within the most severe part of the latest sub-prime financial crisis. The analysis of data and discussions of relevant findings and results of this research are organized and explained as follows:

Statistical Analysis of Volatility and Testing for Non-Normality Patterns

To investigate the statistical properties of the data, we have computed the log returns of each series. Table (1) illustrates the daily volatility of each of the sample indices under regular market and stressed market conditions. Stressed market volatilities are calculated by implementing an empirical distribution of past returns for all stock market indices' time series and, hence, the maximum negative returns (losses), which are witnessed in the historical time series, are selected for this purpose. This approach can aid in overcoming some of the limitations of normality assumption and can provide a better analysis of VaR and especially under severe and illiquid market settings.

From Table (1) we can observe that the index with the highest volatility is the SE All Share Index (under regular market condition) whereas the DFM General Index has demonstrated the highest volatility under stressed market situation.s Annualized volatilities are depicted in Table (1), and this is performed by adjusting (multiplication) the daily volatilities with the square root of 260—assuming there are 260 trading days in the calendar year.

An interesting outcome of the study of sensitivity factors (beta factors for systematic risk) is the manner in which the results are varied across the sample indices as indicated in Table (1). SE All Share Index appears to have the highest systematic risk factor (0.98) vis-à-vis the Shuaa Arab Index (that is the highest systematic risk) and the MSM30 Index seems to have the lowest systematic factor (0.1). Moreover, and in accordance with general beliefs, Shuaa GCC Index (with a sensitivity factor of 1.05) is the best indicator of the entire sample indices that appears to move very closely with respect to the benchmark Shuaa Arab Index (with a beta factor of 1.0).

In another study, the measurements of skewness and kurtosis are achieved on the sample indices. The results are depicted in Table (2). It is seen, in general, that all indices have shown asymmetric behavior (both positive and negative values). Moreover, kurtosis studies have shown similar patterns of

Table 1.Risk analysis dataset: Daily and annual volatility and systematic risk factor (beta)

Stock Market Indices	Daily Volatility (Regular Market)	Daily Volatility (Stressed Market)	Annual Volatility (Regular Market)	Annual Volatility (Stressed Market)	Systematic Risk Factor
DFM General Index	1.93%	12.16%	31.05%	196.03%	0.58
ADSM Index	1.42%	7.08%	22.83%	114.09%	0.40
BA All Share Index	0.59%	3.77%	9.50%	60.76%	0.06
KSE General Index	0.76%	3.74%	12.28%	60.25%	0.14
MSM30 Index	0.84%	8.70%	13.58%	140.27%	0.10
DSM20 Index	1.53%	8.07%	24.65%	130.19%	0.31
SE All Share Index	2.08%	11.03%	33.50%	177.90%	0.98
Shuaa GCC Index	1.45%	8.10%	23.36%	130.56%	1.05
Shuaa Arab Index	1.28%	7.57%	20.62%	122.11%	1.00

Notes: This table illustrates the daily and annual volatility of each stock market index under regular and stressed market conditions and the systematic risk factor (beta sensitivity coefficient) for each market.

Sources: Designed by the author using in-house built software.

Table 2. Risk analysis dataset: Descriptive statistics of daily returns, skewness, kurtosis, and Jarque-Bera test of non-normality

Stock Market Indices	Maximum	Minimum	Median	Arithmetic Mean	Skewness	Kurtosis	Jarque-Bera (JB) Test
DFM General Index	9.9%	-12.2%	0.01%	0.12%	0.01	7.86	955**
ADSM Index	6.6%	-7.1%	0.00%	0.07%	0.12	7.26	734**
BA All Share Index	3.6%	-3.8%	0.00%	0.05%	0.43	10.24	2142**
KSE General Index	5.0%	-3.7%	0.00%	0.09%	-0.18	8.38	1173**
MSM30 Index	5.2%	-8.7%	0.00%	0.12%	-0.57	18.40	9617**
DSM20 Index	6.2%	-8.1%	0.00%	0.06%	-0.11	5.59	273**
SE All Share Index	9.4%	-11.0%	0.07%	0.03%	-0.97	8.47	1361**
Shuaa GCC Index	11.1%	-8.1%	0.00%	0.06%	-0.66	14.00	4949**
Shuaa Arab Index	9.4%	-7.6%	0.00%	0.07%	-0.61	13.79	4758**

Notes: This table desorrstrates descriptive statistics of daily returns and the JB test for non-normality. The JB test cleary indicates that all stock markets exhibit non-normal behavior

Asterisk ** denotes statistical significance at the 0.01 levels.

Sources: Designed by the author using in-house built software.

abnormality (i.e. peaked/flat distributions). Nonetheless, the Jarque-Bera (JB) test shows an obvious general deviation from normality and, thus, rejects the hypothesis that GCC stock markets' time series returns are normally distributed.

Optimization Case studies for the Setting of LVaR Maximum Limits

Optimum risk limits (or risk budgeting) are an important element for any corporate trading/asset management risk management unit and it should be defined clearly and used wisely to ensure control on the trading/investment unit's exposure to risk. All limit-setting and control, monitoring and reporting should be performed by the risk management unit, independently from the front office's traders.

How should we set risk limits to safeguard against maximum loss amounts? These are some of the central questions risk managers must envisage. In this chapter a simplified—however a practical approach—is presented for the setting of optimum LVaR limits. To this end, a variety of optimization case studies with different LVaR calculations have been examined in order to setup procedures for the establishment of optimum LVaR limits and adequate policies for handling situations in which trading/investment units are above the authorized LVaR limits. These LVaR limits procedure and methodology must be analyzed and approved by the board of directors of the financial entity. All trading/investment units need to have such limits of LVaR as practical guidelines and also as a strict policy for their risk takings. Any excess of LVaR beyond the ratified limits must be reported to top management by the risk management unit. Moreover, traders/asset managers need to give full and justified explanations of why their LVaRs are beyond the approved limits.

To this end, Tables (3)-(4) represent four optimization case studies for the setting of realistic and optimum LVaR trading limits. In all four optimization case studies, the effects of various asset allocations (with or without short-selling) are investigated for the purpose of setting of adequate LVaR limits. In all case studies, the optimization is based on the definition of LVaR as the maximum possible loss over a specified time horizon within a given confidence level. The optimization technique solves the problem by finding the market positions that maximize the loss, subject to the fact that all constraints are satisfied within their boundary values. Further, in all cases a liquidation horizon of 10 trading days is assumed. For the sake of simplification of the optimization process and thereafter its analysis, a volume trading limit of AED 100,000,000 is assumed as a constraint—that is the financial entity (or trading unit) must keep a maximum overall market value of stocks of no more than AED100,000,000 (between long and short positions).

While in Optimization Case Study 1 distinct asset allocation percentages are assumed, in Optimization Case Study 2 all equity trading position is concentrated in one market index that has, under severe market conditions, the highest daily return volatility—that is, the Dubai Financial Market (DFM) General Index. Finally, in Optimization Case Study 3 and Optimization Case Study 4 the effect of short-selling of the sample stocks (or indices) is also contemplated by randomly short-selling some of the sample stocks.

The principal effect of diversification on LVaR limits setting is seems to be through Case Study 1; that is with unequal asset allocation percentages. The highest LVaR numbers that are calculated so far is for Optimization Case Study 4, when the trading budget is allocated between long and short equity trading positions. In fact, and in accordance with our previous studies on other financial markets, such as Mexico and Morocco (Al Janabi, 2007a and 2007b), generally speaking we have found that short-selling decreases LVaR figures and, hence, LVaR trading limits. In the case of the GCC stock markets, the above phenomena (of high LVaR figures) can be explained by the nature of the diminutive correlation factors that we have witnessed in the entire GCC stock markets. These tiny correlation factors have led to grand diversification benefit for long equity trading positions and visa-versa for short positions.

Table 3. LVaR maximum daily tracking limits in AED with different correlation factors (ρ) and under regular market settings

Maximum LVaR Limit-Setting	ρ = Empirical	ρ = +1	ρ = 0
Optimization Case study 1	1,763,111	3,103,361	1,424,273
Optimization Case study 2	4,545,602	4,545,602	4,545,602
Optimization Case study 3	6,513,506	2,749,183	6,700,999
Optimization Case study 4	8,180,278	9,230,010	7,129,998

Notes: This table illustrates the optimization results of the maximum daily LVaR trading limits for four optimization case studies with different correlation factors and under regular market settings. As a result, optimization case study 4 denotes the highest LVaR limits for all four cases.
Sources: Designed by the author using in-house built software.

Table 4. LVaR maximum daily tracking limits in AED with different correlation factors (ρ) and under stressed market settings

Maximum LVaR Limit-Setting	ρ = Empirical	ρ = +1	ρ = 0
Optimization Case study 1	8,743,201	14,741,854	7,189,807
Optimization Case study 2	26,051,584	26,051,584	26,051,584
Optimization Case study 3	33,564,189	16,170,835	34,580,452
Optimization Case study 4	41,252,076	48,825,296	35,998,602

Notes: This table illustrates the optimization results of the maximum daily LVaR trading limits for four optimization case studies with different correlation factors and under stressed market settings. As a result, optimization case study 4 denotes the highest LVaR limits for all four cases.
Sources: Designed by the author using in-house built software.

As a conclusion of this study, the board of directors of the financial trading/investment entity can set the maximum daily LVaR limits for the equity trading portfolio as follows:

- Maximum permitted daily LVaR limit under regular market conditions = AED 8,180,278 with empirical correlations.
- Maximum permitted daily LVaR limit under stressed market conditions = AED 41,252,076 with empirical correlations.
- Maximum permitted daily LVaR limit under regular market conditions = AED 9,230,010 with correlations of ones.
- Maximum permitted daily LVaR limit under stressed market conditions = AED 48,825,296 with correlations of ones.
- Maximum permitted daily LVaR limit under regular market conditions = AED 7,129,998 with correlations of zeros.
- Maximum permitted daily LVaR limit under stressed market conditions = AED 35,998,602 with correlations of zeros.
- Maximum permitted total daily trading volume limit = AED 100,000,000 (between long and short-selling trading positions).

It should be noted here that the above optimum approved VaR trading limits are in their converted (or equivalent) UAE dirham (AED) values at the current or prevailing foreign exchange rates of other GCC countries versus the UAE dirham.

CONCLUDING REMARKS

Under special conditions when changes in market risk factors are normally distributed, the LVaR can be calculated using a closed-form parametric approach. For maximum LVaR limits-setting and daily trading risk measurement purposes these assumptions are made for the sake of simplifying the calculation process. However, for an emerging market environment, one needs to supplement the closed-form parametric approach with other analysis such as stress-testing and simulation analysis. This is done with the objective of estimating the impact of assumptions that are made under LVaR approach. Likewise, the effects of illiquidity of trading assets, in emerging markets, must be dealt with more wisely and should be brought into existence within the LVaR framework.

The analyses that are performed in this article include volatility, non-normality tests along with the calculations of optimum LVaR trading limits. Our results suggest that in almost all tests, there are clear asymmetric behaviors in the distribution of returns of the sample indices and the two benchmark indices. The appealing outcome of this study suggests the inevitability of combining LVaR calculations with other methods such as stress-testing and scenario analysis to grasp a thorough picture of other remaining risks (such as, fat-tails in the probability distribution) that cannot be revealed with the plain assumption of normality.

In conclusion, LVaR limits' setting is an important concern as part of daily risk management process for corporate treasury strategic decision-making. To this end, a meaningful procedure for an optimization engine with a robust algorithm is developed to illustrate a practical approach for the setting of maximum VaR limits for a corporate treasury equity-trading-unit. In all case studies, the volume limit in

UAE dirham (AED100,000,000) is assumed constant and is used as a constraint (on the matrix-algebra's complex mathematical function) for the establishment of adequate and practical LVaR limits. For this particular study, VaR limits are established for normal and severe market conditions and under the notion of different correlation factors. To this end, several case studies and simulations are performed with different asset allocations (with or without short-selling) and with the objectives of setting an optimum limits structure for an equity market risk management unit.

CONFLICT OF INTEREST

The author declares no conflict of interest in this chapter.

REFERENCES

Al Janabi, M. A. M. (2005). Trading Risk Management: Practical Applications to Emerging-Markets. In S. Motamen-Samadian (Ed.), *Risk Management in Emerging Markets* (pp. 91–136). Palgrave/MacMillan. doi:10.1057/9780230596368_7

Al Janabi, M. A. M. (2007a). Equity Trading Risk Management: The Case of Casablanca Stock Exchange. *International Journal of Risk Assessment and Management*, *7*(4), 535–568. doi:10.1504/IJRAM.2007.012743

Al Janabi, M. A. M. (2007b). Risk Analysis, Reporting and Control of Equity Exposure: Viable Applications to the Mexican Financial Market. *Journal of Derivatives & Hedge Funds*, *13*(1), 33–58. doi:10.1057/palgrave.jdhf.1850059

Al Janabi, M. A. M. (2008). A Practical Approach to Market Risk Analysis and Control: Empirical Test of the Mexican Foreign Exchange and Stock Markets. *International Journal of Risk Assessment and Management*, *9*(1 & 2), 70–103. doi:10.1504/IJRAM.2008.019314

Al Janabi, M. A. M. (2012). Optimal commodity asset allocation with a coherent market risk modeling. *Review of Financial Economics*, *21*(3), 131–140. doi:10.1016/j.rfe.2012.06.007

Al Janabi, M. A. M. (2013). Optimal and coherent economic-capital structures: Evidence from long and short-sales trading positions under illiquid market perspectives. *Annals of Operations Research*, *205*(1), 109–139. doi:10.100710479-012-1096-3

Al Janabi, M. A. M. (2014). Optimal and investable portfolios: An empirical analysis with scenario optimization algorithms under crisis market prospects. *Economic Modelling*, *40*, 369–381. doi:10.1016/j.econmod.2013.11.021

Al Janabi, M. A. M., Arreola-Hernández, J. A., Berger, T., & Nguyen, D. K. (2017). Multivariate dependence and portfolio optimization algorithms under illiquid market scenarios. *European Journal of Operational Research*, *259*(3), 1121–1131. doi:10.1016/j.ejor.2016.11.019

Amihud, Y., Mendelson, H., & Pedersen, L. H. (2005). Liquidity and Asset Prices. *Foundations and Trends in Finance*, *1*(4), 269–364. doi:10.1561/0500000003

Angelidis, T., & Benos, A. (2006). Liquidity adjusted value-at-risk based on the components of the bid-ask spread. *Applied Financial Economics*, *16*(11), 835–851. doi:10.1080/09603100500426440

Arreola-Hernández, J., Al Janabi, M. A. M., Hammoudeh, S., & Nguyen, D. K. (2015). Time lag dependence, cross-correlation and risk analysis of U.S. energy and non-energy stock portfolios. *Journal of Asset Management*, *16*(7), 467–483. doi:10.1057/jam.2015.33

Arreola-Hernandez, J., Hammoudeh, S., Khuong, N. D., Al Janabi, M. A. M., & Reboredo, J. C. (2016). Global financial crisis and dependence risk analysis of sector portfolios: A vine copula approach. *Applied Economics*, *49*(25), 2409–2427. doi:10.1080/00036846.2016.1240346

Bangia, A., Diebold, F.X., Schuermann, T., & Stroughair, J.D. (2002). *Modeling liquidity risk with implications for traditional market risk measurement and management*. Academic Press.

Berkowitz, J. (2000). *Incorporating Liquidity Risk into VAR Models*. Working Paper. Graduate School of Management, University of California, Irvine.

Berkowitz, J., & O'Brien, J. (2001). *How Accurate are Value-at-Risk Models at Commercial Banks?* Working Paper. US Federal Reserve Board's Finance & Economic.

Cochrane, J. H. (2005). *Asset Pricing*. Princeton, NJ: Princeton University Press.

Garcia, R., Renault, E., & Tsafack, G. (2007). Proper Conditioning for Coherent VaR in Portfolio Management. *Management Science*, *53*(3), 483–494. doi:10.1287/mnsc.1060.0632

Hisata, Y., & Yamai, Y. (2000). *Research toward the practical application of liquidity risk evaluation methods*. Discussion Paper. Institute for Monetary and Economic Studies, Bank of Japan.

Jorion, P. (2001). *Value-at-Risk: The New benchmark for Controlling Market Risk*. Chicago: McGraw-Hill.

Le Saout, E. (2002). *Incorporating liquidity risk in VaR models*. Working Paper. Paris 1 University.

Madhavan, A., Richardson, M., & Roomans, M. (1997). Why do security prices change? A transaction-level analysis of NYSE stocks. *Review of Financial Studies*, *10*(4), 1035–1064. doi:10.1093/rfs/10.4.1035

Madoroba, S. B. W., & Kruger, J. W. (2014). Liquidity effects on value-at-risk limits: Construction of a new VaR model. *Journal of Risk Model Validation*, *8*(4), 19–46. doi:10.21314/JRMV.2014.127

Markowitz, H. (1959). *Portfolio Selection: Efficient Diversification of Investments*. New York: John Wiley.

Meucci, A. (2009). Managing Diversification. *Risk (Concord, NH)*, *22*(5), 74–79.

Morgan Guaranty Trust Company. (1994). *RiskMetrics-Technical Document*. New York: Morgan Guaranty Trust Company, Global Research.

Roch, A., & Soner, H. M. (2013). Resilient price impact of trading and the cost of illiquidity. *International Journal of Theoretical and Applied Finance*, *16*(6), 1–27. doi:10.1142/S0219024913500374

Ruozi, R., & Ferrari, P. (2013). *Liquidity Risk Management in Banks: Economic and Regulatory Issues*. Springer Briefs in Finance; doi:10.1007/978-3-642-29581-2

Sharpe, W. (1963). A simplified Model for Portfolio Analysis. *Management Science*, *9*(2), 277–293. doi:10.1287/mnsc.9.2.277

Takahashi, D., & Alexander, S. (2002). Illiquid Alternative Asset Fund Modeling. *Journal of Portfolio Management*, *28*(2), 90–100. doi:10.3905/jpm.2002.319836

ENDNOTES

1 For other relevant literature on liquidity, asset pricing and portfolio choice and diversification one can refer as well to Ruozi and Ferrari (2013); Roch and Soner (2013); Angelidis and Benos (2006); Bangia, et al. (2002); Berkowitz (2000); Madhavan et al. (1997); Hisata and Yamai (2000); Le Saout (2002); Amihud et al. (2005); Takahashi and Alexander (2002); Arreola-Hernández, et al. (2017); Arreola-Hernández, et al. (2015); Cochrane (2005); and Meucci (2009), among others.

2 The LVaR model applied here is based on that proposed by Al Janabi (2013) and Al Janabi et al. (2017). For further discussion on LVaR literature and models, see Madoroba and Kruger (2014). In their paper, Madoroba and Kruger (2014) review and compare ten liquidity risk VaR models, including Al Janabi model. For further details on the mathematical derivation and rational usefulness of Al Janabi model, refer to Al Janabi (2013) and Al Janabi et al. (2017) research papers.

Chapter 15
The Value of the Company and Sustainable Development

Iwona Dorota Bąk
West Pomeranian University of Technology, Poland

Beata Szczecińska
West Pomeranian University of Technology, Poland

ABSTRACT

The aim of the study is to attempt to systematize the concept of economic value that takes into account elements of sustainable development. At the same time, it is the voice in the ongoing discussion on the purpose and methods of valuation of the company's value. The measure of strength of each enterprise is its value expressed in monetary units. Due to differences in the results of the valuation of enterprises made by groups of experts representing such disciplines as finance, taxes, or marketing, there was a need to identify sources and to analyze more precisely the resulting discrepancies. The values of the enterprise should include both measurable and hard to measure values, which largely differentiate economic units from each other. The need for a wider perspective on the data published by enterprises appeared along with new business models, changes in consumer trends, environmental regulations, or the impact of social media.

INTRODUCTION

The subject matter discussed in the study on determining the category of values in economics is an important subject for at least three reasons. The first of them results from the fact that in the economy, the fundamental meaning is attached to the category of values. Without this category, the economy would not be able to explain the economic process. The second reason is the changes in time when determining this category. It cannot be ruled out that these changes will also occur in the future. The third reason is due to the diversity of this category in terms of defining and determining it.

DOI: 10.4018/978-1-7998-1033-9.ch015

Value is an ambiguous concept and its definition depends on the perspective from which it is considered. It is a very important issue in all fields related to economic sciences, because proper determination of the economic value for an economic entity is necessary to stay on the market, achieve the assumed financial results or adopt the best market strategy (Lewicka, 2014, p. 64). Due to the complexity of the issue and a heterogeneous practical approach thereto, there are major difficulties in its valuation.

The value expressed in monetary units is a measure of the strength of each enterprise, because it can significantly increase its impact on the market environment. The company's drive to maximize profits or to increase the market share often occurs with the violation of social and environmental values. Achieving financial goals must allow for social and ecological aspects as the main areas of sustainable development. The business activity of enterprises disregarding the indicated areas in the long term, is doomed to failure. For this reason, there is a need to design economic processes that include the idea of sustainable development.

The events of recent years, ecological threats in the world and the global economic and financial crisis create a new picture of the functioning of currently operating enterprises. The strength of external impact and the multifaceted approach to running business emphasize the ethical, moral and economic nature of the development and growth of competing enterprises (Jabłoński, 2015). Enterprises based on corporate social responsibility supported by the international community implement the assumptions of building a competitive position taking into account the wishes of all stakeholders and paying attention to the importance of ecological issues. The starting point for the implementation of such a perspective on building a competitive position is the concept of sustainable development.

Sustainable development is currently one of the most frequently discussed problems, important for further development of countries around the world. This is an important area for both scientific considerations and inquiries as well as decisions regarding future strategic directions of development of national economies. In the relevant literature (e.g. Sexton, Barrett, Lu, 2008), it is pointed out that the current stage of the evolution of the idea of sustainable development is primarily its concretisation, the aim of which is to develop the theoretical basis of a new paradigm of development and its integration with other areas of research, including such directions as: sustainable transport, sustainable agriculture (Altieri, 2018), sustainable logistics (Kiba-Janiak, 2015), sustainable finances (Fullwiler, 2015), as well as the sustainable value of the company (Laszlo, 2003).

The assessment of the extent to which the company's activities are sustainable is complex, both due to the complexity of the relationship and the difficulty of their direct measurement. The process of creating a sustainable development strategy to be truly sustainable must take into account all types of stakeholders. That is why it is so important to get an initial understanding of the environment and to identify real stakeholders as well as to define oneself with regard to the key ones from the point of view of the company (Brzozowski, 2010). The enterprises, which adopt a socio-economic policy considering the stakeholders, the local environment and the natural environment should adhere to the principles of sustainable development. The functioning of enterprises compliant with these principles may contribute to the increase of their attractiveness, the strengthening of the competitive position and, consequently, to the improvement of their value.

The aim of the study is to attempt to systematize the concept of economic value that takes into account elements of sustainable development. At the same time, it is the voice in the ongoing discussion on the purpose and methods of valuation of the company's value The work emphasizes the importance of sustainable development in relation to the functioning of enterprises. The stages in the enterprise on the road to sustainable development as well as the benefits and costs resulting therefrom are indicated. Applying the principles of sustainable development in the functioning of enterprises may contribute to the increase of their value, as well as strengthening of the competitive position.

THE COMPANY VALUE

In a market economy, an enterprise is treated as a commodity and subject to the laws and mechanisms regulating the market. Therefore, first of all, one should speak about its useful and exchangeable (commercial) value. The exchange value establishes in the simplest terms the amount of cash that buyers are able to spend on this enterprise. Of course, this value cannot occur without the utility value of an enterprise, just like an enterprise's assets - understood as a certain ability to multiply income - cannot occur in isolation from a real property, i.e. creating its material substance. The relevant literature distinguishes a number of other terms describing the goodwill, e.g. in German literature there is an objective, subjective, arbitrary and decision-making value (e.g. Helbling, 1991). These values remain in relation to each other in specific relationships.

An arbitrary value is a value which is determined only on the basis of the enterprise data characterizing its economic and financial condition. It remains outside the influence of stakeholders and is determined by specially appointed experts. A certain opposite of this value is the decision value, which is determined by the seller or buyer, i.e. the interested party. Thus, it includes the interests of the evaluating party. This value is characterized by the fact that it is determined in a very wide range on the basis of subjective premises. Hence, the goodwill is described as subjective. It is understood as the value established in consideration of a specific objective function. The counterbalance of this value is the objective value, i.e. the value built on the basis of market conditions, without the influence of stakeholders or with their minimal participation. The goodwill is also interpreted as (see Ignaciuk, 1990):

1. The book value resulting from entries in trading books (the balance sheet),
2. The liquidation value as the sum of prices obtained from the sale of individual assets (or the whole) of the enterprise,
3. The replacement value, i.e. the sum of financial outlays necessary to reconstruct individual elements of the company's assets at a given moment,
4. The collateral value, and therefore the value guaranteeing the loan granted,
5. The economic value of the company, which is a reflection of its ability to multiply income (profits),
6. The goodwill as a functioning economic organism, hence resulting from the degree of its organization (the market position, organizational structure, staff qualifications, etc.); it reflects the synergy effect of tangible and intangible properties and the characteristics of the enterprise, regardless of its financial resources,
7. The market value, or the value formed in the process of transactions made on the market.

Similar definitions of types of goodwill and studies of the impact of various factors on this category can be found, for example, in the works of such authors, as: Leland, Toft (1991), Matschke, M. J., Brösel, G., Matschke, X. (2010), Vintilă, Gherghina (2014), Rashid, Islam, Nuryanah (2014), Antwi, Mills, Zhao (2012).

Matschke, and others (2010) emphasize that the whole enterprise is a unique conglomerate of tangible and intangible assets (the factors of production), and its value results from the best possible and effective combination of these production factors. This means that the entirety is more valuable than the sum of its parts, which results in the increase in value (a positive synergy effect).

Research on the relationship between various factors and the goodwill has been the subject of a serious debate, both theoretical and empirical one. In the entire literature of the subject, the research have focused on indicating which factors have the greatest (the most significant) impact on the value of the company. For example, the attempts have been made to prove that the company's goodwill depends on:

- The degree of financial market development in individual countries and the degree of ownership concentration (e.g. Vintilă, Gherghina, 2014);
- The level of indebtedness of enterprises (e.g. Rashid, Islam, Nuryanah, 2014);
- The adopted structure of capitals and the use of the leverage phenomenon (e.g. Myers, 1993; Antwi, Mills, Zhao, 2012; Ogbulu, Emeni, 2012; Ushijima, 2015).

Enterprise Value (EV, FV - Firm Value, CV- Corporate Value) is the ability to create free cash flows and to generate surpluses in relation to the invested capital, which may result in the increase in its price on the organized market (e.g. on the stock exchange). Thus, the concept of company value refers to the future. The most important features of the company's value are (Tomczyk, 2012, p. 61):

- The strategic dimension that relates to maximization of enterprise value as the main purpose of its activities, which may lead to maximization of profits and other benefits for shareholders and other stakeholders of the business;
- The long-term prospect, connected with building value for a long period of time, in order to ensure the confidence of the markets in which the company competes (mainly the market of investors, employees, suppliers and clients);
- Future value expressed in money, which is a measure of the effectiveness of actions aimed at maximization the goodwill, an investor, an employee or a customer will be able to connect with the company when it will expect real benefits for itself in the future.

Creating value in an enterprise is a process that consists of three basic elements (Nogalski, Bors, 2000):

- A skilful combination of organization's mission, strategic goals, as well as strategy and tactics,
- The involvement of all levels of enterprise management in the micro- and macro-organization activities,
- The effective combination of qualitative and material (quantitative) qualities determining value, i.e.: business strategy and corporate finance.

The measure of strength of each enterprise is its value expressed in monetary units. Due to differences in the results of the valuation of enterprises made by groups of experts representing such disciplines as finance, taxes or marketing, there was a need to identify sources and to analyse more precisely the resulting discrepancies. The values of the enterprise should include both measurable and hard to measure values, which largely differentiate economic units from each other.

Global economic crisis has mercilessly revealed shortcomings in the methods used to determine the value of enterprises. These methods are mainly based on the concepts of capital market theory, which is based on the premise of a perfect market and perfect competition in the idealized world of models. In many cases, legitimate business decisions, for example regarding the purchase or sale of an enterprise, cannot be based on these models. Such decisions require models that explicitly allow for the existence of imperfect markets, as well as precise goals, plans and expectations of the entity for whom the value of the enterprise is determined. The literature on the valuation of enterprises is often limited to the calculation of different values and, consequently, focuses on the question which one of them may be the "proper one". The concepts of determining the value of enterprises have changed over the years from various subjective models to an attempt to determine the objective value. Subjective models assume that the company has no single value, and its specific and "proper" one depends on the recipient - there is no "per se" value, only the value "for someone" (Matschke, et al., 2010). The goals of objective valuation of enterprises are not described in a uniform or unambiguous manner, the representatives of this concept agree on the idea of determining the value of the enterprise regardless of a specific person related to or person interested in the valuation based on factors that can be implemented by everybody. A very important aspect of the objective valuation of enterprises is the idea of overcoming the conflict of interest between persons interested in the valuation through.

The variety of presented concepts indicates the multiplicity of elements affecting the value of the enterprise. In addition, it should be remembered that any type of value of a particular company may be subject to changes in place and time.

THE SUSTAINABLE VALUE OF THE ENTERPRISE

Sustainable development is currently one of the most frequently discussed problems, important for the further development of countries around the world. The concept of sustainable development which was first formulated explicitly during the Third UNEP Program in 1975 as

...such a course of inevitable and desirable economic development that would not materially and irreversibly affect the human environment and would not lead to the degradation of the biosphere and would not undermine the laws of nature, economics and culture (UN, 1975),

has since the beginning enjoyed considerable interest among researchers from various fields of science. The inclusion of economic issues in this definition has become the basis for formulating a broader concept of sustainable development. In the Brundtland Briefing Report of the World Commission on Environment and Development UN in 1987, sustainable development was defined as

sustainable development to meet current needs without the risk that future generations will not be able to meet their needs (WCED, 1987; Szopik-Depczyńska et al., 2018).

At the present stage of the implementation of the objectives stipulated by different strategies of sustainable development, including in particular in the latest Global Strategy for Sustainability 2030 (Agenda 2030, 2015), we have to deal with a significant differentiation of the obtained results in various countries of the world. Sustainable development is particularly important for ensuring proper development and environmental security in both highly developed regions and those that do not develop as dynamically. It is important both at the level of regions, institutions and enterprises. Factors at the regional level can contribute to achieving sustainable development and ensure a dynamic development of the whole society (Stefanescu, On, 2012). One of the most important elements of sustainable development are enterprises and the innovations they implement. Their impact on sustainable development - both at the regional and global level - is the subject of scientific research over the past 10-15 years.

In order to achieve the goals of Agenda 2030, it is necessary to establish strategic relations between enterprises and direct and active management thereof. A properly sustainable value creation is the key source of competitive advantage for companies (Buxel, Esenduran, Griffin, 2015; Vandaele, Decouttere, 2013). In the subject literature, a large number of issues are raised in order to make a qualitative or quantitative assessment of the degree of sustainable development in business (e.g. Global Reporting Initiative, 2006; Dow Jones Sustainability Indices, etc.). Problems related thereto were recognized as the main criteria of business value, both for clients and entrepreneurs (Jaramillo, Arimany-Serrat, Vidal, Ferràs-Hernandez, 2018). Often, however, they do not show any particular interest in the issues of sustainable development in the business sector (Berns et al., 2009). Therefore, the result offered by these instruments does not fully meet the needs or expectations that decision-makers are demanding when making decisions (Biju, Shalij, Prabhushankar, 2015).

The ongoing processes of globalization of economies and enterprises and the transformation of economic entities affect not only the sphere of management and technological change, but more and more often the mental issue, referring to changes in the state of awareness of the managerial staff. The awareness changes concern the impact of enterprises on the environment. Beliefs about the fact that this impact is significant belong to the category of truisms, but the need to reorient in taking into account non-business interests becomes noticeable.

Dolan and Garcia (1999) claimed almost 20 years ago that the system of beliefs and values that shaped the management model and organization in the 20th century is insufficient today. There is a need to develop a new model *that will allow the company to operate efficiently and compete in markets that are more and more global, complex, requiring specialization, are constantly changing and are oriented to quality and customer satisfaction* (Dolan, Garcia, 1999, p. 1). In the work, the authors analysed known and widely used management concepts: management by instruction (MBI - developed in the 1920s) and management by objectives (MBO - developed in the 1960s), which was confronted with a new approach, called management through values (MBV), translated by many authors as competence management.

The evolution of these concepts, according to the authors of the MBV concept, followed the emergence of four trends in recent decades, which forced organizations to adapt to remain competitive on increasingly demanding and unpredictable markets. These four trends are:

1. The need for high quality and customer orientation,
2. The need for greater professionalism, autonomy and responsibility,
3. The need to change 'bosses' into real leaders,
4. The need for a more flat and efficient organization structure (Dolan, Garcia, 1999).

The awareness changes are supposed to increase the sensitivity of shareholders and managers to the expectations of the public demanding its needs to be taken into account already at the stage of developing programs and development strategies of emerging and existing corporations and enterprises.

Social responsibility as a challenge comes from many factors, the most important of which are: the strength of societies that expect enterprises to take part in social responsibility resulting from their actions, demanding transparency of procedures and selection of contractors for the company in its supply chain, openness and publicity of the main directions of activities of entities. In the decision-making process, during which losses and profits are estimated, enterprises should take into account the so-called social costs of decisions, responsibility for the natural environment and the local community, including social goals in the area of strategic goals of the company, monitoring and measuring social programs costs, the degree of achievement of achievements, reliable creation and sharing reports on the level of socio-ecological goals and reports on delivery and spending of resources allocated to the company's sustainable development system (Ismail, 2009).

The company's drive at the maximization of profits or the increase market share often occurs with the violation of social and environmental values. Achieving financial goals must allow for social and ecological aspects as the main areas of sustainable development. The business activity of enterprises disregarding the indicated areas in the long term, is doomed to failure. For this reason, there is a need to design economic processes that include the idea of sustainable development. The rational conduct of business contributes to sustainable development, and thus preserves or even improves the ability of the next generations to meet their needs in the future (Trojanowski, 2013, p. 150).

Rogall (2010, p. 37) indicates economic problem areas, which are also a challenge for modern enterprises. The author includes, among others:

- The instability of the national economy, e.g. insufficient employment offer,
- The insufficient satisfaction of basic needs, high prices,
- The inflation, a high degree of concentration and economic power,
- Economic imbalance, dependence on raw materials supply, underdevelopment,
- State indebtedness, insufficient distribution of collective goods and unfair distribution of income.

Enterprises conducting business activity fulfill the objectives set for the entity connected with staying on the market, improving the competitive position, thus increasing its economic value. The company's success is assessed on the basis of financial profit measures, such as the return on investment, assets, sales and equity. However, more and more often, in addition to the economic argument, an ethical argument is given to the conducted activity, which reflects the improvement of social well-being. In this way, it comes to balancing between people and profits. Such considerations were published by Bansal in 2005 in the Ivey Business Journal. She argues that considering these issues as: either economics or ethics, polarizes the discussion and diverts attention from the space in which these concepts converge and where potential solutions exist. This overlapping space is not a compromise. It is a completely real position that uses business models that simultaneously meet economic and ethical goals. The new corporate rules, procedures and programs are able to provide an economic return, while providing the public with a position in which most members of the organization would like to participate. Bansal (2005) argues that there is no room for space overlap by transforming ethical issues in economic terms or in isolation from economic models, but rather in combining social and economic processes.

Similar conclusions were presented by Porter (2012) when formulating the goals of enterprises, taking into account, on the one hand, the social aspect, and on the other economic effects as:

- There is an opportunity to transform thinking and practice about the role of the corporation in society,
- Shared value gives rise to far broader approaches to economic value creation,
- Shared value thinking will drive the next wave of innovation, productivity growth, and economic growth,
- Businesses acting as businesses, not as charitable givers, are arguably the most powerful force for addressing many of the pressing issues facing our society,
- A transformation of business practice around shared value will give purpose to the corporation and represents our best chance to legitimize business again.

The negative externalities of companies' economic activities, such as noise, congestion and pollution, have an impact on those who have no part in the economic transaction and have not consented to it. Because the most critical resources in the world, such as water and air, can not be reasonably priced, they are used in a reckless way. "The Tragedy of the Commons", described by Hardin (1968), shows how the theory of market equilibrium breaks down into common assets, such as ocean fishing, common pastures, air and groundwater resources. Since no one owns the resource, producers believe that fish stocks (or air, water or common land) are without ownership.

Scientific research on the role of people in climate change, as well as many lessons learned from industrial pollution and their negative impact on the environment led to a greater general awareness of the need for sustainability. Customers increasingly demand products to be produced in an environmentally friendly way that reduces the negative impact on land resources (Thorn, Kraus, Parker, 2011). That is why companies face the growing need to consider sustainable development in their business models and marketing activities (Buxel et al., 2015).

It is worth citing, for example, the views of Laszlo (2003), who even believes that ... *an integrated economic, social and ecological approach leads to the development of more durable value for shareholders than the approach focused on quick profits, which deprives one or many stakeholders of value and transfers it to the company's shareholders*. This author describes a set of tools to help create and manage value for stakeholders from many sectors in today's changing competitive environment. The toolkit is based on a large number of consulting and executive working sessions in Fortune 1000 companies that aim to provide managers with the skills to determine how to build sustainable economic value, including elements of sustainable development.

A sustainable company is one that contributes to sustainable development while providing economic, social and environmental benefits. Hart and Milstein (2003) have developed a sustainable value framework that directly links the social challenges of global sustainability with the creation of shareholder value by the company. The framework shows how global challenges related to sustainable development - perceived through a proper business lens - can help to define strategies and practices that contribute to a more sustainable world while improving the value of the company. The "win-win" approach is defined as creating a "lasting value" by the company. There are four basic dimensions of the sustainable development strategy from the point of view of value creation (Figure 1):

1. Pollution prevention focuses on improving the environmental performance of today's products and processes by reducing waste and gas emissions from ongoing operations. Less waste means better use of inputs, which results in lower costs of raw materials utilization and waste disposal as well as an increase in the financial result. However, effective prevention of pollution requires full em-

ployee involvement as well as an effective, functioning quality management system (Hart, 1995). The prevention of pollution is becoming the fastest way to increase the value of the company in the eyes of investors.

2. **Product Management:** While pollution prevention focuses on internal operations, product management goes beyond organizational boundaries, covering the entire product life cycle - from the access to raw material, through production processes, to the product use and the disposal of used products. Product management therefore includes the integration of activities through interaction with external entities: suppliers, clients, regulators, communities, NGOs and the media. Constructive stakeholder engagement increases external trust and affects the company's reputation (Hart, Milstein, 2003).
3. Clean technology does not relate to a gradual improvement connected with pollution prevention but to innovations that will overcome standard procedures (e.g. Vergragt, Van Grootveld, 1994). The emergence of breakthrough technologies, such as: genomics, information technology, nanotechnology and renewable energy sources, create an opportunity to reduce the negative effects of businesses. Solving social and environmental problems is possible through internal development and the acquisition of new skills by companies (McDonough, Braungart, 2002).
4. The vision of sustainable development - the growing gap between the rich and the poor may be a chance for future development, by launching new products on previously unsupported markets. More and more multinational corporations recognize that listening to the voices of the poor can be a source of creativity and innovation. Global enterprises are beginning to take steps to make the most of their skills and resources to meet the basic nutritional, energy, housing and communication needs of the poorest people in the world (Hart, Milstein, 2003).

Every factor of sustainable development and related business strategies and practices correspond to a specific dimension of shareholder value. Considering the full range of challenges and opportunities is the first managerial step towards creating a lasting value.

Creating a sustainable company value should have a long-term dimension. Investigating this value should be included in the business strategy, however many companies still struggle to integrate sustainable development into their strategies and management structures. The authors of the report: Redefining Sustainable Business (Cramer, Allison-Hope, Taylor, Richmond, Bancilhon, 2018), on the basis of interviews with 50 leaders of sustainability and surveys with GlobeScan in 2017 on the state of sustainable business, say that building of a long-term sustainable value should include three steps:

Step 1: Creating a flexible business narrative convincing to create a long-term value that will confirm that sustainability plays the central role in business success;
Step 2: Engaging investors in the vision of creating a long-term value;
Step 3: Getting to know recipients, mainly long-term stakeholders, because they will be interested in greater involvement in matters of good management and value creation.

The results of the survey included in the study From Sustainability to Business Value indicate that companies are fighting above all for transforming the issue of sustainable development into commercial possibilities. Only a small part of them claim that it has introduced significant new business initiatives such as: creating new products, buying a different company and starting operations outside their primary market as a direct result of problems related to sustainable development. The cases of sustainable de-

Figure 1. Sustainable value framework
Source: Hart S. L., Milstein M. B. (2003). Creating sustainable value. Academy of Management Executive, Vol. 17, No. 2, p. 60

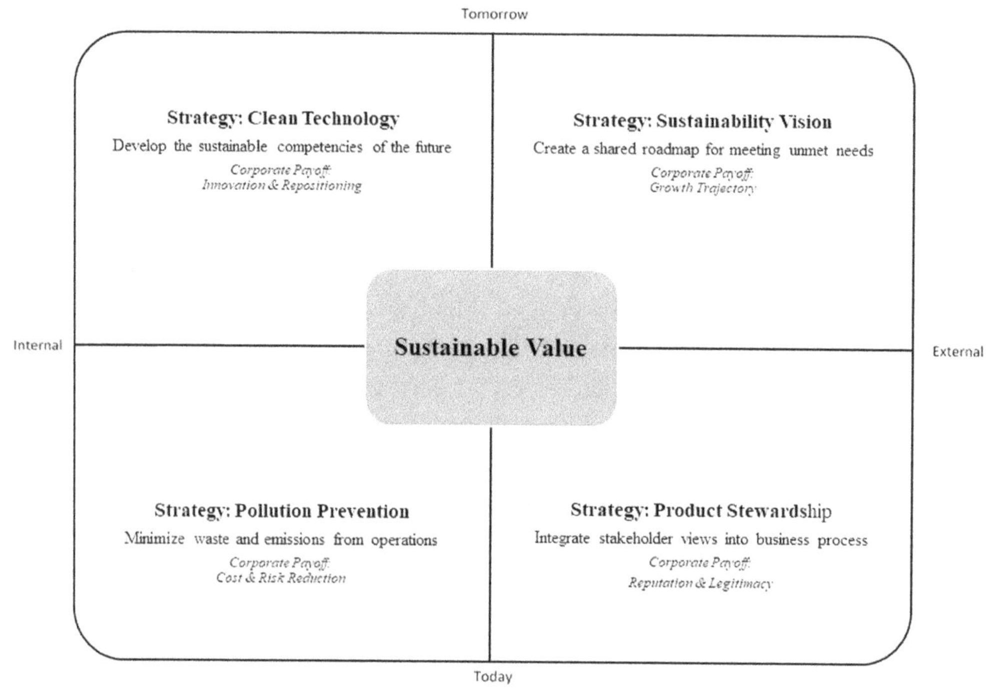

velopment driving strategic business decisions seem to be more widespread among larger international organizations with significant capital reserves than in the case of smaller enterprises. Some of the largest companies in the world have adopted sustainable development as a way to accelerate the growth of their own value. The result of this was, for example, acquiring new customers, and thus increasing sales revenues. In addition, sustainable development is the driving force behind increased innovation activity. Those companies that will bring new ones to the market sooner than competitors will do, will be more effective in further development of the company, and thus their value will increase. More generally, the principle of applying sustainable thinking in all types of strategic decisions becomes increasingly important.

The non-financial results of enterprises have begun to attract the attention of an increasing number of investment specialists because they realize that profitability alone is not sufficient for long-term growth of the company's value. Looking beyond economic, strategic and operational factors, including environmental and social issues helps to increase corporate transparency, strengthens risk management, promotes stakeholder engagement and improves communication with stakeholders. Most companies strive to maximize profits, which is why they defend themselves against introducing elements of sustainable development in their operations as they seem expensive. Researchers around the world are conducting research to show the relationship between sustainable management and the value of enterprises (Table 1). Most studies mainly concern more advanced and mature economies (Berthelot, Coulmont, Serret, 2012), and their results confirm that investors pay attention to the active involvement of enterprises in sustainable development, which improves their value.

The need for a wider perspective on the data published by enterprises appeared along with new business models, changes in consumer trends, environmental regulations or the impact of social media. This trend is confirmed by data published by the S & P 500 Index, indicating that nowadays tangible assets account for only 20% of the total market value of index companies, the rest are intangible assets. It is also important for companies to see a growing interest in investment strategies based on ESG data (E - environment; S - social, G - governance), as shown by financial entities. Sustainable and Responsible Investment (SRI), namely responsible investment, is defined as investment covering every type of investment process that allows to combine investors' financial goals with their care for environmental, social and corporate governance issues (ESG in Equity Analysis ..., 2018). According to the Global Reporting Initiative (GRI), the largest organization dealing with the issue of non-financial data reporting, reporting sustainability issues involves measuring, disclosing and bearing responsibility for internal and external stakeholders for the results and efficiency in addressing these issues .

In recent years, interest in issuing reports with data on sustainable development has been systematically growing. It is visible in the number of publications referring to this term indexed in the years 1987-2015 in the Web of Science database (WoS). The results of that research have been published in 2017 by Zhu and Hua (2017) In that period as many as 59 926 papers on sustainable development, published by authors from 49 countries, have been identified in the WoS database. Also as many as 149 categories of connections with other research areas have been identified. According to the 2011 KPMG (2011) Unsurvey, 95% of the 250 largest companies in the world disclose data on their activities in the field of social and environmental responsibility. Most reports have been published in Japan, then in the United Kingdom and the United States.

Table 1. The examples of studies on measuring sustainable value in an enterprise

Author	Publication	Aim of study	Method	Results
Buxel, Esenduran, & Griffin (2015)	Strategic sustainability: Creating business value with life cycle analysis. *Business Horizons, 58,* 109-122	The environmental impact of the product over its entire life (from raw material extraction, through material processing, production, distribution, use, repair and maintenance, and utilization or recycling).	LCA method as a management tool in an enterprise, supporting decision making, which is of great importance in various areas of product implementation and above all is connected with sustainable development.	This article introduces the LCA method as a management decision tool, and illustrates its value creation potential through multiple industry examples.
Figge, Hahn, (2004)	Sustainable Value Added—measuring corporate contributions to sustainability beyond eco-efficiency. *Ecological Economics, 48,* 173–187	A new approach to measuring the contribution of enterprises to sustainable development called: Balanced added value.	The authors construct equations for the measurement of sustainable added value in an enterprise that also takes into account economic, environmental and social aspects.	Sustainable Value Added as developed in this article provides a new approach to measure corporate contributions to sustainability. However, this paper focuses on method development rather than on the implementation of the method.

continues on following page

Table 1. Continued

Author	Publication	Aim of study	Method	Results
Nicolăescu, Alpopi, Zaharia, (2015)	Measuring Corporate Sustainability Performance. *Sustainability, 7*(1), 851-865	To examine and evaluate the evolving nature of sustainable development management in corporations, the importance of environmental protection and sustainable development, and barriers to the implementation of integrated and strategic development of social responsibility throughout the company.	Surveys via e-mail among directors managing medium-sized enterprises (250-999 employees) who represented 15 sectors from 28 EU countries.	The paper generates insights about the advance of sustainability metrics, the determinants, risks, and chances entailed in making the switch to sustainability, and stakeholders concerned in corporate ES&G management conduct and functioning.
Šimberová, Chvátalová, Kocmanová, Hornungová, Pavláková Dočekalová, (2015)	Sustainable value in measuring of corporate sustainability: approaches and their evaluation. *Journal of Security and Sustainability Issues, 4*(3), 241-259	Measuring sustainable enterprise development based on sustainable value in selected industries.	The presentation of selected models (methods) for measuring sustainable value.	Analysis of this topic brought some interesting ideas for the following areas: firstly, although there are many different initiatives to measure sustainable development, only a few of them are based on an integrated approach to all three aspects of sustainable development, i.e. environmental, economic and social.
Stankevicienea, Nikonorova, (2014).	Sustainable Value Creation in Commercial Banks during Financial Crisis. *Procedia - Social and Behavioral Sciences, 110*, 1197-1208	The proposal of a sustainable value measurement model for commercial banks during the financial crisis.	Research based on data from the 10 largest banks in Lithuania in 2009-2011. A model for determining the permanent value of the bank has been proposed.	The EVA model is more effective in measuring shareholder value, because the main benefit of EVA is that it can be calculated and implemented at all levels of the financial institution.
Loh, Thomas, Wang, (2017)	Sustainability Reporting and Firm Value: Evidencefrom Singapore-Listed Companies. *Sustainability, 9*(11):2112, 1-12	This research aims to investigate the relationship between sustainability reporting and firm value based on listed companies in Singapore.	The research sample consisted of 502 companies listed on the Singapore Exchange (SGX), which had proven activity for sustainable development. The econometric models were evaluated, in which the company's value was explained, and among the explanatory variables, among others the sustainability reporting score of the company.	The results suggest that sustainability disclosure is positively related to the market value of a company, and the better the quality of sustainability reporting, the stronger the linkage.

continues on following page

Table 1. Continued

Author	Publication	Aim of study	Method	Results
Miralles-Quiros M.M, Miralles-Quiros J.L., Arraiano, (2017)	Sustainable Development, Sustainability Leadership and Firm Valuation: Differences across EUROPE. *Business Strategy and the Environment, 26*(7), 1014-1028	Determination of the company's market value.	The Ohlson valuation model and regression models estimated for 10 European countries in 2001-2013 were presented.	Studies have found a significant relation between the market value of equity and non-financial information such as environmental performance or social and environmental reporting.
Husted, Allen, (2007)	Strategic Corporate Social Responsibility and Value Creation Among Large Firms: Lessons from the Spanish Experience. *Long Range Planning, 40*(6), 594-610	An assessment of the influence of Corporate Social Responsibility – CSR on their economic results.	Multiple regression analysis was used.	The results indicate that activities related to CSR give opportunities for innovation and value creation (cost reduction, product differentiation, increased customer loyalty, increased competitive opportunities).
Evans, Fernando, Miying, (2017)	Sustainable Value Creation – From Concept Towards Implementation, In R. G. Stark, & J. Bonvoisin, *Sustainable Manufacturing, Challenges, Solutions and Implementation Perspectives*. Springer, 203-220	This paper seeks to provide understanding of key concepts for and tools that aid practitioners in sustainable value creation in manufacturing. The chapter also provides case studies on how the tools have helped companies improve sustainability.	The following models were presented: Cambridge Value Mapping Tool, Sustainable Value Analysis Tool (SVAT).	The data suggests the company a leader in efficiently and sustainably manufacturing sugar beet, over the past three decades has been able to systematically find failed value exchanges in their system. The company has been able to identify the waste streams (i.e. carbon dioxide, heat) that had value that is not being captured and destroyed in its system (i.e. failed value).

Source: own elaboration

CONCLUSION

The analysis of studies on sustainable value in the company conducted in the chapter shows that business benefits related to the implementation of sustainable development initiatives are becoming more and more obvious. The involvement of enterprises in sustainable development allows us to improve products, which results in greater satisfaction and loyalty of our clients. Greater motivation and commitment of employees translates into increased creativity and innovation. This affects the positive image of the company, and thus improves the situation on the labor market and cooperation with business partners. As a result, it increases sales and gains a competitive advantage resulting from the above aspects.

However, many companies, especially small ones, still do not show any interest in this direction and do not know where to start. In the literature it is possible to find guidelines how to do it in an organized and systematic manner in three stages:

1. **Making Benefits Tangible:** Enterprises are much more likely to take action if they see the benefits of sustainable development. The observation of such sustainability indicators as: resource efficiency, return on investment, is the starting point for a better understanding of why and how sustainability can affect the value of the company.

2. **Integration of Sustainable Development in the Whole Organization:** Companies that have successfully integrated the objectives of sustainable development in the whole organization, are better prepared to apply sustainable thinking in the entire spectrum of decision making: from strategy setting to reviewing supply chains and establishing cooperation with partners.
3. **Inclusion of the Financial Function:** Many initiatives for sustainable development require initial investment, which means it is much easier to start if the financial team is fully involved and understands the benefits. A strong partnership between finance and sustainable development leaders will be the key to building a business case for investment. The development of the green financial market creates opportunities to attract new investors, potentially achieve more favorable financing conditions and shed light on the organization's commitment to sustainable development.

Sustainability management deals with social, environmental and economic issues in an integrated manner to transform organisations in a way that they contribute to a sustainable development of the economy and society within the limits of the ecosystem. Leaders, managers and entrepreneurs are challenged to contribute to sustainable development on the individual, organisational and societal level. Scholars and practitioners are recently increasingly exploring if and how modified and completely new business models can help maintain or even increase economic prosperity by either radically reducing negative or creating positive external effects for the natural environment and society, literature surrounding this area is scarce and still emerging (Evans, Fernando, Miying, 2017).

Politicians in various countries are looking for ways to introduce legal regulations that strengthen the current regulations in the field of sustainable development in business management. Therefore, in view of challenges related to the introduction of sustainable development measures, studies on this subject provide empirical evidence of the benefits of sustainable development and their impact on the value of the company.

REFERENCES

Agenda 2030: Transforming Our World: The 2030 Agenda For Sustainable Development. (2015). United Nations, A/RES/70/. Retrieved from https://sustainabledevelopment.un.org/content/documents/21252030%20Agenda%20for%20Sustainable%20Development%20web.pdf

Altieri, M. A. (2018). *Agroecology: the science of sustainable agriculture. CRC Press, Taylor&Francis. ESG in Equity Analysis and Credit Analysis.* Principles for Responsible Investment. CFA Insitute. doi:10.1201/9780429495465

Antwi, S., Mills, E. F. E. A., & Zhao, X. (2012). Capital Structure and Firm Value: Empirical Evidence from Ghana. *International Journal of Business and Social Science, 3*(22), 103–111.

Bansal, T. (2005). Building sustainable Value through fiscal and social responsibility. *Ivey Business Journal.* Retrieved from https://iveybusinessjournal.com/publication/building-sustainable-value-through-fiscal-and-social-responsibility/

Berns, M., Townend, A., Khayat, Z., Balagopal, B., Reeves, M., Hopkins, M., & Kruschwitz, N. (2009). The Business of Sustainability: Imperatives, Advantages, and Actions. Boston: The Boston Consulting Group (BCG).

Berthelot, S., Coulmont, M., & Serret, V. (2012). Do Investors Value Sustainability Reports? A Canadian Study. *Corporate Social Responsibility and Environmental Management, 19*(6), 355–363. doi:10.1002/csr.285

Biju, P. L., Shalij, P. R., & Prabhushankar, G. V. (2015). Evaluation of customer requirements and sustainability requirements through the application of fuzzy analytic hierarchy process. *Journal of Cleaner Production, 108*, 808–817. doi:10.1016/j.jclepro.2015.08.051

Brzozowski, T. T. (2010). Sustainable Development strategy as a challenge for the processes of transformation in industry and services. *Prace Komisji Geografii Przemysłu, 15*, 219–228.

Buxel, H., Esenduran, G., & Griffin, S. (2015). Strategic sustainability: Creating business value with life cycle analysis. *Business Horizons, 58*(1), 109–122. doi:10.1016/j.bushor.2014.09.004

Cramer, A., Allison-Hope, D., Taylor, A., Richmond, B., & Bancilhon, C. (2018). *Redefining Sustainable Business. Management for a rapidly changing world*. BSR. Retrieved from https://www.bsr.org/reports/BSR_Redefining_Sustainable_Business.pdf

Dolan, S. L., & Garcia, S. (1999). Managing by Values in the Next Millennium: Cultural Redesign for Strategic Organizational Change. *Journal of Economics, 5*, 1–16.

Evans, S., Fernando, L., & Miying, Y. (2017). Sustainable Value Creation – From Concept Towards Implementation, In R. G. Stark, & J. Bonvoisin (Eds.), Sustainable Manufacturing, Challenges, Solutions and Implementation Perspectives. Springer.

Figge, F., & Hahn, T. (2004). Sustainable Value Added—Measuring corporate contributions to sustainability beyond eco-efficiency. *Ecological Economics, 48*(2), 173–187. doi:10.1016/j.ecolecon.2003.08.005

Fullwiler, S. T. (2015). *Sustainable Finance: Building a More General Theory of Finance*. Working Paper, 106. Binzagr Institute for Sustainable Prosperity.

Global Reporting Initiative. (2006). Amsterdam: GRI Sustainability Reporting Guidelines, Version 3 Global Reporting Initiative.

Hardin, G. (1968). The Tragedy of the Commons. *Science, 162*(3859), 1243-1248. Retrieved from http://science.sciencemag.org/content/162/3859/1243

Hart, S. (1995). A natural resource-based view of the firm. *Academy of Management Review, 20*(4), 986–1014. doi:10.5465/amr.1995.9512280033

Hart, S. L., & Milstein, M. B. (2003). Creating sustainable value. *The Academy of Management Executive, 17*(2), 56–69.

Helbling, C. (1991). *Unternehmensbewertung und Steuern*. IDW Verlag.

Husted, B. W., & Allen, D. B. (2007). Strategic Corporate Social Responsibility and Value Creation Among Large Firms: Lessons from the Spanish Experience. *Long Range Planning, 40*(6), 594–610. doi:10.1016/j.lrp.2007.07.001

Ignaciuk, I. (1990). How to determine the value of a company? [in English]. *Organization Review, 6*, 10–14.

Ismail, M. (2009). Corporate social responsibility and its role in community development: An international perspective. *The Journal of International Social Research, 2/9*, 199–209.

Jabłoński, A. (2015). The financial stability of a company and its business model. *Zeszyty Naukowe Uniwersytetu Przyrodniczo-Humanistycznego w Siedlcach, Seria. Administracja i Zarządzanie, 104*(31), 87–96.

Jaramillo, C. H., Arimany-Serrat, N., Vidal, D. M., & Ferràs-Hernandez, X. (2018). Sustainability values for business: A perspective of value alignment in a supplier–client relationship for case aqualogy. *Intangible Capital, 14*(1), 3–24. doi:10.3926/ic.1083

Kiba-Janiak, M. (2015). A Comparative Analysis of Sustainable City Logistics among Capital Cities in the EU. *Applied Mechanics and Materials, 708*, 113–118. doi:10.4028/www.scientific.net/AMM.708.113

KPMG International Survey of Corporate Responsibility Reporting 2011. (2011). KPMG International.

Laszlo, Ch. (2003). *The Sustainable Company: How to Create Lasting Value through Social and Environmental Performance*. Washington, DC: Island Press.

Leland, H. E., & Toft, K. (1991). Optimal Capital structure, Endogenous Bankruptcy, and the Term Structure of credit spreads. *The Journal of Finance, 51*(3), 987–1019. doi:10.1111/j.1540-6261.1996.tb02714.x

Lewicka, H. (2014). Value as a key concept in the field of economic sciences. *Society and Economy, 2*(2), 64–72.

Loh, L., Thomas, T., & Wang, Y. (2017). Sustainability Reporting and Firm Value: Evidencefrom Singapore-Listed Companies. *Sustainability, 9*(11), 1-12. Retrieved from https://www.researchgate.net/publication/321140723_Sustainability_Reporting_and_Firm_Value_Evidence_from_Singapore-Listed_Companies/download

Matschke, M. J., Brösel, G., & Matschke, X. (2010). Fundamentals of Functional Business Valuation. *Journal of Business Valuation and Economic Loss Analysis, 5*(1). doi:10.2202/1932-9156.1097

McDonough, W., & Braungart, M. (2002). *Cradle to Cradle: Remaking the Way We Make Things*. New York: North Point Press.

Miralles-Quiros, M. M., Miralles-Quiros, J. L., & Arraiano, I. C. (2017). Sustainable Development, Sustainability Leadership and Firm Valuation: Differences across EUROPE. *Business Strategy and the Environment, 26*(7), 1014–1028. doi:10.1002/bse.1964

Myers, S. C. (1993). Still Searching for Optimal Capital Structure. *Journal of Applied Corporate Finance, 6*(1), 4–14. doi:10.1111/j.1745-6622.1993.tb00369.x

Nicolăescu, E., Alpopi, C., & Zaharia, C. (2015). Measuring Corporate Sustainability Performance. *Sustainability, 7*(1), 851–865. doi:10.3390u7010851

Nogalski, B., & Bors, K. (2000). Value management. *Organization Review, 4*, 16–21.

Ogbulu, O. M., & Emeni, F. K. (2012). Capital Structure and Firm Value: Empirical Evidence from Nigeria. *International Journal of Business and Social Science*, *3*(19), 252–261. Retrieved from http://www.ijbssnet.com/journals/Vol_3_No_19_October _2012 /29.pdf

Porter, M. E. (2012). *New Opportunities for Company Performance and Purpose: Creating Shared Value*. Presentation for Hitachi Innovation Forum 2012 Conference, Boston, MA. Retrieved from https://www.hbs.edu/faculty/Publication%20Files/20120719%20-%20Hitachi%20Diamond%20CSV%20Presentation%20-%20FINAL_51404d95-3aa3-4572-a270-25dcfecffc29.pdf

Rashid, K., Islam, S. M. N., & Nuryanah, S. (2014). Debt, governance and the value of a firm. *Corporate Ownership & Control*, *11*(2), 180–191. doi:10.22495/cocv11i2c1p4

Rogall, H. (2010). *The economics of sustainable development. Theory and practice*. Poznan: Zysk i S-ka.

Sexton, M. G., Barrett, P. S., & Lu, S. L. (2008). *The evolution of sustainable development. Book Section*. Manchester, UK: University of Salford.

Šimberová, I., Chvátalová, Z., Kocmanová, A., Hornungová, J., & Pavláková Dočekalová, M. (2015). Sustainable value in measuring of corporate sustainability: Approaches and their evaluation. *Journal of Security and Sustainability Issues*, *4*(3), 241–259. doi:10.9770/jssi.2015.4.3(5)

Stankevicienea, J., & Nikonorova, M. (2014). Sustainable Value Creation in Commercial Banks during Financial Crisis. *Procedia: Social and Behavioral Sciences*, *110*, 1197–1208. doi:10.1016/j.sbspro.2013.12.966

Stefanescu, D., & On, A. (2012). Entrepreneurship and Sustainable Development in European Countries Before and During the International Crisis. *Procedia: Social and Behavioral Sciences*, *58*, 889–898. doi:10.1016/j.sbspro.2012.09.1067

Szopik-Depczyńska, K., Cheba, K., Bąk, I., Stajniak, M., Simboli, A., & Ioppolo, G. (2018). The study of relationship in a hierarchical structure of EU sustainable development indicators. *Ecological Indicators*, *90*, 120–131. doi:10.1016/j.ecolind.2018.03.002

Thorn, M., Kraus, J., & Parker, D. (2011). Life cycle assessment as a sustainability management tool: Strengths, weaknesses, and other considerations. *Environmental Quality Management*, *20*(3), 1–10. doi:10.1002/tqem.20285

Tomczyk, P. (2012). Client as a source of company value. In T. Pakulska (Ed.), *Enterprise and surroundings* (pp. 59–78). Warsaw: Oficyna Wydawnicza SGH.

Trojanowski, T. (2013). Aspects of the sustainable management of marketing activities. In J. S. Kardas & J. Brodowska-Szewczuk (Eds.), *Business Development Opportunities*. Siedlce: Wydawnictwo Uniwersytetu Przyrodniczo-Humanistycznego w Siedlcach.

United Nations (UN). (1975). *United Nations Environment Programme*. Report of the Governing Council on the work pf this third session. New York: United Nations.

Ushijima, T. (2015). *Diversification, Organization, and Value of the Firm*. RIETI Discussion Paper Series 15-E-019. Retrieved from https://www.rieti.go.jp/jp/publications/dp/15e019.pdf

Vandaele, N. J., & Decouttere, C. J. (2013). Sustainable R&D portfolio assessment. *Decision Support Systems*, *54*(4), 1521–1532. doi:10.1016/j.dss.2012.05.054

Vergragt, P., & van Grootveld, G. (1994). Sustainable technology development in the Netherlands: The first phase of the Dutch STD programme. *Journal of Cleaner Production*, *2*(3/4), 133–139. doi:10.1016/0959-6526(94)90035-3

Vintilă, G., & Gherghina, S. C. (2014). The impact of ownership concentration on firm value. Empirical study of the Bucharest Stock Exchange listed companies. *Procedia Economics and Finance*, *15*, 271–279. doi:10.1016/S2212-5671(14)00500-0

WCED (World Commission on Environment and Development). (1987). *Our Common Future. Un Documents: Gathering a Body of Global Agreements has been compiled by the NGO Committee on Education of the Conference of NGOs from United Nations web sites with the invaluable help of information & communications technology*. New York: United Nations.

Zhu, J., & Hua, W. (2017). Visualizing the knowledge domain of sustainable development research between 1987 and 2015: A bibliometric analysis. *Scientometrics*, *10*(2), 893–914. doi:10.100711192-016-2187-8

ADDITIONAL READING

Bąk, I., & Cheba, K. (2018). Study of spatial uniformity of sustainable development of the European Union before, during and after the economic crisis. *Przegląd Statystyczny*, *65*(2), 222–246.

Bąk, I., & Cheba, K. (2018). An analysis of dynamic changes in selected areas of sustainable development of the European Union countries. *Folia Oeconomica Stetinensia*, *18*(1), 93–107. doi:10.2478/foli-2018-0008

Szczecińska, B. (2008). The application of the method of logarithm finding in the causal analysis of the financial results of enterprises of the food sector. *Acta Scientiarum Polonorum Oeconomia, 7*(1): Wydawnictwo SGGW Warszawa, 135-139.

Szopik-Depczyńska, K., Cheba, K., Bąk, I., Stajniak, M., Simboli, A., & Ioppolo G. (2018). The study of relationship in a hierarchical structure of EU sustainable development indicators. *Ecological Indicators, 90,* 120-131, IF2017 – 3,983.

Szopik-Depczyńska K., Cheba K., Bąk I., Kiba-Janiak M., Saniuk S., Dembińska I., & Ioppolo G. (2017). The application of relative taxonomy to the study of disproportion in the area of sustainable development of the European Union. *Land Use Policy, 68*C, 481-491, IF2017 – 3,194.

Compilation of References

29. September 1994 - The Accounting Act (uniform text Dz. U. z 2019 r. poz. 351).

Abazid, M., Abdulrahman, A., & Samine, S. (2018). Least Squares Methods to Forecast Sales for Company. *International Journal of Scientific & Engineering Research*, *9*(6), 864–868.

Abu-Bader, S., & Abu-Qarn, A. S. (2003). Government Expenditures, Military Spending and Economic Growth: Causality Evidence from Egypt, Israel, and Syria. *Journal of Policy Modeling*, *25*(6-7), 567–583. doi:10.1016/S0161-8938(03)00057-7

Acemoglu & Autor. (2012). What does human capital do? A review of Goldin and Katz's *The Race between Education and Technology. Journal of Economic Literature, 50*(2), 426–463.

Acemoglu, D. (1998). Why do new technologies complement skills? Directed technical change and wage inequality. *Quarterly Journal of Economics, 113*(4), 1055–89.

Acemoglu, D., & Autor, D. (2011). Skills, tasks and technologies: implications for employment and earnings. In Handbook of Labor Economics (vol. 4). Amsterdam: Elsevier. doi:10.1016/S0169-7218(11)02410-5

Acemoglu, D., Johnson, S., & Robinson, J. A. (2005). Institutions as the fundamental cause of long-run growth. In P. Aghion & S. Durlauf (Eds.), *Handbook of Economic Growth*. Elsevier.

Acemoglu, D., Naidu, S., Restrepo, P., & Robinson, J. A. (2015). Democracy, redistribution and inequality. In A. Atkinson & F. Bourguignon (Eds.), *Handbook of Income Distribution* (Vol. 2). Elsevier.

Acemoglu, D., & Verdier, T. (1998). Property rights, corruption and the allocation of talent: A general equilibrium approach. *Economic Journal (London)*, *108*(450), 1381–1403. doi:10.1111/1468-0297.00347

Adam, A. (2015). Challenges of Public Finance Sustainability in the European Union. *Procedia Economics and Finance*, *23*, 298–302. doi:10.1016/S2212-5671(15)00507-9

Adamchuk, O., & Papchenkova, M. (2017, November 12). Officials figured out how to "weigh" investors. *Vedomosty*.

ADB. (2017). Transcending the middle-income challenge. *Asian Development Outlook 2017*, Part 2.

Adelman & Adelman. (1959, October). The dynamic properties of the Klein-Goldberger model. *Econometrica*.

Adolf, C., & Röhrig, K. (2016). *Communicating Green Own Resources: A New Narrative for the EU Budget*. Brussels: Green Budget Europe.

Afonso, A., Erbert, W., Schuknect, L., & Thone, M. (2005). Quality of Public Finances and Growth. *ECB Working Paper*, *438*, 1-47.

Agenda 2030: Transforming Our World: The 2030 Agenda For Sustainable Development. (2015). United Nations, A/RES/70/. Retrieved from https://sustainabledevelopment.un.org/content/documents/21252030%20Agenda%20for%20Sustainable%20Development%20web.pdf

Aghion, P., & Kharroubi, E. (2013). *Cyclical macroeconomic policy, financial regulation and economic growth*. BIS Working Paper, 434. Basel, Switzerland: Bank for International Settlements.

Aguilera, R. V., Rupp, D. E., Williams, C. A., & Ganapathi, J. (2007). Putting the S back in corporate social responsibility: A multilevel theory of social change in organizations. *Academy of Management Review*, *32*(3), 836–863. doi:10.5465/amr.2007.25275678

Akgun, O., Cournède, B., & Fournier, J. (2017). *The effects of the tax mix on inequality and growth*. OECD Economics Department Working Papers, No. 1447. OECD Publishing. doi:10.1787/c57eaa14-en

Al Janabi, M. A. M. (2005). Trading Risk Management: Practical Applications to Emerging-Markets. In S. Motamen-Samadian (Ed.), *Risk Management in Emerging Markets* (pp. 91–136). Palgrave/MacMillan. doi:10.1057/9780230596368_7

Al Janabi, M. A. M. (2007a). Equity Trading Risk Management: The Case of Casablanca Stock Exchange. *International Journal of Risk Assessment and Management*, *7*(4), 535–568. doi:10.1504/IJRAM.2007.012743

Al Janabi, M. A. M. (2007b). Risk Analysis, Reporting and Control of Equity Exposure: Viable Applications to the Mexican Financial Market. *Journal of Derivatives & Hedge Funds*, *13*(1), 33–58. doi:10.1057/palgrave.jdhf.1850059

Al Janabi, M. A. M. (2008). A Practical Approach to Market Risk Analysis and Control: Empirical Test of the Mexican Foreign Exchange and Stock Markets. *International Journal of Risk Assessment and Management*, *9*(1 & 2), 70–103. doi:10.1504/IJRAM.2008.019314

Al Janabi, M. A. M. (2012). Optimal commodity asset allocation with a coherent market risk modeling. *Review of Financial Economics*, *21*(3), 131–140. doi:10.1016/j.rfe.2012.06.007

Al Janabi, M. A. M. (2013). Optimal and coherent economic-capital structures: Evidence from long and short-sales trading positions under illiquid market perspectives. *Annals of Operations Research*, *205*(1), 109–139. doi:10.100710479-012-1096-3

Al Janabi, M. A. M. (2014). Optimal and investable portfolios: An empirical analysis with scenario optimization algorithms under crisis market prospects. *Economic Modelling*, *40*, 369–381. doi:10.1016/j.econmod.2013.11.021

Al Janabi, M. A. M., Arreola-Hernández, J. A., Berger, T., & Nguyen, D. K. (2017). Multivariate dependence and portfolio optimization algorithms under illiquid market scenarios. *European Journal of Operational Research*, *259*(3), 1121–1131. doi:10.1016/j.ejor.2016.11.019

Al-Amri, K., & Davydov, Y. (2016). Testing the effectiveness of ERM: Evidence from operational losses. *Journal of Economics and Business*, *87*, 70–82. doi:10.1016/j.jeconbus.2016.07.002

Alchian, A. A., & Demsetz, H. (1972). Production, information costs, and economic organization. *The American Economic Review*, *62*(5), 777-795. Retrieved from: http://www.jstor.org/stable/1815199

Alchian, A. A. (1984). Specifity, specialization, and coalitions. *Journal of Institutional and Theoretical Economics*, *140*(1), 6.

Alemanno, A., & Sibony, A. (2015). *Nudge and the law: A European perspective*. Oxford, UK: Hart. doi:10.5040/9781474203463

Alesina, A., & Passalacqua, A. (2015). The political economy of government debt. In Handbook of Macroeconomics (vol. 2A). North Holland. doi:10.3386/w21821

Alesina, A., Omar, B., Favero, C., Giavazzi, F., & Paradisi, M. (2017). *The effects of fiscal consolidations: theory and evidence.* NBER Working Paper No. 23385.

Alesina, A., & Perotti, R. (1994). The political economy of growth: A critical survey of the recent literature. *The World Bank Economic Review*, *8*(3), 350–371. doi:10.1093/wber/8.3.351

Alesina, A., & Rodrik, D. (1994). Distributive politics and economic growth. *The Quarterly Journal of Economics*, *109*(2), 465–490. doi:10.2307/2118470

Alińska, A., Filipiak, B. Z., & Kosztowniak, A. (2018). The Importance of the Public Sector in Sustainable Development in Poland. *Sustainability*, *10*(9), 3278. doi:10.3390u10093278

Altieri, M. A. (2018). *Agroecology: the science of sustainable agriculture. CRC Press, Taylor&Francis. ESG in Equity Analysis and Credit Analysis.* Principles for Responsible Investment. CFA Insitute. doi:10.1201/9780429495465

Altinok, N., Angrist, N., & Patrinos, H. A. (2018). *Global data set on education quality (1965–2015).* Policy Research Working Paper, 8314. Washington, DC: The World Bank Group.

Amihud, Y., Mendelson, H., & Pedersen, L. H. (2005). Liquidity and Asset Prices. *Foundations and Trends in Finance*, *1*(4), 269–364. doi:10.1561/0500000003

Andersen, E. B. (1991). *The statistical analysis of categorial data.* Berlin: Springer-Verlang. doi:10.1007/978-3-642-97353-6

Andersen, M. S. (2007). *Carbon-energy Taxation Contributed to Economic Groth.* National Environmental Research Insitute News.

Andrada, M. G. (2015). Sustainable development and CSR in the financial sector. *Ann. Econ. Ser.*, *1*, 217–221.

Angelidis, T., & Benos, A. (2006). Liquidity adjusted value-at-risk based on the components of the bid-ask spread. *Applied Financial Economics*, *16*(11), 835–851. doi:10.1080/09603100500426440

Angelopoupos, Philippopoulos, & Tsionas. (2008). Does public sector efficiency matter? Revisiting the relation between fiscal size and economic growth in world sample, *Public Choice, 137*(1-2), 245-278.

Antwi, S., Mills, E. F. E. A., & Zhao, X. (2012). Capital Structure and Firm Value: Empirical Evidence from Ghana. *International Journal of Business and Social Science*, *3*(22), 103–111.

APM. (2016). *A social return on investment: A powerful tool for the realisation of benefits.* Available at https://www.apm.org.uk/media/2218/sroi-report-2016-web-final.pdf

Arestis, P. (2006). Financial liberalization and the relationship between finance and growth. In P. Arestis & M. Sawyer (Eds.), *A Handbook of Alternative Monetary Economics* (pp. 346–364). Cheltenham, UK: Edward Elgar Publishing.

Arezki, R., Bolton, P., Peters, S., Samama, F., & Stiglitz, J. (2017). From global savings glut to financing infrastructure. Economic Policy, 32(90), 221-261.

Arnold, V.I. (1979). Catastrophe theory. *Nature*, (10), 54-63.

Arnold, V. I. (1975). Critical points of smooth functions. *Proc. of International Congress of Mathematicians*, 19-40.

Arnold, V., Benford, T., Canada, J., & Sutton, S. G. (2015). Leveraging integrated information systems to enhance strategic flexibility and performance: The enabling role of enterprise risk management. *International Journal of Accounting Information Systems*, *19*, 1–16. doi:10.1016/j.accinf.2015.10.001

Arreola-Hernández, J., Al Janabi, M. A. M., Hammoudeh, S., & Nguyen, D. K. (2015). Time lag dependence, cross-correlation and risk analysis of U.S. energy and non-energy stock portfolios. *Journal of Asset Management*, *16*(7), 467–483. doi:10.1057/jam.2015.33

Arreola-Hernandez, J., Hammoudeh, S., Khuong, N. D., Al Janabi, M. A. M., & Reboredo, J. C. (2016). Global financial crisis and dependence risk analysis of sector portfolios: A vine copula approach. *Applied Economics*, *49*(25), 2409–2427. doi:10.1080/00036846.2016.1240346

Arrow, K. J. (1970). Political and economic evaluation of social effects and externalities. In J. Margolis (Ed.), *The Analysis of Public Output*. New York: Columbia University Press.

Ashford, N. A., & Hall, R. P. (2011). *Technology, Globalization, and Sustainable Development: Transforming the Industrial State*. New Haven, CT: Yale University Press.

Aslan, Ö. & Korap, H. L. (2006). Financial Developments Economic Growth Relationship in Turkey. Muğla University Journal of the Institute of Social Sciences, 17.

Aspey, E. (2015). The Reform to EU utilities Procurement: Smart, Sustainable and Inclusive? In K. V. Thai (Ed.), *International Public Procurement, Innovation and Knowledge Sharing, Public Administration, Governance and Globalization* (pp. 255–270). Springer International Publishing Switzerland. doi:10.1007/978-3-319-13434-5_13

Atkinson, T., & van de Noord, P. (2001). *Managing public expenditure: Some emerging policy issues and a framework for analysis*. OECD Economics Department Working Paper, No. 285. Paris: Organisation for Economic Co-operation and Development.

Atkinson, G. (2008). Sustainability, the capital approach and the built environment. *Building Research and Information*, *36*(3), 241–247. doi:10.1080/09613210801900734

Auerbach, A. J., & Gorodnichenko, Y. (2012). Measuring the output responses to fiscal policy. *American Economic Journal. Economic Policy*, *4*(2), 1–27. doi:10.1257/pol.4.2.1

Ausan, A. A. (2017). Introduction. In *Russia 2025: From Workforce to Talents*. Moscow: Boston Consulting Group, October.

Autor, D. H., Figlio, D. N., Karbownik, K., Roth, J., & Wasserman, M. (2016). School quality and the gender gap in educational achievement. *The American Economic Review*, *106*(5), 289–295. doi:10.1257/aer.p20161074

Autor, D., & Dorn, D. (2013). The growth of low-skill service jobs and the polarization of the US labor market. *The American Economic Review*, *103*(5), 1553–1597. doi:10.1257/aer.103.5.1553

Avkiran, N. K., & Rowlands, T. (2003). How better identify the true managerial performance: State of art using DEA. *Omega International Journal of Management Science*, *36*(2), 317–324. doi:10.1016/j.omega.2006.01.002

Bąk, I. (2010). The use of the correspondence analysis in the research of the tourist activity of university students. *Folia Oeconomica Stetinensia*, *8*(1), 7–18.

Bąk, I., & Cheba, K. (2018). An analysis of dynamic changes in selected areas of sustainable development of the European Union countries. *Folia Oeconomica Stetinensia*, *18*(1), 93–107. doi:10.2478/foli-2018-0008

Bakija, Cole, & Heim. (2012). *Jobs and Income Growth of Top Earners and the Causes of Changing Income Inequality: Evidence from US Tax Return Data*. Williams College, US Department of Treasury and Indiana University.

Balassone, F., & Franco, D. (2000). *Assessing Fiscal Sustainability: A Review of Methods with a View to EMU*. Rome: Bank of Italy. doi:10.2139srn.2109377

Banerjee, A. V., & Newman, A. F. (1993). Occupational choice and the process of development. *Journal of Political Economy*, *101*(2), 274–298. doi:10.1086/261876

Bangia, A., Diebold, F.X., Schuermann, T., & Stroughair, J.D. (2002). *Modeling liquidity risk with implications for traditional market risk measurement and management*. Academic Press.

Bansal, T. (2005). Building sustainable Value through fiscal and social responsibility. *Ivey Business Journal*. Retrieved from https://iveybusinessjournal.com/publication/building-sustainable-value-through-fiscal-and-social-responsibility/

Barrios, S., & Schaechter, A. (2008). The quality of public finances and economic growth. *Economic Papers*, *337*, 2–49.

Barro, R. J. (2001). Human capital and growth. *The American Economic Review*, *91*(2), 12–17. doi:10.1257/aer.91.2.12

Barro, R. J. (2013). Education and economic growth. *Annals of Economics and Finance*, *14*(2), 301–328.

Barton, T. L., Shenkir, W. G., & Walker, P. L. (2002). *Making enterprise risk management pay off*. Upper Saddle River, NJ: Financial Times/Prentice Hall.

Basel Committee on Banking Supervision (Basel). (2003). *Trends in risk integration and aggregation*. Retrieved on 5/6/2018 from https://www.bis.org/publ/joint07.pdf

Basel World Bank. (2016). *Natural Capital Accounting. Brief*. Washington, DC: The World Bank Group.

Bassanini & Scarpetta. (2002). Does human capital matter for growth in OECD countries? A pooled mean-group approach. *Economics Letters*, *74*(3), 399-405. doi:10.10160165-1765(01)00569-9

Bastiat, F. (1864). *Oeuvres Completes* (Vols. 1–7). Paris: Guillaumin.

Batini, N., Eyraud, L., Forni, L., & Weber, A. (2014). Fiscal multipliers: size, determinants, and use in macroeconomic projections. *IMF. Technical Notes and Manuals*, 4.

Bator, F. M. (1960). *The Question of Government Spending: Public Needs and Private Wants*. New York: Harper and Brothers.

Bawerk & Eugen. (1898). *Karl Marx and the Close of His System: A Criticism* (A. M. Macdonald, Trans.). London: T. Fisher Unwin.

Baxter, R., Bedard, J.C., Hoitash, R., & Yezegel, A. (2013). Enterprise Risk Management Program Quality: Determinants, Value Relevance, and the Financial Crisis. *Contemporary Accounting Research*, *30*(4), 1264–1295. doi:10.1111/j.1911-3846.2012.01194.x

Bayar, Y., Şaşmaz, M. Ü., & Öztürk, Ö. F. (2017). Financial Development and Tax Revenues: Evidence from OECD Countries. *Eurasian Academy of Sciences Eurasian Business & Economic Journal*, *12*, 51–63. doi:10.17740/eas.econ.2017-V12-4

Beasley, M. S., Branson, B. C., & Hancock, B. V. (2015b). *2015 Report on the Current State of Enterprise Risk Oversight: Update on Trends and Opportunities*. Retrieved on 13/6/2018 from https://www.aicpa.org/interestareas/businessindustryandgovernment/resources/erm/downloadabledocuments/aicpa_erm_research_study_2015.pdf

Beasley, M. S., Branson, B., & Pagach, D. (2015a). An analysis of the maturity and strategic impact of investments in ERM. *Journal of Accounting and Public Policy*, *34*(3), 219–243. doi:10.1016/j.jaccpubpol.2015.01.001

Beasley, M. S., Pagach, D., & Warr, R. (2008). Information Conveyed in Hiring Announcements of Senior Executives Overseeing Enterprise-Wide Risk Management Processes. *Journal of Accounting, Auditing & Finance*, *23*(3), 311–332. doi:10.1177/0148558X0802300303

Becker, G. S. (1976). Economic analysis and human behavior. In L. Green & J. Kagel (Eds.), *Advances in Behavioral Sciences* (Vol. 1, pp. 3–17). Chicago: University of Chicago Press, PP.

Becker, G. S., & Murphy, K. M. (1988). A theory of rational addiction. The Journal of Political Economy, 96(4), 675–700.

Beneš, J., Ötker-Robe, İ., & Vávra, D. (2009). *Modeling with macro-financial linkages: credit and policy shocks in emerging markets.* IMF Working Paper, WP/09/123.

Berg & Ostry, (2011a). *Inequality and unsustainable growth: two sides of the same coin?* IMF Staff Discussion Note, 11/08.

Berg & Ostry, (2011b). Equality and efficiency. Is there a trade-off between the two or do they go hand by hand? *Finance & Development, 48*(3), 12-15.

Berg, A. G., & Ostry, J. D. (2011b). Equality and efficiency: Is there a trade-off between the two or do they go hand by hand. IMF. Finance & Development, 48(3), 12-15.

Berg, A., Ostry, J. D., & Zettelmeyer, J. (2011). *What makes growth sustained?* EBRD Working Paper, No. 133.

Berg, A.G., & Ostry, J.D. (2011a). *Inequality and unsustainable growth: two sides of the same coin?* IMF Staff Discussion Note, No. 11/08.

Berg, A., Ostry, J. D., & Zettelmeyer, J. (2012). What makes growth sustained? *Journal of Development Economics, 98*(2), 149–166. doi:10.1016/j.jdeveco.2011.08.002

Berkowitz, J. (2000). *Incorporating Liquidity Risk into VAR Models.* Working Paper. Graduate School of Management, University of California, Irvine.

Berkowitz, J., & O'Brien, J. (2001). *How Accurate are Value-at-Risk Models at Commercial Banks?* Working Paper. US Federal Reserve Board's Finance & Economic.

Bernanke, B. S. (2005). The *global savings glue and the US current account deficit.* Remarks at the Sandridge Lecture. Virginia Association of Economists.

Bernanke, B. (2005). *The Global Savings Glut and the U.S. Current Account Deficit.* Remarks at the Homer Jones Lecture.

Bernanke, B. (2015). *Why Are Interest Rates So Low, Part 3: The Global Savings Glut.* Ben Bernanke's Blog.

Berns, M., Townend, A., Khayat, Z., Balagopal, B., Reeves, M., Hopkins, M., & Kruschwitz, N. (2009). The Business of Sustainability: Imperatives, Advantages, and Actions. Boston: The Boston Consulting Group (BCG).

Bertalanffy, L. (1968). *The General System Theory. Foundation, Development, Applications.* New York: George Braziller.

Berthelot, S., Coulmont, M., & Serret, V. (2012). Do Investors Value Sustainability Reports? A Canadian Study. *Corporate Social Responsibility and Environmental Management, 19*(6), 355–363. doi:10.1002/csr.285

Beschorner, T. (2013). Creating Shared Value: The one-trick pony approach. *Business Ethics Journal Review, 1*(17), 106–112. doi:10.12747/bejr2013.01.17

Biju, P. L., Shalij, P. R., & Prabhushankar, G. V. (2015). Evaluation of customer requirements and sustainability requirements through the application of fuzzy analytic hierarchy process. *Journal of Cleaner Production, 108*, 808–817. doi:10.1016/j.jclepro.2015.08.051

Birman, S. V., Pirondi, E. R. E., & Rodin, E. Y. (2003). Application of DEA to Medical Clinics. *Mathematical and Computer Modelling, 37*(9-10), 923–936. doi:10.1016/S0895-7177(03)00108-0

Blanchard, O., & Summers, L. (2017). *Rethinking stabilization policy. Back to the future. Prepared for the "Rethinking macroeconomic policy" Conference*. Washington, DC: Peterson Institute for International Economics.

Boarini, R., Causa, O., Fleurbaey, M., Grimalda, G., & Woolard, I. (2018). Reducing inequalities and strengthening social cohesion through inclusive growth: a roadmap for action. *Economics. Discussion Papers*. Available at: http://www.economics-ejournal.org/economics/journalarticles/2018-63

Bogdanov, A. A. (1934). Tectology or General Organizational Science. Moscow: Academic Press.

Bold, T., Kimenyi, M., Mwabu, G., Ng'ang'a, A., & Sandefur, J. (2016). *Experimental evidence on scaling up education reforms in Kenya*. Economic Development and Institutions Project Working Paper. Stockholm: Institute for International Economic Studies, Stockholm University.

Bonini, S., & Emerson, J. (2005). *Maximizing Blended Value – Building Beyond the Blended Value Map to Sustainable Investing, Philanthropy and Organizations*. Retrieved from https://pdf-max-blendedvalue.pdf

Bootle, R. P. (2009a). Redrawing. Rethinking the role of the state and markets. Finance & Development, 46(1), 34-35.

Bootle, R. P. (2009b). *The Trouble with Markets: Saving Capitalism from Itself*. London: Nicholas Brealey Publishing.

Bosquet, B. (2000). Environmental Tax Reform: Does it Work? A Survey of the Empirical Evidence. *Ecological Economics*, *34*(1), 19–32.

Bostan, I., Onofrei, M., Dascălu, E. D., Fîrțescu, B., & Toderațcu, C. (2016). Impact of Sustainable Environmental Expenditures Policy on Air Pollution Reduction, During European Integration Framework, *Amfiteatru. Economic Journal (London)*, *18*(42), 286–302.

Boulanger, P. M. (2008). Sustainable development indicators: A scientific challenge, a democratic issue. *SAPIENS*, *1*(1), 45–59.

Boushey, H., & Weller, C. (2008). Has growing inequality contributed to rising household economic distress? *Review of Political Economy*, *20*(1), 1–22. doi:10.1080/09538250701661764

Bowen, H. R. (1953). *Social Responsibilities of the businessman*. New York: Harper & Row.

Boyd, R., & Richerson, P. J. (1985). *Culture and the evolutionary process*. Chicago, IL: University of Chicago Press.

Boz & Tesar. (2019). The global financial cycle. *IMF Economic Review, 67*, 1–3. doi:10.105741308-019-00076-2

Bradbury, K., & Triest, R. (2016). Inequality of opportunity and aggregate economic performance. *Russell Sage Foundation Journal of the Social Sciences*, *2*(2), 178–201. doi:10.7758/rsf.2016.2.2.08

Breidbach, C. F., & Maglio, P. P. (2016). Technology-enabled value co-creation: An empirical analysis of actors, resources, and practices. *Industrial Marketing Management*, *56*(1), 73–85. doi:10.1016/j.indmarman.2016.03.011

Breitung, J., & Candelon, B. (2006). Testing for Short and Long-Run Causality: A Frequency-Domain Approach. *Journal of Econometrics*, *132*(2), 363–378. doi:10.1016/j.jeconom.2005.02.004

Broniewicz, E., & Domańska, W. (2016). Rachunki wydatków na ochronę środowiska (EPEA) jako moduł Europejskich Rachunków Ekonomicznych Środowiska, Optimum. *Studia Ekonomiczne*, *1*(79), 165–181. doi:10.15290/ose.2016.01.79.11

Brown & Hunter. (2004). Democracy and human capital formation. *Comparative Political Studies, 37*(7), 842-864. doi:10.1177/0010414004266870

Brue, S. L., McConnell, C. R., & Flynn, S. M. (2013). Essentials of Economics (3rd ed.). New York: McGraw-Hill.

Brueckner, M., Dabla-Norris, E., Gradstein, M., & Lederman, D. (2017). *The Rise of the Middle Class and Economic Growth in ASEAN*. Washington, DC: The World Bank; doi:10.1596/1813-9450-8068

Brzozowski, T. T. (2010). Sustainable Development strategy as a challenge for the processes of transformation in industry and services. *Prace Komisji Geografii Przemysłu, 15*, 219–228.

Buckholtz J. W., Marois, R. (2012). The roots of modern justice: cognitive and neural foundations of social norms and their enforcement. *Nature Neuroscience, 15*(5), 655—661.

Budzier, A., & Flyvbjerg, B. (2012). Overspend? Late? Failure? What the data says about IT project risk in the public sector. In Commonwealth Governance Handbook 2012/13: Democracy, Development, and Public Administration (pp. 145–47). London: Commonwealth Secretariat.

Bunde, A., & Kantelhardt, J. (2011). *Diffusion and Conduction in Percolation. Diffusion in Condensed Matters*. Berlin: Springer.

Buxel, H., Esenduran, G., & Griffin, S. (2015). Strategic sustainability: Creating business value with life cycle analysis. *Business Horizons, 58*(1), 109–122. doi:10.1016/j.bushor.2014.09.004

Buying Green. A Handbook on green public procurement. (2016). (3rd ed.). Publications Office of the European Union.

Buying Social, A Guide to Taking Account of Social Considerations into Public Procurement. (2011). Publications Office of the European Union.

Card & Di Nardo. (2002). Skill-biased technological change and rising wage inequality: some problems and puzzles. *Journal of Labour Economics, 2002*(4).

Carroll, A. B. (2008). A History of Corporate Social Responsibility: Concepts and Practices. *The Oxford handbook of corporate social responsibility*, 19-46. Retrieved from: https://www.academia.edu /860777/A_history_of_corporate_social_responsibility_concepts_and_practices

Carroll, A. B. (1991). The pyramid of corporate social responsibility: Toward the moral management of organizational stakeholders. *Business Horizons, 34*(4), 39–48. doi:10.1016/0007-6813(91)90005-G

Carroll, A. B. (2015). Corporate social responsibility: The centerpiece of competing and complementary frameworks. *Organizational Dynamics, 44*(2), 87–96. doi:10.1016/j.orgdyn.2015.02.002

Carson, R. T., Mitchell, R. C., Hanemann, M., Kopp, R. J., Presser, S., & Ruud, P. A. (2003). Contingent Valuation and Lost Passive Use: Damages from the Exxon Valdez Oil Spill. *Environmental and Resource Economics, 25*(3), 257–286. doi:10.1023/A:1024486702104

Casualty Actuarial Society Enterprise Risk Management Committee (CAS). (2003). *Overview of Enterprise Risk Management*. Retrieved on 4/6/2018 from https://www.casact.org/pubs/forum/03sforum/03sf099.pdf

Cerra, V. (2018). The global financial crises: 10 years on, why many still feel the pain. IMF Research Perspectives, 19(1).

Cerra, V., & Saxena, S. C. (2017). *Booms, crises, and recoveries: a new paradigm of the business cycle and its policy implications*. IMF Working Paper, WP/17/250.

Cescon, F., Costantini, A., & Rossi, G. (2013). *The influence of Business strategy and Ownership on Management accounting innovations and Risk management techniques: An empirical analysis in large manufacturing companies in Italy*. Retrieved on 20/05/2019 from https://www.uniud.it/it/ateneo-uniud/ateneo-uniud-organizzazione/dipartimenti/dies/ricerca/allegati_wp/wp_2013/wp02_2013.pdf

Chapple, W., & Moon, J. (2005). Corporate social responsibility in Asia: A seven country study of CSR website reporting. *Business & Society*, *44*, 415–441. doi:10.1177/0007650305281658

Charnes, A., Cooper, W., & Lewin, A. Y. S. L. (1994). Data Envelopment Analysis – theory, methodology and applications. London: Kluwer Academic Publishers.

Checherita-Westphal, C., & Rother, P. (2012). The impact of high government debt on economic growth and its channels: An empirical investigation for the Euro Area. *European Economic Review*, *56*(7), 1392–1405. doi:10.1016/j.euroecorev.2012.06.007

Chen, G., & Chen, S. (2016). Financial Development, Labor Participation, and Employment in Urban China. *Emerging Markets Finance & Trade*, *52*, 754–764. doi:10.1080/1540496X.2016.1116285

Cheung, S. N. S. (1978). *The Myth of Social Costs. A Critique of Welfare, Economics and the Implications for Public Policy*. London: Institute of Economic Affairs.

Chiu, C.-Y., Gelfand, M. J., Yamagishi, T., Shteynberg, G., & Wan, C. (2010). Intersubjective culture: the role of intersubjective perceptions in cross-cultural research. Perspectives on Psychological Science, 5(4), 482—493 doi:10.1177/1745691610375562

Christiano, L., Eichenbaum, M., & Rebelo, S. (2011). When is the government spending multiplier large? *Journal of Political Economy*, *119*(1), 78–121.

Christiansen, N. (2014). 6 steps to create shared value in your company. *Greenbiz*. Retrieved from: http://www.greenbiz.com/blog/2014/06/20/6-stepsimplement-csv-your-company

Cingano, F. (2014). *Trends in income inequality and its impact on economic growth.* OECD Social, Employment and Migration Working Papers, No. 163. Retrieved from http: // www.oecd-ilibrary.org/docserver/download/5jxrjncwxv6j.pdf?expires=1439464823&id=id&accname=guest&checksum=EA020172B6EE209A3A7A70E3D3FC5D1F.

Cingano, F. (2014). *Trends in income inequality and its impact on economic growth.* OECD Social, Employment, and Migration Working Papers, No. 163.

Clark, D. N. (1997). Strategic management tool usage: A comparative study. *Strategic Change*, *6*(7), 417–427. doi:10.1002/(SICI)1099-1697(199711)6:7<417::AID-JSC281>3.0.CO;2-9

Coase, R. H. (1937). The nature of the firm. Economica, 4(16), 368-405. doi:10.1111/j.1468-0335.1937.tb00002.x

Coase, R. H. (1960). The Problem of Social Cost. *The Journal of Law & Economics*, *3*, 1–44. doi:10.1086/466560

Coase, R. H. (1972). Industrial organization: a proposal for research. In V. Fuchs (Ed.), *Policy Issues and Research Opportunities in Industrial Organization* (Vol. 3, pp. 59–73). Cambridge, MA: NBER.

Coase, R. H. (1993). *The Firm, the Market and the Law*. Chicago: University of Chicago Press.

Cobb, C., Glickman, M., & Cheslog, C. (2001). *The genuine progress indicator 2001 Update*. Edefining Progress Issue Brief. Available online: URL https://www.researchgate.net/profile/Clifford_Cobb/publication/237470296_THE_GENUINE_PROGRESS_INDICATOR_2000_UPDATE/links/56fe2d0a08aee995dde673d1.pdf

Cochrane, J. H. (2005). *Asset Pricing*. Princeton, NJ: Princeton University Press.

Comin, D., & Nanda, R. (2019). Financial development and technology diffusion. *IMF Economic Review*, *67*(2), 395–419. doi:10.105741308-019-00078-0

Committee of the Sponsoring Organizations (COSO). (2004). *Enterprise Risk Management, Integrated Framework (Executive Summary Framework).* Retrived on 11/6/2018 from https://www.coso.org/Documents/COSO-ERM-Executive-Summary.pdf

Committee of the Sponsoring Organizations (COSO). (2017). *Enterprise Risk Management - Integrating with Strategy and Performance Executive Summary.* Retrieved on 11/6/2018 from https://www.coso.org/Documents/2017-COSO-ERM-Integrating-with-Strategy-and-Performance-Executive-Summary.pdf

Commons, J. (1931). Institutional economics. American Economic Review, 21(4), 607-619.

Commons, J. R. (1934). *Institutional Economics. Its Place in Political Economy.* New Brunswick, NJ: Transactions Publishers.

Communication from the Commission to the European Parliament. the Council, the European Economic and Social Committee and the Committee of the Regions Renewed social agenda: Opportunities, access and solidarity in 21st century Europe, COM (2008) 412 final, Brussels.

Communication from the Commission to the European Parliament. the Council, the European Economic and Social Committee and the Committee of the Regions. Public procurement for a better environment COM (2008) 400 final, Brussels.

Communication from the Commission. (2020). *EUROPE 2020 A strategy for smart, sustainable and inclusive growth.* Brussels: COM. (Original work published 2010)

Costa, E., & Pesci, C. (2016). Social impact measurement: Why do stakeholders matter? *Sustainability Accounting. Management and Policy Journal*, *7*(1), 99–124.

Cottarelli, C., & Jaramillo, L. (2013). Walking hand in hand: Fiscal policy and growth in advanced economies. *Review of Economics and Institutions*, *4*(2), 1–25. doi:10.5202/rei.v4i2.113

Cournède, Denk, & Hoeller. (2015). *Finance and inclusive growth.* OECD Economic Policy Papers. No. 14.

Cox, D. R. (1972). Regression Models and Life-tables (with discussion). *Journal of the Royal Statistical Society. Series B. Methodological*, *2*(2), 187–220. doi:10.1111/j.2517-6161.1972.tb00899.x

Coyle, D. (2017). Rethinking GDP. *Finance & Development, 54*(1), 16.

Crafts, N. (2017). Whither economic growth? Finance & Development, 54(1).

Cramer, A., Allison-Hope, D., Taylor, A., Richmond, B., & Bancilhon, C. (2018). *Redefining Sustainable Business. Management for a rapidly changing world.* BSR. Retrieved from https://www.bsr.org/reports/BSR_Redefining_Sustainable_Business.pdf

Crane, A., Palazzo, G., Spence, L. J., & Matten, D. (2014). Contesting the Value of "Creating Shared Value.". *California Management Review*, *56*(2), 130–153.

Crockford, G. N. (1982). The bibliography and history of risk management: Some preliminary observations. *Geneva Papers on Risk & Insurance*, *7*(2), 169–179. doi:10.1057/gpp.1982.10

Cuberes & Teignier. (2016). Aggregate effects of gender gaps in the labor market: a quantitative estimate. *Journal of Human Capital, 10*(1), 1–32.

Cutler, D. M., & Summers, L. H. (1987). *The Costs of Conflict Resolution and Financial Distress: Evidence from the Texaco-Pennzoil Litigation.* NBER Working Paper No. 2418 (Also Reprint No. r1231). Retrieved on 5/6/2018 from http://www.nber.org/papers/w2418

Daly, H. E., & Cobb, J. B. (1989). *For the Common Good. Redirecting the Economy toward Community, Environment, and a Sustainable Future*. Boston, MA: Beacon Press.

Dandan, M. M. (2011). Government expenditures and economic growth in Jordan. *IPEDR, 4*, 467–471.

Dao, M. Q. (2017). Public Policies, Institutions, and Economic Growth in Low-Income and Lower Middle-Income Countries: Further Empirical Evidence. *Adv. Econ. Bus*, *5*(8), 440–447. doi:10.13189/aeb.2017.050802

de Rosa, F. (2007). Zamówienia publiczne a partnerstwo publiczno-prywatne [Public Procurement and public-private partnership]. DIESIS.

De Smedt, B. (2014). Advances in the use of neuroscience methods in research on learning and instruction. *Frontline Learning Research*, *2*(4), 7–14.

De Viti de Marko, A. (1936). First Principles of Public Finance. London: Jonathan Cape.

Deloitte. (2013). *Exploring Strategic Risk*. Retrieved on 2/6/2018 from https://www2.deloitte.com/content/dam/Deloitte/global/Documents/Governance-Risk-Compliance/dttl-grc-exploring-strategic-risk.pdf

Demetriades, O. P., & Hussein, A. K. (1996). Does financial development cause economic growth? Time-series evidence from 16 countries. *Journal of Development Economics*, *51*(2), 387–411. doi:10.1016/S0304-3878(96)00421-X

Demiańczuk, T. (2018). *Powstaje EKOpark w Ursusie*. Retrieved from http://www.um.warszawa.pl/aktualnosci/powstaje-ekopark-w-ursusie

Demirgüç-Kunt, A. (2017). Hot Off The Press. The Global Financial Development Report 2017/2018: Bankers without Borders.

Demsetz, H. (1967). Toward a theory of property rights. American Economic Review, 57(2), 347-359.

Desender, K. (2007). On the Determinants of Enterprise Risk Management Implementation. *Managing Worldwide Operations & Communications with Information Technology, 2007 IRMA International Conference*, 115-118.

Diamond, J. (2003). *Performance-budgeting: Managing the reform proces*. IMF Working Paper, No. 33.

Dickinson, G. (2001). Enterprise Risk Management: Its Origins and Conceptual Foundation. *The Geneva Papers on Risk and Insurance. Issues and Practice*, *26*(3), 360–366. doi:10.1111/1468-0440.00121

DiMaggio, P. J., & Powell, W. W. (1983). The iron cage revisited: Institutional isomorphism and collective rationality in organizational fields. *American Sociological Review*, *48*(2), 147–160. doi:10.2307/2095101

Dinkelman, T. (2011). The effects of rural electrification on employment: New evidence from South Africa. *The American Economic Review*, *101*(7), 3078–3108. doi:10.1257/aer.101.7.3078

Directive 2004/17/EC of the European Parliament and of the Council of 31 March 2004 coordinating the procurement procedures by entities operating in the water, energy, transport and postal services sectors.

Directive 2004/18/EC of the European Parliament and of the Council of 31 March 2004 on the coordination of procedures for the award of public works contracts, public supply contracts and public service contracts.

Directive 2009/33 / EC of the European Parliament and of the Council of 23 April 2009 on the promotion of clean and energy-efficient road transport vehicles.

Directive 2010/30/EU of the European Parliament and of the Council of 19 May 2010 on the indication by labeling and standard product information of the consumption of energy and other resources by energy-related products.

Directive 2014/23/EU of 26 February 2014 on the award of concession contracts.

Directive 2014/24/EC of the European Parliament and of the Council of 26 February 2014 on public procurement and repealing Directive 2004/18/EC.

Directive 2014/25/EU of 26 February 2014 on procurement by entities operating in the water, energy, transport and postal services sectors.

Dixit, A., & Pindyck, R. (1994). *Investment Under Uncertainty*. Princeton, NJ: Princeton University Press.

Do Valle, P. O., Pintassilgo, P., Matias, A., & Andre, F. (2012). Tourist Attitudes Towards an Accommodation Tax Earmarked for Environmental Protection: A Survey in the Algarve. *Tourism Management*, *33*(2), 1408–1416. doi:10.1016/j.tourman.2012.01.003

Doctor, R. N., Newton, D. P., & Pearson, A. (2001). Managing uncertainty in research and development. *Technovation*, *21*(2), 79–90. doi:10.1016/S0166-4972(00)00026-2

Dodd, R. (2007). Subprime: tentacles of a crisis, *Finance & Development, 44,* 15–19.

Dolan, S. L., & Garcia, S. (1999). Managing by Values in the Next Millennium: Cultural Redesign for Strategic Organizational Change. *Journal of Economics*, *5*, 1–16.

Domagała, A. (2009). *Zastosowanie metody Data Envelopment Analysis do badania efektywności europejskich giełd papierów wartościowych*. Uniwersytet Ekonomiczny w Poznaniu.

Draper, N. R., & Smith, H. (1973). *Analiza regresji stosowana*. Warszawa: Państwowe Wydawnictwo Naukowe.

Duflo, E. (2012). Women empowerment and economic development. *Journal of Economic Literature*, *50*(4), 1051–1079. doi:10.1257/jel.50.4.1051

Durusu-Ciftci, D., Ispir, M. S., & Yetkiner, H. (2017). Financial development and economic growth: Sometheory and More Evidence. *Journal of Policy Modeling*, *39*(2), 290–306. doi:10.1016/j.jpolmod.2016.08.001

Dusiński, A. (2003). Zasady etycznego postępowania w firmie. In W. Gasparski, A. Lewicka-Strzałecka, B. Rok, & G. Szulczewski (Eds.), Europejskie standardy etyki i społecznej odpowiedzialności biznesu (pp. 167-177). Warszawa, Poland: Wydawnictwo Wyższej Szkoły Przedsiębiorczości i Zarządzania im. Leona Koźmińskiego.

Easterly, W., Islam, R., & Stiglitz, J. E. (2000). Shaken and stirred: explaining growth volatility. In *Macroeconomic Paradigms for Less Developed Countries*. The World Bank. Retrieved from: http://www.worldbank.org/research/growth/growth%20volatility%20jan%202000.html

EBRD. (2018). *Transition Report 2017-2018: Sustaining Growth*. EBRD.

EBRD. (2018). *Transition Report 2017-2018: Sustaining Growth*. EBRD. Retrieved from http://www.tr-ebrd.com

Eganyan, A. (2015). *Investment in Infrastructure: Money, Projects, Motivation. PPP, Concessions, Project Financing*. Moscow: Alpina Publisher Inc.

Égert, B. (2012). *Public debt, economic growth and nonlinear effects: myth or reality?* OECD Economics Department Working Papers, 993, October. OECD Publishing.

Égert, B. (2015). Public debt, economic growth and nonlinear effects: Myth or reality? *Journal of Macroeconomics*, *43*, 226–238. doi:10.1016/j.jmacro.2014.11.006

Eggertsson, Th. (1990). *Economic Behavior and Institutions: Principles of Neo-institutional Economics*. Cambridge, UK: Cambridge University Press. doi:10.1017/CBO9780511609404

Emerson, J. (2003). The Blended Value Proposition: Integrating social and financial returns. *California Management Review, 45*(4), 36. Retrieved from: https://wuecampus2.uniwuerzburg.de /moodle/pluginfile.php/235946/mod_resource/content/0/Emerson03%20-%20The%20Blended% 20Value%20Proposition%20%20Integrating%20Social%20and%20 Financial%20Returns%20(California%20 Management%20Review).pdf

EPF. (2019). *Sustainable Development Goals*. Retrieved April 10, 2019, from http://www.eu-patient.eu/campaign/access-to-healthcare/sustainable-development-goals/

Epstein, M. J., & Roy, M. J. (2001). Sustainability in Action: Identifying and Measuring the Key Performance Drivers. *Long Range Planning, 34*(5), 585–604. doi:10.1016/S0024-6301(01)00084-X

Erickson, M., Mayhew, B. W., & Felix, W. L. Jr. (2000). Why Do Audits Fail? Evidence from Lincoln Savings and Loan. *Journal of Accounting Research, 38*(1), 165–194. doi:10.2307/2672927

Esteve-Volart, B. (2004). *Gender discrimination and growth: Theory and evidence from India. Development Economics Paper, 42*. Suntory Centre, Suntory and Toyota International Centres for Economics and Related Disciplines, London School of Economics and Political Science.

European Commission. (2017). Sustainability Of Public Finances. *EU Commission*. Available at: Https://Ec.Europa.Eu/Info/Business-Economy-Euro/Economic-And-Fiscal-Policy-Coordination/Eu-Economic-Governance-Monitoring-Prevention-Correction/European-Semester/Thematic-Factsheets/Fiscal-Stability_pl

European Environment Agency. (1996). *Environmental Taxes. Implementation and Environmental Effectiveness*. Author.

Eurostat. (2017). *Energy, Transport and Environment Indicators*. Luxembourg: Publications Office of the European Union.

Eurostat. (2019). *Sustainable development indicators*. Retrieved April 9, 2019, from https://ec.europa.eu/eurostat/web/sdi/main-tables

Evaluation Report "Impact and Effectiveness of EU Public Procurement Legislation". Commission Staff Working Paper, European Commission, DGInternal Market SEC (2011) 853. (n.d.). Functional and Utility Program (PFU) of the public procurement contract. Retrieved from http://zim.lodz.bip-e.pl/zim/zamowienia-publiczne

Evans, S., Fernando, L., & Miying, Y. (2017). Sustainable Value Creation – From Concept Towards Implementation, In R. G. Stark, & J. Bonvoisin (Eds.), Sustainable Manufacturing, Challenges, Solutions and Implementation Perspectives. Springer.

Evans, D. K., & Yuan, F. (2017). Economic returns to interventions that increase learning. In *World Development Report 2018, Background paper*. Washington, DC: The World Bank Group.

Farrell, M., & Gallagher, R. (2014). The Valuation Implications of Enterprise Risk Management Maturity. *The Journal of Risk and Insurance, 82*(3), 625–657. doi:10.1111/jori.12035

Ferreira, L. Lugo, & Ozler. (2014). *Inequality of opportunity and economic growth: a cross-country analysis*. World Bank Policy Research Working Paper, 6915.

Figge, F. (2001). Environmental Value Added: A new measure for measuring eco-efficiency. *Journal of Applied Environmental Research, 14*(1-4), 184–197.

Figge, F., & Hahn, T. (2004). Sustainable Value Added—Measuring corporate contributions to sustainability beyond eco-efficiency. *Ecological Economics, 48*(2), 173–187. doi:10.1016/j.ecolecon.2003.08.005

Figge, F., & Hahn, T. (2004). Value-oriented impact assessment: The economics of a new approach to impact assessment. *Journal of Environmental Planning and Management, 47*(6), 921–941. doi:10.1080/0964056042000284901

Figge, F., & Hahn, T. (2005). The Cost of Sustainability Capital and the Creation of Sustainable Value. *Journal of Applied Environmental Research, 14*(1-4), 184–197.

Fijałkowska, J. (2016). Raportowanie informacji niefinansowych zgodnie z nową dyrektywą UE 2014/95/UE jako wyzwanie dla przedsiębiorstw. In E. Kożuchowska, (Ed.), Rachunkowość na rzecz zrównoważonego rozwoju. Gospodarka - etyka – środowisko (pp. 30-40). Wrocław, Poland: Wydawnictwo Uniwersytetu Ekonomicznego we Wrocławiu.

Filipiak, B. Z. (2014). Challenges of Sustainable Development in the New Financial Perspective—Financial Approach. In H. Witte (Ed.), *Nachhaltigkeit, ökonomiche Gleichgewichte und Wertschöpfung* (pp. 169–192). Bahia Blanca, Argentina: Edi UNS.

Filmer, D., Rogers, H., Angrist, N., & Sabarwal, S. (2018). *Learning-adjusted years of schooling (LAYS): Defining a new macro measure of education.* Policy Research Working Paper, 8591. Washington, DC: World Bank.

Finn, A., & Leibbrandt, M. (2013). *Mobility and inequality in the first three waves of NIDS.* SALDRU Working Paper, No. 120, and NIDS Discussion Paper, No. 2013/2. SALDRU, University of Cape Town.

Florea, R., & Florea, R. (2016). Internal Audit and Risk Management. ISO 31000 and ERM Approaches. *Economy Transdisciplinarity Cognition, 19*(1), 72–77.

Florio, C., & Leoni, G. (2017). Enterprise risk management and firm performance: The Italian case. *The British Accounting Review, 49*(1), 56–74. doi:10.1016/j.bar.2016.08.003

Förster, M., Llena-Nozal, A., & Nafilyan, V. (2014). *Trends in top incomes and their taxation in OECD countries.* OECD Social, Employment and Migration Working Papers, No. 159. doi:10.1787/5jz43jhlz87f-en

Fraser, J. R. S., & Simkins, B. J. (2016). The Challenges of and solutions for implementing enterprise risk management. *Business Horizons, 59*(6), 689–698. doi:10.1016/j.bushor.2016.06.007

Friedman, M. (1962). *Capitalism and Freedom.* Chicago: Chicago University Press.

Frigo, M. L., & Anderson, R. J. (2011). Strategic Risk Management: A Foundation for Improving Enterprise Risk Management and Governance. *Journal of Corporate Accounting & Finance, 22*, 81–88. doi:10.1002/jcaf.20677

Frisch, R. (1933). Propagation Problems and Impulse Problems in Dynamic Economics. In *Economic Essays in Honour of Gustav Cassel.* London: Allen and Urwin.

Fullwiler, S. T. (2015). *Sustainable finance: Building a more general theory of finance.* Binzagr Institute for Sustainable Prosperity, Working Paper No. 106.

Fullwiler, S. T. (2015). *Sustainable Finance: Building a More General Theory of Finance.* Working Paper, 106. Binzagr Institute for Sustainable Prosperity.

G20/OECD/WB. (2018). *Stocktake of tools and instruments related to infrastructure as an asset class.* G20/OECD/WB. Background Report.

Galor, Moav, & Vollrath. (2006). *Inequality in land ownership, the emergence of human capital promoting institutions, and the great divergence.* SSRN-id670883.

Galor, O., & Moav, O. (2004). From physical to human capital accumulation: Inequality and the process of development. *The Review of Economic Studies, 71*(4), 1001–1026. doi:10.1111/0034-6527.00312

Galor, O., & Zeira, J. (1993). Income distribution and macroeconomics. *The Review of Economic Studies, 60*(1), 35–52. doi:10.2307/2297811

Garba, T., & Abdullahi, S. Y. (2013). Public Expenditure and Economic Growth: An Application of Cointegration and Granger Causality Tests on Nigeria. *J. Econ. Soc., 15*, 1–30.

García, J. L., Heckman, J. J., Leaf, D. E., & Prados, M. J. (2016). *The Life-Cycle Benefits of an Influential Early Childhood Program*. NBER Working Paper 22993. National Bureau of Economic Research.

Garcia-Escribano, M., & Liu, C. Y. (2017). *Expenditure assessment tool (EAT). Fiscal Affairs Department Technical Notes and Manuals, 17/06*. Washington, DC: International Monetary Fund.

Garcia, R., Renault, E., & Tsafack, G. (2007). Proper Conditioning for Coherent VaR in Portfolio Management. *Management Science, 53*(3), 483–494. doi:10.1287/mnsc.1060.0632

Garner, S., & Littlejohns, P. (2011). Disinvestment from low value clinical interventions: NICEly done? *BMJ (Clinical Research Ed.), 343*(jul27 2), d4519. doi:10.1136/bmj.d4519 PMID:21795239

Gates, S. (2006). Incorporating strategic risk into enterprise risk management: A survey of current corporate practice. *Journal of Applied Corporate Finance, 18*(4), 81–90. doi:10.1111/j.1745-6622.2006.00114.x

Gatnar, E. (2008). *Multiple-model approach to classification and regression*. Warsaw: PWN.

Gatzert, N., & Martin, M. (2013). *Determinants and Value of Enterprise Risk Management: Empirical Evidence from the Literature*. Working Paper. Department for Insurance Economics and Risk Management, Friedrich-Alexander-University (FAU) of Erlangen-Nürnberg. Retrieved on 5/6/2018 from http://citeseerx.ist.psu.edu/viewdoc/download?doi=10.1.1.888.6403&rep=rep1&type=pdf

Geels, F. (2011). The multi-level perspective on sustainability transitions: Responses to sev-en criticisms. *Environmental Innovation and Societal Transitions, 1*(1), 24–40. doi:10.1016/j.eist.2011.02.002

Geweke, J. (1982). Measurement of Lineer Dependence and Feedback Between Multiple Time Series. *Journal of the American Statistical Association, 77*(378), 304–324. doi:10.1080/01621459.1982.10477803

Giosi, A., Testarmata, S., Brunelli, S., & Staglianň, B. (2012). *Does the Quality of Public Finance Enhance Fiscal Discipline in the European Union? A Cross-Country Analysis*. Milano: McGraw-Hill Education.

Glewwe, P. W., Maiga, E., & Zheng, H. (2014). The Contribution of Education to Economic Growth: A Review of the Evidence, with Special Attention and an Application to Sub-Saharan Africa. *World Development, 59*, 379–393. doi:10.1016/j.worlddev.2014.01.021

Global Footprint Network (2015). *NPV+: Making the Economic Case for Sustainable Investments in Maryland*. Author.

Global Infrastructure Outlook. (2017). *Infrastructure Investment Needs: 50 countries, 7 sectors to 2040. July, A G20 Initiative*. Sydney: Global Infrastructure Hub.

Global Infrastructure Outlook. (2018). *Infrastructure Investment Need in the Compact with Africa countries. Prepared by Oxford Economics for Global Infrastructure Hub. A G20 Initiative*. Sydney: Global Infrastructure Hub.

Global Reporting Initiative. (2006). Amsterdam: GRI Sustainability Reporting Guidelines, Version 3 Global Reporting Initiative.

Goldin, C., & Katz, L. (2008). *The Race between Education and Technology*. Belknap Press for Harvard University Press.

Goldsmith, R. W. (1969). *Financial structure and development*. New Haven, CT: Yale University Press.

Gonzales, C., Jain-Chandra, S., Kochhar, K., Newiak, M., & Zeinullayev, T. (2017). Tackling income inequality. In K. Kochhar, S. Jain-Chandra, & M. Newiak (Eds.), *Women, Work, and Economic Growth: Leveling the Playing Field* (pp. 49–72). Washington, DC: International Monetary Fund.

Goodman, L. A. (1986). Some useful Extensions of the Usual Correspondence Analysis Approach and Usual Log-Linear Models Approach in the analysis of Contingency Tables. *International Statistical Review, 54*(3), 243–309. doi:10.2307/1403053

Gordon, L. A., Loeb, M. P., & Tseng, C. (2009). Enterprise risk management and firm performance: A contingency perspective. *Journal of Accounting and Public Policy, 28*(4), 301–327. doi:10.1016/j.jaccpubpol.2009.06.006

Gouldner, A. (1960). The norm of reciprocity: A preliminary statement. *American Sociological Review, 25*(2), 161–178. doi:10.2307/2092623

Grace, M. F., Leverty, J. T., Phillips, R. D., & Shimpi, P. (2015). The Value of Investing in Enterprise Risk Management. *The Journal of Risk and Insurance, 82*(2), 289–316. doi:10.1111/jori.12022

Graczyk, A. (2009). Ekonomiczne podstawy ochrony środowiska. *Biuletyn Polskiego Towarzystwa Ekonomicznego, 1*(39), 4–11.

Grądalski, F. (2006). *System podatkowy w świetle teorii optymalnego opodatkowania.* Warszawa: Szkoła Główna Handlowa w Warszawie.

Granger, C. W. J. (1969). Investigating Causal Relationship by Econometric Models and Cross-Spectral Methods. *Econometrica, 37*(3), 424–438. doi:10.2307/1912791

Greenacre, M. (1984). *Theory Applications of Correspondence Analysis.* London: Academic Press.

Greenacre, M. (1994). Multiple and Joint Correspondence Analysis. In M. Greenacre & J. Blasius (Eds.), *Correspondence Analysis in Social Sciences. Recent Developments and Applications.* San Diego, CA: Academic Press.

Greenacre, M., & Hastie, T. (1987). The geometric Interpretation of Correspondence Analysis. *Journal of the American Statistical Association, 82*(398), 437–447. doi:10.1080/01621459.1987.10478446

Gruber, J., Milligan, K., & Wise, D. A. (2009). *Social security programs and retirement around the world: the relationship to youth employment, introduction and summary.* NBER Working Paper, No. 14647

Guckenheimer, J. (1973). Bifurcation and catastrophe', Proc. International Sympos. In M. Peixoto (Ed.), *Dynamical Systems.* New York: Academic Press.

Guide to the application of the European Union rules on state aid, public procurement and the internal market to services of general economic interest, and in particular to social services of general interest SWD (2013) 53 final/2, European Commission, Brussels.

Guillemette, Y., & Turner, D. (2018). *The long view: scenarios for the world economy to 2060. OECD. Economic Policy Paper, May, No. 22.* Paris: OECD Publishing.

Gupta, D. K. (1990). *The Economics of Political Violence. The Effect of Political Instability on Economic Growth.* New York: Praeger.

Guzik, B. (2009). *Podstawowe modele DEA w badaniu efektywności gospodarczej i społecznej.* Wydawnictwo Uniwersytetu Ekonomicznego w Poznaniu.

Haibara, T. (2009). Environmental Funds, Public Abatement, and Welfare. *Environmental and Resource Economics, 44*(2), 167–177. doi:10.100710640-009-9276-6

Haken, H. (1977). *Synergetics. An Introduction*. Berlin: Springer - Verlag.

Halpern, D. (2015). *Inside the nudge unit: How small changes can make a big difference*. New York, NY: Random House.

Hanushek, E. A. (1979). Conceptual and empirical issues in the estimation of educational production functions. *Journal of Human Resources, 14*(3), 351–88.

Hanushek, E. A., Lavy, V., & Hitomi, K. (2008). Do students care about school quality? Determinants of dropout behavior in developing countries. *Journal of Human Capital*, *2*(1), 69–105. doi:10.1086/529446

Hanushek, E. A., & Woessmann, L. (2008). The role of cognitive skills in economic development. *Journal of Economic Literature*, *46*(3), 607–668. doi:10.1257/jel.46.3.607

Hanushek, E. A., & Woessmann, L. (2012). Do better schools lead to more growth? Cognitive skills, economic outcomes, and causation. *Journal of Economic Growth*, *17*(4), 267–321. doi:10.100710887-012-9081-x

Hanushek, E. A., & Woessmann, L. (2015). *The Knowledge Capital of Nations: Education and the Economics of Growth*. Cambridge, MA: MIT Press. doi:10.7551/mitpress/9780262029179.001.0001

Hanushek, E., & Woessmann, L. (2010). Education and economic growth. In D. J. Brewer & P. J. McEwan (Eds.), *Economics of Education*. Amsterdam: Elsevier.

Hardin, G. (1968). The Tragedy of the Commons. *Science, 162*(3859), 1243-1248. Retrieved from http://science.sciencemag.org/content/162/3859/1243

Harrington, S. E., Niehaus, G., & Risko, K. J. (2002). Enterprise Risk Management: The Case Of United Grain Growers. *Journal of Applied Corporate Finance*, *14*(4), 71–81. doi:10.1111/j.1745-6622.2002.tb00450.x

Harris, C., Green, S., Ramsey, W., Allen, K., & King, R. (2017). Sustainability in Health care by allocating resources effectively (SHARE) 1: Introducing a series of papers reporting an investigation of disinvestment in a local healthcare setting. *BMC Health Services Research*, *17*(1), 1–13. doi:10.118612913-017-2210-7 PMID:28472962

Hart, S. (1995). A natural resource-based view of the firm. *Academy of Management Review*, *20*(4), 986–1014. doi:10.5465/amr.1995.9512280033

Hart, S. L., & Milstein, M. B. (2003). Creating sustainable value. *The Academy of Management Executive*, *17*(2), 56–69.

Hart, S. L., & Milstein, M. B. (2003). Creating Sustainable Value. *The Academy of Management Executive*, *17*(2), 56–69. doi:10.5465/AME.2003.10025194

Hartwig, R., & Till Grüne-Yanoff, T. (2017). Nudging and Boosting: Steering or Empowering Good Decisions. *Perspectives on Psychological Science*, *12*(6), 1–14. doi:10.1177/1745691617702496 PMID:28792862

Hatzius, J., Hooper, P., Mishkin, F., Schoenholtz, K. L., & Watson, M. W. (2010). *Financial conditions indexes: a fresh look after the financial crisis.* NBER Working Paper Series, 16150. Retrieved from: http://www.nber.org/papers/w16150

Hausmann, R., Pritchett, L., & Rodrik, D. (2005). Growth accelerations. *Journal of Economic Growth, 10*(4), 303–29.

Hausmann, R., Pritchett, L., & Rodrik, D. (2005). Growth accelerations. *Journal of Economic Growth*, *10*(4), 303–329. doi:10.100710887-005-4712-0

Hegel, G. W. F. (1967). *Hegel's Philosophy of Right* (B. T. M. Knox, Trans.). Oxford, UK: Oxford University Press.

Helbling, C. (1991). *Unternehmensbewertung und Steuern*. IDW Verlag.

Helpman, El. (2004). *The Mystery of Economic Growth*. Harvard University Press.

Henderson, V. (2014). *Black–Scholes Model*. Wiley. doi:10.1002/9781118445112.stat04690

Henschel, T. (2010). Typology of risk management practices: An empirical investigation into German SMEs. *International Journal of Entrepreneurship and Small Business*, *9*(3), 264–294. doi:10.1504/IJESB.2010.031922

Hillson, D. (2003). *Effective Opportunity Management for Projects: Exploiting Positive Risk*. Monticello, NY: Marcel Dekker, Inc. doi:10.1201/9780203913246

Hisata, Y., & Yamai, Y. (2000). *Research toward the practical application of liquidity risk evaluation methods*. Discussion Paper. Institute for Monetary and Economic Studies, Bank of Japan.

Hochman & Rodgers. (1969). Pareto optimal redistribution. *American Economic Review, 59*, 542-557.

Hodgson, G. M. (2003). The mystery of the routine. The Darwinian destiny of an evolutionary theory of economic change. Revue Économique, 54(2), 355-384. doi:10.2307/3503007

Hodgson, G. M. (1988). *Economics and Institutions. A Manifesto for a Modern Institutional Economics*. Philadelphia, PA: University of Pennsylvania Press, Polity Press. doi:10.9783/9781512816952

Holzinger, K., Knill, C., & Sommererb, T. (2011). Is there convergence of national environmental policies?An analysis of policy outputs in 24 OECD countries. *Environmental Politics*, *20*(1), 20–35. doi:10.1080/09644016.2011.538163

Homans, G. (1961). *Social Behavior: Its Elementary Forms*. New York: Harcourt Brace Jovanovich.

Honore, A. M. (1961). Ownership. In A. G. Guest (Ed.), *Oxford Essays in Jurisprudence*. Oxford, UK: Oxford University Press.

Hosoya, Y. (1991). The Decomposition and Measurement of the Interdependency Between Second-Order Stationary Processes. *Probability Theory and Related Fields*, *88*(4), 429–444. doi:10.1007/BF01192551

Hoyt, R. E., & Liebenberg, A. P. (2008). *The Value of Enterprise Risk Management: Evidence from the U.S. Insurance Industry*. Society of Actuaries, ERM Monograph Paper. Retrieved on 4/6/2018 from http://citeseerx.ist.psu.edu/viewdoc/download?doi=10.1.1.514.6423&rep=rep1&type=pdf

Hoyt, R. E., & Liebenberg, A. P. (2011). The Value of Enterprise Risk Management. *The Journal of Risk and Insurance*, *78*(4), 795–822. doi:10.1111/j.1539-6975.2011.01413.x

Hsieh, C., Hurst, E., Jones, C. I., & Klenow, P. J. (2013). *The allocation of talent and US economic growth*. NBER Working Paper, No. 18693.

Hsieh, C.-T., & Klenow, P. J. (2010). Development accounting. *American Economic Journal. Macroeconomics*, *2*(1), 207–223. doi:10.1257/mac.2.1.207

Husted, B. W., & Allen, D. B. (2007). Strategic Corporate Social Responsibility and Value Creation Among Large Firms: Lessons from the Spanish Experience. *Long Range Planning*, *40*(6), 594–610. doi:10.1016/j.lrp.2007.07.001

Ignaciuk, I. (1990). How to determine the value of a company? [in English]. *Organization Review*, *6*, 10–14.

Imbs, J., & Méjean, I. (2015). Elasticity optimism. American Economic Journal: Macroeconomics, 7(3), 43-83. doi:10.1257/mac.20130231

IMF Fiscal Monitor, (2018a, October). *Managing Public Wealth*. Washington, DC: IMF.

IMF Fiscal Monitor. (2018a, October). *Managing Public Wealth*. Washington, DC: IMF.

IMF Fiscal Monitor. (2018b, April). *Capitalizing on Good Times*. Washington, DC: IMF.

IMF Fiscal Monitor. (2019). *Curbing Corruption*. Washington, DC: IMF.

IMF. (2016). Financial Development *Database*. IMF.

IMF. (2017). *Fiscal Monitor: Tackling Inequality*. Washington DC: IMF.

IMF. (2017). *Fiscal Monitor: Tackling Inequality*. Washington, DC: International Monetary Fund.

IMF. (2018). *Inequality and poverty across generations in the European Union*. IMF Discussion Note SDN/18/01.

IMF. (2019). *Fiscal Monitor. Curbing Corruption*. Washington, DC: IMF.

Immervoll, H., & Richardson, L. (2011). *Redistribution policy and inequality reduction in OECD countries: what has changed in two decades?* OECD Social, Employment and Migration Working Papers, No. 122. Paris: OECD Publishing. doi:10.1787/5kg5dlkhjq0x-en

InfraONE. (2018). Infrastructure investment: 2018. Analytical Review. Moscow: InfraONE: First Infrastructure Company.

Insel, T. R., & Landis, S. C. (2013). Twenty-five years of progress: The view from Nimh and Ninds. *Neuron*, *80*(3), 561–567. doi:10.1016/j.neuron.2013.09.041 PMID:24183009

Institute for European Environmental Policy (IEEP). (2014). Environmental Tax Reform in Europe: Opportunities for the Future. Annexes to Final Report. Brussels: IEEP.

International Institute for Labour Studies. (2011). *Green Policies in the EU: a Review*. International Labour Organization. EC-IILS Joint Discussion Paper Series, 14.

International Monetary Fund (2019). *Global Financial Stability Report: Vulnerabilities in a Maturing Credit Cycle*. Washington, DC: IMF.

International Monetary Fund. (2008). *Global Financial Stability Report: Containing Systemic Risks and Restoring Financial Soundness*. Washington, DC: IMF.

International Monetary Fund. (2019). *Global Financial Stability Report: Vulnerabilities in a Maturing Credit Cycle*. Washington, DC: IMF.

Interpretative communication of the Commission on the Community law applicable to public procurement and the possibilities for integrating environmental considerations into public procurement. COM (2001) 274 final, Official Journal of the European Communities 28.11.2001.

Interpretative Communication of the Commission on the Community law applicable to public procurement and the possibilities for integrating social considerations into public procurement, COM (2001) 566 final, Official Journal of the European Communities C 333/27, 28.11.2001.

Ismail, M. (2009). Corporate social responsibility and its role in community development: An international perspective. *The Journal of International Social Research*, *2/9*, 199–209.

Iwanicz-Drozdowska, M., Jaworski, W., Szelągowska, A., & Zawadzka, Z. (2017). *Bankowość- Instytucje, operacje, zarzadzanie*. Warszawa, Poland: Poltext.

Jabłoński, A. (2015). The financial stability of a company and its business model. *Zeszyty Naukowe Uniwersytetu Przyrodniczo-Humanistycznego w Siedlcach, Seria. Administracja i Zarządzanie*, *104*(31), 87–96.

Jabłoński, A., & Jabłoński, M. (2014). A modern model of strategic management and value management of the region - key issues (translated from Polish). *Samorząd Terytorialny*, *11*, 22–31.

Jain-Chandra, S., Kochhar, K., Newiak, M., Zeinullayev, T., & Zhuang, L. (2016). Gender inequality around the world. In K. Kochhar, S. Jain-Chandra, & M. Newiak (Eds.), *Women, Work and Economic Growth: Leveling the Playing Field* (pp. 13–30). Washington, DC: International Monetary Fund.

Jakubiec, T. (2018). *Green public procurement as an instrument for the implementation of sustainable development* (PhD Dissertation). University of Lodz, Faculty of Economics and Sociology.

Jaramillo, C. H., Arimany-Serrat, N., Vidal, D. M., & Ferràs-Hernandez, X. (2018). Sustainability values for business: A perspective of value alignment in a supplier–client relationship for case aqualogy. *Intangible Capital*, *14*(1), 3–24. doi:10.3926/ic.1083

Jeanneney, S., & Kpodar, K. (2011). Financial Development and Poverty Reduction: Can There be a Benefit without a Cost? *The Journal of Development Studies*, *47*(1), 143–163. doi:10.1080/00220388.2010.506918

Jensen, R. (2007). The digital provide: information (technology), market performance, and welfare in the South Indian fisheries sector. *The Quarterly Journal of Economics*, *122*, 879-924.

Jensen, M. C. (2001). Value maximization, stakeholder theory, and the corporate objective function. *Applied Corporate Finance*, *14*(3), 8–21. doi:10.1111/j.1745-6622.2001.tb00434.x

Jeucken, M. (2001). *Sustainable finance and banking: The financial sector and the future of the planet*. London: Earthscan Publications Ltd.

Jones, Ch. I., & Klenow, P. J. (2016). Beyond GDP? Welfare across countries and time. *The American Economic Review*, *106*(9), 2426–2457. doi:10.1257/aer.20110236

Jorion, P. (2001). *Value-at-Risk: The New benchmark for Controlling Market Risk*. Chicago: McGraw-Hill.

Joumard, I., Pisu, M., & Bloch, D. (2012). Tackling Income Inequality: The Role of Taxes and Transfers. *OECD Journal: Economic Studies*, *2012*(1). doi:10.1787/eco_studies-2012-5k95xd6l65lt

Kamela-Sowińska, A. (2014). Od rachunkowości do opisu gospodarczego. *Zeszyty Teoretyczne Rachunkowości*, *77*(133), 107–115.

Kamela-Sowińska, A. (2016). Czy rachunkowość to już nauka społeczna? In A. Karmańska (Ed.), *Nauka o rachunkowości na progu gospodarki opartej na wiedzy* (pp. 309–328). Warszawa, Poland: Oficyna Wydawnicza - Szkoła Głowna Handlowa w Warszawie.

Kapelyushnikov, R. I. (1990). Economic Theory of Property Rights (methodology, basic concepts, range of problems). Moscow: Publishing House of Institute of World Economics and International Relations, the USSR Academy of Science.

Kates, R. W., Parris, T. M., & Leiserowitz, A. A. (2005). What is sustainable development? Goals, indicators, values, and practice. *Environ. Sci. Policy Sustain. Dev.*, *47*(3), 8–21. doi:10.1080/00139157.2005.10524444

Kaufmann, L., & Ridder, Ch. (2003). Valuation of biotechnology companies. *Financial Operation*, *7*, 448–456.

Kellogg, D., & Charnes, J. M. (2000). Real option valuation for a biotechnology company. *Financial Analysts Journal*, *56*(3), 76–87. doi:10.2469/faj.v56.n3.2362

Kenworthy, L., & Pontusson, H. J. (2005). Rising inequality and the politics of redistribution in affluent countries. Perspectives on Politics, 3(3), 449-471. doi:10.1017/S1537592705050292

Kerwin, J. T., & Thornton, R. L. (2015). Making the grade: Understanding what works for teaching literacy in rural Uganda. PSC Research Report, 15-842. Population Studies Center, Institute for Social Research, University of Michigan.

Keynes, J. M. (1936). *The General Theory of Employment, Interest and Money*. London: McMillan.

Keynes, J. M. (1937). The "ex ante" theory of the rate of interest. *Economic Journal (London)*, *46*(186), 241. doi:10.2307/2225525

Keynes, J. M. (1939). The process of capital formation. *Economic Journal (London)*, *49*(195).

Khan, M. J., Hussain, D., & Mehmood, W. (2016). Why do firms adopt enterprise risk management (ERM)? Empirical evidence from France. *Management Decision*, *54*(8), 1886–1907. doi:10.1108/MD-09-2015-0400

Kiba-Janiak, M. (2015). A Comparative Analysis of Sustainable City Logistics among Capital Cities in the EU. *Applied Mechanics and Materials*, *708*, 113–118. doi:10.4028/www.scientific.net/AMM.708.113

Kim, J. Y. (2018). The Human Capital Gap: Getting Governments to Invest in People. *Foreign Affairs*. Available at: https://www.foreignaffairs.com/articles /2018-06-14/human-capital-gap

Kindleberger, C. (1993). *A Financial History of Western Europe*. Oxford, UK: Oxford University Press.

Kindleberger, C. P. (1996). *Manias, Panics and Crashes. A History of Financial Crises*. New York: John Willey&Sons, Inc.

King & Rebelo. (1993). Transitional dynamics and economic growth in the neoclassical model. *American Economic Review*, *83*, 908-931.

Kleffner, A. E., Lee, R. B., & McGannon, B. (2003). The Effect of Corporate Governance on the Use of Enterprise Risk Management: Evidence From Canada. *Risk Management & Insurance Review*, *6*(1), 1098–1616. doi:10.1111/1098-1616.00020

Kleiner, G. B. (2004). Evolution of Institutional Systems. Moscow: Russian Academy of Science. Central Economics and Mathematics Institute, Publishing House "Nauka".

Knill, C., Debus, M., & Heichel, S. (2010). Do parties matter in internationalised policy areas? The impact of political parties on environmental policy outputs in 18 OECD countries, 1970-2000. *European Journal of Political Research*, *49*(3), 301–330. doi:10.1111/j.1475-6765.2009.01903.x

Kondratiev, N. D. (1984). The Long Wave Cycle (G. Daniels, Trans.). New York: Richardson and Snyder.

Korhonen, L. (2007). *Economic shocks in large emerging market countries*. Bank of Finland, BOFIT.

Koritsev, M. A. (2009). Institutional Structure and Mechanisms of the Quasi-markets Functioning in the Public Sector. Rostov on Don: Publishing House "Assistance - XXI century."

KPMG International Survey of Corporate Responsibility Reporting 2011 . (2011). KPMG International.

KPMG. (2008). *Climate Changes your Business*. Available at http://www.climatebiz.com/sites/default/files/document/Climatechang_riskreport.pdf

Kramer, M., Kingsbury, T., Mundle, D., & Voûte, J. (2011). Creating Shared Value In Action [PDF Slides]. *FSG*. Retrieved from: https://www.fsg.org/sites/default/files/tools-and-resources/CSV_ Webinar.pdf

Krasodomska, J. (2010). Informacje niefinansowe jako element rocznego raportu spółki. *Zeszyty Naukowe. Uniwersytet Ekonomiczny w Krakowie*, *816*, 45–57.

Krejdl, A. (2006). *Fiscal Sustainability – Definition, Indicators and Assessment of Czech Public Finance Sustainability*. Working Papers No.3. Czech National Bank, Research Department.

Krueger & Lindahl. (2001). Education for growth: why and for whom? *Journal of Economic Literature*, *39*(1), 1011-1136.

Krugman, P. (2009, April 19). How did economists get it so wrong? *The New York Times.*

Kudełko, M. (2016). Korygowanie niekorzystnych efektów zewnętrznych – ujęcie teoretyczne i empiryczne. *Jurnal of Management and Finance*, *14*(3), 339-351.

Kuhlman, T., & Farrington, J. (2010). What is Sustainability? *Sustainability*, *2*(11), 3436–3448. doi:10.3390u2113436

Kuhl, P. K. (2010). Brain mechanisms in early language acquisition. *Neuron*, *67*(5), 713–727. doi:10.1016/j.neuron.2010.08.038 PMID:20826304

Lafferty, W., & Hovden, E. (2003). Environmental policy integration: Towards an analytical framework. *Environmental Politics*, *12*(3), 1–10. doi:10.1080/09644010412331308254

Lam, J. (2017). *Implementing Enterprise Risk Management – From Methods to Applications*. Hoboken, NJ: John Wiley & Sons, Inc. doi:10.1002/9781118922415

Łapacz, D. (2015). Zamówienia publiczne w Unii Europejskiej – analiza porównawcza procedur w wybranych państwach członkowskich [Public Procurement in the European Union - a comparative analysis of procedures in selected Member States]. In *Biznes międzynarodowy w gospodarce globalnej 2015* [International business in the global economy 2015], No. 34. Instytut Biznesu Międzynarodowego, Uniwersytet Gdański.

Laszlo, C. (2008). Sustainable Value. *Problems of Sustainable Development*, *3*(2), 25–29.

Laszlo, Ch. (2003). *The Sustainable Company: How to Create Lasting Value through Social and Environmental Performance*. Washington, DC: Island Press.

Laura, K. (2008). Crises of confidence…and a lot more. Finance & Development, 45(2), 9-13.

Lavinas, L., & Veiga, A. (2013). Brazil's one laptop per child program: Impact evaluation and implementation assessment. *Cadernos de Pesquisa*, *43*(149).

Le Grand, J., & Bartlett, W. (1993). *Quasi-Markets and Social Policy*. London: Macmillan Press. doi:10.1007/978-1-349-22873-7

Le Saout, E. (2002). *Incorporating liquidity risk in VaR models*. Working Paper. Paris 1 University.

Lebart, L., Morineau, A., & Warwick, K. M. (1984). *Multivariate Descriptive Statistical Analysis. Correspondence Analysis and Related Techniques for Large Matrices*. New York: John Wiley & Sons, Inc.

Lechner, P., & Gatzert, N. (2018). Determinants and value of enterprise risk management: Empirical evidence from Germany. *European Journal of Finance*, *24*(10), 867–887. doi:10.1080/1351847X.2017.1347100

Lee, R., & Mason, A. (2017). Cost of aging. Finance & Development, 54(1).

Leeder, S. (2013). Australia's leadership in developing goals for sustainable global health. *The Medical Journal of Australia*, *199*(6), 377. doi:10.5694/mja13.c0916 PMID:24033193

Leiter, A. M., Parolini, A., & Winner, H. (2011). Environmental Regulation and Investment: Evidence from European Industries. *Ecological Economics*, *70*(4), 759–770. doi:10.1016/j.ecolecon.2010.11.013

Leland, H. E., & Toft, K. (1991). Optimal Capital structure, Endogenous Bankruptcy, and the Term Structure of credit spreads. *The Journal of Finance*, *51*(3), 987–1019. doi:10.1111/j.1540-6261.1996.tb02714.x

Lewicka, H. (2014). Value as a key concept in the field of economic sciences. *Society and Economy*, *2*(2), 64–72.

Liebenberg, A.P. & Hoyt, R.E. (2003). The Determinants of Enterprise Risk Management: Evidence From the Appointment of Chief Risk Officers. *Risk Management and Insurance Review*, *6*(1), 37-52. doi:10.1111/1098-1616.00019

Liesen, A., Figge, F., & Hahn, T. (2013). Net Present Sustainable Value: A New Approach to Sustainable Investment Appraisal. *Strategic Change*, *22*(3-4), 175–189. doi:10.1002/jsc.1931

Lindert, P. (2004). *Growing Public Social Spending and Economic Growth since the Eighteenth Century*. Cambridge, UK: Cambridge University Press.

Lindgreen, A., Swaen, V., & Campbell, T. (2009). Corporate Social Responsibility Practices in Developing and Transitional Countries: Botswana and Malawi. *Journal of Business Ethics*, *90*(S3), 429–440. doi:10.100710551-010-0415-3

Loh, L., Thomas, T., & Wang, Y. (2017). Sustainability Reporting and Firm Value: Evidencefrom Singapore-Listed Companies. *Sustainability, 9*(11), 1-12. Retrieved from https://www.researchgate.net/publication/321140723_Sustainability_Reporting_and_Firm_Value_Evidence_from_Singapore-Listed_Companies/download

Lundqvist, S. A. (2014). An Exploratory Study of Enterprise Risk Management: Pillars of ERM. *Journal of Accounting, Auditing & Finance*, *29*(3), 393–429. doi:10.1177/0148558X14535780

Lundqvist, S. A. (2015). Why firms implement risk governance – Stepping beyond traditional risk management to enterprise risk management. *Journal of Accounting and Public Policy*, *34*(5), 441–466. doi:10.1016/j.jaccpubpol.2015.05.002

Lupu, N., & Pontusson, J. (2011). The structure of inequality and the politics of redistribution. American Political Science Review, 105(2), 316-336. doi:10.1017/S0003055411000128

Lutz, W., Butz, W., & Samir, K. C. (2014). *World Population and Human Capital in the Twenty-First Century*. London: Oxford University Press. doi:10.1093/acprof:oso/9780198703167.001.0001

Madhavan, A., Richardson, M., & Roomans, M. (1997). Why do security prices change? A transaction-level analysis of NYSE stocks. *Review of Financial Studies*, *10*(4), 1035–1064. doi:10.1093/rfs/10.4.1035

Madoroba, S. B. W., & Kruger, J. W. (2014). Liquidity effects on value-at-risk limits: Construction of a new VaR model. *Journal of Risk Model Validation*, *8*(4), 19–46. doi:10.21314/JRMV.2014.127

Magun, Rudnev, & Schmidt. (2015b). Russian basic human values through the lens of the European value types. *The Russian Public Opinion Herald Data. Analysis. Discussions. Quarterly*, *3-4*(121), 74-93.

Magun, V., & Rudnev, M. (2015). Basic human values of the Russians: both different from and similar to other Europeans. In *Culture Matters in Russia and Everywhere: Backdrop for the Russia-Ukraine Conflict*. London: Lexington Books.

Magun, V., Rudnev, M., & Schmidt, P. (2015a). 'Within-and between-country value diversity in Europe: A typological approach'. *European Sociological Review*. Available at http://esr.oxfordjournals.org/content/early/2015/08/20/esr.jcv080.full

Maia, I. R. D., & Chaves, G. M. M. (2016). Integration of Risk Management into Strategic Planning: A New Comprehensive Approach. *2016 Enterprise Risk Management Symposium*.

Maleva, T. M. (2014). *The man in the pay-as-you-go pension system*. Paper presented at the Annual Conference. Association of Russian Economic Think-Tanks, Moscow, Russia.

Malina, A. (2005). Research on structural similarities between Poland and EU countries in terms of employment structure. *Argumenta Oeconomica Cracoviensia*, *4*, 57–70.

Manpower Group. (2014). *The Talent Shortage Continues: How the Ever Changing Role of HR Can Bridge the Gap*. Manpower Group.

Markowitz, H. (1952). Portfolio Selection. *The Journal of Finance*, *7*(1), 77–91.

Markowitz, H. (1959). *Portfolio Selection: Efficient Diversification of Investments*. New York: John Wiley.

Marrero & Rodríguez. (2015). *Inequality of opportunity and economic performance*. Economic Mobility Conference. Federal Reserve System Community Development Research.

Marrero, G. A., & Rodríguez, J. G. (2010). *Inequality of opportunity and growth*. ECINEQ. Society for the Study of Economic Inequality. Working Paper Series. ECINEQ WP 2010-154.

Marrero, G. A., & Rodríguez, J. G. (2012). Inequality of opportunity in Europe. *Review of Income and Wealth*, *58*(4), 597–621. doi:10.1111/j.1475-4991.2012.00496.x

Marrero, G. A., & Rodríguez, J. G. (2013). Inequality of opportunity and growth. *Journal of Development Economics*, *104*, 107–122. doi:10.1016/j.jdeveco.2013.05.004

Marrero, G. A., & Rodríguez, J. G. (2016). Inequality … of opportunity and economic performance. In *Economic Mobility: Research & Ideas on Strengthening Families, Communities & the Economy* (pp. 385–420). Federal Reserve Bank of St. Louis and the Board of Governors of the Federal Reserve System.

Marshall, A. (1988). Income distribution, the domestic market and growth in Argentina. *Labour and Society*, *13*(1), 79–103.

Marx, K. (1995). *Capital: A New Abridgement*. Oxford, UK: Oxford University Press.

Mason, A. (1988). 'Savings, economic growth and demographic change. *Population and Development Review*, *14*(1), 113–144. doi:10.2307/1972502

Masztalerz, M. (2014). Wartość dla interesariuszy w zrównoważonym przedsiębiorstwie. *Studia Oeconomica Posnaniensia*, *2*(8), 66–77.

Matschke, M. J., Brösel, G., & Matschke, X. (2010). Fundamentals of Functional Business Valuation. *Journal of Business Valuation and Economic Loss Analysis*, *5*(1). doi:10.2202/1932-9156.1097

McConnell, C., & Brue, S. (2008). *Economics* (17th ed.). New York: McGraw-Hill.

McDonough, W., & Braungart, M. (2002). *Cradle to Cradle: Remaking the Way We Make Things*. New York: North Point Press.

McKinnon, R. I. (1973). *Money and capital in economic development*. Washington, DC: The Brookings Institution.

McKinsey Global Institute. (2013). *Infrastructure productivity: how to save $1 trillion a year. McKinsey Infrastructure Practice*. Washington, DC: McKinsey & Company.

McKinsey Global Institute. (2015). *Debt and (Not Much) Deleveraging*. McKinsey Global Institute.

McKinsey Global Institute. (2016a, June). *Bridging Global Infrastructure Gaps*. McKinsey Global Institute in collaboration with McKinsey's Capital Projects and Infrastructure Practice.

McKinsey Global Institute. (2016b, October). *A Tool Kit to Close California's Housing Gap: 3.5 Million Homes by 2025*. McKinsey Global Institute.

McKinsey Global Institute. (2017). *The New Dynamics of Financial Globalization*. McKinsey Global Institute.

McKinsey Global Institute. (2017a, February). *Reinventing Construction: A Route to Higher Productivity*. McKinsey Global Institute in collaboration with McKinsey's Capital Projects and Infrastructure Practice.

McKinsey Global Institute. (2017b, July). *Improving Construction Productivity*. McKinsey's Capital Projects and Infrastructure Practice.

McKinsey Global Institute. (2017c, September). *Navigating risks in project finance. Interview*. McKinsey's Capital Projects and Infrastructure Practice.

McKinsey Global Institute. (2017d). *Bridging infrastructure gaps. Has the world made progress?* Discussion Paper in Collaboration with McKinsey's Capital Projects and Infrastructure Practice. Washington, DC: McKinsey & Company.

McKinsey Global Institute. (2018). *A decade after the global financial crisis: what has (and hasn't) changed?* Briefing Note. McKinsey Global Institute.

McKinsey Global Institute. (2018a). *Rising corporate debt: peril or promise*? Discussion Paper. McKinsey Global Institute.

McKinsey Global Institute. (2018b). How secure is the global financial system a decade after the crisis? *McKinsey Podcast*.

McShane, M. K., Nair, A., & Rustambekov, E. (2011). Does Enterprise Risk Management Increase Firm Value*? Journal of Accounting, Auditing & Finance*, *26*(4), 641–658. doi:10.1177/0148558X11409160

McSweeney, B. (2006). Net present value: The illusion of certainty. *Strategic Change*, *15*(1), 47–51. doi:10.1002/jsc.746

Mehr, R. I., & Hedges, B. A. (1963). *Risk Management and the Business Enterprise*. Homewood, IL: Irwin.

Ménard, C. (1997). Le pilotâge des formes organisationnelles hybrids. *Revue Economique*, *48*(2), 741-751.

Ménard, C. (2003). The economics of hybrid organizations. *Journal of Institutional and Theoretical Economics*.

Meucci, A. (2009). Managing Diversification. *Risk (Concord, NH)*, *22*(5), 74–79.

Meulbroek, L. K. (2002). *Integrated Risk Management for the Firm: A Senior Manager's Guide*. Retrieved from https://ssrn.com/abstract=301331

Mikes, A., & Kaplan, R. S. (2013). *Towards a Contingency Theory of Enterprise Risk Management*. AAA 2014 Management Accounting Section (MAS) Meeting Paper. Retrieved from https://papers.ssrn.com/sol3/papers.cfm?abstract_id=2311293

Milanovic, B. (2012). *Global income by the numbers in history and now*. World Bank, Working Paper, No. 6259.

Miller, S. J., & Vela, M. A. (2013). *Are Environmentally Related Taxes Effective?* Washington, DC: Inter-American Development Bank. doi:10.2139srn.2367708

Minski, H. P. (1957). Central banking and monetary market changes. *The Quarterly Journal of Economics*, *71*(2).

Minsky, H. P. (1985). The financial instability hypothesis: a restatement. In P. Arestis & T. Skouras (Eds.), *Post-Keynesian Economic Theory: A Challenge Neoclassical Economics*. Brighton, UK: Wheatsheaf.

Minsky, H. P. (1992). Profits, deficits and instability: A policy discussion. In D. B. Paradimitriou (Ed.), *Profits, Deficits and Instability*. London: Macmillan. doi:10.1007/978-1-349-11786-4_2

Minsky, H. P. (2008). *Stabilizing an Unstable Economy*. New York: McGraw-Hill.

Miralles-Quiros, M. M., Miralles-Quiros, J. L., & Arraiano, I. C. (2017). Sustainable Development, Sustainability Leadership and Firm Valuation: Differences across EUROPE. *Business Strategy and the Environment*, *26*(7), 1014–1028. doi:10.1002/bse.1964

Moore, G. (2003). Hives and horseshoes, Mintzberg and McIntyre: What future for corporate social responsibility? *Business Ethics (Oxford, England)*, *12*(1), 41–53. doi:10.1111/1467-8608.00304

Morgan Guaranty Trust Company. (1994). *RiskMetrics-Technical Document*. New York: Morgan Guaranty Trust Company, Global Research.

Morgan, P. J., & Pontines, V. (2014). *Financial Stability and Financial Inclusion.* ADBI Working Paper Series, No.488.

Morrisson & Murtin. (2010). The Kuznets curve of human capital inequality: 1870–2010. *The Journal of Economic Inequality*, *11*(3), 283-301.

Mourougane, A., Botev, J., Fournier, J.-M., Pain, N., & Rusticelli, E. (2016). *Can an increase in public investment sustainably lift economic growth?* OECD Economics Department Working Papers, No. 1351. Paris: OECD. doi:10.1787/a25a7723-en

Musgrave, R. (1959). *The Theory of Public Finance*. New York: McGrow-Hill.

Musgrave, R. (1998). The role of the state in the fiscal theory. In P. B. Sorensen (Ed.), *Public Finance in a Changing World* (pp. 35–50). London: Macmillan. PP. doi:10.1007/978-1-349-14336-8_2

Myers, S. C. (1993). Still Searching for Optimal Capital Structure. *Journal of Applied Corporate Finance*, *6*(1), 4–14. doi:10.1111/j.1745-6622.1993.tb00369.x

Myrdal, G. (1954). *The Political Element in the Development of Economic Theory.* Cambridge, MA: Harvard University Press.

Nestlé. (2014). *Nestlé in society: Creating Shared Value and meeting our commitments 2013.* Retrieved from: http://www.nestle.com

Nicholls, J., et al. (2012), A Guide to Social Return on Investment (SROI). *The SROI Network*, 108.

Nicolăescu, E., Alpopi, C., & Zaharia, C. (2015). Measuring Corporate Sustainability Performance. *Sustainability*, *7*(1), 851–865. doi:10.3390u7010851

Nocco, B. W., & Stulz, R. M. (2006). Enterprise Risk Management: Theory and Practice. *Journal of Applied Corporate Finance*, *18*(4), 8–20. doi:10.1111/j.1745-6622.2006.00106.x

Nogalski, B., & Bors, K. (2000). Value management. *Organization Review*, *4*, 16–21.

Nordhaus, W. D., & Tobin, J. (1973). Is Growth Obsolete? The Measurement of Economic and Social Performance. In National Bureau of Economic Research (pp. 509–532). Columbia University Press.

North, D. (1997). *The process of economic change.* Research Paper 128. World Institute for Development Economics Research.

North, D. (2003). *Understanding the Process of Economic Change*. Princeton, NJ: Princeton University Press.

North, D. C. (1981). *Structure and Change in Economic History.* New York: W. W. Norton & Co.

North, D. C. (1990). *Institutions, Institutional Change and Economic Performance*. Cambridge, UK: Cambridge University Press. doi:10.1017/CBO9780511808678

Novokmet, F., Piketty, T., & Zucman, G. (2017). *From Soviets to oligarchs: inequality and property in Russia, 1905-2016.* WID. World Working Paper Series, No. 2017/09.

Nowak, E. (1990). *Taxonomic methods in the classification of socio-economic objects (translated from Polish).* Warsaw: PWE.

Nunn, N., & Puga, D. (2012). Ruggedness: the blessing of bad geography in Africa. The Review of Economics and Statistics, 94, 20-36.

O'Sullivan, P., Allington, N. F. B., & Esposito, M. (Eds.). (2015). *The Philosophy, Politics and Economics of Finance in the 21st Century. From Hubris to Disgrace* (1st ed.). Cambridge, UK: University of Cambridge. doi:10.4324/9780203797723

OECD Skills Outlook. (2013). *First Results from the Survey of Adult Skills*. Programme for the International Assessment of Adult Competencies (PIAAC). Organisation for Economic Co-operation and Development. Available at: http://www.oecd.org/site/piaac/surveyofadultskills.htm

OECD. (2001). *Environmentally Related Taxes in OECD Countries*. Paris: Issues and Strategies.

OECD. (2003). *The Sources of Economic Growth in OECD Countries*. Paris: OECD Publishing. Available at: https://www.oecd.org

OECD. (2008). *Growing Unequal? Income Distribution and Poverty in OECD Countries*. Paris: OECD Publishing.

OECD. (2010). *PISA 2009. Results, What Students Know and Can Do: Student Performance in Reading, Mathematics, and Science* (Vol. 1). Paris: OECD.

OECD. (2010). *Taxation*. Paris: Innovation and the Environment.

OECD. (2011). *Divided We Stand: Why Inequality Keeps Rising OECD*. OECD Publishing. Retrieved from: http://www.oecd.org/els/soc/dividedwestandwhyinequalitykeepsrising.htm

OECD. (2011). *Divided We Stand: Why Inequality Keeps Rising*. Paris: OECD Publishing; doi:10.1787/9789264119536-

OECD. (2012). *Environmental Tax and Green Growth*. Southeast Asian Economic Outlook 2011/12.

OECD. (2015). *In It Together: Why Less Inequality Benefits All*. Paris: OECD Publishing; doi:10.1787/9789264235120-

OECD. (2017). *Bridging the Gap: Inclusive Growth 2017. Update Report*. Paris: OECD. Available at: http://www.oecd.org/inclusive-growth/Bridging_the_Gap.pdf

OECD. (2018). *A Broken Social Elevator? The framework of policy action on inclusive growth*. Paris: OECD Publishing. Retrieved from: https://www.oecd.org/mcm/documents/C-MIN-2018-5-EN.pdf

OECD. (2018). *The Future of Education and Skills: Education 2030*. Paris: OECD Publishing.

OECD. (2018a). *The Framework for Policy Action on Inclusive Growth*. Paris: OECD Publishing. Available at: http://www.oecd.org/mcm/documents/C-MIN-2018-5-EN.pdf

OECD. (2018b). *A Broken Social Elevator? How to Promote Social Mobility*. Paris: OECD Publishing. doi:10.1787/9789264301085-

OECD. (2019). *Under Pressure: The Squeezed middle Class*. Paris: OECD Publishing.

OECD. (2019a). *Job polarization and the work profile of the middle class*. Cope Policy Brief, April. Available at: http://oe.cd/middle-class-2019

OECD. (2019b). *Under Pressure: The Squeezed Middle Class*. Paris: OECD Publishing. Available at: http://oe.cd/middle-class-2019

Ogbulu, O. M., & Emeni, F. K. (2012). Capital Structure and Firm Value: Empirical Evidence from Nigeria. *International Journal of Business and Social Science*, *3*(19), 252–261. Retrieved from http://www.ijbssnet.com/journals/Vol_3_No_19_October _2012 /29.pdf

Okun, A. (1975). Equality and Efficiency: The Big Tradeoff. Washington, DC: Brookings.

Okun, A. M. (2015). *Equality and Efficiency: The Big Tradeoff*. Washington, DC: Brooking Institution Press.

Organization for Economic Cooperation and Development. (2017). *OECD Corporate Governance Factbook – 2017*. Retrieved from http://www.oecd.org/daf/ca/Corporate-Governance-Factbook.pdf

Orsetta, C., Vindics, A., & Akgun, O. (2018). *An empirical investigation on the drivers of income redistribution across OECD countries*. OECD Economics Department Working Papers, No. 1488.

Ortiz, I., & Cummins, M. (2013). The Age of Austerity: A Review of Public Expenditures and Adjustment Measures in 181 Countries. New York: Academic Press.

Panizza, U., & Presbitero, A. F. (2012). *Public debt and economic growth: is there a causal effect?* Mo.Fi.R. Working Papers, 65.

Panizza, U., & Presbitero, A. F. (2013). Public debt and economic growth in advanced economies: A survey. *Swiss Society of Economics and Statistics*, *149*(2), 175–204. doi:10.1007/BF03399388

Parry, I., & Small, K. (2004). *Does Britain or the United States Have the Right Gasoline Tax?* Discussion Paper 0212 rev. Washington, DC: Resources for the Future.

Pearce, D. W., Markandya, A., & Barbier, E. B. (1989). *Blueprint for a Green Economy*. London: Earthscan.

Pejovich, S. (1981). *Fundamentals of Economics: A Property Rights Approach*. Academic Press.

Pelt, M. J. F., Kuyvenhoven, A., & Nijkamp, P. (1990). Project appraisal and sustainability: Methodological challenges. *Project Appraisal*, *5*(3), 139–158. doi:10.1080/02688867.1990.9726764

Perez, C. (2009). The double bubble at the turn of the century: technological roots and structural implications. *Cambridge Journal of Economics, 33*(4), 779–805.

Persson, T., & Tabellini, G. (1994). Is inequality harmful for growth? Theory and evidence. *The American Economic Review*, *84*, 600–621.

Peterson, C., Rice, S., Short, J., Esler, D., Bodkin, J., Ballachey, B., & Irons, D. (2003). Long-Term Ecosystem Response to the Exxon Valdez Oil Spill. *Science*, *302*(5653), 2082–2086. doi:10.1126cience.1084282 PMID:14684812

Pfitzer, M., Bockstette, V., & Stamp, M. (2013). Innovating for shared value. *Harvard Business Review*, *91*, 100–107.

Pigou, A. (1924). *The Economics of Welfare* (2nd ed.). London: McMillan.

Pigou, A. C. (2010). *Economics of Welfare*. London: Macmillan Publishing.

Piketty, T., Saez, E., & Zucman, G. (2016). *Distributional national accounts: methods and estimates for the United States*. NBER Working Paper Series, No. 22945.

Piketty, Th. (2013). *Le Capital au XXI*[e] *Siecle*. Editions de Seuil.

Pilipenko, A. I. (1997). *Cognitive barriers in teaching physics and methodological principles for overcoming them*. The Dissertation Abstract for a Scientific Degree of Doctor of Pedagogics. Moscow: Russian Academy of Education Publisher.

Pilipenko, A. I., Morosova, E. A., Pilipenko, O. I., & Savenkova, E. V. (2015). *Innovative Models of Education: The Aspect of Psychological and Cognitive Barriers*. Available at SSRN: http://ssrn.com/abstract=2597968

Pilipenko, Z. A. (2012). *Global Financial Shocks' Impact on the World Economy.* Abstract of the Doctoral Thesis in Economics. Moscow: M.V. Lomonosov' Moscow State University Press.

Pilipenko, A. I., Pilipenko, O. I., & Pilipenko, Z. A. (2019). Education and Inclusive Development: Puzzle of Low-learning Equilibrium. In B. S. Sergi (Ed.), *Modeling Economic Growth in Contemporary Russia* (pp. 163–198). London: Emerald Publishing Limited. doi:10.1108/978-1-78973-265-820191006

Pilipenko, A., Dikhtiar, V., Baranova, N., & Pilipenko, Z. (2019). Financial stability: modeling the Russian budgetary and tax policy with fiscal multipliers' attraction. In S. S. Bruno (Ed.), *Modeling Economic Growth in Contemporary Russia* (pp. 63–92). London: Emerald Publishing Limited. doi:10.1108/978-1-78973-265-820191003

Pilipenko, A., & Pilipenko, Z. (2018). Shocks in global economy: Impulse model of macroeconomic cycle. In B. S. Sergi, F. Fidanoski, M. Ziolo, & V. Naumovski (Eds.), *Regaining Global Stability After the Financial Crisis. A volume in the Advances in Finance, Accounting, and Economics (AFAE) Book Series* (pp. 238–256). Hershey, PA: IGI Global. doi:10.4018/978-1-5225-4026-7.ch012

Pinsky, A. A. (1978). Methodology as a science. *Soviet Pedagogy*, 12.

Pociecha, J., Podolec, B., Sokołowski, A., & Zając, K. (1988). *Taxonomic methods in socio-economic research (translated from Polish).* Warsaw: PWN.

Porter, M. E. (2012). *New Opportunities for Company Performance and Purpose: Creating Shared Value.* Presentation for Hitachi Innovation Forum 2012 Conference, Boston, MA. Retrieved from https://www.hbs.edu/faculty/Publication%20Files/20120719%20-%20Hitachi%20Diamond%20CSV%20Presentation%20-%20FINAL_51404d95-3aa3-4572-a270-25dcfecffc29.pdf

Porter, M. E., & Kramer, M. R. (1999). Philanthropy's new agenda: Creating value. *Harvard Business Review*, *77*, 121–131. Retrieved from http://www.fsg.org/publications/philanthropy%E2%80%99s-new-agenda PMID:10662001

Porter, M. E., & Kramer, M. R. (2002). The Competitive Advantage of Corporate Philanthropy. *Harvard Business Review*, *80*(12), 56–68. Retrieved from https://hbr.org/2002/12/the-competitive-advantage-of-corporate-philanthropy PMID:12510538

Posner, R.A. (1998). *Economic Analysis of Law.* Austin, TX: A Division of Aspen Publishers, Inc., A Wolters Kluwer Company.

Posner, R. A. (2009). *A Failure of Capitalism.* Cambridge, MA: Harvard University Press.

PPIAF Annual Report. (2018). *Public-Private Infrastructure Advisory Facility.* PPIAF Annual Report.

Prahalad, C. K., & Ramaswamy, V. (2004). *The Future of Competition.* Boston: Harvard Business School Press.

Presbitero, A. F. (2012). Total public debt and growth in developing countries. *European Journal of Development Research*, *24*(4), 606–626. doi:10.1057/ejdr.2011.62

Pressman, S. (2007). The decline of the middle class: an international perspective. *Journal of Economic Issues*, *41*, 181-200. doi:10.2307/25511161

Pritchett, L. (2000). Understanding patterns of economic growth: Searching for hills among plateaus, mountains, and plains. *The World Bank Economic Review*, *14*(2), 221–250. doi:10.1093/wber/14.2.221

Pritchett, L. (2013). *The Rebirth of Education: Schooling Ain't Learning.* Baltimore, MD: Brookings Institution Press.

Public Procurement Indicators 2015. (2016). European Commission, DG GROW G4 - Innovative and e-Procurement.

Public-Private Partnerships. (2014). *Reference Guide. Version 2.0.* International Bank for Reconstruction and Development/The World Bank, Asian Development Bank, and Inter-American Development Bank.

Quigley, M. (2013). Nudging for health: On public policy and designing choice architecture. *Medical Law Review, 21*(4), 588–621. doi:10.1093/medlaw/fwt022 PMID:24081425

Radula, R., & Keel, K. (2018). *The Effects of Crises and EU Fiscal Governance Reforms on the Budgetary Institutions of Member States* Paper presented at the ECPR SGEU conference, Paris, France.

Rajan, R. G. (2010). *Fault Lines: How Hidden Fractures Still Threaten the World Economy*. Princeton, NJ: Princeton University Press.

Randall, D., & Mills, P. (2008). Outbreak: U.S. subprime contagion. Finance & Development, 45(2), 14-18.

Raportowanie rozszerzonych informacji niefinansowych za rok 2017 – pierwsze doświadczenia i dobre praktyki. (n.d.). Retrieved from https://www.gov.pl/documents/1079560/1080340/Raport_MF.PDF/1b41abe7-a7db-60a8-4641-cbbb0fb35764

Rashid, K., Islam, S. M. N., & Nuryanah, S. (2014). Debt, governance and the value of a firm. *Corporate Ownership & Control, 11*(2), 180–191. doi:10.22495/cocv11i2c1p4

Rasmussen, J. (1983). Skills, rules, and knowledge; signals, signs, and symbols, and other distinctions in human performance models. IEEE Transactions on Systems, Man, and Cybernetics, 13(3), 257-266. doi:10.1109/TSMC.1983.6313160

Rawls, J. (1971). *A Theory of Justice*. Cambridge, MA: Belknap Press of Harvard University Press.

Rawls, J. (1971). *Theory of Justice. Harvard.* Harvard University Press.

Razali, A. R., Yazid, A. S., & Tahir, I. M. (2011). The Determinants of Enterprise Risk Management (ERM) Practices in Malaysian Public Listed Companies. *Journal of Social and Development Sciences, 1*(5), 202–207.

Regulation (EC) No 106/2008 of the European Parliament and of the Council of 15 January 2008 on a Community energy-efficiency labeling program for office equipment.

Regulation (EC) No. 66/2010 of the European Parliament and of the Council of 25 November 2009 on the EU Eco-label.

Reinhart, C. M., & Rogoff, K. S. (2009). *This Time is Different. Eight Centuries of Financial Folly*. Princeton, NJ: Princeton University Press. doi:10.2307/j.ctvcm4gqx

Renda, A., Pelkmans, J., Egenhofer, C., Schrefler, L., Luchetta, G., & Selcuki, C. (2012). *The uptake of green public procurement in the EU27*. Academic Press.

Riad, N. (2017). Education for life: Llabor markets are changing, and millennials must prepare and adjust. *Finance & Development, 54*(2), 16-19.

Risk Management Institute (RIMS). (2017). *ERM Benchmarks*. Retrieved on 28/5/2019 from http://www.rmmagazine.com/2017/12/01/erm-benchmarks/

Risk Management Institute (RIMS). (n.d.). Retrieved on https://www.rims.org/resources/ERM/Pages/WhatisERM.aspx

Ritter, G. (1996). Storia dello Stato Sociale. Rome: Laterza.

Robins, N., & Zadek, S. (Eds.). (2017). *Roadmap for a Sustainable Financial System*. Washington, DC: World Bank and UNEP.

Roch, A., & Soner, H. M. (2013). Resilient price impact of trading and the cost of illiquidity. *International Journal of Theoretical and Applied Finance*, *16*(6), 1–27. doi:10.1142/S0219024913500374

Rockness, H., & Rockness, J. (2005). Legislated Ethics: From Enron to Sarbanes-Oxley, the Impact on Corporate America. *Journal of Business Ethics*, *57*(1), 31–54. doi:10.100710551-004-3819-0

Rogall, H. (2010). *The economics of sustainable development. Theory and practice*. Poznan: Zysk i S-ka.

Romer, P. M. (1986). Increasing returns and long-run growth. *The Journal of Political Economy*, *94*(5), 1002-1037.

Rosiek, J. (2005). *The Impact of Envirronmental Tax Policy on Sustainable Developmentof the EU Economies. DEA Approach.* 11th International Conference of ASECU. Retrieved from asecu.gr/files/11th_conf_files/18.pdf

Rószkiewicz, M. (2011). *Analiza klienta*. Kraków: Wydawnictwo SPSS Polska.

Roszkowska, P. (2011). *Rewolucja w raportowaniu biznesowym. Interesariusze, konkurencyjność,społeczna odpowiedzialność*. Warszawa, Poland: DIFIN.

Rozmainsky, I. V. (2015). Investor myopia and persistence of the global crisis: A Post-Keynesian view. *Montenegrin Journal of Economics*, *11*(1), 107–116.

Ruffing, K. G. (2010). The Role of the Organization for Economic Cooperation and Development. *Environmental Policy Making Review of Environmental Economics and Policy*, *4*(2), 199–210. doi:10.1093/reep/req007

Ruiz-Nunez, F., & Wei, Z. (2015). *Infrastructure investment demands in emerging markets and developing economies*. Policy Research Working Paper, No. 7414. Washington, DC: World Bank.

Ruiz-Nunez, F., & Wei, Z. (2016). *From global savings glut to financing infrastructure: the advent of investment platforms*. IMF Working Paper, WP/16/18.

Ruozi, R., & Ferrari, P. (2013). *Liquidity Risk Management in Banks: Economic and Regulatory Issues*. Springer Briefs in Finance; doi:10.1007/978-3-642-29581-2

Rychen, D. S., & Salganik, L. H. (Eds.). (2001). Defining and Selecting Key Competencies. Paris: OECD DeSeCo Project.

Rychen, D. S., & Salganik, L. H. (Eds.). (2003). Key Competencies for a Successful Llife and a Well-functioning Society. Paris: OECD DeSeCo Project.

Rychen, D. S., Salganik, L. H., & McLaughlin, M. E. (Eds.). (2003). *Contributions to the Second DeSeCo Symposium*. Paris: OECD DeSeCo Project.

Rydzewski, P. (2010). Metody analizy danych w socjologicznych badaniach rozwodów. *Roczniki Nauk Społecznych, 2*(38).

Sachs, J. D., & Larrain, F. B. (1993). *Macroeconomics in the Global Economy*. Englewood Cliffs, NJ: Prentice Hall.

Saez, E. (2018). *Striking it Richer: the Evolution of Top Incomes in the United States*. Berkeley, CA: UC Berkeley. doi:10.4324/9780429494468-9

Sahay, R., Cihak, M., N'Diaye, P., Barajas, A., Bi, R., Ayala, D., … Yousefi, S. R. (2015). *Rethinking financial deepening: stability and growth in emerging markets*. IMF Staff Discussion Note, SDN/15/08.

Sahay, R., Cihak, M., N'Diaye, P., Barajas, A., & Bi, R. (2015). *Rethinking Financial Deepening: Stability and Growth in Emerging Markets*. IMF Staff Discussion Note.

Saint Paul, G., & Verdier, T. (1996). Inequality, redistribution and growth: A challenge to the conventional political economy approach. *European Economic Review*, *40*(3-5), 719–728. doi:10.1016/0014-2921(95)00083-6

Salganik, Rychen, Moser, & Konstant. (1999). *Projects on Competencies in the OECD Context: Analysis of Theoretical and Conceptual Foundations.* Paris: OECD DeSeCo Project.

Schick, A. (2002). Does budgeting have a future? *OECD Journal on Budgeting*, *2*(2), 7–48. doi:10.1787/budget-v2-art8-en

Schinasi, G. J. (2006). *Safeguarding Financial Stability: Theory and Practice.* Washington, DC: IMF.

Schmeisser, W. (2010). Innovation profitability analysis in the assessment of pharmaceutical R&D projects. In *Innovation performance accounting: financing decisions and risk assessment of innovation processes* (1st ed.). New York: Springer. doi:10.1007/978-3-642-01353-9_4

Scholz, M., & De los Reyes, G. (2015). Creating Shared Value: Limits and Suggestions for Further Development. *ZeitschriftfürWirtschafts- und Unternehmensethik, 16*(2), 192-201.

Schularick, M., & Taylor, A. (2012). Credit booms gone bust: monetary policy, leverage cycles, and financial crises, 1870–2008. *American Economic Review, 102.*

Schumpeter, J. A. (1911). *The Theory Of Economic Development: An İnquiry İnto Profits, Capital, Credit, İnterest, and The Business Cycle* (R. Opie, Trans.). Cambridge, MA: Harvard University Press.

Schwab, K. (2015, December 12). The fourth industrial revolution: What It Means and How to Respond. *Foreign Affairs. Science and Technology.*

Schwartz, S. H. (1994). Are there universal aspects in the content and structure of values? *The Journal of Social Issues*, 50.

Schwartz, S. H., Cieciuch, J., Vecchione, M., Davidov, E., Fischer, R., Beierlein, C., ... Konty, M. (2012). 'Refining the theory of basic individual values'. *Journal of Personality and Social Psychology, 103*(4), 663–688. doi:10.1037/a0029393 PMID:22823292

Scott, I. A. (2012). Looking for value in health care. *The Medical Journal of Australia, 197*(10), 538–539. doi:10.5694/mja12.11497 PMID:23163667

Seal, H. L. (1967). Studies in the History of Probability and Statistics. XV The historical development of the Gauss linear model. *Biometrika, 54*(1-2), 1–24. doi:10.1093/biomet/54.1-2.1 PMID:4860564

Sen, A. (1979). Personal utilities and public judgments; or what is wrong with welfare economics? *Economic Journal, 89*, 537-589.

Sen, A. (1999). *Development as Freedom.* Oxford, UK: Oxford University Press.

Sergi, B. S., Fidanoski, F., Ziolo, M., & Naumovski, V. (Eds.). (2018). *Regaining Global Stability After the Financial Crisis.* Hershey, PA: IGI Global.

Sergi, B., Fidanoski, F., Ziolo, M., & Naumovski, V. (2018). *Regaining Global Stability After The Financial Crisis.* IGI Global. doi:10.4018/978-1-5225-4026-7

Sexton, M. G., Barrett, P. S., & Lu, S. L. (2008). *The evolution of sustainable development. Book Section.* Manchester, UK: University of Salford.

Shah, M. M. (2008). Sustainable Development. Encyclopedia of Ecology.

Sharpe, W. (1963). A simplified Model for Portfolio Analysis. *Management Science, 9*(2), 277–293. doi:10.1287/mnsc.9.2.277

Shaw, E. S. (1973). *Financial deepening in economic development.* Oxford, UK: Oxford University.

Shiller, R. (2004). *Irrational Exuberance* (2nd ed.). Princeton, NJ: Princeton University Press.

Shishkin, S. (2000). *Reform of the Russian Health Care Financing*. Moscow: Publishing House of Gaidar Institute for Economic Policy.

Shubik, M. (1999). *Theory of Money and Financial Institutions*. Cambridge, MA: MIT Press.

Šimberová, I., Chvátalová, Z., Kocmanová, A., Hornungová, J., & Pavláková Dočekalová, M. (2015). Sustainable value in measuring of corporate sustainability: Approaches and their evaluation. *Journal of Security and Sustainability Issues*, *4*(3), 241–259. doi:10.9770/jssi.2015.4.3(5)

Simkins, B., & Ramirez, S. A. (2008). Enterprise-Wide Risk Management and Corporate Governance. *Loyola University of Chicago Law Journal. Loyola University of Chicago. School of Law*, *39*, 571–594.

Slutsky, E.E. (1937, April). The summation of random causes as the source of cyclic process. *Econometrica*.

Slutsky, E. E. (2010). *Economic and Statistical Works: Favorites*. Moscow: Eksmo.

Smallman, C. (1996). Risk and organizational behaviour: A research model. *Disaster Prevention and Management: An International Journal*, *5*(2), 12–26. doi:10.1108/09653569610112880

Smith, S. (2007). *Podatki a środowisko naturalne. In Efektywność polityki podatkowej* (pp. 285–344). Warszawa: Wydawnictwo Sejmowe.

Sobel, P. J., & Reding, K. F. (2004). Aligning Corporate Governance with Enterprise Risk Management. *Management Accounting Quarterly*, *5*(2), 29-37.

Solow, R. M. (1957). Technical change and the aggregate production function. *Review of Economics and Statistics, 39*, 312-320.

Spilimbergo, A., Symansky, S., & Schindler, M. (2009). *Fiscal multipliers*. IMF Staff Position Note, No. 11. Retrieved from http://www.imf.org/external/pubs/ft/spn/ 2009/spn0911.pdf

Spilimbergo, A., Symansky, S., & Schindler, M. (2009). *Fiscal multipliers*. IMF Staff Position Note, No. 11. Retrieved from http://www.imf.org/external/pubs/ft/spn/2009/spn0911.pdf

Sprawozdanie Prezesa Urzędu Zamówień Publicznych o funkcjonowaniu systemu zamówień publicznych w 2015 roku . (2016). [Report of the President of the Public Procurement Office on the functioning of the public procurement system in 2015]. Urząd Zamówień Publicznych.

Staff Team from the Fiscal Affairs Department IMF. (2009). *Fiscal Implications of the Global Economic and Financial Crisis*. Washington, DC: IMF.

Stanimir, A. (2005). *Analysis of correspondence as a tool for studying economic phenomena* (translated from Polish). Wroclaw: Wydawnictwo AE we Wroclawiu.

Stankevicienea, J., & Nikonorova, M. (2014). Sustainable Value Creation in Commercial Banks during Financial Crisis. *Procedia: Social and Behavioral Sciences*, *110*, 1197–1208. doi:10.1016/j.sbspro.2013.12.966

Statistics Poland. (2019). *Sustainable Development Goals*. Retrieved March 31, 2019, from http://sdg.gov.pl/

Stefanescu, D., & On, A. (2012). Entrepreneurship and Sustainable Development in European Countries Before and During the International Crisis. *Procedia: Social and Behavioral Sciences*, *58*, 889–898. doi:10.1016/j.sbspro.2012.09.1067

Stevens, P., & Weale, M. (2004). Education and economic growth. In G. Johnes & J. Johnes (Eds.), *International Handbook on the Economics of Education*. Cheltenham, UK: Edward Elgar.

Stewart, J. J., Allison, P. N., & Johnson, R. S. (2001). Putting a price on biotechnology. *Nature Biotechnology, 19*(9), 813–817. doi:10.1038/nbt0901-813 PMID:11533634

Stiglitz, J. E. (2012). *The Price of Inequality: How Today's Divided Society Endangers Our Future*. New York: W.W. Norton and Company.

Stuart, N., & Adams, J. (2007). The Sustainability of Canada's Healthcare System: A Framework for Advancing the Debate. *Healthcare Quarterly, 10*(2), 96–103. doi:10.12927/hcq.2007.18839 PMID:18271106

Study on "Strategic use of public procurement in promoting green, social and innovation policies." (2015). Final Report. European Commission, DG GROW, written by PwC.

Stulz, R. M. (1996). Rethinking Risk Management. *Journal of Applied Corporate Finance, 9*(3), 8–24. doi:10.1111/j.1745-6622.1996.tb00295.x

Subhanij, T., Banerjee, S., & Jian, Z. (Eds.). (2018). *Tax Policy for Sustainable Development in Asia and the Pacifi.* United Nations.

Sustainable development Commission. (2011). *What is sustainable development?* Retrieved from http://www.sd-commission.org.uk/pages/what-is-sustainable-development.html

Świątkowska, S. (2015). *Budki lęgowe dla jerzyków – dokumentacja projektowa.* Retrieved from http://docplayer.pl/9088975-Budki-legowe-dla-jerzykow-dokumentacja-procesu-realizacji-pracy.html

Syska, J. (2014). *Współczesne metody analizy regresji wspomagane komputerowo.* Uniwersytet Śląski. Retrieved from http://el.us.edu.pl/ekonofizyka/images/b/b6/MetodyDoboruModeli.pdf

Szaleniec, M. (2008) *Sieci neuronowe i regresja wieloraka – czyli jak okiełznać złożoność w badaniach naukowych.* Statsoft Polska. Retrieved from https://media.statsoft.pl/_old_dnn/downloads/sieci%20neuronowe.pdf

Szlachta, J. (2011). Odniesienia europejskie nowej generacji programowania rozwoju regionalnego w Polsce [European References of the new generation of regional development programming in Poland]. In J. Szlachta & J. Woźniak (Eds.), *Krajowa Strategia Rozwoju Regionalnego do roku 2020 a strategie rozwoju społeczno-gospodarczego województw* [National Strategy of Regional Development until 2020 and strategies for socio-economic development of voivodships]. Polska Akademia Nauk, Komitet Przestrzennego Zagospodarowania Kraju, Warszawa. Retrieved from http://zim.lodz.bip-e.pl/zim/zamowienia-publiczne

Szopik-Depczyńska, K., Cheba, K., Bąk, I., Stajniak, M., Simboli, A., & Ioppolo, G. (2018). The study of relationship in a hierarchical structure of EU sustainable development indicators. *Ecological Indicators, 90*, 120–131. doi:10.1016/j.ecolind.2018.03.002

Szymkowiak, M., Młodak, A., & Wawrowski, Ł. (2017). Mapping poverty at the level of subregions in Poland using indirect estimation. *Statistics in Transition New Series, 18*(4), 609-635.

Tabarraei, H. R., Rouabah, A., & Pierrard, O. (2019). *Sovereigns and financial intermediaries spillovers.* IMF Working Paper, February, WP/19/43.

Takahashi, D., & Alexander, S. (2002). Illiquid Alternative Asset Fund Modeling. *Journal of Portfolio Management, 28*(2), 90–100. doi:10.3905/jpm.2002.319836

Tanzi & Schuknecht. (1997). Reconsidering the fiscal role of government: the international perspective. *American Economic Review, 87*, 164-168.

Tanzi & Schuknecht. (2000). *Public Spending in the 20th Century*. Cambridge, UK: Syndicate of the Press of the University of Cambridge.

Tanzi, V. (2011). *Government versus Markets: The Changing Economic Role of the State*. Cambridge, UK: Syndicate of the Press of the University of Cambridge.

Tanzi, V., & Schuknecht, L. (2000). *Public Spending in the 20th Century: A Global Perspective*. Cambridge, UK: Cambridge University Press. doi:10.1017/CBO9780511625800

Taş, S., Ağır, H., & İğde, G. (2016). Causality Analysis of the Export and Economic Growth: The Case of Turkey. EconWorld, 2016, Barcelona, Spain.

Thaler, R., & Sunstein, C. R. (2008). *Nudge: Improving decisions about health, wealth and happiness*. New York, NY: Simon & Schuster.

The Act of 11.05.2017 on Statutory Auditors, Audit Firms and Public Oversight (uniform text Dz. U. z 2017 r. poz. 1089).

The Act of The Directive 2014/95/EU of the European Parliament and of the Council of 22 October 2014.

The Economist Intelligence Unit Limited. (2017). *The Worldwide Educating for the Future Index: A Benchmark for the Skills of Tomorrow*. London: The Economist Intelligence Unit Limited.

The International Organization for Standardization (ISO). (n.d.). *ISO/Guide 73:2009(en)*. Retrieved on 9/6/2018 from https://www.iso.org/obp/ui/#iso:std:iso:guide:73:ed-1:v1:en

Thom, R. (1969). Topological models in biology. *Topology*, *8*, 313-36.

Thom, R. (1974). Catastrophe theory: its present state and future perspectives. In Dynamical Systems (pp. 1-75). Berlin: Springer-Verlag.

Thorn, M., Kraus, J., & Parker, D. (2011). Life cycle assessment as a sustainability management tool: Strengths, weaknesses, and other considerations. *Environmental Quality Management*, *20*(3), 1–10. doi:10.1002/tqem.20285

Toda, H. Y., & Yamamoto, T. (1995). Statistical Inference in Vector Autoregressions With Possibly Integrated Processes. *Journal of Econometrics*, *66*(2), 225–250. doi:10.1016/0304-4076(94)01616-8

Tomala, M. (2018). Opodatkowanie ekologiczne narzędziem ochrony środowiska państw nordyckich. Bezpieczeństwo. *Teoria i Praktyka*, *1*, 103–115.

Tomczyk, P. (2012). Client as a source of company value. In T. Pakulska (Ed.), *Enterprise and surroundings* (pp. 59–78). Warsaw: Oficyna Wydawnicza SGH.

Trehan, B., & Walsh, C. (1991). Testing the Intertemporal Budget Constraints: Theory and Applications to U.S. Federal Budget and Current Account Deficits. *Journal of Money, Credit and Banking*, *23*(2), 206–223. doi:10.2307/1992777

Trigeorgis, L. (1995). *Real options in capital investments: models, strategies and applications*. Westport, CT: Praeger.

Trigeorgis, L. (1996). *Real options for managerial flexibility and strategy in resource allocation*. Cambridge, MA: MIT Press.

Trojanowski, T. (2013). Aspects of the sustainable management of marketing activities. In J. S. Kardas & J. Brodowska-Szewczuk (Eds.), *Business Development Opportunities*. Siedlce: Wydawnictwo Uniwersytetu Przyrodniczo-Humanistycznego w Siedlcach.

United Nations (UN). (1975). *United Nations Environment Programme*. Report of the Governing Council on the work pf this third session. New York: United Nations.

United Nations. (2013). *National Transfer Accounts Manual: Measuring and Analyzing the Generational Economy*. New York: ONU Department of Economic and Social Affairs, Population Division.

United Nations. (2018). *Scaling up Finance for the Sustainable Development Goals: Experimenting with Models of Multilateral Development Banking*. United Nations. Available online: http://unctad.org/en/PublicationsLibrary/gdsecidc2017d4_en.pdf

US Congressional Budget Office. (2016). *An Update to the Budget and Economic Outlook, 2016 to 2026*. Available at: www.cbo.gov/publication/51908

Ushijima, T. (2015). *Diversification, Organization, and Value of the Firm*. RIETI Discussion Paper Series 15-E-019. Retrieved from https://www.rieti.go.jp/jp/publications/dp/15e019.pdf

Van der Waldt, G. (2016). The Role of Government in Sustainable Development. *Towards a Conceptual and Analytical Framework for Scientific Inquiry Administratio Publica*, *24*(2), 49–72.

Vandaele, N. J., & Decouttere, C. J. (2013). Sustainable R&D portfolio assessment. *Decision Support Systems*, *54*(4), 1521–1532. doi:10.1016/j.dss.2012.05.054

Vaslavskiy, Y., & Vaslavskaya, I. (2019). Infrastructure Public-Private Partnership projects: budget consolidation policy in Russia and government expenditures' efficiency increase. In B. S. Sergi (Ed.), *Modeling Economic Growth in Contemporary Russia* (pp. 199–228). London: Emerald Publishing Limited. doi:10.1108/978-1-78973-265-820191007

Venetsanos, K., Angelopoulou, P., & Tsoutsos, T. (2002). Renewable energy sources project appraisal under uncertainty: The case of wind energy exploitation within a changing energy market environment. *Energy Policy*, *30*(4), 293–307. doi:10.1016/S0301-4215(01)00096-9

Verboven, H. (2011). Communicating CSR and business identity in the chemical industry through mission slogans. *Business Communication Quarterly*, *74*(4), 415–431. doi:10.1177/1080569911424485

Vergragt, P., & van Grootveld, G. (1994). Sustainable technology development in the Netherlands: The first phase of the Dutch STD programme. *Journal of Cleaner Production*, *2*(3/4), 133–139. doi:10.1016/0959-6526(94)90035-3

Vernadsky, V. I. (1967). The Biosphere and the Noösphere. Moscow: Publishing House "Mysl"

Vintilă, G., & Gherghina, S. C. (2014). The impact of ownership concentration on firm value. Empirical study of the Bucharest Stock Exchange listed companies. *Procedia Economics and Finance*, *15*, 271–279. doi:10.1016/S2212-5671(14)00500-0

Viscelli, T. R., Hermanson, D. R., & Beasley, M. S. (2017). The Integration of ERM and Strategy: Implications for Corporate Governance. *Accounting Horizons*, *31*(2), 69–82. doi:10.2308/acch-51692

Vlasov, S. A., & Deryugina, E. B. (2018). Fiscal multipliers in Russia. *Journal of the New Economic Association*, *38*(2), 104-119.

Voitchovsky, S. (2005). Does the profile of income inequality matter for economic growth? Distinguishing between the effects of inequality in different parts of the income distribution. *Journal of Economic Growth*, *10*(3), 273–296. doi:10.100710887-005-3535-3

Wagner, R.E. (1976). Revenue structure: fiscal illusion and budgetary choice. *Public Choice*, *25*, 45-61.

Walińska, E. (2015). Zintegrowany raport - początek końca sprawozdania finansowego? *Zeszyty Teoretyczne Rachunkowości*, *82*(138), 151–165.

WCED (World Commission on Environment and Development). (1987). *Our Common Future. Un Documents: Gathering a Body of Global Agreements has been compiled by the NGO Committee on Education of the Conference of NGOs from United Nations web sites with the invaluable help of information & communications technology.* New York: United Nations.

WDR. (2018). *World Development Report 2018: Learning to Realize Education's Promise.* Washington, DC: World Bank.

WDR. (2019). *World Development Report 2019: The Changing Nature of Work.* Washington, DC: The World Bank Group.

WEF. (2015). New Vision for Education: Unlocking the Potential of Technology. World Economic Forum.

WEF. (2017). *Sustainable Development Impact Summit.* Geneva: WEF.

WEF. (2018). Creating a Shared Future in a Fractured World. Annual Meeting, 2018. World Economic Forum.

WEF. (2018). *Towards a Reskilling Revolution: A Future of Jobs for All.* World Economic Forum

West, S. E., & Williams, R. C. III. (2004). Estimatesfrom a Consumer Demand System: Implications for the Incidence of Environmental Taxes. *Journal of Environmental Economics and Management, 47*(3), 535–558. doi:10.1016/j.jeem.2003.11.004

White, W. (2009). Modern macroeconomics is on the wrong track. Finance & Development, 46(4).

WHO. (2019). *Universal health coverage (UHC).* Retrieved April 9, 2019, from https://www.who.int/en/news-room/fact-sheets/detail/universal-health-coverage-(uhc)

Wier, M., Birr-Pedersen, K., Jacobsen, H. K., & Klok, J. (2005). Are Co_2 Taxes Regressive? Evidence from the Danish Experience. *Ecologocal Economisc, 52*(2), 239–251. doi:10.1016/j.ecolecon.2004.08.005

William, J. F., & Parker, J. C. (2010). Measuring the sustainable return on investment (SROI) of waste to energy. *Proceedings of the 18th Annual North American Waste to Energy Conference.* 10.1115/NAWTEC18-3552

Williamson, O. (1996). *The Mechanisms of Governance.* Oxford, UK: Oxford University Press.

Wisner, J. D., & Fawcett, S. E. (1991). Linking Firm Strategy to Operating Decisions through Performance Measurement. *Production and Inventory Management Journal, 32*(3), 5–11.

Withana, S., Brink, P., Illes, A., Nanni, S., & Watkins, E. (2014). Environmental Tax Reform in Europe: Opportunities for the future. Institute for European Environmental Policy (IEEP) for the Netherlands Ministry of Infrastructure and the Environment.

Wójcik-Jurkiewicz, M. (2016). Idea społecznie odpowiedzialnego biznesu a kształtowanie wyniku finansowego spółki. *Studia Ekonomiczne: Zeszyty Naukowe Uniwersytetu Ekonomicznego w Katowicach, 253,* 140–150.

Wong Y., A. P., & R. D. (2016). Sustainable development goals, universal health coverage and equity in health systems: The Orang Asli commons approach. *Glob Health Epidemiol Genom, 1.*

World Bank. (2014). *IEG's World Bank Group Support to Public-Private Partnerships. Lessons from Experience in Client Countries, FY02–12 and World Bank Group draft Management Response.* Washington, DC: World Bank.

World Bank. (2017). *Contribution of Institutional Investors. Private Investment in Infrastructure. 2011-H1 2017. World Bank Report. World Bank Group Public-Private Partnerships.* Washington, DC: World Bank.

World Bank. (2018). *Global Financial Development Report 2017/2018.* Washington, DC: Bankers Without Borders.

World Bank. (2018). *Rolling Back Russia's Spatial Disparities: Re-assembling the Soviet Jigsaw under a Market Economy.* Washington, DC: The World Bank Group.

World Bank. (2018). *The Human Capital Project*. Washington, DC: The World Bank Group.

World Bank. (2019). *Global Economic Prospects, January 2019: Darkening Skies*. Washington, DC: World Bank.

World Economic Forum. (2014). *The Global Gender Gap Report 2014*. Insight Report. Author.

World Economic Forum. (2017). *The Inclusive Growth and Development Report, 2017*. Geneva: WEF.

World Economic Forum. (2018). *The Inclusive Development Index 2018. Summary and Data Highlights*. World Economic Forum.

World Economic Outlook. (2018). *Challenges to Steady Growth*. October. Washington, DC: IMF.

World Health Organization. (2016). *Metadata SDG indicator 3.1.2*. Retrieved from https://unstats.un.org/sdgs/metadata

World Health Organization. (2017). *Metadata SDG indicator 3.4.1*. Retrieved from https://unstats.un.org/sdgs/metadata/files/Metadata-03-04-01.pdf

World Health Organization. (2018a). *Metadata SDG indicator 3.1.1*. Author.

World Health Organization. (2018b). *Metadata SDG indicator 3.2.1*. Author.

World Health Organization. (2018c). *Metadata SDG indicator 3.2.2*. Author.

World Health Organization. (2018d). *Metadata SDG indicator 3.3.2*. Author.

World Health Organization. (2018e). *Metadata SDG indicator 3.4.2*. Author.

World Health Organization. (2018f). *Metadata SDG indicator 3.9.2*. Author.

World Health Organization. (2018g). *Metadata SDG indicator 3.a.1*. Author.

World Health Organization. (2018h). *Metadata SDG indicator 3.c.1*. Author.

World Health Organization. (2018i). *Metadata SDG indicator 3.d.1*. Author.

Wykaz jednostek zainteresowania publicznego. (n.d.). Retrieved from https://www.gov.pl/web/finanse/wykaz-jzp-1

Zaleska, M., & Koleśnik, J. (2018). Zarządzanie sytuacją kryzysową - działania pomocowe i gwarancyjne. In M. Zaleska (Ed.), *Świat bankowości*. Warszawa, Poland: DIFIN.

Zeeman, E. C. (1977). *Catastrophe Theory: Selected papers, 1972-1977*. Reading, MA: Addison-Wesley.

Zhang, T. (2017). Toward inclusive growth. Finance & Development, 54(1), 26.

Zhu, J., & Hua, W. (2017). Visualizing the knowledge domain of sustainable development research between 1987 and 2015: A bibliometric analysis. *Scientometrics*, *10*(2), 893–914. doi:10.100711192-016-2187-8

Ziębicki, B. (2014). *Efektywność organizacyjna podmiotów sektora publicznego*. Kraków: UEK.

Zielone zamówienia publiczne; Praktyczny podręcznik dla beneficjentów funduszy europejskich; Nowe drogi rozwoju, człowiek, natura, infrastruktura. (2008). [Green public procurement; A practical manual for beneficiaries of European funds; New ways of development, man, nature, and infrastructure]. Academic Press.

Žižlavský, O. (2014). Net present value approach: method for economic assessment of innovation projects. *Proceedings from 19th International Scientific Conference; Economics and Management*.

About the Contributors

Mazin A. M. Al Janabi is Full Professor of Finance & Banking and Financial Engineering at the EGADE Business School, Tecnologico de Monterrey, Santa Fe Campus, Mexico City, Mexico. Professor Al Janabi holds a Ph.D. degree from the University of London, United Kingdom, and has over 30 years of real-world experience in diverse academic institutions, financial markets & institutions and international finance & banking corporations, and in many different roles. He has worked for top international financial groups (e.g., ING-Barings and BBVA) where he held several senior management positions, such as Director of Global Market Risk Management, Director of Asset & Liability Management, Head of Trading Risk Management, and Head of Trading of Financial Derivative Products. Professor Al Janabi has strong interest for research, publications and developments within emerging economies. He has several publications in refereed international journals, books, book chapters, research methods cases, and business cases. Furthermore, he has participated as guest speaker and presenter in several international conferences and symposiums. He has served as consultant in finance & banking and as advisor for the creation of new financial markets within emerging economies. He has written extensively on contemporary topics in trading, market and counterparty risk management besides modern portfolio management. His research interests and consulting activities address practitioners and regulatory issues in financial risk management, derivative securities, and portfolio management. In addition, his previous and current research & development in quantitative finance and financial engineering have been formally classified in the academic literatures as *"Al Janabi Model"* for Liquidity Risk Management. In fact, *"Al Janabi Model"* can offer practical tools to portfolio managers in many ways and with different uses and applications. His approach to tackling the estimation of liquidity risk in financial markets offers insights to techniques to deal with a major stumbling block to efficient use of assets in portfolios and hedge funds. Professor Al Janabi has published in top-tiered journals such as: *European Journal of Operational Research, International Review of Financial Analysis, Annals of Operations Research, Applied Economics, Economic Modelling, Review of Financial Economics, Journal of Asset Management, Service Industries Journal, Studies in Economics and Finance, International Journal of Financial Engineering, Journal of Emerging Market Finance, Emerging Markets Finance and Trade, Review of Middle East Economics and Finance, Journal of Economic Research, Journal of Risk Finance, Journal of Banking Regulation, Annals of Nuclear Energy, among others.* Before joining EGADE Business School, Professor Al Janabi worked for several years as Full Professor of Finance & Banking and Financial Engineering at UAE University (UAEU) in Abu Dhabi, UAE and also at Al Akhawayn University in Ifrane (AUI), Morocco, among other academic institutions. He received several awards for excellence in teaching, research and service and other awards in recognition of outstanding research publications output in A*/A ranked journals in finance, financial engineering, and operations research. His biography was cited and featured in Who's Who in the World (2013-Present) and in Who's Who in Science and Engineering (2016-Present).

Iwona Bak is an expert in the field of quantitative methods, specializing in analyzes regarding the use of quantitative methods in economic. research, with particular emphasis on international comparisons in the area of sustainable development, competitiveness of the national economy and regional development, with experience in working with advanced statistical packages: STATISTICA, R program, etc. Author and co-author of scientific articles published in scientific journals from the JCR list, also having practical experience in the implementation of projects carried out on behalf of public institutions.

Małgorzata Burchard-Dziubińska (Ph.D.) is a researcher in the field of economics of natural resources and environmental protection. She holds a postdoctoral degree in economics. Currently, she holds the position of an associate professor at the Faculty of Economics and Sociology at the University of Lodz, Poland. She is author and editor of papers and books related to issues of sustainable development and green economy. co-editor of Journal Ekonomia i Środowisko (Economics and Environment). She is President of Polish Association of Environmental and Natural Resources Economists and was President of Polish Economic Society – Lodz Division (2010-2015). She was a manager in several scientific projects and a scholarship holder.

Katarzyna Cheba is an expert in the field of quantitative methods, specializing in analyzes regarding the use of quantitative methods in economic. research, with particular emphasis on international comparisons in the area of sustainable development, competitiveness of the national economy and regional development, with experience in working with advanced statistical packages: STATISTICA, R program, etc. Author and co-author of scientific articles published in scientific journals from the JCR list, also having practical experience in the implementation of projects carried out on behalf of public institutions.

Manipadma Datta has been in management teaching, training and research for more than three decades in India and abroad. His areas of expertise are varied, ranging from - Sustainable Development, Climate Finance, Responsible Investments, Integrated Reporting, Circular Economy Finance, Weather Derivative, to Public Management, CSR, Strategic Management, Sustainability and Creativity, Valuation of Intangibles and so on. Currently he is a Professor in Business and Sustainability in TERI School of Advanced Studies (TERISAS), New Delhi, the pioneer in sustainability research. Prof. Datta has served many institutions of eminence including University of Calcutta, Vidyasagar University, Nirma University, Institute of Management Technology Ghaziabad, Indian Institute of Management Lucknow, International Institute of Management Delhi and Vrije University Brussels. He is a regular contributor to national and international refereed journals and is on their editorial boards. He has co-authored two books and authored an audiovisual one on strategic finance. He is on the PhD adjudicator boards of several universities in India and abroad. A regular consultant to IFC, World Bank, Government of India sponsored research projects, he has developed housing finance models for the poor in Bangladesh and Nepal and a business model for utilizing biodiversity of the Cooperative Republic of Guyana, South America. He holds a Masters Degree and a PhD from the University of Calcutta; he is also a Fellow (FCS) of the Institute of Company Secretaries of India.

Beata Zofia Filipiak graduated from Faculty of Economic of University of Szczecin, Poland, in 1990, and obtained a PhD in economics and financial strategy from Faculty of Transport and Connectivity of the same university in 1995. Scholarship holder of the Flemish governmentat the University of Antwerp in 1999. Beata Zofia Filipiak worked in different financials instytucion and obtained the qualifications of a tax advisor in 1998. She was involved in 24 scientific projects regarding: corporate financial strategies, financial strategies of LGU's and sustainable development. Since 2013 is employed as a full professor at Institute of Finance of University of Szczecin.Beata Zofia Filipiak has authored and coauthored more than 200 publications including thirty monographs. Her research interests span from financial strategies, sustainable finance, financial analysis and financial aspects of sustainable development.

Murat Gündüz, graduated from Mugla University, Department of Statistics and Computer Science. He holds a PhD in numerical methods. His main research interests are econometrics and statistical applications. His research interests include Time Series Analysis, Panel Data Analysis, Causality Analysis, Cointegration Analysis, Total Factor Productivity, Financial Development and Financial Globalization. He is an assistant professor in the Department of Econometrics at Usak University.

Tomasz Jakubiec (Ph.D. in Economics Sciences) in his research focuses on sustainable development and environmental protection. He is the author of several articles about green public procurement and urban issues such as strategic planning processes, metropolitan urban agenda, initiatives engaging citizen in actions on public interest, smart city concept and founding of public investments involving sustainable development based approach. He is experienced senior officer working in municipality office of Lodz City (third biggest city in Poland). He is head of Mayor's Department e.g. responsible for supervising on policy of municipal companies, economic development, etc. For over seven years he was leading Department responsible for preparing and implementing city development strategy and fund-rising based on projects. He was leader and participant of many international projects cofinanced by UE funds e.g. LIFE, Interreg, Horizon 2020, URBACT. He also was organizer of many scientific and municipal events, congresses and conferences, both international and domestic. He is an expert on field of urban agenda and GPP on local, regional and domestic level. In his job and academical research he try to be focused on implementing practical aspects of sustainable development and innovative solutions. He is teaching practical aspects of GPP and sustainable public investments.

Nataliya Sergeevna Makarova teaches on Financial Markets, Public Finance and Social Contracts in the Economics of Emerging Markets at the Russian State University named after A.N. Kosygin. She graduated from Moscow State University of Consumer Cooperatives. In 2005 she got a degree of Candidate of Economics from Volgograd State University. Since then she worked in the financial business, taught as a Senior Lecturer then as an Associate Professor at the Department of Finance and Banking of the Russian State University named after K.G. Rasumovskiy. Now she is an Associate Professor at the Department of Finance and Business Analytics of the Russian State University named after A.N. Kosygin. She has more than 60 publications indexed by RISC (RF). Currently she is working on her doctoral dissertation, titled "Multilevel pension system of the Russian Federation: the basis of the new social contract and factors of public finance sustainability". Her scientific interests include the following issues: intergenerational equity and economic growth, public finance sustainability, income and wealth polarization of the population, the middle class functions on the society.

Katarzyna Miszczyńska, Doctor of Economic Sciences, is an assistant professor in the Department of Public Finance at the University of Lodz, Poland. Doctoral thesis defended in the Faculty of Economics and Sociology in the University of Lodz. Graduate of the University of Lodz. Received master's degree in Information Technology and Econometrics in 2010, and in 2011 her second master's degree in

Finance and Accounting. Since 2010 working at the University of Lodz. Expert in health economics with particular emphasis of public finance and econometric modeling. Author of several academic articles, monograph sections, analytical works. Since 2017 leader of scientific grant Multicriteria assessment of efficiency of public hospitals in Poland and identification of determinants of their indebtedness financed by the National Science Centre in Poland.

Ebru Oydag received her MSc in Shipping, Trade & Finance from the City University, London in 1996 with a Merit (3.7 average). She is a graduate of Istanbul University Business School (English curriculum) in top 3. She is a chartered accountant as a member of ACCA. She also holds ACCA DipIFR. She has more than 20 years of work experience in finance, accounting, auditing, supply chain, strategic management and consulting at various multinational companies. She currently studies towards a PhD degree in management/strategy. Her academic interests include various topics in organisation theory and strategic management. She is a lecturer at Marmara University, Istanbul and also works as a freelance management consultant/trainer.

Yunus Ozyildirim graduated from Inonu University, Department of Econometrics in 2016. In the same year, he started his graduate studies at the Department of Economics at Usak University. He graduated in 2019. He used econometrics and statistics in the financial field and worked on financial inclusion. In addition, he has been attending Inonu University Econometrics Summer Seminars regularly for 3 years and has improved his econometric knowledge from a current perspective.

Andrey Igorevich Pilipenko received his diploma of Higher Education from Leningrad State University (Faculty of Mathematics and Mechanics) in 1972. In 1984 he received his degree of Candidate of Science in Physics and Mathematics from the Institute of Physical Chemistry of the USSR' Academy of Science. In 1998 he received a degree of Doctor of Pedagogical Sciences from Russian Academy of Education. Being full professor For 40 years he has been working as a Professor at many Russian Universities: Lomonosov's Moscow State University, Russian Academy of National Economy under the Government of the Russian Federation, etc. He has been invited as a Professor by Gumilyov' Eurasian National University (Kazakhstan). He is currently a Professor at the Faculty of Marketing and International Cooperation of the Russian Presidential Academy of National Economy and Public Administration. He has about 140 publications, ones, published in 2016-2019 are indexed by Scopus, Doi. His scientific interests lie in the areas of bifurcation effect' modeling in macroeconomics on the base of shocks theory, modeling factors of national financial stability, assessment of interference of monetary and fiscal policies as well as psychological and cognitive barriers in education.

Olga Ivanovna Pilipenko received her diploma of Higher Education from the Moscow State Institute for Foreign Relations (of the USSR' Ministry for Foreign Affairs) in 1975. In 1981 she received her degree of Candidate of Science in Economics from the Institute of Latin America of the USSR' Academy of Science. In 1994 she received a degree of Doctor of Economics from Lomonosov's Moscow State University. Being full professor for 40 years she has been working as a Professor at many Russian Universities: Lomonosov's Moscow State University, Russian Academy of National Economy under the Government of the Russian Federation, etc. She has been invited as a Professor by Hearning Institute (Denmark) and by Aarhus University (Denmark) in the 1990th. She is currently an Invited Professor at the Faculty of Marketing and International Cooperation of the Russian Presidential Academy of National

Economy and Public Administration. She has more than 140 publications; ones, published in 2016, 2019 are indexed by Scopus, Doi. Her scientific interests lie in the areas of bifurcation effect' modeling in global financial markets on the base of shocks theory, modeling factors of global financial stability, of monetary circulation, of public finance, of monetary and fiscal policies interaction, of cyclical development of economic and financial systems.

Zoya Andreevna Pilipenko received her Master's Degree in Economics from Lomonosov's Moscow State University in 2003. In 2004 she received her degree of Candidate of Science in World Economy, Finance, and Banking from Lomonosov's Moscow State University. In 2013 she received her degree of Doctor of Science in World Economy, Finance, and Banking from Lomonosov's Moscow State University. She worked as a financial analyst for the Insurance Company "Gefest," the Joint Stock Company "Sberbank of Russia," the Central Bank of the Russian Federation. She has had teaching and research experience: more than 60 publications including ones, indexed in RISC, Doi, Scopus. She has got certificates in Banking and Finance from practical seminars in Great Britain, Luxembourg, Austria, Italy and France. She is currently a Head of the Group of Rating Agencies and Price Centers, Department of Financial Market Strategic Development, the Central Bank of the Russian Federation. Her scientific interests lie in the area of the shocks theory and the impulse model of cyclical economic development as well as peculiar properties of monetary policy' formation and implementation in connection with definite sectors of financial market.

Ozlem Senvar (PhD in Industrial Engineering) is an Associate Professor at Marmara University in Department of Industrial Engineering. Ozlem Senvar (PhD) officially granted (Ref.2013/327-350) by European Commission for her post doctoral researches in France. She has been author of many peer-reviewed international articles, book chapters, and conference papers. Her research interests involve Operations Management, Advanced Quality Engineering, Statistics, Machine Learning, and Decision Making.

Ria Sinha has the expertise in the areas of Climate Finance, Voluntary Sustainability Standards (VSS) and Business Sustainability with nearly eight years of experience in industry and academia. She holds a PhD in Business Sustainability from TERI School of Advanced Studies (TERI SAS), New Delhi and is a Masters in Economics from University of Calcutta. She was an HSBC Scholar in TERI SAS. As a DAAD-German Indian Climate Change Dialogue Fellow, she spent quite some time in Germany and presented her research at conferences held in Vienna, Berlin and Boston MA. She was also invited as an ICRIER Young Scholar by the National Bureau of Economic Research (NBER) Summer Institute, Massachusetts. At present Dr. Sinha is conducting a research project with the University of Szczecin, Poland. She is attached with Development Alternatives, New Delhi as a Senior Manager and TERI SAS as a Visiting Faculty in the Department of Business and Sustainability.

Anna Spoz, Ph.D, Assistant Professor at the Department of Accountancy at the John Paul II Catholic University of Lublin. Manager, and lecturer of Postgraduate Programs "Accounting and Tax" and "Management and Finance in Public Administration." She combines teaching and scholarly activities with work in the business. Author of publications on finance, accounting, reporting, and management.

Beata Szczecińska is an expert in the field of using methods and techniques which support analysis of management processes. Her scientific and research activity focuses mainly on the assessment of effectiveness, competitive position, capital structure and financial liquidity. Author and co-author of over 60 scientific publications.

Irina Yu. Vaslavskaya has doctoral degrees in economics. She began her professional career as a senior, then a leading researcher of the Department of Scientific Research Institute of Economics, the Russian Academy of Science (2000-2013). She was invited as associate professor by many universities in Moscow, as well as by Kazan Federal University, the Russian Federation (2013-2015). Now she is a head of the Department of Enterprises and Organizations' Economics, Kazan Federal University (the Russian Federation) (2016-2018). She has numerous publications, indexed by RISC (the Russian Federation), Doi, SCOPUS. Her scientific interests lie in the areas of institutional economic theory, public-private partnership' organizational forms in Russia, state and public sector's functions in economic systems as well as factors of slowing economic growth at the globe.

Dorota Wyszkowska graduated Faculty of Economic of University of Bialystok, Poland, in 1999, and obtained a PhD in economics from Faculty of Economic and Management of the same University in 2006. Cooperates with various entities, conducting research on local finances and the silver economy, and preparing studies and reports in this fields. Twice she participated in the research work of the World Bank in the field of local finances in Poland. She was involved in 6 scientific projects regarding: local financial, monitoring of public services, regional development, and silver economy. Since 2007 is employed as a PhD at Department of Economics and Finance of Local Self-government of University of Bialystok. Dorota Wyszkowska has authored and coauthored near about 80 publications. Her research interests span from local financial, sustainable development, financial analysis and financial aspects of sustainable development.

Marian Żukowski is a researcher in the "economics and finance" discipline. More than 35 years of employment at Maria Curie-Sklodowska University in Lublin. During the period of 1994-2004 adviser of the Chairman of the Depositary Credit Commercial Bank in Lublin. Served as Director of the Institute of Economics and Associate Dean of the Faculty of Economics. Since 2010 employed at Catholic University of Lublin. Currently serves as Director of the Institute of Economics and Management. Member of the Financial Sciences Committee of the Polish Academy of Sciences. Specializes in research on the banking system in the countries of Central and Eastern Europe. Author of books on Polish banking system issued in Polish, Ukrainian, Russian and English. (Contact: marian.zukowski@kul.pl.)

Index

G

H

I

L

M

N

O

P

Q

R

S

T

U

W

www.ingramcontent.com/pod-product-compliance
Lightning Source LLC
LaVergne TN
LVHW060008031026
849161LV00025B/2488